Staff of Expert Steering Committee

专家指导委员会

National Key Book Publishing Planning Project of the 13th Five-Year Plan

“十 三 五” 国 家 重 点 图 书 出 版 规 划 项 目

International Clinical Medicine Series Based on the Belt and Road Initiative

“一 带 一 路” 背 景 下 国 际 化 临 床 医 学 丛 书

Performing Statistical Analysis with IBM SPSS 23

IBM SPSS 23 统计软件应用教程

Chief Editor Chen Pingyan Guan Ying

主编 陈平雁 关 颖

ZHENGZHOU UNIVERSITY PRESS

图书在版编目(CIP)数据

IBM SPSS 23 统计软件应用教程 = Performing Statistical Analysis with IBM SPSS 23 :英文/陈平雁,关颖主编. —郑州:郑州大学出版社,2020. 12
(“一带一路”背景下国际化临床医学丛书)
ISBN 978-7-5645-7375-1

Ⅰ. ①I… Ⅱ. ①陈…②关… Ⅲ. ①统计分析-应用软件-英文
Ⅳ. ①C819

中国版本图书馆 CIP 数据核字(2020)第 200528 号

IBM SPSS 23 **统计软件应用教程** = Performing Statistical Analysis with IBM SPSS 23 :**英文**

项目负责人	孙保营　杨秦予	策划编辑	李龙传
责任编辑	张彦勤	装帧设计	苏永生
责任校对	张锦森	责任监制	凌　青　李瑞卿

出版发行	郑州大学出版社有限公司	地　址	郑州市大学路 40 号(450052)
出 版 人	孙保营	网　址	http://www.zzup.cn
经　销	全国新华书店	发行电话	0371-66966070
印　刷	河南文华印务有限公司		
开　本	850 mm×1 168 mm　1/16		
印　张	24.5	字　数	945 千字
版　次	2020 年 12 月第 1 版	印　次	2020 年 12 月第 1 次印刷

书　号	ISBN 978-7-5645-7375-1	定　价	79.00 元

Staff of Editor Steering Committee

编审委员会

Editorial Staff

Chief Editors

Chen Pingyan	Southern Medical University
Guan Ying	Southern Medical University

Vice Chief Editors

Chen Bingwei	Southeast University
Hou Yan	Harbin Medical University
Yang Lin	The Hong Kong Polytechnic University

Editorial board member

Chen Bingwei	Southeast University
Chen Fangyao	Xi'an Jiaotong University
Chen Pingyan	Southern Medical University
Guan Ying	Southern Medical University
Guo Pi	Shantou University
Han Chunlei	Binzhou Medical University
Hou Yan	Harbin Medical University
Peng Zhihang	Nanjing Medical University
Wang ling	Air Force Medical University
Wang Mengqiao	Sichuan University
Wang Shiqi	Inner Mongolia Medical University
Wang Xiling	Fudan University
Wu Ying	Southern Medical University
Yan Fangrong	China Pharmaceutical University
Yang Fang	Central South University
Yang Jun	Jinan University
Yang Lin	Hong Kong Polytechnic University
Zhang Tao	Shandong University

作者名单

主　编

陈平雁　　南方医科大学
关　颖　　南方医科大学

副主编

陈炳为　　东南大学
侯　艳　　哈尔滨医科大学
杨　琳　　香港理工大学

编　委（以姓氏汉语拼音为序）

陈炳为　　东南大学
陈方尧　　西安交通大学
陈平雁　　南方医科大学
关　颖　　南方医科大学
郭　貔　　汕头大学
韩春蕾　　滨州医学院
侯　艳　　哈尔滨医科大学
彭志行　　南京医科大学
王　陵　　空军军医大学
王孟樵　　四川大学
王诗淇　　内蒙古医科大学
王锡玲　　复旦大学
吴　莹　　南方医科大学
言方荣　　中国药科大学
杨　芳　　中南大学
杨　军　　暨南大学
杨　琳　　香港理工大学
张　涛　　山东大学

Preface

At the Second Belt and Road Summit Forum on International Cooperation in 2019 and the Seventy-third World Health Assembly in 2020, General Secretary Xi Jinping stated the importance for promoting the construction of the "Belt and Road" and jointly build a community for human health. Countries and regions along the "Belt and Road" have a large number of overseas Chinese communities, and shared close geographic proximity, similarities in culture, disease profiles and medical habits. They also shared a profound mass base with ample space for cooperation and exchange in Clinical Medicine. The publication of the International Clinical Medicine series for clinical researchers, medical teachers and students in countries along the "Belt and Road" is a concrete measure to promote the exchange of Chinese and foreign medical science and technology with mutual appreciation and reciprocity.

Zhengzhou University Press coordinated more than 600 medical experts from over 160 renowned medical research institutes, medical schools and clinical hospitals across China. It produced this set of medical tools in English to serve the needs for the construction of the "Belt and Road". It comprehensively coversaspects in the theoretical framework and clinical practicesin Clinical Medicine, including basic science, multiple clinical specialities and social medicine. It reflects the latest academic and technological developments, and the international frontiers of academic advancements in Clinical Medicine. It shared with the world China's latest diagnosis and therapeutic approaches, clinical techniques, and experiences in prescription and medication. It has an important role in disseminating contemporary Chinese medical science and technology innovations, demonstrating the achievements of modern China's economic and social development, and promoting the unique charm of Chinese culture to the world.

The series is the first set of medical tools written in English by Chinese medical experts to serve the needs of the "Belt and Road" construction. It systematically and comprehensively reflects the Chinese characteristics in Clinical Medicine. Also, it presents a landmark achievement in the implementation of the "Belt and Road" initiative in promoting exchanges in medical science and technology. This series is theoretical in nature, with each volume built on the mainlines in traditional disciplines but at the same time introducing contemporary theories that guide clinical practices, diagnosis and treatment methods, echoing the latest research findings in Clinical Medicine.

As the disciplines in Clinical Medicine rapidly advances, different views on knowledge, inclusiveness, and medical ethics may arise. We hope this work will facilitate the exchange of ideas, build common ground while allowing differences, and contribute to the building of a community for human health in a broad spectrum of disciplines and research focuses.

Foreign Academician of the Chinese Academy of Engineering
Dean, Academy of Medical Sciences of Zhengzhou University
Director, Barts Cancer Institute, London, UK
6th August, 2020

Foreword

Performing Statistical Analysis with IBM SPSS 23 is written to become an aid in the beginning statistical analysis to students or clinical doctors whose mathematical background is limited to basic algebra. The book puts focus on data file formats, operation steps, results' interpretation, and tries to avoid a deep introduction to programming content and statistical method background. Therefore, the book is mainly aimed at medical students, or students from other healthcare related professions such as pharmacy or public health services who need to face with a lot of data from patients monitoring and laboratory tests.

There are thirteen chapters. Chapter 1: Overview and basic steps in data analysis, Chapter 2: Data management, Chapter 3: Transform, Chapter 4: Analysis of descriptive statistics, Chapter 5: Compare means, Chapter 6: General linear model, Chapter 7: Correlation & regression, Chapter 8: Classify, Chapter 9: Reliability analysis, Chapter 10: Nonparametric tests, Chapter 11: Survival analysis, Chapter 12: Graphs, 13: Comprehensive data analysis.

A number of important features have been made in this book. One of the important features of this book is citing a lot of actual data from medical and biological researches. The examples are close to daily scientific research projects, so this book can work not only as an introductory level textbook, but also as a handbook for clinicians or other healthcare professionals in data analysis. Furthermore, a detailed explanation of the analysis results is another outstanding feature of this book. Detailed and accurate interpretation is particularly helpful for correct understanding and reasonable application of statistical methods for readers. A special section called comprehensive data analysis included in this book is another feature of this book. This new content requires students to work with a dataset to perform various statistical tests, and then summarize the results. We also provide a flow chart to aid readers to choose appropriate analytical method based on the data characters.

It is important to acknowledge the many people whose contributions have gone into the first edition of *performing statistical analysis with IBM* 23. The support from the International School of Southern Medical University is essential for this book. We would also like to thank Chen Liya of Nanfang Hospital for her provision of the index of applications, her exhaustive accuracy check of the page proofs, and her general availability and advice concerning all matters statistics. We also thank the publisher for their helpful advice.

However, due to our limited level, the inadequacies are inevitable. We appreciate any comment and suggestions towards the book so that we can make the book perfect in the second edition. Thanks.

Editors

目　录

Chapter 1

Overview and Basic Steps in Data Analysis

SPSS is the short form of Statistical Product and Service Solutions. It is an integrated software package of computer program for the statistical analysis of social, medicine, educational and other kinds of data. The SPSS software was first released in 1968 by three graduate students Norman H. Nie, Dale H. Bent, and C. Hadlai Hull. The SPSS Inc. was purchased by IBM in 2009 and the software renamed as IBM SPSS software from the version of 17.0. In this book, the software would be call in short, for example, as SPSS 13.0 or IBM SPSS 17.0 separately for convenience.

1.1 The operating environment of IBM SPSS 23

IBM SPSS 23 software has the following requirements for the software and hardware environment of microcomputers:

1) Operating system: Recommended OS including Windows 7, Windows XP, Windows Vista, Linux and, Mac OS.

2) RAM: At least 1 GB.

3) Hard disk space: At least 800 MB.

4) Screen: SVGA (800 pixels×600 pixels) or higher.

5) Network: Support TCP/IP.

1.2 Windows and view

There are four main kinds of windows in IBM SPSS 23 software: Data Editor, Output window (Viewer), Syntax Editor window, and Script window.

1.2.1 Data Editor

There are several ways to activate the Data Editor:

1) The Data Editor will be automatically ready to function when the software is activated.

2) When a new dataset is activated with ongoing dataset unclosed.

3) Activated from File menu:

File

    New

Data

As other window under the Windows Operating System, the Data Editor can be zoomed in or zoomed out, dragged, minimized and maximized. The main function of Data Editor includes establishing new dataset, editing and presenting existed dataset. There are two different and separated views of Data Editor, which are Data View and Variable View(Figure 1-1 and Figure 1-2). Date View is used to edit data and Variable View is used to define, check and modify variable characters.

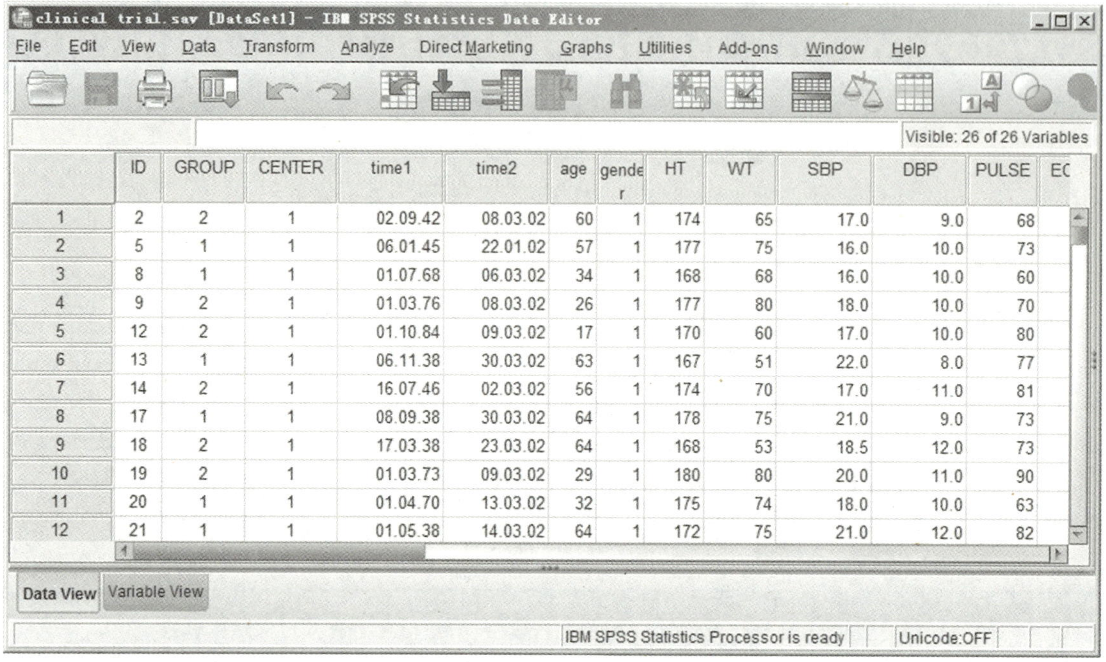

clinical trial.sav [DataSet1] - IBM SPSS Statistics Data Editor

File Edit View Data Transform Analyze Direct Marketing Graphs Utilities Add-ons Window Help

Visible: 26 of 26 Variables

	ID	GROUP	CENTER	time1	time2	age	gender	HT	WT	SBP	DBP	PULSE	EC
1	2	2	1	02.09.42	08.03.02	60	1	174	65	17.0	9.0	68	
2	5	1	1	06.01.45	22.01.02	57	1	177	75	16.0	10.0	73	
3	8	1	1	01.07.68	06.03.02	34	1	168	68	16.0	10.0	60	
4	9	2	1	01.03.76	08.03.02	26	1	177	80	18.0	10.0	70	
5	12	2	1	01.10.84	09.03.02	17	1	170	60	17.0	10.0	80	
6	13	1	1	06.11.38	30.03.02	63	1	167	51	22.0	8.0	77	
7	14	2	1	16.07.46	02.03.02	56	1	174	70	17.0	11.0	81	
8	17	1	1	08.09.38	30.03.02	64	1	178	75	21.0	9.0	73	
9	18	2	1	17.03.38	23.03.02	64	1	168	53	18.5	12.0	73	
10	19	2	1	01.03.73	09.03.02	29	1	180	80	20.0	11.0	90	
11	20	1	1	01.04.70	13.03.02	32	1	175	74	18.0	10.0	63	
12	21	1	1	01.05.38	14.03.02	64	1	172	75	21.0	12.0	82	

Data View | Variable View

IBM SPSS Statistics Processor is ready | Unicode:OFF

Figure 1-1 Data View of Data Editor

If you have more than one data file open, there is a separate Data Editor window for each data file.

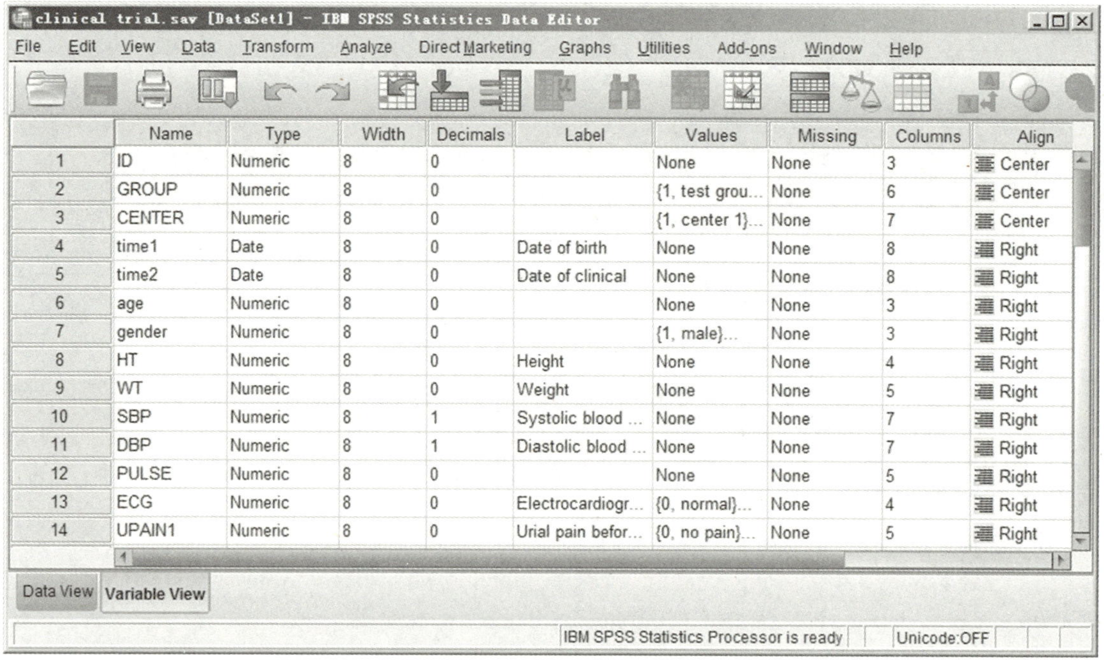

clinical trial.sav [DataSet1] - IBM SPSS Statistics Data Editor

File Edit View Data Transform Analyze Direct Marketing Graphs Utilities Add-ons Window Help

	Name	Type	Width	Decimals	Label	Values	Missing	Columns	Align
1	ID	Numeric	8	0		None	None	3	Center
2	GROUP	Numeric	8	0		{1, test grou...	None	6	Center
3	CENTER	Numeric	8	0		{1, center 1}...	None	7	Center
4	time1	Date	8	0	Date of birth	None	None	8	Right
5	time2	Date	8	0	Date of clinical	None	None	8	Right
6	age	Numeric	8	0		None	None	3	Right
7	gender	Numeric	8	0		{1, male}...	None	3	Right
8	HT	Numeric	8	0	Height	None	None	4	Right
9	WT	Numeric	8	0	Weight	None	None	5	Right
10	SBP	Numeric	8	1	Systolic blood ...	None	None	7	Right
11	DBP	Numeric	8	1	Diastolic blood ...	None	None	7	Right
12	PULSE	Numeric	8	0		None	None	5	Right
13	ECG	Numeric	8	0	Electrocardiogr...	{0, normal}...	None	4	Right
14	UPAIN1	Numeric	8	0	Urial pain befor...	{0, no pain}...	None	5	Right

Data View | Variable View

IBM SPSS Statistics Processor is ready | Unicode:OFF

Figure 1-2 Variable View of Data Editor

1.2.2 Output window (Viewer)

There are two ways to activate the Viewer:

1) Automatically activated at the first time, when you run a procedure that generates output.

2) Activation from File menu.

File

  New

    Output

The analysis results including texts, tables and charts are displayed in the Viewer. All outputs can be edited and saved for later use.

The Output window contents two parts, the "Title window" on the left and the "Result window" on the right (Figure 1-3). If you have more than one Viewer open, there will only be one Viewer window activated.

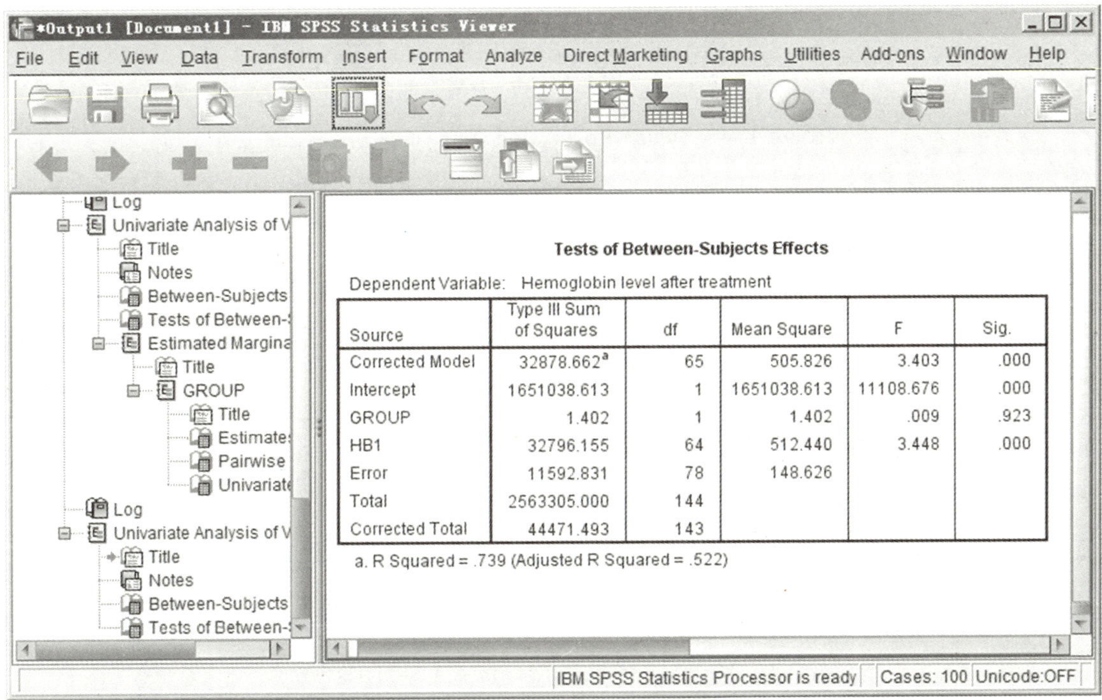

Figure 1-3 Output window for IBM SPSS 23

According to the type of outputs (text, tables or charts), there will be three output editors (Text Output Editor, Pivot Table Editor and Chart Editor) to modify the outputs.

1.2.3 Syntax Editor window

There are two ways to activate the Viewer (Figure 1-4):

1) Click the paste button on the dialog box.

2) Activation from the File menu.

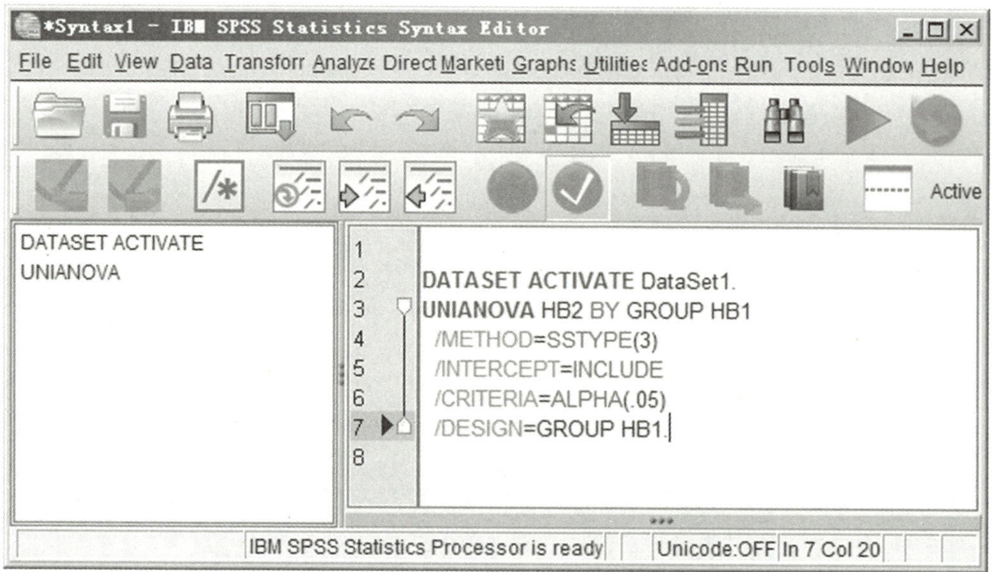

Figure 1-4 Syntax Editor window for IBM SPSS 23

File

New

Syntax

All dialog choices can be pasted into a Syntax window, where all selections made appear in the form of command syntax. Pasted commands can be then saved in a file ended with ". sps" as a suffix. The saved file can be used for future analysis or a subsequent session.

The "Syntax" allows users to conduct special features that are not available through dialog boxes by editing command syntax and avoid repeated procedures when doing large scale analysis.

1.3 Data file creation, import and export

Data files processed by the software can be classified into two categories: new dataset created by the software or existed data created by other software.

1.3.1 Data file creation

The following steps demonstrate how to create a data file with IBM SPSS software.

When the SPSS program is launched, the following window will open (Figure 1-5):

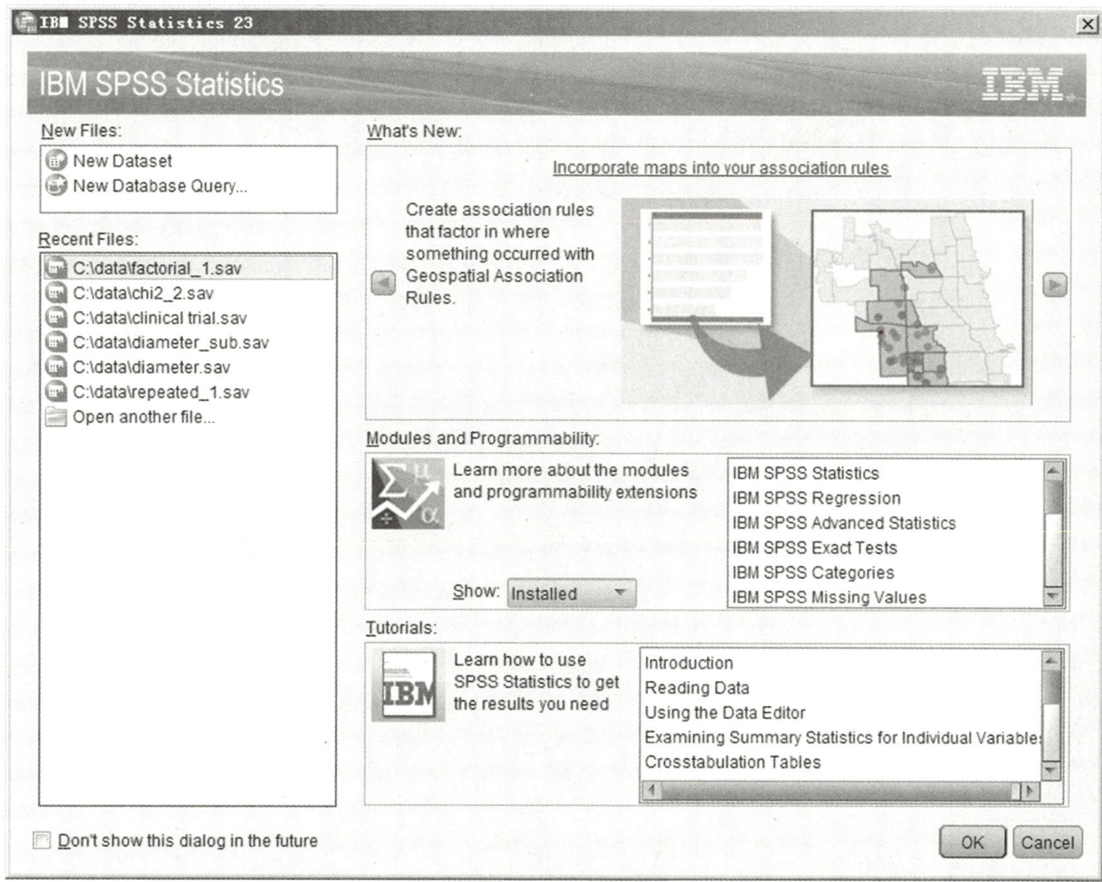

Figure 1-5 Welcome dialog of IBM SPSS 23

Select the "New Dataset" option at the "New Files" section at the left top of the dialog, and click "OK" button at the bottom of the right (Figure 1-6).

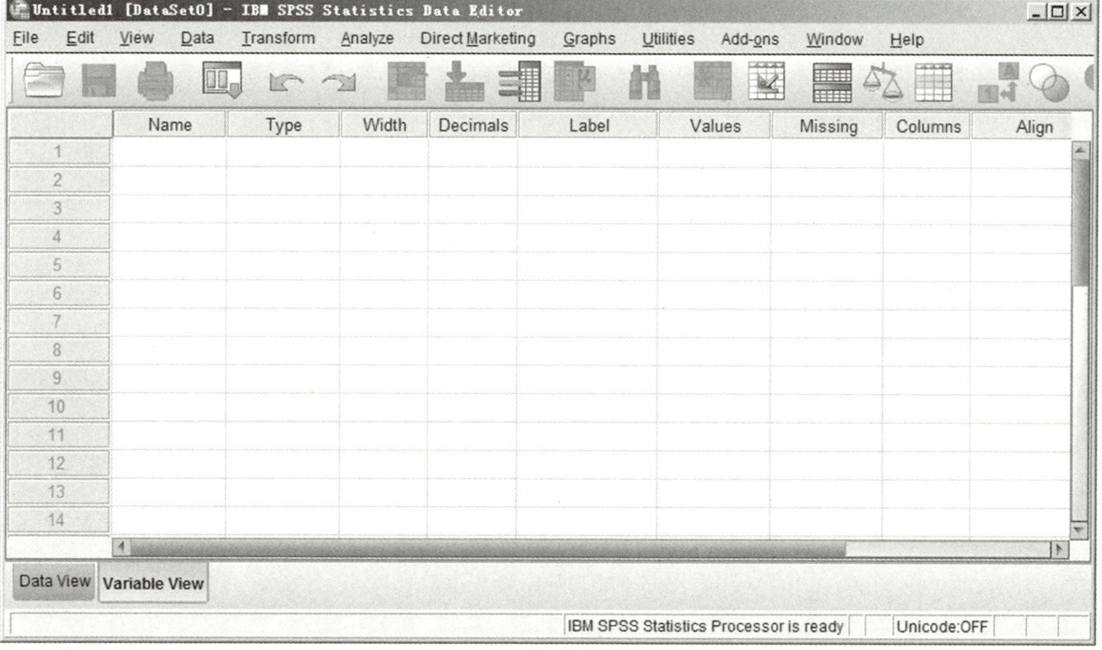

Figure 1-6 IBM SPSS 23 Data Editor

We also can simply open the Data Editor from the File menu:

File

New

Data

The dataset of IBM SPSS 23 follows a two-dimensional row-column structure. Each row stands for an observed case while each column represents a variable.

The first step to create a new dataset is to define the variable. To begin with, activate the "Variable View" by clicking the "Variable View" button at the left bottom of Data Editor. The following characters (Name, Type, Width, Decimals, Label, Values, Missing, Columns, Align, Measure, and Role) are need to be pre-specified (Figure 1-7).

	Name	Type	Width	Decimals	Label	Values	Missing	Columns	Align	Measure	Role
1											
2											
3											
4											
5											

Figure 1-7 Variable characters need to be defined (Variable View)

(1) Name: There are several restrictions for the name of a variable in IBM SPSS software.

1) The length of a variable name should no longer than 64 bites.

2) Variable name must be start with English letter, Chinese character or "@" "#" and "$". Variable name start with @ indicates a macro variable, # a temporary variable and $ system variable (which cannot be defined by users). Legal names should not be ended with "_" or ".".

3) No space or special marks (i. e. "!" "?") is allowed in variable name.

4) No IBM SPSS system key words (AND, ALL, BY, EQ, GE, GT, LE, LT, NE, NOT, OR, TO, WITH) is allowed to be used as variable names.

5) Not case intensive.

(2) Type, Width and Decimals: For the definition of Type, Width and Decimals, left click the right side of the cell located in the Type column and activate the "Variable Type" dialog box (Figure 1-8).

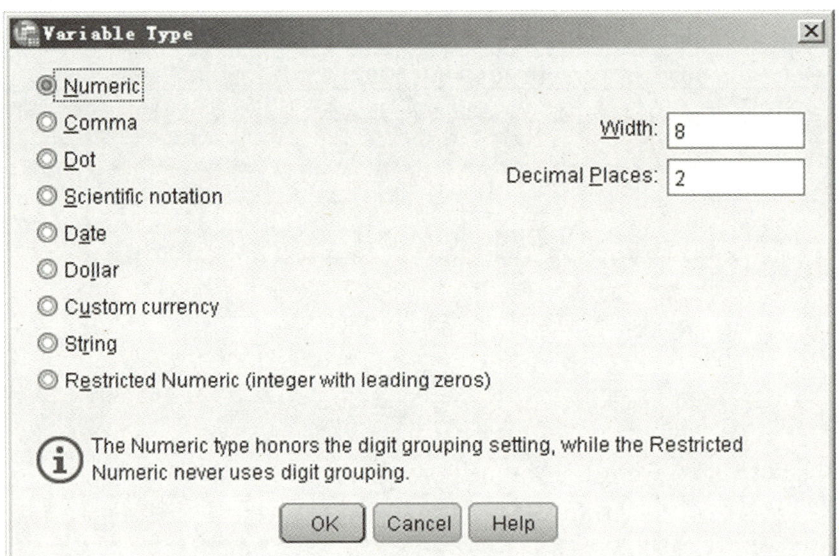

Figure 1-8 The Variable Type dialog box

Width: 8 : The width of the variable. The default width is 8.

⊙Numeric: Standardized numerical variable (system default).

◎Comma: Numeric data expressed in comma numerical variable.

◎Dot: Numeric data expressed in dot numerical variable.

◎Scientific notation: Numeric data expressed in scientific notation.

◎Date: Date variable.

◎Dollar: Numeric variable with " $ ".

◎Custom currency: Custom variable/User-defined variable.

◎String: Characters. Not involved in analysis for most cases.

◎Restricted Numeric (integer with leading zeroes): Variable for integer start with 0.

Decimal Places: 2 : Retained decimal digits. The default value is 2.

(3) Label: Variable name should be as simple as it can while label is the demonstration of the variable. Label is quite important when there are too many variables content in the same dataset especially.

(4) Values: Left click the right side of the cell located in the Value column and activate the "Value Labels" dialog box (Figure 1-9).

◇Value Labels

Value: 2

Label: Female

Entering the number in the "Value" blank and the characters it represents in the "Label" blank. Then click the "Add" button, and the number-character relation would be shown in the section under the Label blank.

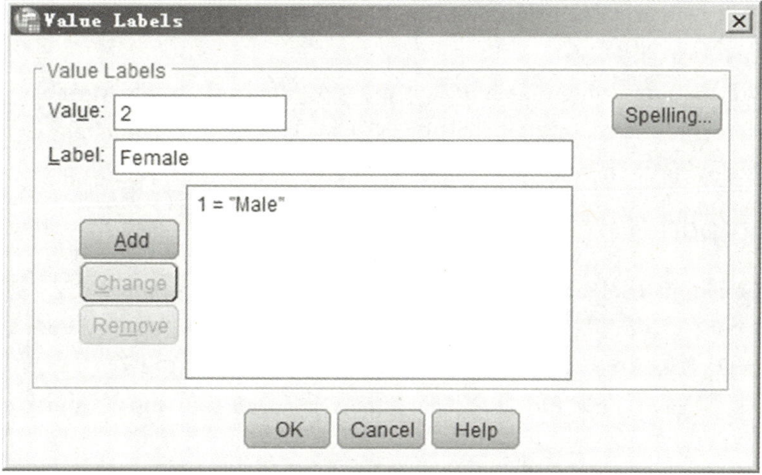

Figure 1-9 The Value Labels dialog box

(5) Missing: Left click the right side of the cell located in the Type column and activate the "Missing Values" dialog box (Figure 1-10).

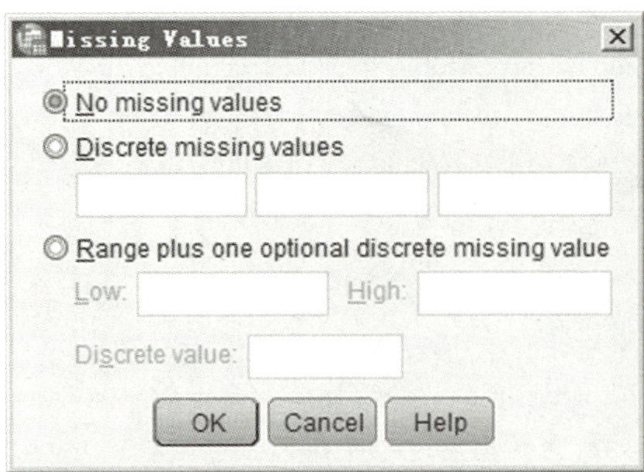

Figure 1-10 The Missing Values dialog box

⊙No missing values: All missing value will be replaced by " · ". Default option.

◎Discrete missing values: [ ] [ ] [ ] : Defined value (3 different values at most) in dataset will be regarded as missing.

◎Range plus one optional discrete missing value:

Low: [2] High: [5]

Discrete value: [7]

Value in the defined range or equal to the discrete value will be regarded as missing.

(6) Columns: Define the width of value displayed (Figure 1-7).

(7) Align: Define the alignment way (left, right or central) (Figure 1-7).

(8) Measure: Mark the variable as Scale, Ordinal or Nominal according to the precision accuracy of the data (Figure 1-7).

(9) Role: Some of the processing dialog accept pre-specified role of the variable. When they are activated, variables satisfy certain role requirement will exist in the dialog. Default role is Input, other roles include Target, Both, None, Partition and Split (Figure 1-7).

1.3.2 Data import

Data type acceptable for IBM SPSS 23 includes SPSS/PC+ (*.sys), Systat (*.syd, *.sys), Protable (*.pro), Excel (*.xls, *.xlsx, *.xlsm), Lotus (*.w*), Sylk (*.slk), dBase (*.dbf), SAS (*.sas7bdat, *.sd7, *.sd2, *.ssd01, *.ssd04, *.xpt), STATA (*.dta), ASCII (*.txt, *.dat) and *etc*.

To import SPSS (*.sav) data file, the data import is located in the "Open" submenu, under the "File" menu:

File

  Open

    Data

Select "SPSS Statistics (*.sav)" at the "Files of type" menu and all files with ".sav" as a suffixare displayed in the file window. Select the data intention to open or enter the name of data file and left click the "Open" button at the right side of the file window, the data will be imported into the Data Editor (Figure 1-11).

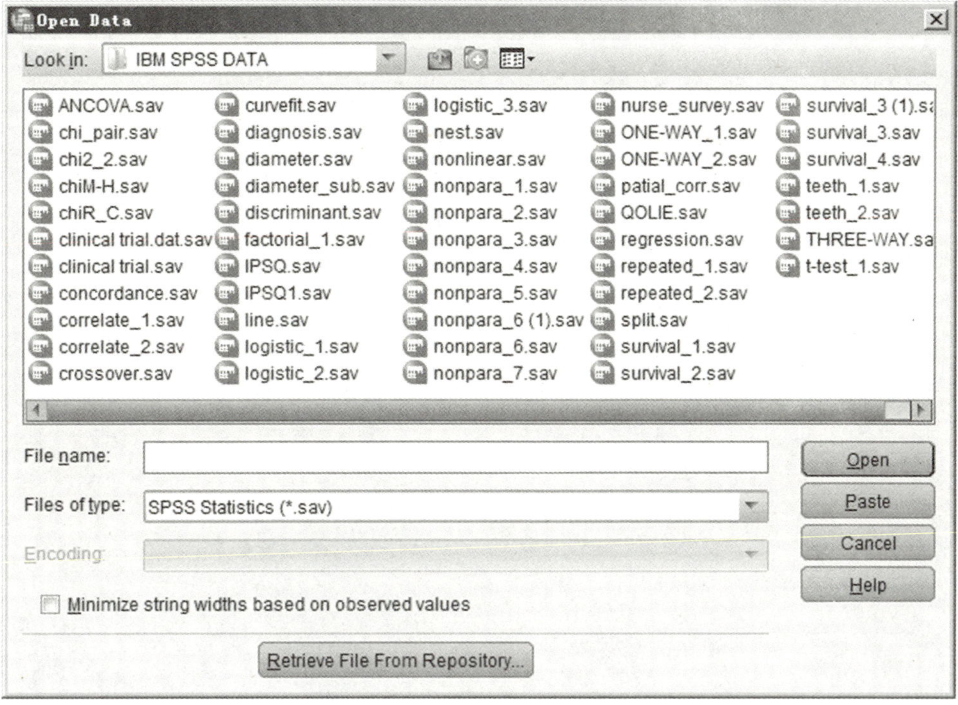

Figure 1-11 The Open Data dialog box of data import

To import ASCII (*.txt, *.dat) data file, the data import is located in the "Read Text Data" submenu, under the "File" menu:

File

Read Text Data

It also can be done through the "Open" submenu, under the "File" menu, switch the type of Files to Text (*.txt, *.dat, *.csv, *.tab) in the Open Data dialog box (Figure 1-12).

Figure 1-12 The Open Data dialog for ASCII files

By selecting the file and clicking the "Open" button, the Text Import Wizard dialog box is activated (Figure 1-13).

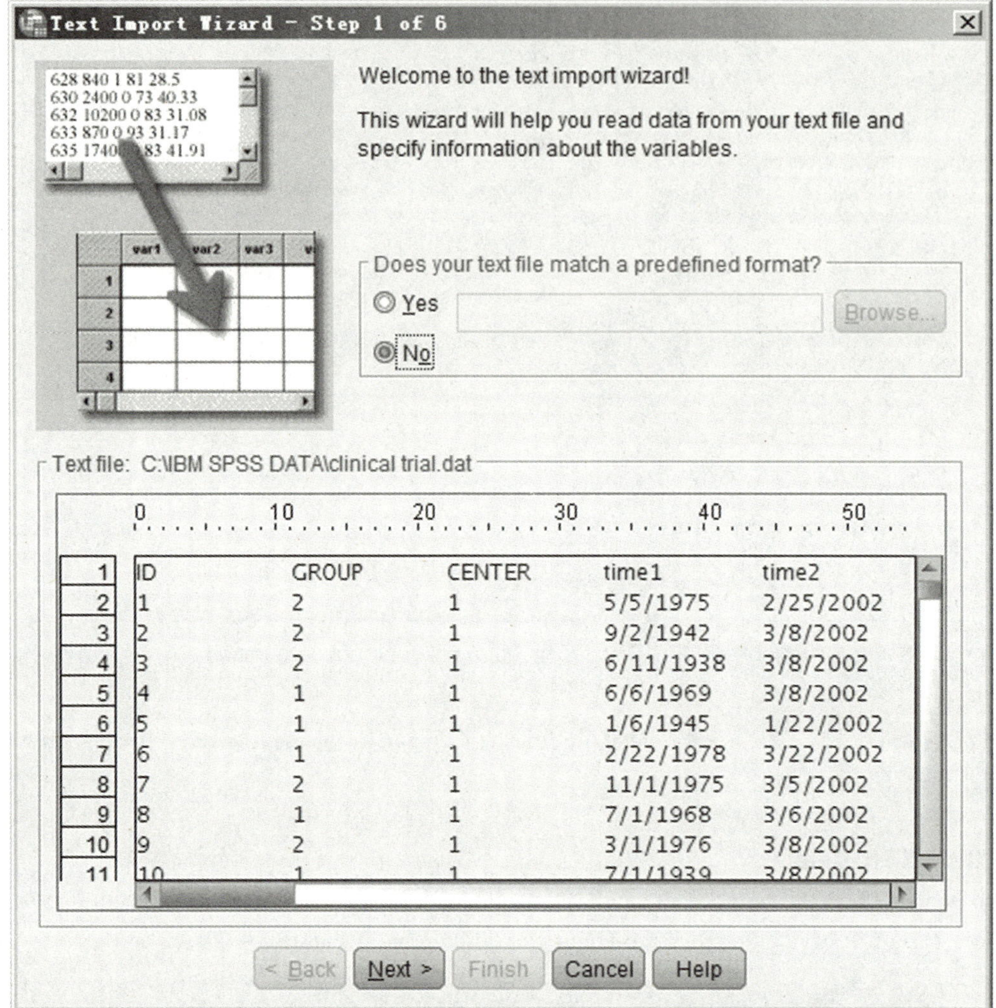

Figure 1-13 The Text Import Wizard dialog box for ASCII files (step 1)

◇Does your text file match a predefined format?

◎Yes: If select, the Brows option will be activated.

⊙No (system default)

There are six steps to import ASCII files. Each step will be done in an isolated dialog. Figure 1-13 illustrates the first step. When the first step is completed, left click the "Next" button and enter the second step (Figure 1-14).

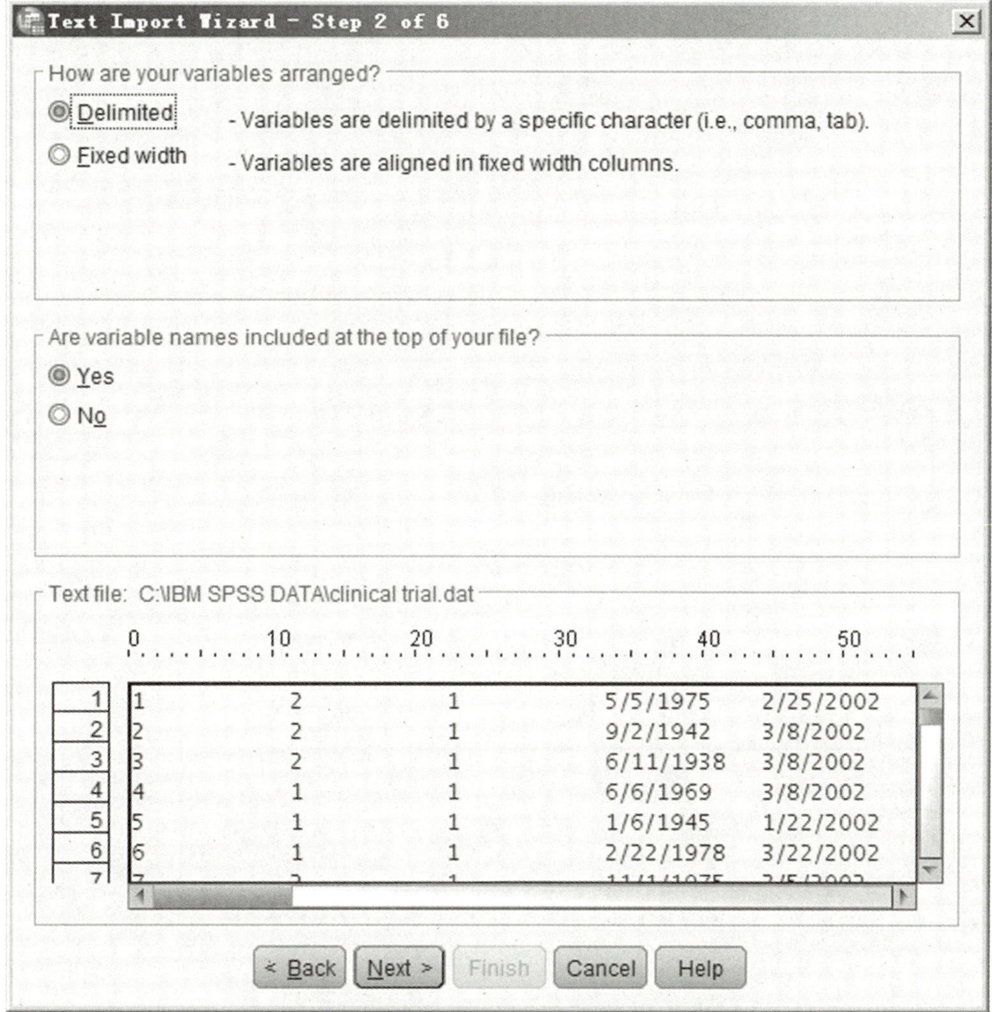

Figure 1-14 The Text Import Wizard dialog box for ASCII files (step two)

◇How are your variables arranged?

⊙Delimited:-Variables are delimited by a specific character (i. e. ,comma,tab).

◎Fixed width:-Variables are aligned in fixed-width columns.

◇Are variable names included at the top of your file?

⊙Yes:If select,the first row will be regarded as the variable names.

◎No(system default):The software will name the variables with V1,V2...automatically.

Complete step two,click the"Next" button and enter step three (Figure 1-15).

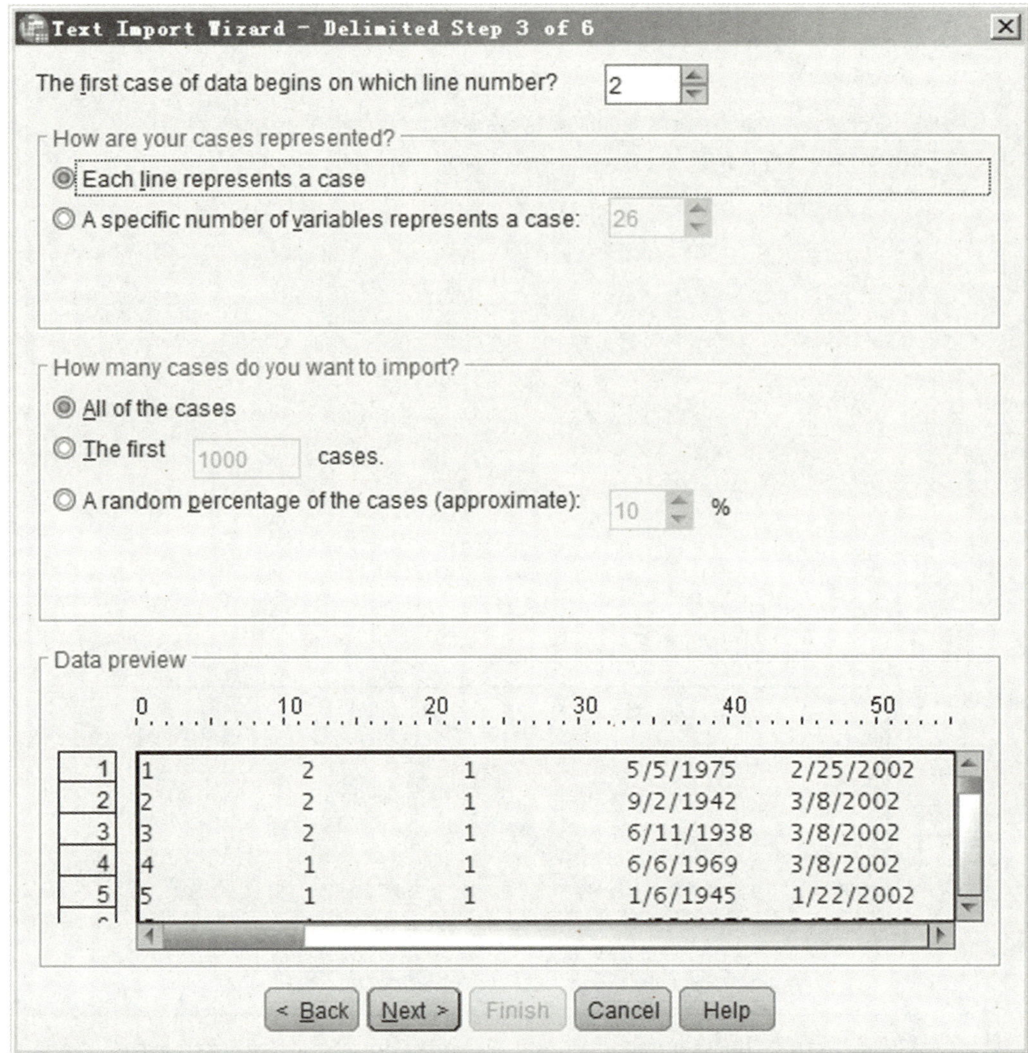

Figure 1-15 The Text Import Wizard dialog box for ASCII files (step three)

The first case of data begins on which line number? [2]: Line data begins, system default as 1. If the first line is variable name, select 2 (as in this example).

◇How are your cases represented?

⊙Each line represents a case (system default): A line for each case.

◎A specific number of variables represents a case: [26]: 26 variables represent 1 case.

◇How many cases do you want to import?

⊙All of the cases (system default): Import all cases.

◎The first [1000] cases: Import first 1 000 cases.

◎A random percentage of the cases (approximate) [10]%: Import randomly selected 10% of all cases.

Complete step three, click the "Next" button and enter step four (Figure 1-16).

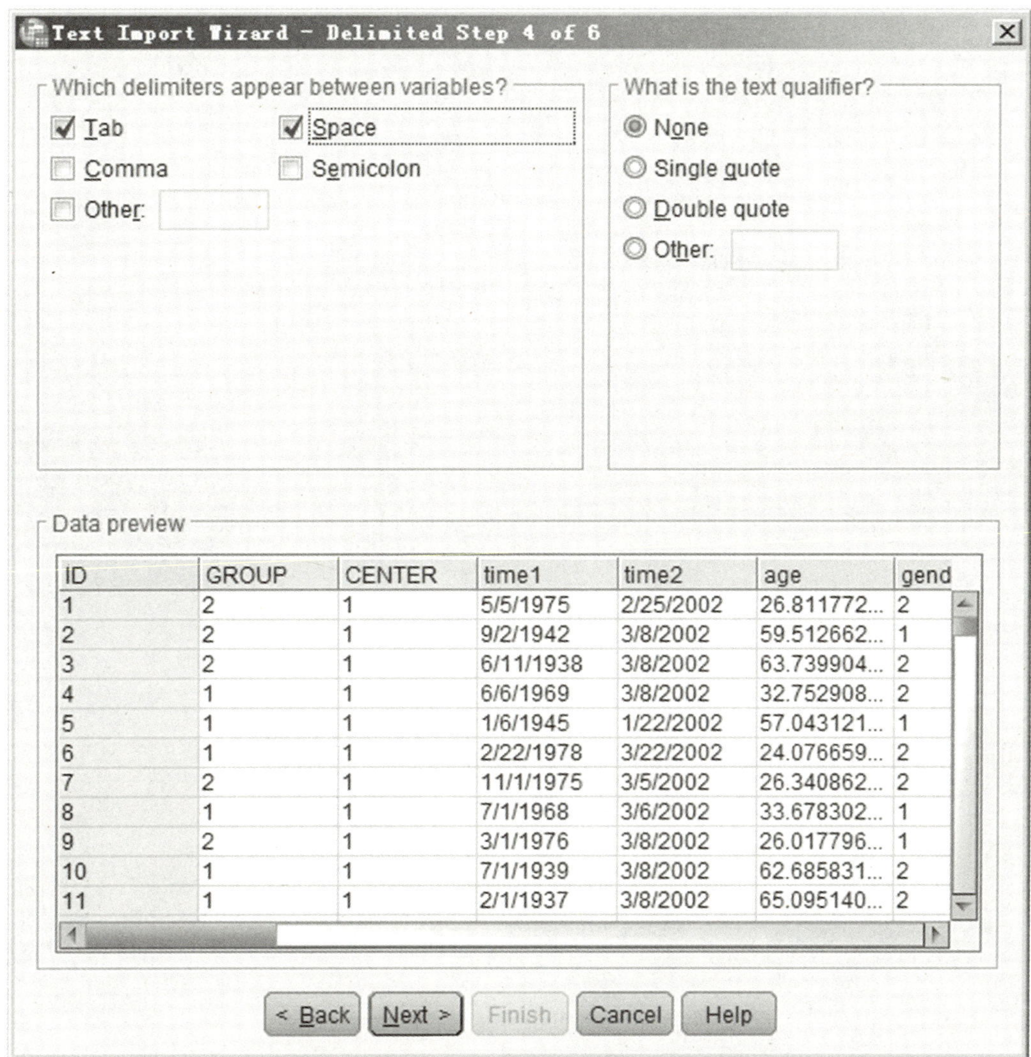

Figure 1-16 The Text Import Wizard dialog box for ASCII files (step four)

◇Which delimiters appear between variables? (Data separated by which mark?)

☑Tab(system default) ☑Space(system default)

□Comma □Semicolon

□Other: □

◇What is the text qualifier? (What is the modifier for character variables?)

⊙None(system default)

◎Single quote

◎Double quote

◎Other: □

Complete step four, click the "Next" button and enter step five (Figure 1-17).

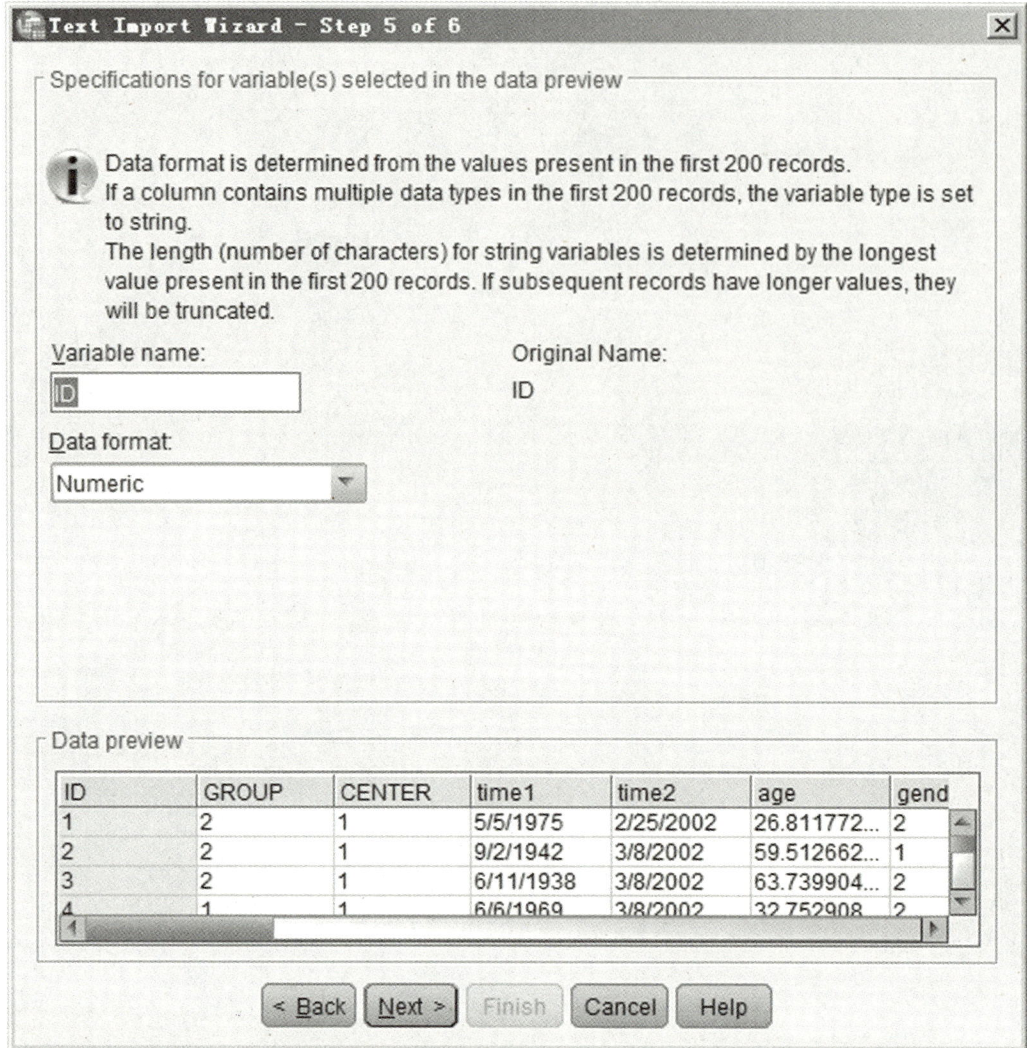

Figure 1-17 The Text Import Wizard dialog box for ASCII files (step five)

◇Specifications for variable(s) selected in the data preview.

Variable name: ID Original Name:

Data format: Numeric ID

User can chose variables need to be modified from the data preview section and make adjustments in the "Specification for variable(s) selected in the data preview" section.

Complete step five, click the "Next" button and enter step six (Figure 1-18).

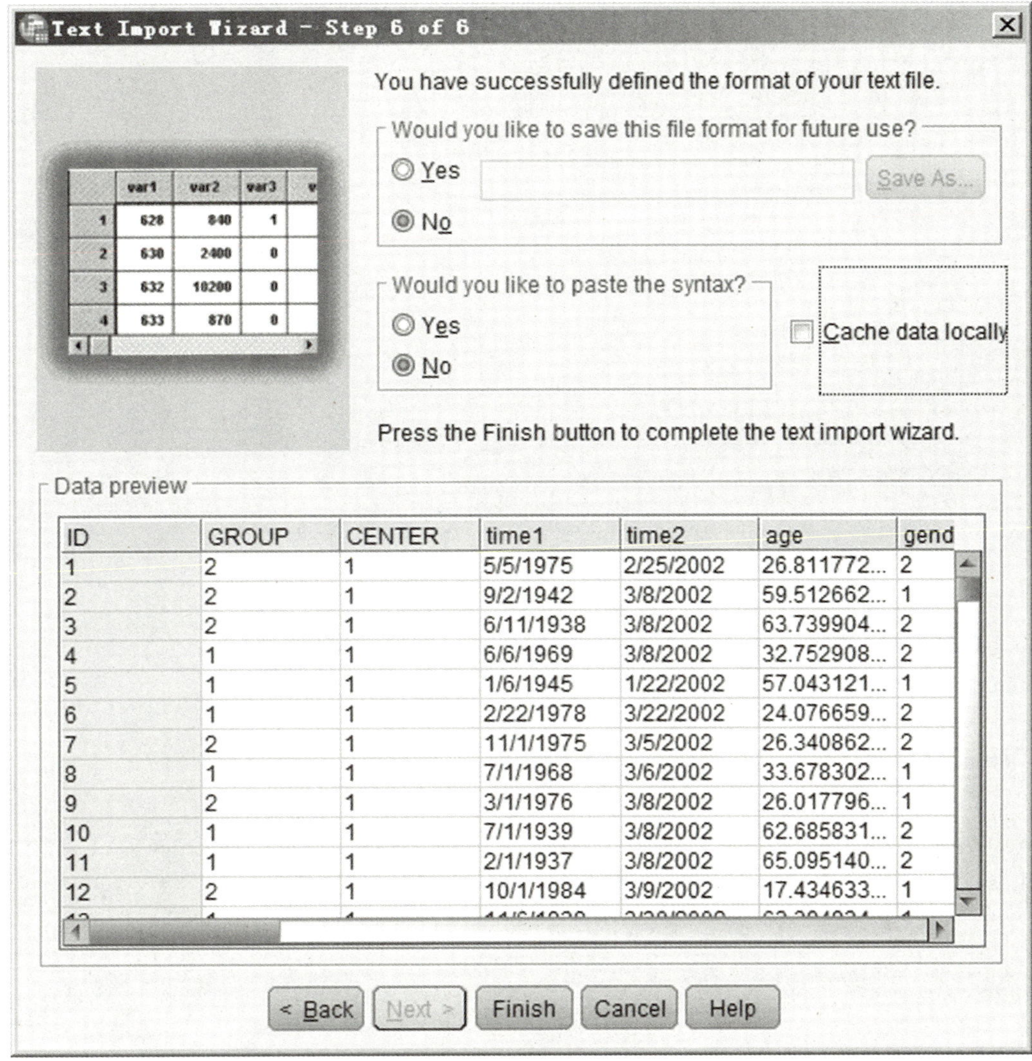

Figure 1-18 The Text Import Wizard dialog box for ASCII files (step six)

◇Would you like to save this file format for future use?

◎Yes: If select, the "Save As" option will be activated.

⊙No(system default)

◇Would you like to paste the syntax?

◎Yes: If select, the imported procedure will be pasted into a syntax file.

⊙No(system default)

□Cache data locally: Caching data locally. System default as selected, in this example it is unnecessary.

Complete step six, click the "Finish" button. The data import procedure has been done, and the data are displayed in the Data Editor(Figure 1-19).

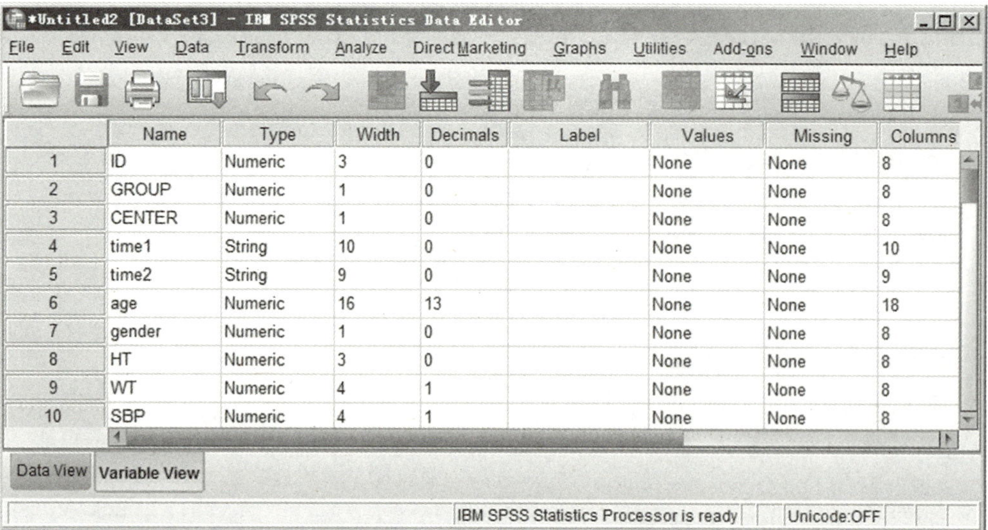

Figure 1-19 The imported ASCII file

To import Excel (*.xls) data file, the data import is located in the "Open" submenu, under the "File" menu:

File

Open

Data

Switch the Files of type to Excel (*.xls, *.xlsx, *.xlsm) in the Open Data dialog (Figure 1-20). Select the file and left click the "Open" button, then the "Opening Excel Data Source" dialog box is activated (Figure 1-21).

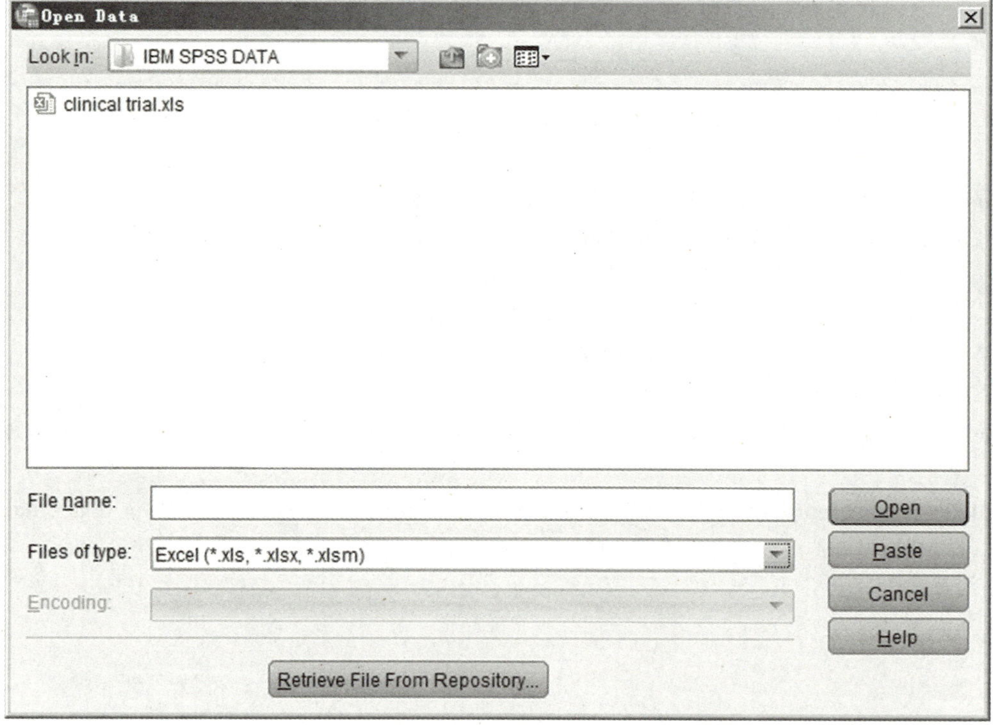

Figure 1-20 Open Data dialog box for excel files

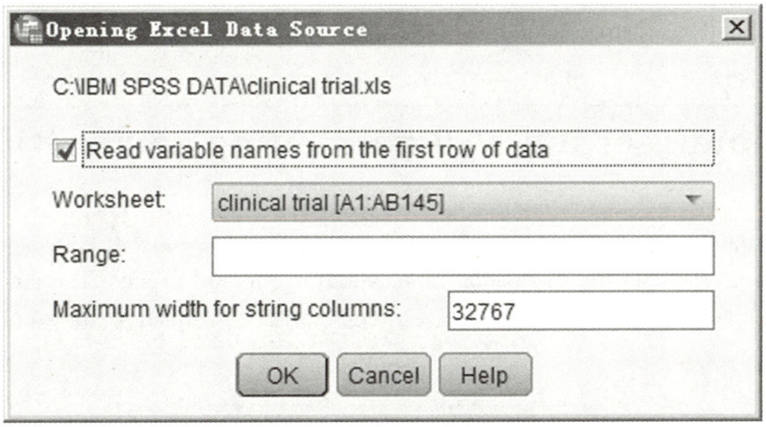

Figure 1-21 Opening Excel Data Source dialog box

☑Read variable names from the first row of data. Regard the first line as variable name. If not select, then the variables will be named with V1, V2... automatically (system default).

Click "OK", and the data will be displayed in the Data Editor.

1.3.3 Data export

IBM SPSS 23 can save data into formats including SPSS Statistics (*. sav), SPSS/PC+ (*. sys), Tab delimited (*. dat), Fixed ASCII (*. dat), Comma delimited (*. csv), Sylk (*. slk), Systat (*. syd, *. sys), SAS (*. sas7bdat, *. sd7, *. sd2, *. ssd01, *. ssd04, *. xpt), STATA (*. dta), 1-2-3 Rel (*. wk3, *. wk1, *. wks) and *etc.*

Data export is located in the "Save/Save As" submenu, under the "File" menu (Figure 1-22):

File

Save/Save As

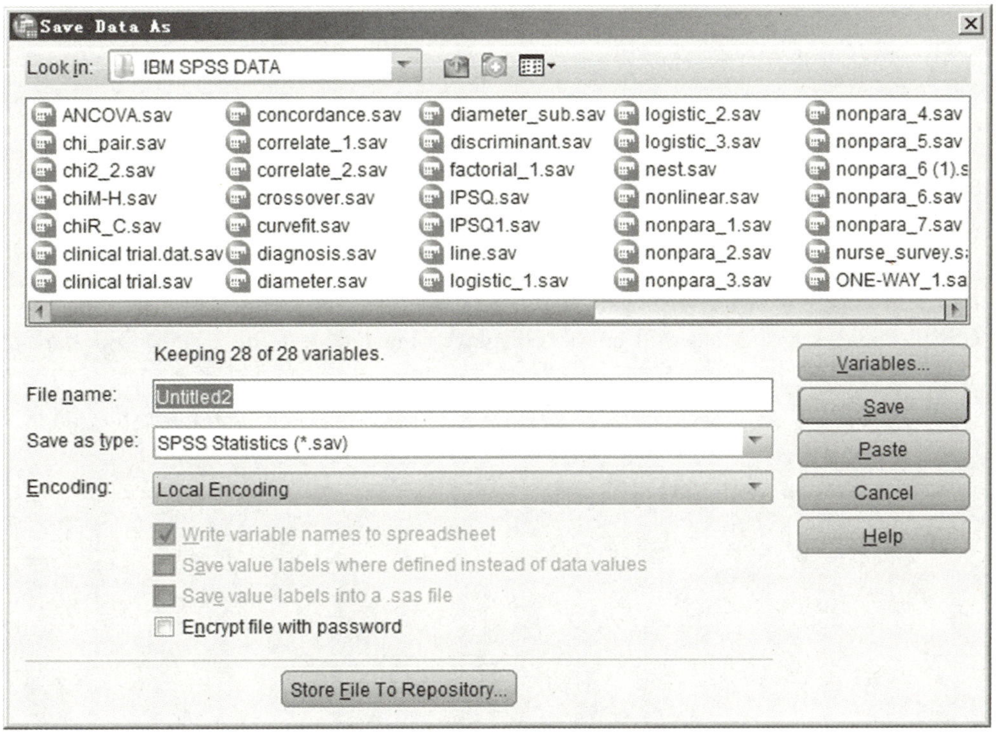

Figure 1-22 Save Data As dialog box

File name: Entering file name of the saved file.
Save as type: Select saved file type.

1.4 Attribute setting of data reading and writing

Restrictions on data reading and writing have been added to the software since version 12.0. It provides ideal protection to the data file in case of unrecovered operations on data. The attribute setting of data reading and writing is located in the "Mark File Read Only/Mark File Read Write" under the "File" menu (Figure 1-23):

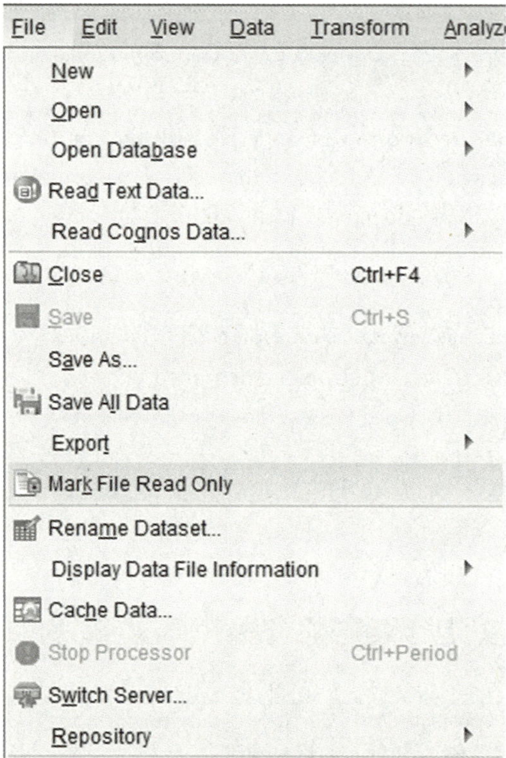

Figure 1-23 Attribute setting of data reading and writing

As shown in Figure 1-23, the current dataset is available for both reading and writing. If click "Mark File Read Only", changes of the data will only be displayed but unable to be saved to the dataset.

Chen Fangyao, Guan Ying

Chapter 2

Data Management

Before you do any data analysis, it is most likely that you need to manage your dataset to make it suitable for subsequent analysis. For example, you may need to derive a new variable from one or several original variables by grouping or calculating percentage, *etc*. Sometime you may need to reformat the dataset through data transpose, or recode variables to facilitate selection of subsets for analysis, or combine the datasets from different source files. Hence, this chapter serves as a foundation for you to know how to use SPSS.

Here we use the file "Clinical trial. sav" as the example. After clicking "Data" in main menu, the "Data" submenu pops out (Figure 2 - 1), which consists of options covering three aspects of data management: data edition, data structure and data selection.

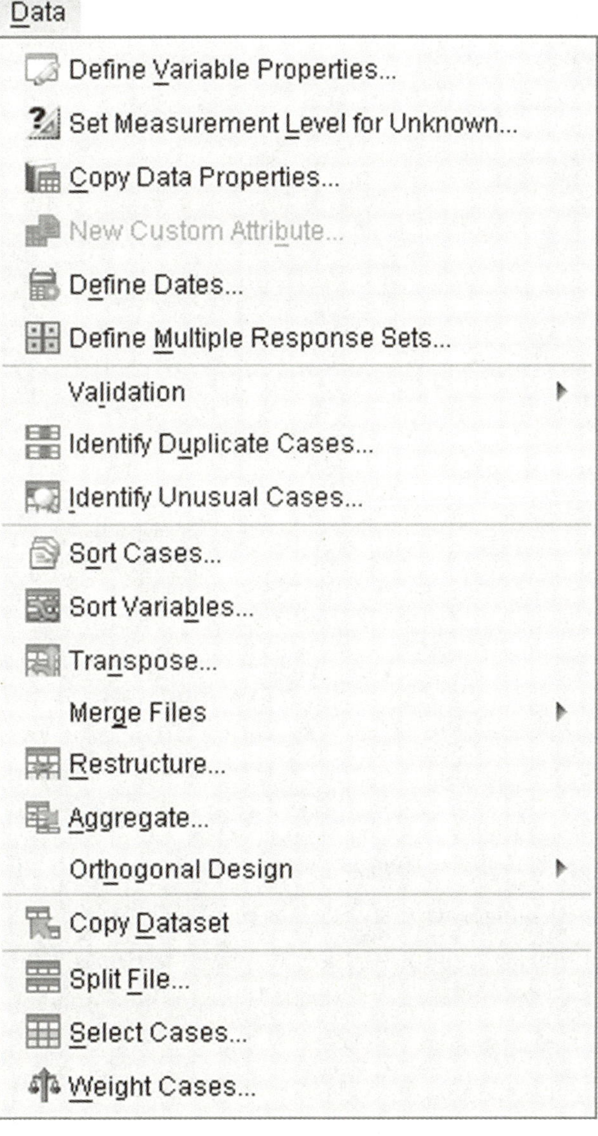

Figure 2-1 The Data submenu

2.1 Data Edition

2.1.1 Define Variable Properties

In "Data View", select from the menu:

Data

Define Variable Properties

The Define Variable Properties dialog box pops out (Figure 2-2), in which we can select variables.

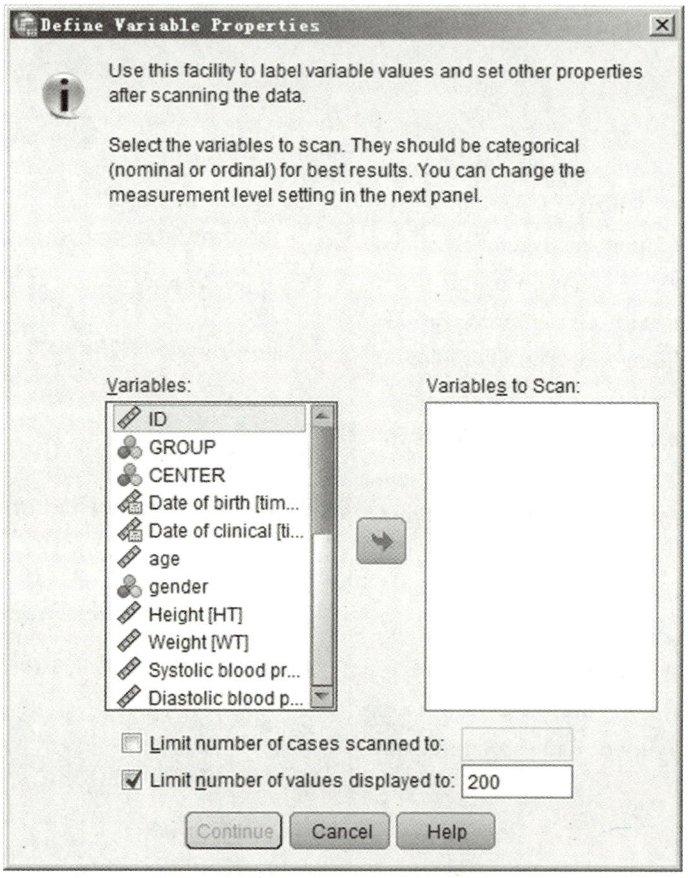

Figure 2-2 The Define Variable Properties dialog box(1)

◇Variables to Scan: Variables that need to scan.

□Limit number of cases scanned to: [ ]: Limit number of cases to scan.

☑Limit number of values displayed to: [200]: Restrict number of displayed values. The default limit is 200, *etc.*, the screen only displays the first 200 different values.

After clicking "Continue", the Define Variable Properties dialog box pops out (Figure 2-3).

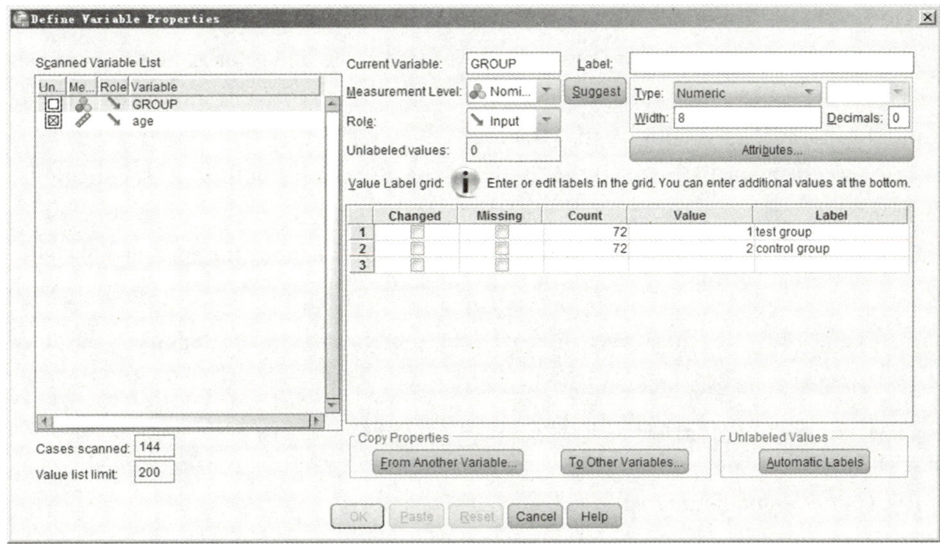

Figure 2-3 The Define Variable Properties dialog box(2)

◇Scanned Variable List:List of scanned variables.

1)Current Variable:The variable currently selected for editing.

2)Label:The label of current variable.

3)Measurement Level:There are three categories, nominal, ordinal and quantitative variables. The system default is quantitative variable. If user are not sure about the measurement level, click "Suggest" to get a detailed explanation (Figure 2-4). In Figure 2-4, the current measurement level of "AGE_G" is an ordinal variable (i. e. this variable has an intrinsic order), and the system suggests either ordinal or nominal variables for users to choose. If user choose the default, the measurement level of the variable "GROUP" is still defined as an ordinal variable after clicking "Continue".

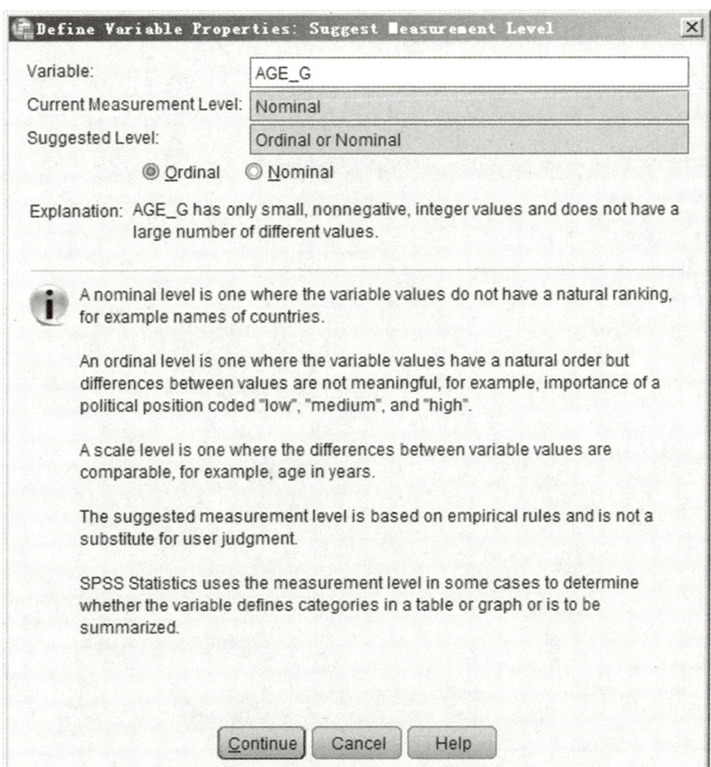

Figure 2-4 The Suggest Measurement Level dialog box

4) Type: The available options are standard numeric variable, comma numeric variable, dot numeric variable, scientific notation, date variable, numerical variable with dollar mark, custom variable (Currency), percent variable, and character variable (String). You can also specify the width and decimal points by entering the integers in the "Width" and "Decimal" boxes.

5) Role: The default option is Input. In addition, there are options Output or Target, Both, None, Partition, and Split.

6) Attributes: Set the variable attribute. Click this button to customize the increase or decrease of variable attributes.

7) Unlabeled values ☐: The values without labels or marks. In the Scanned Variable List, ☐ denotes labeled variables, and ☒denotes unlabeled variables.

8) Changed: If the label is changed, the box under "Changed" is correspondingly shown as ☑.

9) Missing: If a row is selected (☑), the corresponding values in this row is defined as missing values.

10) Count: Count the numbers of each category for variables.

11) Value: Value of a variable.

12) Label: Label a variable.

13) Cases Scanned: [144]: The number of cases that have been scanned. For example, [144] means that 144 cases have been scanned.

14) Value list limit: [200]: Maximum tolerance count of different displayed values, by default, is 200.

15) Copy Properties: The properties can be copied from another variables.

16) Unlabeled Values: You may click "Automatic Labels" to create automatic labels for those unlabeled values.

2.1.2 Set Measurement Level for Unknown

In "Data View", select from the menu:

Data

Set Measurement Level for Unknown

The Set Measurement Level for Unknown dialog box pops out (Figure 2-5). Variables without known measurement level can be selected in the nominal, ordinal or continuous variable box. Then click "OK".

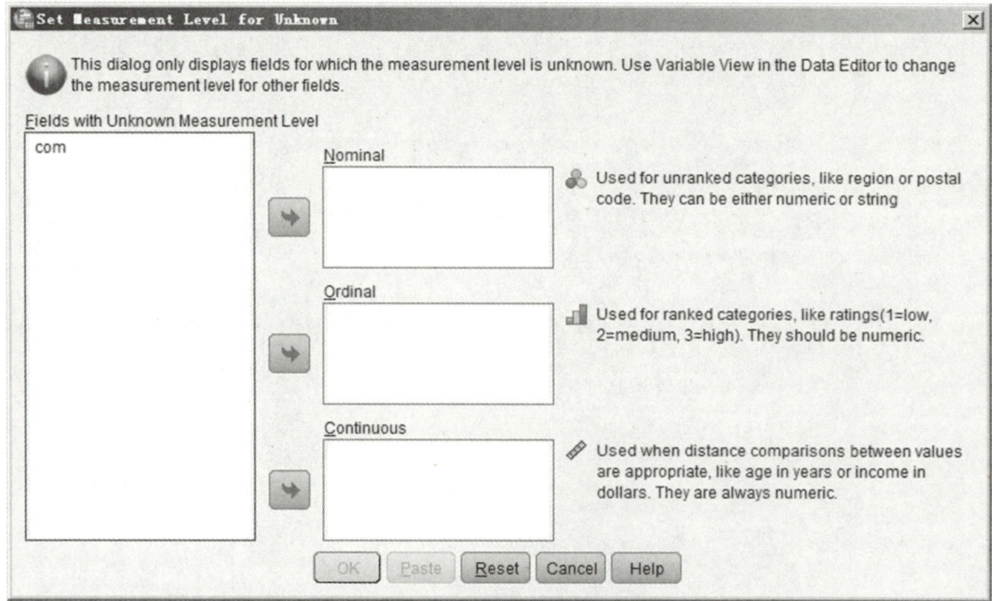

Figure 2-5 The Set Measurement Level for Unknown dialog box

2.1.3 Copy Data Properties

Select from the menu:

Data

Copy Data Properties

The Copy Data Properties dialog box pops out (Figure 2-6). There are five steps, each of which is shown in a separate dialog box.

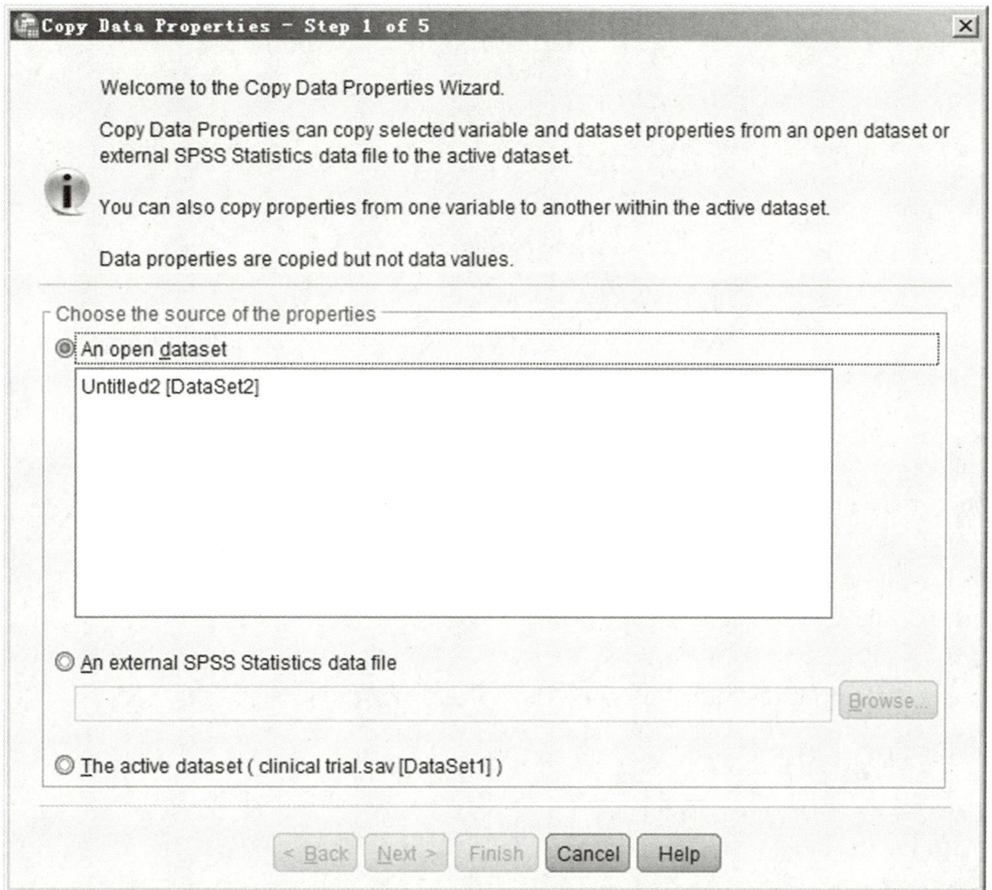

Figure 2-6 The Copy Data Properties dialog box

◇Choose the source of the properties.

⊙An open dataset(sytem default): Choose this if the source of the properties is from a currently open dataset.

◎An external SPSS Statistics data file: Click "Browse" to import data files.

◎The active dataset (clinical trial. sav [DataSet1]): The file name of currently active dataset is "clinical trial. sav". The active dataset can be different from the open dataset.

2.1.4 New Custom Attribute

In "Variable View", select from the menu:

Data

New Custom Attribute

The New Custom Attribute dialog box pops out(Figure 2-7).

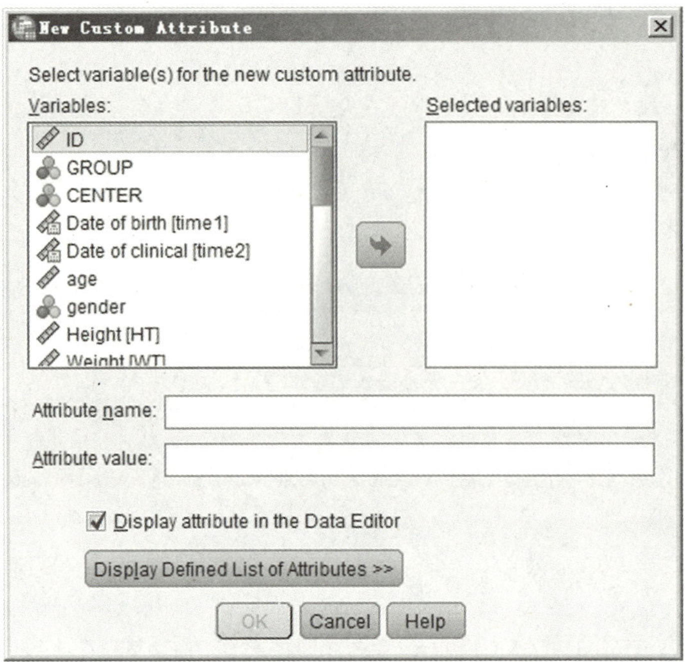

Figure 2-7 The New Custom Attribute dialog box

1) Variables: List of all variables in the dataset.

2) Selected variables: Variables selected for new custom attribute.

3) Attribute name: To set the attribute name of the selected variable.

4) Attribute value: To set the attribute value of the selected variable.

5) ☑Display attribute in the Data Editor.

6) Display Defined List of Attributes/Hide Defined List of Attributes.

2.1.5 Define Dates

In "Data View", select from the menu:

Data

Define Dates

The Define Dates dialog box pops out (Figure 2-8).

1) Cases Are: A list of time format options.

2) First Case Is: Define the start date and time. Here we choose the format of "Years, Quarters, Months" under "Cases Are" and define the start time as the first month of the first quarter in 2004. Note: the quarter cannot be set greater than 4, the month cannot be set greater than 12. The maximum variables are also shown in this dialog box.

After clicking "OK", four columns of new default variables are generated. An underline is added after the original name of each variable to create a new explanatory variable named by default as DATE_.

In this case, the first three columns are YEAR_, QUARTER_, and MONTH_. The fourth column is a character variable DATE_, after combining the first three columns (Figure 2-9).

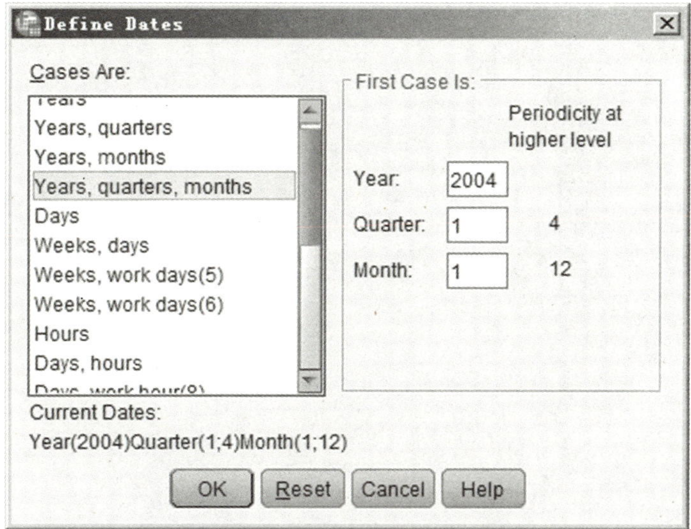

Figure 2-8 The Define Dates dialog box

YEAR_	QUARTER_	MONTH_	DATE_
2004	1	1	JAN 2004
2004	1	2	FEB 2004
2004	1	3	MAR 2004
2004	2	4	APR 2004
2004	2	5	MAY 2004
2004	2	6	JUN 2004
2004	3	7	JUL 2004

Figure 2-9 The tables shown after the Define Dates procedure

2.1.6 Define Multiple Response Sets

In "Data View", select from the menu:

Data

Define Multiple Response Sets

The Define Multiple Response Sets dialog box pops out (Figure 2-10).

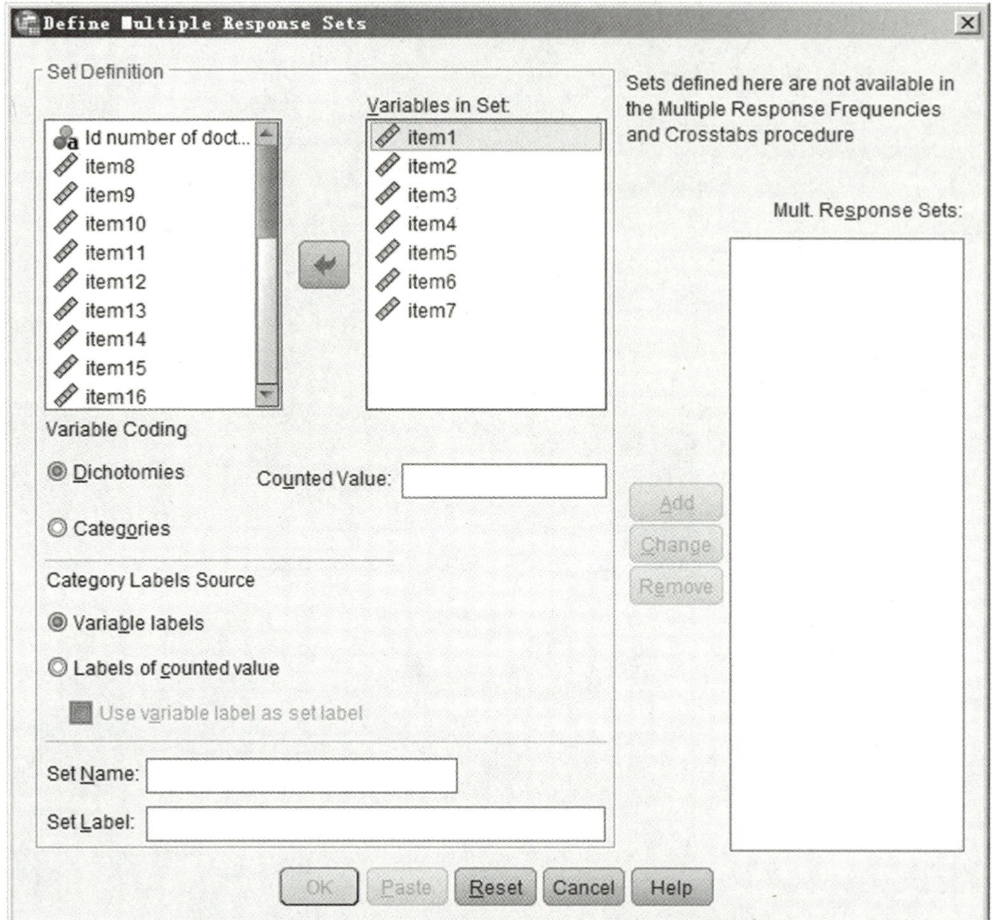

Figure 2-10 The Define Multiple Response Sets dialog box

2.2 Data Validation

By taking the Data Validation procedure, we can quickly check the validity of values and variables, which is particularly useful for data analysis of large clinical trials. Predefined validation rules can be retrieved by clicking "Data/Validation/Load" in the menu. Because predefined rules cannot be universally applied for different data, customized validate rules are more often used in practice. The validation process of single-variable rules and cross-variable rules is described with the data file "clinical trial. sav" as the example. Here we use two sample rules: ①single variable rules: age ranges from 18 to 65 (years old); ②cross-variable rules: female and weight≥70 kg.

Select from menu:

Data

Validation

Define Rules

The Defined Validation Rules dialog box pops out (Figure 2-11), which consists of two check boxes: Single-Variable Rules and Cross-Variable Rules.

◇Rule Definition: Define a rule (Figure 2-11).

1) Name: The name of rule can be imported directly from variable names in dataset or be customized. Here the variable "age" is selected.

2) Type: The variable value can be of three different types: Numeric, Character, and Date. In this example, the variable value is Numeric. For Date variables, different formats can be selected.

3) Valid Values: There are two options for valid values, "Specific value" and "Within a range". Here we select "Within a range", and put 18 and 65 into the Minimum and Maximum boxes, respectively.

☑Allow noninteger values within range: noninteger values will be allowed within the selected range.

☑Allow user-missing values: user-missing values will be allowed.

☑Allow system-missing values: system-missing values will be allowed.

Rules can be managed by clicking New, Duplicate, and Delete.

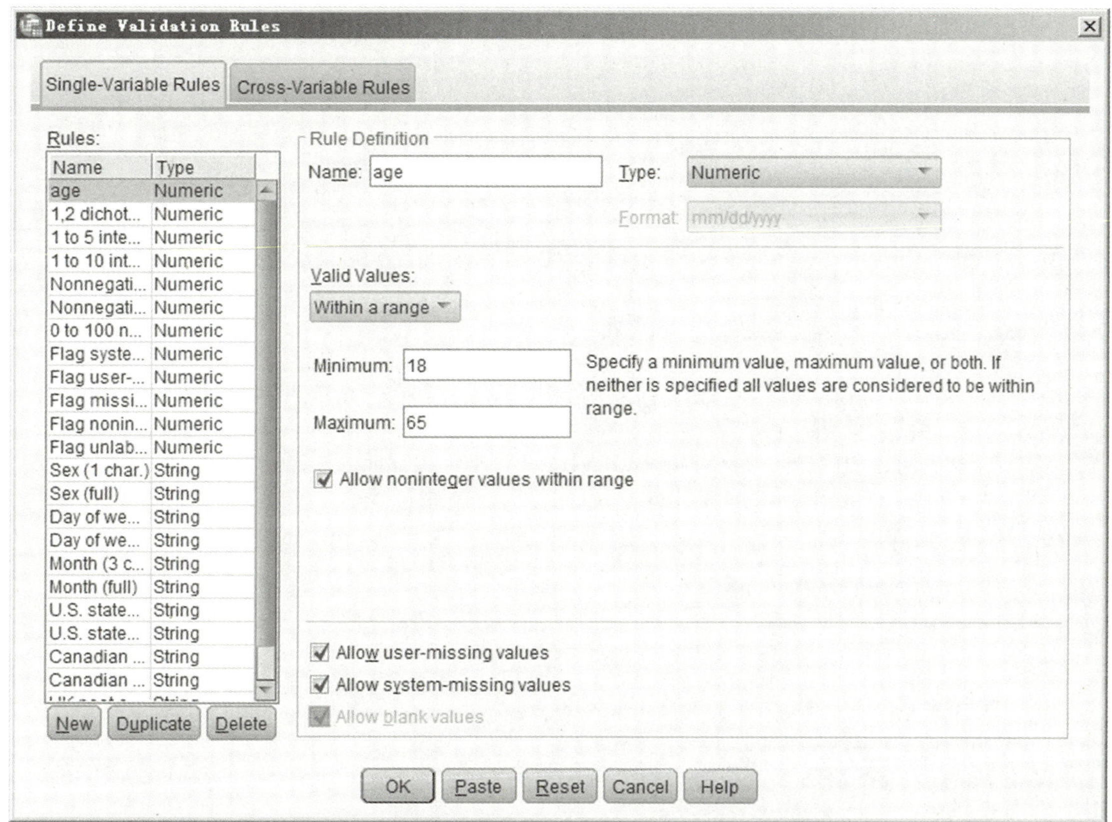

Figure 2-11 The Define Validation Rules Single-variable Rules dialog box

Cross-Variable Rules: The rules are applicable to multiple variables (Figure 2-12).

Logical Expression (should evalvate to 1 for an invalid case): mark the invalid entries as "1". Click "Insert" to select the variable needs to be validated. Then enter "(gender = 2) & (WT >= 70)" in the Logical Expression box.

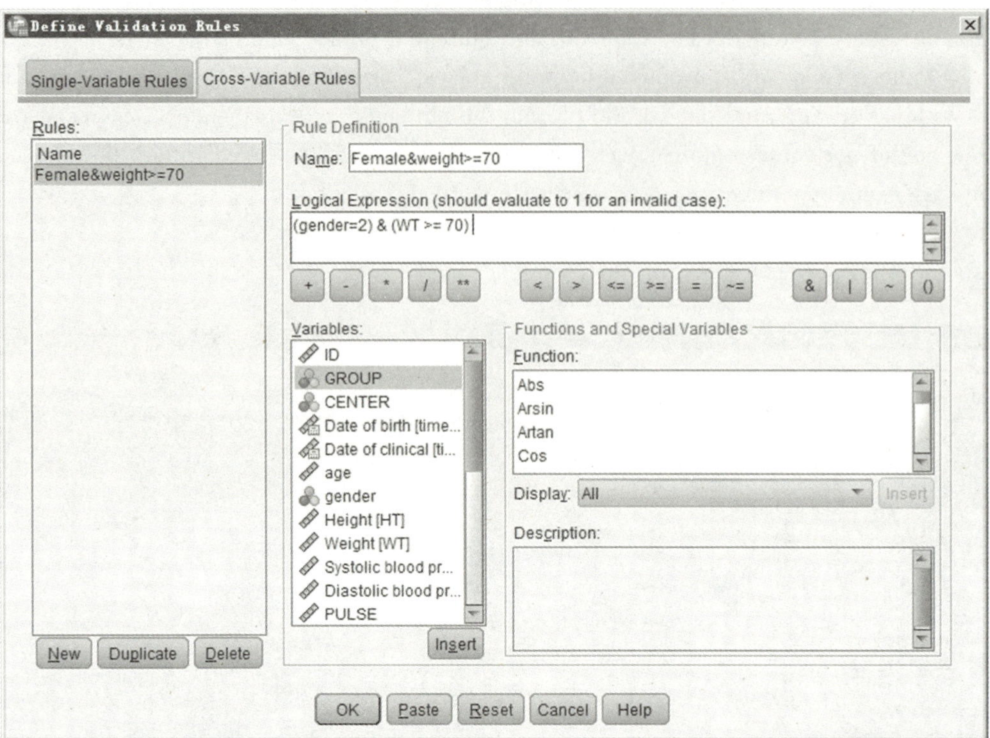

Figure 2-12 The Define Validation Rules: Cross-Variable Rules dialog box

(1) Single-Variable Rules: An age range of 18 to 65 (years old).

The validation process is as follows.

Select from menu:

Data

Validation

Validate Data

The Validate Data dialog box pops out (Figure 2-13).

1) Variables

Analysis Variables: For single variable data, the variables for analyzing can be selected directly into this box. Here "age" is selected.

Case Identifier Variables: Here "ID" and "CENTER" are selected. Check if the unique variable repeats.

2) Basic Check: Click "Basic Checks" and then the Basic Checks dialog box pops out (Figure 2-14).

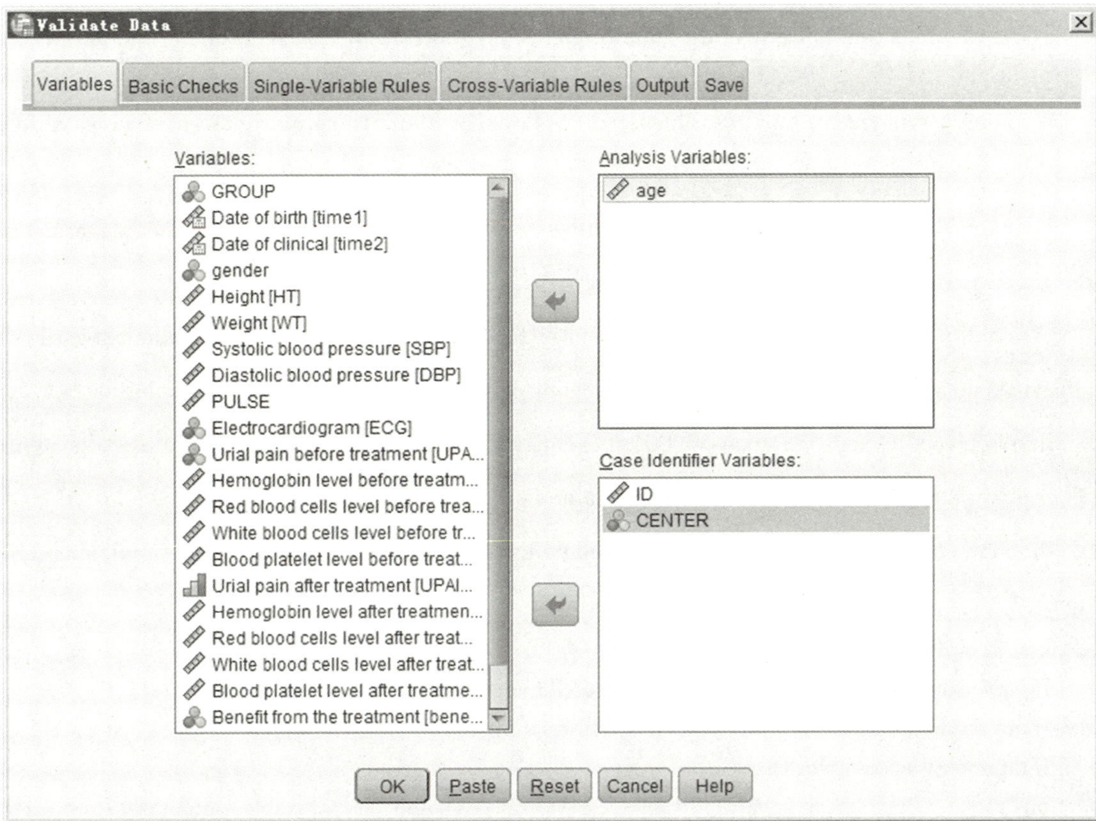

Figure 2-13 The Validate Data dialog box

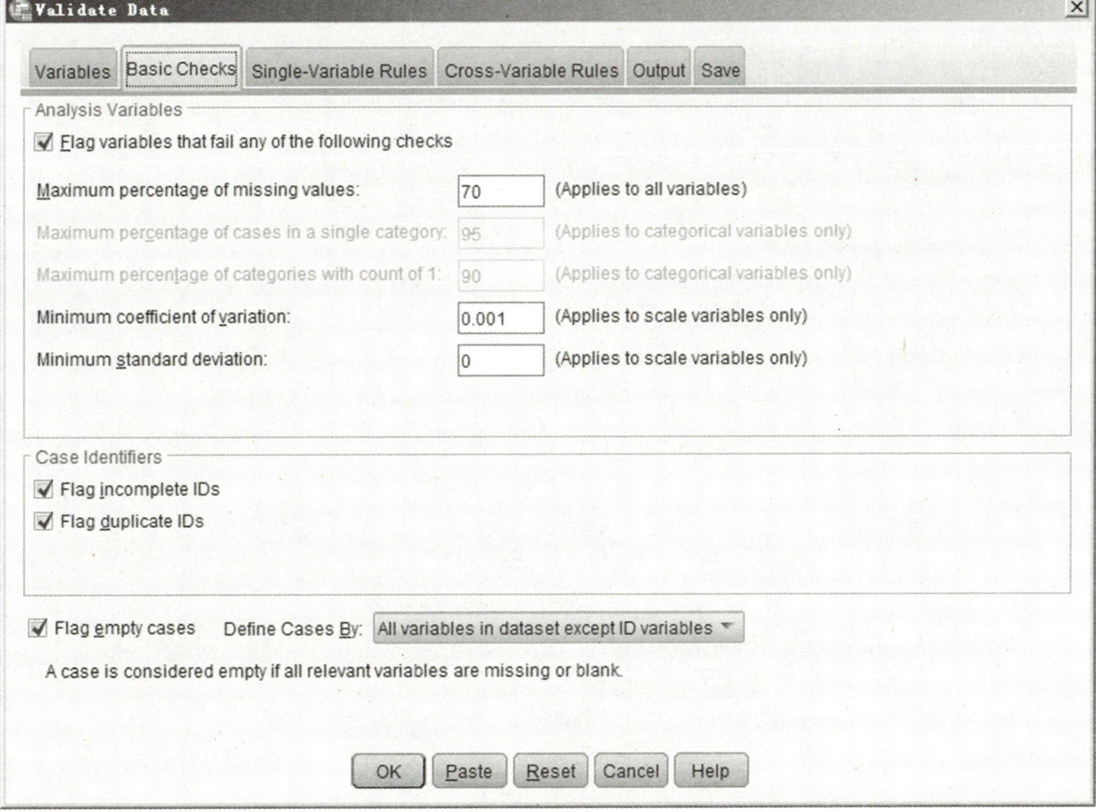

Figure 2-14 The Validate Data: Basic Checks dialog box

◇Analysis Variables: Variables under analysis.

☑Flag variables that fail any of the following checks: The variables false to one of the following conditions will be labeled (i. e. , flagged).

Maximum percentage of missing values: [70]: For all variables, the maximum percentage of missing values is [ ], and the default value is [70].

Maximum percentage of cases in a single category [95]: This code only applies to categorical variables, the maximum percentage for a single category is [ ], and the default value is [95].

Maximum percentage of categories with count of 1: [90]: This code only applies to categorical variables, the maximum percentage of categories with count of 1 is [ ], and the default value is [90].

Minimum coefficientof variation: [0. 001]: This code only applies to scale variables, the minimum coefficient of variation is [ ], and the default value is [0. 001].

Minimum standard deviation: [0]: This code only applies to scale variables, the minimum standard deviation is [ ], and the default value is [0].

◇Case Identifiers.

☑Flag incomplete IDs: The incomplete IDs will be flagged.

☑Flag duplicate IDs: The duplicate IDs will be flagged.

☑Flag empty cases: The cases with empty cells will be flagged.

Options include "All analysis variables except ID variables" and "All variables in dataset except ID variables". Notice that a case is excluded from analysis only if all its relevant variables are missing or blank.

3) Single-Variable Rules: The selected variable names as shown in Figure 2-15, and the Distribution diagram, Maximum value, Minimum value and Validate rule of the variable are displayed. Click "Define Rules" to modify the rules.

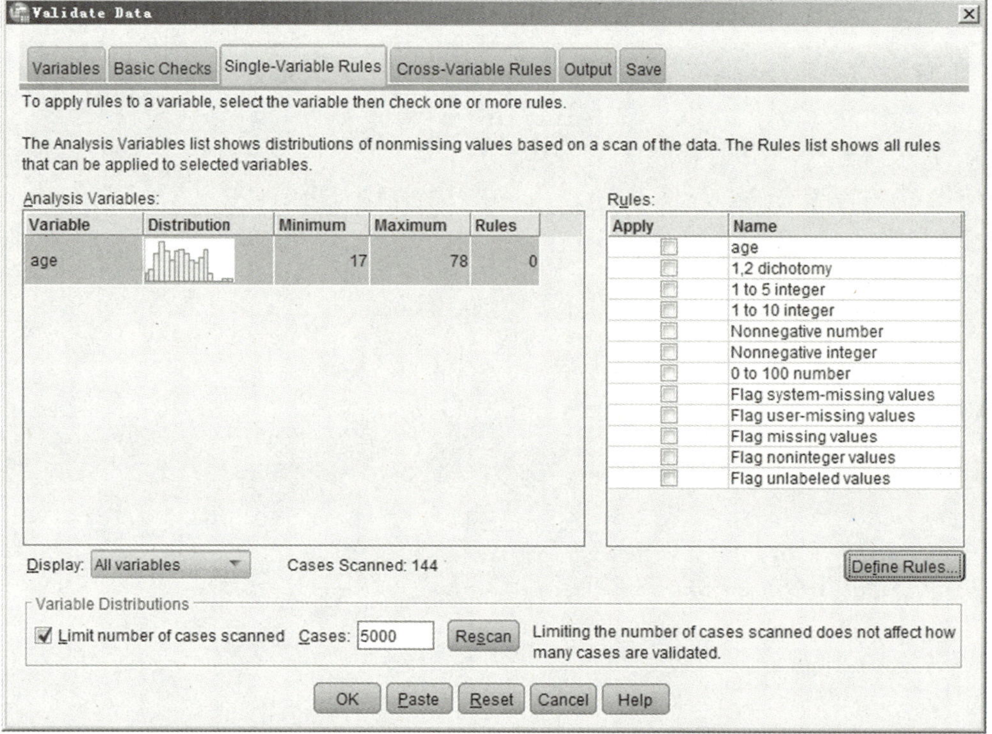

Figure 2-15 The Validate Data: Single-Variable Rules dialog box

Display: Click this cell to display variables. Options include All variables, Numeric variables, Character variables, and Date variables, the default selection is All variables.

Cases Scanned: 144: There are 144 cases scanned in this example.

☑Limit number of cases scanned Cases: 5000 : The default limit number of cases scanned is 5 000. Note that this limit in number of cases scanned does not affect how many cases are validated.

4) Cross-Variable Rules: Set the rules for the cross-related (or associated) variables (Figure 2-14).

5) Output: Define the format of outputs (Figure 2-16).

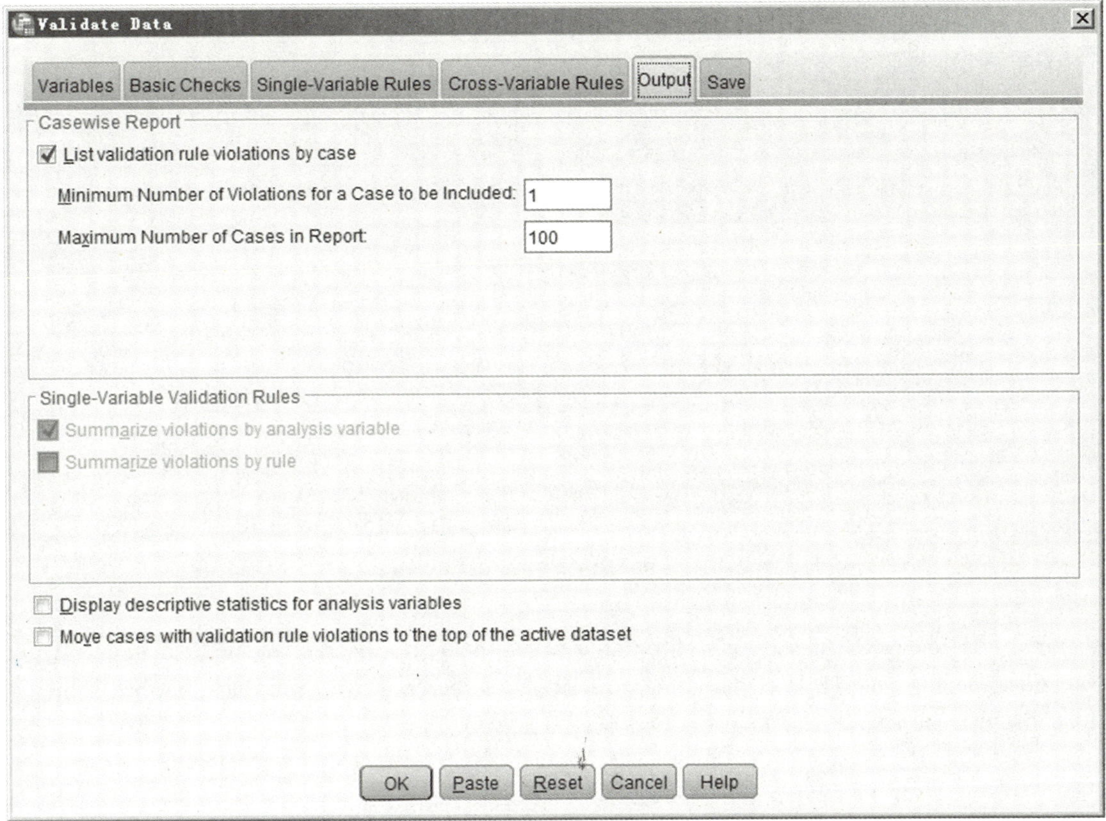

Figure 2-16 The Validate Data: Output dialog box

◇Casewise Report: Report as shown on case basis.

☑List validation rule violations by case.

Minimum Number of Violations for a Case to be included: 1 : The default minimum tolerance count of entries is 1.

Maximum Number of Cases in Report: 100 : The default maximum tolerance count of entries is 100.

◇Single-Variable Validation Rules

☑Summarize violations by analysis variable.

□Summarize violations by rule.

□Display descriptive statistics for analysis variables.

□Move cases with validation rule violations to the top of the active dataset.

6) Save: Click this cell to save Empty Case, Duplicate ID Group, Incomplete ID, and Validation Rule Violations (Figure 2-17).

□Replace existing summary variables.

□Save indicator variables that record all validation rule violations.

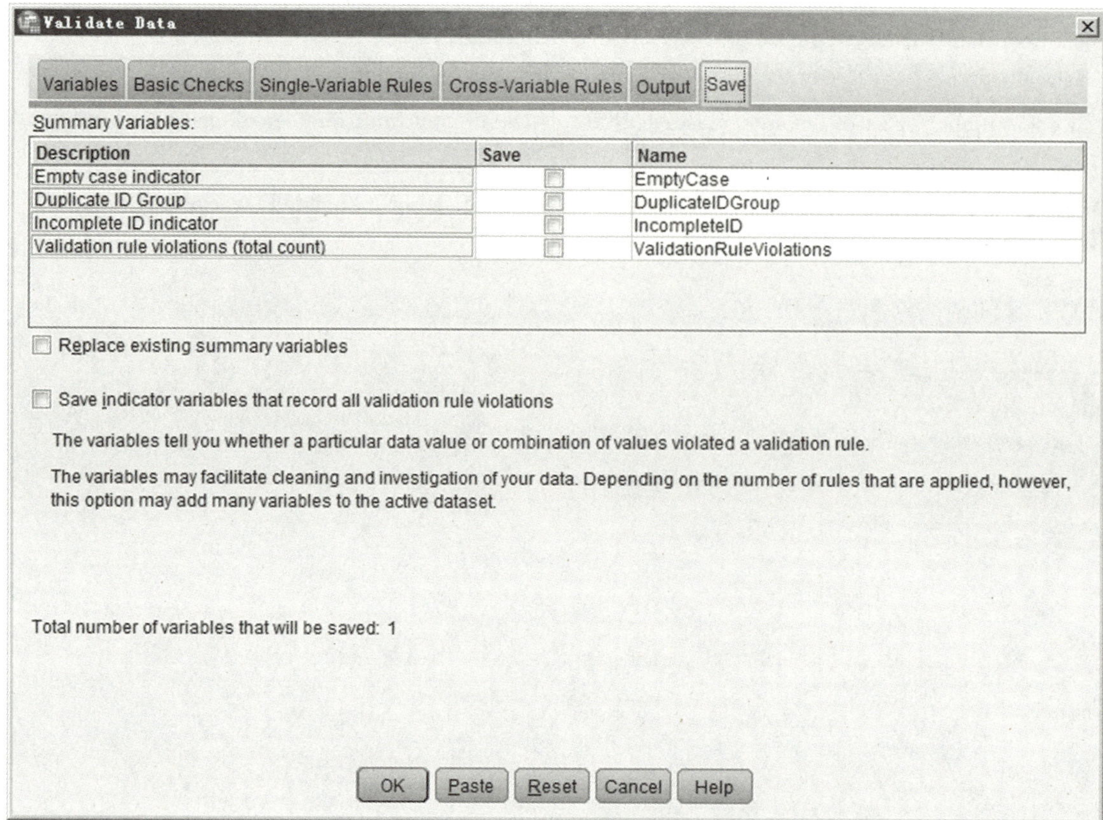

Figure 2-17 The Validate Data:Save dialog box

Figure 2-18 shows the description of validate rules, including the rule name (age), data type, and range of rules, ranging from 18 to 65, *etc*. Figure 2-19 shows the cases with variables that break the validation rules, together with their case numbers and trial centers.

Rule Descriptions

Rule	Description
age	Type: Numeric Domain: Range Flag user-missing values: No Flag system-missing values: No Minimum: 18 Maximum: 65 Flag unlabeled values within range: No Flag noninteger values within range: No $VD.SRule[1]: Rule

Rules violated at least once are displayed.

Figure 2-18 Summary of validation rule descriptions

Case Report

Case	Validation Rule Violations	Identifier	
	Single-Variable[a]	ID	CENTER
5	age (1)	12	center 1
32	age (1)	59	center 2
41	age (1)	72	center 2
100	age (1)	11	center 1
125	age (1)	74	center 2

a. The number of variables that violated the rule follows each rule.

Figure 2–19 Output list of the cases with rule violations

(2) Cross–Variable Rules: Female and weight >= 70 kg.

Select from menu:

Data

Validation

Validate Data

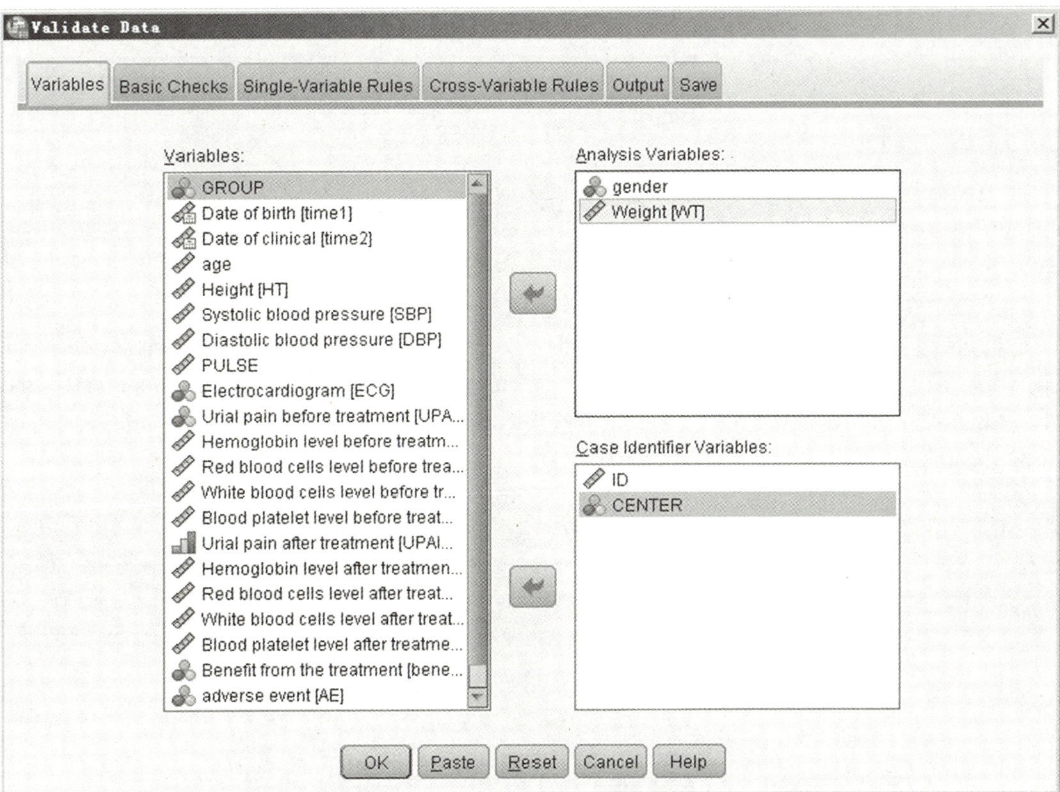

Figure 2–20 The Vandate Data dialog box

The Validate Data dialog box pops out (Figure 2–20). Select "gender" and "Weight[WT]" in the validation variable box and "ID" and "CENTER" in the identification variable box. Click the "Cross–Variable Rules" tab to enter the detailed rules (Figure 2–21).

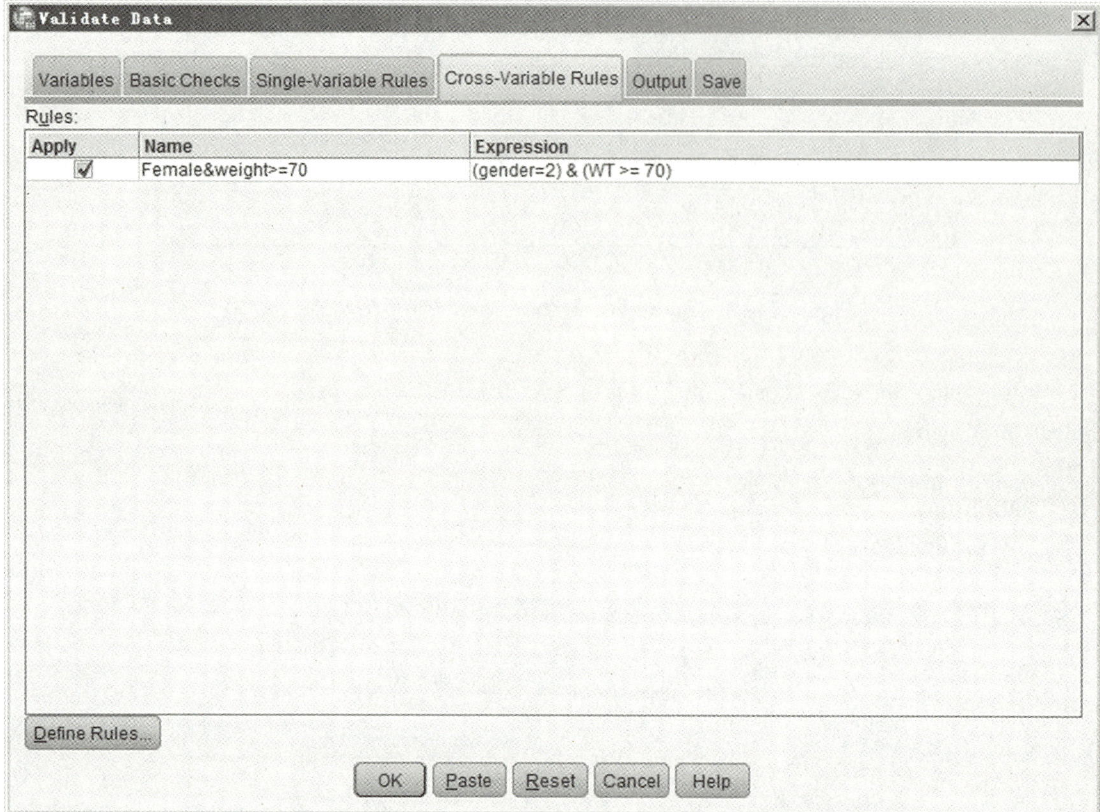

Figure 2-21 The Validate data: Cross-Variable Rules dialog box

The outputs as shown in Figure 2-22 and Figure 2-23. The name of Cross-Variable Rule is "Female and weight >= 70 kg", and there are 9 invalid cases. This rule can be written as "(gender = 2) and (WT >= 70)". Figure 2-23 shows the location, rule identification, case number, and center information of cases that violate the rules.

Cross-Variable Rules

Rule	Number of Violations	Rule Expression
Female&weight>=70	9	(gender=2) & (WT >= 70)

Figure 2-22 Cross-Variable Rule

Case Report

	Validation Rule Violations	Identifier	
Case	Cross-Variable	ID	CENTER
100	Female&weight>=70	11	center 1
110	Female&weight>=70	41	center 1
111	Female&weight>=70	42	center 1
116	Female&weight>=70	47	center 1
124	Female&weight>=70	69	center 2
127	Female&weight>=70	82	center 2
129	Female&weight>=70	89	center 2
132	Female&weight>=70	101	center 2
134	Female&weight>=70	104	center 2

Figure 2-23 Output list of the cases with Rule Violations

2.3 Identify Duplicate Cases

The function is primarily used for checking duplicate data but can also be used to select matching cases in case-control designs.

Select from menu:

Data

Identify Duplicate Cases

The Identify Duplicate Case dialog box pops out(Figure 2-24). Select the matching variable into the "Define matching cases by:". If necessary, select the sorted variables into "Sort within matching groups by:".

◇Variables to Create: Create a variable to label duplicate cases.

☑Indicator of primary cases (1=unique or primary, 0=duplicate): Define variable name for duplicate variables and define primary cases in the duplicate cases. The variable name (system default) is "Primary Last" or "Primary First". Define "1" as the primary case; "0" as the duplicate case.

⊙Last case in each group is primary (system default): The last observation of each duplicate cases is treated as primary case.

◎First case in each group is primary: The first observation of each duplicate cases is treated as primary case.

□Filter by indicator values: Filter the duplicate cases.

□Sequential count of matching case in each group (0=nonmatching case): Generate a new variable, with the default name of "Match Sequence", to provide accumulative count of matching cases in each group.

☑Move matching cases to the top of the file.

☑Display frequencies for created variables.

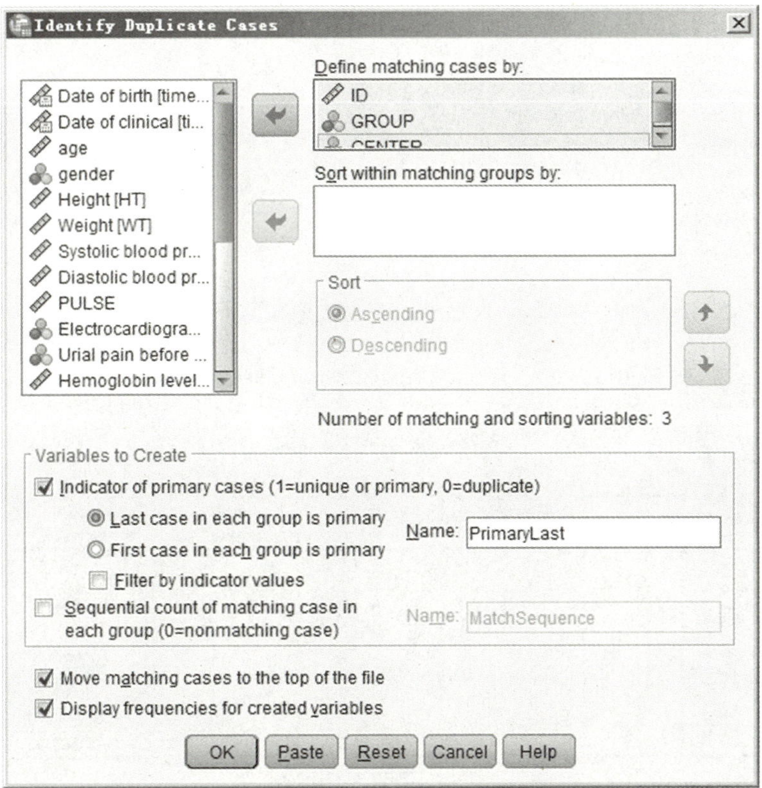

Figure 2-24 The Identify Duplicate Cases dialog box

2.4 Identify Unusual Cases

Select from menu:

Data

Identify Unusual Cases

The Identify Unusual Cases dialog box pops out (Figure 2-25).

Select the variables to analyze into "Analysis Variables", or into "Case Identifier Variable". Percentage of cases with highest anomaly index values: 5, i. e., the default highest percentage is 5%. In this example, the weight variable "Weight[WT]" is selected for checking and "Group" is chosen as case identification variable. As shown in Figure 2-26, Case is the case number in the data, and Group is the identification variable. For example, the first unusual case is 94th with the weight 45 kg in the second group.

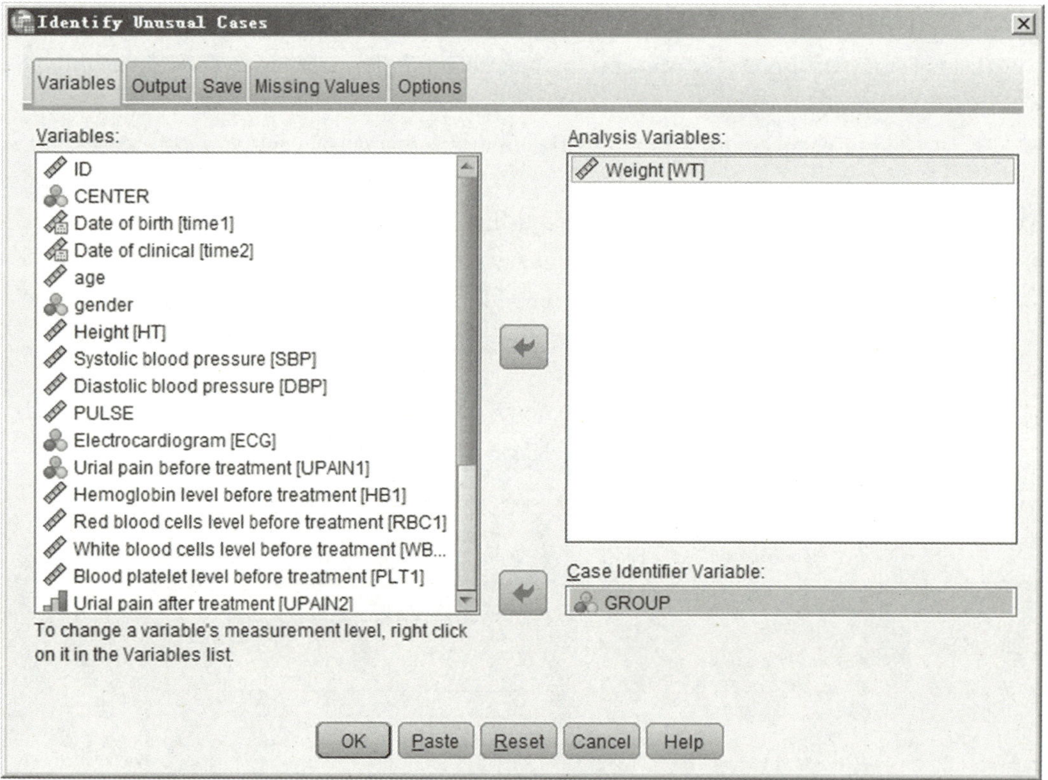

Figure 2-25 The Identify Unusual Cases dialog box

Anomaly Case Reason List

Reason: 1

Case	GROUP	Reason Variable	Variable Impact	Variable Value	Variable Norm
94	2	WT	1.000	45	52.00
88	1	WT	1.000	88	80.23
50	1	WT	1.000	57	60.60
86	1	WT	1.000	87	80.23
91	2	WT	1.000	87	80.23
117	2	WT	1.000	58	60.60
28	1	WT	1.000	76	72.39

Figure 2-26 Output list of unusual cases

2.5 Sort Cases

Select from menu:

Data

Sort Cases

The Sort Cases dialog box pops out(Figure 2-27).

◇Sort by:Sort the selected variables. If more than two variables are selected, sorting will be processed according to their entry sequence in the "Sort by" columns.

◇Sort Order:

⊙Ascending (system default):Numerical variables are ordered in ascending order by their values. Character variables are arranged in alphabetical order of A, B, C, D, *etc*.

◎Descending:Numerical variables are arranged in descending order, and character variables are arranged in reverse alphabetical order of Z, Y, X, *etc*.

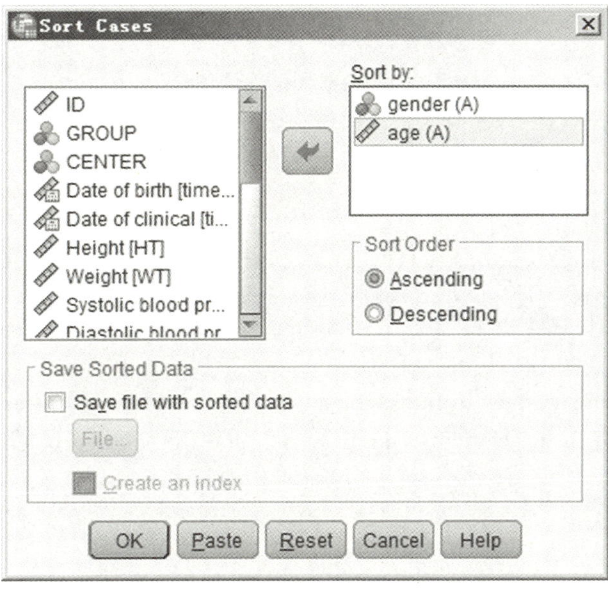

Figure 2-27 The Sort Cases dialog box

2.6 Sort Variables

Select from menu:

Data

Sort Variables

The Sort Variables dialog box pops out(Figure 2-28).

◇Variable View Columns.

◇Sort Order:

⊙Ascending (system default):Numerical variables are sorted in ascending order, and character variables in alphabetical order.

◎Descending:Numerical variables are sorted in descending order, and character variables are arranged in reverse alphabetical order.

☑Save the current (pre-sorted) variable order in a new attribute: Save the current variable order as a new attribute, and you can enter the name in the "Attribute name" box.

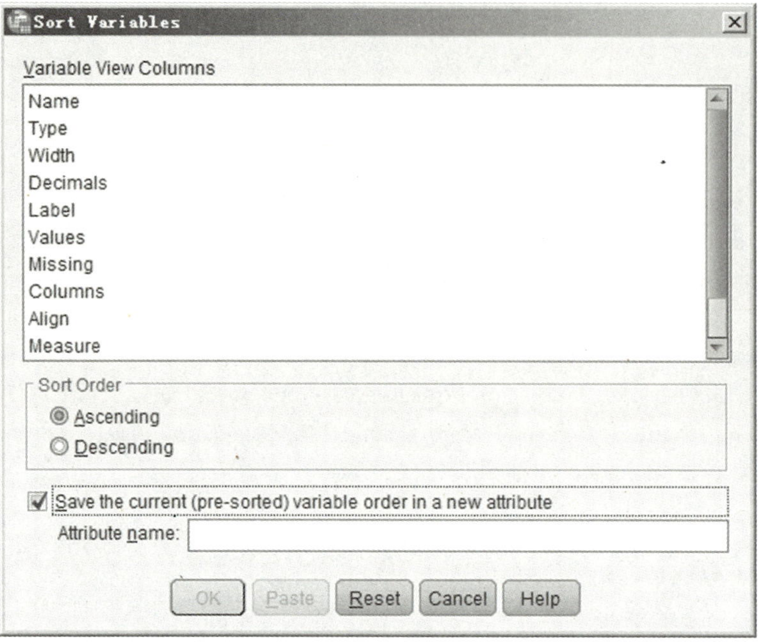

Figure 2-28 The Sort Variables dialog box

2.7 Transpose

In this section, we introduce how to transpose the row and column of the original data, i. e. The row of original dataset is converted to the column of new dataset, and the column of original dataset to the row of new dataset.

Select from menu:

Data

Transpose

The Transpose dialog box pops out (Figure 2-29).

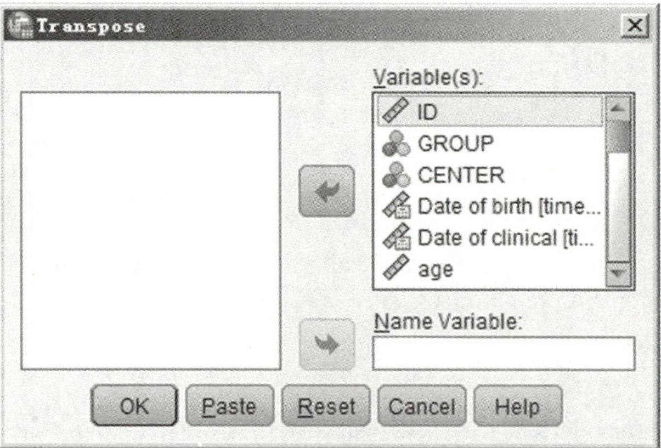

Figure 2-29 The Transpose dialog box

◇Variable(s):Select variables to transpose.

◇Name Variable:Enter the new variable name for the transposed data into the "Name variable" box.

If the original variable is character, the new variable name will be the same as the original character. If the original variable is numeric, the new variable name will begin with the letter V, which is followed by the original value. If the original variable is missing, the new variable name will be automatically generated as "var001" "var002" "var003", *etc*. In addition, another new character variable named "CASE-LBL" will also automatically generated to contain the original data labels.

2.8 Merge Files

2.8.1 Add Cases

In this section, we introduce how to add cases from an external data file to the working data file. The case numbers in the new data file will be the sum of case numbers in these two files.

Select from menu:

Data

Merge Files

Add Cases

Select the data file that need to be added→ Click "Continue"→ the Add Cases From dialog box pops out(Figure 2-30).

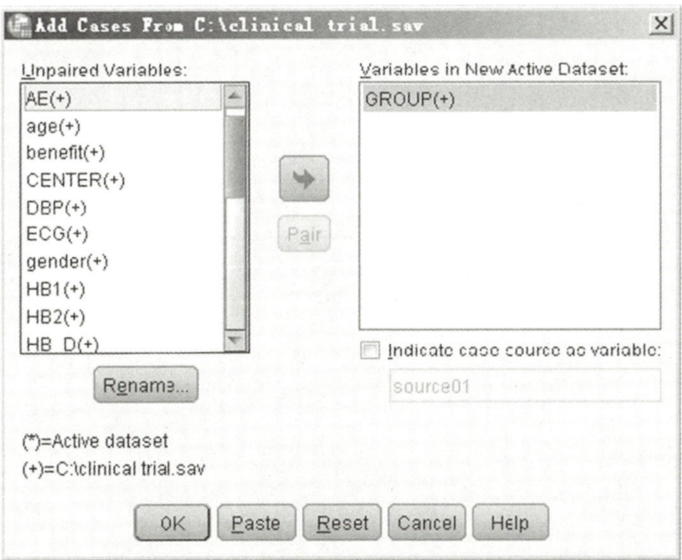

Figure 2-30 The Add Cases Form dialog box

◇Unpaired Variables:Display variables from two data files with name and type that are not exactly the same, i. e. , these variables are not identical to each other.

1) To separate these variables into different columns in the new data file, select this variable and add it into the "Variables in New Active Dataset" box.

2) To merge two certain variables into one column in the new data file, select this pair of variables and click "Pair" to add them into the "Variables in New Active Dataset" box. The merged variable will use the same name as the variable of current working data file.

After one variable is selected, the "Rename" box will be activated to enter new variable name.

The variables imported from the current working data file are labeled " * ".

The variables imported from the external data are labeled "+".

◇Variables in New Active Dataset: Display variables that have the identical name and type from two data files. You can keep these variables in the new data file, or exclude one variable by selecting this variable and adding this variable into the Unpaired Variables box.

□Indicate case source as variable: Use this to label case source. The default is a binary variable named "source01". Here "1" denotes the variable from the external file, and "0" from the current working file.

2.8.2 Add Variables

Add variables from an external data file to the working data file.

Select from menu:

Data

Merge Files

Add Variables

Select an external data file → click "Continue"→ the Add Variables from dialog box pops out (Figure 2-31).

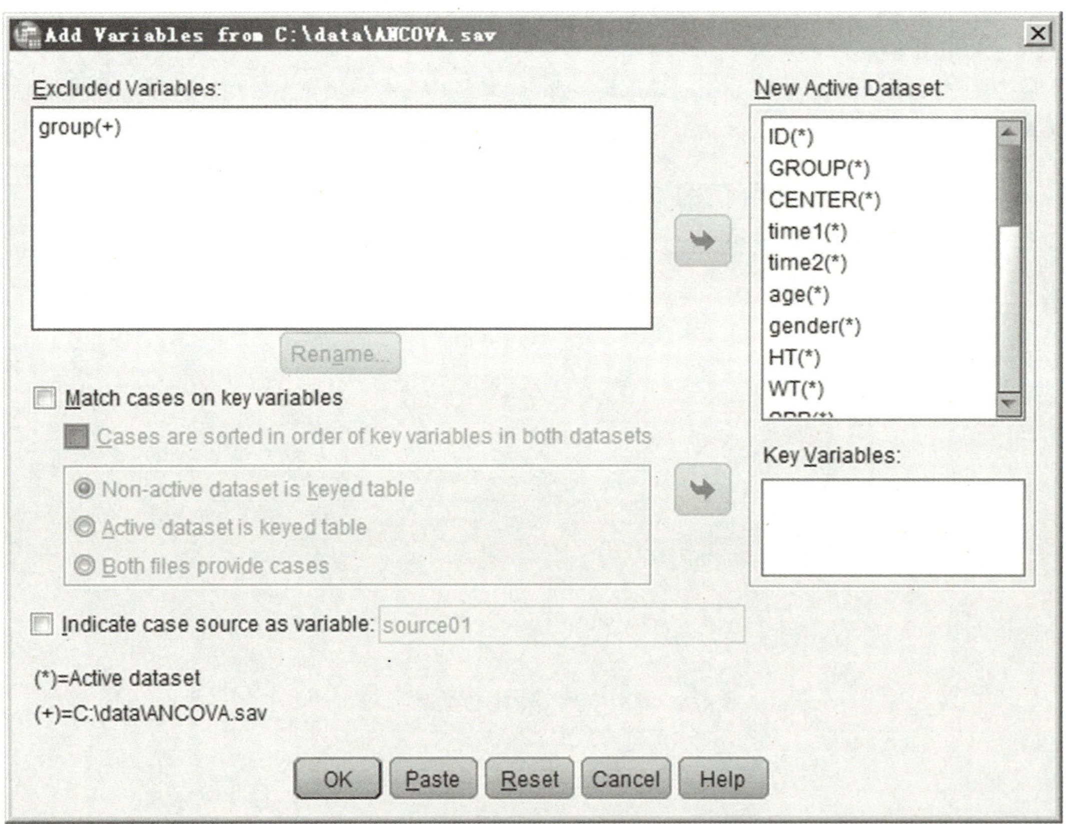

Figure 2-31 The Add Variables dialog box

◇New Active Dataset: Display variables with different names or types in the two data files. You can keep all these variables in a new data file; or exclude some variables by selecting variables and send them to the "Excluded Variables" box.

◇Excluded Variables: For those variables with same name and type from two data files, the variables from the working (i. e., current) file as shown in the New Active Dataset box, and those from the external file in the Excluded Variables box.

The user can click the "Rename" button to rename the variable, in order to allow those variables from the external file to become new variables in the new data file.

To keep two variables that are identical in two data files as one variable in the new data file (i. e. key variables), we need to sort cases (refer to setion 2.5) using the variable in the working file, and then click "Match cases on key variables" to choose the way that cases are selected by key variables.

□Match cases on key variables.

⊙Non-active dataset is keyed table: Keep cases in the working data file, and merge the cases that have the identical key variables from the external file.

◎Active dataset is keyed table: Keep cases in the external data file, and merge the cases that have the identical key variables from the working file.

◎Both files provide cases: Merge cases from both working and external data files.

□Indicate case source as variable: Click this button to label source variable. The default is a binary variable named as source01. Here "1" denotes the variable from the external file, and "0" from the current working file.

You may select the variables from "Excluded Variables" box into the "Key Variables" box and then click "OK" to create a merged new file based on the selected key variables.

2.9 Data Restructure

For more complex data (such as those from clinical trials and large-scale surveys), we often convert the original database into different subsets for sophisticated data analysis. In this section, we will introduce how to achieve this goal through the Restructure process of SPSS.

The data file "repeated_1.sav" is used as the Example 2-1. This dataset has 12 rows and 6 columns, from 6 variables of 12 cases. Among the 6 variables, there is one identification variable (ID), one group variable (GROUP) and the remaining 4 response variables (all are repeated measurement variables). Now combine the four response variables into one new variable "FL"; hence, the original dataset is converted to a new dataset with 48 cases, which is named "repeated_1_trans1.sav".

Select from menu:

Data

Restructure

The Restructure Data Wizard dialog box pops out (Figure 2-32).

⊙Restructure selected variables into cases (system default): An original dataset of m variables from n cases will be converted into a new dataset of k variables from nm/k cases, where $m>k$ and m is an integer multiple of k. For example, the original dataset of 2 cases and 4 variables is converted into a new data file with 8 cases and 1 variable; Figure 2-33 shows the restructure from 2 cases and 6 variables to 6 cases and 2 variables.

◎Restructure selected cases into variables: The reverse procedure of the above option, which converts an original dataset of k variables from nm/k cases into a new dataset of m variables from n cases, where $m \geq k$, and m is an integer multiple of k.

◎Transpose all data: This is equivalent to the data transpose procedure described in the section 2.7. Click the button to transpose all rows and columns, and the procedure of data restructure will end.

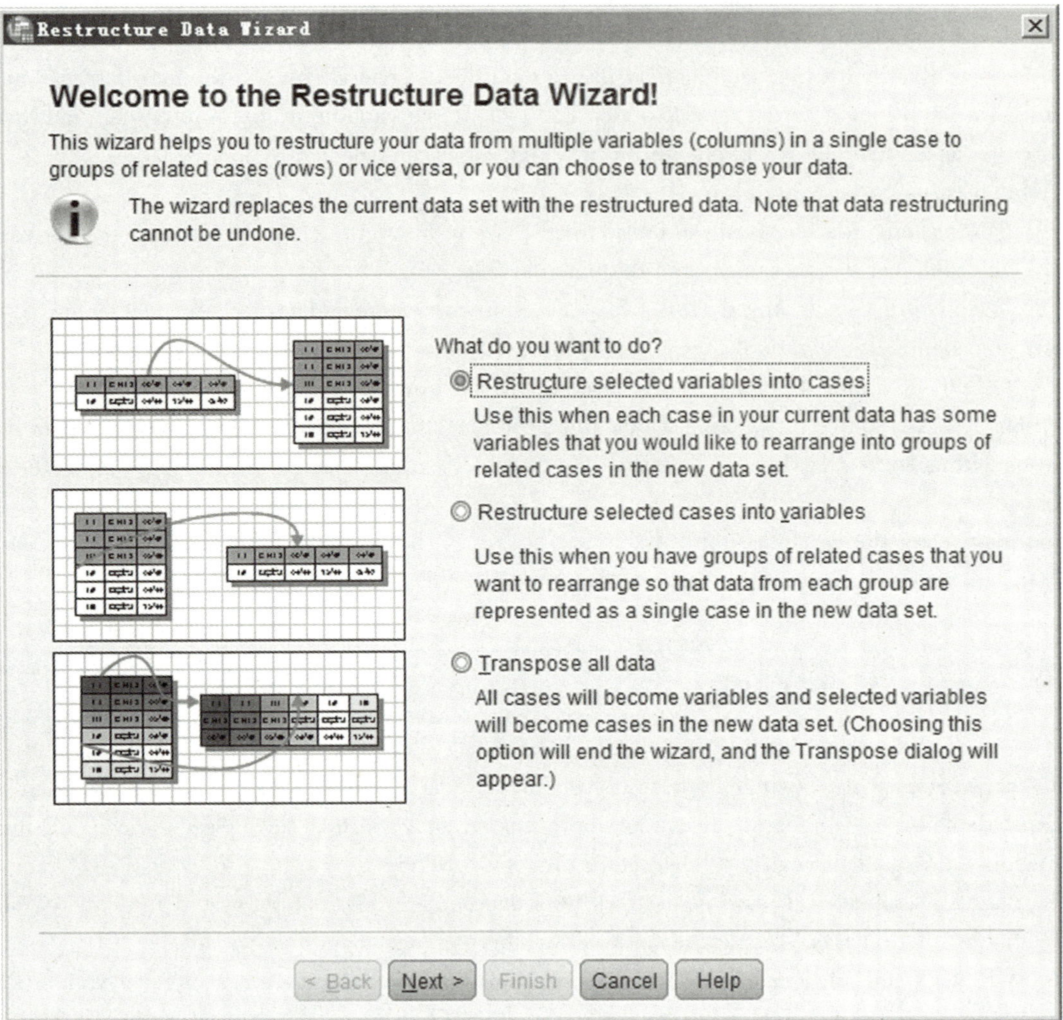

Figure 2-32 The Restructure Data Wizard dialog box

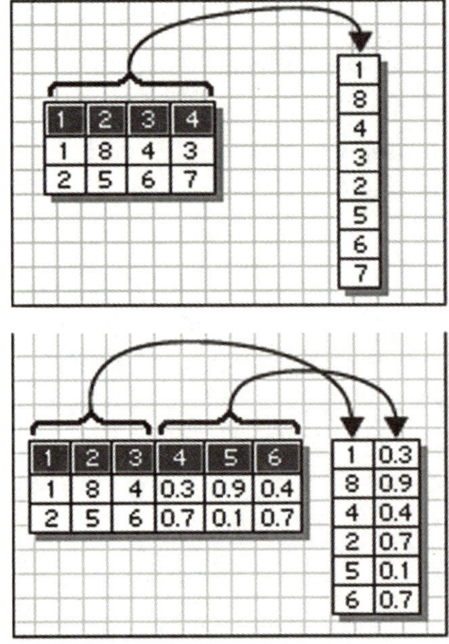

Figure 2-33 The Data Restructure graph

If you choose the first two options, you will need to finish the following six steps:

(1) Click "Next>" in "Restructure Data", and the Restructure Data Wizard–Step 2 of 7 dialog box pops out (Figure 2–34).

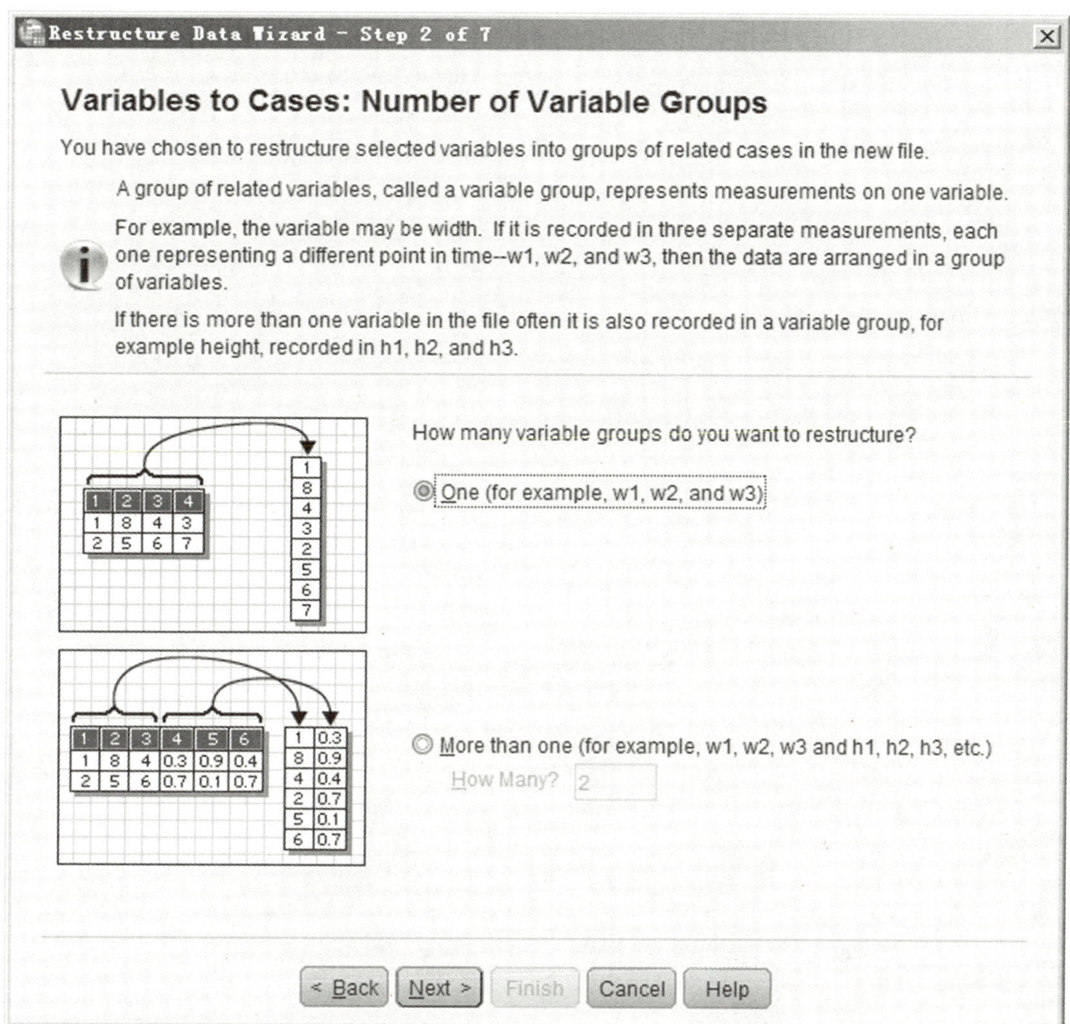

Figure 2–34 The Restructure Data Wizard–Step 2 of 7 dialog box

⊙One (for example, w1, w2, and w3) (system default): Convert the selected m variables to one variable. This option is selected here.

◎More than one (for example, w1, w2, w3 and h1, h2, h3, *etc.*): Convert the selected m variables to k variables, $m>k>1$, and m is an integer multiple of k.

Here the value of k can be set in the "How many?" box, where 2 is the default value.

(2) Click "Next >" in step 2 and the "Restructure Data Wizard–Step 3 of 7" pops out (Figure 2–35).

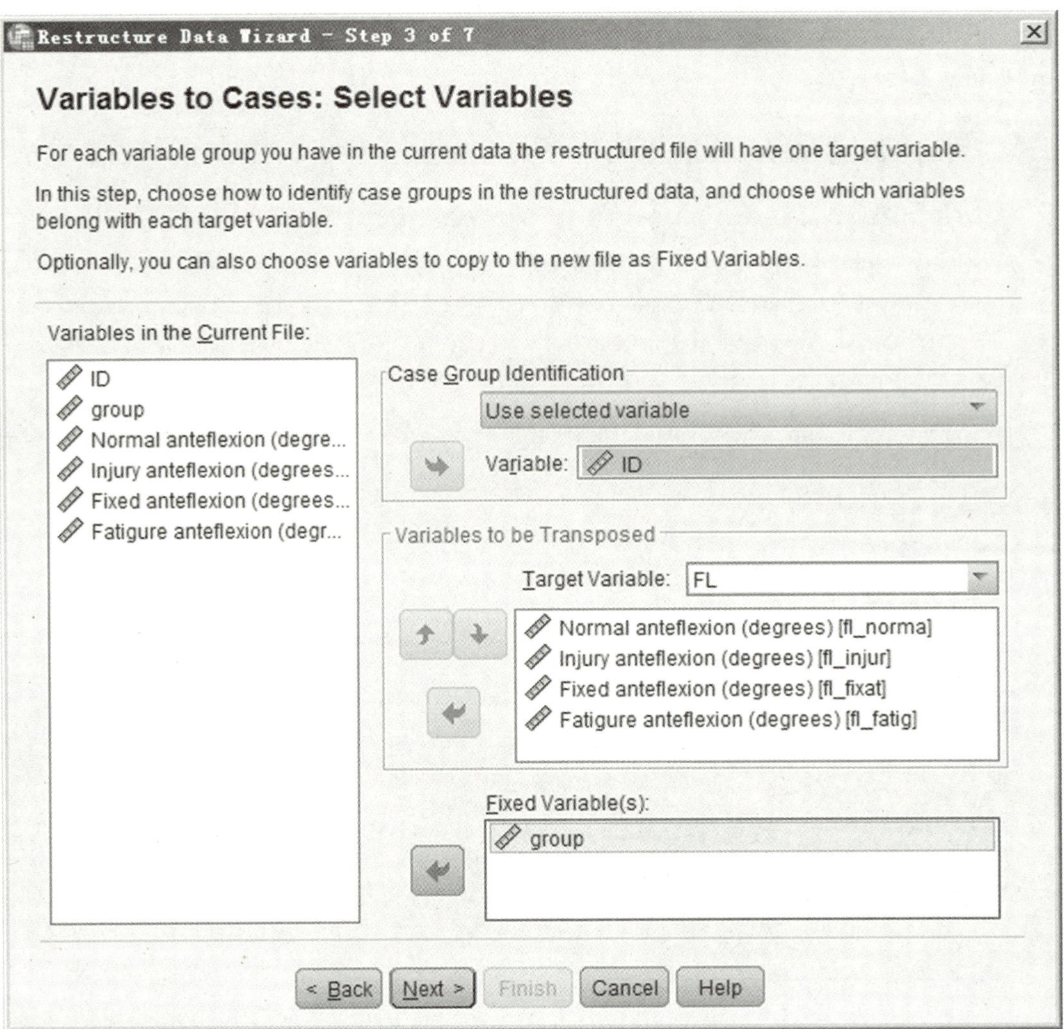

Figure 2-35 The Restructure Data Wizard-Step 3 of 7 dialog box

◇Variables in the Current File: You can select the variables from this list.

◇Case Group Identification: The identification variables in primary cases have three options.

1) Use case number (system default): This is the default option.

2) Use selected variable: Use one variable from the working dataset as the identification variable. Here we choose the variable "ID" as case group identification.

3) None: No identification variables are used.

◇Variables to be Transposed: Select variables to be transposed. Here "fl_normal" "fl_injur" "fl_fixat" and "fl_fatig" are selected.

Target Variable: The default name of target variable is "trans1", and will be "tran2" "trans3", if there are more than one target variables. The variable name can also be customized, here the name "FL" is used. The corresponding original variable is shown in the box below the "Target Variable" box.

Fixed Variable(s): The variable "group" is selected as a fixed variable here.

(3) Click "Next >" and the Restructure Data Wizard-Step 4 of 7 dialog box pops out (Figure 2-36). This step is to create Index Variables, which are often used as group variables.

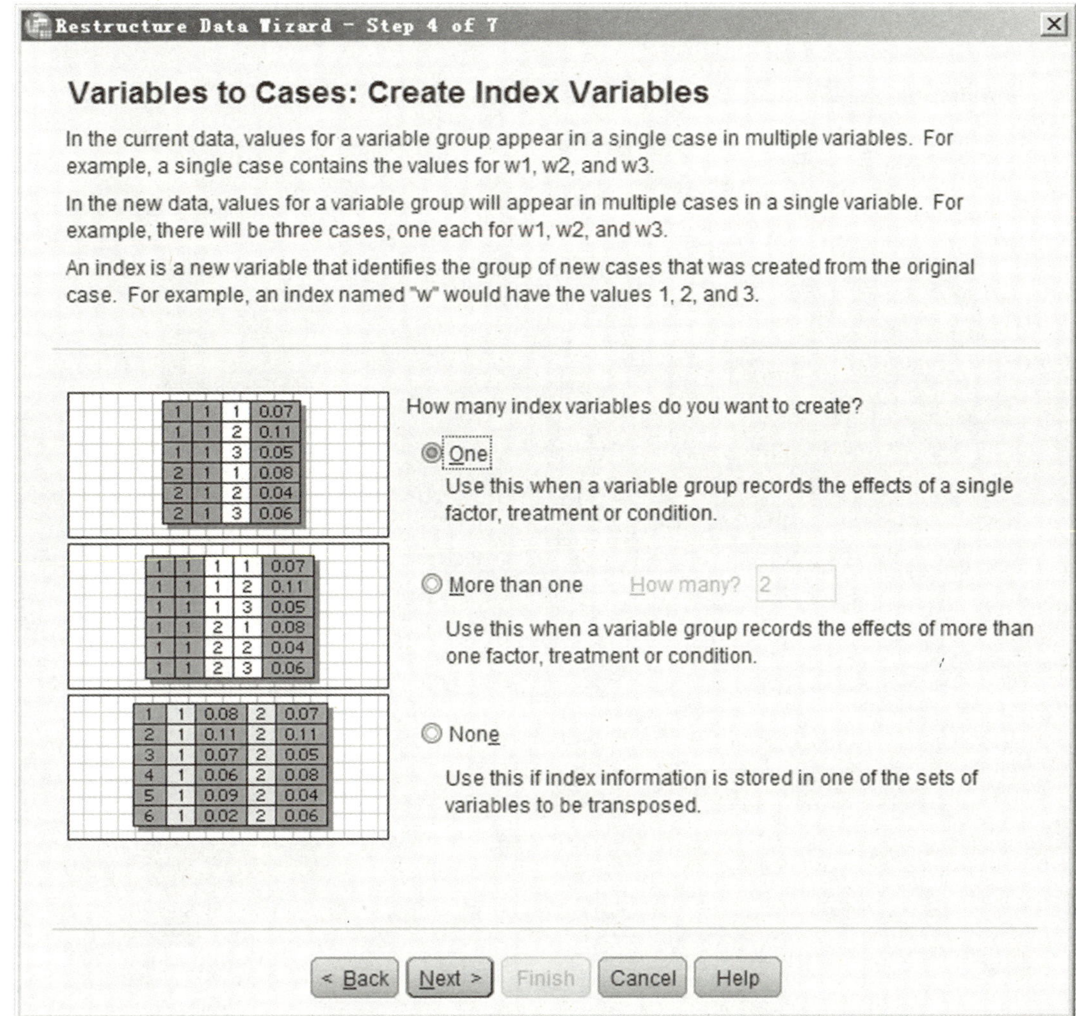

Figure 2-36 The Restructure Data Wizard-Step 4 of 7 dialog box

◇How many index variables do you want to create?

⊙One (system default): Create one index variable.

◎More than one: Create multiple index variables. The number of index variables can be customized by entering an integer in the "How many?" box where the default number is 2.

◎None: Do not create index variables.

(4) Click "Next >" and the Restructure Data Wizard-Step 5 of 7 dialog box pops out (Figure 2-37).

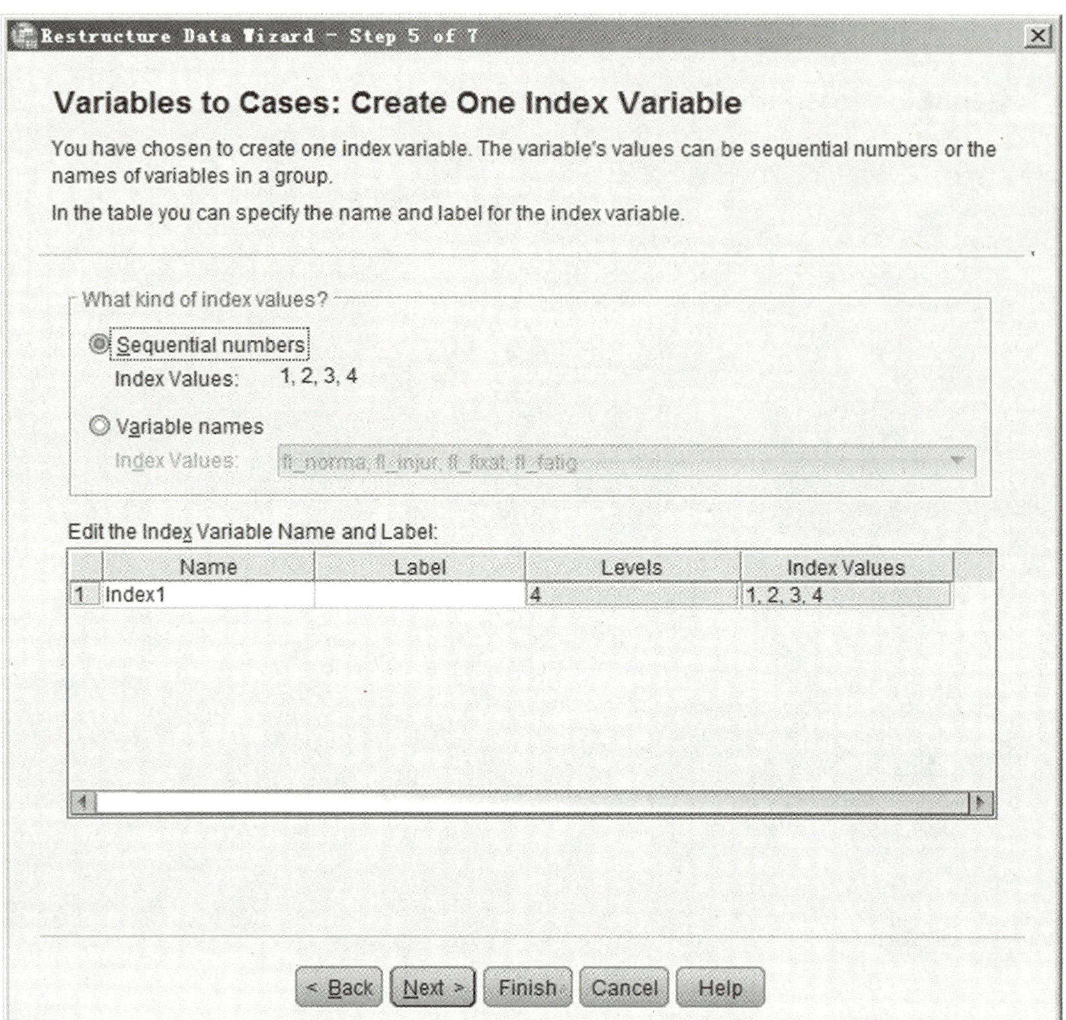

Figure 2-37 The Restructure Data Wizard-Step 5 of 7 dialog box

◇What kind of index values? This defines the format of index value.

⊙Sequential numbers (system default): Index values are continuous digits, such as 1, 2, 3, 4, *etc.*, which represent different levels of index variables corresponding to the values of original variable. The value is given by the order of corresponding original variable.

◎Variable names: Same as the original variable name, here this option is chosen.

Index Values: The values of the index variables, in this example there are four variable values (i. e. four levels): "fl_normal" "fl_injur" "fl_fixat" "fl_fatig", which are ordered according to the order of original variable.

Edit the Index Variable Name and Label: Enter the name and label of the Index Variable.

(5) Click "Next >" and the Restructure Data Wizard-Step 6 of 7 dialog box pops out (Figure 2-38).

◇Handing of Variables not selected.

⊙Drop variable(s) from the new data file (system default): Delete unselected variables. This option is chosen in this example.

◎Keep and treat as fixed variable(s): Keep unselected variables and treat them as fixed variables.

◇System Missing or Blank Values in all Transposed Variables.

⊙Create a case in the new file (system default): Keep missing data in the transposed data file. This option is chosen here.

◎Discard the data: Delete all missing values.

◇Case Count Variable.

□Count the number of new cases created by the case in the current data: Choose whether to create the count variable. The default is not to count as shown here.

Name: Name a count variable.

Label: Label a count variable.

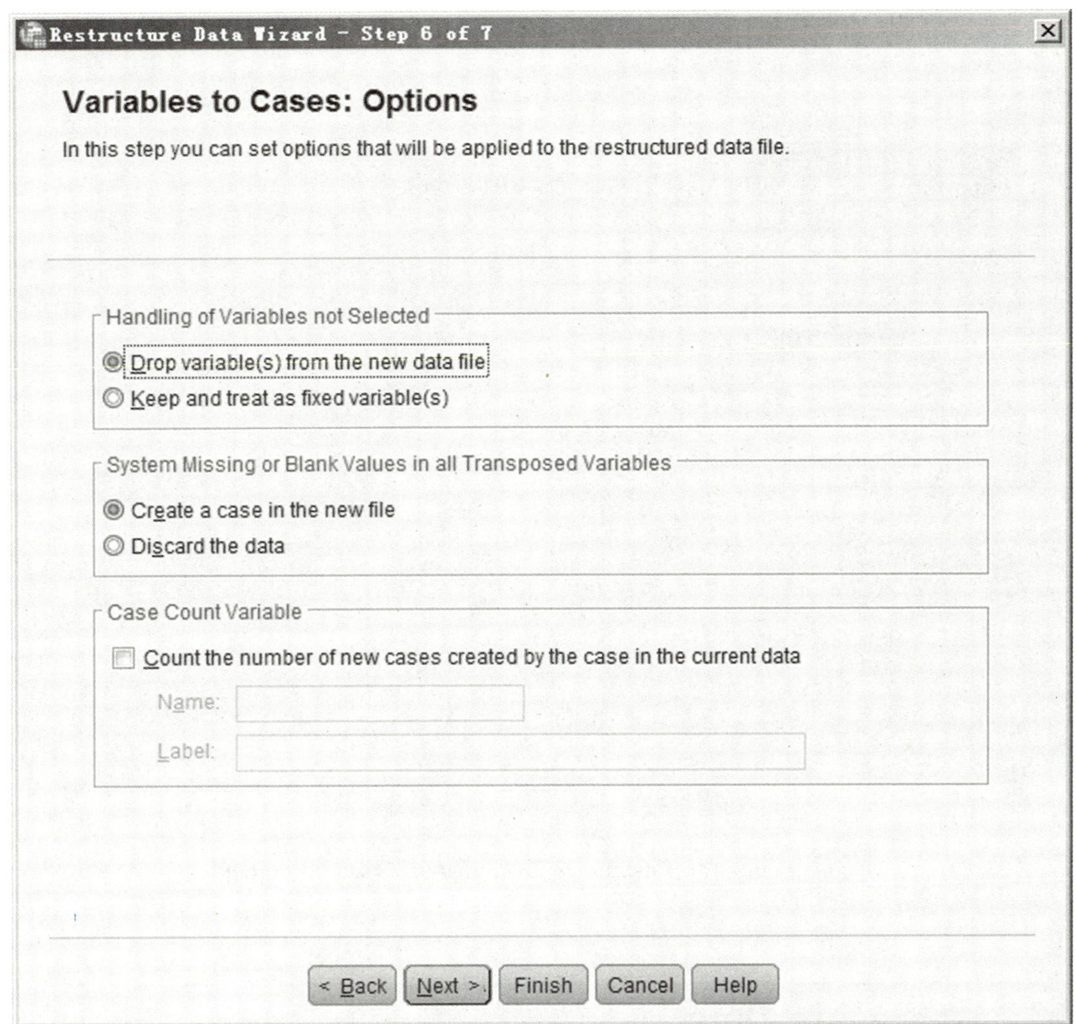

Figure 2–38 The Restructure Data Wizard–Step 6 of 7 dialog box

(6) Click "Next >" in step 6 of 7, the Restructure Data Wizard–Finish box pops out (Figure 2–39).

⊙Restructure the data now (system default): Perform data restructure immediately. Here this option is chosen and the result is saved to "repeated_1_tran1. sav".

◎Paste the syntax generated by the wizard into a program file: Save the syntax of the above restructure procedure into a program file.

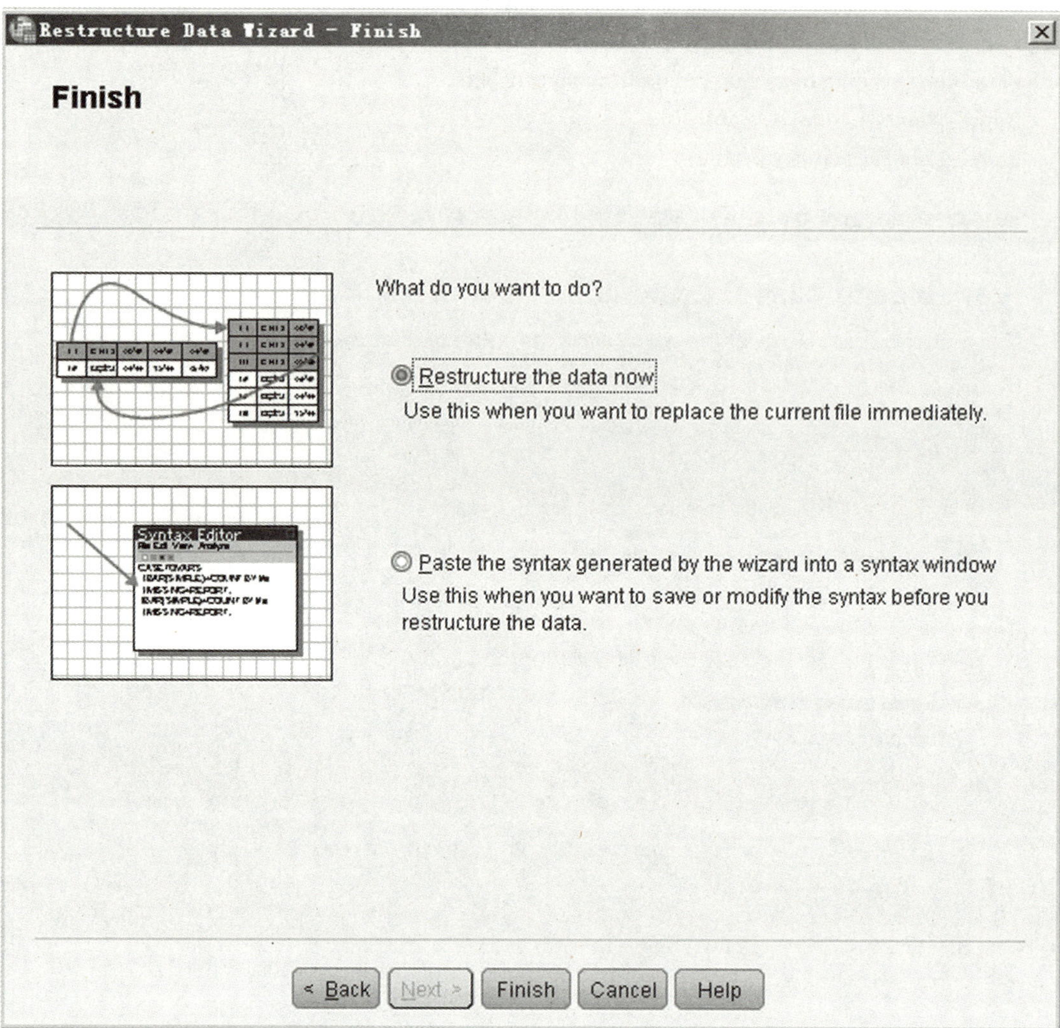

Figure 2-39 The Restructure Data Wizard-Finish dialog box

2.10 Aggregate Data

Sometime we need to combine several intermediate variables (or statistics), such as mean, standard deviation, minimum value, and maximum value, into a new data file. In this section, we will introduce how to aggregate data.

The datafile "diameter. sav" is used as the Example 2-2. To measure the sagittal tube diameter of the human vertebral column, 216 vertebral specimens were separately measured four times, and the original data can be found in the file "diameter. sav". Please put the mean of these four measurements into a new data file "diameter_sub. sav".

Select from menu:

Data

Aggregate

The Aggregate Data dialog box pops out (Figure 2-40).

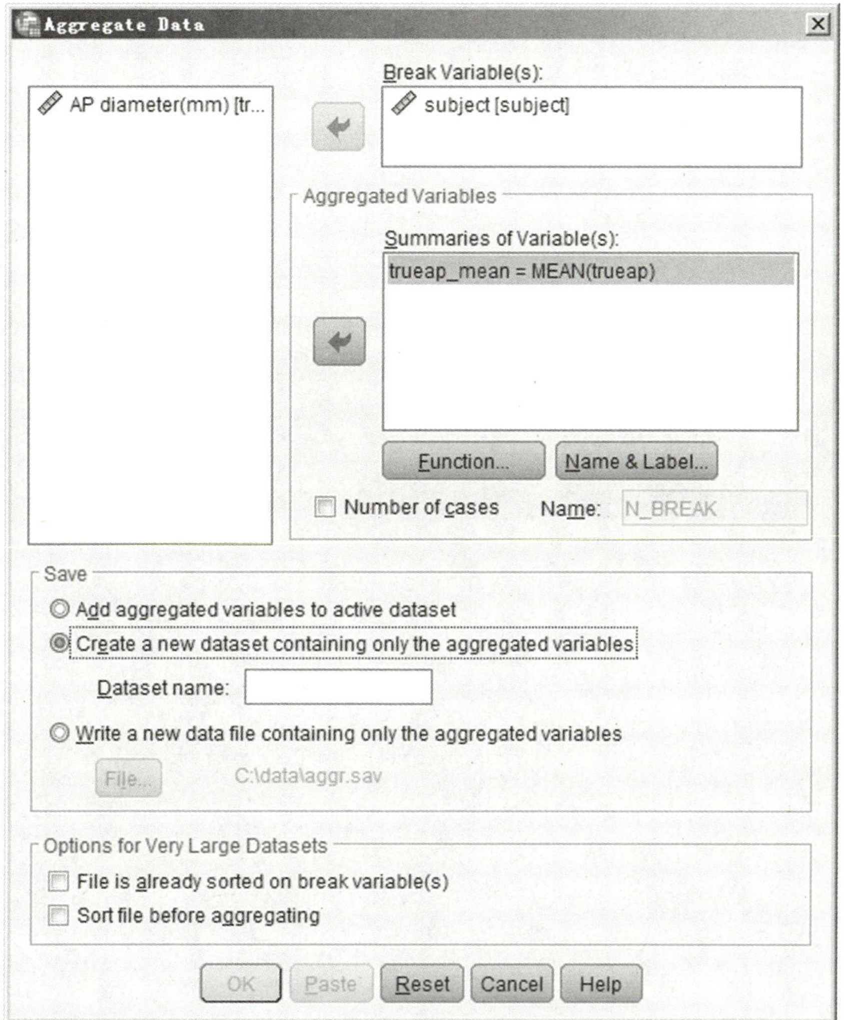

Figure 2-40 The Aggregate Data dialog box

◇Break Variable(s): To be selected from the left box. Here the variable "subject" is selected.

In the new data file (the aggregate file), only one new aggregate value is generated from each level of break variable. The name and feature of break variable are the same as those of original dataset. Break variables can be numeric or character.

◇Aggregated Variables: To be selected from the left box. Here the variable "trueap" is selected.

In the "Aggregate Data" file, the original response variables are aggregated to form a new variable. The default name is same as the original variable name followed by an underscore and the function name. For example, if the aggregate function is calculating the mean, the aggregate variable is then named as "trueap_mean". New variable name can also be modified and labeled.

★Name & Label: Change the name and label of the aggregate variable. Click "Name & Label" to show the Aggregate Data: Variable Name and Label dialog box (Figure 2-41), and then enter the variable name and label to their corresponding boxes.

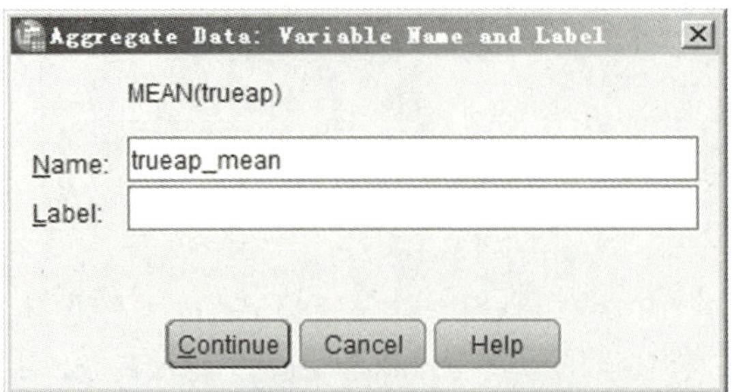

Figure 2 – 41 The Aggregate Data: Variable Name and Label dialog box

★Function: Click "Function" to open the Aggregate Data: Aggregate Function dialog box (Figure 2–42).

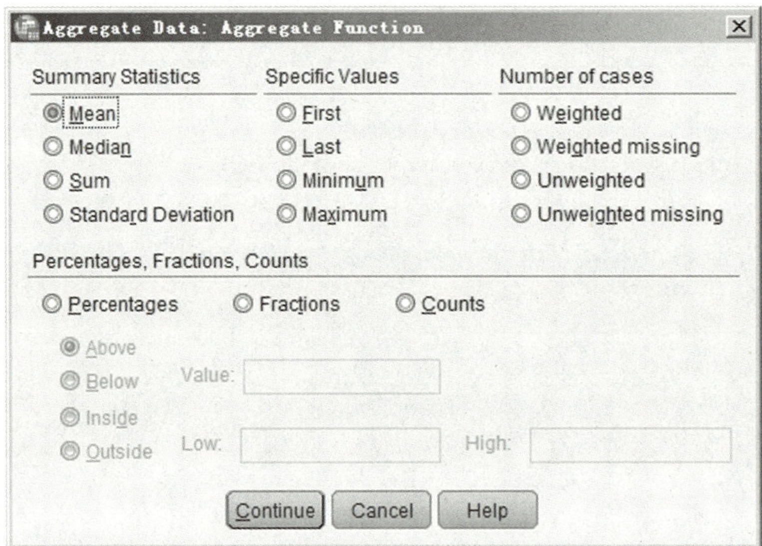

Figure 2–42 The Aggregate Data: Aggregate Function dialog box

There are 20 functions listed under five categories in this dialog box, but you can only choose one option.

1) Summary Statistics

⊙Mean (ststem default): The mean at each classification level of the original variable. This option is selected for this example.

◎Median: The median at each classification level of the original variable.

◎Sum: The sum at each classification levels of the original variable.

◎Standard Deviation: The standard deviation at each classification level of the original variable.

2) Specific Values

◎First: The first observation value at each classification level of the original variable.

◎Last: The last observation value at each classification level of the original variable.

◎Minimum: The minimum value at each classification level of the original variable.

◎Maximum: The maximum value at each classification level of the original variable.

3) Number of cases: The number of observations at each classification level of the original variable.

◎Weighted: The number of weighted observations at each classification level of the original variable.

◎Weighted missing: The number of weighted missing values at each classification level of the original variable.

◎Unweighted: The number of unweighted observations at each classification level of the original variable.

◎Unweighted missing: The number of unweighted missing values at each classification level of the original variable.

4) Percentages

◎Above: The percentage of observations at each classification level of original variable greater than the set value, expressed as a percentage. You need to set the values in the "Value" box.

◎Below: The percentage of observations at each classification level of original variable less than the set value, expressed as a percentage. You need to set the values in the "Value" box.

◎Inside: The percentage of observations at each classification level of original variable between Low and High. You need to set the values in the "Low" and "High" boxes.

◎Outside: The percentage of observations at each classification level of original variable outside Low and High. You need to set the values in the "Low" and "High" boxes.

5) Fractions

◎Above: The proportion of observations at each classification level of original variable greater than the set value, expressed as a decimal. You need to set the values in the "Value" box.

◎Below: The proportion of observations at each classification level of original variable less than the set value, expressed as a decimal. You need to set the values in the "Value" box.

◎Inside: The proportion of observations at each classification level of original variable between Low and High, expressed as a decimal. You need to set the values in the "Low" and "High" boxes.

◎Outside: The proportion of observations at each classification level of original variable beyond Low and High, expressed as a decimal. You need to set the values in the "Low" and "High" boxes.

□Number of cases (Figure 2-40): The number of cases in each classification level, and the default name is "N_BREAK".

◇Save (Figure 2-40).

⊙Add aggregated variables to active dataset (system default): Add aggregated variables to the current data file.

◎Create a new dataset containing only the aggregated variables: Here the data file is renamed "diameter_sub. sav".

◎Write a new data file containing only the aggregated variables: Click on the "File" button to allow the change of file name and path.

◇Options for Very Large Datasets: The following options could increase the calculation speed of processing large data files.

□File is already sorted on break variable(s): Check this if the source file has already been sorted on the break (i. e., classification) variable.

□Sort file before aggregating: Check this if you plan to sort the file on the breaking variables before aggregating data.

2.11 Copy Dataset

Open a data file that needs to be copied and select from the menu:

Data

Copy Dataset

Then you can create a new data file same as the original one.

2.12 Split Files

Data processing sometimes requires analyzing certain break variables in a layered manner, also known as fixed-level analysis. For example, after you split the file by gender, you can do separate analyses of men and women.

Select from menu:

Data

Split Files

The Split Files dialog box pops out (Figure 2-43).

◎ Analyze all cases, do not create groups: Analyze all cases, do not create groups, or restore group files.

⊙Compare groups: Add the variables into the "Groups Based on" box to specify the comparison groups. If more than two variables are selected into the box (note: a maximum of 8 group variables are allowed), they are listed in their selection sequence.

◎ Organize output by groups: This option is similar to the "Compare groups" option, but gives a complete set of results for each combination of group variables in output (note: a maximum of 8 group variables are allowed).

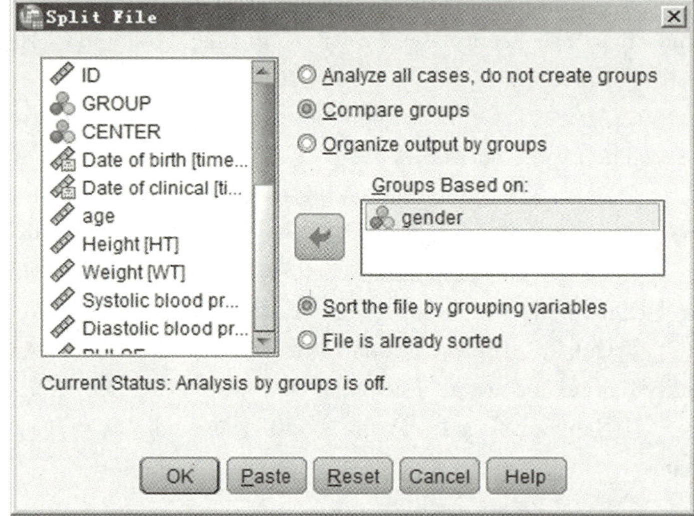

Figure 2-43 The Split File dialog box

◎Sort the file by grouping variables: Sort the data file in ascending order by group variables before splitting the file.

⊙File is already sorted: If you have sorted the observation file in ascending order, click on this to save running time.

2.13 Select Cases

If you are only interested in certain levels (or groups) of data; or plan to use 90% of cases to establish a discriminant function, and the rest 10% to evaluate the performance of this function; or plan to use the data of a certain period or selected number of cases, these objectives can be achieved by the Select Cases function.

Select from menu:

Data

Select Cases

The Select Cases dialog box pops out (Figure 2-44).

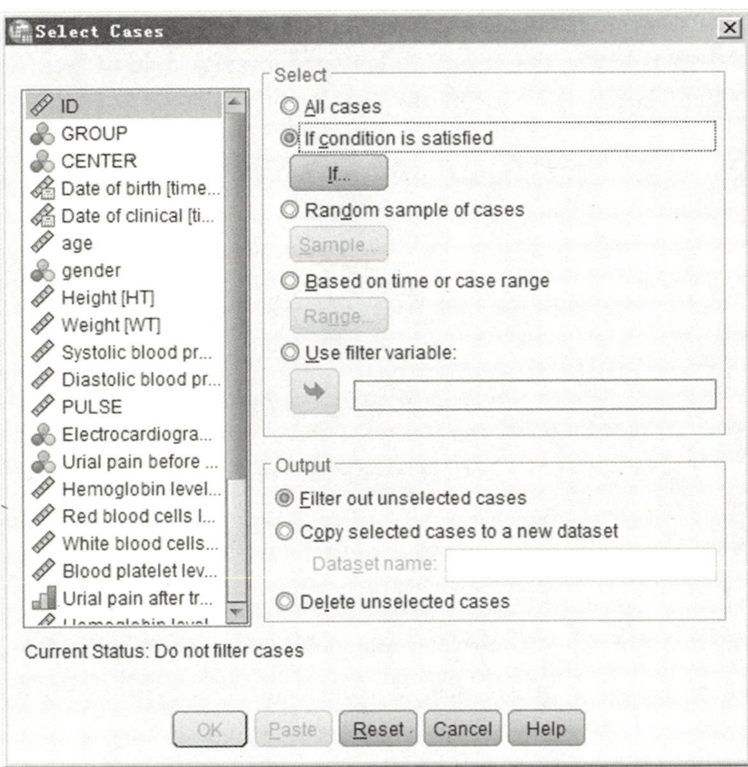

Figure 2-44 The Select Cases dialog box

◇Select: Select some cases.

◎All cases: Select all cases.

⊙If condition is satisfied: Select cases that fulfilled certain conditions. Check this option and click on the "If" button to open the Select Cases: If dialog box (Figure 2-45). Here we use the data file "clinical trial. sav" as an example and select the cases with the variable "gender=1" (i. e., male cases) for further analysis.

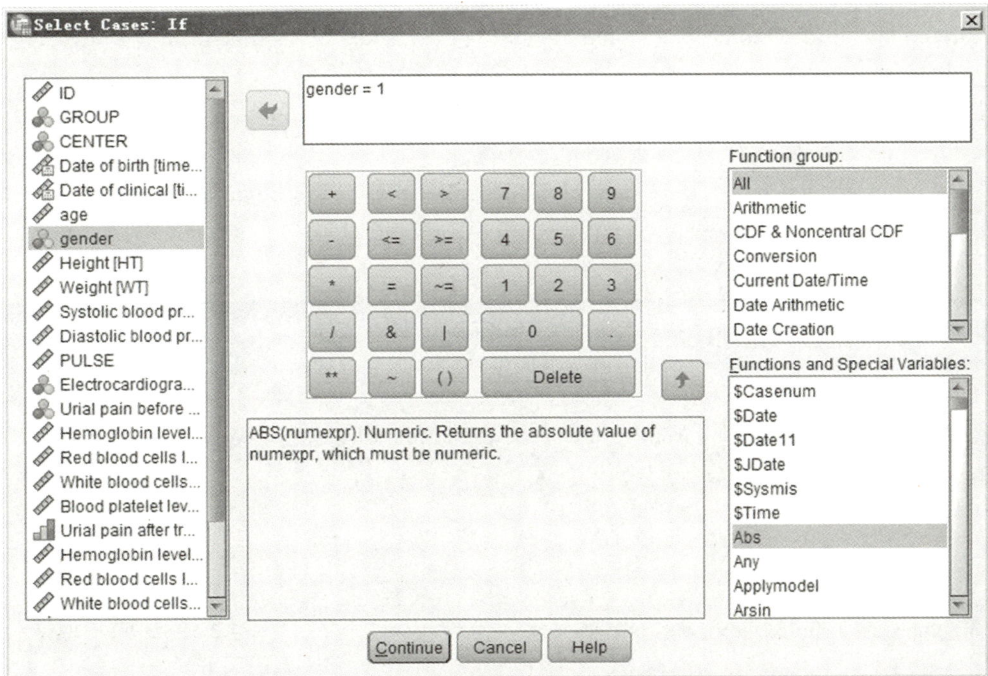

Figure 2-45 The Select Case: If dialog box

◎Random sample of cases(Figure 2-44): Randomly select a certain percentage or number of cases. Check this option and then click on the "Sample" button to open the Select Cases: Random Sample dialog box (Figure 2-46) where the Sample Size can be set.

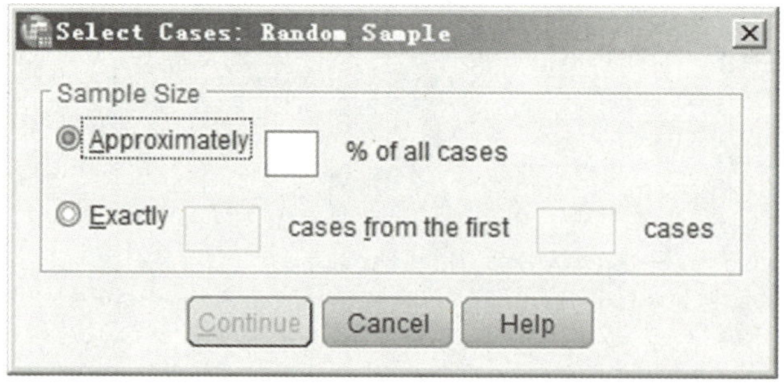

Figure 2-46 The Select Cases: Random Sample dialog box

◇Sample Size:

⊙Approximately [ ] % of all cases: In this box you can enter the approximate proportion of cases you want to randomly select from the dataset. Pay attention to the term "approximate" here. For example, even if [90] is entered in the box, the number of cases randomly selected from a dataset of one hundred cases is not necessarily 90.

◎Exactly [ ] cases from the first [ ] cases: You can enter the exact number of cases that will be randomly selected from the subset of working dataset. For example, if you enter 10 in the first box and 40 in the second, 10 cases will be randomly selected from the first 40 cases.

◎Based on time or case range(Figure 2-44): Select cases by the range of time or case numbers.

◎Use filter variable(Figure 2-44): Except "All Cases", all the options generate a filter variable named "filter_$" in the "Data View" dialog box. In this filter variable, "1" denotes the selected cases and "0" denotes the unselected cases. Check this option to activate the bar below and the filter variables can be selected from the variable list on the left.

◇Output(Figure 2-44).

⊙Filtered out unselected cases (system default): Unselected cases remain in the data file, with a diagonal in their case number cell, and zero in their filter variable cell.

◎Copy selected cases to a new dataset: Copy the selected cases into a new data file. You name this new data files by click on the "Dataset name" option.

◎Deleted unselected cases: Delete unselected cases from the working data file. This option shall be used with caution because the deleted data cannot be restored.

2.14 Weight Cases

Weights to different values of variables are often determined by the frequency of all the combination of certain categorical variable(s).

Select from menu:

Data

Weight Cases

The Weight Cases dialog box pops out(Figure 2-47).

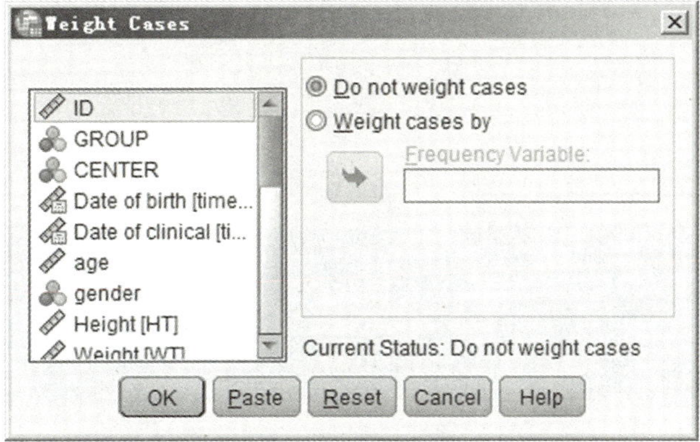

Figure 2-47 The Weight Cases dialog box

◎Do not weight cases: Do not assign any weights to the variables.

⊙Weight cases by (system default): Select a variable from the list as frequency variable, then all cases will be weighted by this frequency variable in subsequent analysis.

Yang Lin

Chapter 3

Transform

In many situations, the raw data are not immediately ready for analyzing, thus requiring appropriate transformation on the data before statistical analysis. SPSS is a powerful software for transforming data. In addition to simple variable computing, shifting and recoding, SPSS can also perform complex statistical functions and logical functions.

When click the main menu "Transform", Submenu under Transform pops out (Figure 3-1). The key features include: Compute Variable, Programmability Transformation, Count Values within Cases, Shift Values, Recode into Same Variables, Recode into Different Variables, Automatic Recode, Create Dummy Variables, Visual Binning, Optimal Binning, Anonymize Variables, Prepare Data for Modeling, Rank Cases, Date and Time Wizard, Create Time Series, Replace Missing Values, Random Number Generators and Run Pending Transforms. In this chapter, we will focus on 10 common features.

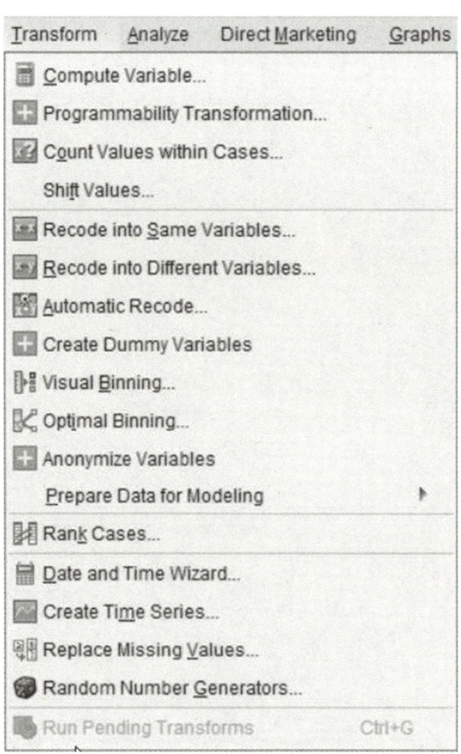

Figure 3-1 Submenu under Transform

3.1 Computing Variable

Computing variable means a variable will be generated after functioning on existing variables. The "Compute Variable" submenu is under "Transform" menu. The dialog box of Compute Variable is presented in Figure 3-2.

Transform

Compute Variable

The "Target Variable" is a new variable or an existing variable. After entering the target variable name, the "Type & Label" button under the "Target Variable" is activated. When you click this button, the dialog box of Compute Variable: Type and Label pops out (Figure 3-3).

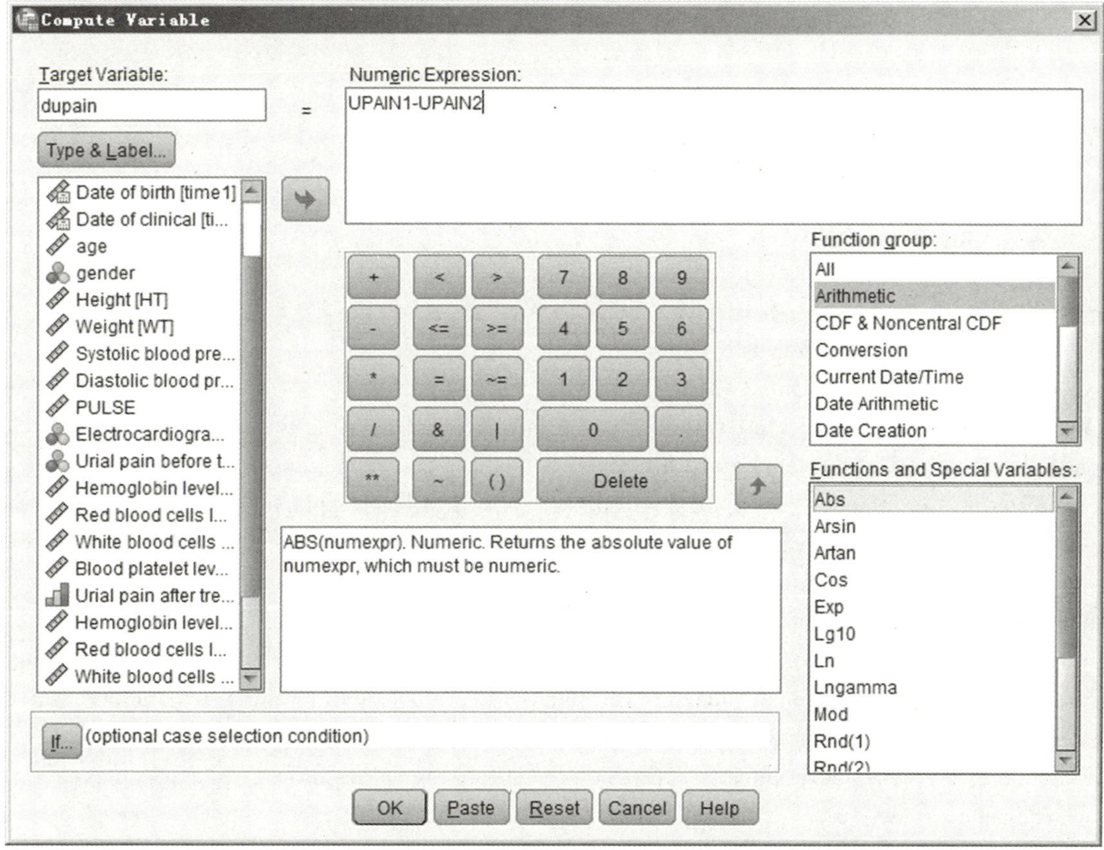

Figure 3-2 The Compute Variable dialog box

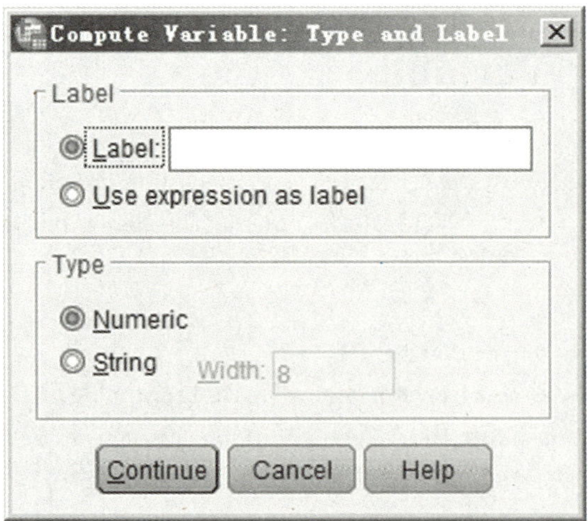

Figure 3-3 The Compute Variable: Type and Label dialog box

◇Label: Label for target variable.

⊙Label [ ]: Enter label in the box.

◎Use expression as label.

◇Type: Type for target variable.

⊙Numeric.

◎String: The default width is 8 bytes.

◇Numeric Expression (Figure 3-2):

You can enter the expression area directly using the keyboard or using the software-supplied calculation pad, or you can select the function in the function box into the expression area. SPSS 23 provides 201 functions listed in the Function and Special Variables box with a brief explanation of each function in the lower-middle box of the main dialog box. Function group box displays 19 different function groups, and the definition and application of various functions can be found in appendix. In numeric expressions, character constants need to be enclosed in single or double quotes.

★If (optional case selection condition, Figure 3-2): Define the case selection condition. When you click the "If" button, a dialog box of Compute Variables: If Cases pops out. If you select "Include if case satisfies condition" button, the expression box is activated (Figure 3-4).

Function expressions and arithmetic expressions treat missing values differently. for example:

□arithmetic expression $(x_1+x_2+x_3)/3$

If at least one of the three variables are missing, the result of the expression is a missing value.

□function expression MEAN(x_1, x_2, x_3)

The result of the expression is missing only if all three variables are missing values.

□function expression MEAN.2(x_1, x_2, x_3)

The result of the expression is not a missing value if two or more variables are not missing.

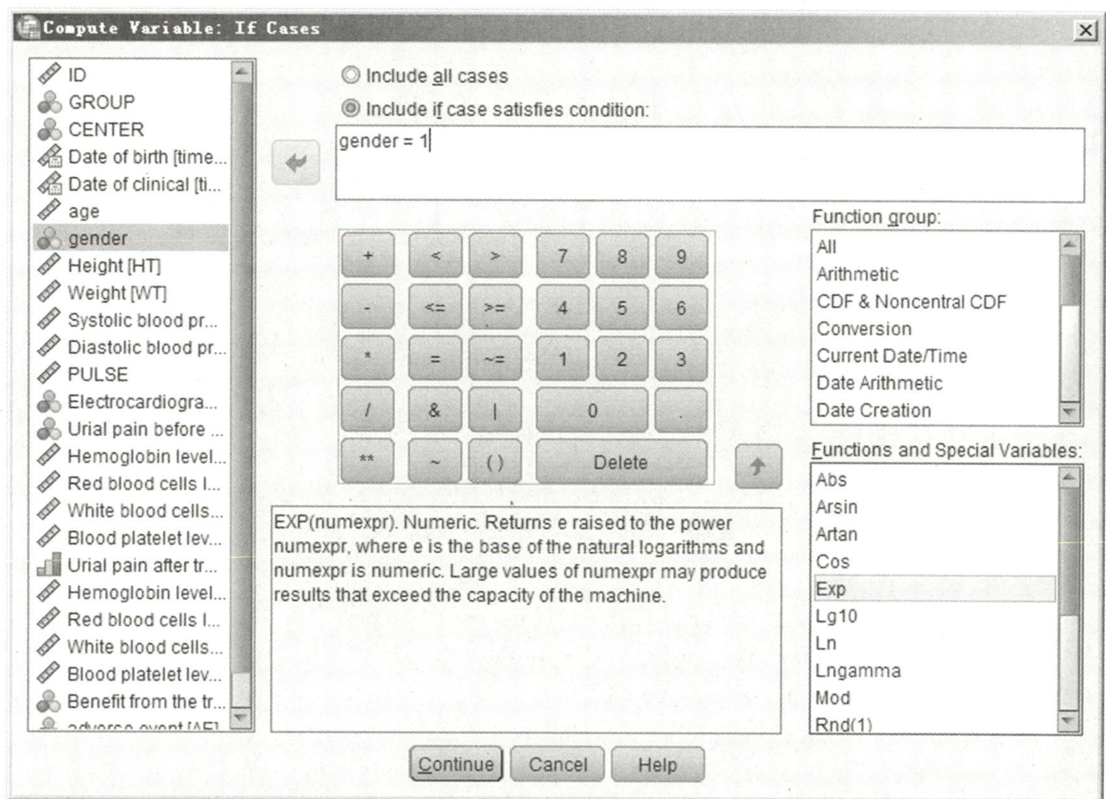

Figure 3-4 The Compute Variable: If Cases dialog box

3.2 Counting Values within Cases

The submenu "Count Values within Cases" under "Transform" can generate new variables that count values within cases.

The data file "IPSQ. sav" is used as the Example 3-1. The file is a satisfactory survey with 20 inpatients. There are 39 questions in the questionnaire, corresponding to 39 variables in the data file (variable names starting with letters acc, c, d, f, h, n, o or s). Each question has 5 options for the answer, namely "very dissatisfied" "dissatisfied" "OK" "satisfied" and "very satisfied" corresponding to scores from 1 to 5. Please count the number of scores from 1 to 5 for each inpatient.

When click the submenu "Count Values within Cases" under the menu "Transform", the dialog box of Count Occurrences of Values within Cases pops out (Figure 3-5).

Transform

Count Values within Cases

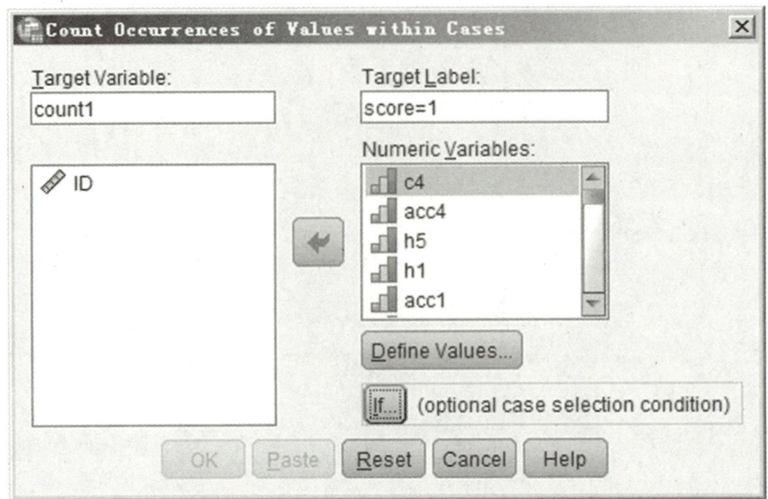

Figure 3-5 The Count Occurrences of Values within Cases dialog box

◇Target Variable: Name of the target variable. Please enter "count1" to "count5" in this example.

◇Target Label: Label of the target variable. Please enter "score=1" to "score=5" in this example.

◇Numeric Variables: Select the variable. Select 2 or more variables of the same type (numeric or string). Please select 39 variables starting with the letters acc, c, d, f, h, n, o or sin this example.

Click "Define Values" button, and the dialog box of Count Values within cases: Values to Count pops out (Figure 3-6).

◇Value: Define the value you want to count.

⊙Value: Enter the defined values into the box (enter 1 to 5 in this example). The "Add" button is activated once you enter the value. Click the button, the defined value is added into the "Values to Count" box. Click the "Continue" button.

◎System-missing: If selected, system-missing values are included when counting.

◎System-or user-missing: If selected, system- or user-missing values are included when counting.

◎Range, ☐ through ☐: Define the range of the value, e. g., from 2 to 4.

◎Range, LOWEST through value: ☐: Define the range of the value, e. g., from the lowest value to 3.

◎Range, value through HIGHEST: ☐: Define the range of the value, e. g., from 4 to the highest value.

★If (optional case selection condition): Define the case selection condition. It is the same to section 3.1.

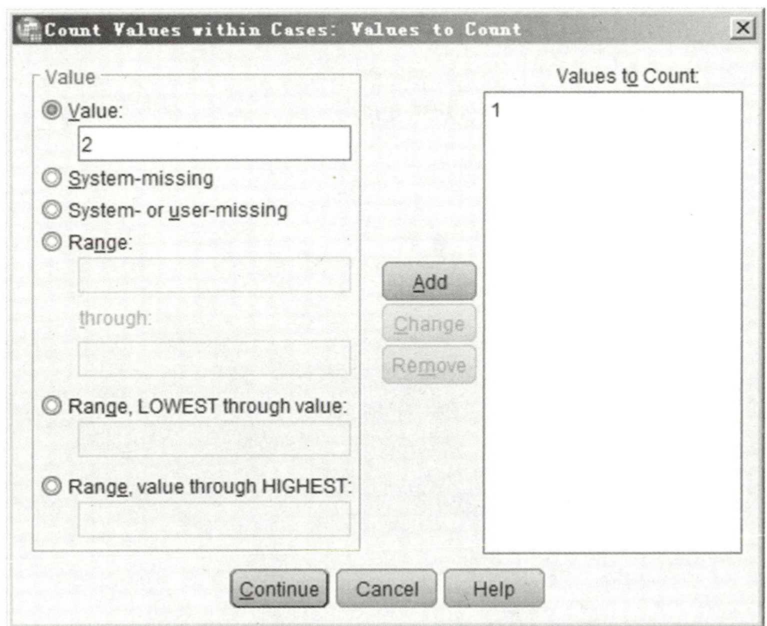

Figure 3-6 The Count Values within Cases: Values to Count dialog box

3.3 Shifting Values

Shift values refer to the generation of a new variable that lags or leads the original data. When click the submenu "Shift Values" under menu "Transform", the dialog box of Shift Values pops out (Figure 3-7).

Transform

Shift Values

◇Variable→New name: Original variable name→new variable name.

◇Name and Method.

Name: d_age4 . New variable name, e. g. , d_age4. Click the "Change" button to display the new variable name in "Variable→New name" box.

Method:

◎Get value from earlier case (Lag): Lag the original data by n observations. If n is 2, the data of new variable is lagged by 2 observations from the original data. The first 2 observations of the new variable are the system-missing values, while the last 2 observations do not appear in the new data.

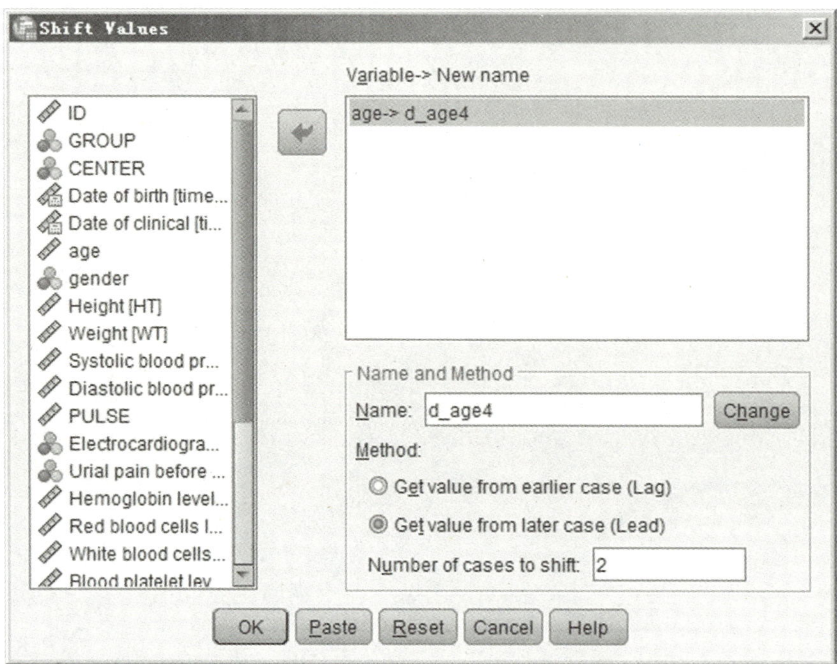

Figure 3-7 The Shift Values dialog box

⊙Get value from later case (Lead): Lead the original data by *n* observations. If *n* is 2, the data of new variable lead by 2 observations from the original data. The last 2 observations of the new variable are the system-missing values, while the first 2 observations do not appear in the new data.

Number of cases to shift: [2]. This is a non-negative integer. Figure 3-7 shows the original variable "age" and the new variable "d_age4" generated by leading the original data by 2 observations.

3.4 Recoding data

In a survey, both positive and negative questions often appear in one questionnaire, leading to inconsistent answer code with actual code. As the data are entered according to the answer code, it is necessary to recode the data. It is common in data processing that we create a new categorical variable to store the recoded data.

The data file "IPSQ. sav" is used as the Example 3-1. Please recode value "1,2,3,4,5" of variable "c2" to values "5,4,3,2,1" accordingly, without changing the variable name. When click the submenu "Recode into Same Variables" under menu "Transform", the dialog box of Recode into Same Variables pops out (Figure 3-8).

Transform

Recode into Same Variables

Select the variable "c2" into the "Numeric Variables" box. If two or more variables are selected at the same time, the type of the selected variables (numeric or string) should be the same. Once you select the variable into the "Numeric Variables" box, the "Old and New Values" button is activated. Click the button, and the dialog box of Recode into Same Variables: Old and New Values pops out (Figure 3-9).

◇Old Value.

⊙Value: Enter a specific numeric code representing an existing category.

◎System-missing: Applies to any system missing values.

◎System–or user–missing: Applies to any system–missing values, or special missing value codes defined by the user in the Variable View window.

◎Range, 2 through 3.9 : Range of the old value, e. g. , from 2 to 3.9.

◎Range, LOWEST through value: 1.9 : Range of the old value, e. g. , ≤1.9.

◎Range, value through HIGHEST: 4 : Range of the old value, e. g. , ≥4.

◎All other values.

◇New Value.

⊙Value: A specific numeric code representing new value.

◎System–missing: System missing value.

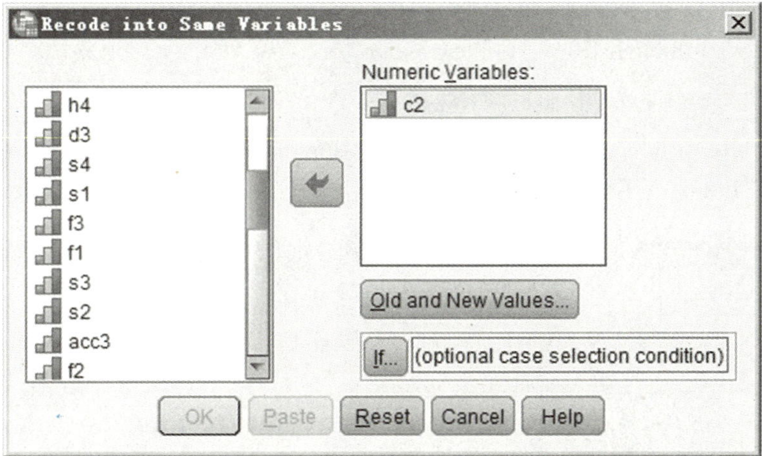

Figure 3–8 The Recode into Same Variables dialog box

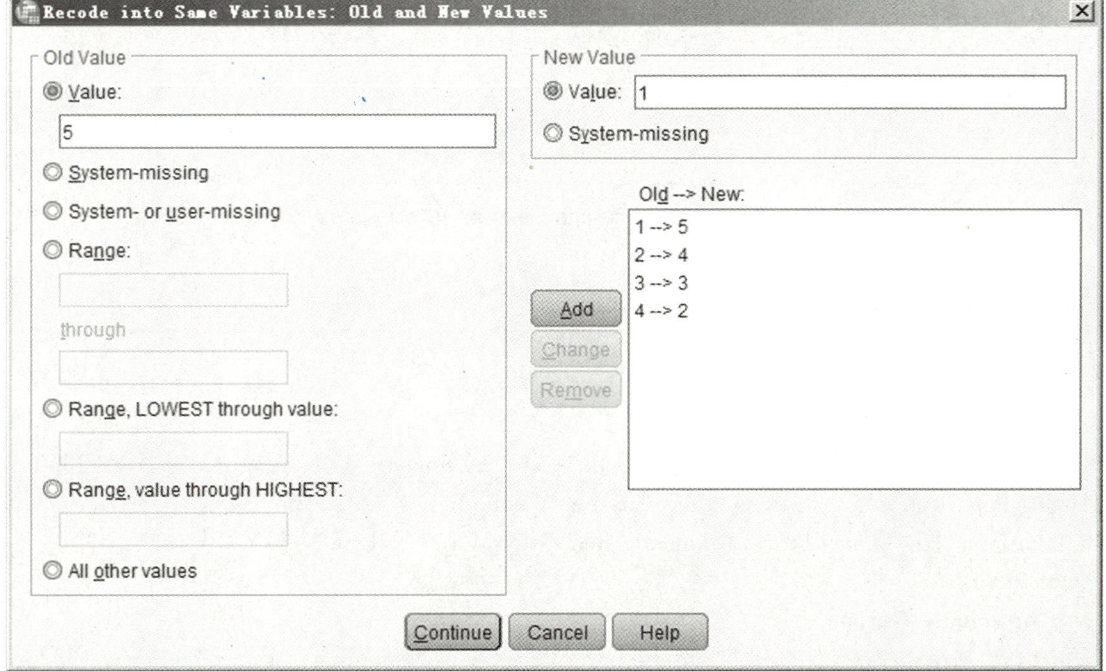

Figure 3–9 The Recode into Same Variables: Old and New Values dialog box

The data file "clinical trial. sav" is used as the Example 3–2. Recode the variable "age" to a new variable "AGE_G" based on the following rules: ≤35 years→1; 36–50 years→2; >50 years→3. When click the submenu "Recode into Different Variables" under menu "Transform", the dialog box of Recode into Different Variables pops out (Figure 3–10).

Transform

Recode into Different Variables

Select the original variable "age" into the box "Numeric Variable → Output Variable" and enter the new variable name "AGE_G" into the box of "Name" under "Output Variable". You may also enter the label for the new variable if needed. When click the "Old and New Values" button, the dialog box of Recode into Different Variables: Old and New Values pops out, which is similar to Figure 3–9. Here are the steps to recode.

◎Old Value: Lowest through [35] → New Value [1] → Add.

◎Old Value: [36] through [50] → New Value [2] → Add.

◎Old Value: [51] through highest → New Value [3] → Add.

After you finish the recoding steps, click "Continue" button to return to the previous dialog box. Click "Change" and "OK" button to finish.

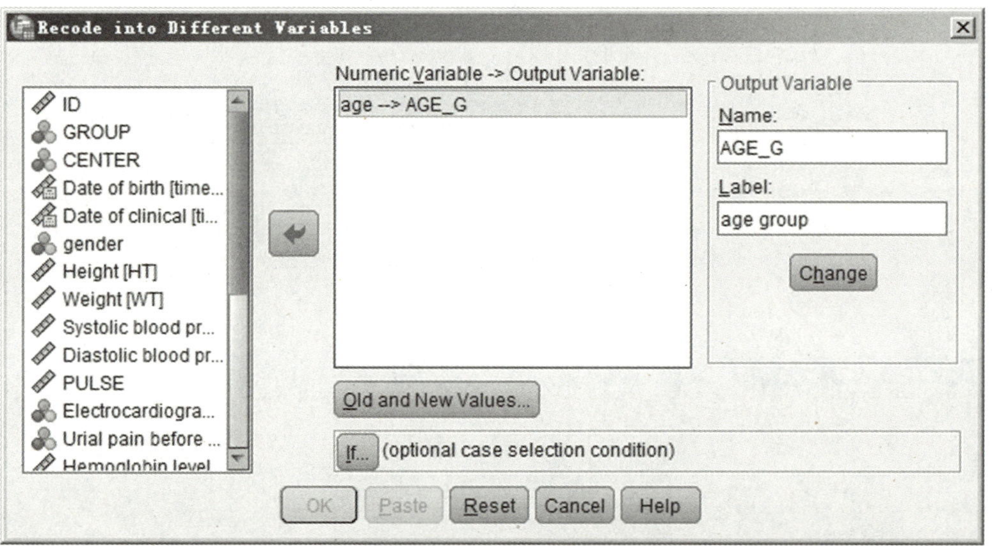

Figure 3–10 The Recode into Different Variables dialog box

3.5 Automatic Recode

Automatic recoding is the process to recode the values of numerical variable or string variable to integers starting from 1, and then saves as a new variable. When click the submenu "Automatic Recode" under menu "Transform", the dialog box of Automatic Recode pops out (Figure 3–11).

Transform

Automatic Recode

Select the original variable "age" into the box "Variable →New Name". Enter the new variable name "age_rank" into the box "New Name", and click the "Add New Name" button to confirm the new variable name.

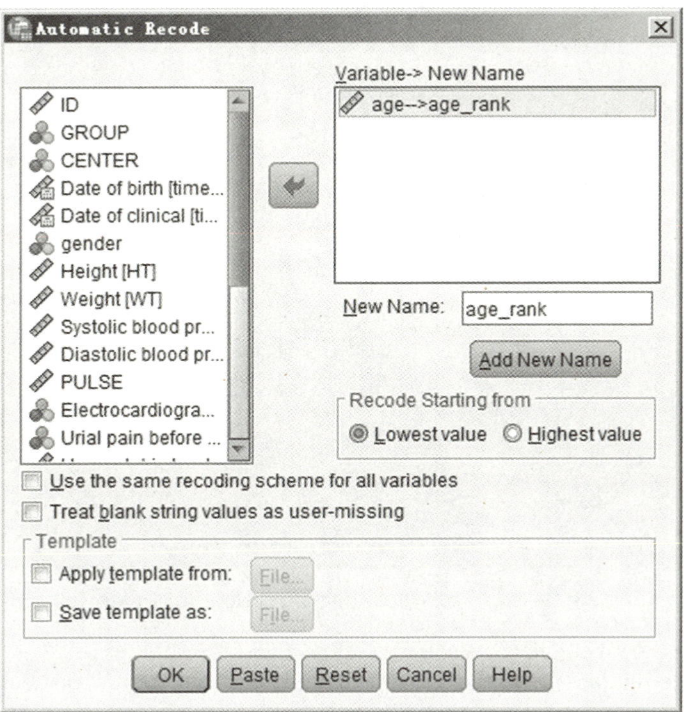

Figure 3-11 The Automatic Recode dialog box

◇Recode Starting from.

⊙Lowest value: Recode from the smallest to the largest value, starting from 1.

◎Highest value: Recode from the largest to the smallest value, starting from 1.

□Use the same recoding scheme for all variables.

□Treat blank string values as user-missing: Treat blank string values as user-missing, and they will be recoded after non-missing values.

◇Template.

□Apply template from File: Click "File" to import template.

□Save template as File: Click "File" to choose the directory to save template.

3.6 Visual Binning

The function of "Visual Binning" is to convert continuous variables into categorical variables. When click the submenu "Visual Binning" under menu "Transform", the dialog box of Visual Binning pops out (Figure 3-12).

Transform

Visual Binning

Select the variables whose values will be grouped into bins to the box "Variables to Bin".

□Limit number of cases scanned to: ☐: Limit number of cases included in the visual binning. If set to 20, only the binning visualization of the first 20 cases is displayed.

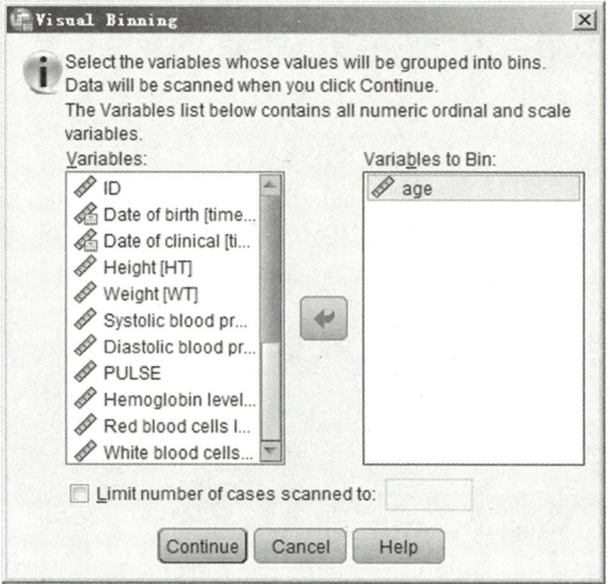

Figure 3-12 The Visual Binning dialog box (step 1)

Click the "Continue" button, the dialog box of Visual Binning at step 2 pops out (Figure 3-13). When the variable in the "Scanned Variable List" is selected, the histogram of the variable is displayed. Click the "Make Cutpoints" button, and the dialog box of Make Cutpoints pops out (Figure 3-14). There are three different methods to make cutpoints, including Equal Width Intervals, Equal Percentiles Based on Scanned Cases and Cutpoints at Mean and Selected Standard Deviations Based on Scanned Cases. After you make cutpoints, click the "Apply" button to return to the previous dialog box. Vertical lines of the classification points will be displayed in the histogram.

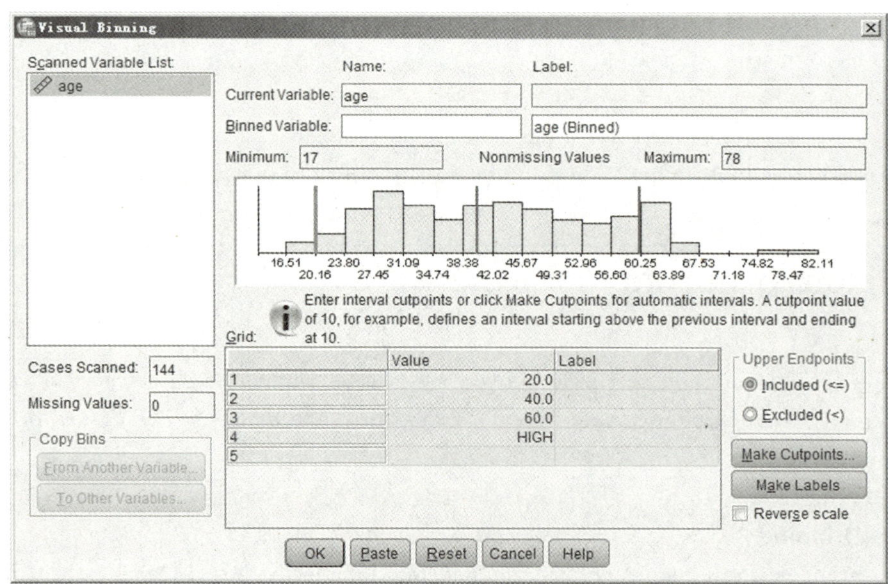

Figure 3-13 The Visual Binning dialog box (step 2)

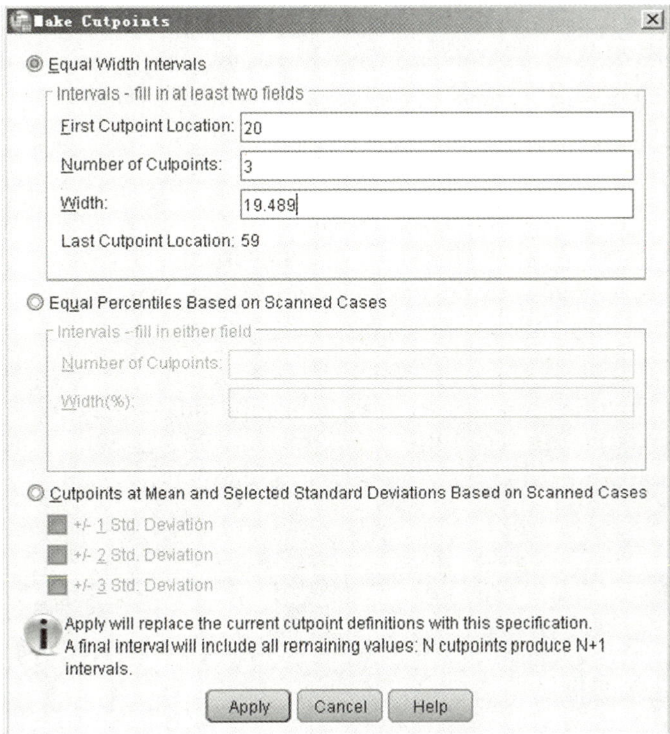

Figure 3-14 The Make Cutpoints dialog box

3.7 Optimal Binning

The function of optimal binning is to classify the values according to the principle of optimization. When click submenu "Optimal Binning" under the menu "Transform", the dialog box of Optimal Binning pops out (Figure 3-15).

Transform

Optimal Binning

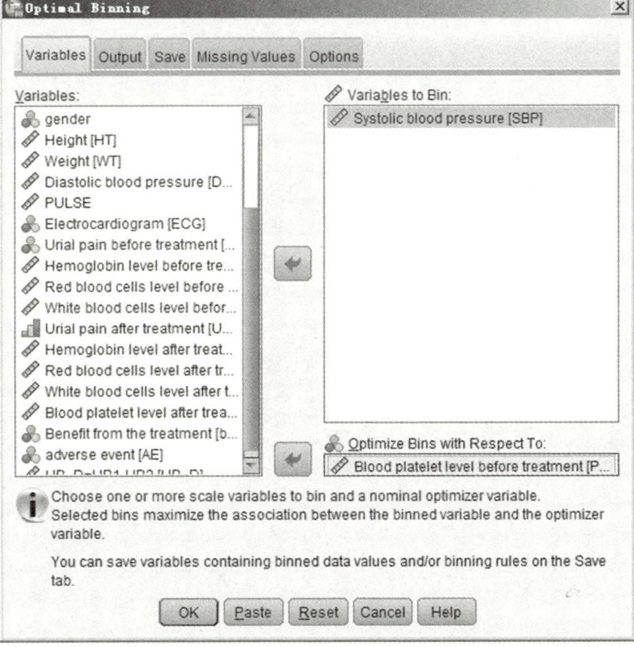

Figure 3-15 The Optimal Binning dialog box

◇Variables to Bin: Variable to bin, e. g. "SBP".

◇Optimize Bins with Respect To: The classification variable that optimal binning respect to, e. g. we select "PLT2" as the classification variable when optimal binning for SBP.

1) Under the menu "Output" in the dialog box of Optimal Binning, you can choose to display endpoints for bins, descriptive statistics for variables that are binned and model entropy for variables that are binned.

2) Under the menu "Save", you can choose to save variables to active dataset by creating variables that contain binned data values, as well as saving the binning rules as syntax.

3) Under the menu "Missing Values", you can choose alternative approaches when dealing with missing values.

4) Under the menu "Options", you can set to exclude or include of bin endpoints. The result of optimal binning is displayed in Figure 3-16. The SBP is classified into 7 categories according to PLT level after treatment, namely <16.0 kPa, <17.0 kPa, <17.2 kPa, <18.5 kPa, <19.8 kPa, <20.4 kPa and 20.4 kPa or over.

	End Point				
Bin	Lower	Upper	83	89	102
1	a	16.0	0	0	0
2	16.0	17.0	0	0	0
3	17.0	17.2	1	0	0
4	17.2	18.5	0	1	0
5	18.5	19.8	0	0	0
6	19.8	20.4	0	0	0
7	20.4	a	0	0	1
Total			1	1	1

Each bin is computed as Lower <= Systolic blood pressure < Upper.

Figure 3-16 Results of optimal binning

3.8 Ranking Cases

The function of "Ranking Cases" is to rank the case values of a variable in ascending or descending order. The process can generate a new variable saving the rank, while the order of original data is unchanged. It differs from "Sort Cases" because "Sort Cases" reorders the original data without generating a new variable. When click the submenu "Rank Cases" under menu "Transform", the dialog box of Rank Cases pops out (Figure 3-17).

Transform

Rank Cases

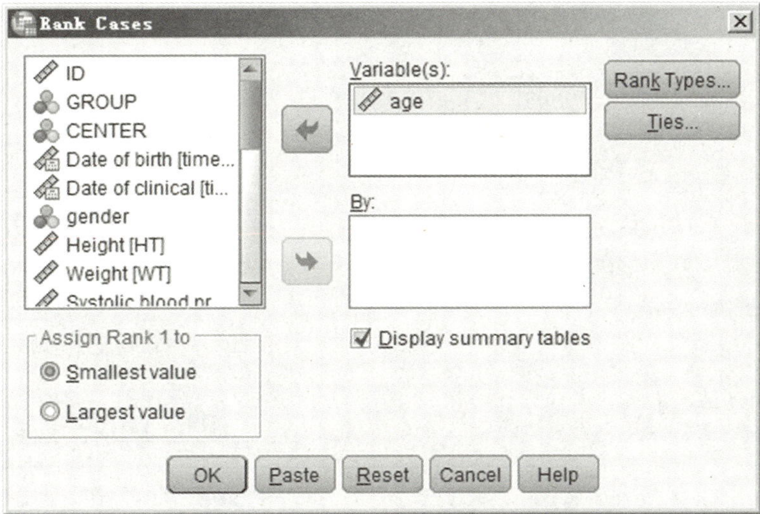

Figure 3-17 The Rank Cases dialog box

◇Variable(s):Select the variables that to rank.

◇By:Select the group variable that ranking will be done respectively.

☑Display summary tables:Output the table of descriptive statistics.

◇Assign Rank 1 to:Rank method.

⊙Smallest value:Rank from the smallest to the largest value.

◎Largest value:Rank from the largest to the smallest value.

★Rank Types. When click the "Rank Types" button, the dialog box of Rank Cases:Types pops out (Figure 3-18).

☑Rank(system default):Simple rank.

□Savage score:Savage score based on exponential distribution.

□Fractional rank:Display in decimals.

□Fractional rank as %:Display in percentages.

□Sum of case weights:Sample size of each group.

□Ntiles: 4 . Number of groups based on percentile. The default value is 4, which means it can categorize into 4 groups based on percentile.

□Proportion estimates:There are four methods, including Blom, Tukey, Rankit and Van der Waerden.

□Normal scores:Score of standard normal distribution, i. e. Z scores.

★Ties:Ranking method when dealing with ties.

When you click the "Ties" button, the dialog box of Rank Cases:Ties pops out (Figure 3-19). Results of case ranking as shown in Table 3-1 for various methods dealing with ties.

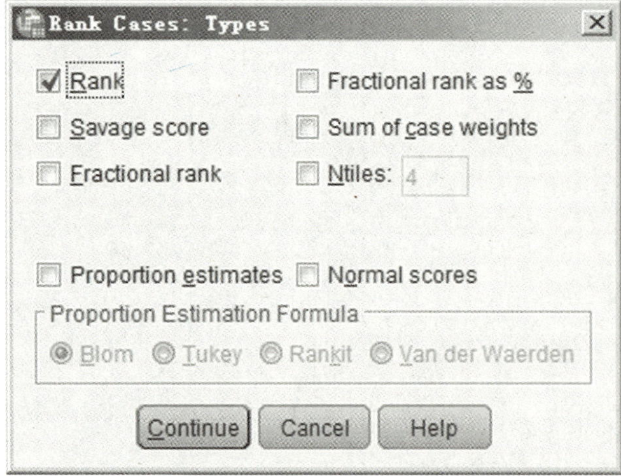

Figure 3-18 The Rank Cases: Types dialog box

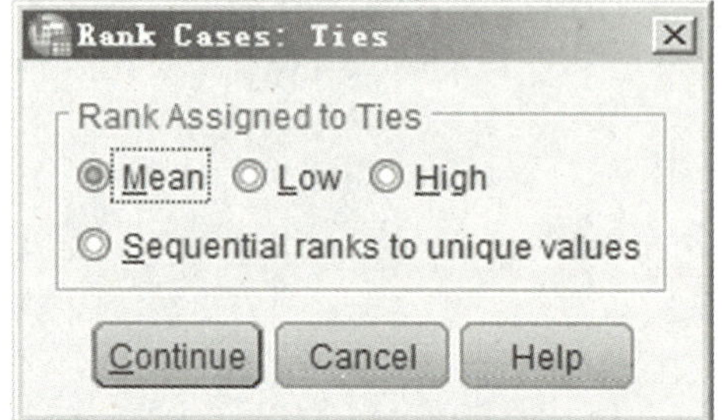

Figure 3-19 The Rank Cases: Ties dialog box

Table 3-1 Results of case ranking for different methods dealing with ties

Value	Mean	Low	High	Sequential
7	1	1	1	1
9	3	2	4	2
9	3	2	4	2
9	3	2	4	2
15	5	5	5	3
21	6	6	6	4

3.9 Replacing missing values

Missing data is a common problem in statistical analysis, such as data from a survey study. Some SPSS statistical functions can not be executed because of missing data, such as times series analysis. Therefore, we should use statistical methods to deal with missing data to make full use of original data and ensure the statistical functions working. When click the submenu "Replace Missing Values" under menu "Transform", the dialog box Replace Missing Values pops out (Figure 3-20).

Transform

Replace Missing Values

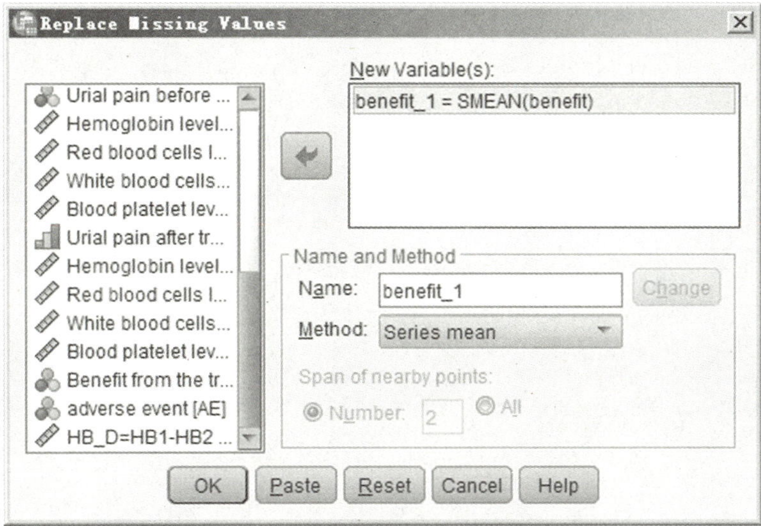

Figure 3-20 The Replace Missing Values dialog box

◇Name and Method: Name of generated variable, and methods to deal with missing value.

Name: Name of generated variable. A new variable can be generated after replacement of missing data. The default variable name is to add "_1" after the original variable name, and users can also define variable names. The original variables names and data are still retained.

Method: Methods to deal with missing data.

1) Series mean: Replace the missing value with the arithmetic mean of the variables.

2) Mean of nearby points: Replace the missing value with the arithmetic mean of the nearby points. If this method is selected, the option for Span of nearby points is activated.

3) Median of nearby points: Replace the missing value by the median of nearby points. If selected, the option for Span of nearby points is activated.

4) Linear interpolation: Linear interpolation method. Replace the missing value with linearly interpolated value of 2 nearby points before and after the missing value.

5) Linear trend at point: Linear trend method. Use linear regression to estimate and replace missing value.

Span of nearby points.

⊙Number: 2 : Replace the missing value with the arithmetic mean of two valid values up and down nearby the missing value.

◎All: Replace the missing value with the arithmetic mean of all valid observations.

3.10 Random number generators

When click the submenu "Random Number Generators" under menu "Transform", the dialog box of "Random Number Generators" pops out (Figure 3-21).

Transform

Random Number Generators

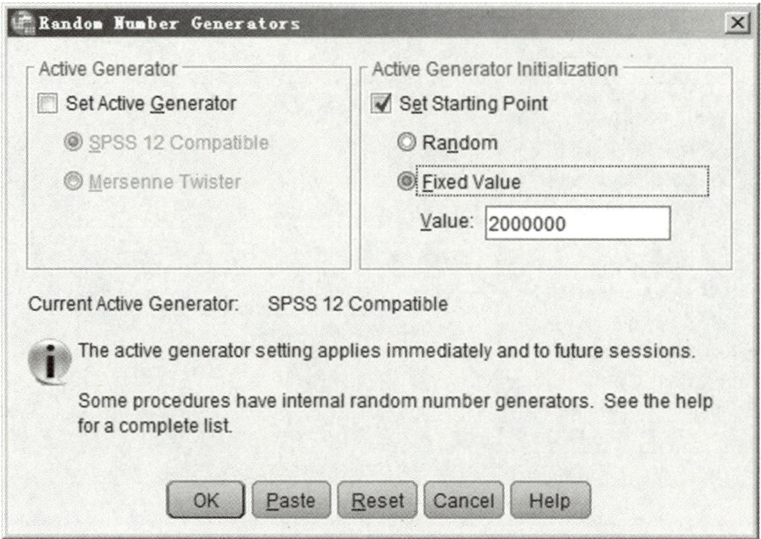

Figure 3–21 The Random Number Generators dialog box

◇Active Generator.

□Set Active Generator.

⊙SPSS 12 Compatible: Random number generator of SPSS 12 and earlier versions.

◎Mersenne Twister: New random number generator, which is more robust than the SPSS 12 and earlier versions.

◇Active Generator Initialization.

☑Set Starting Point.

◎Random: Randomly selected random number seed.

⊙ Fixed Value/Value: 2000000 : Fixed random number seed, and the range is 1 – 2 000 000 000. This option is considered for reproducible of simulation results.

Wand Xiling

Chapter 4

Analysis of Descriptive Statistics

The "Descriptive Statistics"(basic statistical analysis) in the submenu of statistical analysis includes seven processes:Frequencies,Descriptives,Explore,Crosstabs,Ratio,P-P Plots and Q-Q Plots (Figure 4-1).

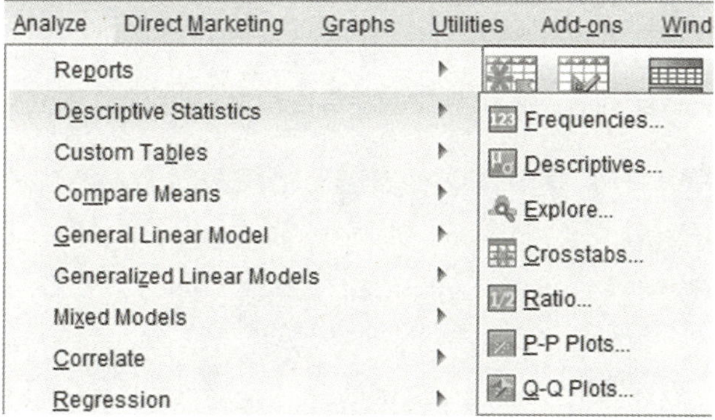

Figure 4-1 Basic statistical analysis menu in statistical analysis Module

4.1 Frequencies

4.1.1 Description

The analysis of frequency distribution mainly describes the distribution characteristics of data by means of frequency distribution table, bar chart and histogram, as well as various statistics of central trendcy and dispersion.

4.1.2 Example

Example 4-1 The data file "diameter_sub. sav" is used as the Example 4-1, which records the sagittal diameter of 216 human spine vertebrae. Try to make a descriptive analysis of the variable "trueap_mean" (sagittal diameter) and draw histograms.

4.1.3 Running the command

Analyze

Descriptive Statistics

Frequencies

The dialog box of Frequencies pops out (Figure 4-2).

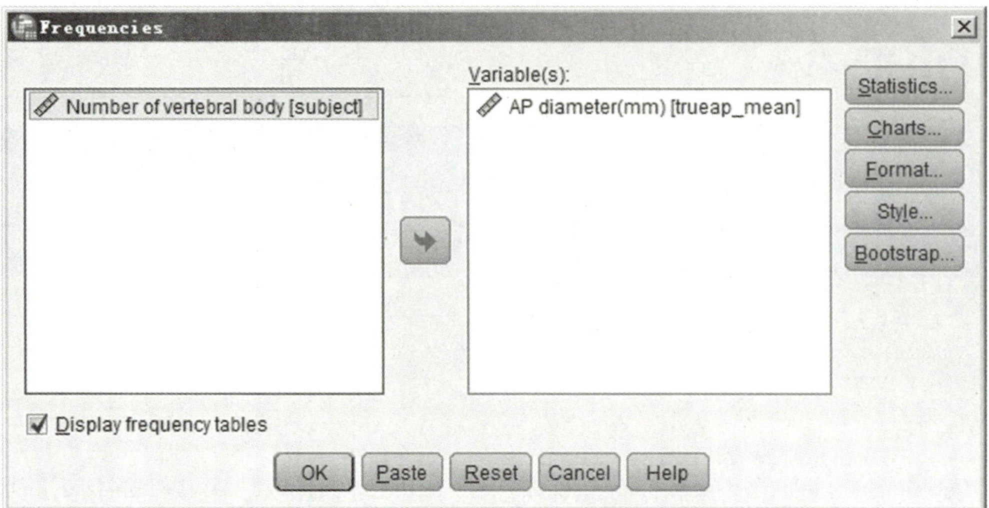

Figure 4-2 The Frequencies dialog box

☑Display frequency tables.

★Statistics: Click "Statistics" button, and the dialog box of Frequencies: Statistics pops out (Figure 4-3).

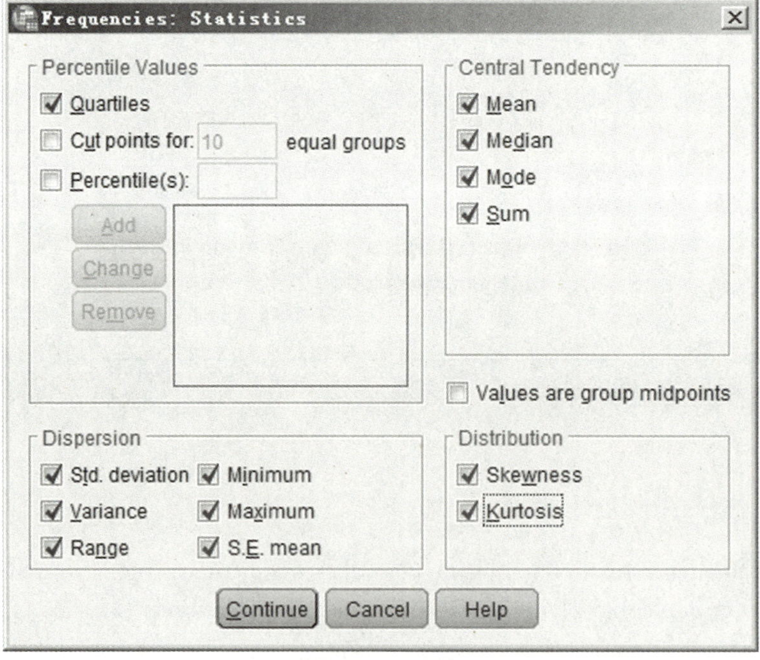

Figure 4-3 The Frequencies: Statistics dialog box

◇Percentile Values.

☑Quartiles.

□Cut points for: [10] equal groups: All observed values are divided equally according to percentile *n*. The default value of the system is 10, that is the output of the value of $P_{10}, P_{20} \ldots P_{90}$.

□Percentile (s) [ ]: Select a custom percentile. The "Add" button is activated after the value is filled in the text box.

◇Central Tendency.

☑Mean.

☑Median.

☑Mode.

☑Sum.

◇Dispersion.

☑Std. deviation. ☑Minimum.

☑Variance. ☑Maximun.

☑Range. ☑S. E. mean.

□Values are group midpoints: When calculating the percentile, it is assumed that the current data has been divided into different groups. The current data is calculated as the group median of each group.

◇Distribution.

☑Skewness.

☑Kurtosis.

★Charts: Click "Charts" button (Figure 4-2), and the dialog box of Frequencies: Charts pops out (Figure 4-4).

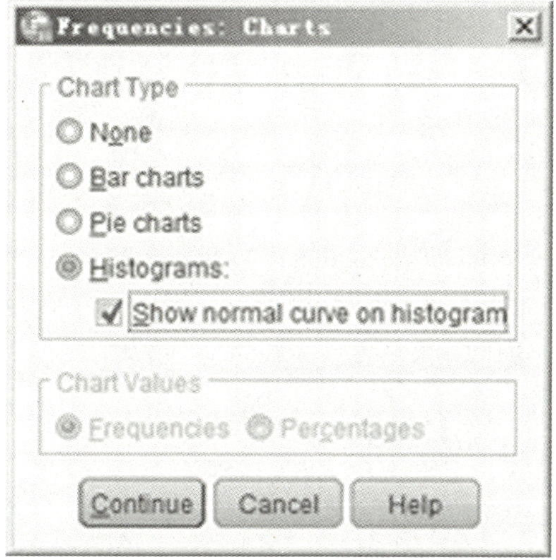

Figure 4-4 The Frequencies: Charts dialog box

◇Chart Type.

◎None.

◎Bar charts.

◎Pie charts.

⊙Histograms: Select this item and activates the following options in the Example 4-1.

☑Show normal curve on histogram.

◇Chart Values: This option is valid only for bar and circle diagrams.

⊙Frequencies. ◎Percentages.

★Format: Click "Format" button (Figure 4-2), and the dialog box of Frequencies: Format pops out (Figure 4-5).

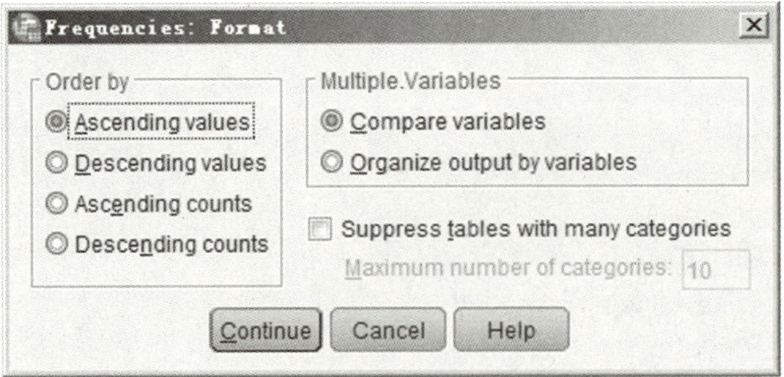

Figure 4-5 The Frequencies: Format dialog box

◇Order by.

⊙Ascending values.

◎Descending values.

◎Ascending counts.

◎Descending counts.

◇Multiple Variables.

⊙Compare variables.

◎Organize output by variables.

□Suppress tables with many categories.

Maximum number of categories: 10.

★Bootstrap: The relevant statistics are calculated by bootstrap method.

Click "Bootstrap" button (Figure 4-2), and the dialog box of Bootstrap pops out (Figure 4-6).

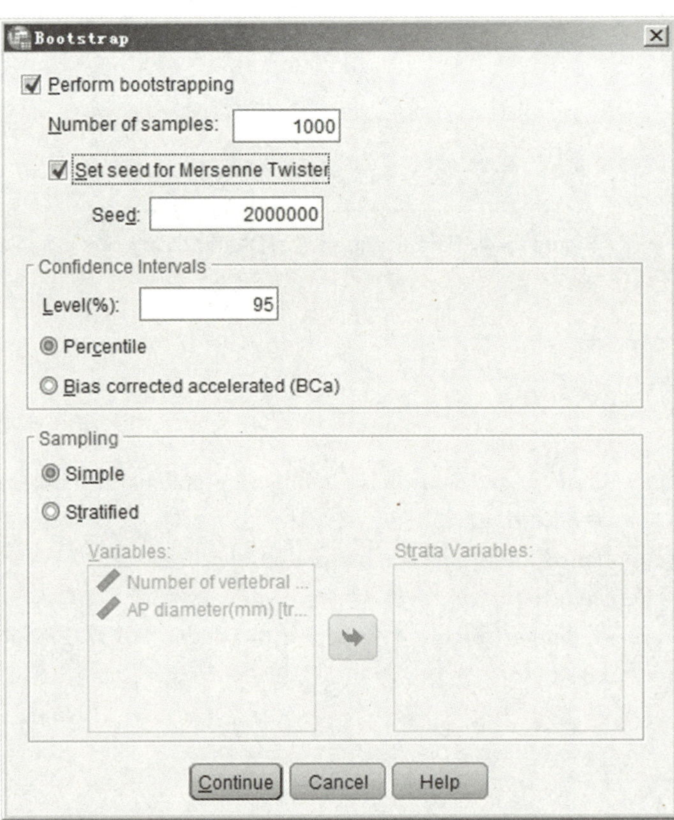

Figure 4-6 The Bootstrap dialog box

☑Perform bootstrapping.

Number of samples: 1000

☑Set seed for Mersenne Twister.

Seed: 2000000 : The positive integer between 1 and 2 000 000 000 is optional. If seed set is not allowed, the result of each run is different. The default number is 2 000 000.

◇Confidence Intervals.

Level (%): 95.

⊙Percentile: The confidence interval is calculated according to the percentile method.

◎Bias corrected accelerated (BCa): The confidence interval can be calculated by the accelerated bootstrap sampling after bias correction.

◇Sampling: Bootstrap sampling method.

⊙Simple: Simple sampling method, namely the currently selected variables as a whole sampling (system default).

◎Stratified: The method of stratified sampling is that bootstrap sampling is carried out independently in each layer according to the stratified variables selected in the "Strata Variables" box.

4.1.4 Reading the output

(1) Without bootstrap sampling, the main results obtained according to the options in the "Statistics" and "Charts" as shown in Figure 4-7 and Figure 4-8. Skewness coefficient and its standard error are -0.189 and 0.166 respectively, and $Z=-0.189/0.166=-1.1386$ ($P=0.2549$). Kurtosis coefficient and its standard error are -0.057 and 0.330 respectively, and $Z=-0.057/0.330=-0.1727$ ($P=0.8629$). Combined with the two results, the data is considered to be normally distributed.

In the Example 4-1, the probability of bilateral (tail) is also can be calculated by using the function of CDF. NORMAL (Z,0,1) in compute variable.

Statistics

AP diameter(mm)

N	Valid	216
	Missing	0
Mean		14.4421
Std. Error of Mean		.04881
Median		14.4875
Mode		14.45
Std. Deviation		.71728
Variance		.514
Skewness		-.189
Std. Error of Skewness		.166
Kurtosis		-.057
Std. Error of Kurtosis		.330
Range		4.18
Minimum		12.25
Maximum		16.43
Percentiles	25	13.9031
	50	14.4875
	75	14.8969

Figure 4-7 Output of the Example 4-1

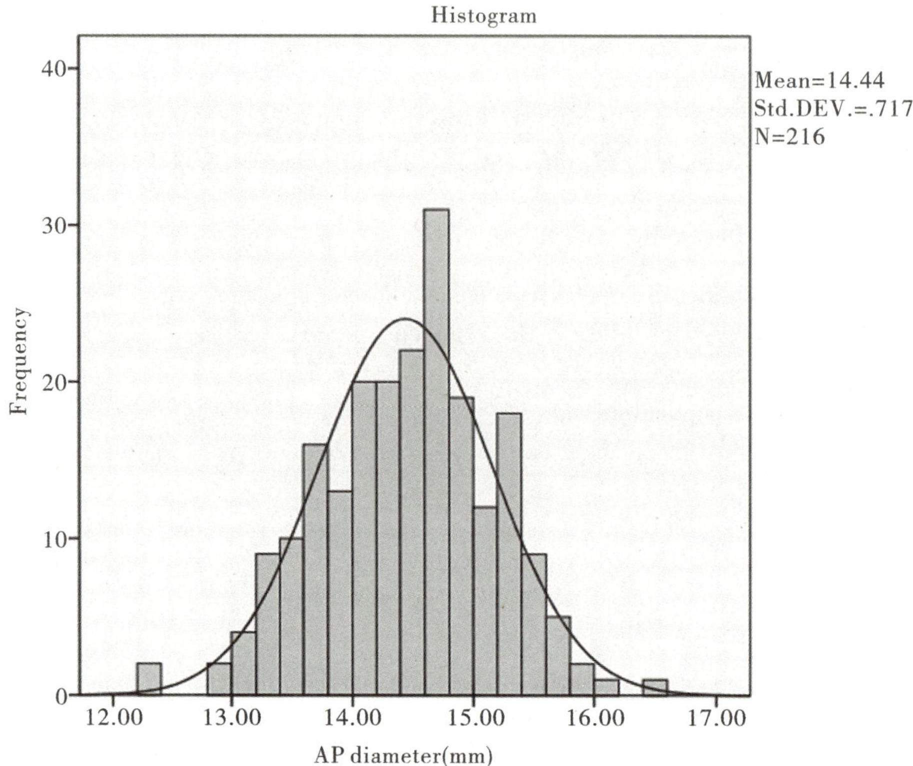

Figure 4-8 Frequency distribution histogram and normal curve

(2) The bootstrap sampling the main output as shown in Figure 4-9. To calculate the mean and standard deviation, for example, according to the bootstrap default option, 95% confidence interval of mean and standard deviation are 14.345 9-14.533 7 and 0.651 37-0.786 66, respectively.

Statistics

AP diameter(mm)

		Statistic	Bootstrap[a]			
			Bias	Std. Error	95% Confidence Interval	
					Lower	Upper
N	Valid	216	0	0	216	216
	Missing	0	0	0	0	0
Mean		14.4421	-.0021	.0479	14.3459	14.5337
Std. Deviation		.71728	-.00210	.03428	.65137	.78666

a. Unless otherwise noted, bootstrap results are based on 1000 bootstrap samples

Figure 4-9 The main output results of bootstrap sampling

4.2 Descriptives

4.2.1 Description

Descriptive statistical analysis is mainly used to calculate all kinds of statistics which describe the trend of central tendency and dispersion. In addition, one important function is to make standardized transformation of variables, namely *Z* transformation.

4.2.2 Example

Example 4–2 The data file "clinical trial. sav" is used as the Example 4–2. Four variables: "HB1" (pre–treatment hemoglobin), "RBC1" (pre–treatment red blood cells), "WBC1" (pre–treatment white blood cells) and "PLT1" (pre–treatment platelet) are in the data file. Please give the descriptives of four variables in the data file.

4.2.3 Running the command

Analyze

Descriptive Statistics

Descriptives dialog box pops out (Figure 4–10). Select the variable "HB1" "RBC1" "WBC1" "PLT1" under the Variable (s) box.

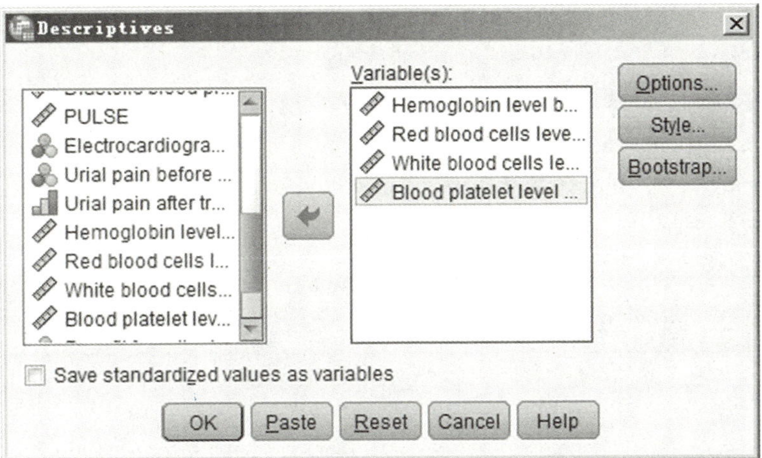

Figure 4–10 The Descriptives dialog box

□Save standardized values as variables: Standardize the analysis variables. This option produces a standardized value (*Z* score) and stores the *Z* score in the data file as a new variable named "*Z*" before the original variable name. *Z* points calculation formula is: $z_i = (x_i - \bar{x})/s$, where $\bar{x}$ for the variable mean, *s* for standard deviation.

★Options: Click "Options" button, and the dialog box of Descriptives: Options pops out (Figure 4–11).

◇Display Order.

◎Variable list.

◎Alphabetic.

◎Ascending means.

◎Descending means.

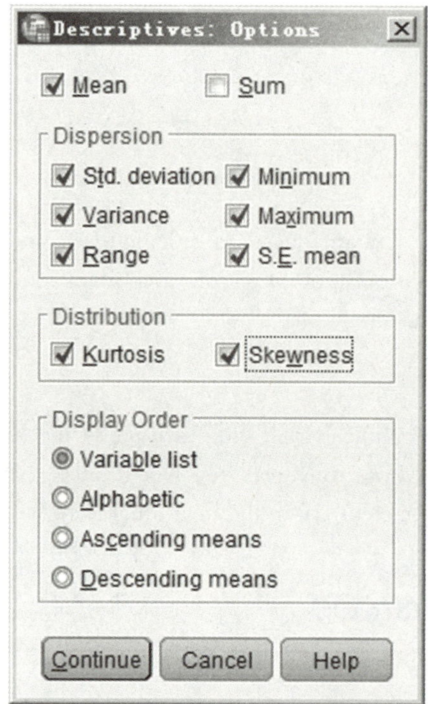

Figure 4-11 The Descriptives: Options dialog box

4.2.4 Reading the output

The output of the Example 4-2 is shown in Figure 4-12, which shows that the descriptive statistical analysis process is exactly the same as the statistics output of the "Frequencies" process. The only difference with the description procedure is that there is an option to generate standardized values (save standardized values as variables).

Descriptive Statistics

	N	Range	Minimum	Maximum	Mean		Std. Deviation	Variance	Skewness		Kurtosis	
	Statistic	Statistic	Statistic	Statistic	Statistic	Std. Error	Statistic	Statistic	Statistic	Std. Error	Statistic	Std. Error
Hemoglobin level before treatment	144	123	70	193	135.40	1.563	18.754	351.709	-.209	.202	1:419	.401
Red blood cells level before treatment	144	4.23	3.09	7.32	4.4817	.04888	.58660	.344	.879	.202	3.390	.401
White blood cells level before treatment	144	12.50	2.90	15.40	6.8238	.16957	2.03483	4.141	1.233	.202	2.526	.401
Blood platelet level before treatment	144	590	83	673	217.85	6.294	75.528	5704.489	2.090	.202	9.344	.401
Valid N (listwise)	144											

Figure 4-12 Output of the Example 4-2

4.3 Explore

4.3.1 Description

Exploratory analyses mainly include the following objectives.

1) Check the data for outliers and(or) extreme values.

2) The premise assumptions, such as normal distribution and homogeneity of variance test, can be tested. When the distribution and variance homogeneity of data are not satisfied, the method of data conversion is suggested, and the parametric method or non-parametric method is adopted.

3) Understanding the characteristics of differences between groups.

4) The statistics, normality test and descriptive statistical diagrams, including stem and leaf diagrams, histogram and box diagram, can be given in the explore process.

4.3.2 Example

Example 4-3 The data file "clinical trial. sav" is used as the Example 4-3. The variable "PLT1" (pre-treatment platelet) in the Example 4-3 is analyzed by grouping variable as "group".

4.3.3 Running the command

Analyze

Descriptive Statistics

Explore

The dialog box of Explore is listed in Figure 4-13.

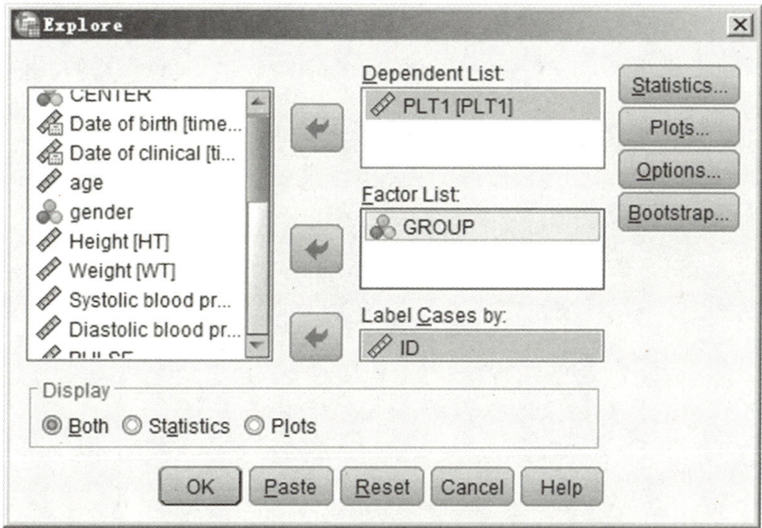

Figure 4-13 The Explore dialog box

◇Dependent List: Optional dependent variables (explanatory variables), that is, exploratory analysis of the variables, generally for the measurement type, can choose one or more. Select the variable "PLT1" in the Example 4-3.

◇Factor List: Options for a category (GROUP) variable, typically a count or class type, with one or more optional. Select the grouping variable "GROUP" in the Example 4-3.

◇Label Cases by: In general, only one classified variable or identification variable can be selected to mark the observation unit. In the Example 4-3, the identification variable "ID" is selected.

◇Display: Output content.

⊙Both ◎Statistics ◎Plots (system default)

★Statistics: Click "Statistics" button, and the dialog box of Explore: Statistics pops out (Figure 4-14). This example is fully selected.

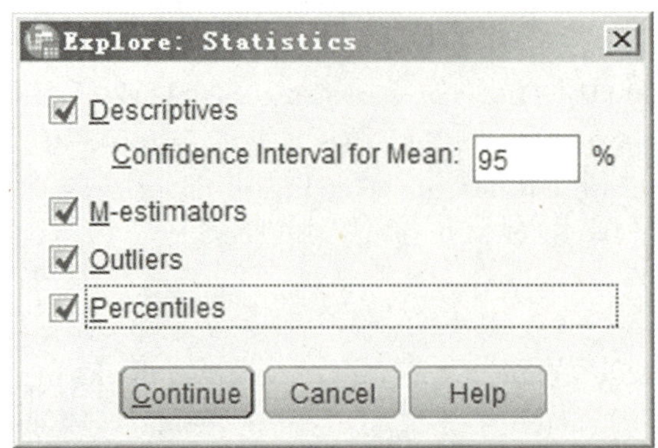

Figure 4-14 The Explore:Statistics dialog box

☑Descriptives:Confidence Interval for Mean 95 %:The confidence interval of the total mean. The system defaults is 95%.

☑M-estimators.

☑Outliers:Displays five maximum and five minimum values.

☑Percentiles.

★Plots:Click "Plots" button(Figure 4-13),and the dialog box of Explore:Plots pops out (Figure 4-15).

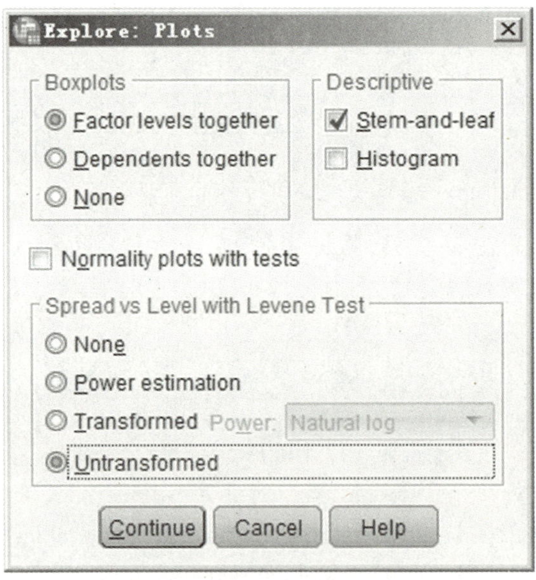

Figure 4-15 The Explore:Plots dialog box

◇Boxplots.

⊙Factor levels together (system default):For each category variable,only one dependent variable is shown per graph. Select this item in the Example 4-3.

◎Dependents together:For each category variable,each graph shows all dependent variables.

◎None.

◇Descriptive.

☑Stem-and-leaf:Stem and leaf diagrams,used to describe the frequency distribution,replace the groups in the frequency table with actual values,and the values are composed of Stem and leaf. Figure 4-16 is one of the analysis results of the Example 4-3. In this case,the stem width is 100,and each leaf represents one case. For example,there are 2 cases with platelet count of 80×10^9/L,1 case with 120×

10^9/L, 3 cases with 130×10^9/L, and so on.

□Histogram.

□Normality plots with tests: The normality test is made and the normal probability diagram is drawn. The Kolmogorov-Smirnov statistic is given and the Shapiro-Wilk statistic is given when the sample size ≤ 50.

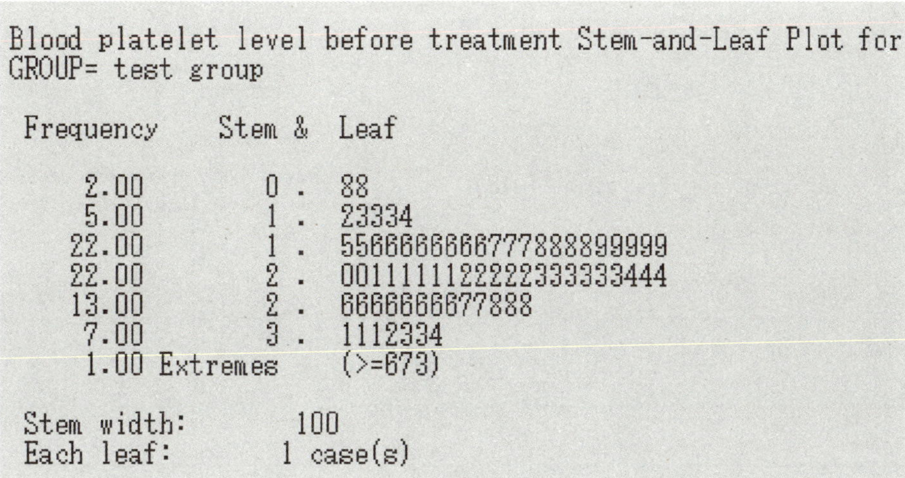

```
Blood platelet level before treatment Stem-and-Leaf Plot for
GROUP= test group

 Frequency    Stem &  Leaf

     2.00        0 .  88
     5.00        1 .  23334
    22.00        1 .  5566666666777888899999
    22.00        2 .  0011111122222333333444
    13.00        2 .  6666666677888
     7.00        3 .  1112334
     1.00 Extremes    (>=673)

 Stem width:       100
 Each leaf:       1 case(s)
```

Figure 4-16 Stem-and-Leaf plots of test group before treatment

◇Spread *vs* Level with Levene Test: Levene variance homogeneity test, there are four options.

1) If no homogeneity test of variance is made, "None" is selected.

2) If we do the homogeneity test of variance, we first select "Untransformed" to test the homogeneity of variance on the original data. If the data satisfy the homogeneity, testing ends here.

3) If the data don't satisfy the homogeneity, we choose "Power estimation" to determine the power transformation method.

4) At last, we try to find a method to satisfy the homogeneity in six power transformation methods. If the above efforts cannot meet the requirement of homogeneity, nonparametric analysis should be considered.

◎None.

◎Power estimation: The best power transformation value can be obtained by power transformation estimation, which provides a reference for selecting the following power transformation methods, in order to achieve the purpose of homogeneity of variance.

◎Transformed Power: Power transformation method. After selection this code, power transformation method box is activated, the following methods are available.

1) Natural log.

2) 1/square root.

3) Reciprocal.

4) Square root.

5) Square.

6) Cube.

7) Untransformed.

★Options: Click "Options" button (Figure 4-13), and the dialog box of Explore: Options pops out (Figure 4-17).

◇Missing Values: Determine how missing values are handled.

⊙Exclude cases listwise (system default): For each observation unit, as long as one variable selected in the analysis is a missing value, the observation unit is regarded as the missing value and does not participate in the analysis process.

◎Exclude cases pairwise: For a unit of observation, only the missing value of the variable and the variable related to the analysis of the variable is considered to be missing.

◎Report values: The observation units with missing values in the classification variables are analyzed separately and the corresponding output results are obtained.

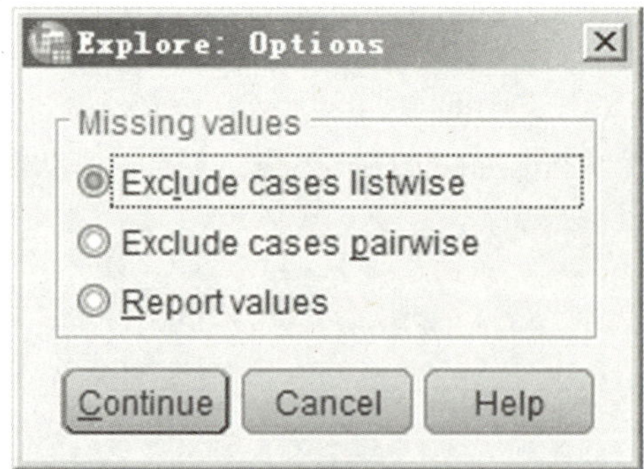

Figure 4-17 The Explore: Options dialog box

4.3.4 Reading the output

(1) Description of the units involved in the analysis process: 72 cases in each group, no missing data (Figure 4-18).

Case Processing Summary

	GROUP	Cases					
		Valid		Missing		Total	
		N	Percent	N	Percent	N	Percent
Blood platelet level before treatment	test group	72	100.0%	0	0.0%	72	100.0%
	control group	72	100.0%	0	0.0%	72	100.0%

Figure 4-18 Description of the unit of observation

(2) Descriptive statistics: Some of the results are as follows (Figure 4-19).

1) 5% Trimmed Mean: The average after the maximum and the smallest observations of 5% are removed.

2) Interquartile Range.

Descriptives

	GROUP			Statistic	Std. Error
Blood platelet level before treatment	test group	Mean		224.00	9.270
		95% Confidence Interval for Mean	Lower Bound	205.52	
			Upper Bound	242.48	
		5% Trimmed Mean		219.29	
		Median		217.50	
		Variance		6186.704	
		Std. Deviation		78.656	
		Minimum		83	
		Maximum		673	
		Range		590	
		Interquartile Range		91	
		Skewness		2.598	.283
		Kurtosis		14.004	.559
	control group	Mean		211.71	8.520
		95% Confidence Interval for Mean	Lower Bound	194.72	
			Upper Bound	228.70	
		5% Trimmed Mean		205.44	
		Median		198.00	
		Variance		5226.012	
		Std. Deviation		72.291	
		Minimum		102	
		Maximum		482	
		Range		380	
		Interquartile Range		79	
		Skewness		1.474	.283
		Kurtosis		3.150	.559

Figure 4-19 Output of descriptive statistics

(3) M-Estimators: M-estimator is a robust estimator of the central tendency, and lists four kinds of M-Estimators: Huber, Tukey, Hampel and Andrews. In addition to giving the estimator, Hagrid deals with the weighted constant of the estimator calculated by different methods (Figure 4-20).

M-Estimators

	GROUP	Huber's M-Estimator[a]	Tukey's Biweight[b]	Hampel's M-Estimator[c]	Andrews' Wave[d]
Blood platelet level before treatment	test group	217.23	216.74	216.68	216.75
	control group	200.70	196.21	199.86	196.20

a. The weighting constant is 1.339.
b. The weighting constant is 4.685.
c. The weighting constants are 1.700, 3.400, and 8.500
d. The weighting constant is 1.340*pi.

Figure 4-20 Output of M-Estimators

(4) Percentiles: The results of weighted average and Tukey method (limited to quartile) are given respectively (Figure 4-21).

Percentiles

		GROUP	Percentiles 5	10	25	50	75	90	95
Weighted Average (Definition 1)	Blood platelet level before treatment	test group	127.80	147.90	170.00	217.50	261.00	311.70	330.70
		control group	116.50	137.20	163.50	198.00	242.75	295.00	376.75
Tukey's Hinges	Blood platelet level before treatment	test group			170.00	217.50	261.00		
		control group			164.00	198.00	242.50		

Figure 4-21 Output of Percentiles

(5) Normality test: The results of Kolmogorov-Smimov method and Shapiro-Wilk method are given in Figure 4-22.

1) Sig. (significance level): *P* value. All *P* values are less than or equal to 0.024, indicating that the platelet counts in both groups are not subject to normal distribution. Generally speaking, the greater the *P* value, the more support data from the normal distribution.

2) df (degrees of freedom).

Tests of Normality

	GROUP	Kolmogorov-Smirnov[a] Statistic	df	Sig.	Shapiro-Wilk Statistic	df	Sig.
Blood platelet level before treatment	test group	.113	72	.024	.814	72	.000
	control group	.123	72	.009	.895	72	.000

a. Lilliefors Significance Correction

Figure 4-22 Output of Normality Test

(6) A normal test Q-Q chart of platelet count distribution in the trial group. If the data follow normal distribution, the distribution of scattered points is close to a straight line. The Example 4-3 does not support normal distribution (Figure 4-23).

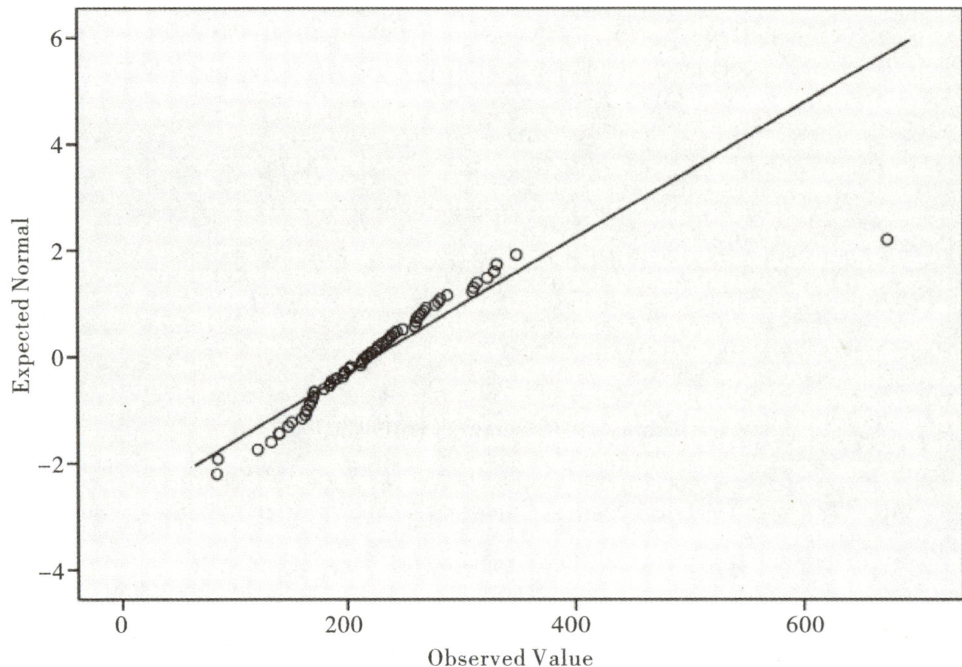

Figure 4-23 Normal Q-Q Plot of Blood platelet level before treatment for test group

(7) Homogeneity test of variance: The results of Levene's homogeneity test of variance are given in Figure 4-24, and four algorithms for calculating Levene statistics are listed.

Test of Homogeneity of Variance

		Levene Statistic	df1	df2	Sig.
Blood platelet level before treatment	Based on Mean	.003	1	142	.960
	Based on Median	.007	1	142	.932
	Based on Median and with adjusted df	.007	1	140.092	.932
	Based on trimmed mean	.001	1	142	.976

Figure 4-24 The results of Levene's homogeneity test of variance

(8) Boxplot and extreme values: In the boxplot (Figure 4-25), five straight lines represent five percentiles, and the height of the box is the quartile range ($=P_{75}-P_{25}$). It should be pointed out that the boxplot is formed after eliminating the outliers and extreme values of variables. The hollow dots (°) in the Figure 4-25 represent outliers, that is, the distance between the observed values and the bottom line or the top line of the box is 1.5 to 3 times of the height of the box, which is regarded as the outlier. The asterisk "*" in the diagram represents the extreme value, that is, when the observed value is more than 3 times the height of the box from the bottom line or top line of the box, it is regarded as the extreme value. Figure 4-26 is the output of option outliers. Each variable lists 5 maximum and 5 minimum values.

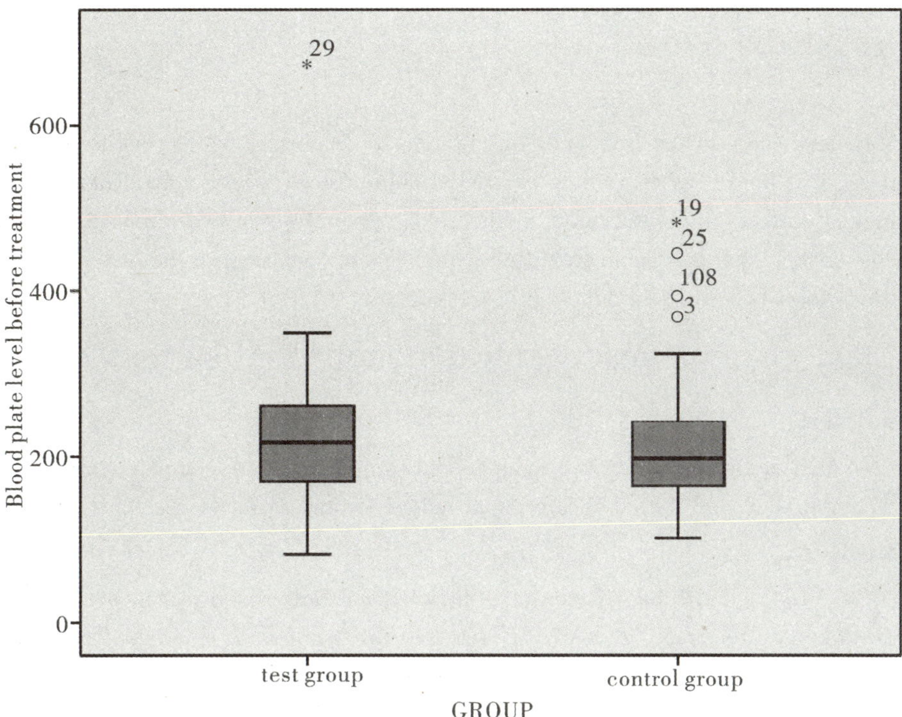

Figure 4-25 The boxplot

Extreme Values

	GROUP			Case Number	ID	Value
Blood platelet level before treatment	test group	Highest	1	19	29	673
			2	50	84	349
			3	17	27	332
			4	43	75	330
			5	54	90	324
		Lowest	1	29	55	83
			2	8	17	84
			3	75	117	120
			4	142	140	132
			5	46	78	139[a]
	control group	Highest	1	10	19	482
			2	15	25	445
			3	66	108	393
			4	95	3	368
			5	5	12	324
		Lowest	1	7	14	102
			2	65	106	106
			3	16	26	110
			4	111	42	120
			5	36	64	120

a. Only a partial list of cases with the value 139 are shown in the table of lower extremes.

Figure 4-26 Output of the option outlier

4.4 Crosstabs

Column table data refers to the frequency distribution table of each level combination of two or more classified variables, also known as frequency crosstabs, abbreviated as crosstabs. This process provides a variety of testing and correlation measurement methods for the analysis of two-dimensional or high-dimensional linked table data. χ^2 test is a commonly used hypothesis test method for the analysis of the data in the column table, which focuses on the introduction of the content.

4.4.1 χ^2 test for comparison of two independent sample rates

4.4.1.1 Description

There are two data formats in which two independent sample rates are compared: One is frequency tabular, as in the Example 4-3 and the other is original record format, as in the Example 4-4.

4.4.1.2 Example

Example 4-4 To compare the efficacy of ultraviolet and antiviral drugs in the treatment of herpes zoster, patients with herpes zosterare randomly divided into two groups. As shown in Table 4-1 for clinical observations. Are there any differences in overall effectiveness between the two groups?

Table 4-1 Comparison of the efficacy of ultraviolet and antiviral drugs in the treatment of herpes zoster

Group	Valid	Invalid	Total	Effective rate(%)
Antiviral group	31	25	56	55.36
Ultraviolet group	55	9	64	85.94
Total	86	34	120	71.67

4.4.1.3 SPSS data format

The data file "chi2_2.sav" is used as the Example 4-4, which includes 4 rows and 3 columns. Three variables are row variables, column variables and frequency variables (Figure 4-27).

1) Classified variable (row variable): Row variable named "group", "1" stands for antiviral group, and "2" stands for ultraviolet group.

2) Classified variable (column variable): The column variable is named "effect", "1" stands for valid and "2" stands for invalid.

3) Frequency variable: Variable named "freq". Enter the four frequencies in the four-cell table.

group	effect	freq
1	1	31
1	2	25
2	1	55
2	2	9

Figure 4-27 Data file format of χ^2 test

4.4.1.4 Running the command`

Select from the menu:

Data

Weight Cases

The dialog box of Weight Cases pops out(Figure 4-28). Select "weight cases by", and select "freq" to specify the variable as a frequency variable.

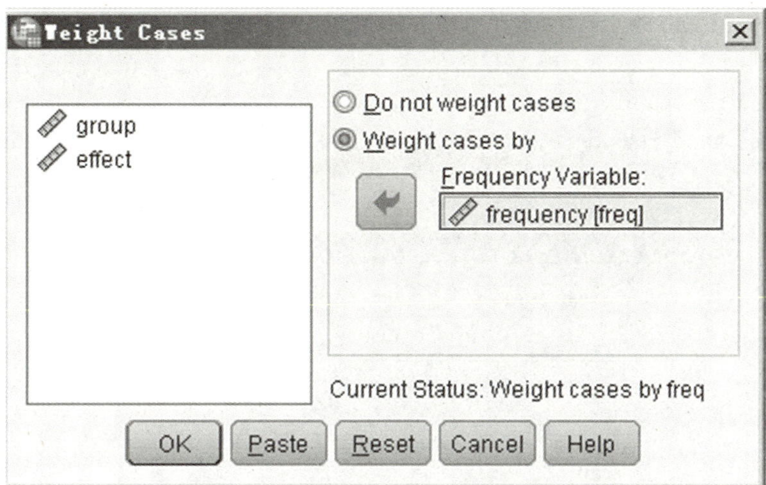

Figure 4-28 The Wight Cases dialog box

Select from the menu:

Analyze

Descriptive Statistics

Crosstabs

The dialog box of Crosstabs is listed in Figure 4-29.

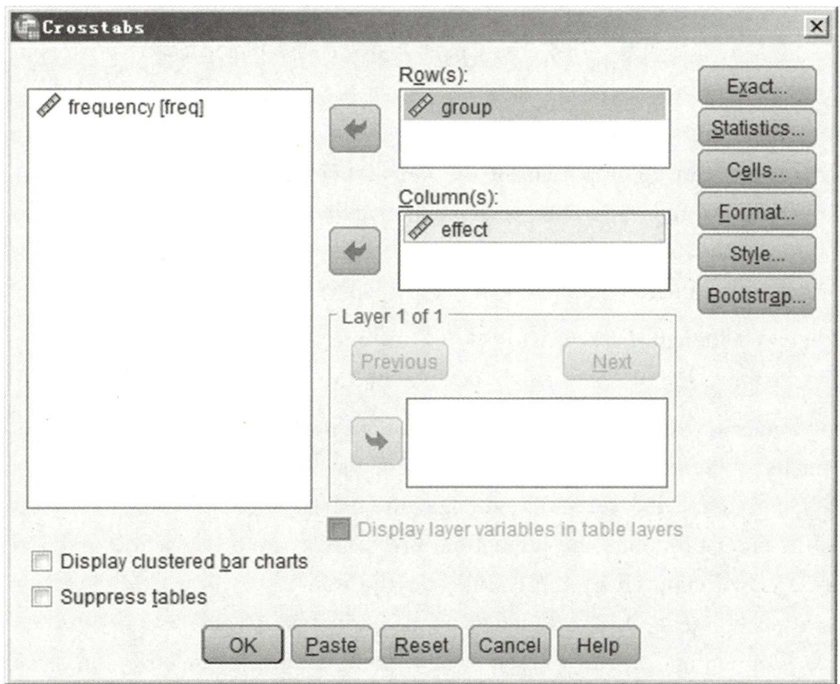

Figure 4-29 The Crosstabs dialog box

◇Row(s):This example is selected as "group".

◇Column(s):This example is selected as "effect".

◇Layer 1 of 1:To control a variable,the variable determines the layer of the frequency distribution table. If you want to add another control variable,click "Next",and then select a variable. Click the "Previous" button to select the previously determined variable.

□Display layer variables in table layers:Used to control whether hierarchical variables are displayed in the frequency table. However,it does not affect the output form of relevant statistics.

□Display clustered bar charts.

□Suppress tables.

★Exact:The exact probability test.

★Statistics:Click the "Statistics" button,and the dialog box of Crosstabs:Statistics pops out (Figure 4-30).

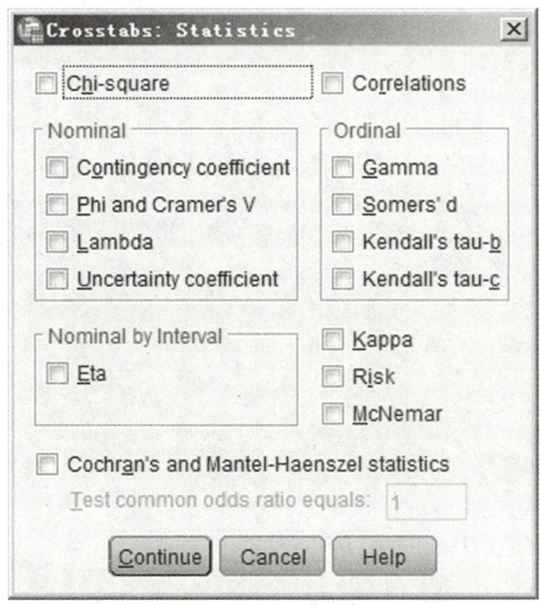

Figure 4-30 The Crosstabs:Statistics dialog box

□Chi-square:The results of Pearson χ^2 test,Likelihood ratio χ^2 test,Yates Continuity Correction χ^2 test and Fisher's exact test can be outputted for the four lattice table data.

□Correlations:Pearson and spearman correlation coefficients are calculated to show the correlation between row variables and column variables.

◇Nominal:Association measurement of two categorical variables.

□Contingency coefficient:$C=\sqrt{\chi^2/(\chi^2+N)}$,where N is the total number of cases. C is between 0 and 1,the greater the value of contingency coefficient,the stronger the correlation of variables.

□Phi and Cramer's V:φ and Cramer column contact number. $\varphi=\sqrt{\chi^2/N}$;$V=\sqrt{\chi^2/(N(k-1))}$. Here k is the smaller number of rows and columns. For the four lattice table data,$\varphi=V$. Both values are between 0 and 1,the greater the value,the stronger the correlation.

□Lambda:In order to reduce the prediction error rate,a value between 0 and 1 is produced,where 1 indicates the best prediction effect and 0 indicates the worst.

□Uncertainty coefficient:It also belongs to the reduction of prediction error rate,which has the same meaning as Lambda and has two kinds of calculation results:symmetric and asymmetric.

◇Ordinal:Correlation degree measurement of two ordered classification variables (rank variables).

□Gamma:Statistics for measuring the correlation between two rank variables. $\gamma=(P-Q)/(P+Q)$.

Here P is Concordant pairs, and Q is Discordant pairs. γ ranges between -1 and $+1$, where $+1$ means perfect positive correlation and -1 means perfect negative correlation. If γ equals 0, it means no correlation at all.

□Somers'd: This statistic is an extension of the Gamma statistic, which is only different from the Gamma statistic in that the denominator is added to the unsymmetrical pairs (Tied pairs). The range and significance of the values are the same as those of Gamma.

□Kendall's tau-b: The formula is $\tau_b = (P-Q)/\sqrt{(P+Q-T_X)(P+Q-T_Y)}$, where T_X is the neutral number of the first variable and T_Y is the neutral number of the second variable.

□Kendall's tau-c: The formula is $\tau_c = 2m(P-Q)/(N^2(m-1))$. Here m is the number of rows and the smaller number of columns; N is the total sample number.

◇Nominal by Interval: The correlation between a qualitative variable and a quantitative variable.

□Eta: Correlation statistics.

□Kappa: κ coefficient is measure of agreement coefficient, used to measure the degree of coincidence between two observers or two observation equipment. κ coefficient ranges from -1 to $+1$. The larger the absolute value of κ coefficient, the higher the degree of coincidence.

□Risk: The risk analysis is only suitable for the four-grid data, and the Relative risk (RR) and Odds ratio (OR) can be given.

□McNemar: χ^2 test of paired counting data.

□Cochran's and Mantel-Haenszel statistics: The Mantel-Haenszel common OR test is used to test whether the two binary variables are independent under the condition of the existence of covariables (hierarchical variables) or after subtracting the influence of covariables. After selecting this item, test common odds ratio equals: [1] is activated. Number 1 is system default, and the difference between common OR value and 1 is statistically significant.

★Cells: The column table displays the contents.

Click the "Cells" button (Figure 4-29), and dialog box of Crosstabs: Cell Display pops out (Figure 4-31).

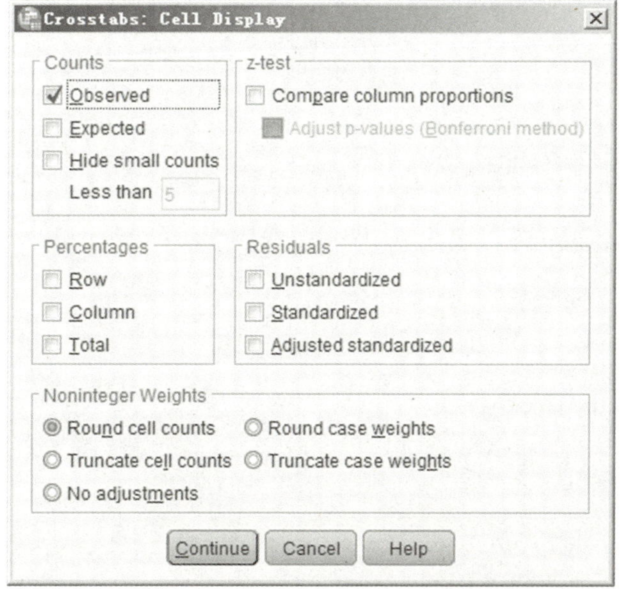

Figure 4-31 The Crosstabs: Cell Display dialog box

◇Counts.

□Observed.

□Expected.

□Hide small counts

Less than [5] :Less than n cases, the system default that less than 5 cases do not have output.

◇z-test: z test based on normal distribution.

□Compare column proportions: The column variables of the row list are used as grouping variables to compare the relative numbers of each row.

□Adjusted P-values (Bonferroni method): If the column variables have three or more categories, the correction of P value should be considered. The method provided here is Bonferroni method.

◇Noninteger Weights: Processing of non-integer frequency variables.

⊙Round cell counts: The frequency per cell is not rounded, but the cumulative frequency is rounded before calculating the statistics.

◎Round case weights: First round all frequencies.

◎Truncate cell counts: The frequency per cell is not rounded, but the cumulative frequency is rounded before calculating the statistics.

◎Truncate case weights: First, all frequencies are rounded.

◎No adjustments.

★Format: Click the "Format" button (Figure 4-29), and the dialog box of Crosstabs: Table Format pops out (Figure 4-32).

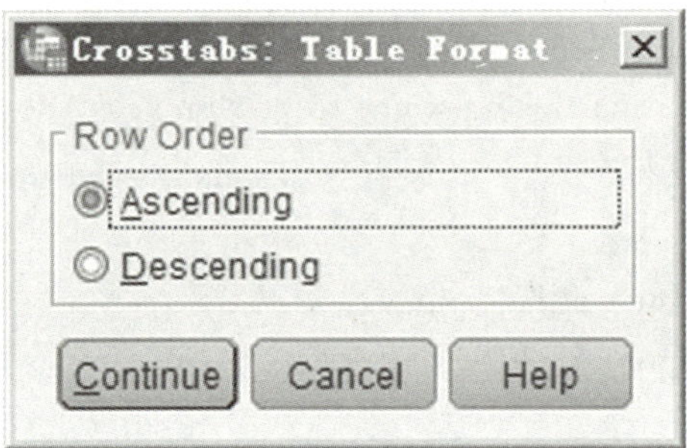

Figure 4-32 The Crosstabs: Table Format dialog box

◇Row order.

⊙Ascending (System default).

◎Descending.

4.4.1.5 Reading the output

The whole process of this example is as follows.

Data

Weight Cases

Weight Cases by: freq

Analyze

Descriptive Statistics

Crosstabs

Row(s): group

Column(s): effect

Statistics

Chi-square

Cells

Observed

Row

(1) Frequency distribution table (Figure 4-33).

(2) Test results (Figure 4-34).

1) Pearson Chi-Square: Uncorrected χ^2 test, suitable for R×C table data.

2) Continuity Correction: The calibration χ^2 test is used only for four lattice table data.

3) Likelihood Ratio: The likelihood ratio χ^2 test is suitable for R×C table data.

4) Fisher's Exact Test: Only the four-cell table data is output by default.

5) Linear-by-Linear Association: A linear trend test is used to analyze whether a classified variable is linearly associated with a hierarchical variable, but other cases can be ignored.

group * effect Crosstabulation

			effect		Total
			effective	invalid	
group	antiviral therapy	Count	31	25	56
		% within group	55.4%	44.6%	100.0%
	ultraviolet irradiation	Count	55	9	64
		% within group	85.9%	14.1%	100.0%
Total		Count	86	34	120
		% within group	71.7%	28.3%	100.0%

Figure 4-33 Frequency distribution table

Chi-Square Tests

	Value	df	Asymp. Sig. (2-sided)	Exact Sig. (2-sided)	Exact Sig. (1-sided)
Pearson Chi-Square	13.755[a]	1	.000		
Continuity Correction[b]	12.290	1	.000		
Likelihood Ratio	14.089	1	.000		
Fisher's Exact Test				.000	.000
Linear-by-Linear Association	13.640	1	.000		
N of Valid Cases	120				

a. 0 cells (0.0%) have expected count less than 5. The minimum expected count is 15.87.

b. Computed only for a 2x2 table

Figure 4-34 Chi-Square test results

6) N of Valid Cases.

7) The theoretical frequency of each lattice is more than 5, and the minimum theoretical frequency is 15.87. $\chi^2 = 13.755$, $v = 1$, $P < 0.001$ (two-tailed test). The difference is statistically significant. It can be concluded that UV treatment of herpes zoster is superior to antiviral drugs. The exchange of row variables and column variables does not change the results of χ^2 test. This conclusion is suitable for χ^2 test in all column tables.

4.4.1.6 Example

Example 4-5 The data file "clinical "trial. sav" is used as the Example 4-5. Try to compare the distribution of gender between the two groups of the classified variable "group". Because of the raw data format, you do not need to specify the frequency variables, the whole process is as follows.

Analyze

Descriptive Statistics

Crosstabs
Row(s):group
Column(s):gender
Statistics
Chi-square
Cells
Observed
Row

The results as shown in Figure 4-35 and Figure 4-36. There is no statistical difference in sex distribution between the two groups ($\chi^2=0.273, P=0.601$).

GROUP * gender Crosstabulation

			gender		Total
			male	female	
GROUP	test group	Count	48	24	72
		% within GROUP	66.7%	33.3%	100.0%
	control group	Count	45	27	72
		% within GROUP	62.5%	37.5%	100.0%
Total		Count	93	51	144
		% within GROUP	64.6%	35.4%	100.0%

Figure 4-35 Gender distribution in both groups

Chi-Square Tests

	Value	df	Asymp. Sig. (2-sided)	Exact Sig. (2-sided)	Exact Sig. (1-sided)
Pearson Chi-Square	.273[a]	1	.601		
Continuity Correction[b]	.121	1	.727		
Likelihood Ratio	.273	1	.601		
Fisher's Exact Test				.728	.364
Linear-by-Linear Association	.271	1	.602		
N of Valid Cases	144				

a. 0 cells (0.0%) have expected count less than 5. The minimum expected count is 25.50.

b. Computed only for a 2x2 table

Figure 4-36 Chi-Square test results

4.4.2 χ^2 test of R×C table data

4.4.2.1 Description

It is mainly used for the comparison of multiple sample rates and two or more sample composition ratios.

4.4.2.2 Example

Example 4-6 The etiological results of 504 pediatric patients in a hospital are as shown in Table 4-2. The etiological positive rate is correlated with age.

Table 4-2 Results of etiological detection in different age groups

Age groups (years)	Etiological detection		Total	Positive rate (%)
	Negative	Positive		
44	30	14	44	31.8
1-	50	60	110	54.4
3-	88	107	195	54.9
6-13	69	86	155	55.5
Total	237	267	504	53.0

4.4.2.3 SPSS data format

Create a data file "chiR_C. sav". Three variables are row variables, column variables and frequency variables (Figure 4-37).

Classified variable (row variable): The row variable is called "age_g", where "1" stands for less than 1 year, "2" stands for 1-3 year, "3" stands for 3-6 years, and "4" stands for 6-13 years old.

Classified variable (column variable): Column variable named "aetiology", where "0" stands for the negative effect, and "1" stands for the positive effect.

Frequency variable: variable named "freq", enter 8 frequencies in Table 4-2.

age_g	aetiology	freq
1	0	30
1	1	14
2	0	50
2	1	60
3	0	88
3	1	107
4	0	69
4	1	86

Figure 4-37 The data file format

4.4.2.4 Running the command

Data

Weight Cases

Weight Cases by: freq

Analyze

Descriptive Statistics

Crosstabs

Row(s): aetiology

Column(s): age_g

Statistics

Chi-square

Cells

Observed

Row

Column

Compare column proportions

Adjusted p-values(Bonferroni method)

4.4.2.5 Reading the output

The frequency distribution table as shown in Figure 4-38, and the test results are as shown in Figure 4-39. Therefore, it can be seen that the pathogeny positive rate is related to age, as the $\chi^2=8.688, v=3$, $P=0.034$ (two-tailed test). Examined the linear trend is statistically significant, $\chi^2 = 3.956, v = 1, P = 0.047$ (two-tailed test). The positive rate of pathogeny increases along with the age increasing trend, but the trend is mainly embodied in"< 1 year old" and "the age of 1-3" the change of the group, after one year of age. The theoretical frequency of all the grids is greater than 5, and the minimum theoretical frequency of the grids is 20.69. Multiple comparisons of the positive rate between different age groups are shown in Figure 4-38. The results showed that the pathogen is positive for those under 1 year old.

aetiology * Age group Crosstabulation

			Age group				Total
			<1 year old	1 year old–	3 years old–	6–13 years old	
aetiology	negative	Count	30a	50a, b	88b	69b	237
		% within Age group	68.2%	45.5%	45.1%	44.5%	47.0%
	positive	Count	14a	60a, b	107b	86b	267
		% within Age group	31.8%	54.5%	54.9%	55.5%	53.0%
Total		Count	44	110	195	155	504
		% within Age group	100.0%	100.0%	100.0%	100.0%	100.0%

Each subscript letter denotes a subset of Age group categories whose column proportions do not differ significantly from each other at the .05 level.

Figure 4-38 Frequency distribution table

Chi-Square Tests

	Value	df	Asymp. Sig. (2-sided)
Pearson Chi-Square	8.688[a]	3	.034
Likelihood Ratio	8.800	3	.032
Linear-by-Linear Association	3.956	1	.047
N of Valid Cases	504		

a. 0 cells (0.0%) have expected count less than 5. The minimum expected count is 20.69.

Figure 4-39 Chi-Square test results

4.4.3 χ^2 test and κ coefficient test for paired counting data

4.4.3.1 Example

Example 4-7 A total of 65 patients with respiratory tract infectionare treated with an antibiotic. The results of bacteriological examination before and after treatment as shown in Table 4-3. Try to analyze whether the antibiotic is effective in the treatment of respiratory tract infections.

Table 4-3 Observation results of antibiotics in the treatment of respiratory tract infections

Bacteriological examination before treatment	Bacteriological examination after treatment		Total
	-	+	
-	20	2	22
+	29	14	43
Total	49	16	65

4.4.3.2 SPSS data format

The data file"chi_pair. sav" is used as the Example 4-7. The file has four rows and three columns. Three variables are row variables, column variables and frequency variables.

Classified variable (row variable): The row variable is called "treat_b", where "0" stands for negative and "1" stands for positive effect.

Classified variable (column variable): The column variable named "treat_a", where "0" stands for negative and "1" stands for positive effect.

Frequency variable: variable named "freq", enter 4 frequencies in Table 4-3.

4.4.3.3 Running the command

Data

Weight Cases

Weight Cases by: freq

Analyze

Descriptive Statistics

Crosstabs

Row(s): treat_b

Column(s): treat_a

Statistics

McNemar

Descriptive:

4.4.3.4 Reading the output

The frequency distribution as shown in Figure 4-40, and the test results as shown in Figure 4-41. The method used is based on the binomial McNemar test. There is a statistical difference ($P<0.001$) that the antibiotic is effective in the treatment of respiratory tract infections.

Bacteriological examination before treatment * Bacteriological examination after treatment Crosstabulation

Count

		Bacteriological examination after treatment		Total
		negative	positive	
Bacteriological examination before treatment	negative	20	2	22
	positive	29	14	43
Total		49	16	65

Figure 4-40 Frequency distribution table

Chi-Square Tests

	Value	Exact Sig. (2-sided)
McNemar Test		.000[a]
N of Valid Cases	65	

a. Binomial distribution used.

Figure 4–41 Chi–Square test results

4.4.3.5 Example 4–8

Example 4–8 The data file "diagnosis. sav" is used as the Example 4–8. The diagnostic results of 116 patients as shown in Table 4–4. Please use κ coefficient method to analyze the coincidence between CT diagnosis and pathological diagnosis.

Table 4–4 Diagnostic results of two examination methods for patients

CT examination	Pathological examination		Total
	Inflammation	Therioma	
inflammation	35	11	46
therioma	3	67	70
Total	38	78	116

4.4.3.6 Running the command

Open the data file "diagnosis. sav". Because it is the raw data, there is no need to define the frequency variables. The process is as follows:

Analyze
- **Descriptive Statistics**
  - **Crosstabs**
  - **Row(s): diag_CT**
  - **Column(s): diag_path**
- **Statistics**
  - **McNemar**
    - **Kappa**

4.4.3.7 Reading the output

McNemar test (Figure 4–42) showed that there is no significant difference in diagnostic results between the two methods ($P=0.057$).

Chi-Square Tests

	Value	Exact Sig. (2-sided)
McNemar Test		.057[a]
N of Valid Cases	116	

a. Binomial distribution used.

Figure 4–42 McNemar test result

The coincidence coefficient of the two diagnostic methods is $k=0.740$ ($P<0.001$), which indicates that the coincidence degree of the two diagnostic methods is statistically significant and strong (Figure 4-43). Generally speaking, $k\geqslant 0.7$ means strong degree of anastomosis; $0.7>k\geqslant 0.4$ is general; $k<0.4$ means weak degree of coincidence.

Symmetric Measures

		Value	Asymp. Std. Error[a]	Approx. T[b]	Approx. Sig.
Measure of Agreement	Kappa	.740	.064	8.060	.000
N of Valid Cases		116			

a. Not assuming the null hypothesis.

b. Using the asymptotic standard error assuming the null hypothesis.

Figure 4-43 The result of measure of agreement

4.4.4 χ^2 test for stratified data

4.4.4.1 Example

Example 4-9 Doll and Hill studied the relationship between smoking and lung cancer in 709 patients with lung cancer and 709 non-tumor patients according to gender. The results follow in Table 4-5. Try to do a case-control analysis of lung cancer.

Table 4-5 Sex and smoking history associated with lung cancer

Smoking history	Male			Female		
	Case	Control	Total	Case	Control	Total
Smoke	647	622	1 269	41	28	69
Not smoke	2	27	29	19	32	51
Total	649	649	1 298	60	60	120

4.4.4.2 SPSS data format

Create a data file "chiM-H. sav", which has eight rows and four columns. Four variables are row variables, column variables, classified variables and frequency variables.

1) The row variable is named "smoke" and marked smoking status. Here, "1" means yes, and "2" means no. Usually row variables are selected for exposure, especially for prospective studies.

2) The list of variables is called "case_ctr", where "1" stands for case group and "2" stands for control group. Variables are usually selected for outcome factors, such as illness or not, especially in prospective studies.

3) The stratified variable is named "gender", where "1" stands for "male" and "2" stands for "female".

4) Frequency variable: variable named "freq", enter the 8 basic frequencies in the above table. The data format as shown in Figure 4-44.

	smoke	case_ctr	gender	freq
1	1	1	1	647
2	1	2	1	622
3	2	1	1	2
4	2	2	1	27
5	1	1	2	41
6	1	2	2	28
7	2	1	2	19
8	2	2	2	32

Figure 4-44 Data format of Example 4-9

4.4.4.3 Running the command`

Select from the menu:

Data

Weight Cases

Weight Cases by: freq (Defining frequency variable)

Analyze

Descriptive Statistics

Crosstabs

Row(s): smoke (Row variable)

Column(s): case_ctr (Column variable)

Layer: gender (Stratified variable)

Statistics

Chi-square

Risk

Cochran's and Mantel-Haenszel statistics

Test common odds ratio equals: 1

Cells

Column

Total

4.4.4.4 Reading the output

(1) Stratified χ^2 test: The results are shown in Figure 4-45 and Figure 4-46. The correlation between smoking and lung cancer is tested according to gender. The results showed that smoking had significant correlation with lung cancer ($P \leqslant 0.016$). The smoking rate in the case group is significantly higher than that in the control group, suggesting that smoking might be a risk factor for lung cancer.

smoke * Case-control study * gender Crosstabulation

gender				Case-control study		Total
				case	control	
male	smoke	yes	% within Case-control study	99.7%	95.8%	97.8%
			% of Total	49.8%	47.9%	97.8%
		no	% within Case-control study	0.3%	4.2%	2.2%
			% of Total	0.2%	2.1%	2.2%
	Total		% within Case-control study	100.0%	100.0%	100.0%
			% of Total	50.0%	50.0%	100.0%
female	smoke	yes	% within Case-control study	68.3%	46.7%	57.5%
			% of Total	34.2%	23.3%	57.5%
		no	% within Case-control study	31.7%	53.3%	42.5%
			% of Total	15.8%	26.7%	42.5%
	Total		% within Case-control study	100.0%	100.0%	100.0%
			% of Total	50.0%	50.0%	100.0%
Total	smoke	yes	% within Case-control study	97.0%	91.7%	94.4%
			% of Total	48.5%	45.8%	94.4%
		no	% within Case-control study	3.0%	8.3%	5.6%
			% of Total	1.5%	4.2%	5.6%
	Total		% within Case-control study	100.0%	100.0%	100.0%
			% of Total	50.0%	50.0%	100.0%

Figure 4-45 Frequency distribution table

Chi-Square Tests

gender		Value	df	Asymp. Sig. (2-sided)	Exact Sig. (2-sided)	Exact Sig. (1-sided)
male	Pearson Chi-Square	22.044[c]	1	.000		
	Continuity Correction[b]	20.316	1	.000		
	Likelihood Ratio	26.140	1	.000		
	Fisher's Exact Test				.000	.000
	Linear-by-Linear Association	22.027	1	.000		
	N of Valid Cases	1298				
female	Pearson Chi-Square	5.763[d]	1	.016		
	Continuity Correction[b]	4.910	1	.027		
	Likelihood Ratio	5.815	1	.016		
	Fisher's Exact Test				.026	.013
	Linear-by-Linear Association	5.715	1	.017		
	N of Valid Cases	120				
Total	Pearson Chi-Square	19.129[a]	1	.000		
	Continuity Correction[b]	18.136	1	.000		
	Likelihood Ratio	19.878	1	.000		
	Fisher's Exact Test				.000	.000
	Linear-by-Linear Association	19.116	1	.000		
	N of Valid Cases	1418				

a. 0 cells (0.0%) have expected count less than 5. The minimum expected count is 40.00.

b. Computed only for a 2x2 table

c. 0 cells (0.0%) have expected count less than 5. The minimum expected count is 14.50.

d. 0 cells (0.0%) have expected count less than 5. The minimum expected count is 25.50.

Figure 4-46 The result of stratified Chi-square test

(2) Stratified risk estimates: The results are shown in Figure 4-47 and are explained below.

1) Odds Radio for: *OR* value and its confidence interval. Combined with Figure 4-47. For example, the *OR* value of the male group is

$$OR = \frac{Smoking\ rate\ in\ case\ group/(1 - Smoking\ rate\ in\ case\ group)}{Smoking\ rate\ in\ control\ group/(1 - Smoking\ rate\ in\ control\ group)}$$

$$= \frac{0.997/0.003}{0.958/0.042} = 14.043.$$

The 95% confidence interval of *OR* value is 3.325-59.301, excluding 1, which is statistically different from 1. The result indicates that smoking is a risk factor for lung cancer in men. The *OR* value of women is 2.466, and the 95% confidence interval is 1.172-5.188, not including 1. The result indicates that smoking is a risk factor for lung cancer in women. The *OR* value of male is significantly greater than that of female, and there is no statistical difference that needs further examination.

2) For cohort: The relative risk *RR* of the cohort study (prospective study) is reported here. This example is a case control study (retrospective study), so this result is meaningless. For the cohort study, it is assumed that the data in this case are divided into smoking group and non-smoking group, and the observation result is whether lung cancer occurs. The incidence of male smoking group = 647/1 269 = 0.510, and that of male non-smoking group = 2/29 = 0.069. The ratio of the two is that the relative risk of lung cancer for men who smoke is $RR = 0.510/0.069 = 7.393$.

It should be pointed out that in the case control study, the *OR* value obtained in the Crosstabs main dialog box is correct whether the case control (case_ctr) variable is selected into the row variable or the column variable. But for the cohort study, the exposure factor must be selected into the row variable and the outcome variable into the column variable, otherwise the reported "for cohort" is wrong.

(3) Consistency test of *OR* values of different genders: the results as shown in Figure 4-48. The results of Breslow-Day and Tarone consistency tests show that there are statistical differences in *OR* values of different genders ($P<0.030$), and male is higher than female.

Risk Estimate

gender		Value	95% Confidence Interval	
			Lower	Upper
male	Odds Ratio for smoke (yes / no)	14.043	3.325	59.301
	For cohort Case-control study = case	7.393	1.939	28.187
	For cohort Case-control study = control	.526	.470	.590
	N of Valid Cases	1298		
female	Odds Ratio for smoke (yes / no)	2.466	1.172	5.188
	For cohort Case-control study = case	1.595	1.063	2.394
	For cohort Case-control study = control	.647	.453	.923
	N of Valid Cases	120		
Total	Odds Ratio for smoke (yes / no)	2.974	1.787	4.949
	For cohort Case-control study = case	1.959	1.352	2.839
	For cohort Case-control study = control	.659	.572	.759
	N of Valid Cases	1418		

Figure 4-47 Stratified risk estimation

Tests of Homogeneity of the Odds Ratio

	Chi-Squared	df	Asymp. Sig. (2-sided)
Breslow-Day	5.215	1	.022
Tarone's	5.175	1	.023

Figure 4-48 Consistency test of *OR* value of the Example 4-9

(4) Covariate analysis: Figure 4-49 shows the test results of Mantel-Haenszel method (MH method) and Cochran improved MH method (CMH method). The principle of the two methods is to test the relationship between smoking and lung cancer with gender as covariate, that is, the relationship between smoking and lung cancer after removing the influence of gender factors. The results showed that smoking is still significantly associated with lung cancer after gender is excluded, further suggesting that smoking is a risk factor for lung cancer.

Tests of Conditional Independence

	Chi-Squared	df	Asymp. Sig. (2-sided)
Cochran's	25.036	1	.000
Mantel-Haenszel	23.626	1	.000

Figure 4-49 Results of MH test and CMH test

(5) Mantel-Haenszel public *OR* value (common odds ratio) estimation: The result as shown in Figure 4-50, which is explained as follows:

1) The public *OR* value is 4.524 with gender as the stratified variable, and the difference is statistically different from 1 ($P<0.001$), and the 95% confidence interval of the combined *OR* value is 2.417-8.467, which does not include 1.

2) In the table, "ln" is the estimated value of natural logarithms, such as ln (4.524) = 1.509; ln (2.417) = 0.883; ln (8.467) = 2.136.

Mantel-Haenszel Common Odds Ratio Estimate

Estimate			4.524
ln(Estimate)			1.509
Std. Error of ln(Estimate)			.320
Asymp. Sig. (2-sided)			.000
Asymp. 95% Confidence Interval	Common Odds Ratio	Lower Bound	2.417
		Upper Bound	8.467
	ln(Common Odds Ratio)	Lower Bound	.883
		Upper Bound	2.136

The Mantel-Haenszel common odds ratio estimate is asymptotically normally distributed under the common odds ratio of 1.000 assumption. So is the natural log of the estimate.

Figure 4-50 Results of estimation of MH common OR value

4.5 Ratio

4.5.1 Description

The ratio analysis process is to analyze the ratio of two quantitative variables, give various statistics of the ratio, and also store the analysis results as data files.

4.5.2 Example

Example 4-10 The data file "clinical trial. sav" is used as the Example 4-10. In this data file, "GROUP" is a grouping variable, various statistics of the ratio of hemoglobin content "HB1" to post-treatment hemoglobin content "HB2" are obtained.

4.5.3 Running the command

Analyze

Descriptive Statistics

Ratio

The dialog box of Ratio Statistics pops out (Figure 4-51).

Select "HB1" into the "Numerator" box, "HB2" into the "Denominator" box and "GROUP" into the "Group Variable" box. After selecting the variables in the box of grouping variables, the "Sort by group variable" option is activated. The output order of ascending and descending order is selected according to the classification level.

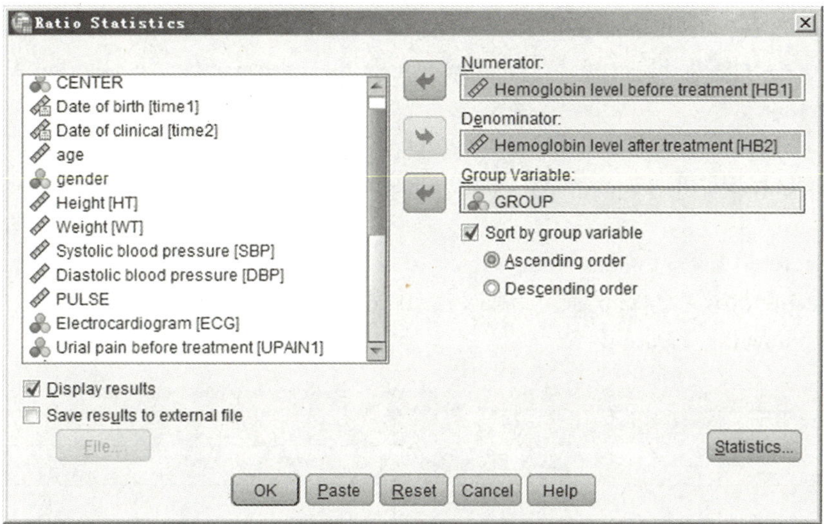

Figure 4-51 The Ratio Statistics dialog box

☑Display results.

☐Save results to external file.

★Statistics: Click "Statistics" button, the dialog box of Ratio Statistics: Statistics pops out (Figure 4-52).

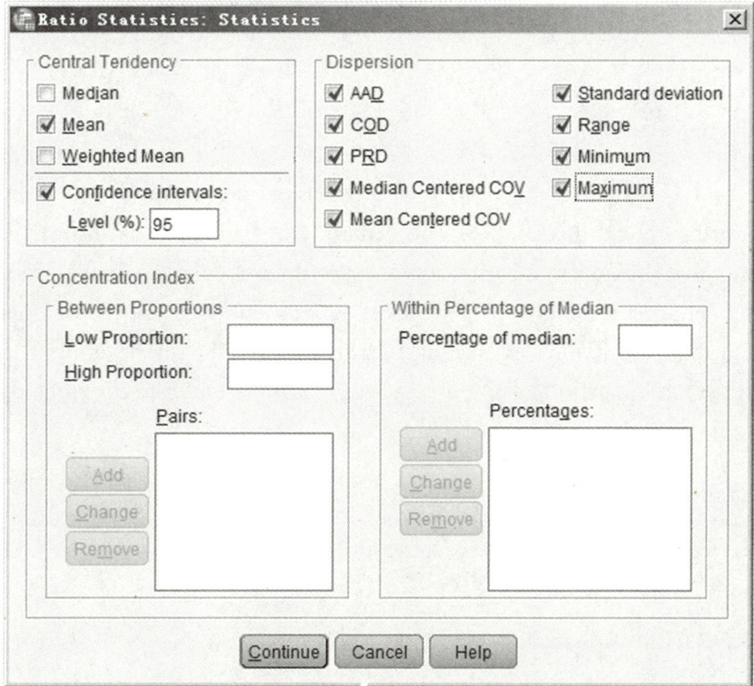

Figure 4-52 The Ratio Statistics: Statistics dialog box

◇Central Tendency.

□Median.

☑Mean.

□Weighted Mean: That is, the mean of the molecule divided by the denominator is equal to the mean calculated by the weight of the denominator.

☑Confidence intervals:

Level(%): 95

◇Dispersion.

☑ADD (average absolute deviation): That is, the sum of absolute values of the median difference between comparisons divided by sample size.

☑COD(coefficient of dispersion): That is, ADD divided by the median compared.

☑PRD(price-related differential): Also known as the return index, that is, the average divided by the weighted average.

☑Median Centered COV (median-centered coefficient of variation): That is, the root mean square of the difference between the comparisons and the median divided by the median and expressed as a percentage.

☑Mean Centered COV (mean-centered coefficient of variation): The coefficient of variation commonly used is divided by the contrast standard deviation by the mean.

The result as shown in Figure 4-53.

Ratio Statistics for Hemoglobin level before treatment / Hemoglobin level after treatment

Group	Mean	95% Confidence Interval for Mean		Minimum	Maximum	Std. Deviation	Range	Average Absolute Deviation	Price Related Differential	Coefficient of Dispersion	Coefficient of Variation	
		Lower Bound	Upper Bound								Mean Centered	Median Centered
test group	1.032	1.001	1.063	.685	1.494	.133	.809	.086	1.007	.086	12.9%	13.7%
control group	1.029	1.000	1.058	.695	1.505	.124	.811	.077	1.006	.076	12.0%	12.4%
Overall	1.030	1.009	1.051	.685	1.505	.128	.820	.082	1.006	.082	12.4%	13.2%

The confidence intervals are constructed by assuming a Normal distribution for the ratios.

Figure 4-53 Output of the Example 4-10

4.6 P-P Plots/Q-Q Plots

4.6.1 Description

Both P-P Plots and Q-Q Plots are used to test whether the probability distribution of a sample is dependent on a certain theoretical distribution. The principle of P-P Plots is to test that the difference between the actual cumulative probability distribution and the theoretical cumulative probability distribution is symmetrical to zero or not. The principle of Q-Q Plots of the axis is to verify whether the actual quartile matches the theoretical quartile. If it is consistent, the divergence should be around a straight line, or the difference between the actual quartile and the theoretical quartile should be distributed in a band symmetrical to the horizontal axis of 0.

4.6.2 Example

Example 4-11 The data file "diameter_sub. sav" is used as the Example 4-11. Please check the normality of the variable "trueap_mean".

4.6.3 Running the command

Select from the menu:

Analyze

Descriptive Statistics

P–P

The dialog box of P–P Plots pops out (Figure 4–54). The same to Q–Q plots.

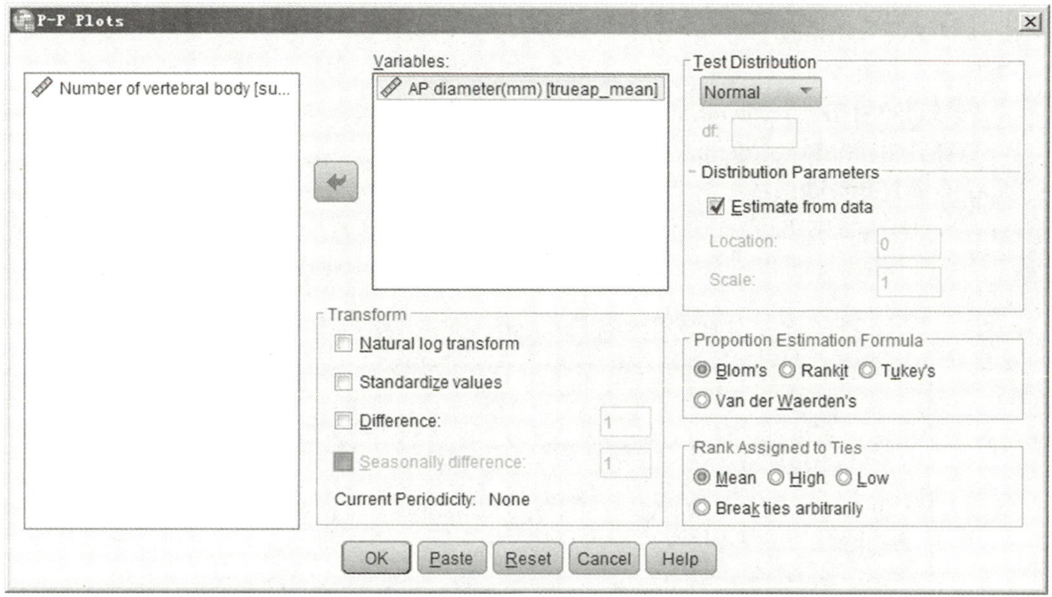

Figure 4–54 The "P–P Plots" dialog box

◇Variables.

◇Test Distribution: There are 13 kinds of distribution to choose from. After selecting a certain distribution, if the distribution involves degrees of freedom, the following df (degree of freedom) frame is activated and filled in.

◇Distribution Parameters: The system defaults Estimate from data. If this is not selected, the "Location" and "Scale" boxes are activated and the corresponding parameters are filled in.

Verifiable distributions are Beta, Chi–Square, Exponential, Gamma, Half – Normal, Laplace, Logistic, t Lognormal, Normal, Pareto, Student T, Weibull and Uniform distribution.

◇Transform.

□Natural log transform.

□Standardize values.

□Difference: Non–seasonal difference transformation, that is, the difference between two consecutive data replaces the original data. Enter a positive integer to determine the difference. If you enter 2, then the first two data systems in the new variable default.

□Seasonally difference: Seasonal difference transformation is used to calculate the data difference between two constant intervals in time series, and the data interval depends on the period.

Current Periodicity: None: The current time period. The system defaults to none.

◇Proportion Estimate Formula: Here are four formulas to choose from.

⊙Blom's: $(r-3/8)/(n+1/4)$. n is the sample size, r is the rank, from 1 to n, the following is the same.

◎Rankit: $(r-1/2)/n$.

◎Tukey's: $(r-1/3)/(n+1/3)$.

◎Van der Waerden's: $r/(n+1)$.

◇Rank Assigned to Ties.

⊙Mean.

◎High.

◎Low.

◎Break ties arbitrarily.

Process:

Analyze

DescriptiveStatistics

P-P

Variables: trueap_mean

Test Distribution: Normal

Estimate from data

The same to Q-Q plots. The results as shown from Figure 4-55 to Figure 4-59. The position parameters of P-P normal probabilistic cumulative probability distribution are 14.4421, and the measured values are 0.71728.

Case Processing Summary

		AP diameter (mm)
Series or Sequence Length		216
Number of Missing Values in the Plot	User-Missing	0
	System-Missing	0

The cases are unweighted.

Figure 4-55 P-P normal probability cumulative probability parameter

After synthesizing the pattern, we can directly infer the data from normal distribution. Accurate statistical inference, however, requires quantitative representation, see the section on normality testing for details.

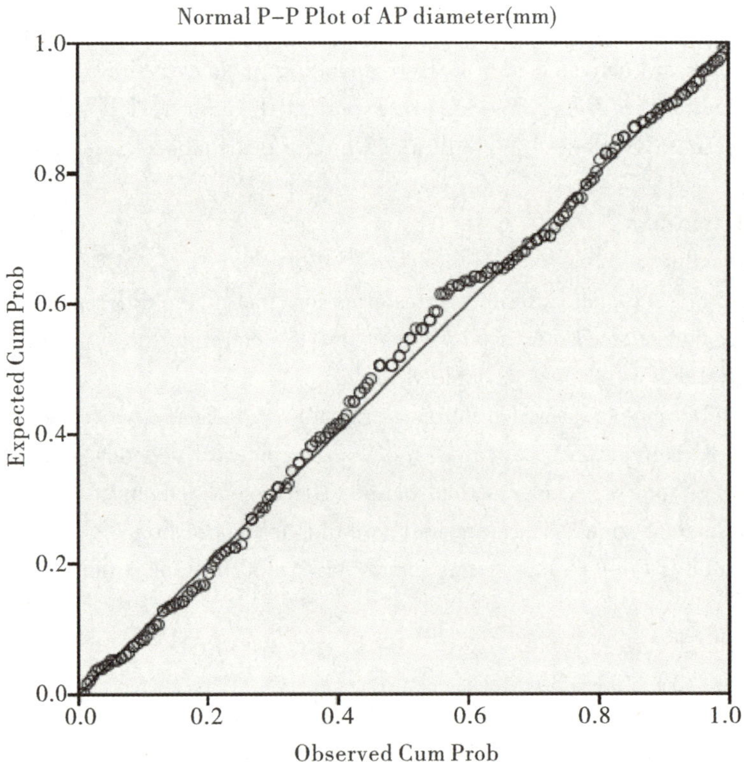

Figure 4-56 Normal P-P Plot

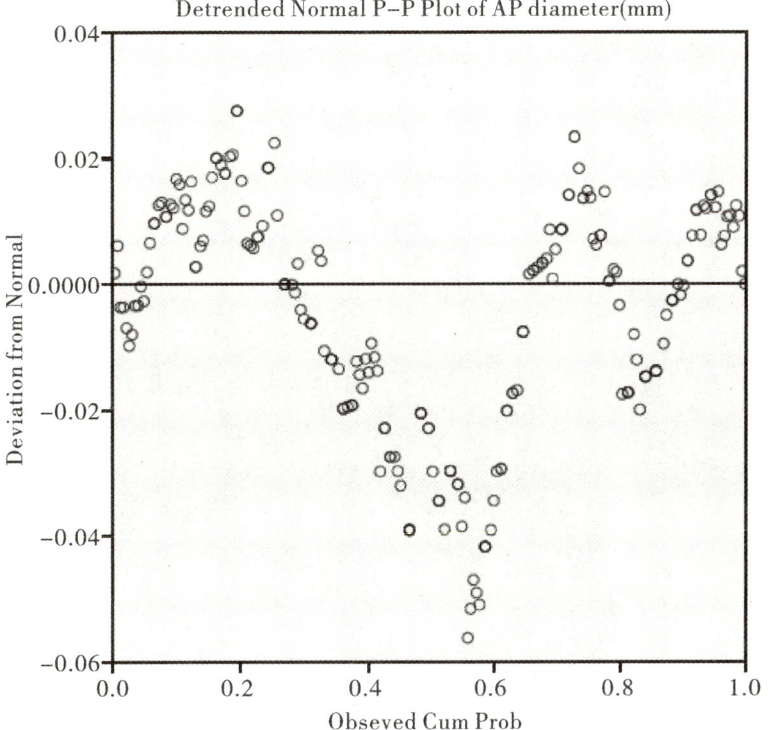

Figure 4-57 Detrended Normal P-P Plot

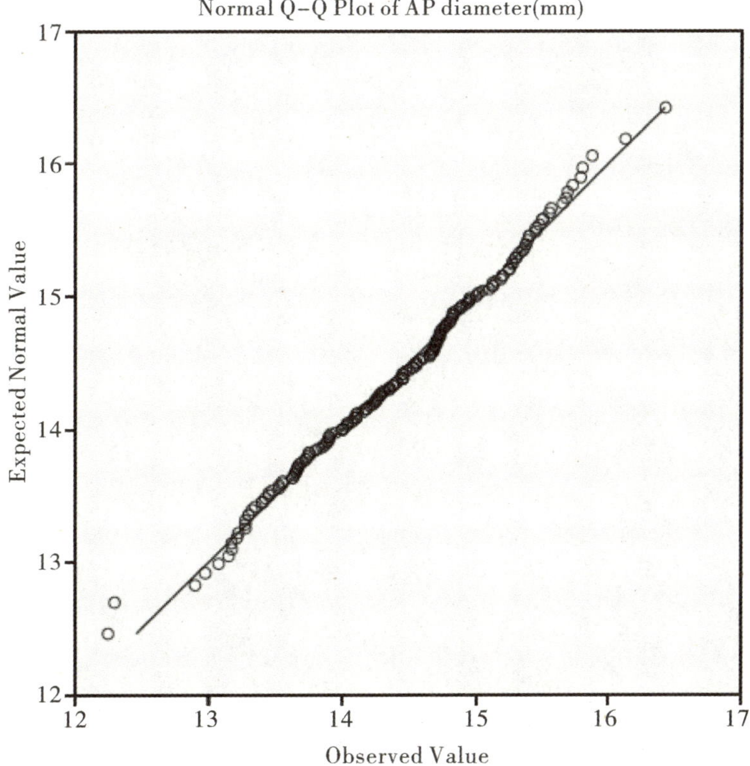

Figure 4-58 Normal Q-Q Plot

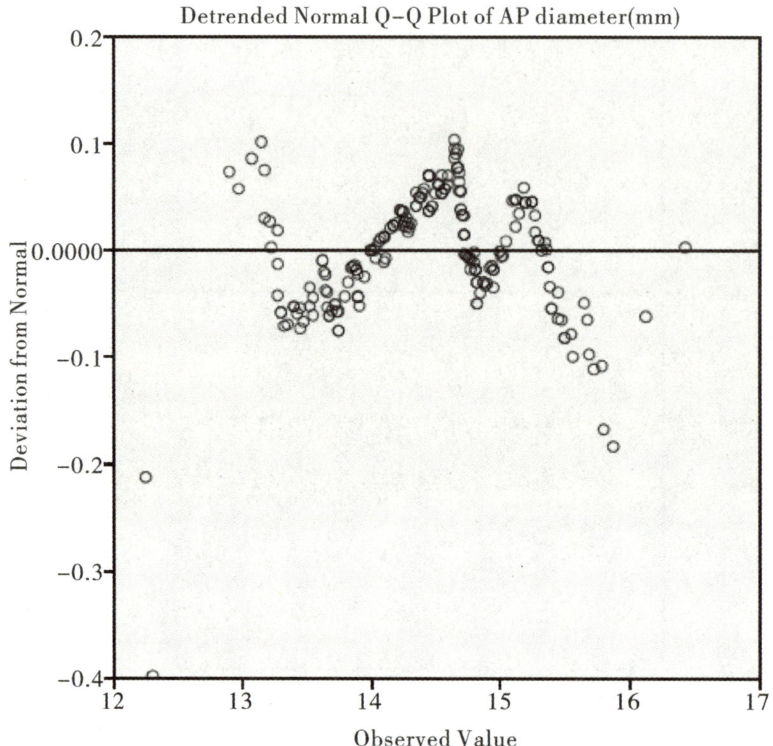

Figure 4-59 Detrended Normal Q-Q Plot

Peng Zhihang

Chapter 5

Compare Means

The "Compare Means" procedure is useful when you want to summarize and compare differences in descriptive statistics across one or more factors, or categorical variables. It consists of five submenus: Means, One-sample T Test, Independent-Samples T Test, Paired-Samples T Test and One-Way ANOVA (Figure 5-1).

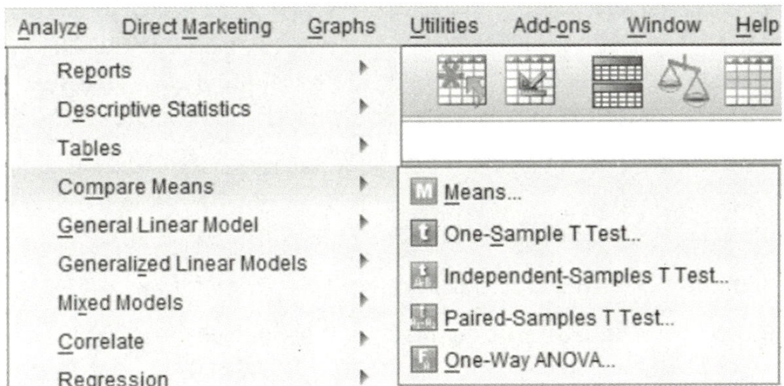

Figure 5-1 The Compare Means procedure and its submenus

5.1 Means

5.1.1 Description

The "Means" procedure is used to summarize and compare differences in descriptive statistics for the quantitative data, across one or more factors, or categorical variables. It is usually used for preliminary analysis of quantitative data. In the "Means" procedure, 21 kinds of statistics can be calculated. Besides, one-way ANOVA (analysis of variance) and test of linear trend can be performed.

5.1.2 SPSS data format

The SPSS data file for the "Means" procedure requires dependent variables and independent variables (if any) in SPSS. The dependent variables represent the set of quantitative data in the sample used to calculate descriptive statistics. The independent variables represent one or more factors, or categorical variables used to group the data.

5.1.3 Example

Example 5–1 The data file "factorial_1. sav" is used as the Example 5–1. In a research on a drug for treatment of liver cancer, the study aims to improve concentration of treat drug in target organs (liver) and lower concentration in the non–target organs (such as heart). A 2×3×2 factorial design is performed with 3 factors.

1) The first factor is the drug ("Drug") with two levels, "mitomycin+polymer material+magnetic material" (Treat, Drug=1) and "mitomycin" =2 (Control, Drug=2).

2) The second factor is time after the treatment ("Time") with three levels, 15 min (Time=1), 30 min (Time=2) and 60 min (Time=3).

3) The third factor is organ ("Organ") with two levels, heart (Organ=1) and liver (Organ=2).

The 60 mice are randomly divided into 12 groups (i. e., 2×3×2 combinations) with 5 mice for each group (i. e., the sample size to repeat is 5 for each group). The observation index (response variable) is the concentration of mitomycin (μg/g) in the tissue. The experiment results of mitomycin concentration in factorial design are shown in Table 5–1.

Table 5–1 Mitomycin concentration (μg/g) in factorial design

Organ	Treat drug group (Drug=1)			Control group (Drug=2)		
	15 min (Time=1)	30 min (Time=2)	60 min (Time=3)	15 min (Time=1)	30 min (Time=2)	60 min (Time=3)
Heart	0.1189	0.3498	0.2404	0.3482	0.6204	0.3968
(Organ=1)	0.1236	0.3227	0.2676	0.3646	0.6544	0.3935
	0.1333	0.3488	0.2505	0.3780	0.6779	0.3942
	0.1031	0.3119	0.2642	0.3562	0.6312	0.3770
	0.0920	0.3270	0.2434	0.3596	0.6221	0.3918
Liver	0.7787	3.6153	0.5643	0.1613	0.3774	0.1194
(Organ=2)	0.7798	3.4654	0.5691	0.1663	0.3566	0.0929
	0.7560	3.4980	0.5799	0.1502	0.3748	0.1050
	0.7745	3.3174	0.5859	0.1124	0.3829	0.0985
	0.7999	3.3617	0.5628	0.1637	0.3942	0.1196

5.1.4 Running the command

Analyze

Compare Means

Means

The main dialog of the Means (Basic analysis of quantitative data) pops out (Figure 5–2).

◇Dependent List: The dependent variable or response variable, i. e. the quantitative variable(s) to be analyzed. In the Example 5–1, choose the quantitative variable "Cons" (Mitomycin Concentration, ug/g).

◇Independent List: The independent variable, i. e. the categorical variable(s) used to subset the dependent variables. Specifying multiple values in the "Layer 1 of 1" box will produce several tables, each with one layer variable. Specify several layers for a single table by clicking "Next" and then entering other categorical variables; this will produce a complex table. In the Example 5-1, Drug, Time and Organ are categorical variables, and all these three variables are chosen into Independent List (Figure 5-2).

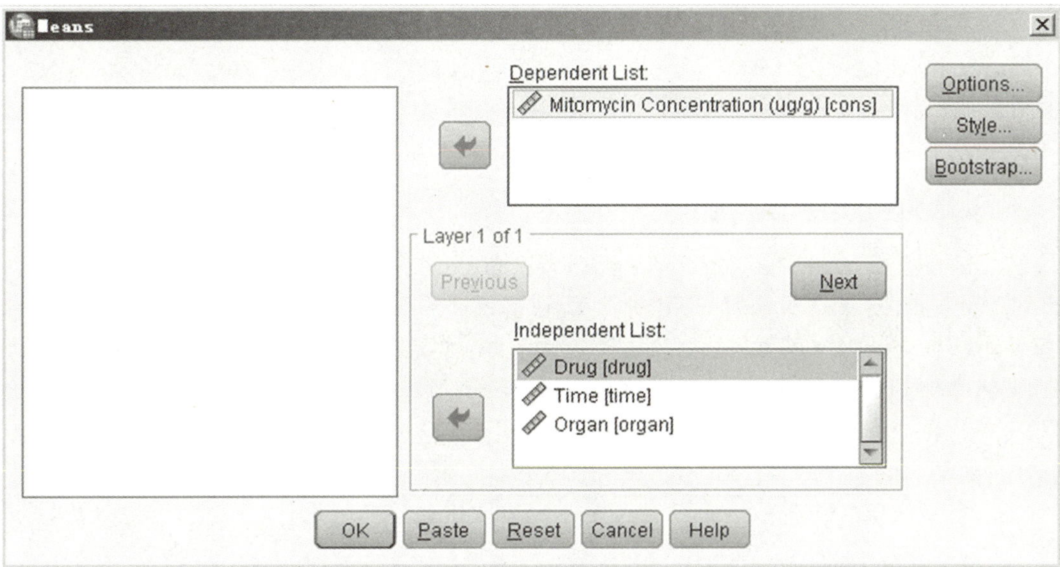

Figure 5-2 The Means dialog box

★ Options

Click "Options" button, and the dialog box of Means: Options pops out (Figure 5-3).

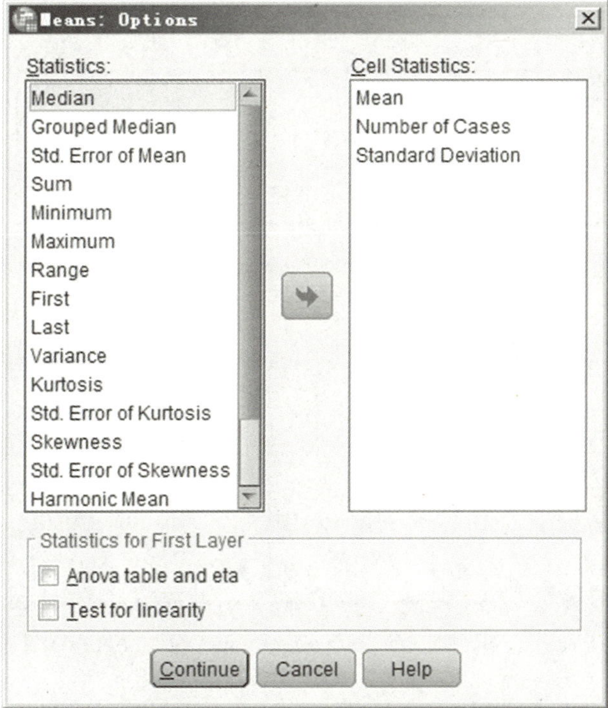

Figure 5-3 The Means: Options dialog box

◇Statistics. Summary statistics available include mean, number of cases, standard deviation, median, grouped median, standard error of mean, sum, minimum, maximum, range, first, last, variance, kurtosis, standard error of kurtosis, skewness, standard error of skewness, harmonic mean, geometric mean, percent of total sum, and percent of total N.

◇Cell Statistics: The statistics is produced in the output. By default, the mean, number of cases, standard deviation will be computed. The user can add additional statistics by clicking and dragging them from the "Statistics" column to the "Cell Statistics" column. Click and drag items in the "Cell Statistics" column to change the order they appear in the output.

◇Statistics for First Layer: Area includes options that will perform One-Way ANOVA and compute linear fit statistics (R, R^2, Eta, and Eta Squared), respectively.

★Bootstrap: Calculate related statistics using Bootstrap.

5.1.5 Reading the output

(1) The descriptive statistics (the layer variableis not defined): In the main dialog of Means procedure, all the three categorical variables "Drug" "Time" and "Organ" are chosen into "Independent List" simultaneously. The layer variable is not defined, so the tables of descriptive statistics are shown for one of three categorical variables separately (as shown from Figure 5-4 to Figure 5-6).

Drug	Mean	N	Std. Deviation
Treat	.916863	30	1.1745367
Control	.338037	30	.1792969
Total	.627450	60	.8826428

Figure 5-4 Mitomycin concentration by drug groups (μg/g)

Organ	Mean	N	Std. Deviation
Heart	.348770	30	.1624495
Liver	.906130	30	1.1823323
Total	.627450	60	.8826428

Figure 5-5 Mitomycin concentration by organ (μg/g)

Time	Mean	N	Std. Deviation
15min	.351015	20	.2711234
30min	1.200495	20	1.3400775
60min	.330840	20	.1765088
Total	.627450	60	.8826428

Figure 5-6 Mitomycin concentration by time (μg/g)

(2) The descriptive statistics (define the layer variable): Three categorical variables Drug, Time and Organ are chosen into "Independent List" successively, each with one layer variable. Specify several layers for a single figure by clicking "Next" button and then entering another categorical variable. Then, a complex table by hybriding three categorical variables is produced (Figure 5-7).

Drug	Time	Organ	Mean	N	Std. Deviation
Treat	15min	Heart	.114180	5	.0165175
		Liver	.777780	5	.0156473
		Total	.445980	10	.3500767
	30min	Heart	.332040	5	.0166926
		Liver	3.451560	5	.1175082
		Total	1.891800	10	1.6460343
	60min	Heart	.253220	5	.0122017
		Liver	.572400	5	.0100891
		Total	.412810	10	.1685534
	Total	Heart	.233147	15	.0942947
		Liver	1.600580	15	1.3590444
		Total	.916863	30	1.1745367
Control	15min	Heart	.361320	5	.0110712
		Liver	.150780	5	.0223150
		Total	.256050	10	.1122001
	30min	Heart	.641200	5	.0245895
		Liver	.377180	5	.0137081
		Total	.509190	10	.1404108
	60min	Heart	.390660	5	.0078453
		Liver	.107080	5	.0121197
		Total	.248870	10	.1497694
	Total	Heart	.464393	15	.1308657
		Liver	.211680	15	.1235002
		Total	.338037	30	.1792969
Total	15min	Heart	.237750	10	.1309271
		Liver	.464280	10	.3309571
		Total	.351015	20	.2711234
	30min	Heart	.486620	10	.1641418
		Liver	1.914370	10	1.6222589
		Total	1.200495	20	1.3400775
	60min	Heart	.321940	10	.0730799
		Liver	.339740	10	.2454704
		Total	.330840	20	.1765088
	Total	Heart	.348770	30	.1624495
		Liver	.906130	30	1.1823323
		Total	.627450	60	.8826428

Figure 5-7 Mitomycin concentration by a factorial design(ug/g)

(3)ANOVA Table:If three categorical variables are not defined as the layer variables, the analysis of variance (ANOVA) is performed for each of three categorical variables. The results are shown in Figure 5-8. If three categorical variables are all defined as the layer variables, the analysis of variance (ANOVA) is only performed for the first layer variable.

ANOVA Table

			Sum of Squares	df	Mean Square	F	Sig.
Mitomycin Concentration (ug/g) * Drug	Between Groups	(Combined)	5.026	1	5.026	7.120	.010
	Within Groups		40.939	58	.706		
	Total		45.964	59			

ANOVA Table

			Sum of Squares	df	Mean Square	F	Sig.
Mitomycin Concentration (ug/g) * Time	Between Groups	(Combined)	9.855	2	4.928	7.779	.001
	Within Groups		36.109	57	.633		
	Total		45.964	59			

ANOVA Table

			Sum of Squares	df	Mean Square	F	Sig.
Mitomycin Concentration (ug/g) * Organ	Between Groups	(Combined)	4.660	1	4.660	6.543	.013
	Within Groups		41.305	58	.712		
	Total		45.964	59			

Figure 5-8 Analysis of variance (ANOVA) the Example 5-1 based on three grouping variables independently

1) Between Groups (Combined): The source of variance between groups.
2) Within Groups: The source of variance within groups, i. e. error term.
3) Total: Total source of variance.
4) Sum of Squares: SS.
5) df: Degree of freedom.
6) Mean Square: SS/df.
7) F: *F* Statistic.
8) Sig: *P* value, or the observed significance level.

5.1.6 Drawing conclusions

The difference of mitomycin concentration between the two drug groups is statistically significant ($P=0.010$). The difference of mitomycin concentration among the three time groups after the treatment is statistically significant ($P=0.001$). The difference of mitomycin concentration between organ groups is statistically significant ($P=0.013$).

Measures of association: The square of eta statistics η^2 are 0.109, 0.214 and 0.101 for three variables Drug, Time and Organ, respectively (from Figure 5-9 to Figure 5-11).

	Eta	Eta Squared
Mitomycin Concentration (ug/g) * Drug	.331	.109

Figure 5-9 Measures of association with Drug

	Eta	Eta Squared
Mitomycin Concentration (ug/g) * Time	.463	.214

Figure 5-10 Measures of association with Time

	Eta	Eta Squared
Mitomycin Concentration (ug/g) * Organ	.318	.101

Figure 5-11 Measures of association with Organ

5.2 One sample *t*-test

5.2.1 Description

One sample *t*-test are typically used to compare a sample mean to a known population mean. It is useful for determining if the current set of data has changed from a long-term value (e. g. ,comparing the current year's temperatures to a historical average to determine if global warming is occurring).

5.2.2 SPSS data format

The SPSS data file for the one sample *t*-test requires a single variable in SPSS. That variable represents the set of scores in the sample that we will compare to the population mean.

5.2.3 Example

Example 5-2 The data file "t-test_1. sav" is used as the Example 5-2. According to nutritional requirements, the calories from daily food intake of adult women is recommended 7 725 kcal (1 cal = 4. 186 8 J). Randomly sampling of 11 adult women aged from 20 to 30, the calories from food intake are listed as followed. If young women aged from 20 to 30 intake enough nutrition?

5 260, 5 470, 5 640, 6 180, 6 390, 6 515, 6 805, 7 515, 7 515, 8 230, 8 770

5.2.4 Running the command

One sample *t*-test is located in the "Compare Means" submenu, under the "Analyze" menu:

Analyze

Compare Means

One-Sample T Test

The dialog box of the One-Sample T Test pops out (Figure 5-12). The dialog box for the One-Sample T Test requires that we transfer the variable representing the current set of scores to the "Test Variable (s)" section. We also enter the population average in the "Test Value" blank. The Example 5-2 is testing the variable calories against a population mean of 7 725.

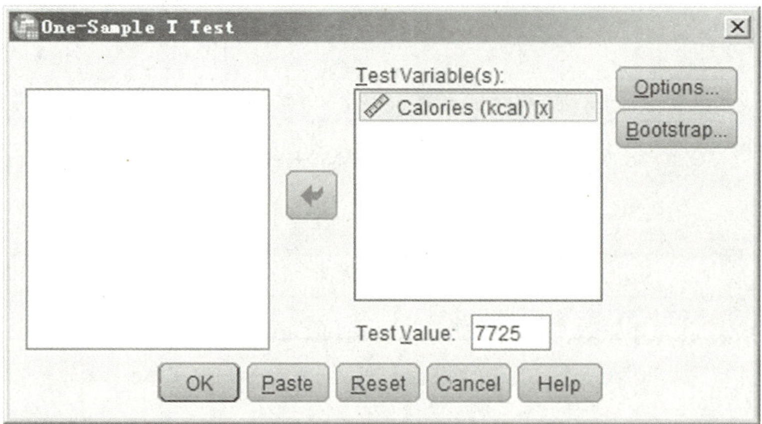

Figure 5-12 The One-Sample T Test dialog box

◇Test Variable(s): Choose the variable "x".

◇Test Value: 7725 .

★Options:

Click "Options" button, and the dialog box of One-Sample T Test: Options pops out.

◇Confidence Interval Percentage: 95 %: 95% confidence interval for the difference between sample mean and population mean (Figure 5-13).

◇Missing Values.

⊙Exclude cases analysis by analysis.

◎Exclude case listwise.

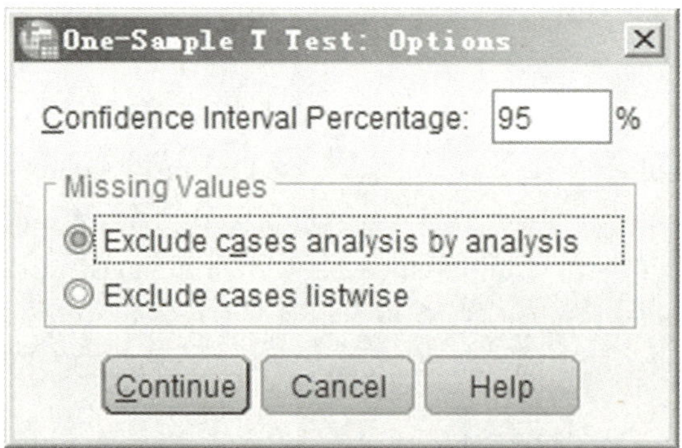

Figure 5-13 The One-Sample T Test: Options dialog box

5.2.5 Reading the output

(1) The output for the one sample t-test consists of two sections. The first section lists the sample variable and some basic descriptive statistics. From the result, we know that the sample size, mean, standard deviation, and standard error are 11, 6 753.64, 1 142.123 and 344.363, respectively (Figure 5-14).

	N	Mean	Std. Deviation	Std. Error Mean
Calories (kcal)	11	6753.64	1142.123	344.363

Figure 5-14 Basic descriptive statistics of the Example 5-2

(2) The second section of output contains the results of the one sample t-test (Figure 5-15). The ex-

ample presented above indicates at value of −2.821 ($t=-2.821$), with 10 degrees of freedom ($\nu=10$). The mean difference of −971.364 is the difference between the sample average (6 753.64) and the population average (7 725). The 95% confidence interval of the difference between the sample average and the population mean is (−1 738.65, −204.07).

One-Sample Test

	Test Value=7725					
					95% Confidence Interval of the Difference	
	t	df	Sig. (2-tailed)	Mean Difference	Lower	Upper
Calories (kcal)	-2.821	10	.018	-971.364	-1738.65	-204.07

Figure 5-15 The result of One Sample t-test of the Example 5-2

5.2.6 Drawing conclusions

1) A significant difference is found [$t=-2.821$, $\nu=10$, $P=0.018$ (two-tailed test)]. The sample mean (6 753.64) is significantly less than the population average (7 725), indicating adult women intake of inadequate calories.

2) The difference between sample mean and population mean is −971.364 with 95% confidence interval (−1 738.65, −204.07). The 95% confidence interval doesnot involve 0, so there is a significant difference between two populations.

5.3 Independent samples *t*-test

5.3.1 Description

An independent samples t-test is used to compare means from independent groups. It is also called two sample t-test, which is used to test whether there are statistical differences in the population mean of two independent samples.

5.3.2 SPSS data format

The SPSS data file for the Independent samples t-test requires dependent variables and independent variables in SPSS. The dependent variables represent the set of quantitative data in the sample used to calculate statistical indicators. The independent variables represent the factors or categorical variables with two levels used to compare the data.

5.3.3 Example

Example 5-3 The data file "clinical trial. sav" is used as the Example 5-3. In order to test the balance of the randomized cohorts in this example, "age", "HT" (height), "WT" (weight), "SBP" (systolic blood pressure), "DBP" (diastolic blood pressure) and "PULSE" (heart rate) are analyzed using the Independent samples t-test.

5.3.4 Running the command

Analyze

Compare Means

Independent-Samples T Test

The main dialog box of Independent-Samples T Test (two-sample t-test) pops out (Figure 5-16).

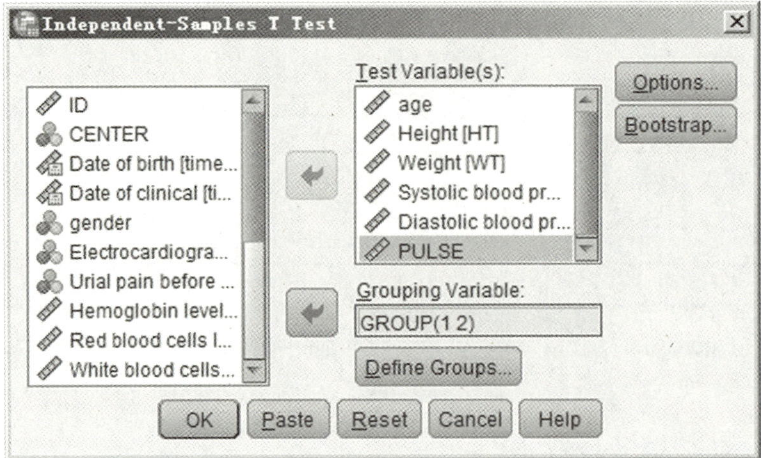

Figure 5-16 The Independent-Samples T Test dialog box

◇Test Variable(s): The dependent variable(s). The variables in this example are "age" "HT" "WT" "SBP" "DBP" and "PULSE".

◇Grouping Variable: The independent variable. Only one variable can be selected. In this example, the variable "group" is selected. After the group variable is selected, the "Define Groups" button is activated. Clicking this button brings up the Define Groups dialog box (Figure 5-17).

⊙Use specified values: Using this function, when grouping variable is categorical. Enter the group variable value of the categories in 2 boxes respectively, which means that you can only compare the two groups. In the Example 5-3, the values of the input group variable "group" are number 1 and 2, respectively.

◎Cut point: Using this function, when grouping variable is numeric and continuous (such as the current Example 5-4). When you set the cut point, grouping variables is automatically divided into two groups at the cut point. One set equal to or greater than the set value, the other set is less than the set value.

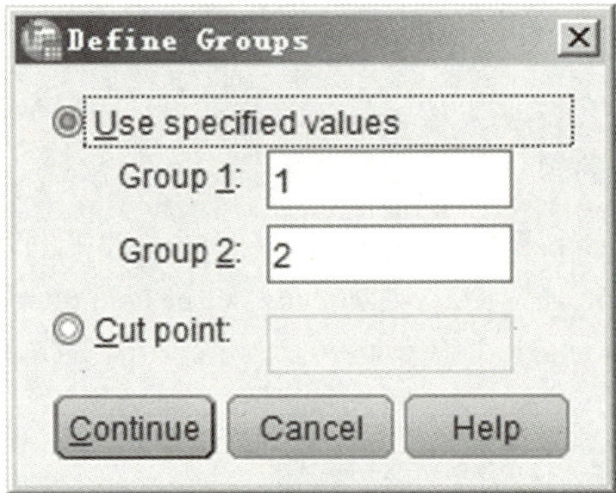

Figure 5-17 The Independent-Samples T Test: Define Groups dialog box

★Options: It is the same as one sample *t*-test.

5.3.5 Reading the output

The output for the independent samples *t*-est consists the basic descriptive statistics (Figure 5-18) and the values of the independent samples *t*-est (Figure 5-19).

Group Statistics

	GROUP	N	Mean	Std. Deviation	Std. Error Mean
age	test group	72	44.36	13.600	1.603
	control group	72	41.08	13.451	1.585
Height	test group	72	169.29	6.955	.820
	control group	72	168.46	6.954	.820
Weight	test group	72	68.07	9.050	1.067
	control group	72	66.66	9.127	1.076
Systolic blood pressure	test group	72	16.719	2.6211	.3089
	control group	72	16.304	2.2299	.2628
Diastolic blood pressure	test group	72	10.249	1.3232	.1559
	control group	72	9.953	.9946	.1172
PULSE	test group	72	72.93	6.092	.718
	control group	72	71.79	6.920	.816

Figure 5-18 Basic descriptive statistics

Independent Samples Test

		Levene's Test for Equality of Variances		t-test for Equality of Means						
									95% Confidence Interval of the Difference	
		F	Sig.	t	df	Sig. (2-tailed)	Mean Difference	Std. Error Difference	Lower	Upper
age	Equal variances assumed	.089	.766	1.457	142	.147	3.285	2.254	-1.171	7.741
	Equal variances not assumed			1.457	141.983	.147	3.285	2.254	-1.171	7.741
Height	Equal variances assumed	.155	.695	.719	142	.473	.833	1.159	-1.458	3.125
	Equal variances not assumed			.719	142.000	.473	.833	1.159	-1.458	3.125
Weight	Equal variances assumed	.066	.798	.931	142	.354	1.410	1.515	-1.585	4.404
	Equal variances not assumed			.931	141.990	.354	1.410	1.515	-1.585	4.404
Systolic blood pressure	Equal variances assumed	3.794	.053	1.024	142	.308	.4153	.4056	-.3864	1.2170
	Equal variances not assumed			1.024	138.444	.308	.4153	.4056	-.3866	1.2172
Diastolic blood pressure	Equal variances assumed	6.959	.009	1.516	142	.132	.2958	.1951	-.0898	.6815
	Equal variances not assumed			1.516	131.815	.132	.2958	.1951	-.0901	.6817
PULSE	Equal variances assumed	.231	.632	1.048	142	.296	1.139	1.086	-1.009	3.287
	Equal variances not assumed.			1.048	139.753	.296	1.139	1.086	-1.009	3.287

Figure 5-19 The results of the Independent-Samples T Test

(1) Levene's Test for Equality of Variances: The results for levene's test. First, calculate the absolute value of the difference between each observed value and the group mean value of the group in which it is measured. Then the absolute value will be analyzed by ANOVA based on the grouping variables and the F value is Levene F statistics. If P value is larger than 0.05, the homogeneity of variance is considered. This method is more reliable in the case of non-normal distribution of data.

(2) Equal variances assumed: t-test results under the condition of heterogeneity of variance using Welch-Satterthwaite approximate t-test. The method calculates the t value according to the independent variance and corrects the degree of freedom, the calculation formula is as follows:

$$t' = \frac{|\overline{X}_1 - \overline{X}_2|}{\sqrt{\dfrac{S_1^2}{n_1} + \dfrac{S_2^2}{n_2}}}, v = \frac{(S_1^2/n_1 + S_2^2/n_2)^2}{\dfrac{(S_1^2/n_1)^2}{n_1 - 1} + \dfrac{(S_2^2/n_2)^2}{n_2 - 1}}. \qquad (5-1)$$

In the Example 5-3, the diastolic pressure of the two groups is not homogeneous ($F = 6.959$, $P = 0.009$). The results as follows: $t = 1.516$, $\nu = 131.815$, $P = 0.132$. The results also contain the difference between the mean of two groups (Mean Difference), the standard error (Std. Error Difference) and 95% confidence interval (95% Confidence Interval of the Difference) for two groups of mean difference.

5.3.6 Drawing conclusions

The difference of the six indexes between the two groups is not statistically significant ($P>0.05$). It suggests that random grouping is balanced.

5.3.7 Example

Example 5-4 The data file "clinical trial. sav" is used as the Example 5-4. Here, the age ("age") is divided into two groups by the age of 50 to compare the systolic blood pressure ("SBP") differences between the two age groups.

5.3.8 Running the command

The Independent-Samples T Test is located in the "Compare Means" submenu, under the "Analyze" menu.

Analyze

Compare Means

Independent-Samples T Test

▸**Test Variable(s): SBP**

▸**Grouping Variable: age**

Define Groups

⊙**Cut Point** 50

5.3.9 Reading the output

The output results are shown in Figure 5-20 and Figure 5-21. The conclusion is that the population variance of the two groups is not homogeneous, and the systolic pressure in the group over 50 years old is significantly higher than that of the group under the age of 50 ($P<0.001$).

Group Statistics

	age	N	Mean	Std. Deviation	Std. Error Mean
Systolic blood pressure	>= 50	42	17.710	2.4815	.3829
	< 50	102	16.019	2.2460	.2224

Figure 5-20 Basic descriptive statistics

Independent Samples Test

		Levene's Test for Equality of Variances		t-test for Equality of Means					95% Confidence Interval of the Difference	
		F	Sig.	t	df	Sig. (2-tailed)	Mean Difference	Std. Error Difference	Lower	Upper
Systolic blood pressure	Equal variances assumed	.923	.338	3.981	142	.000	1.6909	.4247	.8513	2.5304
	Equal variances not assumed			3.819	70.087	.000	1.6909	.4428	.8078	2.5740

Figure 5-21 The results of the Independent-Samples *t*-test

5.4 Paired samples *t*-test

5.4.1 Description

Paired samples t-test, also paired t-test, is used to compare two related means. It tests the null hypothesis that the difference between two related means is 0 when the data are related to each other.

5.4.2 SPSS data format

The SPSS data file for the paired samples t-test requires two variables (represented in columns) in SPSS. The two variables should represent the paired variables for each subject (row).

5.4.3 Example

Example 5-5 The data file "clinical trial. sav" is used as the Example 5-5. Compare the 4 pairs of blood test indicators of the experimental group and placebo group before and after treatment respectively. The indicators include hemoglobin content ("HB1" and "HB2"), red blood cell count ("RBC1" and "RBC2"), white blood cell count ("WBC1" and "WBC2") and platelet count ("PLT1" and "PLT2"). In the variables mentioned above, "1" means indicators before treatment while "2" means after treatment.

5.4.4 Running the command

◇Split Files: Firstly, split the data into experimental group and placebo group. Two ways are available.

(1) "Split Files" Process: The "Split Files" Process is located under the "Data" menu.

Data

  Split File

The dialog box of the Split File is listed in Figure 5-22. Choose "Compare groups" and then put the group variable "GROUP" into the dialog box Groups Based on.

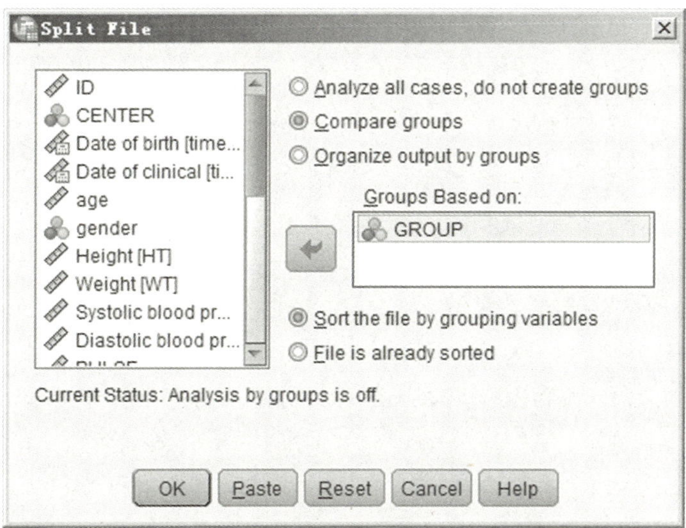

Figure 5-22 The Split File dialog box

(2) "Select Cases" process: The "Select Cases" process is also located under the "Data" menu:

Data

  Select Cases

The dialog box of the Select Cases process is listed in Figure 5-23. Choose "If condition is satisfied" option. Click "IF…" button and set "GROUP=1" in the Select Cases: If dialog box when we analyze the experimental group. Reset "GROUP=2" when we analyze the placebo group. The dialog box for the Select Cases: If is listed in Figure 5-24.

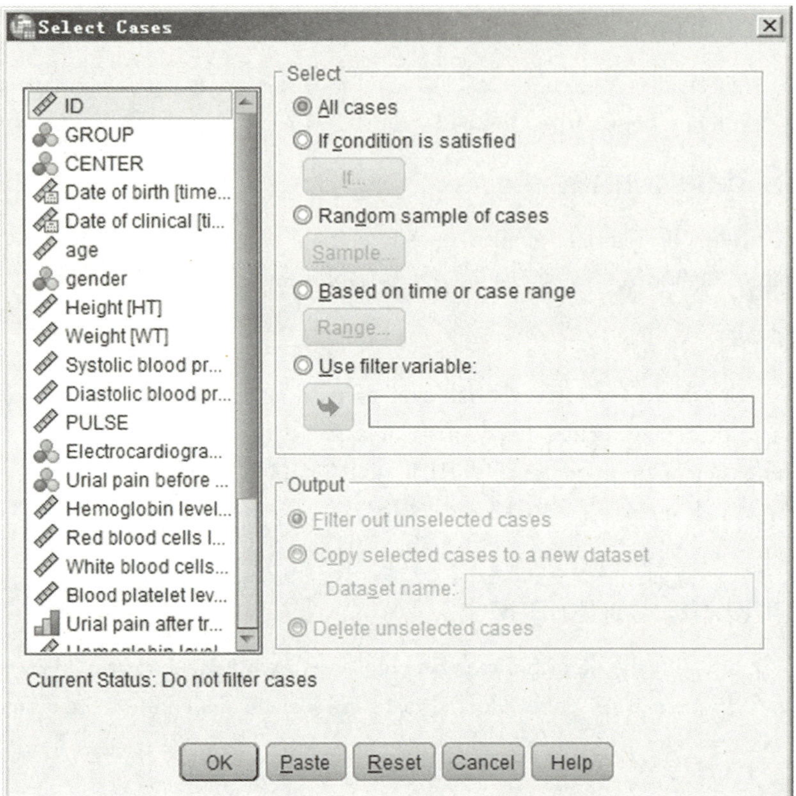

Figure 5-23 The Select Cases dialog box

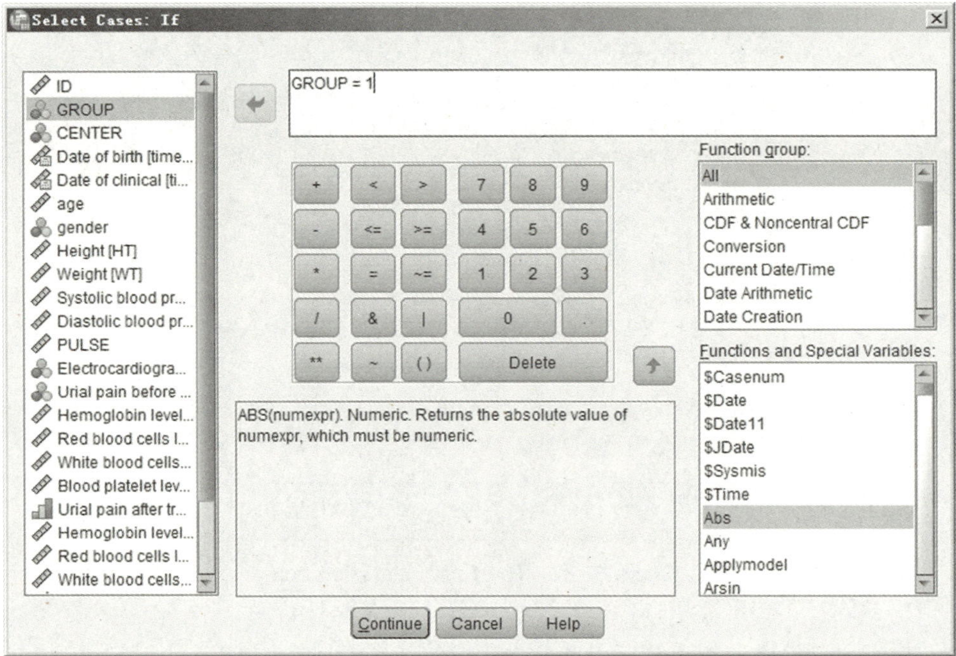

Figure 5-24 The Select Cases: If dialog box

(3) Paired samples t-test:

Analyze

Compare Means

Paired-Samples T Test

The dialog box for the Paired-Samples T Test is listed in Figure 5-25. Select the paired variables from the left box and click the right-arrow button to put the variables into the "Paired Variables" blank. The first variable of the two paired variables is placed in the "Variable 1" column while the second in the "Variable 2" column. Repeat this step until all the variables to be compared are selected.

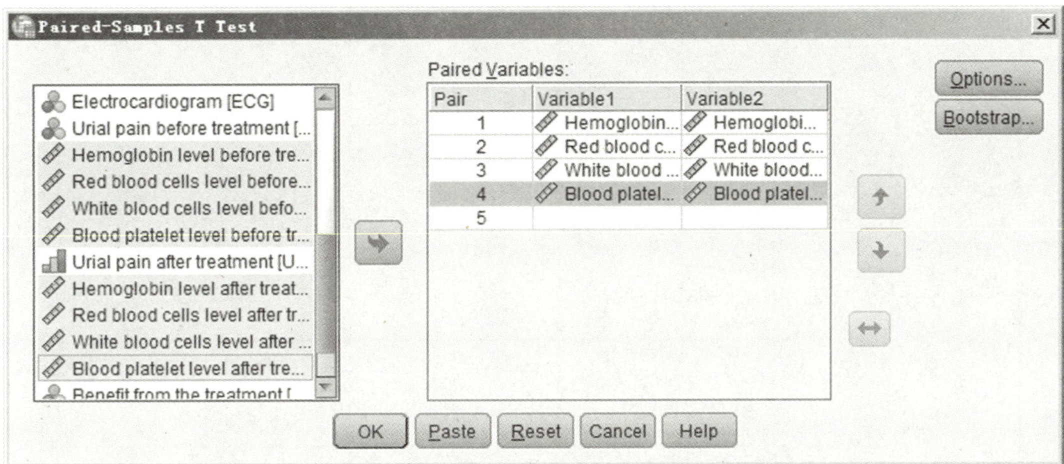

Figure 5-25 The Paired-Samples T Test dialog box

★ Options: The options are the same as one sample t-test.

5.4.5 Reading the output

The output for the paired samples t-test consists of three sections.

(1) Basic descriptive statistics: The first section lists some basic descriptive statistics. From the result, we know the mean, sample size, standard deviation, and standard error of each group (Figure 5-26).

Paired Samples Statistics

GROUP			Mean	N	Std. Deviation	Std. Error Mean
test group	Pair 1	Hemoglobin level before treatment	136.28	72	18.156	2.140
		Hemoglobin level after treatment	133.01	72	17.014	2.005
	Pair 2	White blood cells level before treatment	6.9064	72	2.21117	.26059
		White blood cells level after treatment	7.1907	72	2.02988	.23922
	Pair 3	Red blood cells level before treatment	4.4699	72	.54855	.06465
		Red blood cells level after treatment	4.4211	72	.52186	.06150
	Pair 4	Blood platelet level before treatment	224.00	72	78.656	9.270
		Blood platelet level after treatment	225.67	72	71.381	8.412
control group	Pair 1	Hemoglobin level before treatment	134.51	72	19.420	2.289
		Hemoglobin level after treatment	131.50	72	18.323	2.159
	Pair 2	White blood cells level before treatment	6.7411	72	1.85373	.21846
		White blood cells level after treatment	7.2217	72	2.15189	.25360
	Pair 3	Red blood cells level before treatment	4.4935	72	.62598	.07377
		Red blood cells level after treatment	4.4886	72	.85905	.10124
	Pair 4	Blood platelet level before treatment	211.71	72	72.291	8.520
		Blood platelet level after treatment	223.72	72	78.476	9.248

Figure 5-26 Basic descriptive statistics of the Example 5-5

(2) Correlation analysis: The second section lists the results of correlation analysis between the indicators before and after treatment (Figure 5-27). From the result, we can get the coefficient of product-moment correlation (r) and its P value. The differences between the indicators are significant ($P<0.001$), except for the control group pair 2 ($r=0.145$, $P=0.225$). The correlation of blood platelet level before and after treatment is the strongest ($r=0.729$) among these indicators.

(3) Paired samples t-test: The third section lists the result of the paired samples t-test (Figure 5-28). From the result, the mean, standard deviation, standard error mean, 95% confidence interval of the difference, t value, degree of freedom and 2-tailed P value are shown. The differences we test are all non-significant ($P>0.05$).

Paired Samples Correlations

GROUP			N	Correlation	Sig.
test group	Pair 1	Hemoglobin level before treatment & Hemoglobin level after treatment	72	.571	.000
	Pair 2	White blood cells level before treatment & White blood cells level after treatment	72	.420	.000
	Pair 3	Red blood cells level before treatment & Red blood cells level after treatment	72	.494	.000
	Pair 4	Blood platelet level before treatment & Blood platelet level after treatment	72	.729	.000
control group	Pair 1	Hemoglobin level before treatment & Hemoglobin level after treatment	72	.722	.000
	Pair 2	White blood cells level before treatment & White blood cells level after treatment	72	.145	.225
	Pair 3	Red blood cells level before treatment & Red blood cells level after treatment	72	.554	.000
	Pair 4	Blood platelet level before treatment & Blood platelet level after treatment	72	.520	.000

Figure 5-27 Correlation analysis of the Example 5-5

Paired Samples Test

			Paired Differences					t	df	Sig. (2-tailed)
						95% Confidence Interval of the Difference				
GROUP			Mean	Std. Deviation	Std. Error Mean	Lower	Upper			
test group	Pair 1	Hemoglobin level before treatment - Hemoglobin level after treatment	3.267	16.314	1.923	-.567	7.100	1.699	71	.094
	Pair 2	White blood cells level before treatment - White blood cells level after treatment	-.28431	2.28871	.26973	-.82213	.25351	-1.054	71	.295
	Pair 3	Red blood cells level before treatment - Red blood cells level after treatment	.04875	.53868	.06348	-.07783	.17533	.768	71	.445
	Pair 4	Blood platelet level before treatment - Blood platelet level after treatment	-1.667	55.620	6.555	-14.737	11.403	-.254	71	.800
control group	Pair 1	Hemoglobin level before treatment - Hemoglobin level after treatment	3.014	14.097	1.661	-.299	6.326	1.814	71	.074
	Pair 2	White blood cells level before treatment - White blood cells level after treatment	-.48056	2.62906	.30984	-1.09835	.13724	-1.551	71	.125
	Pair 3	Red blood cells level before treatment - Red blood cells level after treatment	.00485	.73110	.08616	-.16695	.17665	.056	71	.955
	Pair 4	Blood platelet level before treatment - Blood platelet level after treatment	-12.014	74.039	8.726	-29.412	5.384	-1.377	71	.173

Figure 5-28 Paired Samples T Test

5.5 One-way ANOVA

5.5.1 Description

One-way ANOVA process ("analysis of variance") compares the means of two or more independent groups in order to determine whether there is statistical evidence that the associated population means are significantly different.

5.5.2 Example

Example 5-6 The data file "ONE-WAY_1. sav" is used as the Example 5-6. Twenty-seven three-month-old female SD rats are randomly divided into three groups, with 9 SD rats for each group. Three groups are blank control group, ovariectomy group and estrogen group, respectively. After 90 days, the rats are killed and bone changes are measured. The percentage of trabecular area is used to evaluate the results. The results as shown in Table 5-2. Do the effects of the three treatments on skeletal development of rats differed?

Table 5-2 The trabecular area percentage observation of SD rats after 90 days(%)

Control	Ovariectomy	Estrogen
10.28	10.01	28.88
31.35	8.28	12.77
31.23	6.12	27.56
30.44	10.78	15.50
30.04	9.98	26.46
22.78	5.80	16.42
23.46	7.51	27.33
30.36	14.26	22.37
30.61	10.41	12.44

5.5.3 SPSS data format

This data file has 27 rows and 2 columns. Two columns are defined as a category variable and a dependent variable.

(1) Category variable: To illustrate the group (class) to which each subject belongs, in this case the variable named as "group". The variable is labeled as: 1 = "control group", 2 = "ovariectomy group", 3 = "estrogen group".

(2) Dependent variables (response variables): Quantitative variables, in this case the variable named as "tbar" (trabecular is a percentage).

5.5.4 Running the command

The one-way ANOVA test is located in the "Compare Means" submenu, under the "Analyze" menu.

Analyze

  Compare Means

    One-Way ANOVA

The dialog box of the One-Way ANOVA is listed in Figure 5-29.

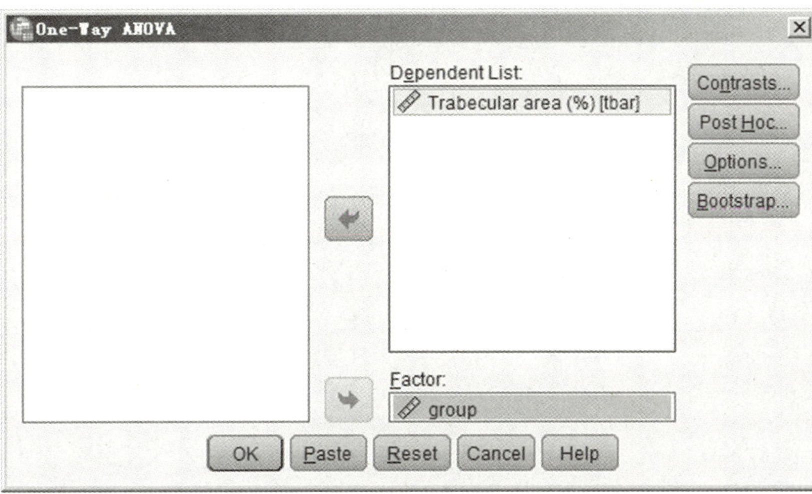

Figure 5-29 The One-Way ANOVA dialog box

◇Dependent List: Select the one or more dependent variables. The variable "tbar" is chosen in the Example 5-6.

◇Factor: Select a categorical variables (factor). Select "group" in the Example 5-6.

★Contrasts: Contrasts of linear combination. Click "Contrasts" button (Figure 5-25), and the dialog box for the One-Way ANOVA: Contrasts (Contrasts of linear combination) pops out (Figure 5-26). Contrast is a linear function of the parameters or statistics used to test the relationship between the means, including the differences and linear trend. Contrast can be expressed as:

$$\alpha_1, \mu_1 + \alpha_2, \mu_2 + \cdots + \alpha_k, \mu_k = 0; \alpha_i \text{ satisfy } \alpha_1 + \alpha_2 + \cdots + \alpha_k = 0. \quad (5\text{-}2)$$

In Formula 5-2, α_i is the linear combination coefficient; μ_i is the overall mean; k is the number of categorical variables. For example, when $k=4$, there are 4 processing groups A, B, C and D. If only B and D are compared, the linear combination coefficients are 0, −1, 0, 1; if group C is compared with the average of the other three groups, then the linear combination coefficient are −1, −1, 3, −1, and so on. The linear combination factors should be entered in the "Coefficients" box in Figure 5-30. For the average trend test, there are five Polynomial options, Linear, Quadratic, Cubic, 4th, and 5th polynomials.

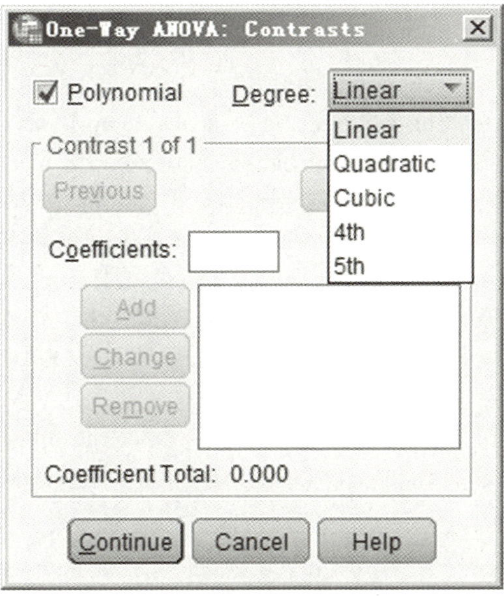

Figure 5-30 The One-Way ANOVA: Contrasts dialog box

★ Post Hoc: Multiple comparisons of means in each group.

Click "Post Hoc" button (Figure 5-29), the dialog box of One-Way ANOVA: Post Hoc Multiple Comparisons (multiple comparisons) pops out (Figure 5-31).

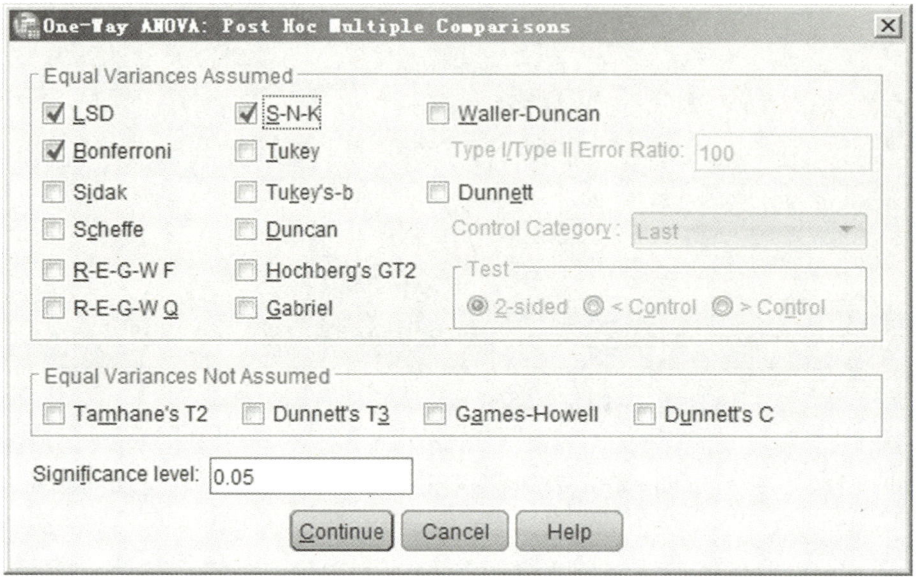

Figure 5-31 The One-Way ANOVA: Post Hoc Multiple Comparisons dialog box

◇Equal Variances Assumed: Multiple comparisons methods to meet equal variances.

Fourteen kinds of multiple comparison methods are available to meet the requirement of equal variances. Commonly used methods are least-significant difference (LSD) method, Scheffe method, S-N-K (Student's Neuman-Keuls) method, Tukey's-b method, Duncan method and Bonferroni method. Among them, LSD method is the most sensitive, Scheffe method is less sensitive, and S-N-K method or Bonferroni method is widely applied. Multiple comparisons are generally used when ANOVA analysis is significant. When variance analysis is not significant, multiple comparisons should not be adopted.

The last of these 14 methods, Dunnett's method, is the only one used to compare multiple treatment groups with one control group. Select this item to activate the "Control Category" column. Set the first group or the last group as the control group. Test column to determine one or two-tailed test.

◇Test.

⊙2-sided: two-tailed test (system default).

◎<Control: One-tailed test. The mean of the compare group is less than that of the control group.

◎>Control: One-tailed test. The mean of the compare group is more than that of the control group.

◇ Equal Variances Not Assumed: Multiple comparisons that do not satisfy the equal variances.

□Tambane's T2: A conservative multiple comparison method based on t-test.

□Dunnett's T3: Multiple comparison method based on student maximal.

□Games-Howell: Non-parametric multiple comparison method.

□Dunnett's C: A multiple comparison method based on studentization range is a method of confidence intervals.

Choose one or more methods from above four analysis, enter the test significance level in the Significance level. [0.05] box, the system default value is 0.05.

★Options:

Click "Options" button (Figure 5-29), and the dialog box of One-Way ANOVA: Options pops out (Figure 5-32).

◇Statistics:

☑Descriptive: Descriptive statistics.

□Fixed and random effects: The standard deviation, standard error and 95% confidence interval of the fixed effect model, as well as the standard error and 95% confidence interval of the random effect model are given.

☑Homogeneity of variance test.

□Brown–Forsythe: Brown–Forsythe approximate variance analysis, a robust test method.

□Welch: Welch approximate variance analysis, a robust test method.

□Means plots: The mean line graph, which horizontal axis is the classification variable, and the vertical axis is the response variables.

◇Missing Values: Missing value processing.

⊙Exclude cases analysis by analysis (system default): Excluding the observation units with missing values in the variables involved in the analysis.

◎ Exclude cases listwise: Remove all observations with missing values in the selected variables.

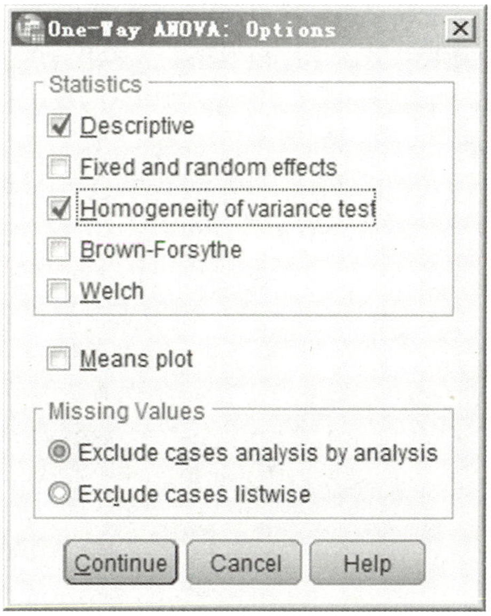

Figure 5–32 The One–Way ANOVA: Options dialog box

5.5.5 Reading the output

In summary, the whole process of this example is as follows:

Analyze

Compare Means

One–Way ANOVA

▸Dependent List: tbar

▸Factor: group

Post Hoc

☑Dunnett's T3

☑Dunnett's C

Options

☑Descriptive

☑Homogeneity of variance test

☑Brown–Forsythe

☑Welch

The main results are listed:

(1) Descriptive statistics: Sample size, Mean, Standard Deviation, Standard Error, 95% Confidence Interval, Minimum and Maximum are listed in Figure 5–33.

(2) Homogeneity of variance test: Levene test equal variances not assumed ($F=4.810, P=0.018$) in Figure 5–34.

(3) Analysis of variance: Although the approximate F test Welch and Brown–Forsythe methods are chosen for varying degrees of variance, the results of the Fisher variance analysis must be included in the results, as shown in Figure 5–35. In the figure, "Between Groups" represents between processing group items; "Within Groups" represents inside processing group items, that is, error items; "Total" represents total items; "Sum of Squares" represents the sum of squares of deviations; "Mean Square" represents the mean squares. After running the program, the statistics is listed ($F=21.086, P<0.001$). From Figure 5–36, the Welch method is based on the F distribution, corrected F values and degrees of freedom ($F=$

31.110, ν=13.134, P<0.001); Brown–Forsythe method is based on the distribution of F and corrected only the degrees of freedom (F=21.086, ν=18.213, P<0.001). Although all three methods are concordant, all of them are significant (P<0.001). However, the latter two methods based on uneven variance should prevail.

In the Example 5–6, there are statistical differences among the mean of the groups, and further multiple comparisons are needed.

Descriptives

Trabecular area (%)

	N	Mean	Std. Deviation	Std. Error	95% Confidence Interval for Mean		Minimum	Maximum
					Lower Bound	Upper Bound		
control group	9	26.7278	6.99503	2.33168	21.3509	32.1046	10.28	31.35
ovariectomy group	9	9.2389	2.63543	.87848	7.2131	11.2647	5.80	14.26
estrogen group	9	21.0811	6.79208	2.26403	15.8603	26.3020	12.44	28.88
Total	27	19.0159	9.30265	1.79030	15.3359	22.6959	5.80	31.35

Figure 5–33 Basic statistics and confidence intervals of the Example 5–6

Test of Homogeneity of Variances

Trabecular area (%)

Levene Statistic	df1	df2	Sig.
4.810	2	24	.018

Figure 5–34 Homogeneity of variance test result of the Example 5–6

ANOVA

Trabecular area (%)

	Sum of Squares	df	Mean Square	F	Sig.
Between Groups	1433.953	2	716.976	21.086	.000
Within Groups	816.067	24	34.003		
Total	2250.020	26			

Figure 5–35 ANOVA table when equal variances assumed of the Example 5–6

Robust Tests of Equality of Means

Trabecular area (%)

	Statistic[a]	df1	df2	Sig.
Welch	31.110	2	13.134	.000
Brown-Forsythe	21.086	2	18.213	.000

a. Asymptotically F distributed.

Figure 5–36 Approximate ANOVA when equal variances not assumed of the Example 5–6

(4) Multiple Comparisons: Figure 5–37 shows multiple comparison methods based on unequal variance, Dunnett's T3 and Dunnett's C. Dunnett's T3 has only interval estimates. Results from both methods are

consistent. There is statistical difference between ovariectomy group with control group and estrogen group ($P<0.001$ and $P=0.002$, respectively). There is no significant difference between control group and estrogen group ($P=0.265$). For the results of the confidence interval, if the confidence interval does not contain 0, then there is a statistical difference at the significant level of 0.05. Combining with the basic statistics in Figure 5-32, the overall conclusion is that the skeletal development of the ovariectomy group is significantly worse than that of the other two groups, with no statistical difference between the other two groups. However, from the view of mean value, the estrogen group (21.081 1) is lower than the control group (26.727 8). Figure 5-37 gives explanation of other results:

1) Dependent Variable: a% that is, the response variable is "tbar".

2) Mean Difference (I-J): Mean difference between groups.

3) Std. Error: The standard error of the mean difference.

Multiple Comparisons

Dependent Variable: Trabecular area (%)

	(I) group	(J) group	Mean Difference (I-J)	Std. Error	Sig.	95% Confidence Interval Lower Bound	95% Confidence Interval Upper Bound
Dunnett T3	control group	ovariectomy group	17.48889*	2.49167	.000	10.4678	24.5100
		estrogen group	5.64667	3.25001	.265	-2.9667	14.2600
	ovariectomy group	control group	-17.48889*	2.49167	.000	-24.5100	-10.4678
		estrogen group	-11.84222*	2.42849	.002	-18.6705	-5.0139
	estrogen group	control group	-5.64667	3.25001	.265	-14.2600	2.9667
		ovariectomy group	11.84222*	2.42849	.002	5.0139	18.6705
Dunnett C	control group	ovariectomy group	17.48889*	2.49167		10.3691	24.6087
		estrogen group	5.64667	3.25001		-3.6400	14.9334
	ovariectomy group	control group	-17.48889*	2.49167		-24.6087	-10.3691
		estrogen group	-11.84222*	2.42849		-18.7815	-4.9030
	estrogen group	control group	-5.64667	3.25001		-14.9334	3.6400
		ovariectomy group	11.84222*	2.42849		4.9030	18.7815

*. The mean difference is significant at the 0.05 level.

Figure 5-37 The results of four multiple comparison methods

5.5.6 Example

Example 5-7 The data file "ONE-WAY_2" is used as the Example 5-7. In the context of Example 5-7, four response variables list, namely "tbn" (trabecular number, /mm^2), "tbsp" (trabecular space, μm), "Lpm" (% of fluorescent marker perimeter), "bfr" (bone formation rate, μm/d × 100). Try and analyze if there are difference for number of trabecular and trabecular space among three groups.

5.5.7 Running the command

First perform the homogeneity of variance test and analysis of variance, the results show the homogeneity of the variance, and the overall comparison between the groups are statistically different. The process is as follows:

Analyze

Compare Means

One-Way ANOVA

▸Dependent List: tbn / tbsp

▸Factor: group

Post Hoc

☑LSD

☑SNK

☑Bonferroni

Options

☑**Descriptive**
☑**Homogeneity-of-variance test**

5.5.8 Reading the output

The results as shown from Figure 5-38 to Figure 5-43, explained as follows.

Descriptives

		N	Mean	Std. Deviation	Std. Error	95% Confidence Interval for Mean		Minimum	Maximum
						Lower Bound	Upper Bound		
Trabecular number (#/mm2)	control group	9	4.4989	1.33624	.44541	3.4718	5.5260	1.29	5.88
	ovariectomy group	9	1.6256	.42951	.14317	1.2954	1.9557	.88	2.41
	estrogen group	9	3.8344	.96061	.32020	3.0961	4.5728	2.56	5.15
	Total	27	3.3196	1.56737	.30164	2.6996	3.9397	.88	5.88
Trabecular space(μm)	control group	9	208.8056	183.70662	61.23554	67.5961	350.0150	118.49	694.50
	ovariectomy group	9	603.9689	206.73451	68.91150	445.0587	762.8791	356.34	1069.23
	estrogen group	9	223.5433	81.37482	27.12494	160.9931	286.0936	140.97	341.87
	Total	27	345.4393	245.58860	47.26355	248.2876	442.5909	118.49	1069.23

Figure 5-38 Basic statistics

(1) Test of Homogeneity of variance (Figure 5-39): Variance between the two response variables in the three groups are equal (P=0.121 and P=0.346).

Test of Homogeneity of Variances

	Levene Statistic	df1	df2	Sig.
Trabecular number (#/mm2)	2.314	2	24	.121
Trabecular space(μm)	1.110	2	24	.346

Figure 5-39 Test of Homogeneity of Variance

(2) ANOVA (Figure 5-40): There is astatistical difference (P<0.001) between the two response variables in the three groups for overall comparison, and multiple comparisons are needed.

ANOVA

		Sum of Squares	df	Mean Square	F	Sig.
Trabecular number (#/mm2)	Between Groups	40.730	2	20.365	21.120	.000
	Within Groups	23.142	24	.964		
	Total	63.872	26			
Trabecular space(μm)	Between Groups	903284.596	2	451642.298	16.303	.000
	Within Groups	664873.142	24	27703.048		
	Total	1568157.738	26			

Figure 5-40 Output of ANOVA table

(3) Multiple comparisons (Figure 5-41): The multiple comparisons results between the LSD and Bonferroni methods are consistent. For the two indicators, there are statistical differences between ovariectomy and control group, as well as between the ovariectomy and estrogen group (P<0.001), but no significant difference between the control group and the estrogen group (P>0.05). However, from the size of P value, LSD method is more sensitive than Bonferroni method.

Multiple Comparisons

Dependent Variable		(I) group	(J) group	Mean Difference (I-J)	Std. Error	Sig.	95% Confidence Interval	
							Lower Bound	Upper Bound
Trabecular number (#/mm2)	LSD	control group	ovariectomy group	2.87333*	.46290	.000	1.9179	3.8287
			estrogen group	.66444	.46290	.164	-.2909	1.6198
		ovariectomy group	control group	-2.87333*	.46290	.000	-3.8287	-1.9179
			estrogen group	-2.20889*	.46290	.000	-3.1643	-1.2535
		estrogen group	control group	-.66444	.46290	.164	-1.6198	.2909
			ovariectomy group	2.20889*	.46290	.000	1.2535	3.1643
	Bonferroni	control group	ovariectomy group	2.87333*	.46290	.000	1.6820	4.0647
			estrogen group	.66444	.46290	.492	-.5269	1.8558
		ovariectomy group	control group	-2.87333*	.46290	.000	-4.0647	-1.6820
			estrogen group	-2.20889*	.46290	.000	-3.4002	-1.0175
		estrogen group	control group	-.66444	.46290	.492	-1.8558	.5269
			ovariectomy group	2.20889*	.46290	.000	1.0175	3.4002
Trabecular space(μm)	LSD	control group	ovariectomy group	-395.16333*	78.46166	.000	-557.1002	-233.2264
			estrogen group	-14.73778	78.46166	.853	-176.6747	147.1991
		ovariectomy group	control group	395.16333*	78.46166	.000	233.2264	557.1002
			estrogen group	380.42556*	78.46166	.000	218.4886	542.3625
		estrogen group	control group	14.73778	78.46166	.853	-147.1991	176.6747
			ovariectomy group	-380.42556*	78.46166	.000	-542.3625	-218.4886
	Bonferroni	control group	ovariectomy group	-395.16333*	78.46166	.000	-597.0955	-193.2312
			estrogen group	-14.73778	78.46166	1.000	-216.6699	187.1944
		ovariectomy group	control group	395.16333*	78.46166	.000	193.2312	597.0955
			estrogen group	380.42556*	78.46166	.000	178.4934	582.3577
		estrogen group	control group	14.73778	78.46166	1.000	-187.1944	216.6699
			ovariectomy group	-380.42556*	78.46166	.000	-582.3577	-178.4934

*. The mean difference is significant at the 0.05 level.

Figure 5-41 Multiple comparisons results

4) S-N-K Multiple Comparisons (Figure 5-42, Figure 5-43): The S-N-K test results are indistinctive, with no statistically significant comparisons in the same column. In this case, both variables showed that the control group and the estrogen group are in the same column, that is, there is no statistical difference between the two groups ($P=0.164$ and $P=0.853$, respectively). Except for the groups that difference is not statistically significant, the rest of the groups are statistically significant (significance level = 0.05), such as ovariectomy group in a single column, which means that the group is significantly different from the other two groups. There is only one group in a column ($P=1.000$) because it is compared with itself. In addition to the line of P value, the remaining values listed in each row is the average of each group.

Trabecular number (#/mm2)

	group	N	Subset for alpha = 0.05	
			1	2
Student-Newman-Keuls[a]	ovariectomy group	9	1.6256	
	estrogen group	9		3.8344
	control group	9		4.4989
	Sig.		1.000	.164

Means for groups in homogeneous subsets are displayed.

a. Uses Harmonic Mean Sample Size = 9.000.

Figure 5-42 SNK multiple comparisons result for "tbn"

According to expressions of SPSS multiple comparisons, there are differential mode (such as LSD method and Bonferroni method) and non-differential mode (such as S-N-K method). Tukey'b method and Duncan method are also expressed in a non-differential manner; Scheffe method and Tukey HSD method are differential and non-differential expressed.

Trabecular space(μm)

	group	N	Subset for alpha = 0.05	
			1	2
Student-Newman-Keuls[a]	control group	9	208.8056	
	estrogen group	9	223.5433	
	ovariectomy group	9		603.9689
	Sig.		.853	1.000

Means for groups in homogeneous subsets are displayed.

a. Uses Harmonic Mean Sample Size = 9.000.

Figure 5-43 S-N-K multiple comparisons result for "tbsp"

Zhang Tao

Chapter 6

General Linear Model

In this chapter, we focus on the analysis with the general linear model (GLM) in SPSS. GLM is widely applied in modern statistics: it can analyze the main effects of individual factors on the dependent variable, and the interaction effects between or among combinations of factors. GLM can be applied to the analysis for both balanced and non-balanced design data; it can also be used in the regression analysis. Many types of experimental designs adopt the GLM univariate analysis, and share common procedures. Before we get to the individual sections of this chapter, it is worthwhile to introduce the common process for the general linear model. From the menu, select:

Analyze

General Linear Model

Univariate

Then the Univariate dialog box pops out (Figure 6-1).

◇Dependent Variable: Also called response variable, only one quantitative variable is selected.

◇Fixed Factor(s): Used for the fixed-effects model, one or more qualitative variables are selected.

◇Random Factor(s): Used for the random-effects or mixed-effects model.

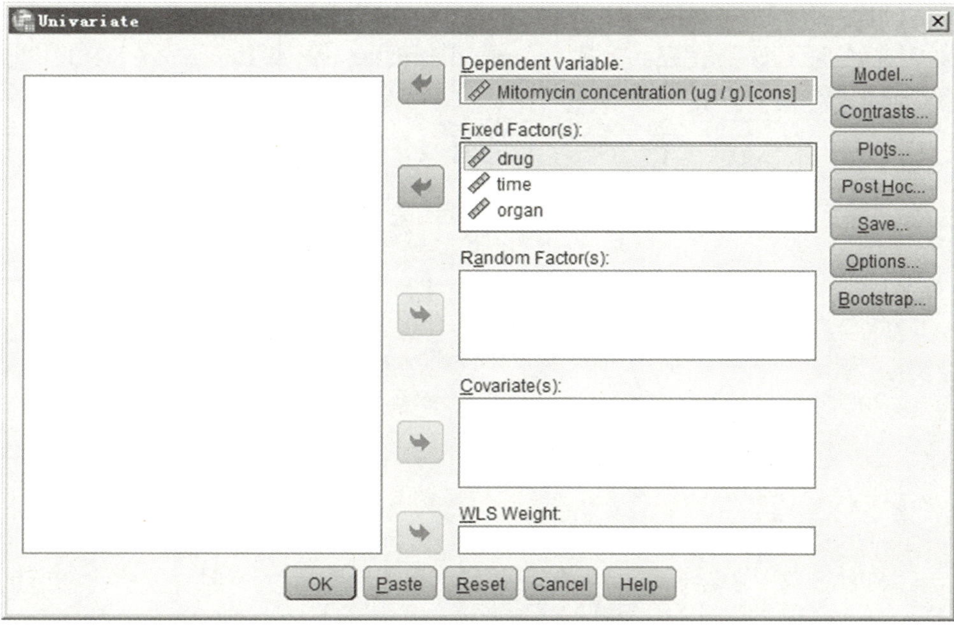

Figure 6-1 The Univariate dialog box

◇Covariate(s): Used in ANCOVA, one or more quantitative variables are selected.

◇WLS Weight: Assignment of weights to the variables in Weighted Least Squares.

★Model:

Click "Model" button, and the dialog box of Univariate: Model pops out (Figure 6-2).

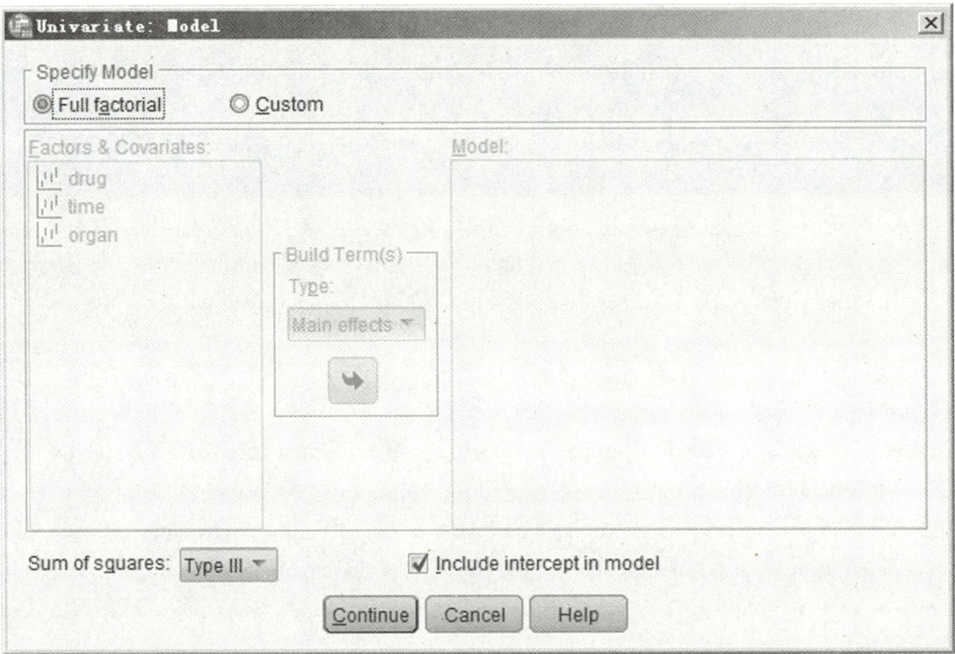

Figure 6-2 The Univariate: Model dialog box

◇Specify Model.

⊙Full factorial: The default model which contains both the main effects and the interaction effects.

◎Custom: The model defined for the specific terms to be included. When selected, the "Factors & Covariates" "Model" and "Build Term(s)" options become available to define the custom model.

◇Sum of squares: The method for calculating the sum of squares; four types (Type Ⅰ, Type Ⅱ, Type Ⅲ, and Type Ⅳ) are available, with "Type Ⅲ" being the default.

☑Include intercept in model: When selected, the model includes the intercept term.

★Plots: Click "Plots" button (Figure 6-1), and the dialog box of Univariate: Profile Plots pops out (Figure 6-3), and refer to subsection 6.3.4.

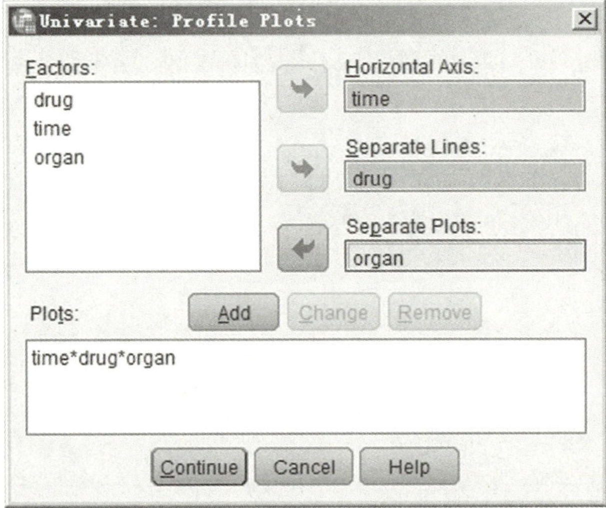

Figure 6-3 The Univariate: Profile Plots dialog box

★Post Hoc: Click "Post Hoc" button (Figure 6-1), and the dialog box of Univariate: Post Hoc Multiple Comparisons for Observed Means pops out. This is used for multiple comparisons (Figure 6-4), and refer to Chapter 5 for detail information.

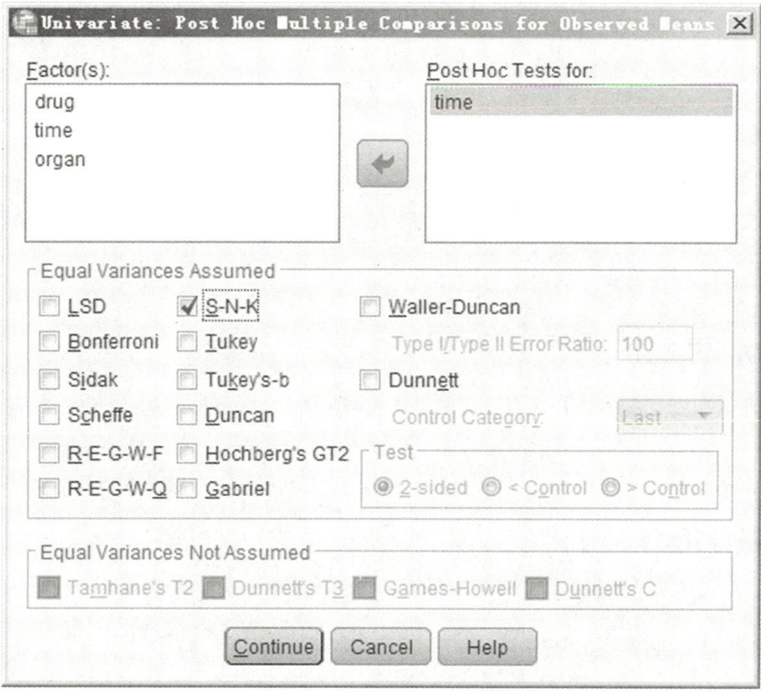

Figure 6-4 The Univariate: Post Hoc dialog box

★Options: Click "Options" button (Figure 6-1), and the dialog box of Univariate: Options pops out (Figure 6-5).

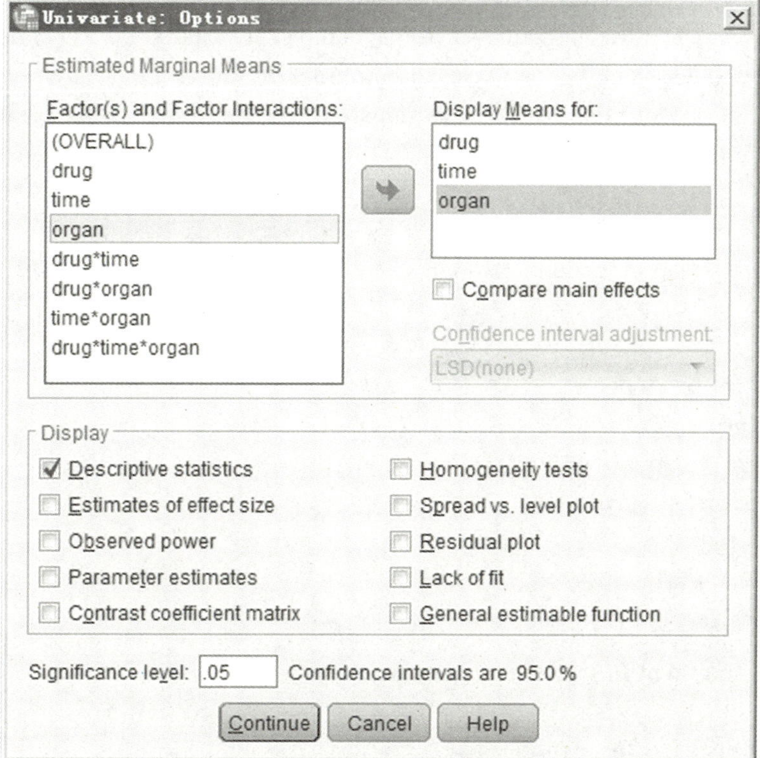

Figure 6-5 The Univariate: Options dialog box

◇Estimated Marginal Means: Use "Factor(s) and Factor Interactions" to select the ones for "Display Means for", which output the mean, standard error, and confidence interval.

◇Display: Options for outputs.

□Descriptive statistics: Mean, standard deviation and sample size.

□Homogeneity tests: Variance equality tests.

◇Significance level: [0.05] Confidence intervals are 95.0% as the default, which corresponds to the 95% confidence intervals.

6.1 Variance analysis of completely randomized design

6.1.1 Description

Completely randomized design aims to study the effects of one primary factor. The design randomly assigns experimental units to the levels of the primary factor, and compares the values of the dependent variable among those groups. The model and analysis are also called one-way ANOVA.

6.1.2 SPSS data format

The data file "ONE-WAY_2. sav" is used, which has 27 rows and 6 columns. Only two variables are used in this analysis: a dependent variable and a grouping variable.

1) Dependent variable: Quantitative, "bfr".

2) Grouping variable (treatment): Qualitative, "group". There are 3 levels, and the labels are: 1 = "control group", 2 = "ovariectomy group", 3 = "estrogen group".

6.1.3 Example

Example 6-1 The data file "ONE-WAY_2. sav" is used as the Example 6-1. Twenty-seven 3-month-old female mice are randomly assigned to 3 groups (1-"control", 2-"ovariectomy", 3-"estrogen"), with a balanced-design of 9 mice in each group. After 90 days, all mice are sacrificed to assay their bone formation. Is there any difference in the dependent variable of "bfr" [Bone formation rate (μm/d×100)] among the 3 groups?

6.1.4 Running the command

To answer this question, we perform a variance analysis of completely randomized design.

Procedure:

Analyze

General Linear Model

Univariate

▸Dependent Variable: bfr

▸Fixed Factor(s): group

Model

⊙Full factorial

Sum of squares: [Type Ⅲ]

☑Include intercept in model

Post Hoc

▸Post Hoc Tests for: group

☑Bonferroni

Options

Estimated Marginal Means

▸Display Means for: group

Display

☑**Descriptive statistics**

☑**Homogeneity tests**

Significance level: 0.05

6.1.5 Reading the output and drawing the conclusions

(1) Descriptive statistics (Figure 6-6): The 3 groups each have 9 mice and their mean "bfr" values are 13.94, 26.75, and 13.75, respectively; for all 27 mice, the mean "bfr" is 18.15. Standard deviation is also shown in the corresponding column.

Descriptive Statistics

Dependent Variable: Bone formation rate (μm/d×100)

group	Mean	Std. Deviation	N
control group	13.9433	7.48787	9
ovariectomy group	26.7522	10.82992	9
estrogen group	13.7456	2.93341	9
Total	18.1470	9.71819	27

Figure 6-6 Output of descriptive statistics

(2) Homogeneity tests (Figure 6-7): Levene's homogeneity test reports a P value of 0.167. We do not reject the null hypothesis and thus accept that variances in all 3 groups are equal.

Levene's Test of Equality of Error Variances[a]

Dependent Variable: Bone formation rate (μm/d×100)

F	df1	df2	Sig.
1.929	2	24	.167

Tests the null hypothesis that the error variance of the dependent variable is equal across groups.

a. Design: Intercept + group

Figure 6-7 Output of Levene's homogeneity test

(3) ANOVA (Figure 6-8): The "Corrected Total" row is the aggregate of the "group" and "Error" rows, and the ANOVA table containing these three rows is the same as the one-way ANOVA table in Chapter 5. The other three rows named "Corrected Model" "Intercept" and "Total" are expressions regarding the related linear model, and the readers can safely ignore them for the current analysis. In the footnote, "R Squared" and "Adjusted R Squared" are given, and their definitions and meanings can be explained in Chapter 7 (simple linear regression). Please refer to that section to understand the meanings of the "R Squared" and "Adjusted R Squared" values reported there. Note: the various ANOVA tables in this chapter can follow similar output format as Figure 6-8.

In the Example 6-1, for the treatment effect ("group" factor), the F statistic has a value of 8.242, and the corresponding P value equals 0.002. Therefore, the mean "bfr" is not identical among the 3 groups. Multiple comparisons are then required to differentiate which groups have different mean "bfr".

Tests of Between-Subjects Effects

Dependent Variable: Bone formation rate (μm/d×100)

Source	Type III Sum of Squares	df	Mean Square	F	Sig.
Corrected Model	999.840[a]	2	499.920	8.242	.002
Intercept	8891.504	1	8891.504	146.595	.000
group	999.840	2	499.920	8.242	.002
Error	1455.681	24	60.653		
Total	11347.025	27			
Corrected Total	2455.522	26			

a. R Squared = .407 (Adjusted R Squared = .358)

Figure 6-8 Output of ANOVA table

(4) Estimated marginal means (Figure 6-9): In comparison to Figure 6-6, additional information of 95% confidence intervals for the mean of each group are reported. Note that the "Std. Error" refers to the standard error for the Error term, which is calculated as:

$$2.596 = \sqrt{MS_E/n} = \sqrt{60.653/9}.$$

group

Dependent Variable: Bone formation rate (μm/d×100)

group	Mean	Std. Error	95% Confidence Interval	
			Lower Bound	Upper Bound
control group	13.943	2.596	8.585	19.301
ovariectomy group	26.752	2.596	21.394	32.110
estrogen group	13.746	2.596	8.388	19.103

Figure 6-9 Output of estimated marginal means of the Example 6-1

(5) Multiple comparisons (Figure 6-10): Regarding the mean "bfr", the differences between "ovariectomy group" and "control group", and between "ovariectomy group" and "estrogen group", are of statistical significance ($P=0.006$ and $P=0.005$, respectively); in contrast, the difference between "control group" and "estrogen group" is non-significant ($P=1.000$). In conclusion, the mean "bfr" of the "ovariectomy group" is higher than that of the other two groups.

Multiple Comparisons

Dependent Variable: Bone formation rate (μm/d×100)

Bonferroni

(I) group	(J) group	Mean Difference (I-J)	Std. Error	Sig.	95% Confidence Interval	
					Lower Bound	Upper Bound
control group	ovariectomy group	-12.8089*	3.67131	.006	-22.2575	-3.3603
	estrogen group	.1978	3.67131	1.000	-9.2509	9.6464
ovariectomy group	control group	12.8089*	3.67131	.006	3.3603	22.2575
	estrogen group	13.0067*	3.67131	.005	3.5580	22.4553
estrogen group	control group	-.1978	3.67131	1.000	-9.6464	9.2509
	ovariectomy group	-13.0067*	3.67131	.005	-22.4553	-3.5580

Based on observed means.
The error term is Mean Square(Error) = 60.653.

*. The mean difference is significant at the .05 level.

Figure 6-10 Output of multiple comparisons (Bonferroni) of the Example 6-1

6.2 Variance analysis of randomized block design

6.2.1 Description

Typically, a blocking factor is a source of variability not of primary interest but may have an effect on the dependent variable. By blocking on such nuisance factors, this source of variability is controlled for, and the block effect can be removed, thus leading to greater accuracy. The model and analysis are also called two-way ANOVA.

6.2.2 SPSS data format

The data file "teeth_1. sav" is used, which has 30 rows and 3 columns. Among the 3 variables: one is the dependent variable and the other two are grouping variables.

(1) Dependent variable: Quantitative, "pull".

(2) Grouping variable (treatment): Qualitative, "group". There are 3 levels, and the labels are: 1 = "ordinary dental clasp", 2 = "RPI dental clasp", 3 = "Y-type dental clasp".

(3) Grouping variable (block): Qualitative, "teeth". There are 10 levels, and the labels are 1 to 10 as the corpse index.

6.2.3 Example

Example 6-2 The data file "teeth_1. sav" is used as the Example 6-2. Dental clasps are used for the purpose of teeth stabilization. It is of interest if 3 types of dental clasps (1-"ordinary", 2-"RPI", 3-"Y-type") are different in pull force (measured in Newton unit). To investigate this question, 30 teeth from 10 recently deceased bodies are measured. Each corpse is seen as a block, and the 3 teeth from each corpse are randomly assigned to the 3 types of dental clasps for pull force test. The results are shown in Table 6-1. Is there any difference in pull force among the 3 types of dental clasps?

Table 6-1 Measurement of pull force for the 3 types of dental clasps

Corpse #	ordinary dental clasp	RPI dental clasp	Y-type dental clasp
1	4.3	6.4	5.0
2	10.2	9.7	8.1
3	6.5	7.7	6.7
4	9.2	10.9	7.8
5	5.7	7.1	6.0
6	7.1	8.9	6.7
7	4.4	5.6	4.2
8	11.3	13.0	10.9
9	8.7	10.6	8.4
10	7.3	8.2	7.5

6.2.4 Running the command

To answer this question, we perform a variance analysis of randomized block design.

Procedure:

Analyze

General Linear Model

Univariate

▸Dependent Variable: pull

▸Fixed Factor(s): group / teeth

Model

⊙Custom

▸Model: group / teeth

Sum of squares: **Type III**

☑Include intercept in model

Post Hoc

▸Post Hoc Tests for: group

☑S-N-K

Options

Estimated Marginal Means

▸Display Means for: group

Display

☑Descriptive statistics

Significance level: 0.05

In the above process, we do not select "Homogeneity tests" because in the "Univariate" analysis, the software can not provide any homogeneity test output when the model contains 2 or more factors and no repeated measurements are conducted. Therefore, in order to perform homogeneity tests for the treatment factor and the block factor, we can conduct one-way ANOVA for individual factors, as seen in Chapter 5. In the Example 6-2, both the treatment factor (Figure 6-11) and the block factor (Figure 6-12) pass homogeneity tests ($P=0.634$ and $P=0.637$, respectively).

Test of Homogeneity of Variances

Force(Newton unit)

Levene Statistic	df1	df2	Sig.
.463	2	27	.634

Figure 6-11 Test of Homogeneity of variances of the treatment factor

Test of Homogeneity of Variances

Force(Newton unit)

Levene Statistic	df1	df2	Sig.
.780	9	20	.637

Figure 6-12 Test of Homogeneity of variances of the block factor

6.2.5 Reading the output and drawing the conclusions

(1) Descriptive statistics: the mean and standard deviation ($\bar{X} \pm S$) for the pull force in the 3 types of dental clasps are: 7.47 ±2.37, 8.81 ±2.27, and 7.13 ±1.89, respectively (Figure 6–13).

group

Dependent Variable: Force (Newton unit)

group	Mean	Std. Error	95% Confidence Interval	
			Lower Bound	Upper Bound
ordinary dental clasp	7.470	.172	7.109	7.831
RPI dental clasp	8.810	.172	8.449	9.171
Y-type dental clasp	7.130	.172	6.769	7.491

Figure 6–13 Output of the Example 6–2

(2) ANOVA (Figure 6–14): The explanations are as follows.

1) Treatment factor: "group" (F=26.687, P<0.001), thus there is statistically significant differences in pull force among the 3 types of dental clasps.

2) Block factor: "teeth" (F=46.496, P<0.001), thus there is statistically significant difference in pull force among the 10 corpses. Blocking is effective in taking into consideration of the difference among teeth sources.

3) In the Example 6–2, if we do not consider the block factor, we can perform a completely randomized design ANOVA as described in section 6.1. Then, for the treatment factor "group" (Figure 6–15, F = 1.651, P=0.211), suggesting that there is no statistically significant difference in pull force among the 3 types of dental clasps. The results from one–way ANOVA are contradictory to the above results from two–way ANOVA, further confirming that the inclusion of the block factor ("teeth") is effective and warranted.

Tests of Between-Subjects Effects

Dependent Variable: Force (Newton unit)

Source	Type III Sum of Squares	df	Mean Square	F	Sig.
Corrected Model	139.488[a]	11	12.681	42.894	.000
Intercept	1826.760	1	1826.760	6179.219	.000
group	15.779	2	7.889	26.687	.000
teeth	123.710	9	13.746	46.496	.000
Error	5.321	18	.296		
Total	1971.570	30			
Corrected Total	144.810	29			

a. R Squared = .963 (Adjusted R Squared = .941)

Figure 6–14 Output of ANOVA table

ANOVA

Force(Newton unit)

	Sum of Squares	df	Mean Square	F	Sig.
Between Groups	15.779	2	7.889	1.651	.211
Within Groups	129.031	27	4.779		
Total	144.810	29			

Figure 6–15 One–way ANOVA of the treatment factor

(3) Multiple comparisons (Figure 6-16): Using the S-N-K method, we observe that two dental clasps reside in Subset column-1 and one dental clasp resides in Subset column-2. Therefore, "RPI dental clasp" has significantly higher pull force than the other two types, while there is no statistically significant difference between the "ordinary dental clasp" and the "Y-type dental clasp" ($P=0.179$).

Force (Newton unit)

Student-Newman-Keuls[a,b]

group	N	Subset	
		1	2
Y-type dental clasp	10	7.130	
ordinary dental clasp	10	7.470	
RPI dental clasp	10		8.810
Sig.		.179	1.000

Means for groups in homogeneous subsets are displayed.
Based on observed means.
The error term is Mean Square(Error) = .296.
a. Uses Harmonic Mean Sample Size = 10.000.
b. Alpha = .05.

Figure 6-16 Output of multiple comparisons (S-N-K)

6.3 Variance analysis of factorial design

6.3.1 Description

Two-way ANOVA such as that shown in section 6.2 allows the effects from more than one factor to be considered together. However, it does not give us any information about the dependence or independence of the multiple factors. For such cases, we resort to ANOVA of factorial design which allows the study of both the main effects and the interaction effects.

6.3.2 SPSS data format

The data file "factorial_1.sav" is used, which has 60 rows and 4 columns. Among the 4 variables: one is the dependent variable and the other three are grouping variables.

1) Dependent variable: Quantitative, "cons".

2) Grouping variable: Qualitative, "drug". There are 2 levels, and the labels are: 1 = "test group", 2 = "control group".

3) Grouping variable: Qualitative, "time". There are 3 levels, and the labels are: 1 = "15 min", 2 = "30 min", 3 = "60 min".

4) Grouping variable: Qualitative, "organ". There are 2 levels, and the labels are: 1 = "heart", 2 = "liver".

6.3.3 Example

Example 6-3 The data file "factorial_1.sav" is used as the Example 6-3. In a research project on drug discovery for liver cancer, a 2×3×2 factorial design is conducted on 3 factors to study the drug effect: the first factor "drug" refers to the test or control groups (with or without the drug studied); the second factor "time" refers to the time after taking the drug; the third factor "organ" corresponds to "heart" or "liver", to differentiate the non-targeted *vs.* targeted organs. Sixty mice are randomly assigned to 12 groups

(2×3×2 combinations of the 3 factors), with each group containing 5 mice. After the experiment, the mice are sacrificed and their individual tissue samples are assayed for the mitomycin concentration ($\mu g/g$) (it is the dependent variable). How do data from this type of factorial design get analyzed?

6.3.4 Running the command

To answer this question, we perform a variance analysis of factorial design (Figure 6-17).

Procedure:

Analyze

General Linear Model

Univariate

▸Dependent Variable: cons

▸Fixed Factor(s): drug / time / organ

Model

⊙Full factorial

Sum of squares: Type Ⅲ

☑Include intercept in model

Post Hoc

▸Post Hoc Tests for: time

☑S-N-K

Options

Estimated Marginal Means

▸Display Means for: drug / time / organ

Display

☑Descriptive statistics

Significance level: 0.05

Plots

▸Horizontal Axis: time

▸Separate Lines: drug

▸Separate Plots: organ

★Plots: interaction-effect plots

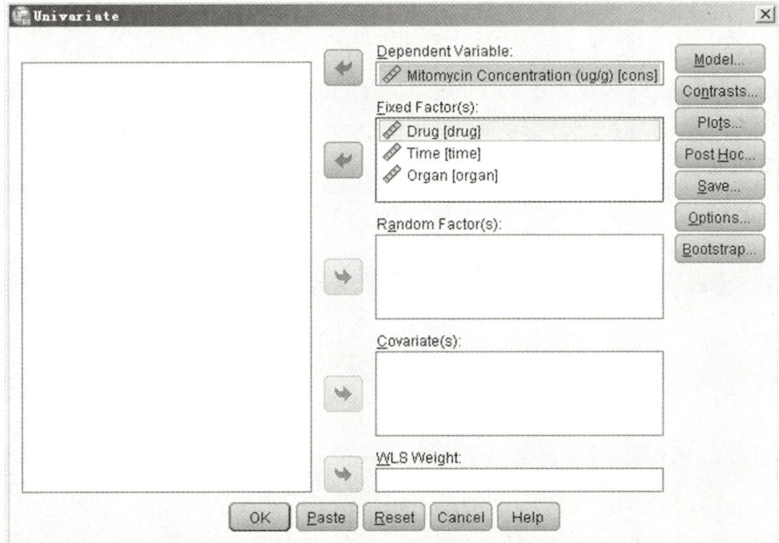

Figure 6-17 The Univariate dialog box

Click "Plots" button, and the dialog box of Univariate: Profile Plots pops out (Figure 6-18).

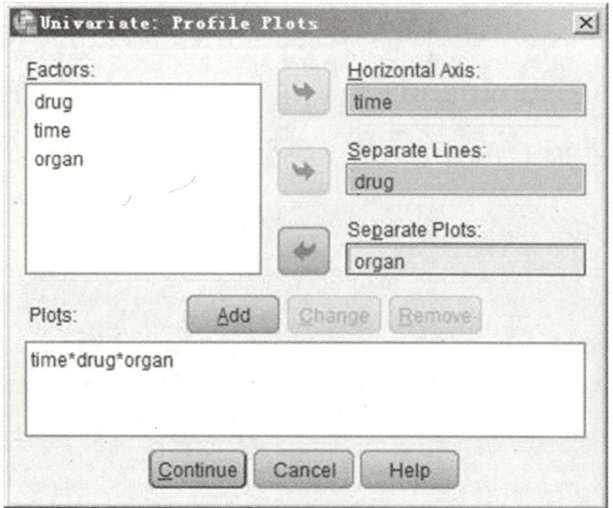

Figure 6-18 The Univariate: Profile Plots dialog box

Interaction-effect plot is a two-dimensional visualization of the interaction effects, displaying the mean of dependent variable at combinations of various factors. Each interaction-effect plot can hold two factors, plotted respectively on the X-axis and separate lines. The Y-axis reflects the dependent variable. In Example 6-3, "Horizontal Axis" (X-axis) selects the "time" factor; "Separate Lines" selects the "drug" factor; "Separate Plots" (also called facets) selects the "organ" factor. Then click "Add" button and the Plots box displays "time * drug * organ", completing the settings for the interaction-effect plot.

6.3.5 Reading the output and drawing the conclusions

(1) Descriptive statistics (Figure 6-19): The mean, standard error, and 95% confidence interval are reported for the "drug" "time" and "organ" factors.

(2) ANOVA results (Figure 6-20): The explanations are listed.

1) Factor: "drug" (F=3 660.158, P<0.001), thus the mitomycin concentration in the "test group" is higher than in the "control group".

2) Factor: "time" (F=3 588.885, P<0.001), thus there is statistically significant difference in dependent variable among the groups. Together with the output in Figure 6-18, it can be concluded that higher mitomycin concentration is observed in the "30 min group" than in the other two groups. There is no statistically significant difference between "15 min group" and "60 min group".

3) Factor: "organ" (F=3 393.707, P<0.001), thus the mitomycin concentration in the "liver group" is higher than in the "heart group".

4) All four combinations of factors have statistically significant interaction effects (P<0.001), which can also be observed in the interaction-effect plots.

5) The ANOVA model with interactions fits the data quite well, with adjusted R^2 = 0.998.

1. drug

Dependent Variable: Mitomycin concentration (ug / g)

drug	Mean	Std. Error	95% Confidence Interval	
			Lower Bound	Upper Bound
test group	.917	.007	.903	.930
control group	.338	.007	.324	.352

2. time

Dependent Variable: Mitomycin concentration (ug / g)

time	Mean	Std. Error	95% Confidence Interval	
			Lower Bound	Upper Bound
15min	.351	.008	.334	.368
30min	1.200	.008	1.184	1.217
60min	.331	.008	.314	.347

3. organ

Dependent Variable: Mitomycin concentration (ug / g)

organ	Mean	Std. Error	95% Confidence Interval	
			Lower Bound	Upper Bound
heart	.349	.007	.335	.362
liver	.906	.007	.893	.920

Figure 6-19 Output of estimated marginal means

Tests of Between-Subjects Effects

Dependent Variable: Mitomycin concentration (ug / g)

Source	Type III Sum of Squares	df	Mean Square	F	Sig.
Corrected Model	45.899[a]	11	4.173	3038.908	.000
Intercept	23.622	1	23.622	17203.664	.000
drug	5.026	1	5.026	3660.158	.000
time	9.855	2	4.928	3588.885	.000
organ	4.660	1	4.660	3393.707	.000
drug * time	4.847	2	2.424	1765.111	.000
drug * organ	9.843	1	9.843	7168.881	.000
time * organ	5.791	2	2.895	2108.711	.000
drug * time * organ	5.876	2	2.938	2139.914	.000
Error	.066	48	.001		
Total	69.586	60			
Corrected Total	45.964	59			

a. R Squared = .999 (Adjusted R Squared = .998)

Figure 6-20 Output of ANOVA table

(3) Multiple comparisons (Figure 6-21): For the 3 factors studied, "drug" and "organ" both have two levels, thus only the "time" factor, which has three levels needs to be checked. Higher mitomycin concentration is observed in the "30 min group" than in the other two groups, while there is no statistically significant difference between "15 min group" and "60 min group" ($P=0.092$).

Mitomycin concentration (ug / g)

Student-Newman-Keuls[a,b]

time	N	Subset 1	Subset 2
60min	20	.330840	
15min	20	.351015	
30min	20		1.200495
Sig.		.092	1.000

Means for groups in homogeneous subsets are displayed.
Based on observed means.
The error term is Mean Square(Error) = .001.

a. Uses Harmonic Mean Sample Size = 20.000.

Figure 6-21 Output of multiple comparisons (SNK)

(4) Interaction-effect plots.

1) Two separate plots are displayed for the two levels of the "organ" factor (Figure 6-22) referring to "heart" and referring to "liver" (Figure 6-23). In each plot, Y-axis is used for the dependent variable of mitomycin concentration; X-axis is used for the "time" factor; two differently colored lines are used for the "drug" factor.

2) The two lines for "test group" and "control group" are not parallel, especially in the "liver" facet (Figure 6-23), suggesting the existence of an interaction effect between the "drug" factor and the "time" factor.

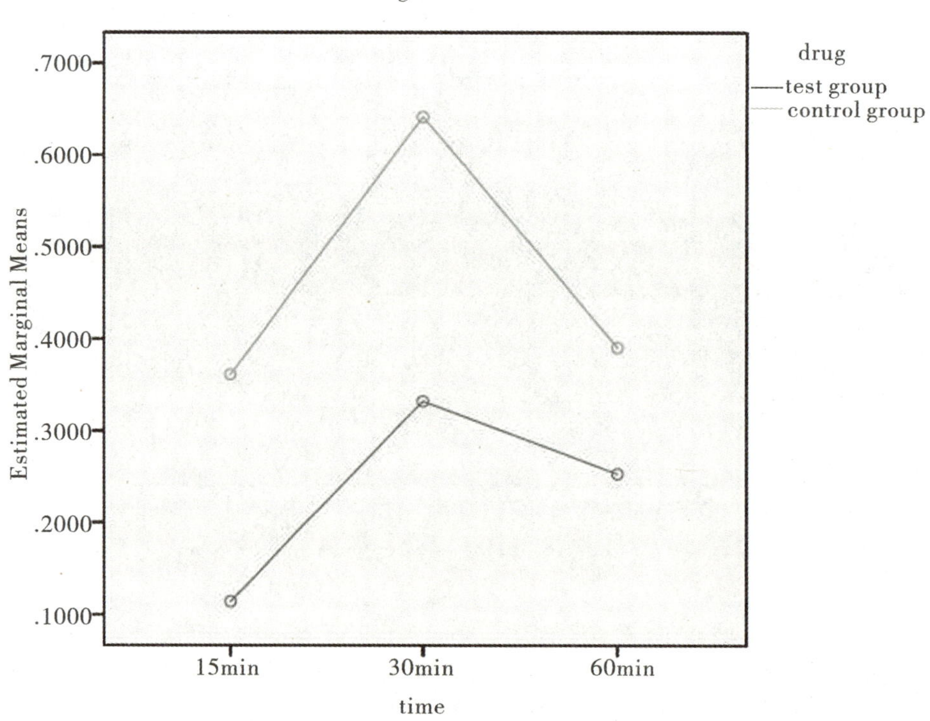

Figure 6-22 Interaction-effect plot output of the "organ" factor (heart)

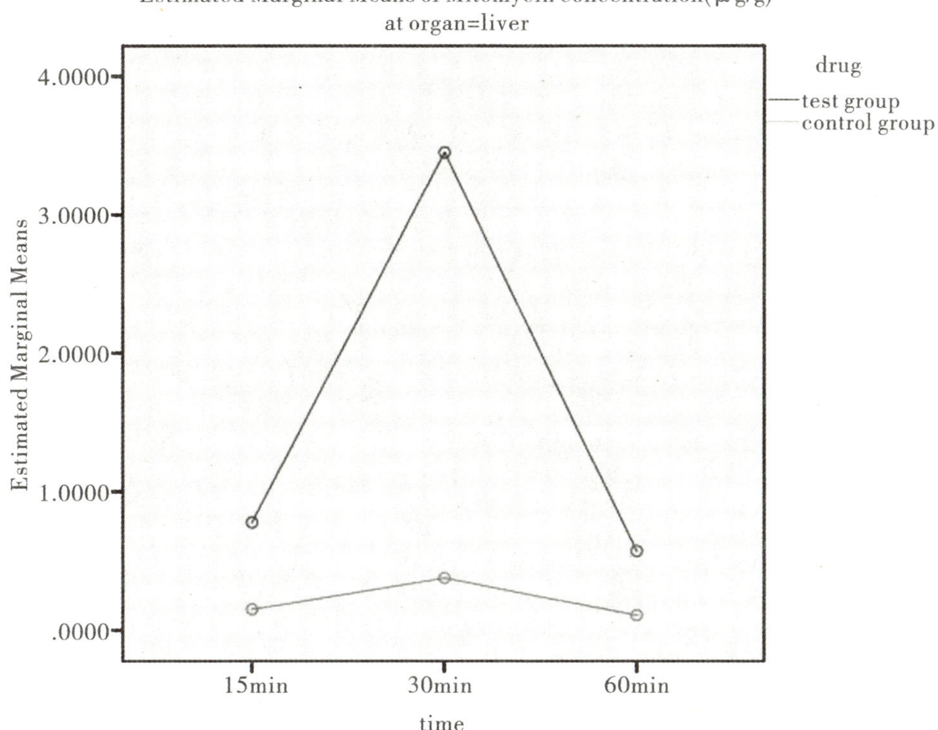

Figure 6-23 Interaction-effect plot output of the "organ" factor (liver)

3) It is easy to identify the condition for the maximal or minimal mean of the dependent variable from the plot.

6.4 Analysis of covariance

6.4.1 Description

Analysis of covariance (ANCOVA) is a statistical method that combines linear regression with analysis of variance (ANOVA) for the comparison of means. The basic idea is to compare different treatment factors of different levels and analyze the interactions between the various treatment factors, after subtracting the linear effects of one or more covariate factors from the dependent variable. For example, to compare the differences in vital capacity among three groups of professional athletes, college students and young laborers, we should deduct the linear effect of chest porch (covariate) on vital capacity before comparing their vital capacity difference.

In addition to satisfying the requirements of the normal distribution and the homogeneity of variances, ANCOVA also requires that the overall regression coefficients between each covariate and the dependent variable are identical but not zero.

6.4.2 SPSS data format

The data file "ANCOVA. sav" is used, which has 56 rows and 3 columns. Three variables are defined: one grouping variable, one dependent variable, and one covariate.

(1) Grouping variable: The variable name is "group" with two levels, 1 = "control group" and 2 = "test group".

(2) Dependent variable: The variable name is "ALP2" (post-treatment ALP).

(3) Covariate: The variable name is "ALP1" (pre-treatment ALP).

6.4.3 Example

Example 6-4 The data file "ANCOVA. sav" is used as the Example 6-4. 56 cases of periodontal disease are randomly divided into two groups of 28 cases. One is the experimental group with minocycline plus basic treatment, and the other is the control group with basic treatment. ALP (alkaline phosphatase) in gingival crevicular fluid is measured to evaluate the therapeutic effect. The lower concentration the ALP is, the better the effect is. Using ANCOVA method, with pre-treatment ALP as a covariate, compare if there is a difference of post-treatment ALP level between the two groups.

6.4.4 Running the command

To answer this question, we perform an ANCOVA.

Procedure:

Analyze

General Linear Model

Univariate

▸Dependent Variable: ALP2

▸Fixed Factor(s): group

▸Covariate(s): ALP1

Model

⊙Full factorial

Sum of squares: Type Ⅲ

☑Include intercept in model

Option

▸Display Means for: group

Significance level: 0.05

6.4.5 Reading the output and drawing the conclusions

(1) Estimated marginal means: Figure 6-24 shows the basic statistics of Means process, without adjustment of the level of pre-treatment ALP1. Figure 6-25 shows the estimation of means for ALP2 after adjustment with the aggregated mean of pre-treatment ALP1 at 691.684 5. The means reported in the two figures are different.

Report

Post-treatment alkaline phosphatase (ALP)

group	Mean	N	Std. Deviation
control group	435.6950	28	344.48918
test group	412.4789	28	549.91891
Total	424.0870	56	454.80871

Figure 6-24 Basic statistics for unadjusted ALP2

group

Dependent Variable: Post-treatment alkaline phosphatase (ALP)

group	Mean	Std. Error	95% Confidence Interval	
			Lower Bound	Upper Bound
control group	484.238[a]	27.342	429.398	539.078
test group	363.936[a]	27.342	309.096	418.776

a. Covariates appearing in the model are evaluated at the following values: Pre-treatment alkaline phosphatase (ALP) = 691.6845.

Figure 6–25 The ALP2 mean estimates after adjustment with ALP1

(2) ANOVA (Figure 6–26): After adjustment with the effect of pre-treatment ALP1, there is a statistically significant difference in post-treatment ALP2 between the two groups (control group and test group, $F=9.618$, $P=0.003$). Together with data from Figure 6–25, we conclude that the test group has better effect (lower post-treatment ALP2) than the control group. In addition, the effect of the covariate "ALP1" on the dependent variable "ALP2" is also significant ($F=493.647$, $P<0.001$).

Tests of Between-Subjects Effects

Dependent Variable: Post-treatment alkaline phosphatase (ALP)

Source	Type III Sum of Squares	df	Mean Square	F	Sig.
Corrected Model	10274499.9[a]	2	5137249.951	247.005	.000
Intercept	267143.666	1	267143.666	12.845	.001
ALP1	10266954.10	1	10266954.10	493.647	.000
group	200045.215	1	200045.215	9.618	.003
Error	1102303.287	53	20798.175		
Total	21448389.37	56			
Corrected Total	11376803.19	55			

a. R Squared = .903 (Adjusted R Squared = .899)

Figure 6–26 ANOVA table for covariance analysis

If we use two sample t-test, that is: Analyze → Compare Means → Independent-Two-Samples T Test. The ALP levels in the two groups before and after treatment are compared respectively. There is no statistical difference between the two groups before treatment ($t=-0.833$, $P=0.408$) and no significant difference after treatment ($t=0.189$, $P=0.851$). It is obvious that the two different approaches (ANCOVA *vs.* two sample t-test) lead to the opposite conclusions.

6.5 Variance analysis of repeated measures

6.5.1 Description

Repeated measurement of data refers to situations when each experimental unit is measured under at least two different treatments or measured multiple times under the same treatment. If such data are misinterpreted using variance analysis of randomized block design, it results in the increase of Type Ⅰ error.

6.5.2 ANOVA of single repeated measures

6.5.2.1 SPSS data format

The data file "repeated_1. sav" is used, which has 12 rows and 5 columns. Five variables are defined: One for grouping variable and four for repeated measures (4 levels).

(1) Grouping variable: The variable name is "group" with two levels, 1 = "SHENG" and 2 = "CD".

(2) Repeated measure variables: Quantitative variables, measured at 4 states ("normal" "injured" "fixed" and "fatigue").

6.5.2.2 Example

Example 6-5 The data file "repeated_1. sav" is used as the Example 6-5. To study the effects of two fixation devices on spinal flexion, 12 vertebral bone specimens are randomly divided into two groups: the SHENG group (5 cases, fixed with SHENG device), and the CD group (7 cases, fixed with CD equipment). The maximal forward flexion (in degree) of each specimen is measured under 4 states ("normal" "injured" "fixed" and "fatigue") respectively. Try to analyze the data (Table 6-2).

Table 6-2 The maximum flexion of 2 fixation devices measured under 4 states

Specimen	Fixation device	Spine status			
		Normal	Injured	Fixed	Fatigue
1	SHENG	5.81	13.53	2.54	5.75
2	SHENG	6.32	13.39	1.72	1.50
3	SHENG	7.08	16.03	10.41	1.95
4	SHENG	7.72	17.80	4.82	5.00
5	SHENG	8.20	11.35	2.35	6.32
6	CD	6.00	10.86	2.73	2.92
7	CD	8.22	22.04	4.03	1.98
8	CD	5.05	15.90	1.88	3.76
9	CD	9.44	17.21	2.54	1.24
10	CD	5.61	10.32	0.89	1.31
11	CD	6.58	15.64	3.05	2.72
12	CD	8.40	19.79	3.27	5.15

6.5.2.3 Running the command

To answer this question, we perform an ANOVA of single repeated measures.

Procedure:

Analyze

General Linear Model

Repeated Measures

The Repeated Measures Define Factor(s) dialog box pops out (Figure 6-27).

◇Within-Subject Factor Name: The system default is "factor1". In the Example 6-5, we filled in "status". Note that the name cannot be identical to any existing variable name.

◇Number of Levels: The number of levels for the repeated measure factor. In the Example 6-5, we filled in "4" because there are 4 levels of the "status" factor. Click "Add" button and activate the "Define" button.

◇Measure Name: When there are more than one set of measure (for example, simultaneous measurement of blood pressure and temperature), they need to be labeled with different names. Note that the name cannot be identical to any existing variable name. In the Example 6-5, there is only one set of measure (flexion), so it does not need to be defined here.

Click "Define" button and the dialog box of Repeated Measures pops out (Figure 6-28).

◇Within-Subject Variables (status): The levels of the repeated measure factor. The Example 6-5 has 4 levels of the "status" factor ("fl_norma" "fl_injur" "fl_fixat" and "fl_fatig"). The number in brackets [eg. "(1)"] refers to the index of each level, and would be used to represent the levels in the later analysis output.

◇Between-Subjects Factor(s): Group factors, select "group".

◇Covariates: The Example 6-5 has no covariates.

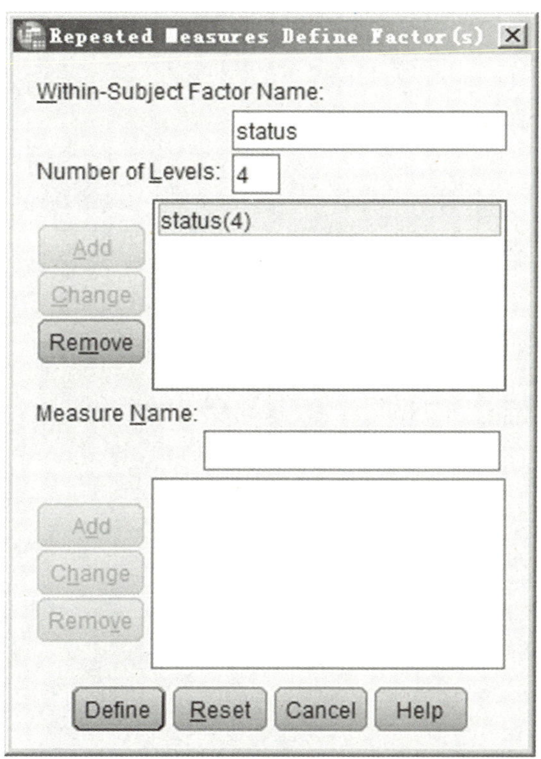

Figure 6-27 The Repeated Measures Define Factors dialog box

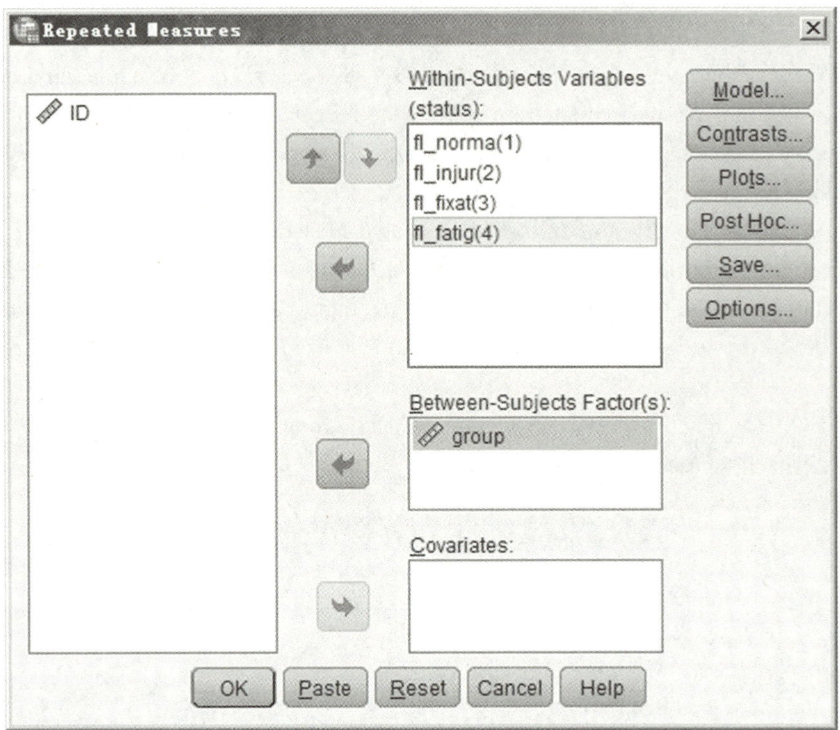

Figure 6-28　The Repeated Measures dialog box

★Model: Click "Model" button and the dialog box of Repeated Measures: Model pops out (Figure 6-29).

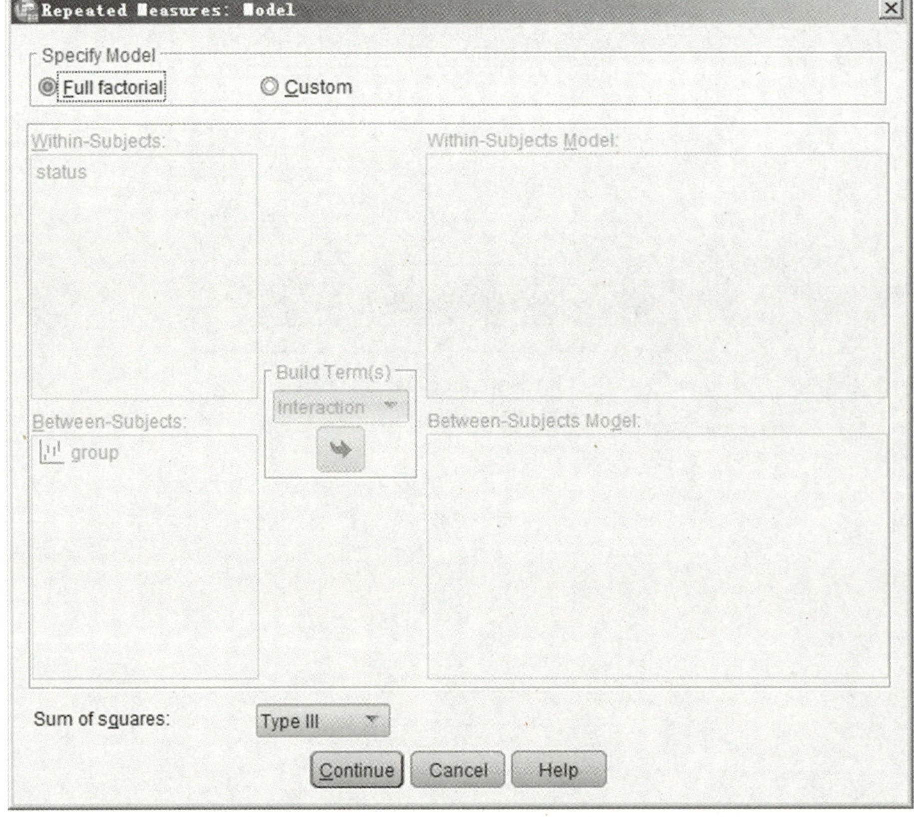

Figure 6-29　The Repeated Measures: Model dialog box

◇Specify Model.

⊙Full factorial: The model with all factors to analyze all main effects and interaction effects. This is the default setting.

◎Custom: The model with user-customized factors to analyze the corresponding main effects and interaction effects.

In the "Within-Subject Model" box, select the repeated measure factor in the model, and in the "Between-Subjects Model" box, select the group factors in the model.

★Contrasts (Figure 6-28): Difference between levels within the factor compared.

★Plots (Figure 6-28): Interaction profile. For more details, please refer to subsection 6.3.5.

★Post Hoc (Figure 6-28): Multiple comparisons of grouping factors.

★Save (Figure 6-28): Save the intermediate results. Residuals, predicted values, Cook distances, *etc.* can be saved as new variables in the data file.

★Options (Figure 6-28): Click "Options" button, and the dialog box of Repeated Measures: Options pops out (Figure 6-30).

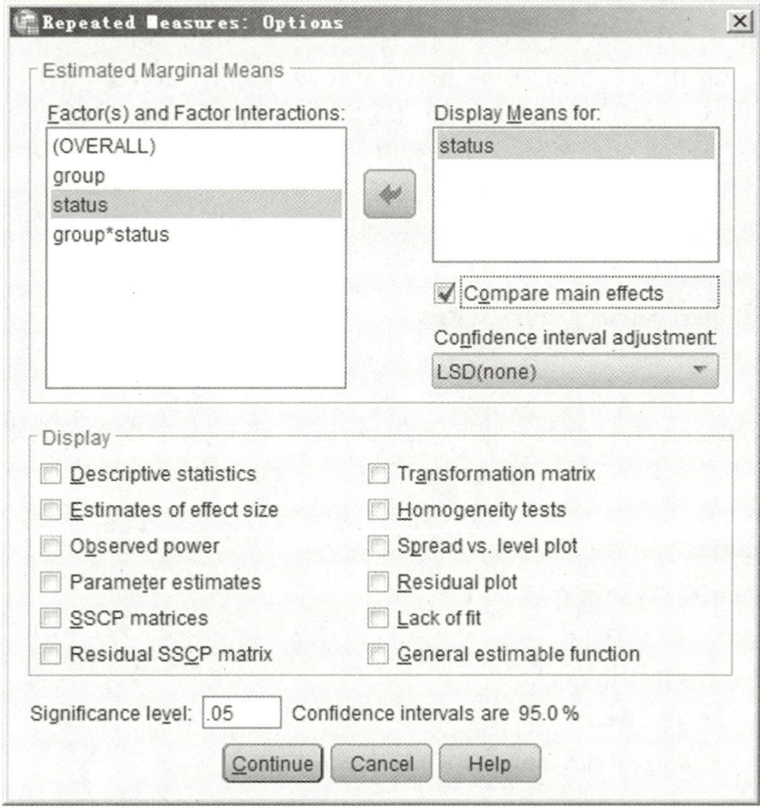

Figure 6-30 The Repeated Measures: Options dialog box

Estimated Marginal Means.

◇Factor(s) and Factor Interactions: Select the factors of main effects and interaction effects in the Model.

◇Display Means for: Output the mean, standard error and confidence interval for the selected factor in the output box.

□Compare main effects: Multiple comparisons of the main effects of different levels of the repeated measure factor. When "Display Means for" box is selected, this option is activated. Note that it does not allow for multiple comparisons between interactions.

◇Confidence interval adjustment: There are 3 multiple comparison methods to choose from: the "LSD (none)""Bonferroni"and "Sidak",with LSD(none) as the system default.

◇Display.

□Descriptive statistics: Mean, standard deviation and sample size.

□Estimates of effect size: Estimating the effect size.

□Observed power: Observe the test efficiency, derived from the sample, and the test performance is different.

□Parameter estimates: It includes regression coefficients, eta statistics and non-center parameters.

□SSCP matrices: Sums of squares and cross-product matrices.

□Residual SSCP matrix: Sums of squares and cross-product matrices of residuals.

□Transformation matrix: Matrix is transposed.

□Homogeneity tests: Levene's variance homogeneity test.

□Spread *vs.* level plot: Scatter plots of mean and standard deviation (variance) for different combinations of factors.

□Residual plot: Residuals, observations and predicted three-variable scatter plot.

□Lack of fit: Misconduct test to test whether the model fitting is meaningful.

□General estimable function: The general linear combination functions of horizontal comparison.

◇Significance level: [0.05] Confidence intervals are 95%. Significance level can be set by oneself (system default of 0.05). The confidence interval system is set to 95% and cann't be set by oneself.

Overall procedure:

Analyze

General Linear Model

Repeated Measures

▸Within-Subject Factor Name: status

▸Number of Levels: 4

Define

▸Within-Subjects Variables (status): fl_norma / fl_injur / fl_fixat / fl_fatig

▸Between-Subjects Factor (s): group

Model

⊙Full factorial

Sum of squares: [Type Ⅲ]

Options

▸Display Means for: status

☑Compare main effects

Confidence interval adjustment: [LSD (none)]

Display

☑Descriptive statistics

Significance level: [0.05]

6.5.2.4 Reading the output and drawing the conclusions

(1) Estimated marginal means (Figure 6-31): Here, 1, 2, 3 and 4 under the status column represent the four states of "normal""injured""fixed" and "fatigue", and the result shows the mean, standard error and 95% confidence interval.

Estimates

Measure MEASURE_1

status	Mean	Std. Error	95% Confidence Interval	
			Lower Bound	Upper Bound
1	7.034	.415	6.109	7.960
2	15.193	1.081	12.783	17.602
3	3.498	.701	1.936	5.059
4	3.415	.520	2.255	4.574

Figure 6-31 The estimated marginal means

(2) Comparison of effect size between groups (Figure 6-32): There was no significant difference in the effect of fixation of both instruments on spinal flexion ($F=0.179, P=0.681$).

Tests of Between-Subjects Effects

Measure: MEASURE_1

Transformed Variable: Average

Source	Type III Sum of Squares	df	Mean Square	F	Sig.
Intercept	2476.609	1	2476.609	251.283	.000
group	1.767	1	1.767	.179	.681
Error	98.558	10	9.856		

Figure 6-32 Comparison of effects between groups

(3) Mauchly's Test of Sphericity: Also known as the ball symmetry test (Figure 6-33).

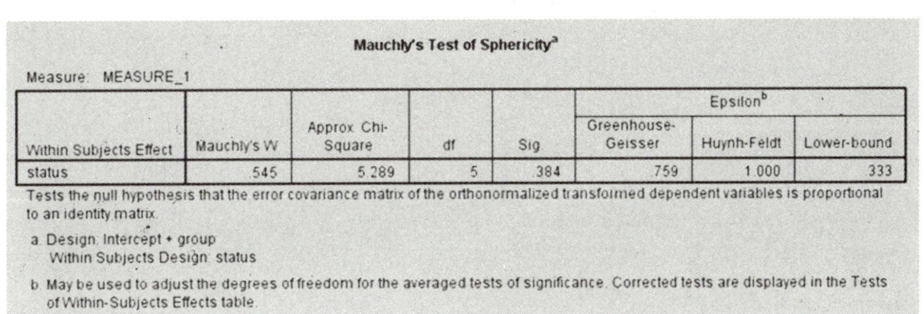

Mauchly's Test of Sphericity[a]

Measure: MEASURE_1

Within Subjects Effect	Mauchly's W	Approx. Chi-Square	df	Sig.	Epsilon[b]		
					Greenhouse-Geisser	Huynh-Feldt	Lower-bound
status	.545	5.289	5	.384	.759	1.000	.333

Tests the null hypothesis that the error covariance matrix of the orthonormalized transformed dependent variables is proportional to an identity matrix.

a. Design: Intercept + group
Within Subjects Design: status

b. May be used to adjust the degrees of freedom for the averaged tests of significance. Corrected tests are displayed in the Tests of Within-Subjects Effects table.

Figure 6-33 The Spherical Test

1) Mauchly's Spherical Test statistic: $W=0.545$, $P=0.384$, without rejecting spherical assumptions, apply Univariate test Law without (epsilon) correction.

2) ε (Epsilon) correction factor: The table lists the three kinds of epsilon correction factor, namely Greenhouse-Geisser, Huynh-Feldt and Lower-bound ε correction factor. When the data do not satisfy the spherical assumption (e.g. $P<0.05$ or $P<0.10$), it is required to use the ε correction factor to correct the degree of freedom.

(4) Comparison of intra-group (repeated) effects and interaction effects (Univariate test): The explanation is listed (Figure 6-34).

1) The information satisfies the spherical assumptions, so the result of "Sphericity Assumed" shall prevail.

2) There are significant differences among the four different levels of repetitive factors (4 states) ($P<0.001$).

3) There is no interaction between status and instrument ($P=0.282$).

4) There are four methods listed in Figure 6-34, which are the same as one column of mean squares. The remaining degrees of freedom, mean square, F values and P values are all different, and are derived from the corrected degrees of freedom. For example, the degree of freedom within the Greenhouse-Geisser method is $2.278 = 3 \times 0.75945$ (0.759 45 is the Greenhouse-Geisser correction factor) and the corresponding mean square, F and P values change (Figure 6-34).

(5) Multiple comparisons (Figure 6-35): There is no statistical difference in flexion between "fixed" and "fatigue" among the four states of "normal" "injured" "fixed" and "fatigue" ($P=0.934$), the rest of the statuses are statistically different ($P \leqslant 0.001$).

Tests of Within-Subjects Effects

Measure: MEASURE_1

Source		Type III Sum of Squares	df	Mean Square	F	Sig.
status	Sphericity Assumed	1072.395	3	357.465	73.009	.000
	Greenhouse-Geisser	1072.395	2.278	470.689	73.009	.000
	Huynh-Feldt	1072.395	3.000	357.465	73.009	.000
	Lower-bound	1072.395	1.000	1072.395	73.009	.000
status * group	Sphericity Assumed	19.583	3	6.528	1.333	.282
	Greenhouse-Geisser	19.583	2.278	8.595	1.333	.286
	Huynh-Feldt	19.583	3.000	6.528	1.333	.282
	Lower-bound	19.583	1.000	19.583	1.333	.275
Error(status)	Sphericity Assumed	146.885	30	4.896		
	Greenhouse-Geisser	146.885	22.784	6.447		
	Huynh-Feldt	146.885	30.000	4.896		
	Lower-bound	146.885	10.000	14.688		

Figure 6-34 Comparison of repetitive and interactive effects

Pairwise Comparisons

Measure: MEASURE_1

(I) status	(J) status	Mean Difference (I-J)	Std. Error	Sig.[b]	95% Confidence Interval for Difference[b] Lower Bound	Upper Bound
1	2	-8.158*	.913	.000	-10.193	-6.124
	3	3.537*	.721	.001	1.929	5.144
	4	3.620*	.645	.000	2.181	5.058
2	1	8.158*	.913	.000	6.124	10.193
	3	11.695*	.971	.000	9.532	13.859
	4	11.778*	1.173	.000	9.165	14.391
3	1	-3.537*	.721	.001	-5.144	-1.929
	2	-11.695*	.971	.000	-13.859	-9.532
	4	.083	.974	.934	-2.087	2.252
4	1	-3.620*	.645	.000	-5.058	-2.181
	2	-11.778*	1.173	.000	-14.391	-9.165
	3	-.083	.974	.934	-2.252	2.087

Based on estimated marginal means

*. The mean difference is significant at the .05 level.

b. Adjustment for multiple comparisons: Least Significant Difference (equivalent to no adjustments).

Figure 6-35 Multiple comparison results under different conditions

6.5.3 ANOVA of two repeated measures

6.5.3.1 SPSS data format

The data file "repeated_2. sav" is used in this analysis procedure. Except for the column labeled "cats" with 6 rows and 14 columns, i. e. the complete combination of two repeated variables: the variable name "time1A" represents the ALP of the ischemic pre-ischemic center; "time4B" represents the Asp in the contralateral mirror phase 6 h after ischemia, and so on. This example has 2 repeated measurement factors, one is the time factor, with 7 levels of namely time1-time7, respectively representing before and 1 h, 3 h, 6 h, 12 h, 18 h, 24 h after ischemia; the other is the brain region, with two levels of namely A and B, respectively referring to the ischemic center and the opposite side mirror phase area.

6.5.3.2 Example

Example 6-6 The data file "repeated_2. sav" is used as the Example 6-6. Six cats were used for cerebral ischemic experiments. Before and 1 h, 3 h, 6 h, 12 h, 18 h and 24 h after ischemia, measure the excitatory amino acid (Asp) changes were measured respectively in the ischemic center and in the opposite side of the mirror district. The results are displayed in Table 6-3, try to analyze the data.

Table 6-3 Asp (IU/g) in different brain regions before and after cat cerebral ischemia

Brain region	Cat number	Before ischemia	1 h after ischemia	3 h after ischemia	6 h after ischemia	12 h after ischemia	18 h after ischemia	24 h after ischemia
Ischemic center area	1	9.64	146.25	187.31	208.05	294.32	314.57	263.85
	2	10.08	144.05	185.64	213.25	298.09	315.46	264.38
	3	9.87	145.32	186.35	213.02	298.66	314.54	261.03
	4	9.96	145.05	185.64	213.55	296.04	314.07	266.09
	5	9.76	140.31	186.37	211.66	293.45	314.04	265.53
	6	9.64	140.58	186.09	210.11	298.61	314.33	262.84
The opposite side of the mirror area	1	9.72	20.46	33.37	39.83	15.37	11.59	8.45
	2	9.99	22.54	34.05	38.45	16.87	11.55	9.04
	3	9.98	22.05	33.14	38.56	17.81	11.04	9.11
	4	9.99	22.43	33.41	39.18	15.97	10.99	9.05
	5	9.89	22.58	34.61	38.45	17.01	11.42	9.23
	6	9.87	20.65	33.04	36.66	18.07	11.21	9.03

6.5.3.3 Running the command

To analyze the data, we perform an ANOVA of two repeated measures.

Procedure:

Analyze

General Linear Model

Repeated Measures

▸**Within-Subject Factor Name: time**

▸**Number of Levels**: 7

▸**Within-Subject Factor Name: spot**

▸**Number of Levels**: 2

Define

▸**Within-Subjects Variables (time, spot): time1A / time1B / time2A / time2B / time3A / time3B / time4A / time4B / time5A / time5B /time6A / time6B / time7A / time7B**

Model

⊙**Full Factorial**

Sum of squares: Type Ⅲ

Plot

▶**Horizontal Axis: time**

▶**Separate Lines: spot**

Options

▶**Display Means for: time/spot**

☑**Compare main effects**

Confidence interval adjustment: LSD(none)

Display

☑**Descriptive statistics**

Significance level: 0.05

6.5.3.4 Reading the output and drawing the conclusions

(1) Estimated marginal means (Figure 6-35): The output includes descriptive statistics. The output given by compare main effects (including the standard errors and confidence intervals) is not shown here.

(2) Analysis of variance (Univariate test) for repeated effects and interaction effects: when there are more than one repeated measures. The statistics and P values for the SPSS spherical test are no longer given, but the correction factor ε is given (Figure 6-37). The main and interaction effects of the two repeated measures as shown in Figure 6-38, so there is statistically significant difference between time and spot ($P<0.001$), and interaction between time and spot ($P<0.001$). Interaction-effects plot in Figure 6-39 can directly reflect such conclusions.

Descriptive Statistics

	Mean	Std. Deviation	N
Pre-operation-A	9.8250	.17774	6
Pre-operation-B	9.9067	.10558	6
Post-operation1h-A	143.5933	2.53890	6
Post-operation 1h-B	21.7850	.97285	6
Post-operation 3h-A	186.2333	.61905	6
Post-operation 3h-B	33.6033	.60609	6
Post-operation 6h-A	211.6067	2.16182	6
Post-operation 6h-B	38.5217	1.06044	6
Post-operation 12h-A	296.5283	2.27629	6
Post-operation 12h-B	16.8500	1.03931	6
Post-operation 18h-A	314.5017	.52029	6
Post-operation 18h-B	11.3000	.25799	6
Post-operation 24h-A	263.9533	1.84550	6
Post-operation 24h-B	8.9850	.27245	6

Figure 6-36 The mean estimates

Mauchly's Test of Sphericity[a]

Measure: MEASURE_1

Within Subjects Effect	Mauchly's W	Approx. Chi-Square	df	Sig.	Epsilon[b]		
					Greenhouse-Geisser	Huynh-Feldt	Lower-bound
time	.000	.	20	.	.431	.935	.167
spot	1.000	.000	0	.	1.000	1.000	1.000
time * spot	.000	.	20	.	.380	.717	.167

Tests the null hypothesis that the error covariance matrix of the orthonormalized transformed dependent variables is proportional to an identity matrix.

a. Design: Intercept
Within Subjects Design: time + spot + time * spot

b. May be used to adjust the degrees of freedom for the averaged tests of significance. Corrected tests are displayed in the Tests of Within-Subjects Effects table.

Figure 6-37 The correction factor ε

Tests of Within-Subjects Effects

Measure: MEASURE_1

Source		Type III Sum of Squares	df	Mean Square	F	Sig.
time	Sphericity Assumed	199827.025	6	33304.504	17551.721	.000
	Greenhouse-Geisser	199827.025	2.588	77203.749	17551.721	.000
	Huynh-Feldt	199827.025	5.610	35619.139	17551.721	.000
	Lower-bound	199827.025	1.000	199827.025	17551.721	.000
Error(time)	Sphericity Assumed	56.925	30	1.898		
	Greenhouse-Geisser	56.925	12.942	4.399		
	Huynh-Feldt	56.925	28.051	2.029		
	Lower-bound	56.925	5.000	11.385		
spot	Sphericity Assumed	707987.307	1	707987.307	570594.639	.000
	Greenhouse-Geisser	707987.307	1.000	707987.307	570594.639	.000
	Huynh-Feldt	707987.307	1.000	707987.307	570594.639	.000
	Lower-bound	707987.307	1.000	707987.307	570594.639	.000
Error(spot)	Sphericity Assumed	6.204	5	1.241		
	Greenhouse-Geisser	6.204	5.000	1.241		
	Huynh-Feldt	6.204	5.000	1.241		
	Lower-bound	6.204	5.000	1.241		
time * spot	Sphericity Assumed	201767.741	6	33627.957	21292.078	.000
	Greenhouse-Geisser	201767.741	2.282	88401.496	21292.078	.000
	Huynh-Feldt	201767.741	4.303	46887.665	21292.078	.000
	Lower-bound	201767.741	1.000	201767.741	21292.078	.000
Error(time*spot)	Sphericity Assumed	47.381	30	1.579		
	Greenhouse-Geisser	47.381	11.412	4.152		
	Huynh-Feldt	47.381	21.516	2.202		
	Lower-bound	47.381	5.000	9.476		

Figure 6-38 Analysis of variance for repeated effect and interaction effects

(3) Multiple comparisons of time level (Figure 6-38): There are statistical differences across all levels ($P<0.001$).

Pairwise Comparisons

Measure MEASURE_1

(I) time	(J) time	Mean Difference (I-J)	Std. Error	Sig.[b]	95% Confidence Interval for Difference[b]	
					Lower Bound	Upper Bound
1	2	-72.823	.516	.000	-74.149	-71.497
	3	-100.052	.197	.000	-100.560	-99.545
	4	-115.198	.432	.000	-116.308	-114.089
	5	-146.823	.608	.000	-148.386	-145.260
	6	-153.035	.141	.000	-153.398	-152.672
	7	-126.603	.375	.000	-127.567	-125.639
2	3	-27.229	.584	.000	-28.730	-25.728
	4	-42.375	.410	.000	-43.430	-41.320
	5	-74.000	.886	.000	-76.278	-71.722
	6	-80.212	.530	.000	-81.573	-78.851
	7	-53.780	.680	.000	-55.527	-52.033
3	4	-15.146	.545	.000	-16.546	-13.746
	5	-46.771	.754	.000	-48.709	-44.832
	6	-52.982	.193	.000	-53.480	-52.485
	7	-26.551	.389	.000	-27.550	-25.552
4	5	-31.625	.782	.000	-33.634	-29.616
	6	-37.837	.505	.000	-39.135	-36.539
	7	-11.405	.505	.000	-12.704	-10.106
5	6	-6.212	.627	.000	-7.824	-4.599
	7	20.220	.911	.000	17.879	22.561
6	7	26.432	.430	.000	25.327	27.536

Based on estimated marginal means

b. Adjustment for multiple comparisons: Least Significant Difference (equivalent to no adjustments).

Figure 6-39 Multiple comparison (LSD) results at different times

(4) Interaction–effect plot (Figure 6–40): The explanation is listed as below.

1) There are statistical differences at different time levels, mainly in the role of ischemic center. Asp in the central ischemic area has been increasing since the onset of ischemia, reaching its peak at 6th time point (18 h after ischemia) and then decreasing. The changes in the contralateral mirror phase region are relatively flat, rising from ischemia to peak at the 4th time point (6 h after ischemia), and then gradually decreased. It should be noted that the horizontal axis of the contour plot is a categorical variable, so the 7th time point in the figure is equidistant, although the actual time is not at intervals.

2) There are statistical differences between different sites ($P<0.001$), and the ischemic center is higher than the opposite side of the mirror area.

3) There is interaction effect between time and location ($P<0.001$), and the change trend of the two is significantly different.

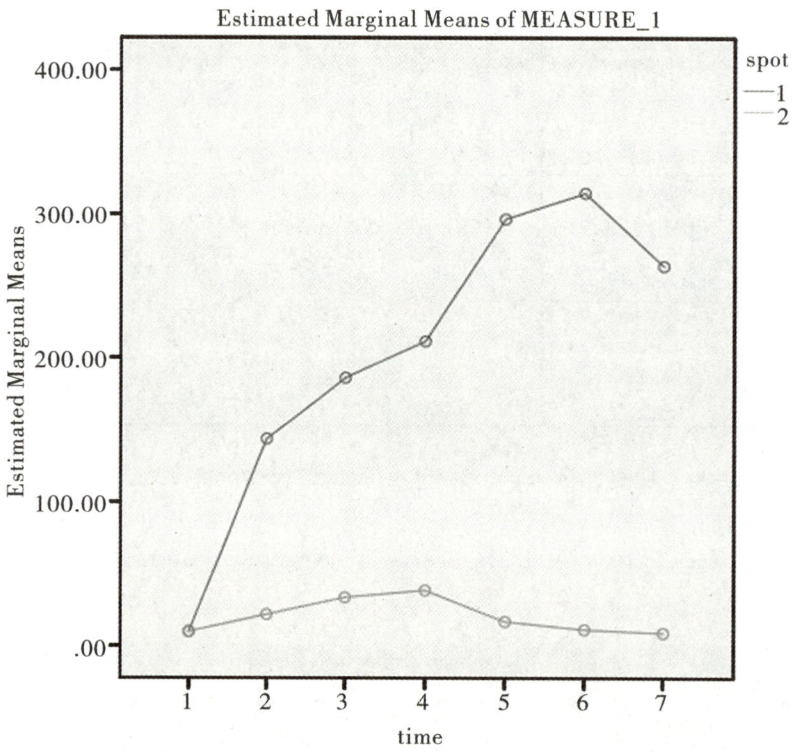

Figure 6–40 Interaction–effect plot output

Yan Fangrong, Wang Mengqiao

Chapter 7

Correlation & Regression

7.1 Bivariate correlation analysis

7.1.1 Description

When both Y and X are random variables, a correlation model can be used. When checking an association between pairs of variables, bivariate correlation analysis can be used. In the procedure, values of X are not pre-selected but occur at random, depending on the unit of association selected in the sample. Pearson correlation coefficient can be used when two variables follow a normal distribution; otherwise, Spearman/Kendall correlation coefficient can be used, for example, non-normal distribution or ordinal variables. Correlation coefficients range in value from −1 (a perfect negative relationship) and +1 (a perfect positive relationship). A value of 0 indicates no linear correlation relationship. When interpreting the results, we should be careful not to draw any cause-and-effect conclusions due to a significant correlation.

7.1.2 SPSS data format

The SPSS data file for the bivariate correlation analysis requires two, numerically measured, continuous variables (e. g., between an independent and a dependent variable or between two independent variables).

7.1.3 Example

Example 7-1 The data file "correlate_1. sav" is used as the Example 7-1, which has 2 columns and 123 rows. Randomly selected 123 people in different age groups to detect telomere restricted fragment (trf), please explore whether "trf" is related by "age". The data describe 2 numeric variables and 123 units, and these two variables named as "age" and "trf".

The requirements for using bivariate correlation analysis is listed.

(1) Linearity and normality are the most important requirements. If the relationship between two variables is not linear, then the model is not valid. In that case, you may need to do data transformation in order to meet the linearity and normality requirements.

(2) With regard to normality, we concern about this only if we want confidence interval or significance tests and if the sample size is small. If the assumptions are met (linear and normality), Pearson correlation coefficient can be used. While, if assumptions are not met or data are ordinal, you may choose Kendall's tau-b (τ_b) or Spearman correlation coefficient, which measure the association between rank-order data. A

bootstrap method can be used to compute the confidence interval without worrying about data distribution.

7.1.3.1 Running the commands

To analyze the data, we preform a bivariate cowelation analysis:

Analyze

Correlate

Bivariate

The dialog box of Bivariate Correlations pops up (Figure 7-1). The dialog box of the Bivariate Correlation requires that we transfer independent variable ("age") and outcome ("trf") to the "Variables" section. Pearson or Kendall's tau-b or Spearman is used to calculate correlation coefficients which mainly selected by the distribution of variables. In the Example 7-1, the sample size is 123 which can be seen as a big sample, so we firstly select Pearson correlation coefficient.

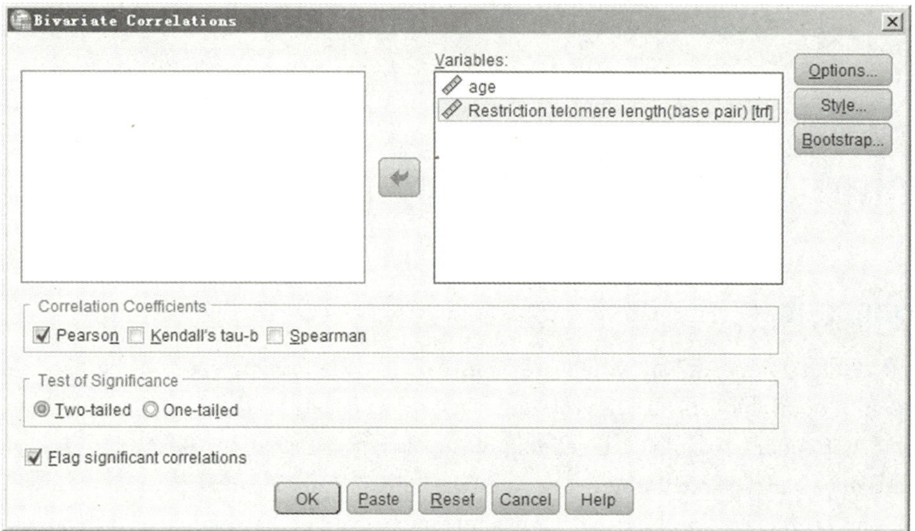

Figure 7-1 The Bivariate Correlation dialog box

◇Variables: Choose the variables "age" and "bp[trf]".

◇Correlation Coefficients: Calculate correlation coefficients.

☑Pearson (system default): Pearson product-moment correlation coefficient, parameter method.

□Kendall's tau-b: Kendall rank correlation coefficient, non-parameter method.

□Spearman: Spearman rank correlation coefficient, non-parameter method.

◇Test of Significance: Select one or two-tailed test.

⊙Two-tailed (system default): Two-tailed test.

◎One-tailed: One-tailed test.

If the direction of association is known in advance, select One-tailed test. Otherwise, select Two-tailed test.

☑Flag significant correlations: Significant mark. Correlation coefficients significant at the 0.05 level are identified with a single asterisk, and those significant at the 0.01 level are identified with two asterisks.

★Options: Click "Options" button, and the dialog box of Bivariate correlations: Options pops out (Figure 7-2).

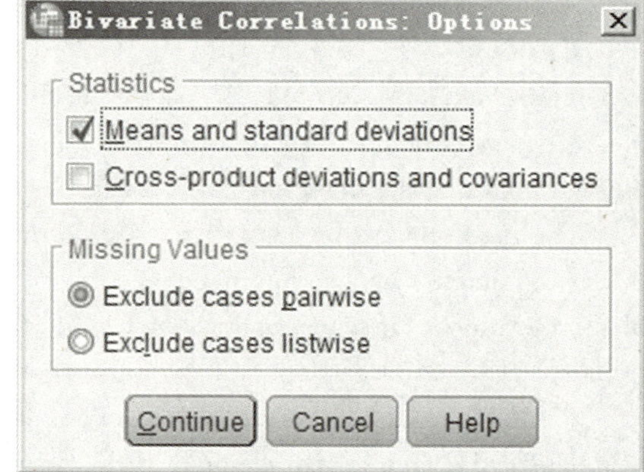

Figure 7-2 The Bivariate Correlations: Options dialog box

◇Statistics.

☑Means and standard deviations: Output mean and standard deviation of each variable.

□Cross-product deviations and covariances: Output Cross-product deviations and covariances of each variable.

◇Missing Values.

⊙Exclude cases pairwise(system default): Remove missing values from pair variables.

◎Exclude case listwise: Remove all units, which includes missing values.

★Bootstrap(Figure 7-1): Perform bootstrapping to estimate standard error and 95% confidence interval of correlation coefficient.

7.1.3.2 Reading the output

(1) The output for the bivariate correlation consists of two sections. The first section lists the sample variable and some basic descriptive statistics. The results show the mean, standard deviation and sample size of participants "age" and "trf" are 31.60, 20.968, 123, and 12.525 0, 1.345 52, 123, respectively (Figure 7-3).

Descriptive Statistics

	Mean	Std. Deviation	N
age	31.60	20.968	123
telomere restriction fragment length(bp)	12.5250	1.34552	123

Figure 7-3 Basic descriptive statistic of participants'age and trf

(2) The second section of output contains matrix results of the bivariate correlation test (Figure 7-4). The correlation coefficient of "age" with "trf" is -0.732 (P<0.001), which indicate a negative relationship between "age" and "trf" in the test population.

Correlations

		age	telomere restriction fragment length(bp)
age	Pearson Correlation	1	-.732**
	Sig. (2-tailed)		.000
	N	123	123
telomere restriction fragment length(bp)	Pearson Correlation	-.732**	1
	Sig. (2-tailed)	.000	
	N	123	123

**. Correlation is significant at the 0.01 level (2-tailed).

Figure 7-4 The result of Pearson correlation analysis

Theoretically speaking, the normality should be checked before computing correlation coefficient. For testing data distribution, the procedure is listed:

Analyze

Descriptive statistics

Explore

Plots (click Normality plots with tests)

The output shows "age" is not a normal distribution. So, Spearman correlation analysis is more suitable for the Example 7 - 1. To obtain Spearman correlation coefficient, simply select the appropriate box (Spearman). There is a minor difference between pearson correlation coefficient (r=-0.732, Figure 7-4) and spearman correlation coefficient (r_s = −0. 748 , Figure 7−5) , which indicate that normality or not will not affect final results in big sample size data. However, for small sample size dataset, pearson and spearman correlation coefficients may have a big difference.

Correlations

			age	telomere restriction fragment length(bp)
Spearman's rho	age	Correlation Coefficient	1.000	-.748**
		Sig. (2-tailed)	.	.000
		N	123	123
	telomere restriction fragment length(bp)	Correlation Coefficient	-.748**	1.000
		Sig. (2-tailed)	.000	.
		N	123	123

**. Correlation is significant at the 0.01 level (2-tailed).

Figure 7−5 The output of Spearman correlation results

7.1.3.3 Drawing conclusions

(1) A significant difference is found [r_s = −0. 748 , n = 123 , P<0. 001 (2−tailed test)].

(2) Significant value is below the significant level (0. 05) , indicating a statistically significant relationship between "age" and "trf". The null hypothesis is rejected and there is a negative correlation relationship between "age" and "trf".

7.1.4 Example

Example 7−2 The data file "correlate _2. sav" is used as the Example 7−2. A data of 278 corpse anatomy information as shown in Table 7−1. Please explore whether age and Coronary arteriosclerosis grade are related to each other.

Table 7−1 Age and Coronary arteriosclerosis

Age	Coronary atherosclerosis grade				Total
	−	+	++	+++	
20−	70	22	4	2	98
30−	27	24	9	3	63
40−	16	23	13	7	59
≥50	9	20	15	14	58
Total	122	89	41	26	278

Here, "Age" and "Coronary arteriosclerosis grade" are ordinal categorical variable, so we select non-parameter analysis to explore the relationship between these two variables. For variable "age_g" (age group), 4 dummy variables are created: 1 = "20−", 2 = "30−", 3 = "40−", 4 = "50−"). For variable "AA" (Coronary arteriosclerosis grade), 4 dummy variables are created: 1 = "−", 2 = "+", 3 = "++" 4 = "+++"). There is one frequency variable "freq" (16 frequency data).

7.1.4.1 Running the commands

As this data frame is a frequency table data, defining the frequency variable should come first, then do the correlation analysis.

Data

Weight Cases

Weight Cases by

▶Frequency Variable: freq Analyze

Correlate

Bivariate

▶Variables: AA/age_g

☑Kendall's tau-b

☑Spearman

7.1.4.2 Reading the output

The results show two non-parameter methods. Kendall correlation coefficient is 0.425 ($P<0.001$), and spearman correlation coefficient is 0.488 ($P<0.001$) (Figure 7-6).

Correlations

			Age group	Coronary arteriosclerosis
Kendall's tau_b	Age group	Correlation Coefficient	1.000	.425**
		Sig. (2-tailed)	.	.000
		N	278	278
	Coronary arteriosclerosis grade	Correlation Coefficient	.425**	1.000
		Sig. (2-tailed)	.000	.
		N	278	278
Spearman's rho	Age group	Correlation Coefficient	1.000	.488**
		Sig. (2-tailed)	.	.000
		N	278	278
	Coronary arteriosclerosis grade	Correlation Coefficient	.488**	1.000
		Sig. (2-tailed)	.000	.
		N	278	278

**. Correlation is significant at the 0.01 level (2-tailed).

Figure 7-6 The output of rank correlation results

7.1.4.3 Drawing conclusions

There is a significant positive relationship between "Age" and "Coronary Arteriosclerosis grade", but the relationship is not so strong which r is above zero but smaller than 0.5.

7.2 Linear regression

7.2.1 Description

The regression analysis aims to determine how, and to what extent, the criterion variables vary as a function of changes in the predictor variables. Linear regression analysis which always used for exploring a linear relationship between one or more independent variable(s) x and a dependent variable y, and also used for regression diagnostic analysis.

7.2.2 SPSS data format

The SPSS data file for linear regression requires only one dependent variable and multiple independent variables. Dependent variable can be measured on a continuous scale. Independent variables an be either continuous or categorical.

7.2.3 Example

Example 7-3 The data file"regression. sav" is used as the Example 7-3, which has 97 cases. The file has 12 columns, which has 11 different explanatory variables and 1 identification variable ("no"). The 11 biochemical blood indicators which are "rbc" (red blood cells), "hb" (hemoglobin), "wbc" (white blood cells), "plt" (platelets), "tbil" (total bilirubin), "dbil" (direct bilirubin), "alt" (alanine aminotransferase), "ast" (aspartate transaminase), "alp" (alkaline phosphatase), "bun" (Urea nitrogen) and "cr" (Creatinine). In order to test the relationship between "hb" and other variables, "hb" is set as dependent variable and others as explanatory variables.

7.2.3.1 Running the commands

Analyze

Regression

Linear

The dialog box of Linear Regression pops out (Figure 7-7).

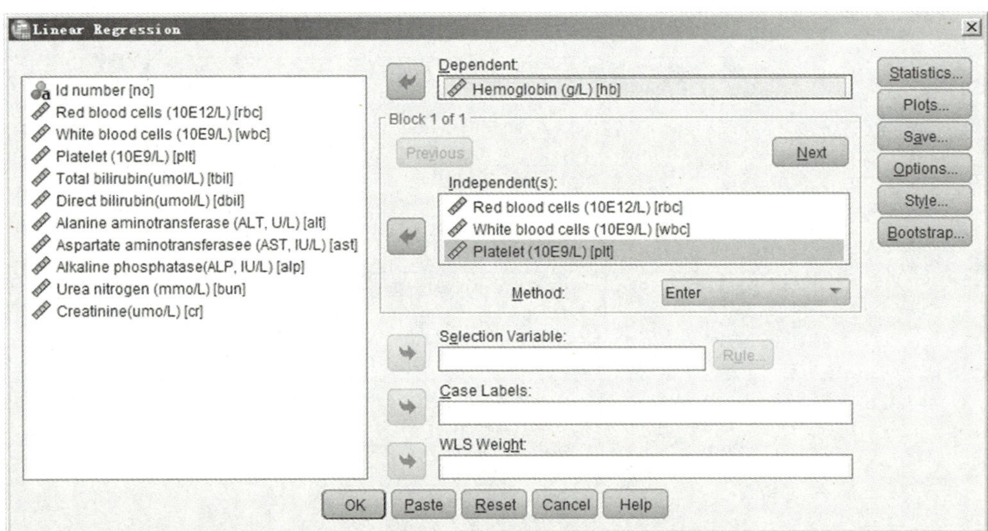

Figure 7-7 The Linear Regression dialog box

◇Dependent: Place dependent variable or outcome variable. "hb" is chosen as the dependent variable in the Example 7-3.

◇Block 1 of 1: Blocks are used to enter specific variables which are predictors or covariates into the model in chunks. The use of blocks allows us to separate the influence of these specific variables based on the predictive model and the relative contribution of variables in each block. If you do not block your independent variables or use stepwise regression, this column should list all of the independent variables that you specified. In the Example 7-3, we firstly highlight 3 blood routine variables "rbc" "wbc" "plt" and use the second arrow button to move them to the "Independent(s)" box. Then, click "Next" button. That is the first block. Then place 5 liver function variables "tbil" "dbil" "alt" "ast" "alp" to the "Independent(s)" box and click "Next" button. That is the second block. Finally, select last two renal function variables as the third block. Then, we have three blocks now. If we choose analysis method of "Enter", the output will show 3 different regression equations (3 predictors, 8 predictors, and 10 predictors regression models) and their analysis results. The "Previous" button is used to check or modify previous block content.

◇Independent(s): Place independent variable(s) or predictor(s). All variables except "no" is chosen as the independent variables in the Example 7-3 (Figure 7-7).

◇Method: Methods of regression. Method selection allows you to specify how independent variables are entered into the analysis. Using different methods, you can construct a variety of regression models from the same set of variables. There are 5 different ways could be chosen.

1) Enter: Forced entry (system default). All selected variables are forced into the model simultaneously. Some researchers maintain that "enter" method is the only appropriate method for theory testing.

2) Stepwise: Stepwise regressions. Each time a predictor is added to the equation, and the predictor is being reassessed constantly to see whether any redundant predictor can be removed.

3) Remove: Forced remove. Remove predictor according to set conditions.

4) Backward: The opposite of the forward method. Placing all predictors in the model and then calculating the contribution of each one by looking at the significance value of the t test for each predictor. The significance value is compared against a removal criterion. If a predictor meets the removal criterion, it is removed from the model, and the model is reestimated for the remaining predictors till no more predictor are removed from the equation.

5) Forward: An initial model is defined that contains only the constant. Each time a variable is added to the equation according to set criterion in Options dialog box, until no other variables are added into the regression equation.

◇Selection Variable: Cases defined by specifying a selection rule are included in the analysis. Choose a selection variable (select only one variable each time), then active "Rule" button to set rule in Linear Regression: set Rule dialog box (Figure 7-8) and specify the condition. For a numerical variable, there are 6 ways could to be select.

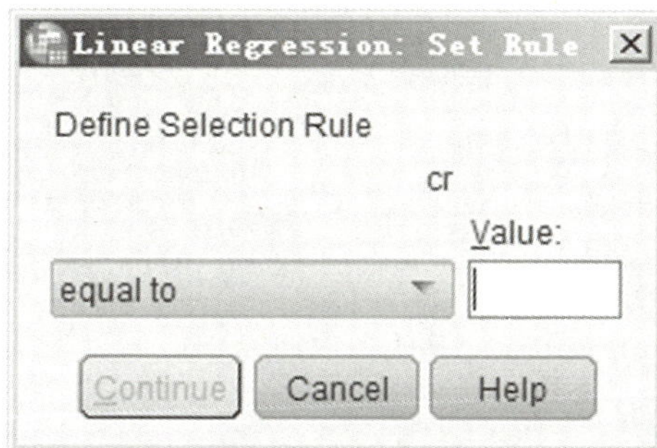

Figure 7-8 The Linear Regression: Set Rule dialog box

◇Define Selection Rule: Define a selection rule for selecting a subset of cases for analysis (Figure 7-8). The name of the selected variable appears on the left. Only met criterion predictor can be analyzed. Put value in "Value" box.

1) equal to: Equal to setting value.

2) not equal to: Not equal to setting value.

3) less than: Less than setting value.

4) less than or equal to: Less than or equal to setting value.

5) greater than: Greater than setting value.

6) greater than or equal to: Greater than or equal to setting value.

String variable choose first two options, "equal to" or "not equal to".

★Statistics: Click "Statistics" button (Figure 7-7) to activate the dialog box of Linear Regression: Statistics (Figure 7-9).

◇Regression Coefficients: The slope of the line and the intercept of the line.

☑Estimates: Display Regression Coefficient B, standard error of B, standardized coefficient beta, t

value for B, and a two-tailed significance level of t.

☑Confidence intervals: 95% confidence interval of regression coefficients with confidence for each regression coefficient or a covariance matrix.

☐Covariance matrix: Displays a variance-covariance matrix of regression coefficients with covariances of variances on the diagonal. A correlation matrix is also displayed.

☑Model fit: The variables entered and removed from the model are listed, and the following goodness-of-fit statistics are displayed: multiple R, R^2 and adjusted R^2, standard error of the estimate, and an analysis of variance table.

☐R squared change: The change in the R^2 statistic that is produced by adding or deleting an independent variable. If the R^2 change associated with a variable is large, the variable is a good predictor of the dependent variable.

☑Descriptives: Provides the number of valid cases, the mean, and the standard deviation for each variable in the analysis. A correlation matrix with a one-tailed significance level and the number of cases for each correlation are also displayed.

☐Part and partial correlations: Part correlation also be called as semi-partial correlation.

☐Collinearity diagnostics: Multicollinear diagnose shows eigenvalues of the scaled and uncentered cross-products matrix, condition indices, and variance-decomposition proportions, along with variance inflation factors (VIF) and tolerances for individual variables.

◇Residuals: The differences between the predicted value and the observed data.

☐Durbin-Watson: Durbin-Watson test for serial correlation of the residuals.

☐Casewise diagnostics: Information for the cases meeting the selection criterion shows residual, predicted value, standardized residual and standard error of predicted value. After a click, it will activate these options.

⊙Outliers outside: 3 standard deviations. A outlier has a large residual. All casewise residual above $\bar{x} \pm ns$ for individual variables will be seen as outliers. System default n as 3. The output will show outlier residual, standardized residual and standard error of predicted value.

◎All cases: Show all residual, standard error of predicted value and predicted values of all observed data.

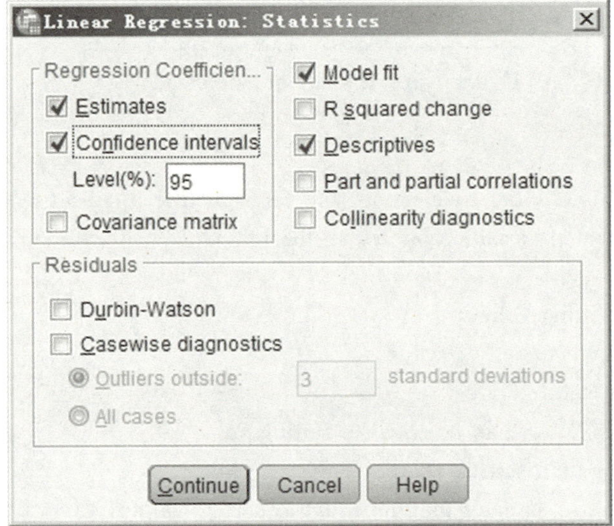

Figure 7-9 The Linear regression: Statistics dialog box

★Plots (Figure 7-7): Give residual scatter plot, normal probability plot, outlier plot and histogram.

★Options: Click "Options" button (Figure 7-7) to activate the dialog box of Linear Regression:

Options (Figure 7-10).

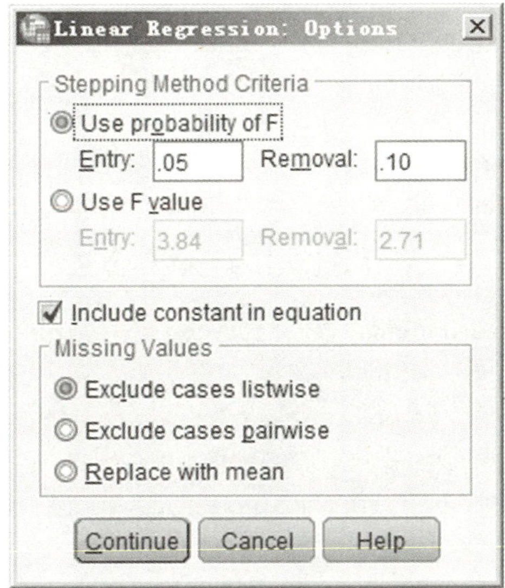

Figure 7-10 The Linear Regression: Options dialog box

◇Stepping Method Criteria.

⊙Use probability of F: The significance level of its F value is variable's entered or removed criterion (System default method).

Entry: 0.05 : Significance level of entry. System default as 0.05. A variable is entered into the model if its $P \leqslant 0.05$.

Removal: 0.10 : Significance level of removal. System default as 0.10. A variable is removed from the model if its $P \geqslant 0.10$. Note: Significance level of removal should bigger than significance level of entry.

◎Use F value: F value of sum of square due to regression test is variable's entered or removed criterion.

Entry: 3.84 . The F boundary value of entered variable, system default as 3.84. A variable is entered into the model if its $F \geqslant 3.84$.

Removal: 2.71 . The F boundary value of removal variable, system default as 2.71. A variable is removed from the model if its $F \leqslant 2.71$.

☑Include constant in equation.

◇Missing values: Dealing with missing values, 3 different ways are following.

⊙Exclude cases listwise: Only cases with valid values for all variables are included in the analyses.

◎Exclude cases pairwise: Cases with complete data for the pair of variables being correlated are used to compute the correlation coefficient on which the regression analysis is based. Degrees of freedom are based on the minimum pairwise N.

◎Replace with mean: All cases are used for computations, with the mean of the variable substituted for missing observations.

★Save: In linear Regression dialog box, click "Save" (Figure 7-7) to add selected options to new variables or new files, each selection adds one or more new variables to active data file (Figure 7-11).

◇Predicted Values: Values that the regression model predict for each case.

☑ Unstandardized: The value the model predicts for the dependent variable.

□Standardized: A transformation of each predicted value into its standardized form.

□Adjusted: The predicted value for a case when that case is excluded from the calculation of the regression coefficients.

□S. E. of mean predictions: Standard errors of the predicted values.

◇Residuals: The actual value of the dependent variable minus the value predicted by the regression equation.

□Unstandardized: The difference between an observed value and the value predicted by the model.

□Standardized: The residual divided by an estimate of its standard deviation. Standardized residuals, which are also known as Pearson residuals, have a mean of 0 and a standard deviation of 1.

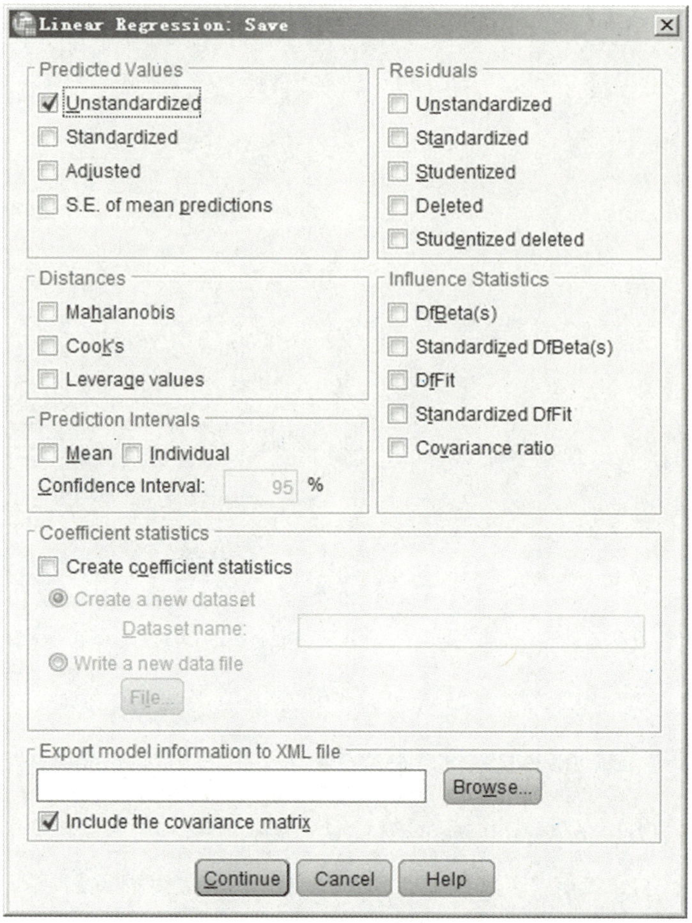

Figure 7-11 The Linear Regression: Save dialog box

□Studentized: The residual divided by an estimate of its standard deviation that varies from case to case, depending on the distance of each case's values on the independent variables from the means of the independent variables.

□Deleted: The residual for a case when that case is excluded from the calculation of the regression coefficients.

□Studentized deleted: The deleted residual for a case divided by its standard error.

◇Distances: Measures to identify cases with unusual combinations of values for the independent variables and cases that may have a large impact on the regression model.

□Mahalanobis: A measure of how much a case's values on the independent variables differ from the average of all cases.

□Cook's: A measure of how much the residuals of all cases can change if a particular case is excluded from the calculation of the regression coefficients.

□Leverage values: Measures the influence of a point on the fit of the regression.

◇Influence Statistics: New variables/ file linear regression saving dialog box "Influence statistics". The change in the regression coefficients (DfBeta[s]) and predicted values (DfFit) that results from the exclusion of a particular case. Standardized DfBetas and DfFit values are also available along with the covariance ratio.

□DfBeta(s): The difference in beta value is the change in the regression coefficient that results from the exclusion of a particular case.

□Standardized DfBeta(s): Standardized difference in beta value.

□DfFit: The difference in fit value is the change in the predicted value that results from the exclusion of a particular case.

□Standardized DfFit: Standardized difference in fit value.

□Covariance ratio: The ratio of the determinant of the covariance matrix with a particular case excluded from the calculation of the regression coefficients to the determinant of the covariance matrix with all cases included.

◇Prediction intervals: The range (from lower to higher) for both mean and individual interval.

□Mean: The confidence interval of a mean of the predicted value.

□Individual: The confidence interval of the dependent variable for an individual case.

Confidence interval: 95 % : Typical confidence interval is 90%, 95%, and 99%, but 95% is systematic default. Note: Mean or Individual must be selected before entering this value.

◇Coefficient statistics:

□Create coefficient statistics:

⊙Create a new dataset: Save correlation coefficient to a new dataset or a data frame. Operator can name for the new dataset.

◎Write a new data file.

◇Export model information to XML file: Parameter estimation and (optionally) their covariance are exported to the specified file in XML (PMML) format. You can use this model file to apply the model information to other data files for scoring purpose.

☑Include the covariance matrix. When options Covariance matrix (Figure 7-9) and include the Covariance matrix (Figure 7-9) was selected at the same time, the results will show covariance matrix after exporting information to XML file.

So mainly analysis processes are like below:

Analyze

Regression

Linear

▸Dependent: hb

▸Indepentent: rbc/wbc/plt/tbil/dbil/alt/ast/alp/bun/cr

Method: Enter/ Stepwise

Statistics

☑Estimates

☑Confidence interval

Level(%): 95

☑Mode fit

☑Descriptives

Options

Missing values

⊙Exclude cases pairwise

7.2.3.2 Reading the output

(1) Basic statistics (Figure 7-12): The variable "alp" has 1 outlier.

(2) Bivariate correlation coefficient matrix and testing results (from Figure 7-13 to Figure 7-15). In this figure, pearson product-moment correlation coefficient is on above, the P value of the correlation coefficient single-tailed test is in the middle, and the sample size is below.

Descriptive Statistics

	Mean	Std. Deviation	N
Hemoglobin (g/L)	131.78	24.735	97
Red blood cells (10e12/l)	4.4685	.85936	97
White blood cells (10e9/l)	9.6819	4.51952	97
Platelet (10e9/l)	253.06	129.903	97
Total bilirubin(umol/L)	11.616	6.3826	97
Direct bilirubin(umol/L)	3.322	2.7448	97
alt (u/l)	34.66	59.596	97
ast (u/l)	36.43	58.377	97
alp (iu/l)	80.327	62.7156	96
Urea nitrogen (mmo/L)	5.096	2.5189	97
Creatinine(umo/L)	82.06	22.407	97

Figure 7-12 Basic statistics

Correlations

		Hemoglobin (g/L)	rbc (10E12/L)	wbc (10E9/L)	plt (10E9/L)	tbil (umol/L)	dbil (umol/L)	alt (U/L)	ast (U/L)	alp (IU/L)	bun (mmo/L)	cr (umo/L)
Pearson Correlation	Hemoglobin (g/L)	1 000	810	-256	-256	217	143	062	096	-083	108	066
	rbc (10E12/L)	810	1 000	-139	-049	200	103	087	106	-036	128	007
	wbc (10E9/L)	-256	-139	1 000	574	-041	-165	-011	002	-018	150	-050
	plt (10E9/L)	-256	-049	574	1 000	-208	-315	-054	-076	-028	-095	-080
	tbil (umol/L)	217	200	-041	-208	1 000	709	016	005	-052	076	-126
	dbil (umol/L)	143	103	-165	-315	709	1 000	062	046	-006	002	014
	alt (U/L)	062	087	-011	-054	016	062	1 000	948	037	432	062
	ast (U/L)	096	106	002	-076	005	046	948	1 000	045	450	069
	alp (IU/L)	-083	-036	-018	-028	-052	-006	037	045	1 000	-072	-058
	bun (mmo/L)	108	128	150	-095	076	002	432	450	-072	1 000	360
	cr (umo/L)	066	007	-050	-080	-126	014	062	069	-058	360	1 000

Figure 7-13 Bivariate correlation coefficient matrix and testing results (Pearson product-moment correlation coefficient)

Correlations

		Hemoglobin (g/L)	rbc (10E12/L)	wbc (10E9/L)	plt (10E9/L)	tbil (umol/L)	dbil (umol/L)	alt (U/L)	ast (U/L)	alp (IU/L)	bun (mmo/L)	cr (umo/L)
Sig. (1-tailed)	Hemoglobin (g/L)		000	006	006	016	081	273	174	211	145	260
	rbc (10E12/L)	000		087	316	025	158	200	151	363	106	472
	wbc (10E9/L)	006	087		000	345	053	458	493	431	071	314
	plt (10E9/L)	006	316	000		020	001	301	230	394	177	217
	tbil (umol/L)	016	025	345	020		000	439	481	309	231	109
	dbil (umol/L)	081	158	053	001	000		274	328	476	490	447
	alt (U/L)	273	200	458	301	439	274		000	360	000	273
	ast (U/L)	174	151	493	230	481	328	000		332	000	252
	alp (IU/L)	211	363	431	394	309	476	360	332		244	287
	bun (mmo/L)	145	106	071	177	231	490	000	000	244		000
	cr (umo/L)	260	472	314	217	109	447	273	252	287	000	

Figure 7-14 Bivariate correlation coefficient matrix and testing results (one-tailed test)

Correlations

		Hemoglobin (g/L)	rbc (10E12/L)	wbc (10E9/L)	plt (10E9/L)	tbil (umol/L)	dbil (umol/L)	alt (U/L)	ast (U/L)	alp (IU/L)	bun (mmo/L)	cr (umo/L)
N	Hemoglobin (g/L)	97	97	97	97	97	97	97	97	96	97	97
	rbc (10E12/L)	97	97	97	97	97	97	97	97	96	97	97
	wbc (10E9/L)	97	97	97	97	97	97	97	97	96	97	97
	plt (10E9/L)	97	97	97	97	97	97	97	97	96	97	97
	tbil (umol/L)	97	97	97	97	97	97	97	97	96	97	97
	dbil (umol/L)	97	97	97	97	97	97	97	97	96	97	97
	alt (U/L)	97	97	97	97	97	97	97	97	96	97	97
	ast (U/L)	97	97	97	97	97	97	97	97	96	97	97
	alp (IU/L)	96	96	96	96	96	96	96	96	96	96	96
	bun (mmo/L)	97	97	97	97	97	97	97	97	96	97	97
	cr (umo/L)	97	97	97	97	97	97	97	97	96	97	97

Figure 7-15 Bivariate correlation coefficient matrix and testing results (sample size)

(3) Enter and removed variables in the regression equation: Use "Enter" option to do a full model test, and 5 variables are included in the equation (Figure 7-16). Using stepwise option, place "rbc" into an equation in the first step, then, place "plt" into that equation in the second step (Figure 7-17).

Variables Entered/Removed[a]

Model	Variables Entered	Variables Removed	Method
1	cr (umo/L), rbc (10E12/L), alp (IU/L), plt (10E9/L), alt (U/L), tbil (umol/L), bun (mmo/L), wbc (10E9/L), dbil (umol/L), ast (U/L)[b]	.	Enter

a. Dependent Variable: Hemoglobin (g/L)

b. All requested variables entered.

Figure 7-16 Full model regression independent variables entered

Variables Entered/Removed[a]

Model	Variables Entered	Variables Removed	Method
1	rbc (10E12/L)	.	Stepwise (Criteria: Probability-of-F-to-enter <= .050, Probability-of-F-to-remove >= .100).
2	plt (10E9/L)	.	Stepwise (Criteria: Probability-of-F-to-enter <= .050, Probability-of-F-to-remove >= .100).

a. Dependent Variable: Hemoglobin (g/L)

Figure 7-17 Stepwise regression independent variables entered

(4) Model testing.

1) Full model test (Enter option): (Figure 7-18, Figure 7-19). Interpretation of results.

①Predictors include constant and other 10 variables: rbc, wbc, plt, tbil, dbil, alt, ast, alp, bun, cr. ②Dependent variable: hb (Hemoglobin content). ③R square: $R^2 = 0.714$, which means that all predictors account for 71.4% of the variation in outcome ("hb" level). ④Adjusted R square: Adjusting R value according to the number of variables in order to avoid bias. It is used in comparing models with different number of independent variables (Formula 7-1). ⑤Equation testing: $F = 21.240$ ($P < 0.001$), which is significant with a probability of less than 0.001.

$$R^2_{adj} = R^2 - \frac{K \times (1 - R^2)}{N - K - 1} = 0.714 - \frac{10 \times (1 - 0.714)}{96 - 10 - 1} = 0.681. \tag{7-1}$$

Model Summary

Model	R	R Square	Adjusted R Square	Std. Error of the Estimate
1	.845[a]	.714	.681	13.980

a. Predictors: (Constant), creatinine(umo/l), red blood cells (10e12/l), alkaline phosphatase(iu/l), platelet (10e9/l), alanine aminotransferase (u/l), total bilirubin(umol/l), urea nitrogen (mmo/l), white blood cells (10e9/l), direct bilirubin(umol/l), aspartate aminotransferasee (u/l)

Figure 7-18 Coefficient of determination in regression equation

ANOVA[a]

Model		Sum of Squares	df	Mean Square	F	Sig.
1	Regression	41509.392	10	4150.939	21.240	.000[b]
	Residual	16611.265	85	195.427		
	Total	58120.657	95			

a. Dependent Variable: hemoglobin (g/l)

b. Predictors: (Constant), creatinine(umo/l), red blood cells (10e12/l), alkaline phosphatase (iu/l), platelet (10e9/l), alanine aminotransferase (u/l), total bilirubin(umol/l), urea nitrogen (mmo/l), white blood cells (10e9/l), direct bilirubin(umol/l), aspartate aminotransferasee (u/l)

Figure 7-19 Variance analysis in regression equation

2) Stepwise regression (Stepwise option) (Figure 7-20, Figure 7-21): In stepwise regression, there are two models.

In model 1, only "rbc" is used as a predictor; while, "rbc" and "plt" are predictors in model 2. In model 1, $R^2=0.657$, which means that "rbc" accounts for 65.7% of the variation in "hb". However, when "plt" is included besides, the value increases to 0.704 or 70.4% of the variance in "hb". Hence, if "rbc" accounts for 65.7%, it means "rbc" and "plt" account for an additional 4.7%. So, the inclusion of the two new predictors has explained a few amounts of variation in "hb" change. In model 1, $R^2_{adj}=0.653$ ($F=179.954$, $P<0.001$). While, in model 2, $R^2_{adj}=0.697$ ($F=110.369$, $P<0.001$), which both are significant with a probability less than 0.001 (Figure 7-20, Figure 7-21).

Model Summary

Model	R	R Square	Adjusted R Square	Std. Error of the Estimate
1	.810[a]	.657	.653	14.565
2	.839[b]	.704	.697	13.610

a. Predictors: (Constant), red blood cells (10e12/l)

b. Predictors: (Constant), red blood cells (10e12/l), platelet (10e9/l)

Figure 7-20 Coefficient of determination Stepwise regression equation

ANOVA[a]

Model		Sum of Squares	df	Mean Square	F	Sig.
1	Regression	38178.102	1	38178.102	179.954	.000[b]
	Residual	19942.556	94	212.155		
	Total	58120.657	95			
2	Regression	40895.177	2	20447.588	110.396	.000[c]
	Residual	17225.480	93	185.220		
	Total	58120.657	95			

a. Dependent Variable: Hemoglobin (g/L)

b. Predictors: (Constant), Red blood cells (10E12/L)

c. Predictors: (Constant), Red blood cells (10E12/L), Platelet (10E9/L)

Figure 7-21 Variance analysis in Stepwise regression equation

(5) Parameters estimation.

1) All variables regression analysis (Enter) (Figure 7-22): Interpretation of results.

• In the column Standardized Coefficients (Beta), influences of independent variables to the dependent variable ("hb") from high to low are rbc>plt>ast >alt>cr>tbil>alp>dbil>bun>wbc.

Coefficients[a]

Model		Unstandardized Coefficients		Standardized Coefficients	t	Sig.	95.0% Confidence Interval for B	
		B	Std. Error	Beta			Lower Bound	Upper Bound
1	(Constant)	38.415	10.916		3.519	.001	16.711	60.120
	rbc (10E12/L)	22.698	1.759	.789	12.905	.000	19.201	26.195
	wbc (10E9/L)	-.167	.415	-.031	-.402	.688	-.993	.659
	plt (10E9/L)	-.038	.015	-.199	-2.591	.011	-.067	-.009
	tbil (umol/L)	.235	.341	.061	.691	.492	-.442	.913
	dbil (umol/L)	-.435	.789	-.048	-.551	.583	-2.002	1.133
	alt (U/L)	-.060	.077	-.145	-.785	.435	-.213	.092
	ast (U/L)	.066	.079	.156	.838	.405	-.091	.223
	alp (IU/L)	-.023	.023	-.059	-1.004	.318	-.069	.023
	bun (mmo/L)	-.449	.739	-.046	-.607	.545	-1.918	1.021
	cr (umo/L)	.069	.072	.063	.960	.340	-.074	.213

a. Dependent Variable: Hemoglobin (g/L)

Figure 7-22 Parameters estimation of regression equation

• General regression equation:

$$hb = 38.415 + 22.698rbc - 0.167wbc - 0.038plt + 0.235tbil - 0.435dbil - 0.060alt + 0.066ast - 0.023alp - 0.449bun + 0.069cr .$$

• Tests of individual regression coefficients in the equation. Predictors "rbc" and "plt" have a significant effect on dependent variable "hb" ($P<0.001$ and 0.01, separately).

2) Stepwise regression (Figure 7-23): Interpretation of results.

• Regression equation: $hb = 39.344 + 23.021rbc - 0.041plt$.

• Stepwise regression is more appropriate in method selection compare with full model regression. One reason is that the number of dependent variables decrease from 10 to 2; the model is more concise and easy to use. The other reason is that stepwise regression R^2_{adj} (adjusted R^2) = 0.697 is larger than full model regression R^2_{adj} = 0.681.

Coefficients[a]

Model		Unstandardized Coefficients		Standardized Coefficients	t	Sig.	95.0% Confidence Interval for B	
		B	Std. Error	Beta			Lower Bound	Upper Bound
1	(Constant)	27.545	7.911		3.482	.001	11.837	43.253
	rbc (10E12/L)	23.328	1.739	.810	13.415	.000	19.875	26.780
2	(Constant)	39.344	8.008		4.913	.000	23.441	55.247
	rbc (10E12/L)	23.021	1.627	.800	14.151	.000	19.791	26.252
	plt (10E9/L)	-.041	.011	-.216	-3.830	.000	-.063	-.020

a. Dependent Variable: Hemoglobin (g/L)

Figure 7-23 Stepwise regression equation parameter estimation

7.2.4 Drawing conclusions

After model testing by using enter and stepwise method, the full model with all variables are statistical significance. The full model equation is valid. Linear regression analysis answers research question of the relationship between "hb" and other variables. Hemoglobin (hb) changes contribute to rbc, plt, ast, alt, cr, tbil, alp, dbil, bund and wbc. Among 10 predictors, some are positive influence to hb (rbc, tbil, ast), while others negative influence to hb (wbc, dbil, alt, alp, bun), but only rbc and plt are statistic significant. In regression analysis method comparison part, stepwise may be more convince and simple than others.

7.3 Nonlinear regression

7.3.1 Description

Nonlinear regression is a method of finding a nonlinear model of the relationship between the dependent variable and a set of independent variables. Unlike traditional linear regression, which is restricted to estimating linear models, nonlinear regression can estimate models with arbitrary relationships between independent and dependent variables. The data are fitted by iterative estimation algorithms.

Linear regression analysis can be used if variables including independent variable(s) x and dependent variable y can be expressed by a linear function after transformed. However, it cannot ensure the residual sum of squares minimized with y transformed. Nonlinear regression analysis is needed when the dependent variable is transformed to build a linear relationship with independent variable(s) or linear relationship cannot be built with any transformation.

7.3.2 SPSS data format

The SPSS data file for nonlinear regression requires only one dependent variable and one or more independent variables. All variables should be continuous. If independent variable is categorical, it should be converted into binary dummy variable.

7.3.3 Example

Example 7-4 The data file "nonlinear. sav" is used as the Example 7-4. A data of 21 records of S78-3 mouse sarcoma volume growth trend over time. Try to build a regression model between volume and time.

7.3.4 Running the commands

The process is as follows:

Analyze

Regression

Nonlinear

▶**Dependent**: *y*

▶**Model Expression**: **a * EXP(b * x)**

▶**Parameters**: **a**(0.0042); **b**(0.1659)

The main dialog box of Nonlinear Regression pops up (Figure 7-24).

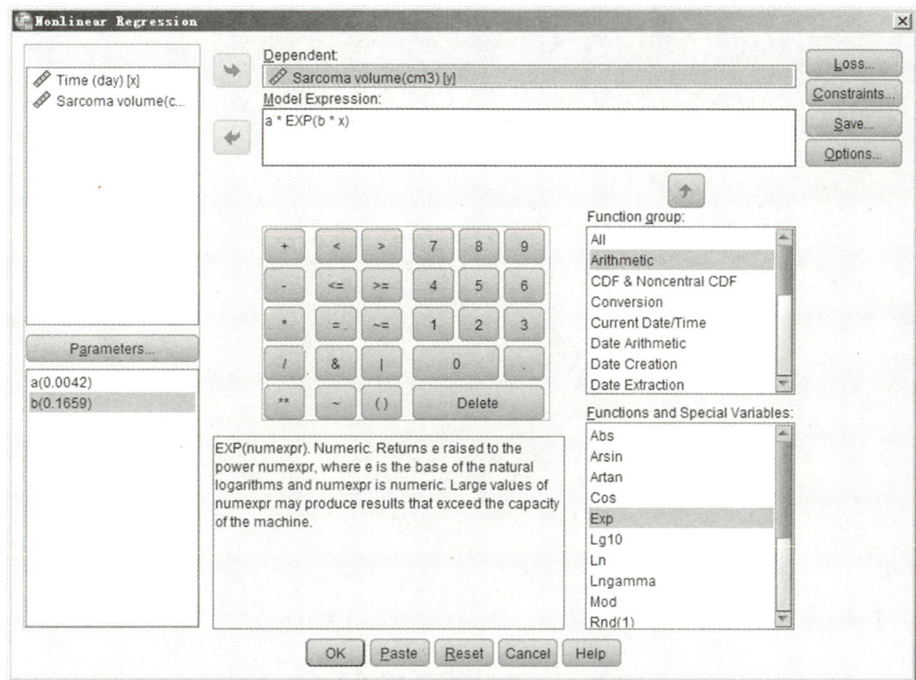

Figure 7–24 The Nonlinear Regression dialog box

◇Dependent: Place dependent variable y.

◇Model Expression: Model expression should be built with at least one independent variable from the source variable box on the left, defined parameters from the parameters box on the bottom left, calculator panel and function box below.

A segmented model using conditional logical expression also can be specified when necessary. To use conditional logic expression within a model expression or a loss function, the sum of a series of terms is formed with one for each condition. Each term consists of a logical expression (in parentheses) multiplied by the expression when that logical expression is true. For example, to a segmented model:

$$f(X) = \begin{cases} 0 & X \leqslant 0 \\ X & 0 < X < 1 \\ 1 & X \geqslant 1 \end{cases},$$

its expression is listed below:

$$(X <= 0) \times 0 + (X > 0 \;\&\; X < 1) \times X + (X >= 1) \times 1 .$$

The logical expression value in parentheses can only be 1 (true) or 0 (false), thus, the model expression equals to $1 \times 0 + 0 \times X + 0 \times 1 = 0$ when $X <= 0$, $0 \times 0 + 1 \times X + 0 \times 1 = X$ when $X > 0$ & $X < 1$, and $0 \times 0 + 0 \times X + 1 \times 1 = 1$ when $X >= 1$.

Character string variable can also be used in the logical expression, such as

(*city* = "*New York*") × *costliv* + (*city* = "*Washington*") × 0.59 × *costliv* .

Commonly used nonlinear models as shown in Table 7–2 and the choice depends on the data character.

Table 7-2 Common nonlinear models

Name	Model expression
Asymptotic Regression	$b_1 - (b_2 * b_3^x)$
Asymptotic Regression	$b_1 + b_2 * exp(b_3 * x)$
Density	$(b_1 + b_2 * x)^{(-1/b_3)}$
Gauss	$b_1 * (1 - b_3 * exp(-b_2 * x^2))$
Gompertz	$b_1 * exp(-b_2 * exp(-b_3 * x))$
Johnson-Schumacher	$b_1 * exp(-b_2/(x + b_3))$
Log-Modified	$(b_1 + b_3 * x)^{b_2}$
Log-Logistic	$b_1 - ln(1 + b_2 * exp(-b_3 * x))$
Metcherlich Law of Diminishing Returns	$b_1 + b_2 * exp(-b_3 * x)$
Michaelis Menten	$b_1 * x/(x + b_2)$
Morgan-Mercer-Florin	$(b_1 * b_2 + b_3 * x^{b_4})/(b_2 + x^{b_4})$
Peal-Reed	$b_1/(1 + b_2 * exp(-(b_3 * x + b_4 * x^2 + b_5 * x^3)))$
Ratio of Cubics	$(b_1 + b_2 * x + b_3 * x^2 + b_4 * x^3)/(b_5 * x^3)$
Ratio of Quadratics	$(b_1 + b_2 * x + b_3 * x^2)/(b_4 * x^2)$
Richards	$b_1/((1 + b_3 * exp(-b_2 * x))^{(1/b_4)})$
Verhulst	$b_1/(1 + b_3 * \exp(-b_2 * x))$
Von Bertalanffy	$(b_1^{(1-b_4)} - b_2 * exp(-b_3 * x))^{(1/(1-b_4))}$
Weibull	$b_1 - b_2 * exp(-b_3 * x^{b_4})$
Yield Density	$(b_1 + b_2 * x + b_3 * x^2)^{-1}$

★Parameters. Click "Parameters" button (Figure 7-24), and the dialog box of Nonlinear Regression: Parameters pops out (Figure 7-25).

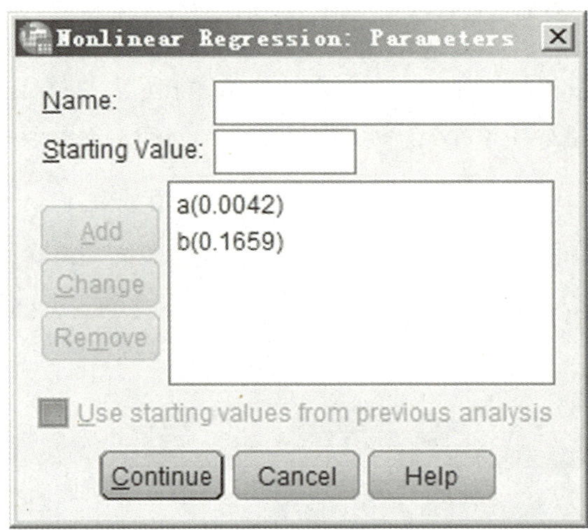

Figure 7-25 The Nonlinear Regression: Parameters dialog box

◇Name: Parameter name. The name must be a valid SPSS variable name and must be used in the model expression in the main dialog box.

◇Starting Value: Staring value will be set for each parameter, as close to the final value as possible. In appropriate starting value will result in failure to converge or in convergence on a solution that is local (rather than global). After the parameter's name and starting value set, click "Add" button, transfer it into the parameter box below. Please edit and delete parameter by the "Change" and "Remove" button.

□Use starting values from previous analysis: Starting value will be obtained from previous nonlinear regression analysis at the last time. If the model is changed, we have to cancel this option.

★Loss: Loss function is the one which should be minimized by iteration in nonlinear regression analysis. The loss function also can be expressed by subsections when necessary.

Click "Loss" button (Figure 7-24) to activate Nonlinear Regression: Loss Function dialog box (Figure 7-26).

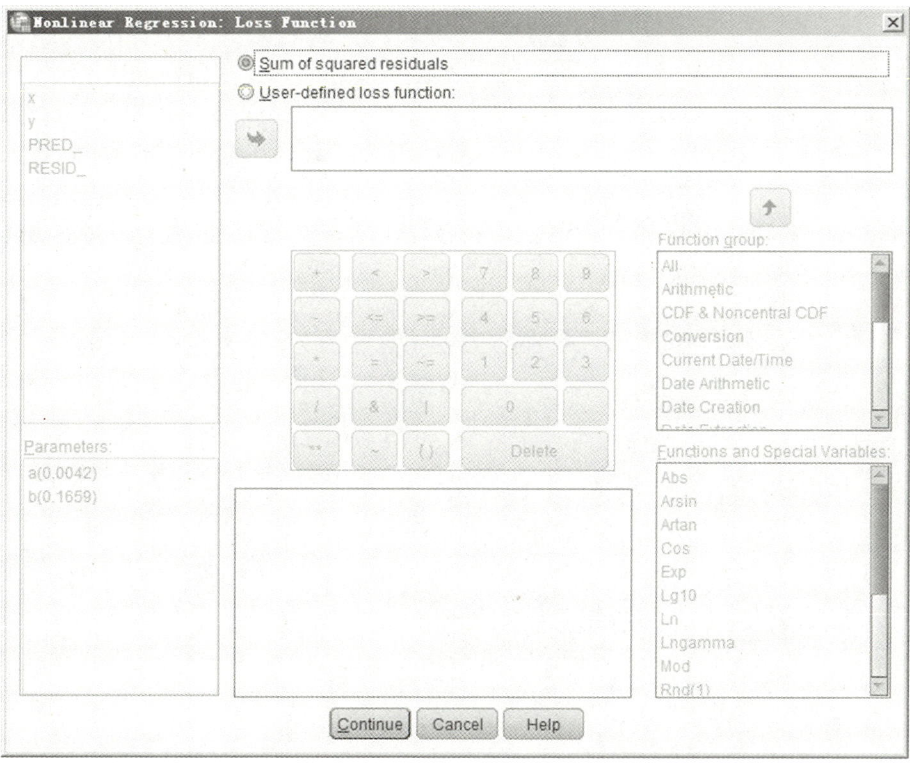

Figure 7-26 The Nonlinear Regression: Loss Function dialog box

⊙Sum of squared residuals: Default loss function which is used in this example.

◎User-defined loss function: User-defined loss function can be built with residuals (RESID_), predicted value (PRED_) and variables from the source variable box on the left, defined parameters from the parameters box on the bottom left, calculator panel and function box below. The model also can be expressed by subsections when necessary.

★Constraints. Click "Constraints" button (Figure 7-24) to activate Nonlinear Regression: Parameter Constraints dialog box (Figure 7-27).

⊙Unconstrained: Default option which is selected in this example.

◎Define parameter constraint: Constraint can be made not only to single parameter but also to the expression composed by parameters. Choose appropriate logical operator (<=, =, >=), and enter a user-defined constant, then click "Add" button, transfer it into the parameter box below. Edit and delete parameter or expression by the "Change" and "Remove" bottom.

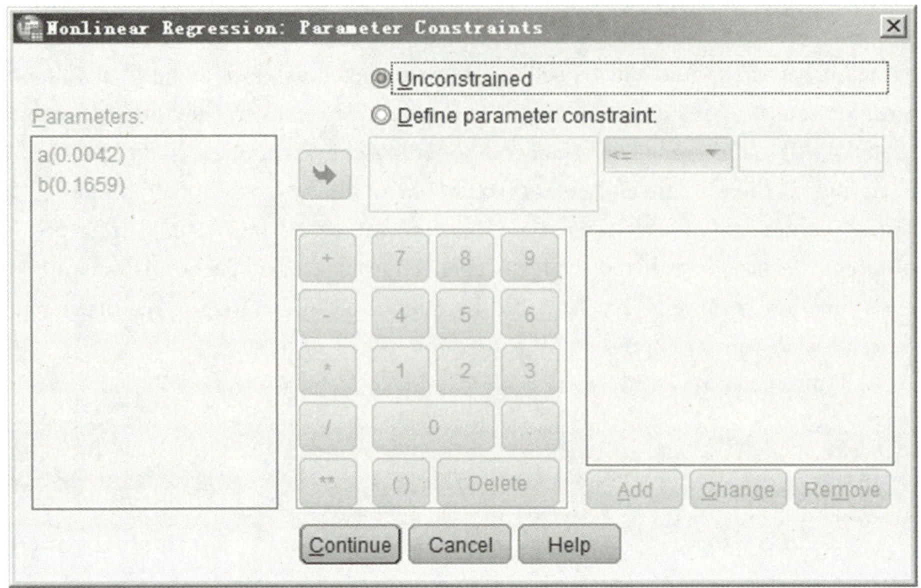

Figure 7-27 The Nonlinear Regression: Parameter Constraints dialog box

★Save: Save as new variable. Click "Save" button (Figure 7-24) and Nonlinear Regression: Save New Variables dialog box pops out (Figure 7-28).

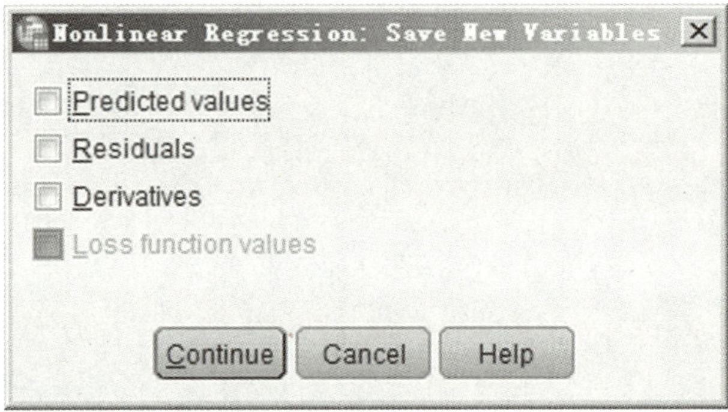

Figure 7-28 The Nonlinear Regression: Save New Variables dialog box

□Predicted values: Save predicted values as new variable "pred".

□Residuals: Save residuals as new variable "Residua".

□Derivatives: Save a derived variable for each parameter in the model with alphabet *d* before corresponding parameter name as variable name.

□Loss function values: Save Loss function values as new variable "loss".

★Options.

Click "Options" button (Figure 7-24) and the dialog box of Nonlinear Regression: Options pops out (Figure 7-29).

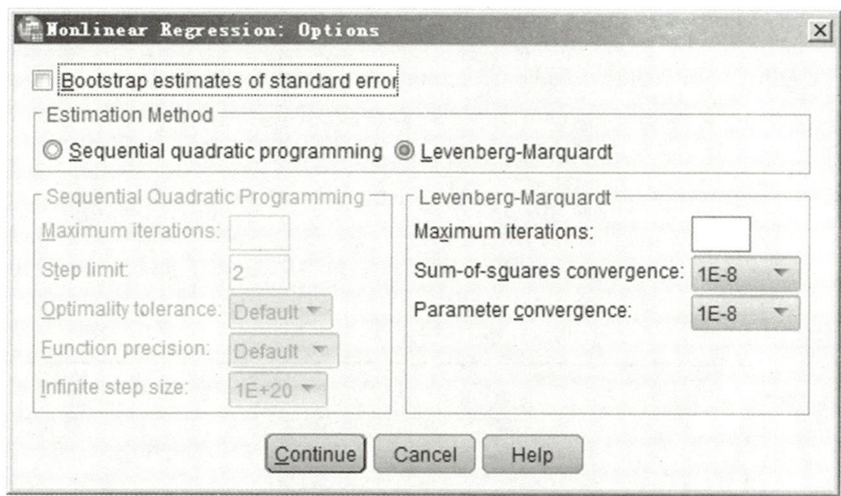

Figure 7–29 The Nonlinear Regression: Options dialog box

□Bootstrap estimates of standard error: If check this option, only estimation method of sequential quadratic programming can be selected below.

◇Estimation method.

◎Sequential quadratic programming: This option will be selected automatically if "Constraint" model or "Loss" function has been defined or "Bootstrap estimates of standard error" option has been checked.

1) Maximum iterations.

2) Step limit: The maximum allowed variation of parameter vector length with a positive value.

3) Optimality tolerance: It can be deemed as the final objective function valid place. For example, if it is set as 0.000 001, the final objective function valid place should be six. The optimal tolerance value must be larger than objective function precision.

4) Function precision: Objective function precision is deemed as a relative precision index with larger function value and absolute precision index with the smaller function value.

5) Infinite step size: If parameter variation is larger than the infinite step size, it is considered that an appropriate result cannot be obtained, then the operation will stop. A positive value should be set for the infinite step size.

⊙Levenberg–Marquardt: Non–Constraint model. Default option which is selected in the Example 7–4. This option cannot be selected if "Constraint" model or "Loss" function has been defined or Bootstrap estimates of standard error option has been checked.

1) Maximum iterations.

2) Sum–of–squares convergence: If a sum–of–squares variation is less than the convergence criterion, then the process will stop.

3) Parameter convergence: If parameter variation is less than the convergence criterion, then process will stop.

In the Example 7–4, scatter plot can be used to determine the model type and parameter starting value as follows:

Graphs

Legacy Dialogs

Scatter/Dot

Simple Scatter

Define

▶**Y Axis**: *y*

▶**X Axis**: *x*

The results (Figure 7-30) show there is a exponential relationship between volume and time ($y = a * e^{b*x}$). Choosing two representative points from the data set. These two dots are far away from each other, for example (0, 0.004 2) and (45, 7.346 1). Listing equation set:

$0.0042 = a * e^{b*0}$

$7.3461 = a * e^{b*45}$

After solving the equation, the starting values of "a" and "b" are obtained, which $a = 0.0042$, $b = 0.1659$.

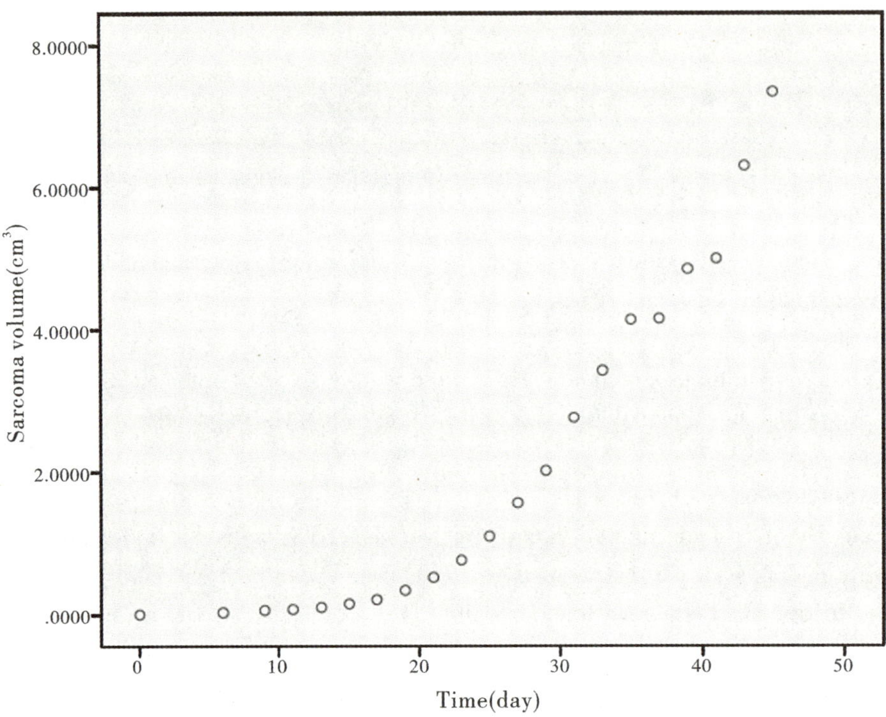

Figure 7-30 Scatter plot of sarcoma volume and time

In addition, to the method above, curve estimation method can also be applied to determine the starting value by fitting exponential function model.

7.3.5 Reading the output

(1) According to parameter estimates results (Figure 7-31), the regression equation is $y = 0.161e^{0.086x}$.

Parameter Estimates

Parameter	Estimate	Std. Error	95% Confidence Interval	
			Lower Bound	Upper Bound
a	.161	.035	.088	.234
b	.086	.005	.075	.097

Figure 7-31 The output of parameter estimates

(2) As shown in Figure 7-32, correlation coefficients matrix among parameters is calculated by a non-parameter method based on outcomes of all iteration steps. The correlation coefficient between "a" and "b" is −0.990.

Correlations of Parameter Estimates

	a	b
a	1.000	-.990
b	-.990	1.000

Figure 7-32 The correlations of parameter estimates

(3) Nonlinear regression ANOVA table as shown in Figure 7-33. Mean square of residual in this table is not the unbiased estimation of error; therefore, the ANOVA cannot be applied for nonlinear regression hypothesis testing. In fact, the goodness of model fit is judged by determination coefficient as follow:

$$R^2 = 1 - \frac{Residual\ sum\ of\ squares}{Corrected\ tatal\ sum\ of\ squares} = 1 - \frac{3.510}{108.796} = 0.968 .$$

It is considered that the model is well fitted with $R^2 = 0.968$. The value of R^2 may be negative with a poor model fitting.

ANOVA[a]

Source	Sum of Squares	df	Mean Squares
Regression	201.543	2	100.771
Residual	3.510	19	.185
Uncorrected Total	205.053	21	
Corrected Total	108.796	20	

Dependent variable: Sarcoma volume(cm3)

a. R squared = 1 - (Residual Sum of Squares) / (Corrected Sum of Squares) = .968.

Figure 7-33 The ANOVA table of nonlinear regression

7.3.6 Drawing conclusions

Nonlinear regression is fitted well with $R^2 = 0.968$ which is close to 1, and the regression equation is exponential that $y = 0.161e^{0.086x}$.

7.4 Binary logistic regression

7.4.1 Description

Logistic regressionis are well used in lots of areas. If the outcome is a categorical variable or ordinal variable, Logistic regression (also called risk factors analysis) can be used for analysis one to more predictors effect on the outcome. Logistic regression also is used to measure category of outcome and control confounders. In contrast to Fisher linear discrimination analysis, Logistic regression doesn't need predictor distribution prerequisites, which means, the independent variable can be continuous variable or discrete variables. While linear regression analysis needs independent variables to follow multiple normal distributions.

When we try to predict membership of only two categorical outcomes, the analysis is known as binary logistic regression. When we hope to predict membership of more than two categories, we use multinomial (or polychotomous) logistic regression. In this section, we mainly introduce binary logistic regression analysis.

7.4.2 SPSS data format

Dependent variable should be two categories.

7.4.3 Example

Example 7-5 The data file "logistic_1. sav" is used as the Example 7-5, which has 422 rows (samples) and 29 columns (variables), which contain 1 dependent variable and 28 independent variables. In order to explore risk factors for acute renal failure (ARF) death, 422 ARF inpatients from 1900 to 2000 in one hospital for a retrospective investigation are selected. There are 29 variables which are "sex, age, social support, chronic_disease, operation, diabetes, tumor, arteriosclerosis, organ transplantation, creatinine (cr), hemoglobin (hb), nephrotoxicity, oliguria, lbp, jaundice, coma, auxiliary respiration, heart failure, liver failure, hemorrhage, respiratory failure, organ failure, pancreatitis, dic, septicemia, infection, hbp, dialysis method and death". Among them, "dialysis method" is a 4 levels multi-categorical variable; "age" "cr" "hg" and "heart failure" are quantitative variables; other variables are binary variables.

(1) Dependent variable: "Death", a two categorical variable. It should be entered as coding variable to represent categories [0 = N (not death), 1 = Y (death)].

(2) Independent variable: Quantitative or qualitative variables. In the Example 7-5, the other 28 variables are predictor, among them, one variable is a multi-categorical variable.

7.4.3.1 Running the commands

The process is listed.

Analyze

Regression

Binary Logistic

Logistic Regression dialog box pops out (Figure 7-34). All variables are listed on the left-hand side.

◇Dependent: Dependent variable, place only one variable each time and it should be a two categorical variable.

◇Covariates: Independent variable(s) or predictor(s), you can place any number of variables you want, and also place the interaction variable(s). Select one more variable at the same time on the left-hand side, the ">a * b>" command is activated. Then, click ">a * b>" button to move variables to the "Covariates" box to put an interaction. "Previous" and "Next" buttons can be used for selecting variables.

◇Method.

1) Enter: Full model.

2) Forward: Conditional. Forward selection method based on conditional parameter estimates.

3) Forward: LR. Forward selection method based on the maximum partial likelihood estimates.

4) Forward: Wald. Forward selection method based on the probability of the Wald statistic.

5) Backward: Conditional. Backward selection method based on conditional parameter estimates.

6) Backward: LR. Backward selection method based on the maximum partial likelihood estimates.

7) Backward: Wald. Backward selection method based on the probability of the Wald statistic.

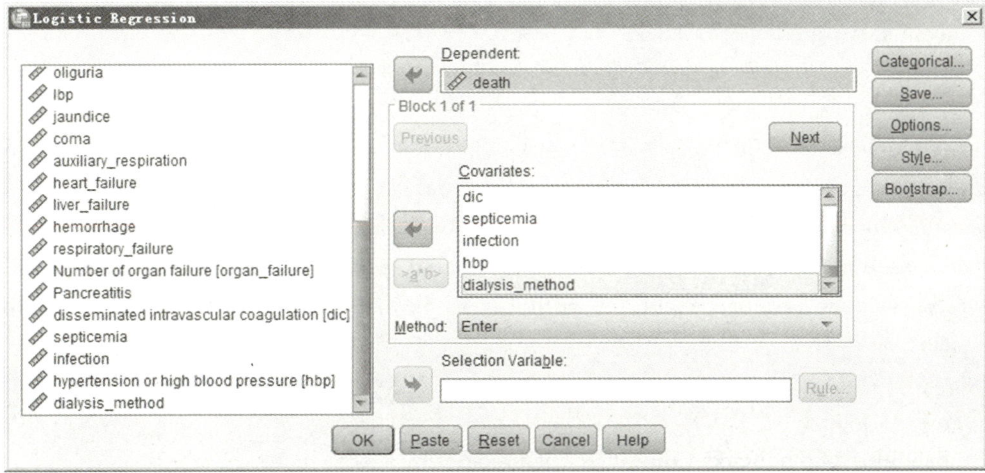

Figure 7-34 The Logistic Regression dialog box

◇Selection Variable: Drag a variable (always categories) to this box, active "Rule" button and click it, definite selection rule of the level value of the variable.

★Categorical: Multi-categorical variable comparison. Click "Categorical" button to activate the dialog box of Logistic Regression: Define Categorical Variables (Figure 7-35).

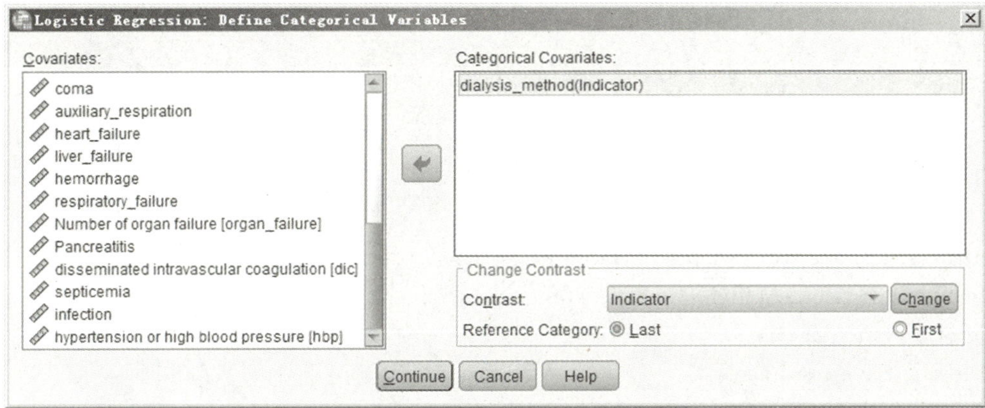

Figure 7-35 The Logistic Regression: Define Categorical Variables dialog box

◇Categorical Covariates: Character variable are automatically set as multi-categorical variable.

◇Change Contrast: Selection and modification of contrast method of different levels in a multi-categorical variable.

Contrast: Different contrast methods.

1) Indicator: When an indicator contrast is used, each category will contrast to reference category. And the reference category is represented in the contrast matrix as a row of zeros.

2) Simple: First or last category as a reference category, and each category is compared to the reference category.

3) Difference: Each category except the first category is compared to the average effect of previous categories (also called reverse Helmert contrast).

4) Helmert: Each category except the last category is compared to the average effect of subsequence categories.

5) Repeated: Each category of the predictor variable except the first category is compared to the previous one.

6) Polynomial: Orthogonal polynomial contrasts. This method assumes each category is equal space, used in the quantitative predictor variable.

7) Deviation: Each category of the predictor variable except reference category is compared with entire effect.

Reference Category: First or last category can be chosen as category baseline. Above all contrast method, "Deviation" "Simple" or "Indicator" can select first or last category as the reference category of the predictor variable. In the Example 7-5, select "Indicator contrast" and set first category as the reference category, that is each category of dialysis method is compared to the first category ("not dialysis").

★Save: Save a new variable (Figure 7-34). Click "Save" and Logistic Regression: Save dialog box pops out (Figure 7-36).

◇Predicted Values: Calculating predicted values of a logistic regression model.

☑Probabilities: A predicted value of event probability. In the Example 7-5, a probability is predicted a value of "death".

☑ Group membership: Groups of predict unit belongs to. In the Example 7-5, groups are "not death" and "death".

◇Influence: Measure the influence of cases on predicted values. Available methods are "Cook's" "Leverage values" and "DfBeta(s)".

☐Cook's: Cook's influence statistic. A measure of how much the residual of all cases will change if a particular observation unit is excluded.

☐Leverage values: The relative influence of each observation on the model's fit.

☐DfBeta(s): The difference in beta value is the change in the regression coefficient which is altered by removing of a particular case.

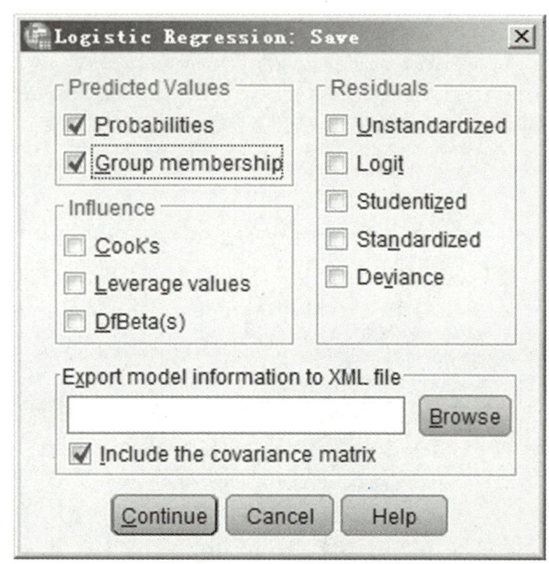

Figure 7-36 The Logistic Regression: Save dialog box

◇Residuals: Save residuals.

☐Unstandardized: Same as unstandardized residual in linear regression.

☐Logit: The residual for the case if it is predicted in the logit scale. The logit residual is the residual divided by the predicted probability times 1 minus the predicted probability.

☐Studentized: The change in the model deviance if a case is excluded.

☐Standardized: Same as a standardized residual in linear regression.

☐Deviance: Residuals based on the model deviance.

◇Export model information to XML file: To export model information (parameter estimates, their covariances) to file in XML format.

☑Include the covariance matrix: List covariance matrices.

★Option: Click "Options" button (Figure 7-34) and Logistic Regression: Options dialog box pops out (Figure 7-37).

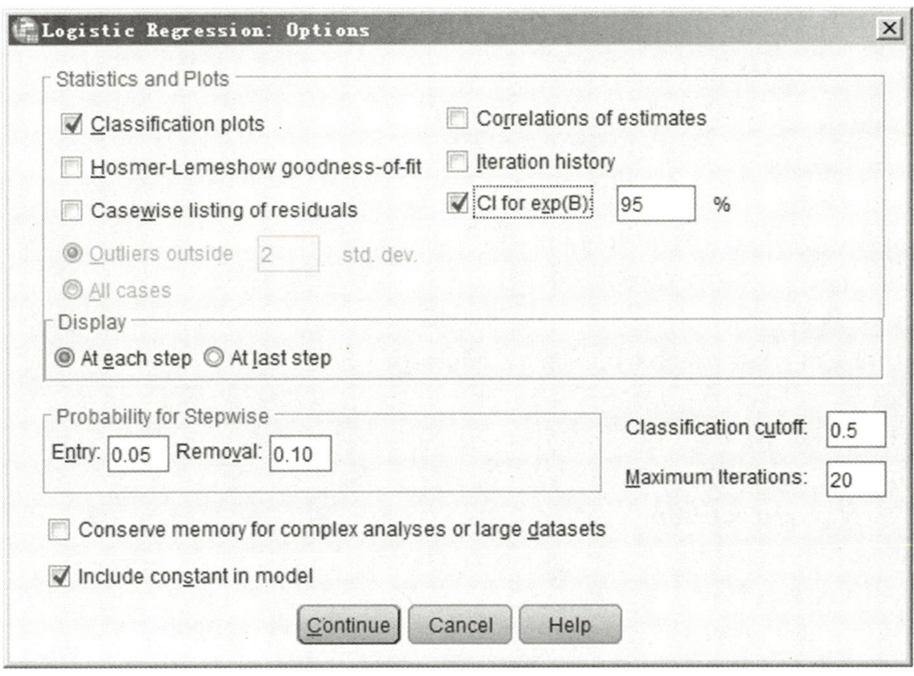

Figure 7-35 The Logistic Regression:Options dialog box

◇Statistics and Plots.

☑Classification plots: Histograms of the actual and predicted values of the outcome variable. A classification plot is used to evaluate the fit of the model to the observed data.

□Hosmer–Lemeshow goodness–of–fit: Which is used to assess how well the chosen model fits the data.

□Casewise listing of residuals: List all indicators of predicted probability, actual and predicted group, temporary variables [unstandardized residuals, standardized residual (Z Resid)] of each observed case.

□Correlations of estimates: Correlation coefficient matrix.

□Iteration history: The progress of the clustering process at each step.

☑CI for exp(B): 95 % :95% confident interval for odd ratio.

⊙Outliers outside 2 std. dev: Only list indicators of those cases for which the standardized residual is greater than 2 times deviation.

◎All cases: List indicators of all cases.

◇Display.

⊙At each step (system default): Display all graphs, tables and statistics at each stage of analysis.

◎At last step: Display all graphs, tables and statistics only after the final model has been fitted (select this item in Example 7-5).

◇Probability for Stepwise.

Entry: 0.05 . Variables inclusion criteria as $P \leq 0.05$ (system default).

Removal: 0.10 . Variables exclusion criteria as $P \geq 0.10$ (system default).

◇Classification cutoff: 0.5 . Determine the cut point for classifying cases as 0.5 (system default).

◇Maximum Iterations: 20 . The maximum number of times that model iterates before terminating.

□Conserve memory for complex analyses or large datasets.

☑Include constant in model: Display constant in model.

7.4.3.2 Running the commands

The process is listed:

Analyze

Regression

Binary Logistic

▶**Dependent: death**

▶**Covariates: sex/ age/…/ infection/ hbp**

▶**Method: Enter/ Forward LR**

Categorical:

▶**Categorical Covariates: dialysis method (indicator (first))**

Save

Predicted Values

☑**Probability**

☑**Group membership**

Options:

Statistics and Plots

☑**Classification plots**

☑**Iteration history**

☑**CI for exp 95%**

Display

⊙**At last step**

☑**Include constant in model**

Note: This analysis process does not consider the interactions among independent variables.

7.4.3.3 Reading the output

(1) Full model (Enter)

1) A contrast of levels to its reference level in the categorical variable. Dummy variables are created in Figure 7-38. The multi-categorical variable dialysis method has 4 categories and its frequency distribution shows in "Frequency" column. "Parameter coding" represents a mixed coding contrast. For example, "not dialysis" is the baseline, so it does not have a parameter coding. In this case, sense of (1), (2), (3) under "Parameter coding" columns is the comparison between this particular dialysis method group and the baseline category (not get treatment).

Categorical Variables Codings

		Frequency	Parameter coding (1)	(2)	(3)
dialysis_method	0	270	1.000	.000	.000
	1	137	.000	1.000	.000
	2	7	.000	.000	1.000
	3	8	.000	.000	.000

Figure 7-38 Categorical variables coding table

2) Model checking. The output (Figure 7-39) summaries a complex computer process that reappraises the predictions of group membership in a successive number of times until the estimates converge to a point where they become almost constant and stabilized, the initial -2 Log likelihood (-2LL) is 562.992.

Figure 7-40 output includes Chi-square statistics (which is related to -2LL) for the overall model. The Chi-square equals to 344.490 ($P<0.001$) which is significant. The Chi-square statistic is the difference between the current -2LL (218.495) and the baseline -2 LL (562.992).

Figure 7-41 shows summary statistics of -2LL for the current model. Nagelkerke's R^2 is 0.757 which indicates that the model is good. Cox & Snell's R^2 interpret this as 55.8% probability of death is explained by the logistic model.

Iteration History[a,b,c]

Iteration		-2 Log likelihood	Coefficients Constant
Step 0	1	562.992	-.455
	2	562.985	-.463
	3	562.985	-.463

a. Constant is included in the model.

b. Initial -2 Log Likelihood: 562.985

c. Estimation terminated at iteration number 3 because parameter estimates changed by less than .001.

Figure 7-39 Only constant model testing

Omnibus Tests of Model Coefficients

		Chi-square	df	Sig.
Step 1	Step	344.490	30	.000
	Block	344.490	30	.000
	Model	344.490	30	.000

Figure 7-40 Overall model summary statistic

Model Summary

Step	-2 Log likelihood	Cox & Snell R Square	Nagelkerke R Square
1	218.495[a]	.558	.757

a. Estimation terminated at iteration number 20 because maximum iterations has been reached. Final solution cannot be found.

Figure 7-41 Summary statistics for the model

- Block: The Example 7-5 describes the model before dialysis method is included. The block -2LL is the change from the current block model to the previous one.
- Step: The difference of -2LL between the current step model and the previous one is the step. When you select full mode, the "step value" is the same as the block -2LL.
- Cox and Snell's and Nagelkerke's R^2 are 0.558 and 0.757, which have same implication as multi-categorical correlation coefficients. That is, these values are on a scale of 0 to 1. Cox and Snell's and Nagelkerke's correlation coefficients indicate how much the regression model can explain the variance of the dependent variable.

3) Parameter estimation and hypothesis testing (Figure 7-42).

- Predictors of "Tumor" "cr" "coma" "organ failure" "Pancreatitis" are statistically significant in the current model ($P<0.005$), which interpreted that they play important roles in outcome.
- B: Regression coefficient.
- SE: Standard error of regression coefficient.

• Wald: Wald statistics is used to test whether or not a regression coefficient for a predictor in a logistic regression is significantly different from zero. It has a Chi-square distribution when df = 1. Wald statistics equals to regression coefficient (B) divided by standard errors (SE).

• Exp(B): Odds ratio is equal to the exponential of B.

• According to the direction of each value in column B, "coma" "liver failure" are risk factors and "cr" "Pancreatitis" are protective factors.

• After comparing, there is no difference among different categories of the predictor; so they will not be considered for analysis in step regression analysis.

		B	S.E.	Wald	df	Sig.	Exp(B)	95% C.I.for EXP(B)	
								Lower	Upper
Step 1[a]	sex	-.182	.413	.193	1	.660	.834	.371	1.874
	age	.016	.014	1.352	1	.245	1.016	.989	1.045
	social_support	-.171	.748	.052	1	.819	.843	.194	3.654
	chronic_disease	-.094	.453	.043	1	.836	.911	.375	2.214
	operation	.063	.619	.010	1	.919	1.065	.316	3.581
	diabetes	1.284	.723	3.158	1	.076	3.612	.876	14.888
	tumor	1.587	.569	7.777	1	.005	4.887	1.602	14.906
	arteriosclerosis	-.424	.622	.464	1	.496	.655	.194	2.215
	organ_transplantation	-3.270	2.150	2.312	1	.128	.038	.001	2.573
	cr	-.001	.001	5.912	1	.015	.999	.997	1.000
	hg	-.046	.063	.536	1	.464	.955	.844	1.080
	nephrotoxicity	.005	.465	.000	1	.991	1.005	.404	2.499
	oliguria	1.069	.697	2.355	1	.125	2.914	.743	11.419
	lbp	.771	.445	2.999	1	.083	2.163	.903	5.177
	jaundice	.921	.544	2.869	1	.090	2.511	.865	7.288
	coma	1.574	.497	10.016	1	.002	4.827	1.821	12.796
	auxiliary_respiration	.897	.734	1.493	1	.222	2.452	.582	10.340
	heart_failure	-.518	.787	.433	1	.510	.596	.127	2.785
	liver_failure	18.432	6686.732	.000	1	.998	101114208.549	.000	.
	hemorrhage	-.146	.610	.057	1	.811	.864	.261	2.856
	respiratory_failure	.479	.643	.555	1	.456	1.615	.458	5.693
	organ_failure	1.643	.456	12.978	1	.000	5.169	2.115	12.634
	Pancreatitis	-2.413	1.054	5.242	1	.022	.090	.011	.707
	dic	1.694	1.288	1.729	1	.189	5.442	.436	67.983
	septicemia	-.605	.619	.953	1	.329	.546	.162	1.839
	infection	.449	.420	1.141	1	.285	1.567	.687	3.572
	hbp	-.529	.889	.354	1	.552	.589	.103	3.365
	dialysis_method			2.687	3	.442			
	dialysis_method(1)	-.132	1.252	.011	1	.916	.877	.075	10.202
	dialysis_method(2)	-.817	1.223	.447	1	.504	.442	.040	4.851
	dialysis_method(3)	-.855	1.977	.187	1	.666	.425	.009	20.502
	Constant	-2.767	1.856	2.223	1	.136	.063		

Figure 7-42 Individual parameter estimation and detection

a. Variable(s) entered on step 1: sex, age, social_support, chronic_disease, operation, diabetes, tumor, arteriosclerosis, organ_transplantation, cr, hg, nephrotoxicity, oliguria, lbp, jaundice, coma, auxiliary_respiration, heart_failure, liver_failure, hemorrhage, respiratory_failure, organ_failure, Pancreatitis, dic, septicemia, infection, hbp, dialysis_method.

4) Discriminant effect on outcome classification. The output (Figure 7-43) is a cross-tabulation of dialysis with outcome status ("death" or "not death"). Use a predictive probability of 0.5 as cut point, then the sensitivity of death is 85.9%, the specificity of death is 94.2% and the overall accuracy of classification is 91% [(244+140)/422 = 0.91].

Classification Table[a]

Observed			Predicted: death no	Predicted: death yes	Percentage Correct
Step 1	death	no	244	15	94.2
		yes	23	140	85.9
	Overall Percentage				91.0

a. The cut value is .500

Figure 7-43 Discrimination of effect

5) Classification plot (Figure 7-44). This plot is a histogram of the predicted probabilities of patient death and it has a similar function of Figure 7-44. Both of them answer the question of "How accurate is our model in classifying individual cases?". In this plot, the vertical axis is predicted the frequency and the horizontal axis is predicted probability of the event occur.

This plot shows the frequency of categorizations for different predicted probabilities and whether they are "death" (Yes) or "not death" (No) categorizations. If the model perfectly fits the data, all of the cases who death should appear on the right-hand side, and all those who are not dead should appear on the left.

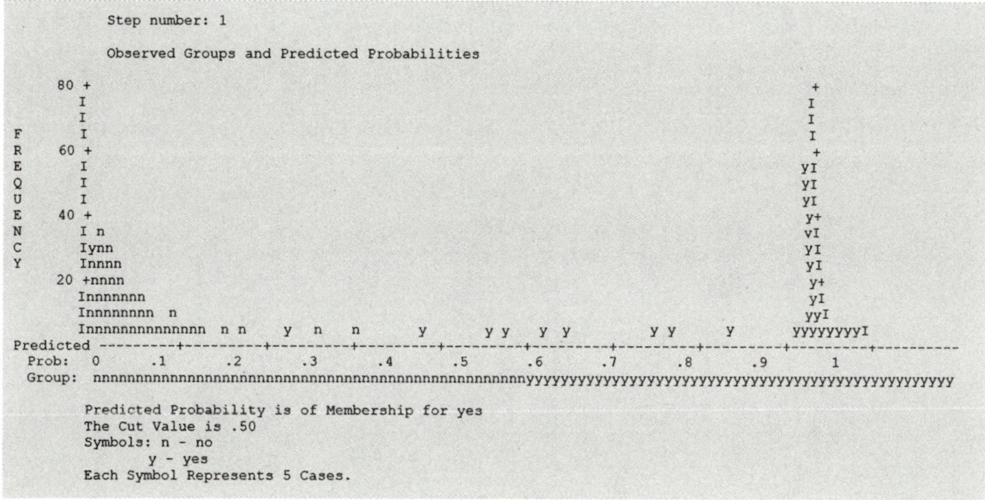

Figure 7-44 Classification plot

(2) Stepwise Logistic Regression (Forward LR). Forward LR method based on partial maximum likelihood ratio. Here only interpret the final step of 9 steps.

1) Model testing (Figure 7-45, Figure 7-46). The difference of 9 steps outputs is the change in the Chi-square resulting (which is related to -2LL) from adding variables to the model. In this case, we only defined 1 block, so the statistics of block and model is same. And the value of R^2 gradually increased by adding variables.

Omnibus Tests of Model Coefficients

		Chi-square	df	Sig.
Step 9	Step	4.063	1	.044
	Block	324.686	9	.000
	Model	324.686	9	.000

Figure 7-45 Stepwise regression model testing

Model Summary

Step	-2 Log likelihood	Cox & Snell R Square	Nagelkerke R Square
9	238.299[b]	.537	.729

a. Estimation terminated at iteration number 5 because parameter estimates changed by less than .001.

b. Estimation terminated at iteration number 6 because parameter estimates changed by less than .001.

Figure 7-46 Stepwise regression model summary

2) Discriminant effect on outcome classification. Classification results with a sensitivity of distinguishing death 85.3% ,a specificity 93.8% and with 90.5% are listed in Figure 7-47. A discriminant analysis is better in classifying data correctly.

Classification Table[a]

Observed		Predicted		
		death		Percentage Correct
		no	yes	
Step 9		243	16	93.8
		24	139	85.3
				90.5

a. The cut value is .500

Figure 7-47 Stepwise regression discriminant effect

3) Parameter estimation (Figure 7-48). Predictors of "diabetes" "tumor" "cr" "lbp" "jaundice" "coma" "auxiliary respiration" "organ failure" "Pancreatitis" are 9 statistically significant in the current model ($P<0.005$). Among these predictors, "cr" and "Pancreatitis" are protective factors, and others are risk factors.

Variables in the Equation

Variables in the Equation

		E	S.E.	Wald	df	Sig.	Exp(B)	95% C.I.for EXP(B)	
								Lower	Upper
Step 9[i]	diabetes	1.239	.633	3.832	1	.050	3.452	.999	11.933
	tumor	1.738	.481	13.061	1	.000	5.684	2.215	14.585
	cr	-.002	.000	9.510	1	.002	.998	.998	.999
	lbp	1.098	.368	8.883	1	.003	2.998	1.456	6.172
	jaundice	1.115	.482	5.344	1	.021	3.051	1.165	7.855
	coma	1.557	.414	14.172	1	.000	4.743	2.109	10.667
	auxiliary_respiration	1.326	.586	5.113	1	.024	3.765	1.193	11.878
	organ_failure	1.581	.241	42.909	1	.000	4.861	3.029	7.802
	Pancreatitis	-2.755	.949	8.436	1	.004	.064	.010	.408
	Constant	-2.386	.413	33.320	1	.000	.092		

i Variable(s) entered on step 9: diabetes.

Figure 7-48 Stepwise logistic regression variables in the equation estimation and testing

4) Stepwise logistic regression summary (Figure 7-49)

- Improvement: From step 1 to step 9, the Chi-square gradually decrease which interpret the iterative effect is gradually increase ($P<0.05$).
- Model: Full model testing which is statistically significant ($P<0.001$).
- Correct Class % : Model classified discriminant.

Step Summary[a,b]

Step	Improvement			Model			Correct Class %	Variable
	Chi-square	df	Sig.	Chi-square	df	Sig.		
1	247.929	1	.000	247.929	1	.000	82.9%	IN: organ_failure
2	28.955	1	.000	276.883	2	.000	88.4%	IN: coma
3	10.266	1	.001	287.149	3	.000	98.4%	IN: lbp
4	8.927	1	.003	296.076	4	.000	88.9%	IN: tumor
5	10.193	1	.001	306.268	5	.000	90.0%	IN: cr
6	5.009	1	.025	311.277	6	.000	89.8%	IN: Pancreatitis
7	5.089	1	.024	316.366	7	.000	89.6%	IN: jaundice
8	4.257	1	.039	320.623	8	.000	88.9%	IN: auxiliary_respiration
9	4.063	1	.044	324.686	9	.000	90.5%	IN: diabetes

a. No more variables can be deleted from or added to the current model.

b. End block: 1

Figure 7-49 Stepwise logistic regression summary

7.4.3.4 Drawing conclusions

Binary logistic regression results show that 9 variables: "diabetes" "tumor" "cr" "Ibp" "jaundice" "coma" "auxiliary respiration" "organ failure" "Pancreatitis influence acute renal failure" (ARF) death. However, "cr" and "Pancreatitis" are protective factors, and others are risk factors.

7.4.4 Example

Example 7-6 The data file "chiM-H. sav" is used as an Example 7-6 to explore whether smoking is a risk factor for lung cancer.

7.4.4.1 Running the commands

Firstly, we need to distinguish the frequency variable, and then, start a logistic regression analysis.

Data

Weight cases

⊙Weight cases by:freq

Analyze

Regression

Binary Logistic

▸Dependent:case_ctr

Covariates:smoke/gender

Method:Enter

Options

☑CI for exp 95%

☑Include constant in model

7.4.4.2 Reading the output

Model testing is showed in Figure 7-50, Chi-square equals to 26.217 ($P<0.001$), the model is statistically significant.

Omnibus Tests of Model Coefficients

		Chi-square	df	Sig.
Step 1	Step	26.217	2	.000
	Block	26.217	2	.000
	Model	26.217	2	.000

Figure 7-50 The result of model testing

Parameters estimation and testing as showed in Figure 7-51. "gender" is significant and positive associated with "lung cancer", indicating females is 0.561 times more likely than males to achieve lung cancer. That is to say, male have more risk than female ($P=0.014$) to achieve lung cancer from the Example 7-6. After excluding effect from gender (control the confounder of gender), "smoke" is still a risk factor for lung cancer ($OR=4.255$, 95% CI (2.348-7.711), $P<0.001$). All outputs are similar with MH Chi-square test results. In this case, it displays that logistic regression can also be used for categorical data and also convenient to use for multi-categorical data analysis and interaction analysis.

Variables in the Equation

		B	S.E.	Wald	df	Sig.	Exp(B)	95% C.I.for EXP(B)	
								Lower	Upper
Step 1[a]	smoke	1.448	.303	22.785	1	.000	4.255	2.348	7.711
	gender	-.578	.234	6.083	1	.014	.561	.354	.888
	Constant	-.898	.293	9.385	1	.002	.407		

a. Variable(s) entered on step 1: smoke, gender.

Figure 7-51 Parameter estimation and testing

7.4.4.3 Drawing conclusions

Smoking is a risk factor on lung cancer by adjusting for gender. And male get more risks compare with female.

7.5 Multinomial logistic regression

7.5.1 Description

Corresponding to binary logistic regression, multinomial logistic regression is used when the dependent variable y has more than two categories.

If y has K categories, one of the K categories will be considered as baseline or reference category, and then $K-1$ non-redundant logit transformation model will be generated. The other $K-1$ categories are compared with the baseline category respectively. For example, $y = j$ is selected as a baseline category, to $y = i$ $(i \neq j)$, its logit transformation model is as follow:

$$g = \log \frac{P(y=i)}{P(y=j)} = B_{i0} + B_{i1}X_1 + B_{i2}X_2 + \ldots + B_{iP}X_P.$$

whereas to $y = j$, all coefficients it the logit transformation model are zero.

7.5.2 SPSS data format

The SPSS data file for multinomial logistic regression requires only one dependent variable and one or more independent variables. Dependent variable should have more than two categories.

7.5.3 Example

Example 7-7 The data file "logistic_2. sav" is used as the Example 7-7, which has 280 rows and 13 columns. The data describe 280 records and 13 variables, and these 13 variables including 1 dependent variable and 12 independent variables (Table 7-3).

In order to explore risk factors for different coronary plaque formation, 280 subjects are randomly sampled in one study to receive 64-slice spiral CT coronary screening. Then, whether plaque have or not and plaque type are recorded, relative influence factors are surveyed such as "age", "gender", body mass index (BMI), family-history of coronary heart disease("family-history"), high blood pressure("hbp"), "diabetes", "smoking", "total cholesterol", high-density lipoprotein ("hdlp"), "triglyceride", "glucose" and "creatinine".

Table 7-3 Descriptions of all variables in data file "logistic_2. sav"

Variable	Assignment	Variable	Assignment
age	continuous (unit: year)	total_cholesterol	1: high; 2: normal
gender	1: female; 2: male	hdlp	1: high; 2: normal
BMI	continuous	triglyceride	1: high; 2: normal
family_history	1: yes; 2: no	glucose	1: high; 2: normal
hbp	1: yes; 2: no	creatinine	1: high; 2: normal
diabetes	1: yes; 2: no	plaque	0: no; 1: non-calcified 2: mixed; 3: calcified
smoking	1: yes; 2: no		

(1) Dependent variable: Multinomial variable, in the Example 7-7, i. e. "plaque" with four categories (0= "no plaque"; 1= "non-calcified plaque"; 2= "mixed plaque"; 3="calcified plaque").

(2) Independent variable: Quantitative or qualitative variables. In the Example 7-7, other 12 variables are independent, among them "age" and "BMI" are quantitative variables and the other 10 variables are

qualitative.

7.5.4 Running the commands

The "Multinomial Logistic Regression" analysis is located in the "Regression" submenu, under the "Analyze" menu:

Analyze

Regression

Multinomial Logistic

▶**Dependent: plaque (First)**

▶**Factor(s)**: gender / family_history / hbp / diabetes / smoking / total_cholesterol / hdlp /triglyceride / glucose / creatinine

▶Covariates: "age" and "BMI"

Model: ⊙Custom/Stepwise

Stepwise Terms

▶Main effects: all variables

Stepwise Methods: Forward stepwise

☑Include intercept in model

Statistics

☑Case processing summary

Model

☑Model fitting information

☑Classification table

☑Goodness of fit

Parameters

☑Estimates Confidence interval(%): 95

☑Likelihood ratio test

The main dialog box of Multinomial Logistic Regression is listed in Figure 7-52.

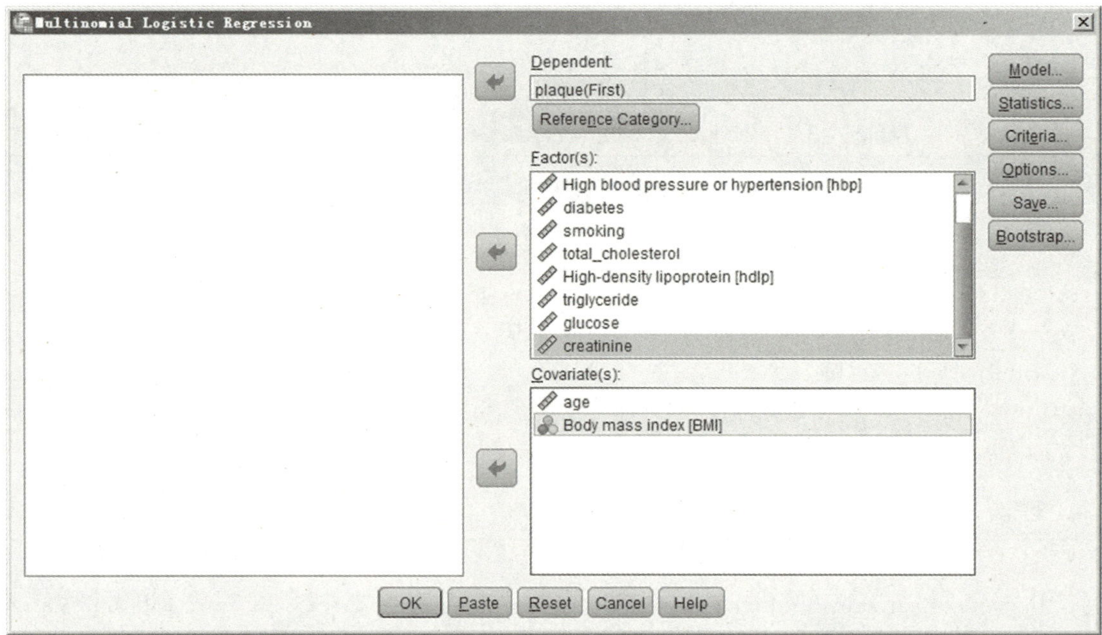

Figure 7-52 The Multinomial Logistic Regression dialog box

◇Dependent: Only one multinomial dependent variable can be placed here. In the Example 7-7, i. e. "plaque".

★Reference Category: Click "Reference Category" button, and the dialog box of Multinomial Logistic Regression: Reference Category pops out (Figure 7-53).

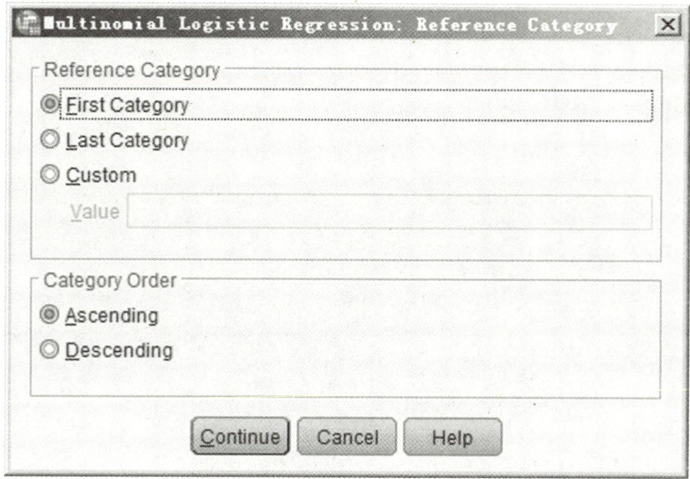

Figure 7-53 The Multinomial Logistic Regression: Reference Category dialog box

◇Reference Category.

⊙First Category: Set the first category as a reference category, such as Example 7-7.

◎Last Category (system default): Set the last category as a reference category.

◎Custom: Enter reference category value in the Value box below.

◇Category Order.

⊙Ascending: Variable values are sorted by ascending order, that is to say, the lowest value is set as the first category and the highest value is set as the last category (system default).

◎Descending: Variable values are sorted by descending order, that is to say, the highest value is set as the first category and the lowest value is set as the last category.

◇Factor(s): Character or numeric variable (Figure 7-52).

◇Covariate(s): Quantitative variable.

★Model: Click "Model" button (Figure 7-52), and the dialog box of Multinomial Logistic Regression: Model pops out (Figure 7-54).

◇Specify model.

◎Main effects: Main effects of all factors and covariates.

◎Full factorial: Main effects of all factors and covariates and interactions of all factors, except for interactions of covariates.

⊙Custom/Stepwise: Customized model. Independent variables can be selected by stepwise regression method, which is used in the Example 7-7.

◇Factors & Covariates: All independent variables are listed below.

◇Build Terms: Build interactions or main effects of terms into the "Forced Entry Terms" box or "Stepwise Terms" box on the right.

The selected factors and covariates as follow. Interaction: Creates the highest-level interaction term of all selected variables. This is the default. Main effects: Creates a main-effects term for each variable selected.

1) All 2-way: Creates all possible two-way interactions of the selected variables.

2) All 3-way: Creates all possible three-way interactions of the selected variables.

3) All 4-way: Creates all possible four-way interactions of the selected variables.

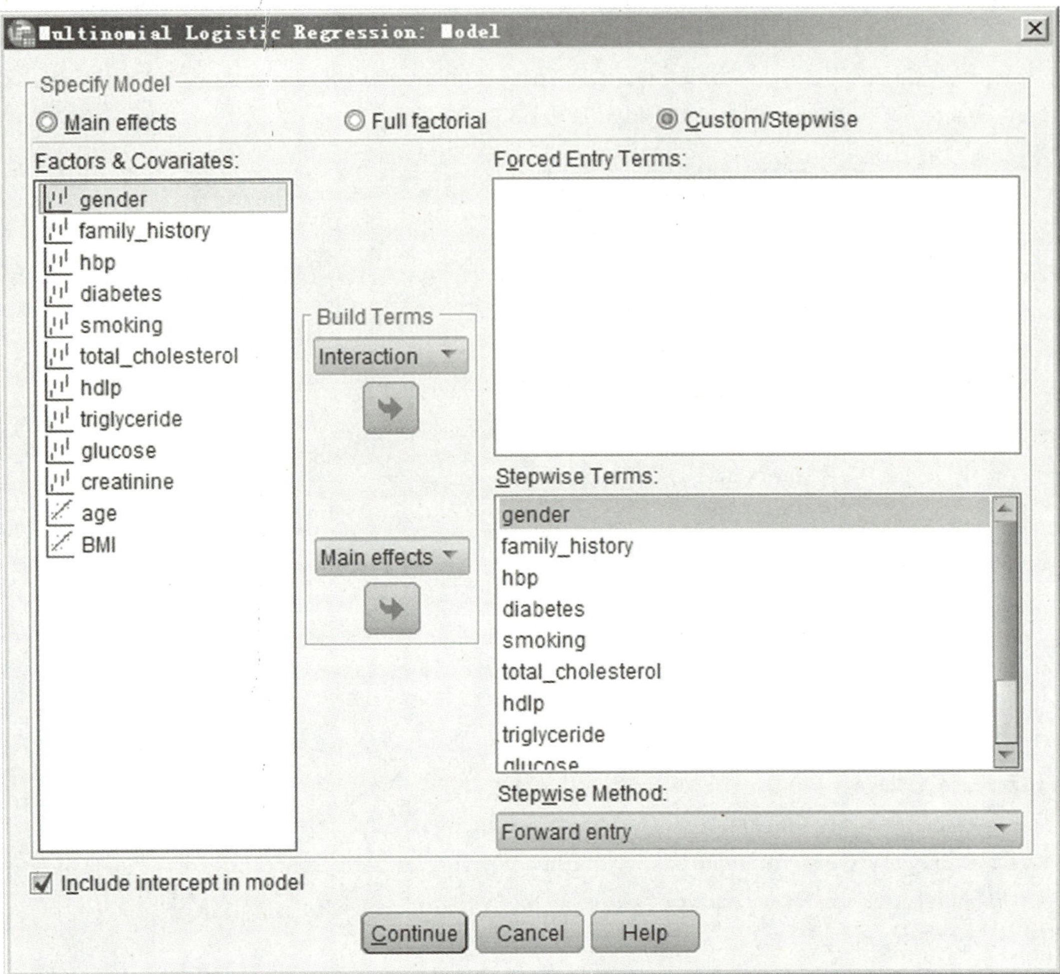

Figure 7-54 The Multinomial Logistic Regression: Model dialog box

4) All 5-way: Creates all possible five-way interactions of the selected variables.

◇Forced Entry Terms: Independent variables added in this box are always included in the model regardless of their influences.

◇Stepwise Terms: Independent variables added to the stepwise list are included in the model according to one of the following user-selected "Stepwise Methods".

◇Stepwise Method.

1) Forward entry: This method begins with no stepwise terms in the model. At each step, the most significant term is added to the model until none of the stepwise terms left out of the model.

2) Backward elimination: This method begins by entering all terms specified on the stepwise list into the model. At each step, the least significant stepwise term is removed from the model until all of the remaining stepwise terms have a statistically significant contribution to the model.

3) Forward stepwise: This method begins with the model that would be selected by the forward entry method. From there, the algorithm alternates between backward elimination on the stepwise terms in the model and forward entry on the terms left out of the model. This continues until no terms meet the entry or removal criteria. The method is selected in the Example 7-7.

4) Backward stepwise: This method begins with the model that would be selected by the backward elimination method. From there, the algorithm alternates between forward entry on the terms left out of the model and backward elimination on the stepwise terms in the model. This continues until no terms meet the entry or removal criteria.

☑Include intercept in model: Default option which is used in the Example 7-7.

★Statistics: Click "Statistics" button (Figure 7-52), and the dialog box of Multinomial Logistic Regression: Statistics pops out (Figure 7-55).

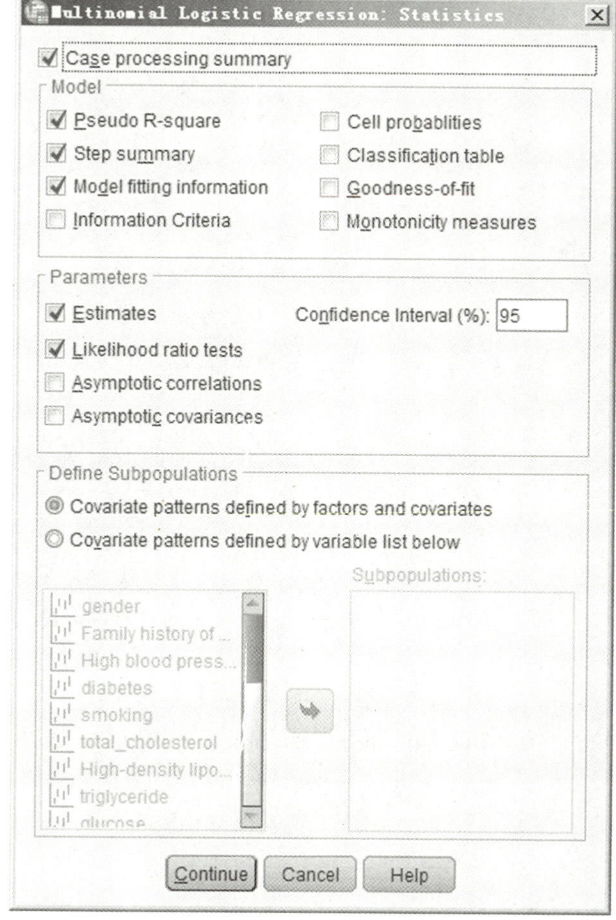

Figure 7-55 The Multinomial Logistic Regression: Statistics dialog box

☑ Case processing summary: This table contains information about the specified categorical variables. Checked by default.

◇Model.

☑Pseudo R-square: This table prints the "Cox" and "Snell" "Nagelkerke" and "McFadden R^2" statistics. Checked by default.

☑Step summary: This table summarizes the effects entered or removed at each step in a stepwise method. It is not produced unless a stepwise model is specified in the Model dialog box. Checked by default.

☑Model fitting information: This table compares the fitted and intercept-only models. Checked by default.

□Information Criteria: Akaike's information criterion (AIC) and Schwarz's Bayesian information criterion (BIC) will be printed if this option is checked.

□Cell probabilities: A table of the observed and expected frequencies (with residual) and proportions by covariate pattern and response category will be printed if this option is checked.

□Classification table: A table of the observed versus predicted responses will be printed if this option is checked.

□Goodness-of-fit: This table prints "Pearson" and "Deviance Chi-square" statistics. The two statistics are similar for a large sample.

□Monotonicity measures: A table with information on the number of concordant pairs, discordant pairs, tied pairs, Somers' D, Goodman and Kruskal's Gamma, Kendall's tau-a, and concordance index C will be printed if this option is checked.

◇Parameters: Statistics related to the model parameters.

☑Estimates: This table prints estimates of the model parameters, with a user-specified level of confidence. Checked by default.

☑Likelihood ratio tests: This table prints likelihood-ratio tests for the model partial effects. The null hypothesis is that all parameters of that effect are 0. Checked by default.

☑Asymptotic correlations: This table prints the parameter correlation matrix.

☑Asymptotic covariances: This table prints the parameter covariance matrix.

◇Define Subpopulations: To select a subset of the factors and covariates in order to define the covariate patterns used by "Cell probabilities" and the "Goodness-of-fit" tests.

⊙Covariate patterns defined by factors and covariates: Checked by default.

◎Covariate patterns defined by variable list below.

★Criteria: To define iteration convergence criteria. Click "Criteria" button (Figure 7-52), and the dialog box of Multinomial Logistic Regression: Convergence Criteria pops out (Figure 7-56).

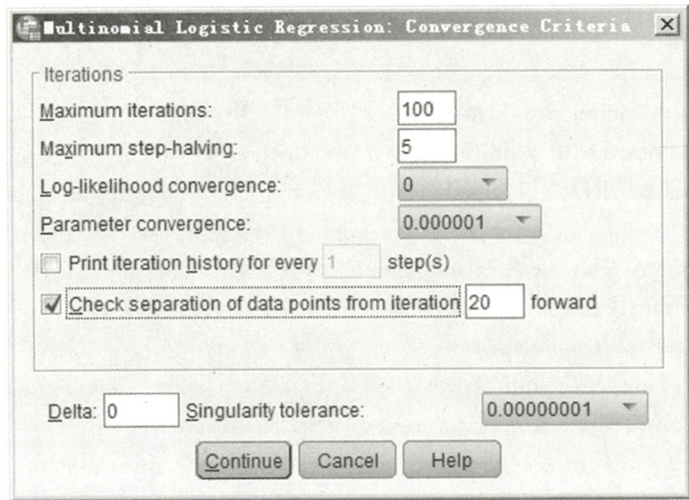

Figure 7-56 The Multinomial Logistic Regression: Convergence Criteria dialog box

◇Iterations: To define iteration parameters.

1) Maximum iterations: The default value is 100.

2) Maximum step-halving: The default value is 5.

3) Log-likelihood convergence: Convergence is assumed if the absolute change in the log-likelihood function is less than the specified value. If there is no change, process will stop by default. Specify a non-negative value.

4) Parameter convergence: Convergence is assumed if the absolute change in the parameter estimates is less than this value. If there is no change, process will stop by default. Specify a non-negative value.

□Print iteration history for every [1] step(s): The default value is 1.

☑Check separation of data points from iteration [20] forward: The default value is 20.

◇Delta [0]: This value is added to each empty cell of the cross tabulation of response category by covariate pattern. This helps to stabilize the algorithm and prevent bias in the estimates. Specify a non-negative value less than 1.

◇Singularity tolerance: [ ] Specify the tolerance used in checking for singularities.

★Options: Click "Options" button (Figure 7-52), and the dialog box of Multinomial Logistic Regression: Options pops out (Figure 7-57).

◇Dispersion Scale: The dispersion scaling value is used to correct the estimate of the parameter covariance matrix. Deviance estimates the scaling value using the deviance function (likelihood-ratio Chi-square) statistic. Pearson estimates the scaling value using the Pearson Chi-square statistic.

◇Stepwise Options: These options are ignored unless a stepwise model is specified in the Model dialog box.

1) Entry Probability: [0.05]. This is the probability of entry test statistic for variable entry. The larger the specified probability, the easier it is for a variable to enter the model. The default value is $P \leqslant 0.05$. This criterion is ignored unless the forward entry, forward stepwise, or backward stepwise method is selected.

2) Entry Test: This is the method for entering terms in stepwise methods. Choose between the

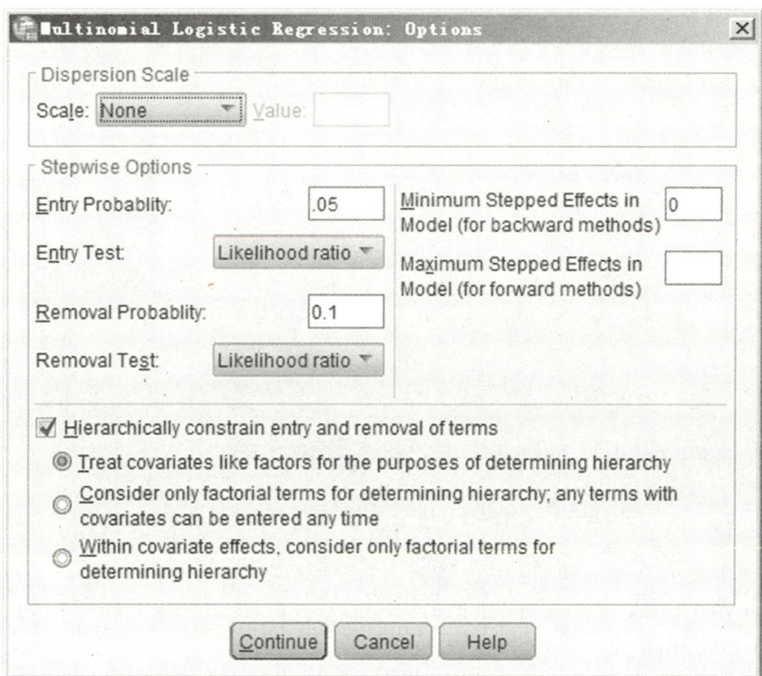

Figure 7-57 The Multinomial Logistic Regression:Options dialog box

likelihood-ratio test and score test. This criterion is ignored unless the forward entry, forward stepwise, or backward stepwise method is selected.

3) Removal Probability [0.1]: This is the probability of removal test statistic for variable removal. The larger the specified probability, the easier it is for a variable to remain in the model. The default value is $P \geqslant 0.10$. This criterion is ignored unless the backward elimination, forward stepwise, or backward stepwise method is selected.

4) Removal Test: This is the method for removing terms in stepwise methods. Choose between the likelihood-ratio test and Wald test. This criterion is ignored unless the backward elimination, forward stepwise, or backward stepwise method is selected.

5) Minimum Stepped Effects in Model (for backward methods): When using the backward elimination or backward stepwise methods, it specifies the minimum number of terms to include in the model. The intercept is not counted as a model term.

6) Maximum Stepped Effects in Model (for forward methods): When using the forward entry or forward stepwise methods, it specifies the maximum number of terms to include in the model. The intercept is not counted as a model term.

☑Hierarchically constrain entry and removal of terms: This option is checked by default to place restrictions on the inclusion of model terms. Hierarchy requires induding all lower order terms in the model first. For example, if the hierarchy requirement is in effect, the factors "BMI" and "Gender" must both be in the model before the "BMI * Gender" interaction can be added. The role of covariates in determining hierarchy is as follows:

⊙Treat covariates like factors for the purposes of determining hierarchy.

◎Consider only factorial terms for determining hierarchy; any terms with covariates can be entered any time.

◎Within covariate effects, consider only factorial terms for determining hierarchy. th

★Save: Save as new variable. Click "Save" button (Figure 7-52), and the dialog box of Multinomial Logistic Regression: Save pops out (Figure 7-58).

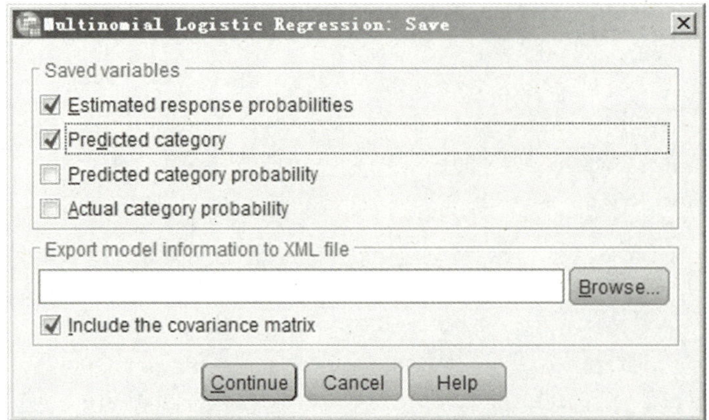

Figure 7-58 The Multinomial Logistic Regression: Save dialog box

◇ Saved variables.

☑Estimated response probabilities: These are the estimated probabilities of classifying a factor/covariate pattern into the response categories. There are as many estimated probabilities as there are categories of the response variable.

☑Predicted category: This is the response category with the largest expected probability for a factor/covariate pattern.

□Predicted category probability: This is the maximum of the estimated response probabilities.

□Actual category probability: This is the estimated probability of classifying a factor/covariate pattern into the observed category.

◇Export model information to XML file.

☑Include the covariance matrix: Checked by default.

7.5.5 Reading the output

(1) Frequencies and percentages of each category for the specified categorical variables as shown in Figure 7-59. There are 262 valid records be included in the following analysis with 18 missing records exclude.

(2) This table prints Pearson and Deviance Chi-square statistics for goodness-of-fit tests (Figure 7-60). Pearson statistic is used to test the agreement of observed frequencies and expected frequencies. The larger the P value of the Pearson Chi-square test, the better the goodness-of-fit. Deviance function (likelihood-ratio Chi-square) statistic is used to test the deviation of the current model to saturated model. The less the D value of the likelihood-ratio Chi-square test, the larger the P value. The fitted model is significant with both larger P values.

Case Processing Summary

		N	Marginal Percentage
plaque	no plaque	166	63.4%
	non-calcified plaque	12	4.6%
	mixed plaque	38	14.5%
	calcified plaque	46	17.6%
gender	female	122	46.6%
	male	140	53.4%
Family history of coronary heart disease	yes	36	13.7%
	no	226	86.3%
High blood pressure or hypertension	yes	80	30.5%
	no	182	69.5%
diabetes	yes	9	3.4%
	no	253	96.6%
smoking	yes	90	34.4%
	no	172	65.6%
total_cholesterol	high	113	43.1%
	normal	149	56.9%
High-density lipoprotein	high	172	65.6%
	normal	90	34.4%
triglyceride	high	106	40.5%
	normal	156	59.5%
glucose	high	35	13.4%
	normal	227	86.6%
creatinine	high	6	2.3%
	normal	256	97.7%
Valid		262	100.0%
Missing		18	
Total		280	
Subpopulation		262[a]	

a. The dependent variable has only one value observed in 262 (100.0%) subpopulations.

Figure 7-59 Case processing summary

Goodness-of-Fit

	Chi-Square	df	Sig.
Pearson	782.585	771	.378
Deviance	431.473	771	1.000

Figure 7-60 Goodness-of-Fit tests

(3) Model Fitting Information table (Figure 7-61) shows that the fitted model is significant with $P<0.001$. Individual tests of terms included in the final model are shown in Likelihood Ratio Tests table (Figure 7-62). The variables "gender" "hdlp" "triglyceride" and "age" variables enter the final model with significant influences on the plaque formation ($P\leq 0.015$).

Model Fitting Information

Model	Model Fitting Criteria	Likelihood Ratio Tests		
	-2 Log Likelihood	Chi-Square	df	Sig.
Intercept Only	532.303			
Final	431.473	100.830	12	.000

Figure 7-61 Model fitting information

Likelihood Ratio Tests

Effect	Model Fitting Criteria	Likelihood Ratio Tests		
	-2 Log Likelihood of Reduced Model	Chi-Square	df	Sig.
Intercept	431.473[a]	.000	0	.
gender	444.370	12.897	3	.005
hdlp	447.475	16.002	3	.001
triglyceride	441.985	10.512	3	.015
age	481.246	49.774	3	.000

The chi-square statistic is the difference in -2 log-likelihoods between the final model and a reduced model. The reduced model is formed by omitting an effect from the final model. The null hypothesis is that all parameters of that effect are 0.

a. This reduced model is equivalent to the final model because omitting the effect does not increase the degrees of freedom.

Figure 7-62 Likelihood ratio tests

(4) Parameter estimates result (Figure 7-63).

1) Set the first category of plaque as the reference category, i. e. "no plaque".

2) *B* is partial regression coefficient. Category with the maximum assignment is automatically set as the reference category for each influence factor, and the corresponding *B* value is 0.

3) Exp(*B*) represents the exposure odds ratio of each category to the reference category, i. e. *OR*. The influence size and direction are reflected by *OR* value.

4) To non-calcified plaque formation, significant influence factors are "gender" and "triglyceride" with *P* values for *B* lower than 0.05. The higher the triglyceride, the easier non-calcified plaque formation (*OR* =5.411, 95% *CI*: 1.275-22.970). Compared with male, non-calcified plaque formation unlikely happen for female (*OR*=0.100, 95% *CI*: 0.012-0.819).

5) To mixed plaque formation, significant influence factors are "gender" "hdlp" "triglyceride" and "age" with *P* values for *B* lower than 0.05. The higher the triglyceride and the older, the easier mixed plaque formation. Compared with male and people with normal "hdlp", mixed plaque formation unlikely happen for female and people with higher "hdlp".

6) To calcified plaque formation, significant influence factors are "gender" and "hdlp" with *P* values for *B* lower than 0.001. The older, the easier it is for calcified plaque formation. Compared with normal people, calcified plaque formation unlikely happen for people with higher "hdlp".

Parameter Estimates

plaque[a]		B	Std. Error	Wald	df	Sig.	Exp(B)	95% Confidence Interval for Exp(B) Lower Bound	Upper Bound
non-calcified plaque	Intercept	-3.799	2.931	1.680	1	.195			
	[gender=1]	-2.304	1.074	4.606	1	.032	.100	.012	.819
	[gender=2]	0[b]	.	.	0	.	.	.	.
	[hdlp=1]	-.344	.691	.247	1	.619	.709	.183	2.749
	[hdlp=2]	0[b]	.	.	0	.	.	.	.
	[triglyceride=1]	1.688	.738	5.240	1	.022	5.411	1.275	22.970
	[triglyceride=2]	0[b]	.	.	0	.	.	.	.
	age	.020	.055	.140	1	.708	1.021	.917	1.136
mixed plaque	Intercept	-10.480	2.071	25.595	1	.000			
	[gender=1]	-1.100	.434	6.424	1	.011	.333	.142	.779
	[gender=2]	0[b]	.	.	0	.	.	.	.
	[hdlp=1]	-1.088	.439	6.131	1	.013	.337	.142	.797
	[hdlp=2]	0[b]	.	.	0	.	.	.	.
	[triglyceride=1]	1.030	.426	5.840	1	.016	2.800	1.215	6.455
	[triglyceride=2]	0[b]	.	.	0	.	.	.	.
	age	.170	.036	21.980	1	.000	1.185	1.104	1.272
calcified plaque	Intercept	-11.290	2.005	31.712	1	.000			
	[gender=1]	-.347	.387	.804	1	.370	.707	.331	1.510
	[gender=2]	0[b]	.	.	0	.	.	.	.
	[hdlp=1]	-1.547	.417	13.793	1	.000	.213	.094	.482
	[hdlp=2]	0[b]	.	.	0	.	.	.	.
	[triglyceride=1]	.561	.402	1.948	1	.163	1.753	.797	3.856
	[triglyceride=2]	0[b]	.	.	0	.	.	.	.
	age	.190	.035	29.639	1	.000	1.209	1.129	1.295

a. The reference category is: no plaque.

b. This parameter is set to zero because it is redundant.

Figure 7-63 Parameter estimates

(5) Discriminant effects as shown in Figure 7-64. The total correct percent is 67.9% for discriminont. Classification table can only provide limited information for model goodness-of-fit. When the observed frequencies of each dependent variable category are different, the algorithm will more likely classify the observed to specific category with a larger sample.

Classification

Observed	Predicted: no plaque	non-calcified plaque	mixed plaque	calcified plaque	Percent Correct
no plaque	156	0	6	4	94.0%
non-calcified plaque	10	0	1	1	0.0%
mixed plaque	23	0	7	8	18.4%
calcified plaque	24	0	7	15	32.6%
Overall Percentage	81.3%	0.0%	8.0%	10.7%	67.9%

Figure 7-64 Classification

7.5.6 Drawing conclusions

A significant model is fitted with four independent variables "gender" "hdlp" "triglyceride" and "age", and the influence of each variable on the plaque formation is significant.

The higher the triglyceride, the easier it is for non-calcified or mixed plaque formation. The older, the mixed or calcified plaque formation. Compared with male, non-calcified or mixed plaque formation unlikely happen for female. Compared with normal people, mixed or calcified plaque formation unlikely happen for people with higher "hdlp".

7.6 Curve fit

7.6.1 Description

Relationships among many variables in medicine are usually curvilinear, and thus quantitative relations need to be described by curvilinear equation. Such process is called curve fit in statistics.

The "Curve Estimation" procedure in SPSS produces curve estimation regression statistics and related plots for 11 different curve estimation regression models, with predicted values, residuals, and prediction intervals saved as new variables.

7.6.2 SPSS data format

The SPSS data file for "Curve Estimation" procedure requires at least two relative variables, and all of them are quantitative.

7.6.3 Example

Example 7-8 The data file "curvefit. sav" is used as the Example 7-8, which has 23 rows and 2 columns representing 23 records and two relative variables x and y. In order to explore antibacterial effect of antibiotic cefoperazone on bacillus subtilis, cefoperazone concentration x (unit: μg/ml) and inhibition zone diameter y (unit: mm) are recorded in one experiment.

7.6.4 Running the commands

The "Curve Estimation" analysis is located in the "Regression" submenu, under the "Analyze" menu:

Analyze

Regression

CurveEstimation

▶**Dependent**: y

▶**Independent** ⊙**Variable**: x

☑**Include constant in equation**

☑**Plot models**

▶**Models**

☑**Linear** ☑**Quadratic** ☑**Compound** ☑**Growth**

☑**Logarithmic** ☑**Cubic** ☑**S** ☑**Exponential**

☑**Inverse** ☑**Power** ☑**Logistic**

Saves

☑**Predicted values**

The main dialog box of Curve Estimation is listed in Figure 7-65.

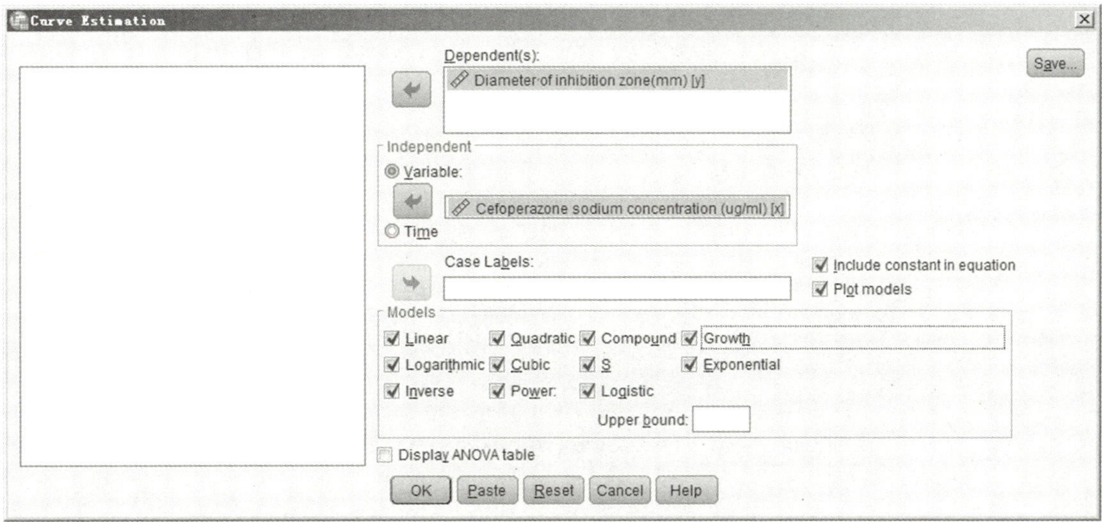

Figure 7-65 The Curve Estimation dialog box

◇Dependent(s):One or more dependent variables should be selected in this box.

◇Independent.

⊙Variable:Selected by default. One independent variable can be placed here.

◎Time:If "Time" is selected, a time variable will be generated where the length of time between cases is uniform. The dependent variable should be a time-series measure.

◇Case Labels:Select a variable for labeling cases in scatter plots.

☑Include constant in equation:This option is checked by default.

☑Plot models: To plot the values of the dependent variable and each selected model against the independent variable.

◇Models.

☑Linear: $Y = b_0 + (b_1 * x)$.

☑Logarithmic: $Y = b_0 + b_1 * ln(x)$.

☑Inverse: $Y = b_0 + b_1/x$.

☑Quadratic: $Y = b_0 + b_1 * x + b_2 * x^2$.

☑Cubic: $Y = b_0 + b_1 * x + b_2 * x^2 + b_3 * x^3$.

☑Power: $Y = b_0 * (x^{b1})$.

☑Compound: $Y = b_0 * (b_1^x)$.

☑S: $Y = e^{[b_0+(b_1/x)]}$.

☑Logistic: $Y = 1/[1/u + b_0 * (b_1{}^x)]$. where u is the upper boundary value. After selecting Logistic, specify the upper boundary value to use in the regression equation. The value must be a positive number that is greater than the largest dependent variable value.

☑Growth: $Y = e^{(b_0+(b_1 * x))}$.

☑Exponential: $Y = b_0 * e^{(b_1 * x)}$.

□Display ANOVA table.

★Save:Save as new variable. Click "Save" button, and the dialog box of Curve Estimation:Save pops out (Figure 7-66).

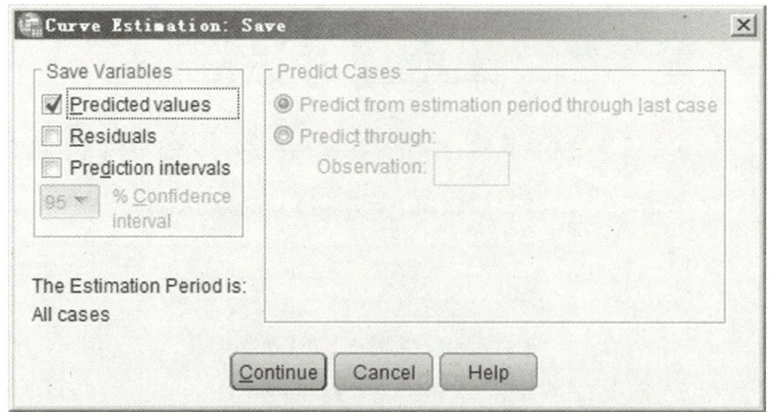

Figure 7–66 The Curve Estimation: Save dialog box

◇Save Variables.

☑Predicted values.

☑Residuals: Observed value of the dependent variable minus the model predicted value.

☑Prediction intervals: Intervals estimation of predicted values, including tolerance interval of individual values and confidence interval of the mean. The default interval is 95%.

◇Predict Cases.

⊙Predict from estimation period through last case: Values for all cases in the file are predicted based on the cases in the estimation period. The estimation period, displayed at the bottom of the dialog box, is defined with the Range sub dialog box of the Select Cases option on the Data menu. If no estimation period has been defined, all cases are used to predict values.

◎Predict through: Observation: ☐. Values through the specified observation number are predicted based on the cases in the estimation period.

7.6.5 Reading the output

(1) All 11 models are significant ($P<0.001$) (Figure 7–65). The two highest R^2 are 0.987 and 0.984 for power and cubic models respectively. Power model is selected according to the scatter plot in this example with the regression equation: $\hat{y} = 5.726x^{0.229}$.

Model Summary and Parameter Estimates

Dependent Variable: Diameter of inhibition zone(mm)

	Model Summary					Parameter Estimates			
Equation	R Square	F	df1	df2	Sig	Constant	b1	b2	b3
Linear	.850	118.900	1	21	.000	9.966	.058		
Logarithmic	.975	804.741	1	21	.000	3.359	2.835		
Inverse	.616	33.660	1	21	.000	15.638	-30.250		
Quadratic	.961	244.134	2	20	.000	8.245	.137	.000	
Cubic	.984	378.853	3	19	.000	7.299	.219	-.002	5.050E-6
Compound	.768	69.363	1	21	.000	9.947	1.004		
Power	.987	1572.400	1	21	.000	5.726	.229		
S	.726	55.693	1	21	.000	2.747	-2.637		
Growth	.768	69.363	1	21	.000	2.297	.004		
Exponential	.768	69.363	1	21	.000	9.947	.004		
Logistic	.768	69.363	1	21	.000	.101	.996		

The independent variable is Cefoperazone sodium concentration (ug/ml).

Figure 7–67 The output of model summary and parameter estimates

(2) Change the models selection with only power left, then repeat previous operation, the fitted curve is shown below with perfect performance (Figure 7-68).

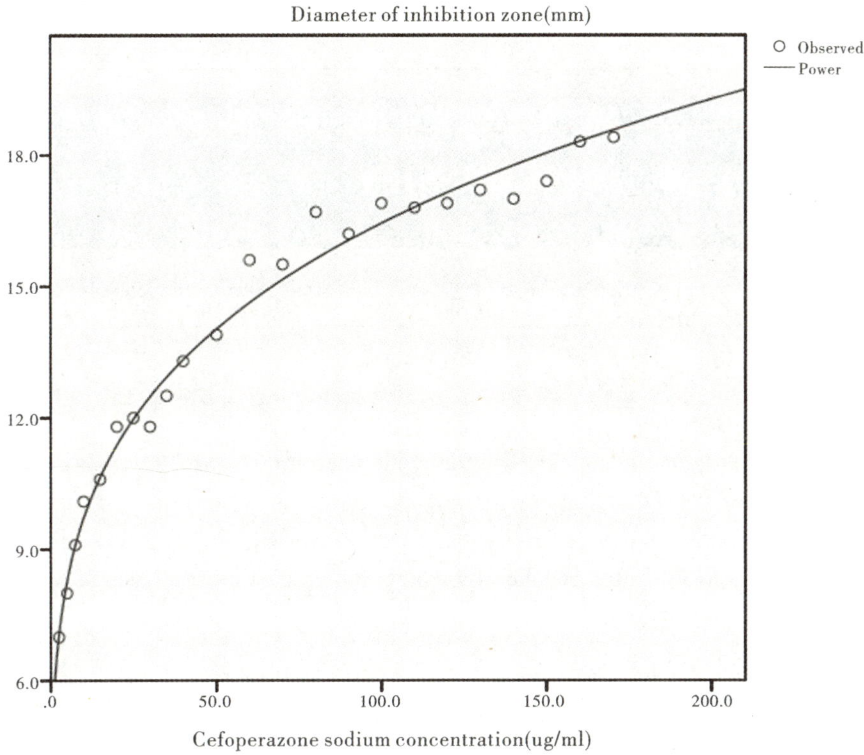

Figure 7-68 Curve fit of power model

7.6.6 Drawing conclusions

Power model is the most appropriate to describe the relationship of cefoperazone concentration x and inhibition zone diameter y.

Wang Ling, Wang Shiqi

Chapter 8

Classify

Classification is an important component of virtually all scientific researches. Statistical techniques concerned with classification are essentially comprised of two types, cluster analysis and discriminant analysis. Cluster analysis aims to uncover groups of observations from unclassified data, while discriminant analysis works with classified data to derive rules for classifying new individuals on the basis of their observed variable values.

8.1 Hierarchical cluster analysis

8.1.1 Description

Cluster analysis is a set of tools for building clusters from multivariate data objects. The aim of cluster analysis is to construct groups with homogeneous properties. The objects in the same cluster should be as similar as possible, and as dissimilar as possible to those in other clusters. SPSS offers three methods for the cluster analysis: *K*-Means Cluster, Hierarchical Cluster, and Two-Step Cluster. Here, only hierarchical cluster is introduced.

According to choosing cluster cases or choosing cluster variables, hierarchical cluster contains case clustering and variable clustering. The agglomeration schedule is as follows.

First, it sets n cases (or variables) as n clusters, and then combine the two clusters with the smallest distance (or largest correlation coefficient), leading to $n-1$ clusters remained.

Second, find the closest two clusters and combine them again leading to $n-2$ clusters, and then repeat. This process continues until all cases (or variables) are in one cluster.

Generally, cluster analysis can be divided into two steps. First, choosing proximity measure. A proximity measure is defined to measure the "closeness" of the objects (cases or variables). The "closer" the objects are, the more homogeneous they are. Then, selecting cluster-building algorithm. Measure the objects that are assigned to clusters on the basis of the proximity. Therefore, the differences between clusters can become large and objects in a group can become as close as possible.

SPSS can output vertical dendrogram, horizontal dendrogram or tree structure diagram, *etc.*, to indicate the categorical results.

8.1.2 Example

Example 8-1 The data file "regression. sav" is used as the Example 8-1. Use "Cluster analysis" to analyze 11 full blood counts and blood biochemical markers ("rbc" "hb" "wbc" "plt" "tbil" "dbil" "alt" "ast" "alp" "bun" and "cr").

8.1.3 Operational Process

(1) Step-by-step process.

Analyze

Classify

Hierarchical Cluster

Click "Analyze" from the menu bar, then "Classify" from the pull-down menu, "Hierarchical Cluster" from the second pull-down menu to open Hierarchical Cluster Analysis main dialog box (Figure 8-1).

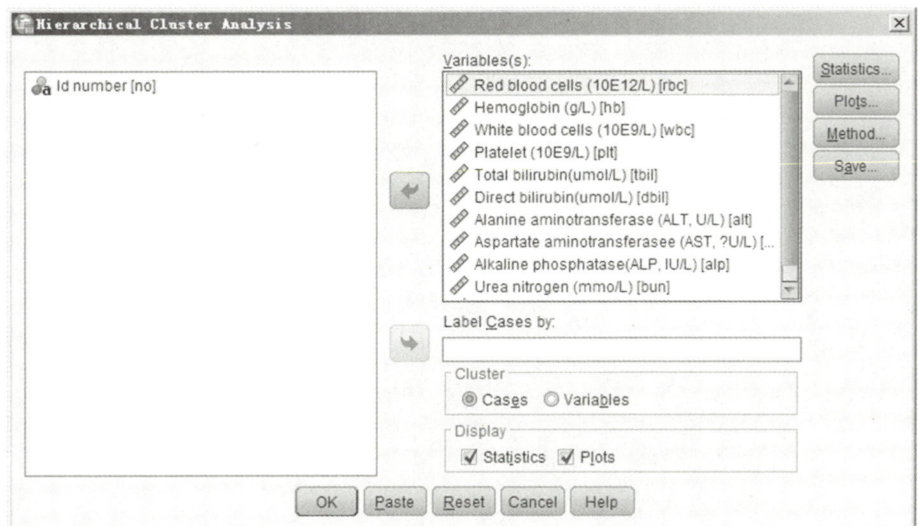

Figure 8-1 The Hierarchical Cluster Analysis dialog box

◇Variable(s): Select 11 variables "rbc" "hb" "wbc" "plt" "tbil" "dbil" "alt" "ast" "alp" "bun" and "cr" from variable list box and move them to "Variable(s)" box as analysis variables.

◇Label Cases by: It is an option to label cases, and can be helpful to read the output. If no variable is chosen, it will use row numbers as output. Only use for cases classification.

◇Cluster: Clustering type.

◎Cases (system default): Case clustering.

⊙Variables: Variable clustering. This item is selected in the Example 8-1.

◇Display: Output options.

☑Statistics: Statistics. ☑Plots: Clustering plots.

★Statistics. Click "Statistics" button, and the dialog box of Hierarchical Cluster Analysis: Statistics pops out (Figure 8-2).

☑Agglomeration schedule: The table you can see what's happening at each step of the clustering procedure, it shows the distance or similarity between the individuals or clusters.

□Proximity matrix: The distance or similarity matrix between cases or variables.

◇Cluster Membership: Display the cluster to which each case is assigned at one or more stages in the combination of clusters.

⊙None (system default): Do not show clustering membership.

◎Single solution: Display clustering membership by a fixed number of clusters. If you fill with "3", each case of 3 clusters is displayed.

◎Range of solutions: Display clustering membership by a range of clusters.

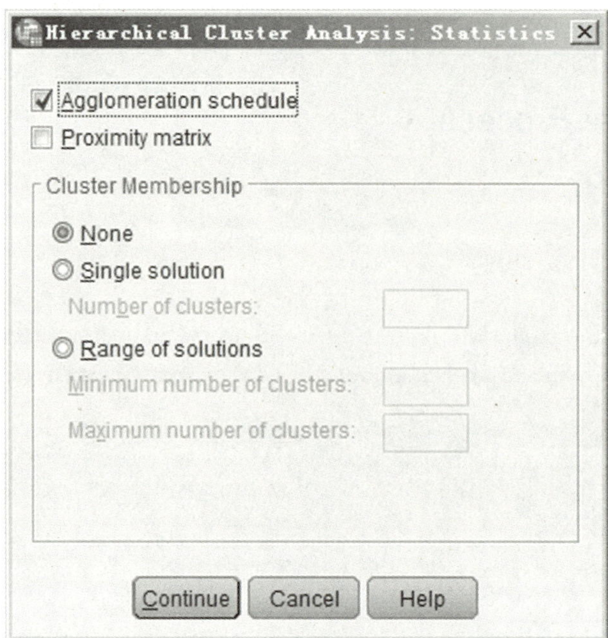

Figure 8-2 The Hierarchical Cluster Analysis:Statistics dialog box

★Plots:Plots button(Figure 8-1) allows you to select the outputs that will illustrate the cluster solution (Figure 8-3).

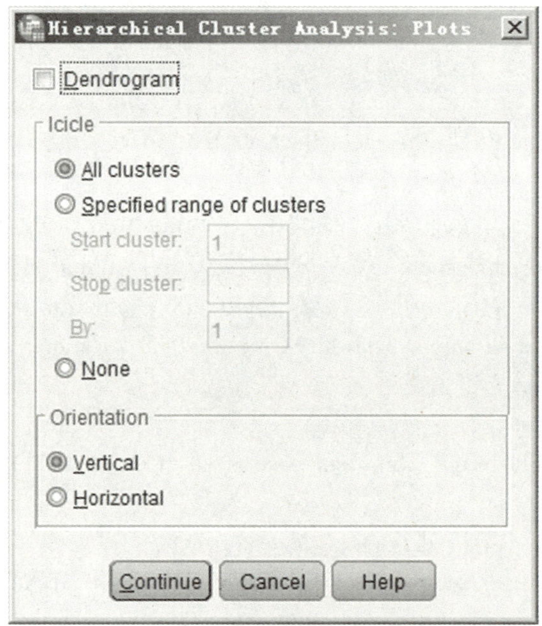

Figure 8-3 The Hierarchical Cluster Analysis: Plots dialog box

□Dendrogram:A tree graph which displays the clusters merges at each step and the values of the coefficients.

◇Icicle.

⊙All clusters (system default):SPSS can generate icicle plot automatically.

◎Specified range of clusters:Show a specified range of icicle plots. For example, we fill with "Start cluster" with 1, "Stop cluster" with 5, "By" with 2, the results show the icicle plots of 1 cluster, 3 clusters and 5 clusters.

◎None: Do not show icicle plot.

◇Orientation: The orientation of icicle plot. If you have a large number of cases (variables) to cluster, you can make a horizontal icicle plot.

⊙Vertical (system default): Vertical icicle plot.

◎Horizontal: Horizontal icicle plot.

★Method: Click "Method" (Figure 8-1), and the dialog box of Hierarchical Cluster Analysis: Method pops out (Figure 8-4).

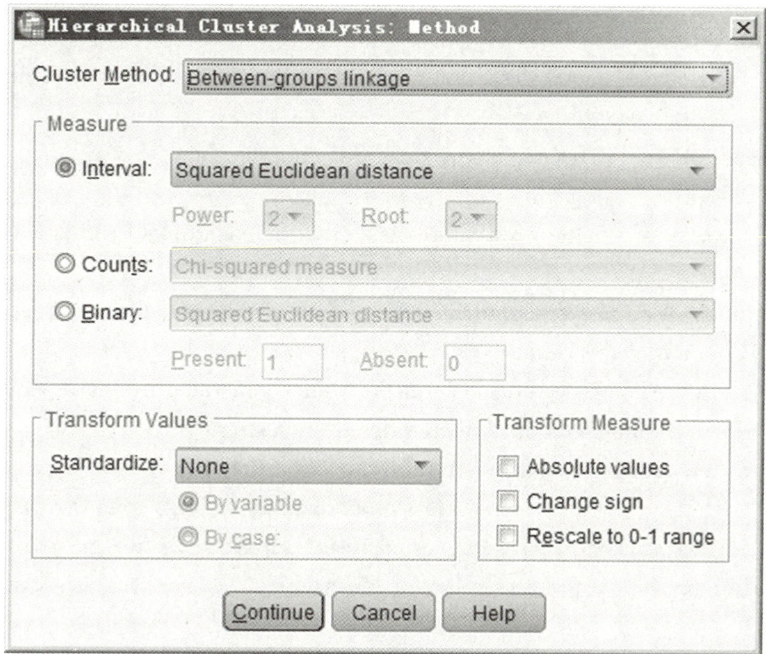

Figure 8-4 The Hierarchical Cluster Analysis: Method dialog box

Cluster Method: It defines the distance between two clusters (cluster A and cluster B).

1) Between-groups linkage: The distance as the average distance found between one case from the cluster A and one case from the cluster B.

2) Within-groups linkage: The distance as the average of all the distances between the cases within a single new cluster determined by combining cluster A and cluster B.

3) Nearest neighbor: The distance as the minimum distance found between one case from cluster A and one case from cluster B.

4) Furthest neighbor: The distance as the maximum distance found between one case from cluster A and one case from cluster B.

5) Centroid clustering: The distance as the distance between the centroid of cluster A and the centroid of cluster B.

6) Median clustering: The distance as the distance between median of cluster A and the median of cluster B.

7) Ward's method: The distance as the distance of all clusters to the grand average of the sample.

◇Measure: The method of measuring distance.

⊙Interval: Continuous variable (quantitative variable). Available alternatives are "Euclidean distance" "Squared Euclidean distance" "Cosine" "Pearson correlation" "Chebychev" "Block" and "Minkovskiand Customized". Cosine measures is the cosine angle of the two vectors. Block means absolute distance. For customized distance, selecting this option to activate the following boxes: Power and Root.

◎Counts: Discrete variable (count variable). Including Chi-square (χ^2) measure and Phi-square (Φ^2) measure.

◎Binary: Provided nearly 30 kinds of measure methods including "Euclidean distance" and "squared Euclidean distance".

◇Transform Values.

Standardize: Standardized transform of data.

1) None: No transform.

2) Z scores: Values are standardized to z scores, with a mean of 0 and a standard deviation of 1.

3) Range from −1 to 1: Values are standardized to a range from −1 to 1, that is, each value is divided by the range of the values.

4) Range 0 to 1: Values are standardized to a range from 0 to 1, that is, each value subtracts minimum value and then divides by the range.

5) Maximum magnitude of 1: The maximum standardized value is 1, that is, each value is divided by the maximum of the values.

6) Mean of 1: The mean of standardized values is 1, that is, each value is divided by the mean of the values.

7) Standard deviation of 1: The standard deviation of standardized values is 1, that is, each value is divided by standard deviation of the values.

◇Transform Measures: Allows you to transform the values generated by the distance measure.

□Absolute values. It eliminates the direction of the linkage.

□Change sign: We change the sign of the distance measures.

□Rescale to 0–1 range: The measures are standardized to a range from 0 to 1.

★Save: "Save" dialog is used to save clustering results in the data file, only used for cases cluster. Click "Save" button (Figure 8–1), the dialog box of Hierarchical Cluster Analysis: Save pops out (Figure 8–5).

◇Cluster Membership: We save cluster membership label for each case. Saved variables can then be used in subsequent analyses to explore other differences between groups.

⊙None (system default): No output.

◎Single solution: Only one variable about cluster membership label is generated when the numbers of clusters is determined.

◎Range of solutions: 2 or more variables about cluster membership label is generated, the number of clusters is determined by a sequence of cluster solutions.

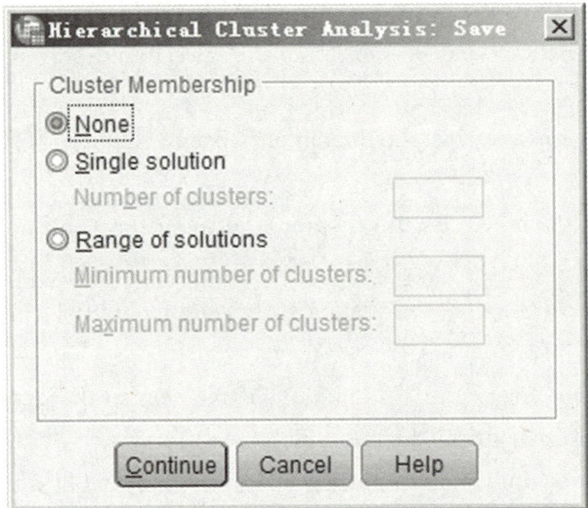

Figure 8–5 The Hierarchical Cluster Analysis: Save dialog box

(2) Process.

Analyze

Classify

Hierarchical Cluster

▸**Variable(s): rbc / hb / wbc / plt / tbil / dbil / alt / ast / alp / bun / cr**

Cluster

⊙**Variables**

Display

☑**Statistics**

☑**Plots**

Statistics

☑**Agglomeration schedule**

☑**Proximity Matrix**

Plots

☑**Dendrogram**

Icicle

⊙**All clusters**

Orientation

⊙**Vertical**

Method

Cluster: Between-groups linkage

Measure:

⊙**Interval: Pearson correlation**

8.1.4 Main output results

SPSS first produce a "Case Processing Summary" which lists the number of valid cases, the number of missing cases. The proximity matrix is the second table in the output if requested.

(1) Agglomeration Schedule (Figure 8-6): The agglomeration schedule follows proximity matrix. The number of steps in the agglomeration schedule is the number of variables (cases) subtracting 1. In the Example 8-1, "rbc" "hb" "wbc" "plt" "tbil" "dbil" "alt" "ast" "alp" "bun" and "cr" represent as 1-11 variables. There are 10 steps because 11 variables are used to analyze. As shown in Figure 8-6, variable 7 and variable 8 ("alt" and "ast") are combined at the first stage because their Pearson correlation coefficient ($r=0.949$) is the highest. The pairs with smaller coefficient are more heterogeneous than previous combinations. Here, the first five steps of the clustering are listed.

Step1: Variable 7 and Variable 8 ("alt" and "ast").

Step2: Variable 1 and Variable 2 ("rbc" and "hb").

Step3: Variable 5 and Variable 6 ("tbil" and "dbil").

Step4: Variable 3 and Variable 4 ("wbc" and "plt").

Step5: Variable 7, Variable 8 and Variable 10("alt" "ast" and "bun").

Agglomeration Schedule

Stage	Cluster Combined		Coefficients	Stage Cluster First Appears		Next Stage
	Cluster 1	Cluster 2		Cluster 1	Cluster 2	
1	7	8	.949	0	0	5
2	1	2	.812	0	0	6
3	5	6	.710	0	0	6
4	3	4	.554	0	0	9
5	7	10	.442	1	0	7
6	1	5	.174	2	3	8
7	7	11	.164	5	0	8
8	1	7	.048	6	7	10
9	3	9	-.023	4	0	10
10	1	3	-.076	8	9	0

Figure 8-6 Agglomeration Schedule of hierarchical clustering analysis

(2) Vertical icicle plot (Figure 8-7): Like the agglomeration schedule, Icicle Plot displays the homogeneity between two cases. Each grey bars (i. e. column) in the plot is one variable (case), each row represents a cluster solution with different numbers of clusters. You can read the figure from the top to down, as following.

1 cluster: ("rbc" "hb" "wbc" "plt" "tbil" "dbil" "alt" "ast" "alp" "bun" "cr").

2 clusters: ("alp" "plt" "wbc") ("rbc" "hb" "tbil" "dbil" "alt" "ast" "bun" "cr").

3 clusters: ("alp") ("plt" "wbc") ("rbc" "hb" "tbil" "dbil" "alt" "ast" "bun" "cr").

4 clusters: ("alp") ("plt" "wbc") ("cr" "bun" "alt" "ast") ("tbil" "dbil" "hb" "rbc").

5 clusters: ("alp") ("plt" "wbc") ("cr") ("bun" "alt" "ast") ("tbil" "dbil" "hb" "rbc").

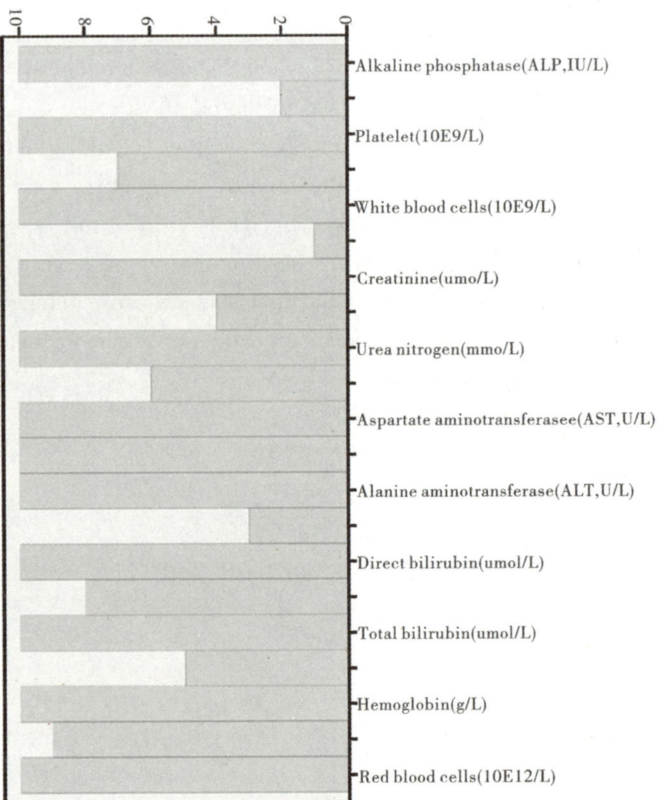

Figure 8-7 Vertical icicle plot of hierarchical cluster analysis

(3) Dendrogram (Figure 8-8): The dendrogram is a visual display of clustering process. The distances are rescaled from 0 to 25, the ratio of the rescaled distances is same as the ratio of distance. From left to right, clusters are getting more similar. In the Example 8-1, corresponding to the smallest rescaled distance, variable 7 and variable 8 are the most similar among all pairs. What you see in this plot gives the similar information as the results from the agglomeration schedule and icicle plot.

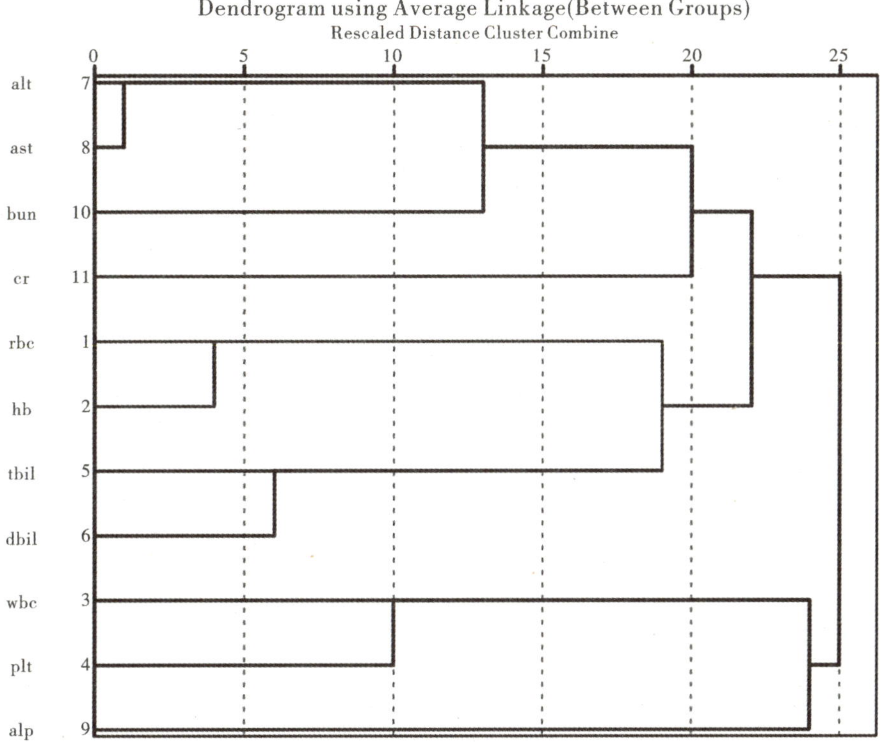

Figure 8-8 Dendrogram of hierarchical cluster analysis

8.2 Discriminant analysis

8.2.1 Description

In medical research, we often encounter problems on determining the classification of subjects. For example, a medical researcher may record different variables relating to patients' backgrounds (clinical signs, symptoms, laboratory parameters, *etc.*) in order to find out which variables can predict the type of the disease best.

Discriminant analysis (also known as discriminant function analysis) is a powerful classificatory technique. A set of discriminant functions are established from a sample of cases where group membership is known, and then classification rules (i. e., weights and linear combination resulting from the discriminant functions) are used in the classificatory analysis to assign new cases to the pre-existing groups.

The data used in discriminant analysis involve multiple variables. The assumptions required for a discriminant analysis are multivariate normality and homogeneity of variance-covariance matrices. The discriminant analysis can be done by discriminant analysis module of SPSS software.

8.2.2 Example

Example 8-2 The data file "discriminant. sav" is used as the Example 8-2, which has 23 observations (rows) and 6 variables (columns). To investigate the role of some electrocardiographic parameters in identifying healthy people, patients with aortic atherosclerosis and patients with coronary heart disease, ECG data about 23 patients who had been diagnosed are collected. The variables are: "x1" "x2" "x3" "x4" "x5" and "category". Five variables are independent variables, and "category" is grouping variable. The codes for the grouping variables are as following: 1 = "healthy", 2 = "aortic sclerosis", 3 = "coronary heart disease".

8.2.3 Operation Process

(1) Step-by-step process

Analyze

Classify

Discriminant

Click "Analyze" from the menu bar, then click "Classify" from the pull-down menu, "Discriminant" from the second pull-down menu to open Discriminant Analysis main dialog box (Figure 8-9).

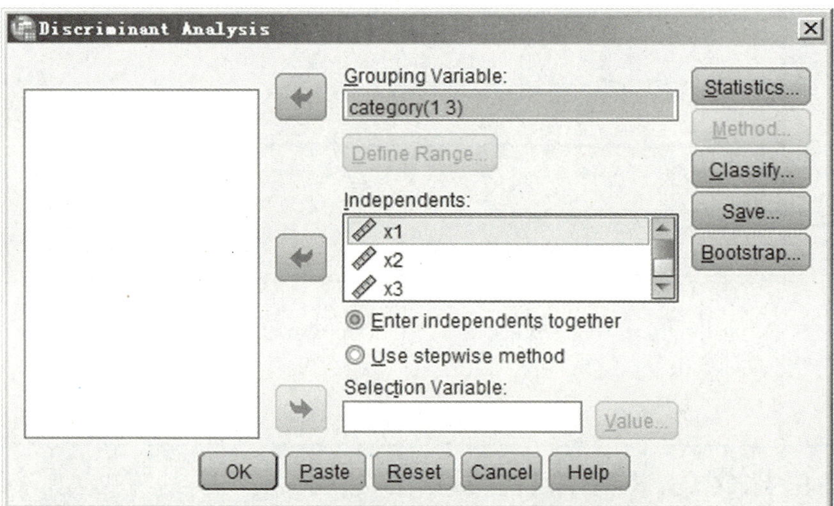

Figure 8-9 The Discriminant Analysis dialog box

◇Grouping Variable: Click grouping variable "category" and then click the right arrow button to move into the "Grouping Variable" box, then "Define Range" box is activated. Click this button, then open the Discriminant Analysis: Define Range dialog box, input the minimum and the maximum of the grouping variables respectively. In the Example 8-2, the minimum and maximum values of the grouping variable "category" are number 1 and number 3, respectively.

◇Independents: move "x1" "x2" "x3" "x4" and "x5" into "Independents box".

⊙Enter independents together (system default): All the independent variables enter the discriminant equation simultaneously.

◎Use stepwise method: Stepwise discriminant analysis. When you have a lot of independent variables, the stepwise method can be useful by automatically select the "best" variables to use in the model. The stepwise method starts with a model that doesn't include any of the independent variables. At each step, the independent with the largest "F-to-Enter" value that exceeds the entry criteria is added to the model, and the "F-to-Move" value is smaller than that of the remove criteria should be excluded from the model.

◇Selection Variable:Select cases. The "Value" button is activated after the variable are selected into "Selection Variable" box (the grouping variable and the selected independent variables in model cannot be selected). Click "Value" button and fill with the selected value, only selected cases are involved in analysis. If not selected, all cases are involved in discriminant analysis.

★Statistics. Click "Statistics" button, and the dialog box of Discriminant Analysis:Statistics pops out (Figure 8-10).

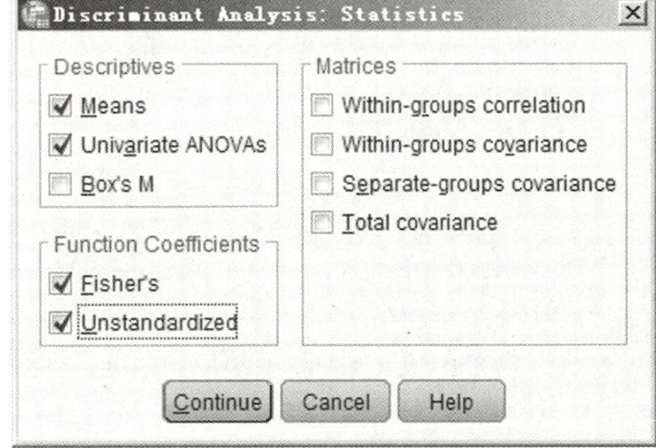

Figure 8-10 The Discriminant Analysis:Statistics dialog box

◇Descriptive:Descriptive statistics.

☑Means.

☑Univariate ANOVAs.

☐Box's M: Box test of homogeneity of covariance matrices.

◇Matrices.

☐Within-groups correlation: Displays a pooled within-groups correlation matrix that is obtained by averaging the separate covariance matrices for all groups.

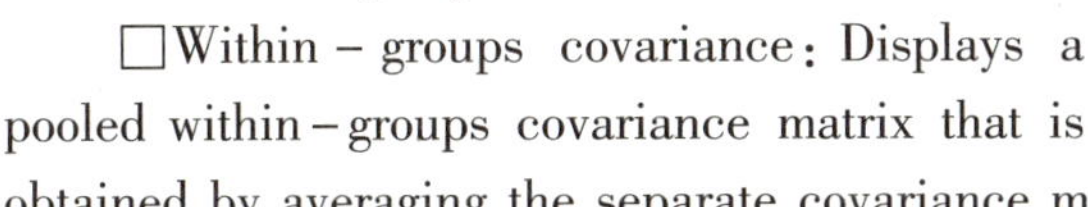

☐Within-groups covariance: Displays a pooled within-groups covariance matrix that is obtained by averaging the separate covariance matrices for all groups.

☐Separate-groups covariance:Displays separate covariance matrices for each group.

☐Total covariance:Displays a covariance matrix from all cases as a single sample.

◇Function Coefficients.

☑Fisher's:Displays Fisher's classification function coefficients.

☑Unstandardized:Displays the unstandardized discriminant function coefficients.

★Method: Only used for stepwise discriminant analysis. When we choose "Use stepwise method", "Method" is activated. Click "Method" button (Figure 8-9), and the dialog box of "Discriminant Analysis:Stepwise Method" pops out (Figure 8-11).

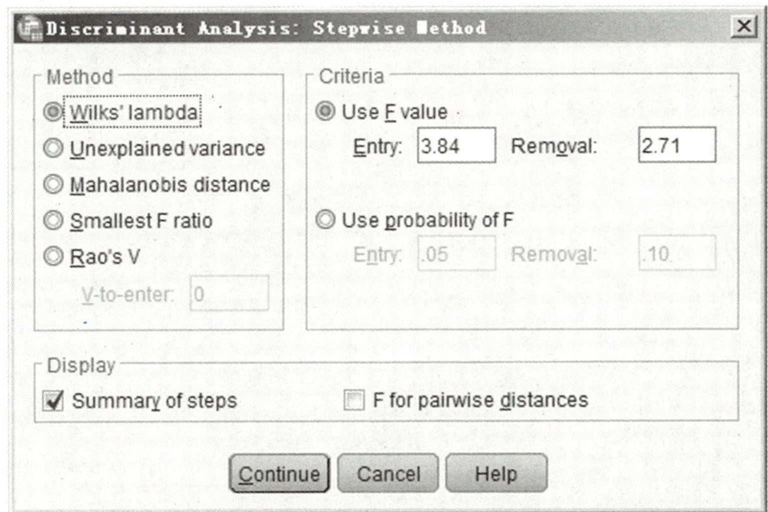

Figure 8-11 The Discriminant Analysis:Stepwise Method dialog box

◇Method:Select the statistic to be used for entering or removing new variables for stepwise discriminant analysis.

⊙Wilks' lambda: The variable that minimizes the overall Wilks' lambda is entered (system default).

◎Unexplained variance: The variable that minimizes the sum of the unexplained variation between groups is entered.

◎Mahalanobis distance: The variable that maximizes Mahalanobis distance is entered.

◎Smallest F ratio: The variable that maximizes F ratio computed from the Mahalanobis distance between groups is entered.

◎Rao's V: Maximize Rao V.

V-to-enter [0]: The increase in Rao's V is entered.

The variable that maximizes the increase in Rao's V is entered.

◇Criteria: Criteria for entering and removing variables.

⊙Use F value: Take F value as Entry value and Removal value.

Entry [3.84]: Entry value of F, the default value is 3.84. A variable will be entered into the model if its F value is greater than 3.84.

Removal [2.71]: Removal value of F, the default value is 2.71. A variable will be removed if the F value is less than 2.71.

◎Use probability of F: Use probability of F as Entry value and Removal value.

Entry [0.05]: Entry value of probability, the default value is 0.05. A variable will be entered into the model if its probability of F is not greater than 0.05.

Removal [0.10]: Removal value of probability, the default value is 0.1. A variable is removed if its probability of F is not less than 0.1.

◇Display: Displays options.

☑Summary of steps: Display statistics for all variables at each step.

☐F for pairwise distances: Display matrix of F value and P value for pairwise group comparisons.

★Classify: Classification parameters. Click "Classify" button (Figure 8-9), and the dialog box of Discriminant Analysis: Classification pops out (Figure 8-12).

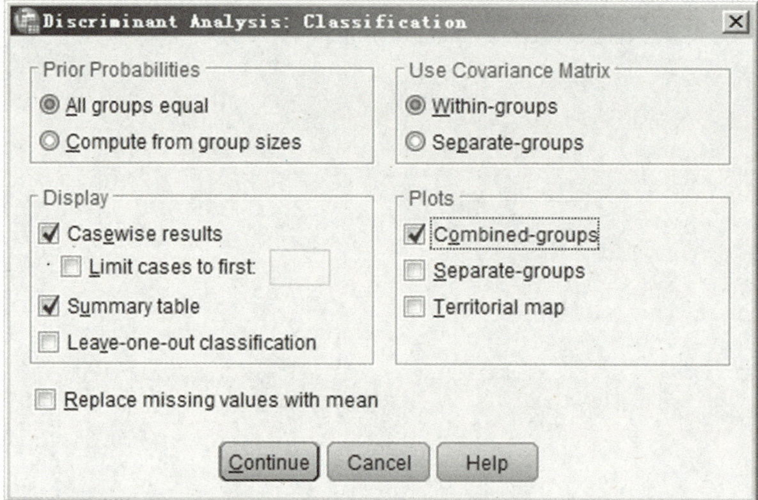

Figure 8-12 The Discriminant Analysis: Classification dialog box

◇Prior Probabilities: Set a priori probability.

⊙All groups equal (system default): Probabilities of all groups are equal.

◎Compute from group sizes: The percentage of samples in each group is the prior probability.

◇Display: Displays options.

☑Casewise results: Actual group, predicted group, posterior probabilities, and discriminant scores are displayed for each case.

□Limit cases to first: [ ] : Only list casewise results of first few specified cases.

☑Summary table: The crosstab of actual group and predicted group.

□Leave-one-out classification: Each case in the analysis is classified by the functions derived from all cases other than that case.

◇Use Covariance Matrix.

⊙Within-groups: System default.

◎Separate-groups.

◇Plots.

☑Combined-groups: Create an all-groups scatter plot of the first two discriminant function values.

□Separate-groups: Create separate-group scatter plots of the first two discriminant function values.

□Territorial map: A plot of the boundaries used to classify cases into groups based on function values.

□Replace missing values with mean.

★Save (Figure 8-9): Save dialog is used to save predicted group membership, discriminant scores and probabilities of group membership into data file. Click "Save" button, and the dialog box of Discriminant Analysis: Save pops out (Figure 8-13).

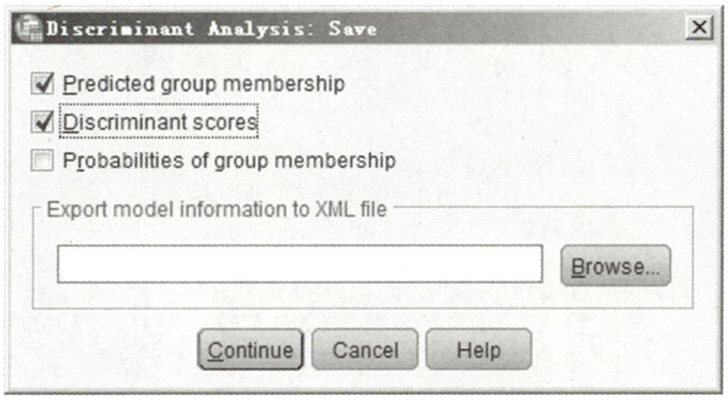

☑Predicted group membership: Only one single variable.

☑Discriminant scores: One variable is generated for each unstandardized discriminant function.

Figure 8-13 The Discriminant Analysis: Save dialog box

□Probabilities of group membership: One variable for each group.

We can export model information to the specified XML file.

(2) Process.

Analyze

Classify

Discriminant

Grouping Variable: category (1,3)

Independents: x1/x2/x3/x4/x5

⊙Enter independents together

Statistics

Descriptive

☑Means

☑Univariate ANOVAs

Function Coefficients

☑Fisher's

☑Unstandardized

Classify

Prior Probabilities

⊙All groups equal

Display

☑**Casewise results**
☑**Summary table**
Plots
☑**Combined groups**
Save
☑**Predicted group membership**
☑**Discriminant scores**

8.2.4 Main output results

(1) Add new variables to data file: Three new variables have been saved as new variables to the data file "Discriminant": Predicted group membership (Dis_1), Discrimination scores D1 (Dis1_1), Discrimination scores D2 (Dis2_1).

(2) Group Statistic: The "Group Statistics" table gives the descriptive outputs. It displays means, standard deviations and sample size of each sub-group of each variable, as well as the overall statistics of each variable (Figure 8-14).

Group Statistics

Actual groups		Mean	Std. Deviation	Valid N (listwise)	
				Unweighted	Weighted
Healthy	x1	7.4373	2.33287	11	11.000
	x2	238.5555	45.03975	11	11.000
	x3	13.8918	2.88074	11	11.000
	x4	5.5236	.44747	11	11.000
	x5	7.6736	1.80803	11	11.000
aortic atherosclerosis	x1	6.8886	2.14427	7	7.000
	x2	342.8471	77.58641	7	7.000
	x3	14.9971	3.79894	7	7.000
	x4	5.2586	.42188	7	7.000
	x5	9.2471	1.42264	7	7.000
coronary heart disease	x1	5.2540	1.82185	5	5.000
	x2	310.2360	68.15144	5	5.000
	x3	18.1760	3.39008	5	5.000
	x4	4.8880	.43814	5	5.000
	x5	10.4920	2.47790	5	5.000
Total	x1	6.7957	2.25388	23	23.000
	x2	285.8791	75.46847	23	23.000
	x3	15.1596	3.56056	23	23.000
	x4	5.3048	.48843	23	23.000
	x5	8.7652	2.12169	23	23.000

Figure 8-14 The statistics of the actual groups

(3) One-way ANOVA of each variable (Figure 8-15): One-way ANOVA is carried out for each independent variable, and the results are shown below.

1) The differences of the variables x2, x4, and x5 among the three groups are statistically significant.

2) Wilk's lambda is used to test for significant differences between groups, the null hypothesis is that the means of the groups are equal. The values of Wilks' λ are between 0 and 1, the smaller λ, the smaller P value is.

Tests of Equality of Group Means

	Wilks' Lambda	F	df1	df2	Sig.
x1	.853	1.729	2	20	.203
x2	.598	6.711	2	20	.006
x3	.773	2.939	2	20	.076
x4	.731	3.675	2	20	.044
x5	.701	4.272	2	20	.029

Figure 8-15 One-way ANOVA table of the actual group

(4) Canonical discriminant function.

Canonical discriminant function is displayed as follows (Figure 8-16):

D1 = −13.788+0.292x1−0.025x2−0.053x3+2.452x4+0.783x5.

D2 = 0.010−0.111x1−0.016x2+0.138x3−0.188x4+0.488x5.

Canonical Discriminant Function Coefficients

	Function	
	1	2
x1	.292	-.111
x2	-.025	-.016
x3	-.053	.138
x4	2.452	-.188
x5	.783	.488
(Constant)	-13.788	.010

Unstandardized coefficients

Figure 8-16 Canonical discriminant function unstandardized coefficients

It is the list of coefficients of the unstandardized discriminant equation. It is the unstandardized scores concerning the independent variables. Discriminant scores D1 and D2 can be calculated by those functions (Figure 8-17), with three variables "Dis_1" "Dis1_1" and "Dis2_1" generated and added into file data by selecting "Save" dialog. According to Dis1_1 and Dis2_1, predicted group can be estimated (Figure 8-18).

Category 1 (Healthy, Dis_1 = 1): If Dis1_1>0.

Category 2 (aortic atherosclerosis, Dis_1 = 2): If Dis1_1<0 and Dis2_1<0.

Category 3 (coronary heart disease, Dis_1 = 3): If Dis1_1<0 and Dis2_1 ≥0.

It indicates the average discriminant scores for subjects in the three groups.

Functions at Group Centroids

Actual groups	Function 1	Function 2
Healthy	1.139	-.055
aortic atherosclerosis	-1.148	-.710
coronary heart disease	-.900	1.115

Unstandardized canonical discriminant functions evaluated at group means

Figure 8-17 Functions at group centroids

	x1	x2	x3	x4	x5	category	Dis_1	Dis1_1	Dis2_1
1	8.11	261.10	13.23	6.00	7.36	1	1	1.72	-.83
2	9.36	185.39	9.02	5.66	5.99	1	1	2.33	-.93
3	9.85	249.58	15.61	6.06	6.11	1	1	1.56	-1.13
4	2.55	137.13	9.21	6.11	4.35	1	1	1.37	-.25
5	6.01	231.34	14.27	5.21	8.79	1	1	.99	.88
6	9.64	231.38	13.03	4.88	8.53	1	1	1.10	.24
7	4.11	260.25	14.72	5.36	10.02	1	1	1.01	1.25
8	8.90	259.51	14.16	4.91	9.79	1	1	1.17	.63
9	7.71	273.81	16.01	5.15	8.79	1	1	.17	.25
10	7.51	303.59	19.14	5.70	8.53	1	1	.33	-.01
11	8.06	231.03	14.41	5.72	6.15	1	1	.77	-.71
12	6.80	308.90	15.11	5.52	8.49	2	2	-.27	-.55
13	8.68	258.69	14.02	4.79	7.16	2	2	-1.22	-.61
14	5.67	355.54	15.13	4.97	9.43	2	2	-2.40	-.62
15	8.10	476.69	7.38	5.32	11.32	2	2	-2.02	-3.06
16	3.71	316.12	17.12	6.04	8.17	2	2	-.44	-.30
17	5.37	274.57	16.75	4.98	9.67	2	3	-.30	1.06
18	9.89	409.42	19.47	5.19	10.49	2	2	-1.39	-.88
19	5.22	330.34	18.19	4.96	9.61	3	3	-1.94	.35
20	4.71	331.47	21.26	4.30	13.72	3	3	-.68	2.94
21	4.71	352.50	20.79	5.07	11.00	3	3	-1.43	1.07
22	3.36	347.31	17.90	4.65	11.19	3	3	-2.42	1.07
23	8.27	189.56	12.74	5.46	6.94	3	1	1.96	.14

Figure 8-18 Discriminant scoresand predicted group

(5) Prior probabilities for groups: Equal prior probabilities are assumed for all groups, and it has no effect on the coefficients (Figure 8-19).

Classification Function Coefficients

	Actual groups		
	Healthy	aortic atherosclerosis	coronary heart disease
x1	7.455	6.859	6.729
x2	-.479	-.411	-.447
x3	.266	.297	.536
x4	101.358	95.875	96.139
x5	29.598	27.488	28.573
(Constant)	-366.979	-335.715	-339.229

Fisher's linear discriminant functions

Figure 8-19 The prior probability for groups

(6) Fisher's linear discriminant functions (Figure 8-20): The Fisher discriminant function coefficients, Fisher's linear discriminant functions are listed as follows:

$Z1 = -366.979 + 7.455x1 - 0.479x2 + 0.266x3 + 101.358x4 + 29.598x5$

$Z2 = -335.715 + 6.859x1 - 0.411x2 + 0.297x3 + 95.875x4 + 27.488x5$

$Z3 = -339.229 + 6.729x1 - 0.447x2 + 0.536x3 + 96.139x4 + 28.573x5$

The discriminant functions are used to classify observed units into three categories. Substitute the observed values into these discriminant functions, we can get the discriminant function scores *Z*1, *Z*2 and *Z*3. According to *Z*1, *Z*2 and *Z*3, the case belonging to the predicted group has the largest scores. The classification results are the same with the results of the canonical discriminant function.

Classification Function Coefficients

	Actual groups		
	Healthy	aortic atherosclerosis	coronary heart disease
x1	7.455	6.859	6.729
x2	-.479	-.411	-.447
x3	.266	.297	.536
x4	101.358	95.875	96.139
x5	29.598	27.488	28.573
(Constant)	-366.979	-335.715	-339.229

Fisher's linear discriminant functions

Figure 8-20 Fisher discriminant function coefficients

(7) Classification results (Figure 8-21): The table is a simple summary of the number and percent of subjects classified correctly and incorrectly. The rows are the actual (original) group and the columns are the predicted categories. When prediction is perfect, all cases will lie on the diagonal line. The classification results show that overall predictive accuracy is 91.3% (21/23). One hundred percent of the healthy are classified correctly into healthy group, while 85.7% and 80% are classified correctly into coronary heart disease group and aortic atherosclerosis group, respectively.

Classification Results[a]

		Actual groups	Predicted Group Membership: Healthy	Predicted Group Membership: aortic atherosclerosis	Predicted Group Membership: coronary heart disease	Total
Original	Count	Healthy	11	0	0	11
		aortic atherosclerosis	0	6	1	7
		coronary heart disease	1	0	4	5
	%	Healthy	100.0	.0	.0	100.0
		aortic atherosclerosis	.0	85.7	14.3	100.0
		coronary heart disease	20.0	.0	80.0	100.0

a. 91.3% of original grouped cases correctly classified.

Figure 8-21 Classification Results

(8) Plot of Discriminant Classification (Figure 8-22): Combined-group plots of discriminant classification create an all-case scatter plot of the first two discriminant function values. While the X-axis is the first canonical discriminant function scores Dis1_1, the Y-axis is the second canonical discriminant function scores Dis2_1. "■" represents groups centroid, which is the center of there groups. If Dis1_1>0 then case is predicted as "healthy", if Dis1_1<0 and Dis2_1<0 then case is predicted as "aortic atherosclerosis", and if Dis1_1<0 and Dis2_1≥0 then case is predicted as "coronary heart disease". Only two cases are misclassified, which are number 17 and 23.

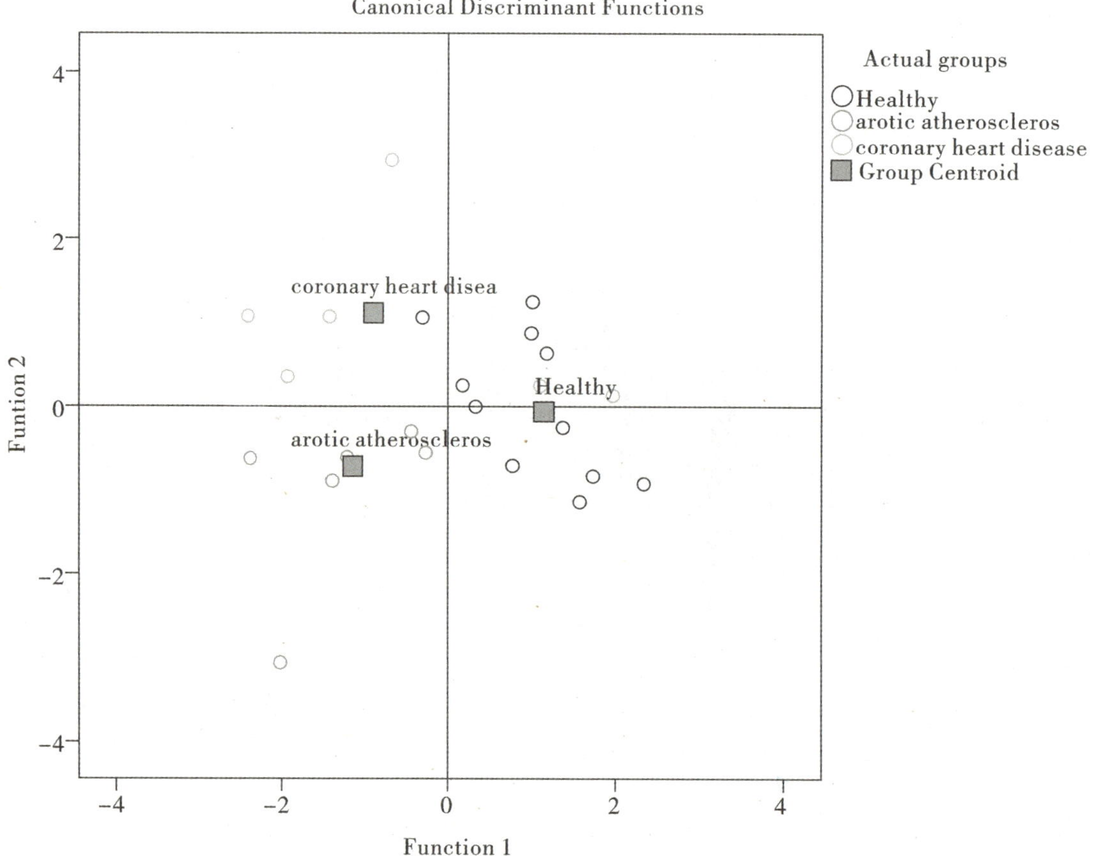

Figure 8-22 Plot of Canonical Discriminant Functions

8.3 Exploratory factor analysis

8.3.1 Description

Exploratory factor analysis (EFA) is a data reduction technique, which attempts to use underlying unobservable variables (namely common factors) to explain the variance of a relatively large set of observed variables, and thus it can be used to identify the underlying relationship between factors and measured variables. It is assumed that each observable variable is linearly related to the common factors, and the number of factors (k) is less than or equal to the number of original variables (p). It is commonly used by researchers when developing scales or questionnaires.

Exploratory factor analysis consists of four main steps: reliable measurements, the number of factors, factor rotation and factor scores.

Step 1: Is the data suitable for factor analysis? Kaiser–Meyer–Olkin measure of sampling adequacy (KMO–test) and Bartlett's test of sphericity are used to test whether the sample size is enough or variables are inter–correlated.

Step 2: How many factors? Principal components analysis can be used to help decide the number of factors. Some rules are listed as follows.

(1) Cumulative variance explained: Keep the factors of which the cumulative variance exceeds 70% of the total variance.

(2) Eigenvalues: Keep the factors of which the eigenvalues are greater than 1 (Kaiser–Guttman rule).

(3) Scree plot: Keep all factors before the breaking point.

(4) Individual variance explained: Keep the factors of which the eigenvalue exceeds 5% (or 10%) of the total variance.

(5) Comprehensibility: According to the study, for example, take the dimension of the scale factor as the number of factors.

Step 3: Factor rotation. It might be difficult to interpret and name the factors according to the basis of their factor loading. A solution for this difficulty is factor rotation, which can improve interpretation of the factors.

Step 4: Factor scores. The factor scores can be useful for these reasons.

(1) If we use orthogonal rotation, the factor scores are uncorrelated, and then they can be used to solve multicollinearity problems in multiple regression.

(2) It can be found out that "whether groups or clusters of subjects can be distinguished that behave similarly in scoring on a test battery, the latent, underlying variables are considered to be more fundamental than the original variables".

8.3.2 Example

Example 8–3 The data file "IPSQ1. sav" is used as the Example 8–3, which has 193 observations (rows) and 27 items (columns). Each item is a variable. During the development of inpatient satisfaction scale, the original scale consists of 5 domains, 27 items, which are "Doctor service" (7 items, d1 – d7), "Food supply" (4 items, f1 – f4), "Auxiliary department services" (6 items, h1 – h6), "Nursing" (6 items, n1 – n6) and "Medical environment and facilities" (4 items, s1 – s4).

8.3.3 Operation Process

(1) Step–by–step process.

Analyze

Dimension Reduction

Factor

Click "Analyze" from the menu bar, then "Dimension Reduction" from the pull-down menu, "Factor" from the second pull-down menu to open factor analysis main dialog box (Figure 8-23).

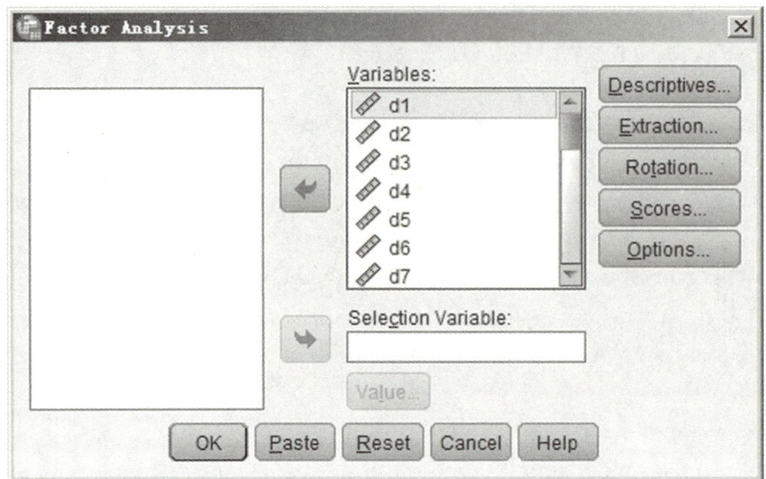

Figure 8-23 The Factor Analysis dialog box

Choose all 27 variables and move them into "Variables" box.

★Descriptives: Descriptive statistics. Click "Descriptives" button, and the dialog box of Factor Analysis: Descriptives pops out (Figure 8-24).

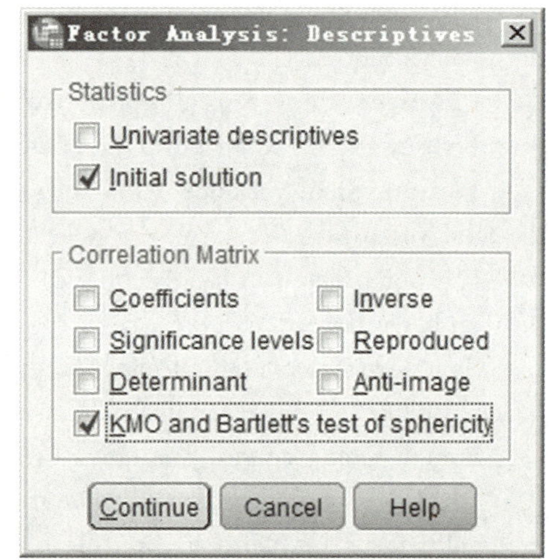

Figure 8-24 The Factor Analysis: Descriptives dialog box

◇Statistics.

□Univariate descriptives: Displays mean, standard deviation and sample size.

□Initial solution: Displays initial communalities, eigenvalues and the percentage of variance explained.

◇Correlation Matrix.

□Coefficients: Display Pearson correlation coefficient matrix.

□Significance levels: Display significance levels of correlation matrix.

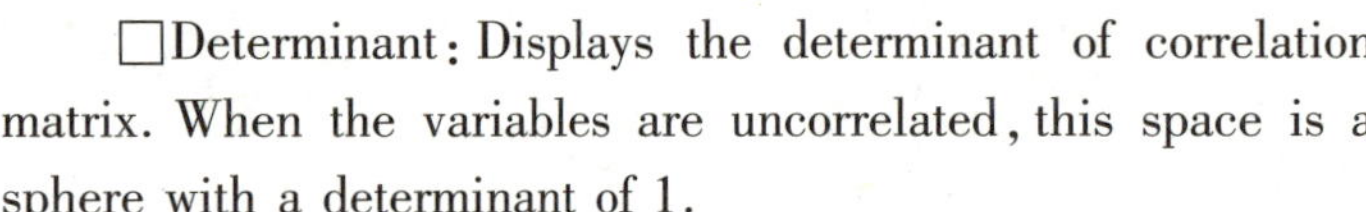

□Determinant: Displays the determinant of correlation matrix. When the variables are uncorrelated, this space is a sphere with a determinant of 1.

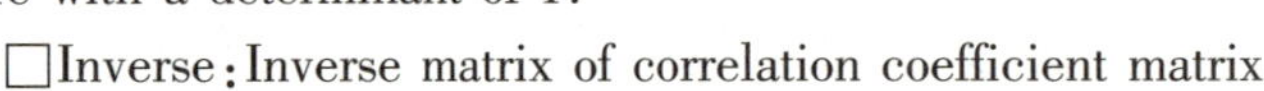

□Inverse: Inverse matrix of correlation coefficient matrix.

□Reproduced: The estimated correlation matrix from the factor solution. Residuals (difference between estimated correlations and observed correlations) are also displayed.

□Anti-image: The anti-image correlation matrix and anti-image covariance matrix. Most of the off-diagonal elements are small in a good factor model. The measure of sampling adequacy for a variable is displayed on the diagonal of the anti-image correlation matrix.

☑KMO and Bartlett's test of sphericity.

1) Kaiser-Meyer-Olkin measure: The reliability of factor analysis is affected by sample size, and it may be fluctuating in small sample size. The Kaiser-Meyer-Olkin measure of sampling adequacy (KMO-test) is used to test whether the sample is adequate. KMO values larger than 0.8 are considered good, while those of less than 0.6 indicate that the sample size is not adequate.

2) Bartlett's test of sphericity: It tests the hypothesis that your correlation matrix is an identity matrix. The identity matrix is a matrix of which all diagonal elements are 1 and all off-diagonal elements are 0, indicating the correlations between variables. The test statistics is χ^2 distribution, and if you don't reject the hypothesis ($P>0.05$) according to the results, the data is not suitable for factor analysis.

★ Extraction: Specify the method of factor extraction. Click "Extraction" button (Figure 8-23), and the dialog box of Factor Analysis: Extraction pops out (Figure 8-25).

◇ Method: There are seven methods of factor extraction.

1) Principal components: System default.

2) Unweighted least square.

3) Generalized least square.

4) Maximum likelihood.

5) Principal axis factoring.

6) Alpha factoring.

7) Image factoring.

◇ Analyze: Analysis matrix.

⦿ Correlation matrix: system default.

◎ Covariance matrix.

◇ Display.

☑ Unrotated factor solution: Displays unrotated factor loadings, communalities, and eigenvalues for the factor solution.

☑ Scree plot: The X-axis of the scree plot is the factor number and the Y-axis is eigenvalue. This plot is used to determine the number of factors that should be kept.

◇ Extract.

⦿ Based on Eigenvalue.

Eigenvalues greater than: [1] : Retain all factors whose eigenvalues exceed a specified value, the default value is 1.

◎ Fixed number of factors.

Factors to extract: Retain a specific number of factors. Positive integer must be input into the box.

Maximum Iterations for Convergence: [25] : The default is 25.

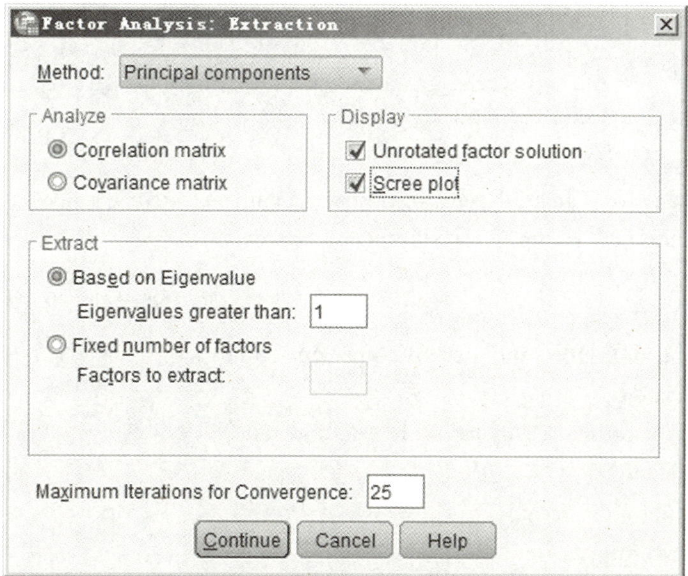

Figure 8-25 The Factor Analysis: Extraction dialog box

★Rotation: Click "Rotation" button (Figure 8-23), and the dialog box of Factor Analysis: Rotation pops out (Figure 8-26).

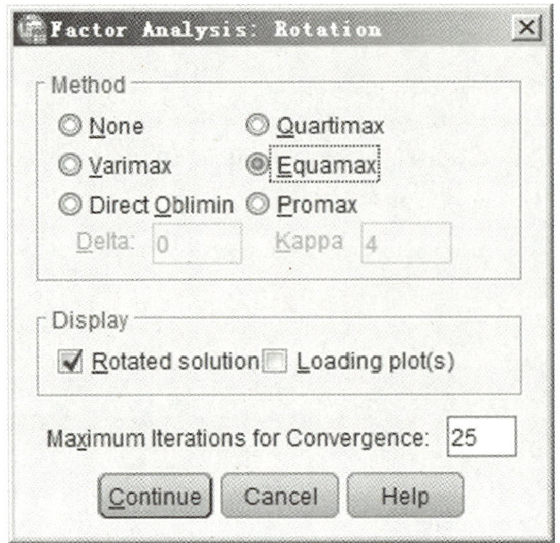

Figure 8-26 The Factor Analysis: Rotation dialog box

◇Method: To select the method of factor rotation.

◎None: No rotation.

◎Varimax: Maximum variance rotation, an orthogonal rotation method

◎Direct Oblimin: A method for oblique rotation. If you select this, you will activate Delta dialog, and then fill in delta value, which is 0 by default.

◎Quartimax: A method for orthogonal rotation, which is used to maximize the sum of all loadings raised to power 4 in the rotated factor structure matrix.

⊙Equamax: A method for orthogonal rotation, which is used to maximize the variance of the squared loadings in each factor in the rotated factor structure matrix.

◎Promax: An oblique rotation, which allows factors to be correlated. If you select this item, you will activate "Kappa" dialog, which is 4 by default.

◇Display: Output.

☑Rotated solution.

□Loading plot(s).

Maximum Iterations for Convergence: [25]: The default value is 25. Fill in a positive integer.

★Scores: Factor Scores. Click "Scores" button (Figure 8-23), and the dialog box of "Factor Analysis: Factor Scores" pops out (Figure 8-27).

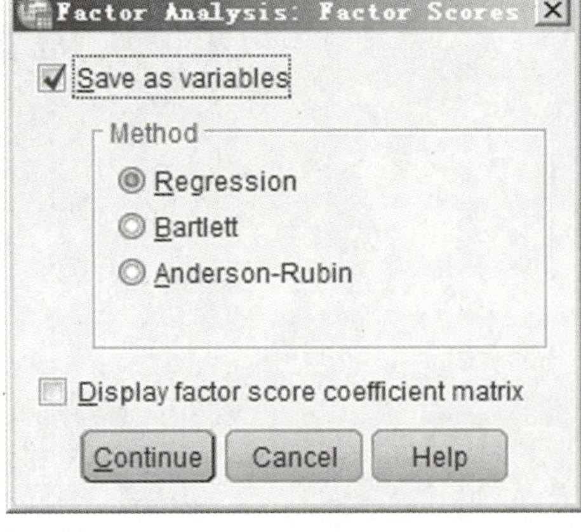

Figure 8-27 The Factor Analysis: Factor Scores dialog box

☑Save as variables: If selected, factor scores will be saved as a new variable in the data file, and at the same time, the "Method" dialog is activated.

◇Method: Methods of estimating factor score coefficients.

⊙Regression: By default.

◎Bartlett.

◎Anderson-Rubin.

□Display factor score coefficient matrix.

★Options: Click "Options" button (Figure 8-23), and the dialog box of Factor Analysis: Options pops out (Figure 8-28).

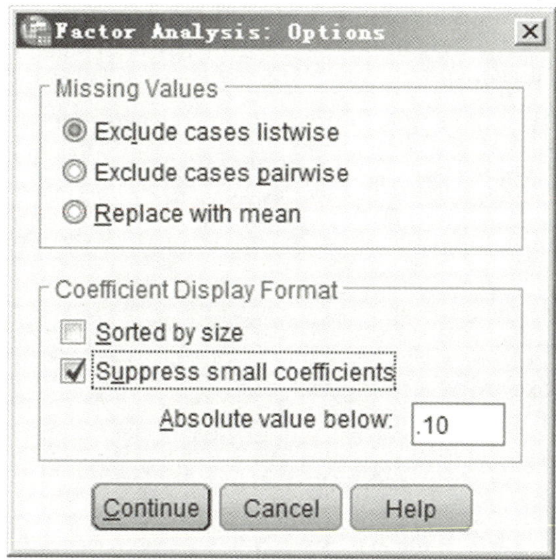

Figure 8-28 The Factor Analysis:Options dialog box

◇Missing Values.

⊙Exclude cases listwise:Remove cases if there is a missing value on any of the variables. Selected by default.

◎Exclude cases pairwise:Remove only the specific missing values from the analysis, not the entire case. For correlation coefficient matrix, it ignores only those missing values if they exist on some variables. Pairwise deletion will result in different sample sizes for each correlation analysis.

◎Replace with mean:Replace missing values with variable's mean.

◇Coefficient Display Format.

□Sorted by size.

☑Suppress small coefficients.

Absolute value below: [0.10] :The default is 0.10.

(2)Process.

Analyze

Dimension Reduction

Factor

▸Variables:d1 ~ d7 / f1 ~ f4 / h1 ~ h6 / n1 ~ n6 / s1 ~ s4

Descriptives

☑Initial solution

☑KMO and Bartlett's test of sphericity

Extraction

Method:Principal components

⊙Correlation matrix

☑Unrotated factor solution

⊙Based on Eigenvalue

Eigenvalues greater than: [1]

Maximum Iterations for Convergence: [25]

Method

Principal axis factoring

⊙Correlation matrix

☑Unrotated factor solution

☑Scree plot

⊙Fixed number of factors

Factors to extract: 5

Maximum Iterations for Convergence: 25

Rotation

Method

⊙Equamax

☑Rotated solution

Maximum Iterations for Convergence:25

Scores

☑Save as variables

Method

⊙Regression

Options

Missing Values

⊙Exclude cases listwise

Coefficient Display Format

☑Suppress small coefficients

Absolute values below: 0.30

8.3.4 Main output results

(1) KMO and Bartlett's Test (Figure 8-29): KMO statistic value is 0.892, indicating the adequate sample size. Bartlett's Test of Sphericity shows $\chi^2 = 1\ 646.130$ ($P<0.001$), which shows that the data is suitable for factor analysis.

KMO and Bartlett's Test

Kaiser-Meyer-Olkin Measure of Sampling Adequacy.		.892
Bartlett's Test of Sphericity	Approx. Chi-Square	1646.130
	df	351
	Sig.	.000

Figure 8-29 Results of KMO and Bartlett's Test

(2) Eigenvalues (Figure 8-30): Total column gives the eigenvalues in decreasing order, with 6 factors of which the eigenvalues are greater than 1. The first factor explains about 38.952% of the total variance, while each of the first 4 factors explains more than 5% of the total variance. The combination of the first 4 factors explains 57.125%, and that of the first 5 or 6 factors explains 61.402% or 65.265%, respectively.

Total Variance Explained

Component	Initial Eigenvalues			Extraction Sums of Squared Loadings		
	Total	% of Variance	Cumulative %	Total	% of Variance	Cumulative %
1	10.517	38.952	38.952	10.517	38.952	38.952
2	1.844	6.828	45.780	1.844	6.828	45.780
3	1.645	6.094	51.874	1.645	6.094	51.874
4	1.418	5.251	57.125	1.418	5.251	57.125
5	1.155	4.277	61.402	1.155	4.277	61.402
6	1.043	3.863	65.265	1.043	3.863	65.265
7	.972	3.602	68.867			
8	.877	3.248	72.114			
9	.766	2.837	74.952			
10	.705	2.611	77.563			
11	.675	2.500	80.062			
12	.648	2.401	82.464			
13	.565	2.092	84.556			
14	.500	1.853	86.409			
15	.489	1.809	88.218			
16	.464	1.718	89.936			
17	.420	1.557	91.493			
18	.380	1.406	92.899			
19	.350	1.297	94.196			
20	.294	1.090	95.286			
21	.273	1.010	96.296			
22	.243	.900	97.196			
23	.196	.725	97.920			
24	.179	.662	98.582			
25	.157	.580	99.162			
26	.132	.488	99.650			
27	.094	.350	100.000			

Extraction Method: Principal Component Analysis.

Figure 8-30 Variance contribution of factor

(3) Scree plot (Figure 8-31): According to the scree plot above, the biggest change can be found between 1 and 2. Perhaps there is only 1 factor, or maybe as much as 4 or 5 factors? It might lead you to a slightly different conclusion among 4 factors to 5 factors. We can choose 5 factors by the structure of the scale.

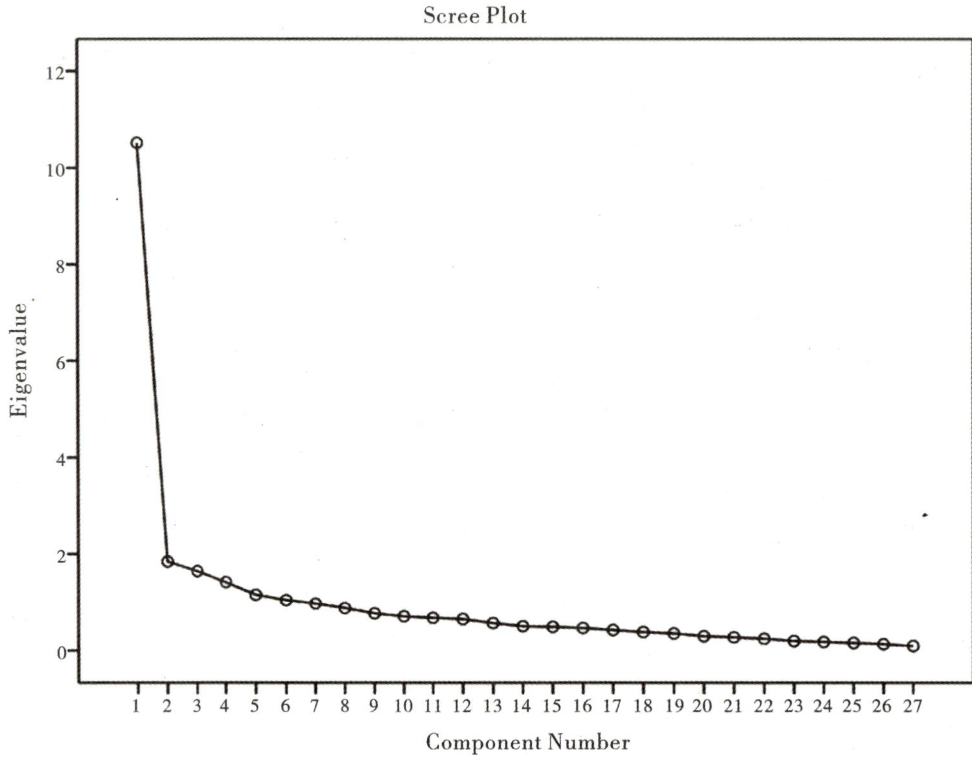

Figure 8-31 Screen plot of factor analysis

(4) Component Matrix (Figure 8-32): Principal axis factoring is used in factor analysis, and factor loadings are shown in Figure 8-32. The matrix of loadings called the component matrix in SPSS is comprised of 27 rows and 8 columns, and we only list the elements of which the factor loadings are more than 0.3 by selecting small coefficients option in SPSS. It is difficult to interpret and name 5 factors on the basis of their factor loadings without factor rotation.

Factor Matrix[a]

	Factor				
	1	2	3	4	5
d1	.799				
d2	.800				
d3	.789				
d4	.383				
d5	.674				
d6	.819				
d7	.738				
f1	.394			.473	
f2	.492			.377	
f3	.568			.359	
f4	.448				
h1	.434				
h2	.498		.437		
h3	.391				
h4	.410		.478		
h5	.438		.306		
h6	.372		.504		
n1	.828				.332
n2	.777				
n3	.375				
n4	.676				
n5	.741				
n6	.763				.408
s1	.603	.479			
s2	.604	.329			
s3	.435	.641			
s4	.681	.313			

Extraction Method: Principal Axis Factoring.

a. 5 factors extracted. 9 iterations required.

Figure 8–32 Component Matrix without rotation

(5) Rotated component Matrix (Figure 8–33): Equamax method is used in factor rotation, and the rotated component matrix shows the factor loadings for each variable. We only list factor loadings greater than 0.3. Based on these factor loadings, the factors represent as follows: Factor 1 to "Doctor service", Factor 2 to "Nursing", Factor 3 to "Auxiliary department services", Factor 4 to "Food supply", and Factor 5 to "Medical environment and facilities".

Rotated Factor Matrix[a]

	Factor				
	1	2	3	4	5
d1	.683	.304		.351	
d2	.657	.363			
d3	.603	.343			
d4	.441				
d5	.516				
d6	.707	.323			
d7	.620	.374			
f1				.672	
f2				.558	
f3				.607	
f4				.446	
h1					.417
h2					.595
h3					.316
h4					.577
h5					.474
h6					.603
n1		.739			.326
n2	.367	.601			
n3		.362			
n4	.338	.511	.339		
n5	.338	.444	.433		
n6		.808			
s1			.696		
s2			.585		
s3			.778		
s4			.662		

Extraction Method: Principal Axis Factoring.
Rotation Method: Equamax with Kaiser Normalization.

a. Rotation converged in 13 iterations.

Figure 8-33 Rotated component matrix

(6) Factor Scores: Factor scores for each case are saved as new variables in the data file and are automatically named with "FAC1_1" "FAC2_1" "FAC3_1" "FAC4_1" "FAC5_1" and "FAC6_1". We selected "exclude cases listwise" for missing data, therefore, factor scores of these cases are missing too.

Chen Bingwei

Chapter 9

Reliability Analysis

9.1 Description

Scales or questionnaires are widely used for evaluating the general population's quality of life, such as the Apgar scale for newborn baby's evaluation, SF-36 scale for evaluating the general population's quality of life. Also, they are used for marketing research or for patients' satisfaction of medical services. In these occasions, the role of the scale is a measurement tool.

It is well known that, a good-quality sphygmomanometer can accurately reflect the true blood pressure level of a subject investigated no matter what time and place, what medical person operate, or what subjects are measured. Similarly, as a measurement tool, scales also should have the dependability and effectiveness. The two indicators called reliability and validity, which are used to evaluate the dependability and effectiveness of the scales or questionnaires, respectively. This chapter mainly introduces the method of reliability evaluation using the SPSS software.

9.2 The general procedure of reliability analysis

The data file "QOLIE. sav" is used as the Example 9-1. When do the reliability analysis, select from the menu as following:

Analyze

Scale

Reliability Analysis

The Reliability Analysis dialog box pops out (Figure 9-1).

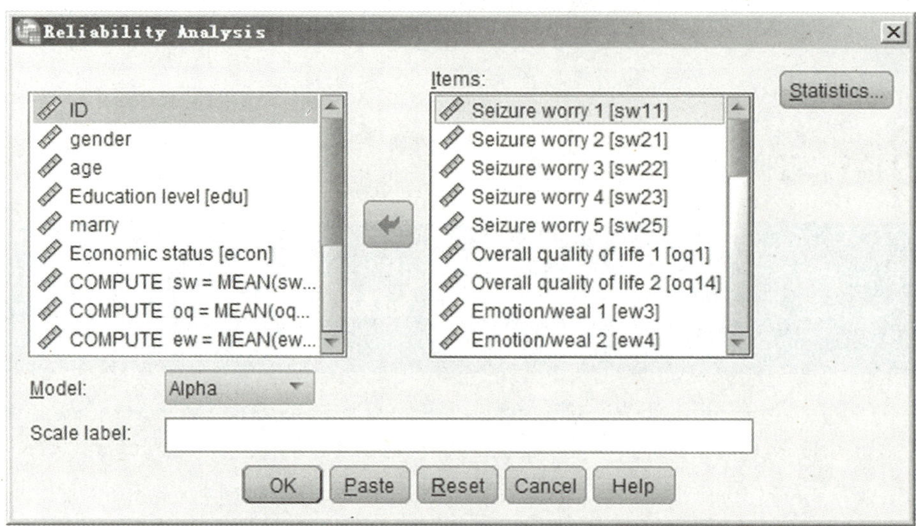

Figure 9-1 The Reliability Analysis dialog box

◇Items: Choose items. Select items to be analyzed in this box.

◇Model: Choose models for reliability calculation. There are five models that can be chosen.

1) Alpha: It is called the Cronbach α coefficient, also called the internal consistency coefficient, which is obtained by the following formula:

$$\alpha = \frac{k \bullet \overline{\text{cov}} / \overline{\text{var}}}{1 + (k - 1)\ \overline{\text{cov}} / \overline{\text{var}}}. \tag{9-1}$$

In the Formula 9-1, k is the number of items, $\overline{\text{cov}}$ is the average covariance between items, $\overline{\text{var}}$ is the average variance of items. If items are standardized to having the same variance, the upper formula can be simplified as the Formula 9-2:

$$\alpha = \frac{k \bullet \bar{r}}{1 + (k - 1)\bar{r}}. \tag{9-2}$$

Here, $\bar{r}$ is the mean correlation coefficient between items, that is, the average of the product-moment correlation coefficient between two of them for all items. The Cronbach α coefficient is the most widely used index for reliability evaluation. The value of this index is between 0 and 1, and the greater its value, the higher the reliability. Generally, a scale has a good reliability when cronbach α coefficient is greater than 0.7. One basic assumption for calculating the Cronbach α coefficient is that there is a positive correlation relationship between items. If there is a negative correlation relationship between items, there is a significant error in the item design of the scale. At this time, the Cronbach α coefficient may be negative.

It can be seen from the above formula that Cronbach α coefficient is determined by the number of items and the correlation relationship between items. Therefore, when evaluating the reliability, it should not only observe the value of Cronbach α coefficient, but also the number of items. For example, the Cronbach α coefficient of a scale is large (such as greater than 0.9), but the scale has too many repeated items. In this case, the reliability of the scale may be not as high as we expected.

When the variance of each item is normalized to 1, the obtained Cronbach α coefficient is called the standardized Cronbach α coefficient (standardized item α). The greater the variance difference between items, the greater the difference between Cronbach α coefficient and standardized Cronbach α coefficient.

The Cronbach α coefficient is equivalent to the Kuder-Richardson 20 (KR20) coefficient when the response variable of each item is binary.

2) Split-half: Split-half reliability. All items in the questionnaire are randomly divided into two equal

parts, and the correlation between the two half tables of the questionnaire represents the split-half reliability. The split-half reliability is based on the calculation of the product moment correlation coefficient between two half-tables, and then adjusted by the Spearman-Brown formula, also known as the Spearman-Brown coefficient. However, the split-half reliability is less used in reality with two reasons. Firstly, due to too many ways to randomly divide the items into two-half tables, especially when the number of items is relatively large, the estimated value of the split-half reliability is usually unstable. Secondly, the Spearman-Brown coefficient is the average of all possible split-half reliability based on the way of dividing the items into two half-tables. Therefore, the Spearman-Brown coefficient can represent split-half reliability.

3) Guttman: Guttman split-half reliability. It is similar to the Spearman-Brown coefficient, but there is no need to meet the preconditions that the reliability and variance of two half tables are homogeneous required by Spearman-Brown coefficient.

4) Parallel: Parallel model. That is, under the condition that the variance homogeneity of all items and the variance homogeneity of error are satisfied, the maximum likelihood estimation of reliability is calculated.

5) Strict Parallel: Strictly parallel model. That is the unbiased estimation of reliability under the contion that the variance homogeneity of all items, the variance homogeneity of errors and the same mean are satisfied.

◇Scale label: Display the labels of items.

★Statistics: Click "Statistics" button, and the dialog box of Reliability Analysis: Statistics pops out (Figure 9-2).

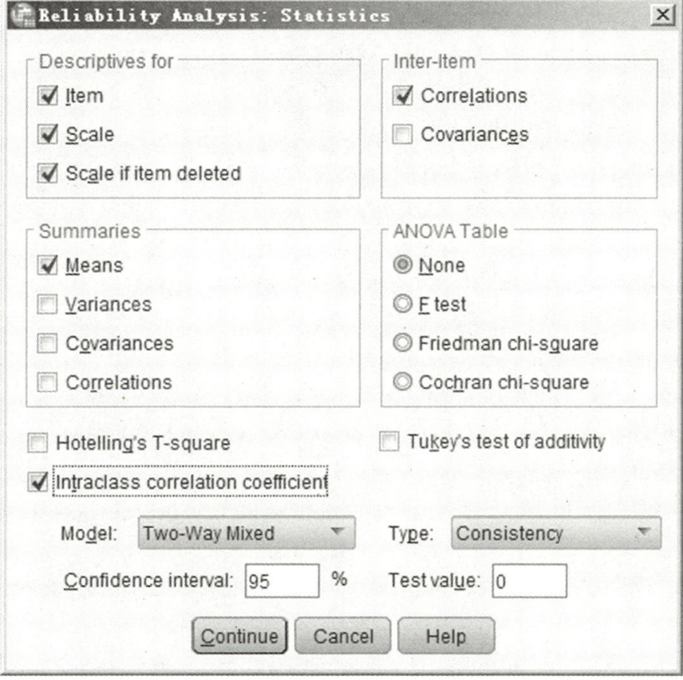

Figure 9-2 The Reliability Analysis: Statistics dialog box

◇Descriptives for.

☑Item: Descriptive statistics for each item, including mean, standard deviation and sample size.

☑Scale: Descriptive statistics for the whole scale, including the mean, variance, standard deviation and number of items in the total item score.

☑Scale if item deleted: Descriptive statistics for the whole scale when the current item is removed, which is essential for a sensitivity analysis. This options includes the following process.

1) Scale Mean if Item Deleted: The mean of the total score of the scale when the current item is removed.

2) Scale Variance if Item Deleted: The variance of the total score of the scale when the current item is removed.

3) Corrected Item-Total Correlation: Pearson correlation coefficient between the score of current item and the total score of the scale when the current item is removed.

4) Squared Multiple Correlation: The coefficient of determination, denoted R^2, which is the proportion of the variance in the current item as the dependent variable that is predictable from the other items as independent variables.

5) Cronbach's Alpha if Item Deleted: The Cronbach α coefficient of the scale when the current item is removed.

◇Inter-Item: The correlation matrix and covariance matrix between items.

☑Correlations: The correlation matrix between items.

☐Covariances: The covariance matrix between items.

◇Summaries: Descriptive statistics, including the mean, minimum and maximum values, range, the ratio of the maximum value to the minimum value, variance.

☑Means: Descriptive statistics of the mean.

☐Variances: Descriptive statistics of the variance.

☐Covariances: Descriptive statistics of the covariance.

☐Correlations: Descriptive statistics of the Pearson correlation coefficient.

◇ANOVA Table: List the table of analysis of variance (ANOVA).

⊙None: Does not list the ANOVA table, which is the default option.

◎F test: List the repeated measurement ANOVA table.

◎Friedman chi-square: List the statistics of Friedman χ^2 and Kendall concordance coefficient, which is suitable for ranked data analysis.

◎Cochran chi-square: List the Cochran Q statistics, which is suitable for binary data analysis.

☐Hotelling's T-square: Hotelling T^2 test, which assumes that the population means of each item are equal.

☐Tukey's test of additivity: The additivity test, which assumes that there are no multiple interactions between items.

☑Intraclass correlation coefficient: Intra-group correlation coefficient (ICC).

◇Model: The effect model, which is an algorithm that determines the ICC, and has three options.

1) Two-Way Mixed: The two-factor mixed effect model, in which the observer and the items are modeled as random and fixed effects, respectively.

2) Two-Way Random: The two-factor random effects model, in which both of the observers and items are modeled as random effects.

3) One-Way Random: The one-factor random effect model, in which the observer is modeled as a random effect.

◇Type: The method of ICC definition. There are two options as following.

1) Consistency: Relative consistency ICC, which is obtained by removing the variance between items from the total variance of the denominator when calculating the ICC.

2) Absolute Agreement: Absolute consistency ICC, which is obtained by retaining the variance between items in the total variance of the denominator when calculating the ICC.

◇Confidence interval: [95%]: 95% confidence interval (system default).

◇Test value [0]: Set a test constant, which is used to compare with the calculated ICC. The range for the constant is between 0 and 1, and the system default value is 0.

9.3 A real example of reliability analysis

9.3.1 Example

Example 9-1 The data file"QOLIE. sav" is used as the Example 9-1, and its structure of the scale as shown in Table 9-1. This example is based on a study that used the Quality of Life in Epilepsy Inventory (QOLIE-33) to investigate the quality of life of 198 epilepsy patients. Please try to analyze the general reliability of the scale and that for each factor.

Table 9-1 Factors and the composition of items and their scoring

Factors	Items (Variable name)	Number of items	Summation	
			Variable name	Calculation
Seizure worry (*sw*)	sw11, sw21, sw22, sw23, sw25	5	sw	Σswi / 5
Overall quality of life (*oq*)	oq1, oq14	2	oq	Σoqi / 2
Emotion/weal (*ew*)	ew3, ew4, ew5, ew7, ew9	5	ew	Σewi / 5
Energy/fatigue (*ef*)	ef2, ef6, ef8, ef10	4	ef	$\Sigma ef\ i$/ 4
Cognition (*cog*)	cog12, cog15, cog16, cog17, cog18, cog26	6	cog	$\Sigma cogi$ / 6
Medical effect (*me*)	me24, me29, me30	3	me	Σmei / 3
Social function (*sf*)	sf13, sf19, sf20, sf27, sf28	5	sf	Σsfi / 5
China negotiation (*cn*)	cn31, cn32	2	cn	Σcni / 2
Overall healthy status (*os*)	os33	1		
Total (Exclude*os*33)		32	sum	-*

* sum=0.07sw+0.12oq+0.14ew+0.11ef+0.24cog+0.03me+0.19sf+0.10cn.

9.3.2 Data files and data processing

9.3.2.1 Data Format

The structure of the original data contains 198 lines and 39 columns, which is made up of 39 variables. Among the first 6 variables, except the first indicator variable "ID", the rest of the 5 variables "gender" "age" "edu" "marry" "econ" are used for the analysis of demographic characteristics. The other 33 variables "sw11"-"os33" represent the 33 items of the scale.

9.3.2.2 Data Processing

For further analysis, the first thing is to calculate the scores of each factor and the whole scale. According to the calculation method of the scale score in Table 9-1, by using the process of "Transform" → "Compute Variable", 9 new variables denoting the scores of 8 factors and the total score of the scale are generated. For example, the generation process of the score for the factor "sw" is as follows:

Transform

Compute Variable

▸Target Variable: sw

Type&Label Use expression as label

▸Numeric Expression: MEAN(sw11, sw21, sw22, sw23, sw25)

The generation process of the scores for the other 7 factors is similar. The generation process of the total score of the scale is as follows:

Transform

Compute Variable

▸Target Variable: sum

Type&Label ⊙Use expression as label

▸Numeric Expression:

0.07 * **sw**+0.12 * **oq**+0.14 * **ew**+0.11 * **ef**+0.24 * **cog**+0.03 * **me**+0.19 * **sf**+0.1 * **cn**

9.3.2.3 Operational Procedure

Analyze

Scale

Reliability Analysis

▸Items: sw11 / sw21 / sw22 / sw23 / sw25 / … **cn**31 / **cn**32

(a total of 32 variables, the item "*os*" (overall healthy status) is not included here and will be used for validity evaluation)

Model: Alpha

Statistics

Descriptive statistics for

☑Item

☑Scale

☑Scale if item deleted

Summaries

☑Means

☑Correlations

Inter-Item

☑Correlations

ANOVA Table

⊙F test

☑Hotelling's T-square

☑Tukey's test of additivity

9.3.2.4 Main Results.

(1) Cronbach α coefficient.

1) Scale's Cronbach α coefficient: The scale is consist of 32 items, and the value of the general Cronbach α coefficient for the scale is 0.939. The value of Cronbach α coefficient based on standardized items is 0.941, indicating the internal consistency reliability of the whole scale is superior (Figure 9-3).

Reliability Statistics

Cronbach's Alpha	Cronbach's Alpha Based on Standardized Items	N of Items
.939	.941	32

Figure 9-3 General Cronbach α coefficient of the Example 9-1

2) Factor's Cronbach α coefficient: In order to calculate the values of Cronbach α coefficients for each factor, all the items corresponding to each factor should be selected into the entry box in the main dialog box every time. With the factor "sw" as an example, the process of calculating the Cronbach α coefficient for the factor is listed below, and the process is applicable to other factors.

Select from the menu:

Analyze

Scale

Reliability Analysis

▸**Items**: sw11 / sw21 / sw22 / sw23 / sw25

Model: **Alpha**

The Cronbach α coefficients of 8 factors of the scale are obtained through 8 similar processes mentioned above (the output details are not shown). The main output results are as follows: seizure worry ("sw", 0.883); overall quality of life ("oq", 0.751); emotion/weal ("ew", 0.780); energy/fatigue ("ef", 0.758); cognition ("cog", 0.870); medical effect ("me", 0.804); social function ("sf", 0.849); China negotiation ("cn", 0.576). Except for the factor "cn", the coefficient values of all the other factors are greater than 0.70, suggesting the internal consistency reliability of each factor is superior.

(2) Descriptive statistics: The descriptive statistics of the items as shown in Figure 9-4. The descriptive statistics of the scale such as the mean (1 696.03), the variance (317 079.300) and the standard deviation (563.098) of the total scores of 32 items (the sum of the scores of the 32 items) of the subjects as shown in Figure 9-5.

(3) Sensitivity analysis of the items: Figure 9-6 shows the result of sensitivity analysis, which analyzes the effect of each item on the relevant statistics. The basic idea of the sensitivity analysis is to observe the changes in the relevant statistics after removing the current item. The explanation is as followed.

1) Scale Mean if Item Deleted: The average of the total scores of the scale after removing the current item. For example, the value of 1 652.30 is the average of the total scores for the other 31 items after removing the item "Seizure worry 1".

2) Scale Variance if Item Deleted: The variance of the total scores of the scale after removing the current item. For example, the value 294 214.998 is the variance of the total scores for the other 31 items after removing the item "Seizure worry 1".

3) Corrected Item-Total Correlation: The Pearson correlation coefficient between the score of the current item and the total score of the scale in which the current item is removed. For example, the value of 0.646 is the correlation coefficient between the score of the current item "Seizure worry 1" and the total score of the other 31 items after removing "Seizure worry 1".

4) Squared Multiple Correlation: The coefficient of determination R^2 is calculated by regression, where the current item works as the dependent variable, and the other items work as independent variables. For example, the value of 0.706 is the coefficient of determination R^2, where the current item "Seizure worry 1" is the dependent variable, and other items after removing "Seizure worry 1" as independent variables.

5) Cronbach's Alpha if Item Deleted: The Cronbach α coefficient of scale in which the current item is removed. For example, the value of 0.936 is the Cronbach α coefficient of the score of the other 31 items after removing the item "Seizure worry 1". In general, this value can be used as an important reference for adjusting items. If the value is larger, the corresponding item should be considered to be modified at first. In the Example 9-1, the item "China negotiation 2" has the largest value of 0.940, indicating that the item should be modified. However, the Cronbach α coefficient of the factor "cn" is low (0.576), supporting the modification of the item "China negotiation 2".

(4) Correlation matrix: The result is not given here. Based on the correlation matrix, the large correlation coefficient is notable. If the correlation coefficient is too large, it indicates that the content of the corresponding items may be repetitive. So, the correlation matrix results can be regarded as a basic reference for

items choice.

Item Statistics

	Mean	Std. Deviation	N
Seizure worry 1	43.74	31.222	198
Seizure worry 2	50.24	32.778	198
Seizure worry 3	44.19	34.599	198
Seizure worry 4	41.92	34.413	198
Seizure worry 5	37.25	30.514	198
Overall quality of life 1	57.12	20.209	198
Overall quality of life 2	54.80	15.802	198
Emotion/weal 1	64.65	25.858	198
Emotion/weal 2	58.89	26.290	198
Emotion/weal 3	57.98	24.925	198
Emotion/weal 4	65.15	32.301	198
Emotion/weal 5	55.96	29.130	198
Energy/fatigue 1	49.39	23.900	198
Energy/fatigue 2	55.66	25.156	198
Energy/fatigue 3	65.35	25.522	198
Energy/fatigue 4	62.93	25.200	198
Cognition 1	55.15	28.795	198
Cognition 2	46.30	30.152	198
Cognition 3	55.15	29.423	198
Cognition 4	58.59	30.859	198
Cognition 5	67.68	28.170	198
Cognition 6	43.03	29.854	198
Medical effect 1	34.50	29.359	198
Medical effect 2	40.15	31.926	198
Medical effect 3	45.45	32.330	198
Social function 1	54.75	34.386	198
Social function 2	56.34	31.086	198
Social function 3	58.33	37.952	198
Social function 4	39.90	33.968	198
Social function 5	44.95	32.353	198
China negotiation 1	67.42	34.713	198
China negotiation 2	63.13	34.233	198

Figure 9-4 Descriptive statistics of the items

Scale Statistics

Mean	Variance	Std. Deviation	N of Items
1696.03	317079.300	563.098	32

Figure 9-5 Descriptive statistics of the scale

Item-Total Statistics

	Scale Mean if Item Deleted	Scale Variance if Item Deleted	Corrected Item-Total Correlation	Squared Multiple Correlation	Cronbach's Alpha if Item Deleted
Seizure worry 1	1652.30	294214.998	.646	.706	.936
Seizure worry 2	1645.80	291278.179	.699	.806	.935
Seizure worry 3	1651.84	293432.767	.599	.696	.936
Seizure worry 4	1654.12	290555.642	.683	.834	.935
Seizure worry 5	1658.79	297179.371	.570	.658	.937
Overall quality of life 1	1638.91	304621.344	.540	.646	.937
Overall quality of life 2	1641.24	307583.545	.528	.648	.938
Emotion/weal 1	1631.39	302259.684	.498	.527	.937
Emotion/weal 2	1637.14	305355.162	.380	.469	.938
Emotion/weal 3	1638.05	304189.376	.446	.649	.938
Emotion/weal 4	1630.88	292912.206	.661	.762	.936
Emotion/weal 5	1640.07	297758.191	.581	.748	.937
Energy/fatigue 1	1646.64	299110.271	.666	.645	.936
Energy/fatigue 2	1640.38	301429.770	.544	.648	.937
Energy/fatigue 3	1630.68	300428.503	.572	.728	.937
Energy/fatigue 4	1633.10	301851.058	.527	.675	.937
Cognition 1	1640.88	295155.851	.674	.734	.936
Cognition 2	1649.74	296527.887	.598	.747	.936
Cognition 3	1640.88	295540.745	.646	.799	.936
Cognition 4	1637.45	296698.616	.578	.615	.937
Cognition 5	1628.36	297321.992	.617	.680	.936
Cognition 6	1653.00	297171.902	.584	.663	.937
Medical effect 1	1661.53	302172.780	.435	.662	.938
Medical effect 2	1655.88	302359.191	.390	.840	.939
Medical effect 3	1650.58	300154.596	.448	.827	.938
Social function 1	1641.29	294566.036	.571	.649	.937
Social function 2	1639.70	294780.886	.632	.777	.936
Social function 3	1637.70	295806.086	.480	.719	.938
Social function 4	1656.13	291791.903	.658	.771	.936
Social function 5	1651.08	290923.117	.719	.810	.935
China negotiation 1	1628.61	299863.158	.421	.556	.939
China negotiation 2	1632.90	306101.557	.259	.483	.940

Figure 9-6 Sensitivity analysis of items

(5) ANOVA of items: Since different scale items belong to repeated measurement variables, the comparisons between the means of item are based on the repeated measurement ANOVA, which is shown in Figure 9-7. There is a significant difference between the means of the 32 items ($F=28.836$, $P<0.001$). In addition, it is notable that the inter variation is decomposed by the error term of the objects. This decomposition method helps to calculate the intra-group correlation coefficient using two different definitions.

(6) Multiple interaction test and equal mean test: The results as shown in Figure 9-8 and Figure 9-9. It is explained as follows.

1) Tukey Multiplex interaction test: The Tukey estimation is 1.433 with the test statistics ($F=18.471$, $P<0.001$), suggesting that there are multiple interactions among items.

2) Hotelling's T^2 test: The test statistics ($T=1\ 251.387$, $F=34.220$, $P<0.001$) shows that the means of items are not all the same. In this case, a strict parallel model for calculating reliability cannot be used.

3) There are significant differences between the means of the 32 items ($F=28.836$, $P<0.001$), which is consistent with the results shown in Figure 9-7.

ANOVA

		Sum of Squares	df	Mean Square	F	Sig
Between People		1952019.443	197	9908.728		
Within People	Between Items	542356.313	31	17495.365	28.836	.000
	Residual	3705299.266	6107	606.730		
	Total	4247655.580	6138	692.026		
Total		6199675.023	6335	978.639		

Grand Mean = 53.00

Figure 9-7 The output of ANOVA table

ANOVA with Tukey's Test for Nonadditivity

			Sum of Squares	df	Mean Square	F	Sig
Between People			1952019.443	197	9908.728		
Within People	Between Items		542356.313	31	17495.365	28.836	.000
	Residual	Nonadditivity	11175.014[a]	1	11175.014	18.471	.000
		Balance	3694124.252	6106	604.999		
		Total	3705299.266	6107	606.730		
	Total		4247655.580	6138	692.026		
Total			6199675.023	6335	978.639		

Grand Mean = 53.00

a. Tukey's estimate of power to which observations must be raised to achieve additivity = 1.433.

Figure 9-8 Multiple interaction test of items

Hotelling's T-Squared Test

Hotelling's T-Squared	F	df1	df2	Sig
1251.387	34.220	31	167	.000

Figure 9-9 Equal mean test of items

(7) Correlation analysis of construct validity (structural validity): Spearman correlation analysis for all the items and factors, and the results as shown in Table 9-2 and Table 9-3. In Table 9-2, the correlation coefficient (0.79) between the factor "EF" and total score "SUM" is larger than the internal consistency coefficient of "EF" (0.76). However, the other internal consistency coefficient of each factor is larger than the correlation coefficient between this factor and other factors. Table 9-3 shows that the correlation coefficients between each item and the factor to which the item belonged are larger than the coefficients between the item and other factors to which the item not belonged. These two points suggest that the construct validity is large.

Table 9-2 Results of correlation analysis and Cronbach α coefficient between factors

Factor	Factor									SUM
	SW	OQ	EW	EF	COG	ME	SF	CN	OS33	
SW	(0.88)									
OQ	0.41	(0.75)								
EW	0.45	0.62	(0.78)							
EF	0.56	0.47	0.73	(0.76)						
COG	0.56	0.48	0.62	0.62	(0.87)					
ME	0.55	0.28	0.25	0.34	0.28	(0.80)				
SF	0.60	0.42	0.48	0.57	0.69	0.35	(0.85)			
CN	0.36	0.33	0.35	0.32	0.25	0.20	0.28	(0.58)		
OS33	0.57	0.58	0.47	0.56	0.49	0.35	0.52	0.21	(-)	
SUM	0.74	0.66	0.78	0.79	0.86	0.44	0.83	0.51	0.63	(0.94)

* The Cronbach α coefficients are listed in brackets.

Table 9-3 The correlation matrix between items and factors

Item	Factor							
	SW	OQ	EW	EF	COG	ME	SF	CN
sw11	0.833	0.417	0.441	0.520	0.422	0.448	0.478	0.232
sw21	0.909	0.314	0.392	0.467	0.499	0.492	0.556	0.329
sw22	0.772	0.307	0.259	0.389	0.451	0.386	0.542	0.400
sw23	0.918	0.341	0.382	0.470	0.477	0.506	0.519	0.301
sw25	0.688	0.298	0.408	0.459	0.470	0.449	0.366	0.222
Oq1	0.369	0.924	0.545	0.408	0.425	0.310	0.390	0.282
Oq14	0.361	0.873	0.567	0.437	0.438	0.170	0.359	0.318
Ew3	0.404	0.388	0.680	0.451	0.439	0.214	0.269	0.261
Ew4	0.199	0.278	0.624	0.295	0.413	0.063	0.303	0.203
Ew5	0.298	0.540	0.666	0.534	0.308	0.178	0.267	0.219
Ew7	0.451	0.472	0.853	0.664	0.551	0.216	0.484	0.323
Ew9	0.284	0.562	0.802	0.684	0.506	0.238	0.400	0.240
Ef2	0.492	0.549	0.559	0.739	0.606	0.276	0.523	0.258
Ef6	0.318	0.386	0.621	0.768	0.482	0.130	0.440	0.186
Ef8	0.457	0.246	0.502	0.767	0.475	0.276	0.434	0.247
Ef10	0.430	0.251	0.544	0.770	0.334	0.352	0.330	0.283
Cog12	0.499	0.415	0.537	0.558	0.778	0.180	0.641	0.163
Cog15	0.304	0.500	0.557	0.506	0.794	0.122	0.478	0.345
Cog16	0.401	0.441	0.541	0.522	0.857	0.135	0.560	0.234
Cog17	0.480	0.229	0.442	0.414	0.735	0.283	0.511	0.076
Cog18	0.475	0.383	0.433	0.530	0.771	0.231	0.564	0.058
Cog26	0.472	0.275	0.368	0.379	0.743	0.355	0.463	0.286

Continue to Table 9-3

Item	Factor							
	SW	OQ	EW	EF	COG	ME	SF	CN
Me24	0.611	0.199	0.234	0.308	0.192	0.734	0.230	0.288
Me29	0.341	0.222	0.190	0.248	0.280	0.908	0.283	0.109
Me30	0.464	0.277	0.218	0.309	0.238	0.893	0.371	0.122
Sf13	0.384	0.343	0.437	0.510	0.525	0.114	0.776	0.222
Sf19	0.446	0.347	0.355	0.471	0.555	0.309	0.882	0.195
Sf20	0.365	0.274	0.357	0.386	0.421	0.176	0.751	0.042
Sf27	0.552	0.315	0.355	0.412	0.581	0.434	0.764	0.342
Sf28	0.640	0.383	0.401	0.465	0.654	0.372	0.796	0.324
Cn31	0.332	0.457	0.411	0.327	0.266	0.223	0.269	0.840
Cn32	0.276	0.095	0.165	0.208	0.151	0.112	0.198	0.836

Guo Pi

Chapter 10

Nonparametric Tests

The nonparametric tests module in the main menu (nonparametric tests) consists of two parts: Legacy Dialogs and the new intelligent analysis module. The former refers to the content, operation and expression under the nonparametric tests module. The latter mainly reflects the function of intelligent analysis. The eight processes of the former part are summarized into three processes, namely One Sample, Independent Samples and Related Samples nonparametric tests analysis. In this chapter, only the Legacy Dialogs for all analyses are introduced.

10.1 Two independent samples test

10.1.1 Description

Nonparametric tests for two independent samples is used to test whether the two independent samples have the same distribution. Two independent samples may do not follow normal distribution.

10.1.2 SPSS data format

There are two variables in two independent samples test: one is a group variable, the other is a test variable.

10.1.3 Measurement data

10.1.3.1 Example

Example 10-1 The data file "nonpara_3. sav" is used as the Example 10-1. For 10 patients with lung cancer and 12 patients with silicosis, X ray plates are used to measure the right margin of the lung gate transverse diameter (cm), and the results are listed in Table 10-1. Try to find whether the RD values differ between the two populations.

Table 10-1 The RD values of the two populations (cm)

Lung Cancer	2.78	3.23	4.20	4.87	5.12	6.21	7.18	8.05	8.56	9.60		
Silicosis	3.23	3.50	4.04	4.15	4.28	4.34	4.47	4.64	4.75	4.82	4.95	5.10

10.1.3.2 Running the command

The two independent samples test is located in the "Nonparametric Tests" submenu, under the "Analyze" menu.

Analyze

Nonparametric Tests

Legacy Dialogs

2 Independent Samples

The dialog box of Two-Independent-Samples Tests is listed in Figure 10-1.

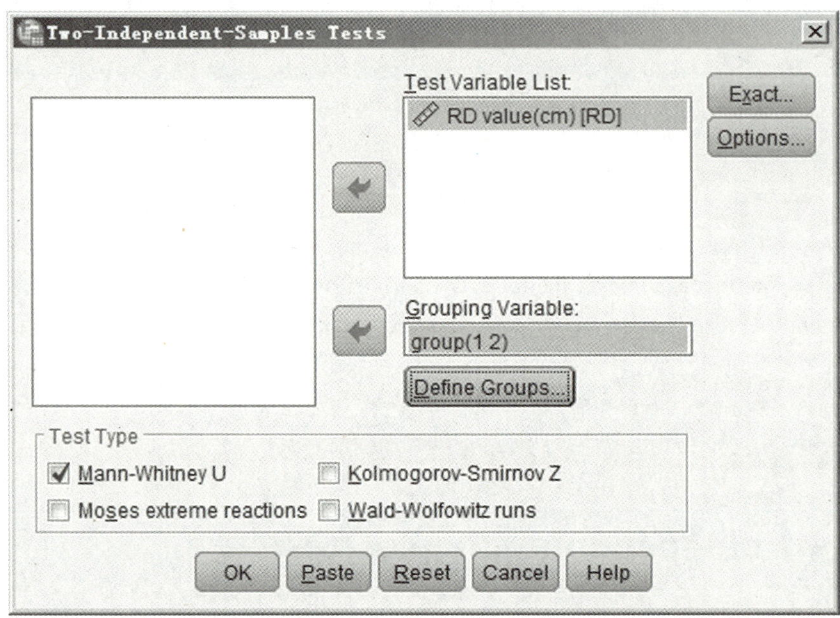

Figure 10-1 The Two-Independent-Samples Tests dialog box

◇Test Variable List: Select the test variable. In the Example 10-1, the variable "RD" is selected.

◇Grouping Variable: Select the grouping variables. In the Example 10-1, the variable "group" is selected and the "Define Groups" (defined grouping variable) dialog box is activated, inputting 1 and 2 in "Define Groups" respectively.

◇Test Type: Four methods can be selected.

☑Mann-Whitney U: This method is used to test whether the location differs between the two-sampling population, which is equivalent to the Wilcoxon rank sum test and the Kruskal-Wallis test of the two groups.

□Kolmogorov-Smirnov Z: The method is used to test whether the location and the shape of the sampling population are different at the same time.

□Moses extreme reactions: After eliminating the maximum and minimum of 5%, compare the differences between the two groups.

□Wald-Wolfowitz runs: It is based on Runs Test after the rank.

10.1.3.3 Reading the output

The mean rank of lung cancer patients is 14.15 (141.50/10), and the mean rank of silicosis workers is 9.29 (111.50/12) (Figure 10-2). Mann-Whitney U statistic is 33.500, Wilcoxon W statistic is 111.50, and the Z-test statistic of the two methods is completely consistent, which is $Z=-1.748$ ($P=0.080$, two-tailed test). The P value of the exact probability test is 0.080. There are no significant differences in RD values between the two groups (Figure 10-3).

Ranks

	group	N	Mean Rank	Sum of Ranks
RD value(cm)	lung cancer patients	10	14.15	141.50
	silicosis workers	12	9.29	111.50
	Total	22		

Figure 10-2 Rank statistics

Test Statistics [a]

	RD value(cm)
Mann-Whitney U	33.500
Wilcoxon W	111.500
Z	-1.748
Asymp. Sig. (2-tailed)	.080
Exact Sig. [2*(1-tailed Sig.)]	.080[b]

a. Grouping Variable: group

b. Not corrected for ties.

Figure 10-3 Results of the Example 10-1

10.1.4 Hierarchical data

10.1.4.1 Example

Example 10-2 The data file "nonpara_4. sav" is used as the Example 10-2. The expression results of HLA-A,B and C of HBV (HBV) DNA are listed in Table 10-2. Do the expression intensity of HLA-A,B and C differ between DNA positive group (DNA^+) and DNA-negative group (DNA^-)?

Table 10-2 The expression of HLA-A,B and C of HBV DNA in serum

Expression Intensity of HLA-A、B、C	DNA^+	DNA^-	Total
-	17	7	24
±	10	15	25
+	9	16	25
Total	36	38	74

10.1.4.2 Runningthe command

First,we describe the frequency variable "freq" by the "Weight Cases" procedure (Figure 10-4), under the "Data" menu as the Figure 10-1.

Data

Weight Cases

▶⊙Weight cases by:"freq"

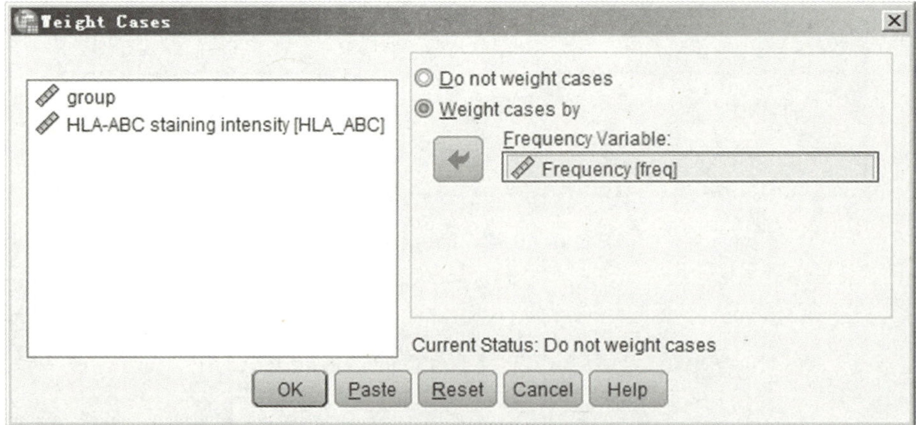

Figure 10-4 The Weight Cases dialog box

The two independent samples test is located in the "Nonparametric Tests" submenu, under the "Analyze" menu, as the Figure 10-1.

Analyze

Nonparametric Tests

LegacyDialogs

2 **Independent Samples**

Select the "Test Variable" in the "Test Variable List" box. This example is the variable "HLA_ABC". Select "group" as "Grouping Variable" in the "Grouping Variable" box. Mann-Whitney U is selected for the Example 10-2.

10.1.4.3 Reading the output

The mean rank of DNA$^+$ group is 31.68, and the mean rank of DNA$^-$ group is 43.01 (Figure 10-5). Mann-Whitney U statistic is 474.500, Wilcoxon W statistic is 1 140.500, and Z-test statistic is $Z=-2.403$ ($P=0.016$, two-tailed test). There is significantly different rank in expression intensity of HLA_ABC between the two groups, with a bigger rank in DNA$^-$ group (43.01>31.68) (Figure 10-6).

Ranks

	group	N	Mean Rank	Sum of Ranks
HLA-ABC staining intensity	DNA+	36	31.68	1140.50
	DNA-	38	43.01	1634.50
	Total	74		

Figure 10-5 Rank statistics

Test Statistics [a]

	HLA-ABC staining intensity
Mann-Whitney U	474.500
Wilcoxon W	1140.500
Z	-2.403
Asymp. Sig. (2-tailed)	.016

a. Grouping Variable: group

Figure 10-6 Results of the Example 10-2

10.2 *K* independent samples test

10.2.1 Description

In the nonparametric test of *K* independent samples, Kruskal–Wallis H test is mainly used to compare the differences of multiple samples.

10.2.2 SPSS data format

The SPSS data file for *K* independent samples test contains multiple grouping variables.

10.2.3 Measurement data

10.2.3.1 Example

Example 10–3 The data file "nonpara_5. sav" is used as the Example 10–3. In order to compare the effects of the three drugs on killing oncomelania, each time we use one of the three drugs to kill 200 oncomelania and record the killing rates. The results are listed in Table 10–3. Are there any differences in the rates of killing oncomelania among the three drugs?

Table 10–3 The killing rates of three drugs (%)

Drug A	Drug B	Drug C
32.5	16.0	6.5
35.5	20.5	9.0
40.5	22.5	12.5
46.0	29.0	18.0
49.0	36.0	24.0

10.2.3.2 Running the command

The nonparametric test of *K* independent samples is located in the submenu of "Nonparametric Tests", under the "Analyze" menu:

Analyze

Nonparametric Tests

Legacy Dialogs

K Independent Samples

The dialog box of K Independent Samples is listed in Figure 10–7. The dialog box of the test requires us to transfer the variables that represent the current killing rates of three drugs to the "Test Variable List" section, and to transfer the grouping variables to the "Grouping Variable" section.

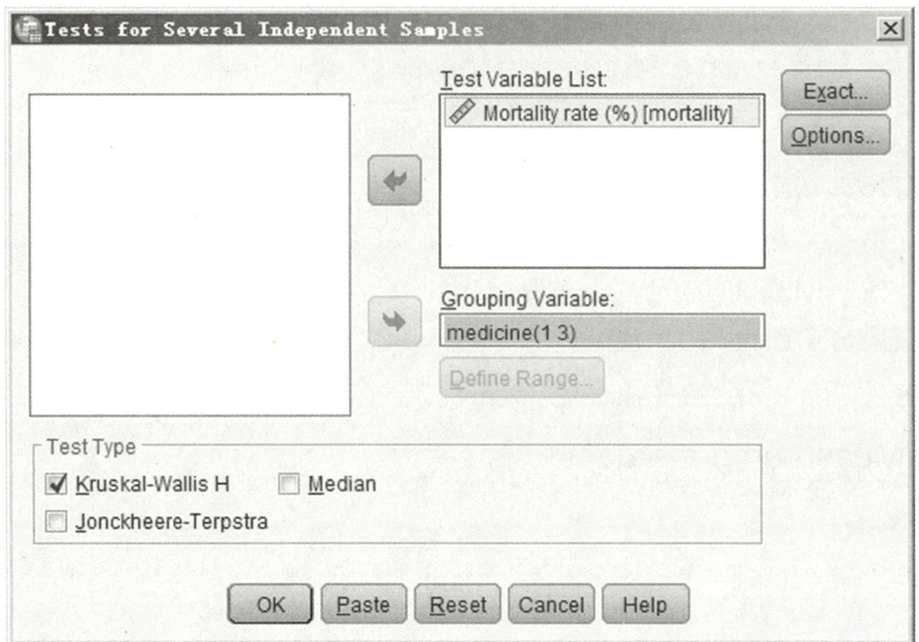

Figure 10-7 The Tests for Several Independent Samples dialog box

◇Test Variable List: In the Example 10-3, the variable "Mortality rate" is chosen as the test variable.

◇Grouping Variable: There are three groups in variable "medicine", which are 1 = "drug A", 2 = "drug B", 3 = "drug C". Click the "Define Range" button, and the dialog box of several independent samples: Define Range pops out (define the range of grouping variable). Fill 1 and 3 in Minimum and Maximum value, respectively, representing the comparison among groups from the first to the third.

◇Test Type: Three methods can be selected.

☑Kruskal-Wallis H: The nonparametric test of K independent samples.

☐Median: Multiple median test.

☐Jonckheere-Terpstra: To test whether multiple samples come from the same distribution. This method is more efficient than Kruskal-Wallis H test for ranked data.

10.2.3.3 Reading the output

The results are listed in Figure 10-8 and Figure 10-9.

Ranks

	medicine	N	Mean Rank
Mortality rate (%)	drug A	5	12.60
	drug B	5	7.60
	drug C	5	3.80
	Total	15	

Figure 10-8 Rank statistics of the Example 10-3

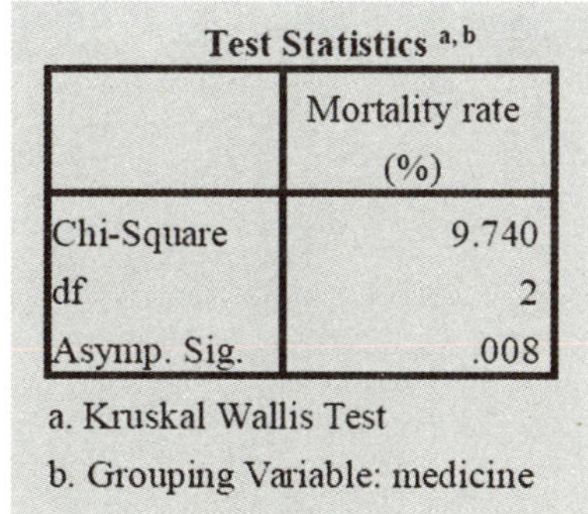

Test Statistics [a,b]

	Mortality rate (%)
Chi-Square	9.740
df	2
Asymp. Sig.	.008

a. Kruskal Wallis Test

b. Grouping Variable: medicine

Figure 10-9 Results of the Example 10-3

The Kruskal-Wallis H test obeys the χ^2 distribution, so the statistic is represented by the χ^2 value. There are significant differences among the 3 groups in this example ($\chi^2 = 9.740$, $v = 2$, $P = 0.008$) (Figure 10-9). Therefore, it can be concluded that the killing rates of different drugs on oncomelania are significantly different. According to the effect of mean ranks, drug A is the best, drug B is the next, and drug C is the worst one (Figure 10-8).

10.2.4 Hierarchical data

10.2.4.1 Example

Example 10-4 The data file "nonpara_6. sav" is used as the Example 10-4. The efficacy values of different internal fixation screws for treating fracture are listed in Table 10-4. Are there any differences in the efficacy value of different treating methods?

Table 10-4 The efficacy of different treating methods

Efficacy	Internal Fixation Nails			Total
	Three wing nails	Rough screws	Fine screws	
Excellent	13	20	20	53
Nonunion	5	4	2	11
Necrosis	7	6	3	16
Total	25	30	25	80

10.2.4.2 Running the command

Before doing the Kruskal-Wallis H test, weight cases should be defined. The dialog box of Weight Cases is under "Data" menu (Figure 10-10) and "freq" is chosen in the "Frequency Variable" section.

Data

Weight Cases

▶⊙Weight cases by: "freq"

The nonparametric test of K independent samples is located in the "Nonparametric Tests" submenu, under the "Analyze" menu (Figure 10-11):

Analyze

Nonparametric Tests

Legacy Dialogs

K Independent Samples

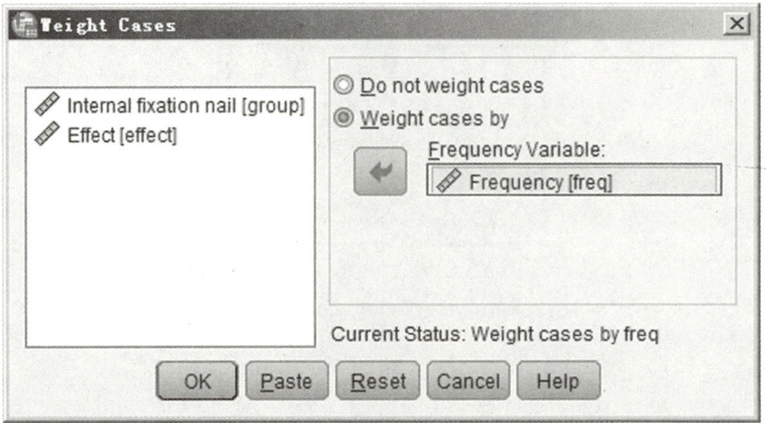

Figure 10-10 The Weight Cases dialog box

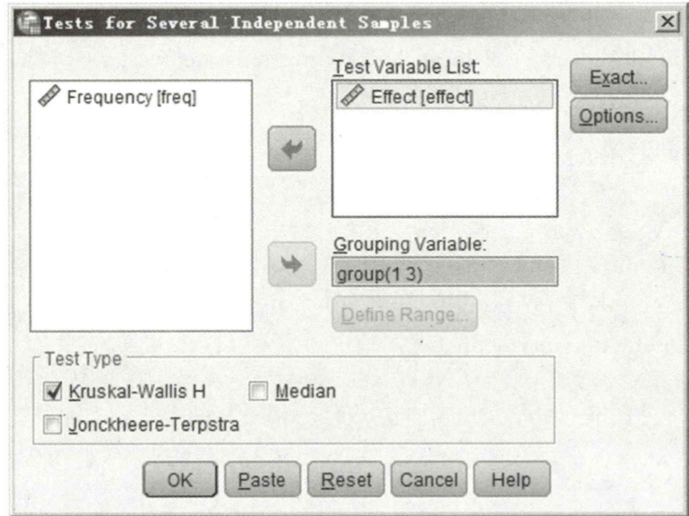

Figure 10-11 The Tests for Several Independent Samples dialog box

◇Test Variable List: "effect". There are three kinds of test variables in "effect", which are coded as 1 = "Excellent", 2 = "Nonunion", 3 = "Necrosis".

◇Grouping Variable: "group(1,3)". In the Example 10-4, there are three groups in the variable "group", which are coded as 1 = "three wing nails", 2 = "rough screws", 3 = "fine screws".

☑Kruskal-Wallis H: The nonparametric test of K independent samples.

10.2.4.3 Reading the output

The outputs are listed in Figure 10-12 and Figure 10-13. From the outputs, there are no significant differences among the efficacy value of three internal fixation screws ($\chi^2 = 4.099$, $\nu = 2$, and $P = 0.129$).

Ranks

	Internal fixation nail	N	Mean Rank
Effect	three wing nails	25	46.14
	rough screws	30	40.37
	fine screws	25	35.02
	Total	80	

Figure 10-12 Rank statistics

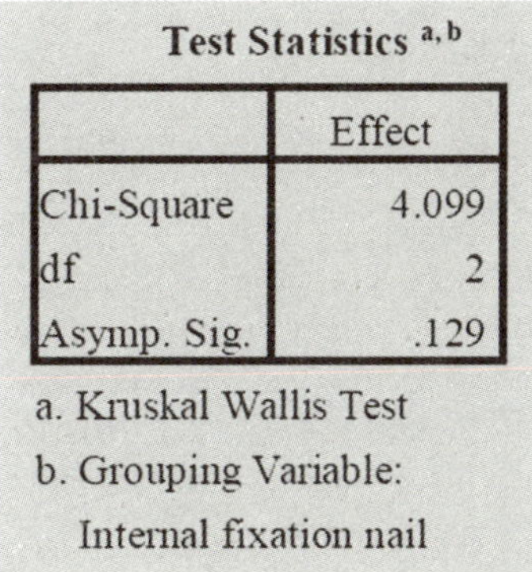
Test Statistics [a,b]

	Effect
Chi-Square	4.099
df	2
Asymp. Sig.	.129

a. Kruskal Wallis Test
b. Grouping Variable: Internal fixation nail

Figure 10-13 Results of the Example 10-4

10.3 Two related samples test

10.3.1 Description

In the two related samples test, Wilcoxon Signed Ranks test is used to compare the differences between the median of matched samples' differences and zero. It can be also used to compare the differences between the median of a single sample and the population.

10.3.2 Example

Example 10-5 The data file "clinical trial. sav" is used as the Example 10-5. The hemoglobin level before and after treatment among 72 samples are listed in Table 10-5. Are there any differences in hemoglobin level before treatment ("HB1") and after treatment ("HB2") in the trial group (GROUP = 1)?

Table 10-5 The hemoglobin level before and after treatment among 72 samples

Samples	HB1	HB2
1	126	107
2	156	156
3	156	156
…	…	…
70	129	126
71	149	140
72	131	130

10.3.3 Running the command

Before doing the two related samples test, we should select cases that need to be analyzed. The "Select Cases" submenu is under the "Data" menu. The dialog box of Select Cases is listed in Figure 10-14. Select button "If condition is satisfied", then click "if" button, and the dialog box of Select Cases: if pops out (define the grouping variables). Then, edit formula "group = 1", which means trial group:

Data

Select Cases

▸⊙**If condition is satisfied:GROUP**=1

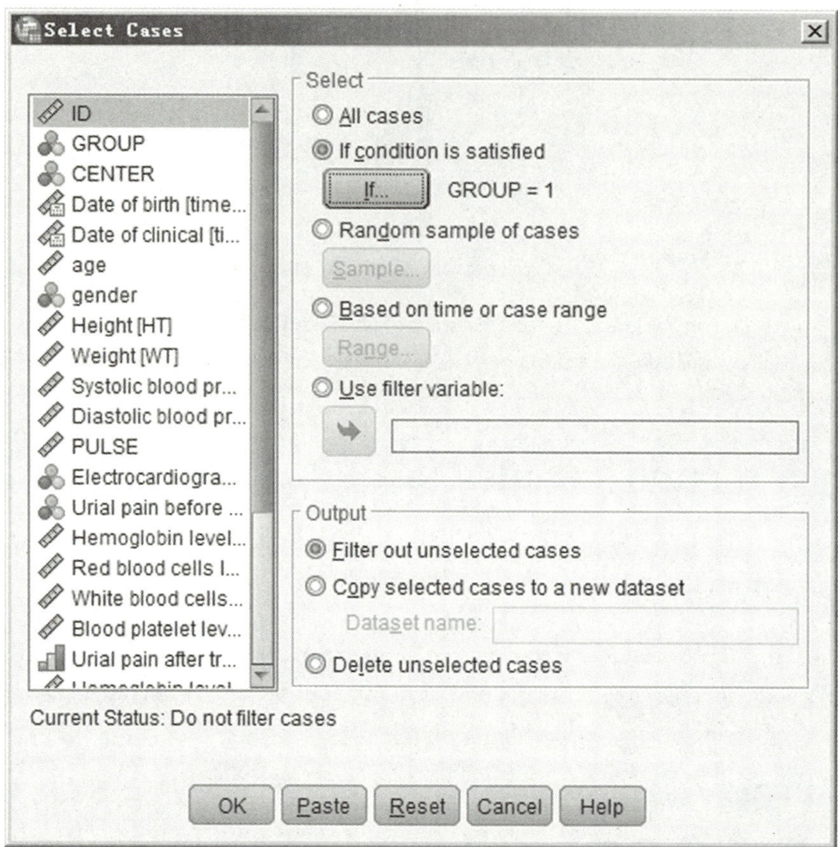

Figure 10-14 The Select Cases dialog box

The two related samples test is located in the "Nonparametric Tests" submenu, under the "Analyze" menu:

Analyze

Nonparametric Tests

Legacy Dialogs

2 **Related Samples Test**

The dialog box of Two-Related-Samples Tests is listed in Figure 10-15.

◇Test Pairs: Select paired variables. In the Example 10-5, the paired variables are "HB1" and "HB2".

◇Test Type: Four methods can be selected.

☑Wilcoxon: Wilcoxon Signed Ranks Test or Wilcoxon One Sample Test. This method is used in this example.

☐Sign: Signed Test. When the sample sizes of two groups are below 25, select the binomial distribution method; otherwise, select the normal distribution method.

☐McNemar: The method is used for comparison of paired enumeration data. It is only used for binary data and each pair of data has the same classification.

☐Marginal Homogeneity: The Marginal Homogeneity test is used for comparison of the two related ordinal samples, and it is an extending method of McNemar test from two to multiple ordinal classified samples.

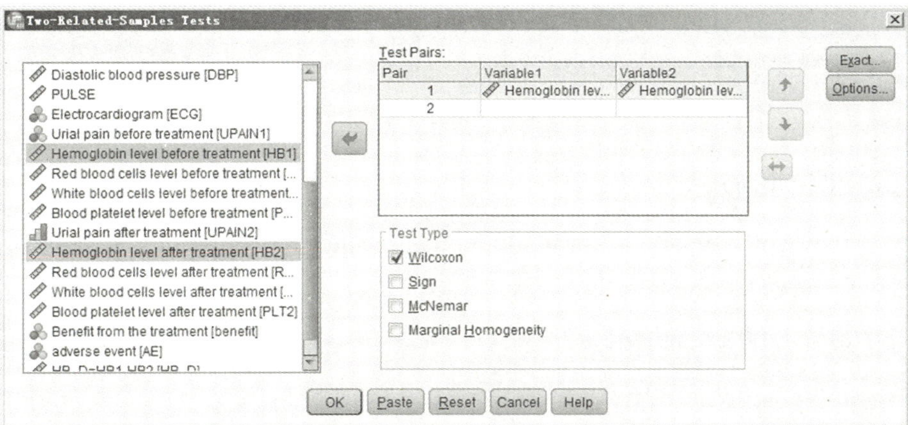

Figure 10-15 The Two-Related-Samples Tests dialog box

10.3.4 Reading the output

Ranks: The sign of the rank is determined by "HB2 – HB1". There are 31 cases in negative ranks, 25 cases in positive ranks and 16 cases in ties ranks. The mean rank of the negative ranks is 31.74 and the mean rank of the positive ranks is 24.48. That is to say, the hemoglobin level decreases after treatment (Figure 10-16). There are no significant differences between before and after treatment ($Z=-1.518$, $P=0.129$) (Figure 10-17).

Ranks

		N	Mean Rank	Sum of Ranks
HB2 - HB1	Negative Ranks	31[a]	31.74	984.00
	Positive Ranks	25[b]	24.48	612.00
	Ties	16[c]		
	Total	72		

a. HB2 < HB1

b. HB2 > HB1

c. HB2 = HB1

Figure 10-16 Ranks statistics

Test Statistics[a]

	HB2 - HB1
Z	-1.518[b]
Asymp. Sig. (2-tailed)	.129

a. Wilcoxon Signed Ranks Test

b. Based on positive ranks.

Figure 10-17 Results of the Example 10-5

10.4 *K* related samples test

10.4.1 Description

Friedman's test is mainly used to compare the differences of distributions among three or more related samples group when randomizing block designed.

10.4.2 SPSS data format

The SPSS data file for the *K* related samples test requires four or more variables in SPSS. One of the variables represents the identified variable of the match groups, and the others are processing group variables. We compare the differences of population distributions among the processing groups.

10.4.3 Example

Example 10-6 The data file "teeth_2. sav" is used as the Example 10-6. In the Example 10-6, try to compare the fixed effect of the three kinds of dental clasps by using nonparametric tests. Their information on tensile strength is listed in Table 10-6.

Table 10-6 Information about tensile strength of 3 dental clasps of 10 samples (N)

Samples	Pull_gen	Pull_RPI	Pull_Y
1	4.3	6.4	5.0
2	10.2	9.7	8.1
3	6.5	7.7	6.7
4	9.2	10.9	7.8
5	5.7	7.1	6.0
6	7.1	8.9	6.7
7	4.4	5.6	4.2
8	11.3	13.0	10.9
9	8.7	10.6	8.4
10	7.3	8.2	7.5

10.4.4 Running the command

The "*K* Related Samples" test is located in the "Nonparametric Tests" submenu, under the "Analyze" menu:

Analyze

Nonparametric Tests

Legacy Dialogs

K Related Samples

The dialog box of Tests for Several Related Samples is listed in Figure 10-18.

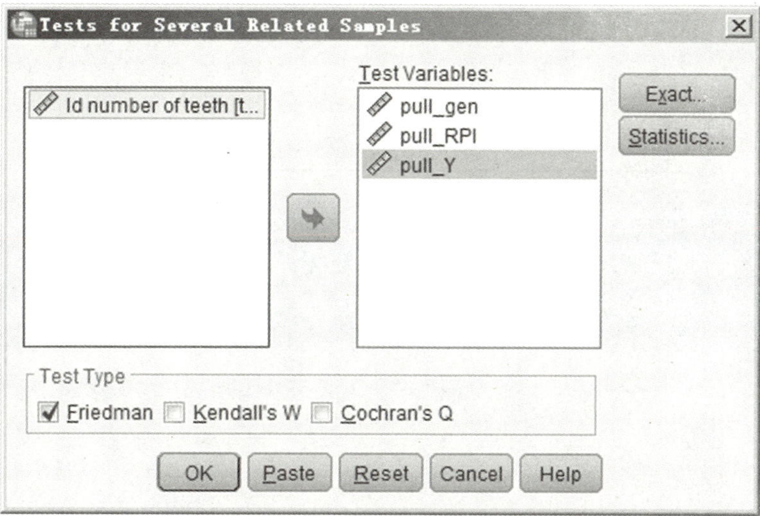

Figure 10-18 The Tests for Several Related Samples dialog box

◇Test Variables: Choose these 3 variables: "pull_gen" "pull_RPI" and "pull_Y".

◇Test Type: Three methods can be selected.

☑Friedman: It is a nonparametric test method for the single sample repeated quantitative measurement data or compatibility group data or hierarchical data. The test hypothesis is that *K* samples are from the same population. It is used in this example.

☐Kendall's W: It is a statistical normalization result of Friedman's test, which is called the coefficient of concordance. Its value ranges between 0 and 1, and it can measure the degree of consistency among different surveyors. The closer to 1, the coefficient of concordance is, the greater the degree of consistency is.

☐Cochran's Q: It is a special case of Friedman's test that all reaction variables are binary classification data and it is also a promoted test of McNemar's test for multiple samples.

10.4.5 Reading the output

The output for the Friedman's test consists of two sections. The first section lists the sample variable and the mean ranks. From the results, the mean ranks of the 3 variables are 1.70, 2.90 and 1.40, respectively (Figure 10-19).

The second section of the output contains the test statistics of Friedman's test (Figure 10-20). The Example 10-6 indicates a significant difference ($\chi^2=12.600, \nu=2, P=0.002$). Then, it can be concluded that RPI is the strongest tensile strength of the dental clasps ($N=2.90$), the second is the ordinary dental clasps, and the "Y" is the smallest tensile strength of the dental clasps.

Ranks

	Mean Rank
pull_gen	1.70
pull_RPI	2.90
pull_Y	1.40

Figure 10-19 Ranks statistics

Test Statistics[a]

N	10
Chi-Square	12.600
df	2
Asymp. Sig.	.002

a. Friedman Test

Figure 10-20 Results of the Example 10-6

Yang Fang

Chapter 11

Survival Analysis

Many applications in biostatistics involve the modeling of lifetime data. In these applications the response variable is the survival time, until some "critical event" occurs, of all subjects including some censored cases. Such survival time data is usually non-normally distributed. According to different research objects and data types, different survival analysis methods can be used. For example, life tables can be used to estimate survival rates such as the postoperative five-year survival rate. Life tables and the Kaplan-Meier method can be used to estimate median survival times. Kaplan-Meier method can be used to compare survival times of patients with different values of a single risk factor. The Cox regression model can be used to analyze the relate survival to a collection of risk factors. In this chapter, several frequently used survival analysis methods are introduced. Since IBM SPSS does not provide a specialized module for conditional logistic analysis, the corresponding implementation by using the module for Cox regression analysis is also provided in this chapter.

11.1 Life tables

11.1.1 Description

Life tables are used to describe the survival pattern of a community. This approach can be used not only when we know the exact survival time of each individual, but also when we only know the number of individuals who survive at a succession of time points.

11.1.2 SPSS data format

The SPSS data file for a life table requires two variables in SPSS. One is the response variable representing the observed survival time or censoring time of individuals in the sample (named "time" in the following example). The other is a classification variable representing the corresponding status recording whether the subject experienced the event of interest within the interval (named "status" in the following example). The classification variable's value has and only has two levels, and the recommended format is using dummy variables (0 = "censoring" and 1 = "death").

11.1.3 Example

Example 11-1 The data file "survival_1.sav" is used as the Example 11-1. Table 11-1 shows the survival time of 20 patients with stage Ⅲ or stage Ⅳ melanoma after treatment in weeks. The final time point is end of the study. Please calculate the cumulative chance of surviving to week 100.

Table 11-1 Survival of patients with stage Ⅲ or stage Ⅳ melanoma after treatment (weeks)

12.8,	15.6,	24.0+,	26.4,	29.2,	30.8+,	39.2,	42.0,	58.4+,	72.0+,
77.2,	82.4,	87.2+,	94.4+,	97.2+,	106.0+,	114.8+,	117.2+,	140.0+,	168.0+

"+" indicates a censored case.

11.1.4 Running the command

The Life Tables is located in the "Survival" submenu, under the "Analyze" menu:

Analyze

Survival

Life Tables

The dialog box of Life Tables is listed in Figure 11-1. The dialog box for the life tables requires that we transfer the variable representing the survival time to the "Time" section and the variable representing the status to the "Status" section. By clicking "Define Event" button to define at least one event value.

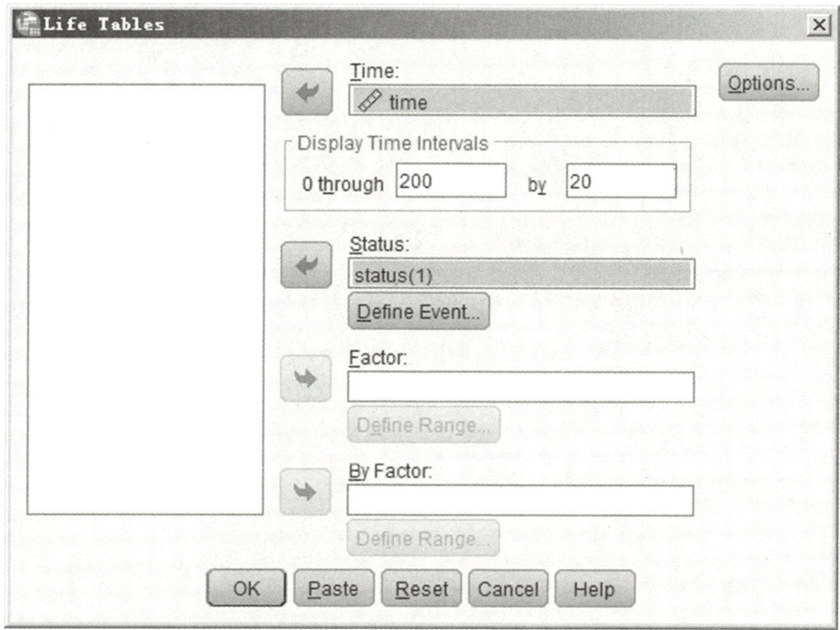

Figure 11-1 The Life Tables dialog box

◇Time: Choose the variable representing survival time. In the Example 11-1, the "time" variable is chosen.

◇Display Time Intervals: The intervals of survival time and the class width. Specify the upper limit of survival by entering a value in the box before "by" and specify the width of each survival time interval by entering a value in the box after "by". In the Example 11-1, 200 and 20 are entered respectively to ensure that the interval of "100-" is shown in the output.

◇Status: Select a survival status variable and then define events. After the "Status" variable being selected, the "Define Event" button is activated. Click this button, and the dialog box of Life Tables: Define Event for Status Variable pops out (Figure 11-2).

◇Value(s) Indicating Event Has Occurred: Indicate that the terminal event has occurred for those cases.

⊙Single value: 1 :Enter a single value that identifies the event of interest.

◎Range of values: ______ through ______ :Enter a range of values that identify the event of interest.

For dichotomous data, the observed death, relapse, disease process and so on are usually defined as the event of interest. In the Example 11-1, "death" is defined as the event of interest and coded as a single value "1". Therefore "1" is entered in the box. All other cases are considered to be censored.

◇Factor(Figure 11-1):define a first-order factor.

◇By Factor:define a second-order factor.

★Options. Click "Options" button (Figure 11-1), and the dialog box of Life Tables: Options dialog box pops out (Figure 11-3).

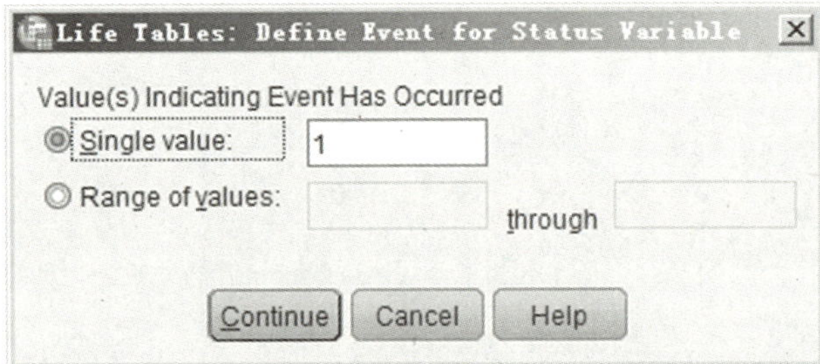

Figure 11-2 The Life Tables: Define Event for Status Variable dialog box

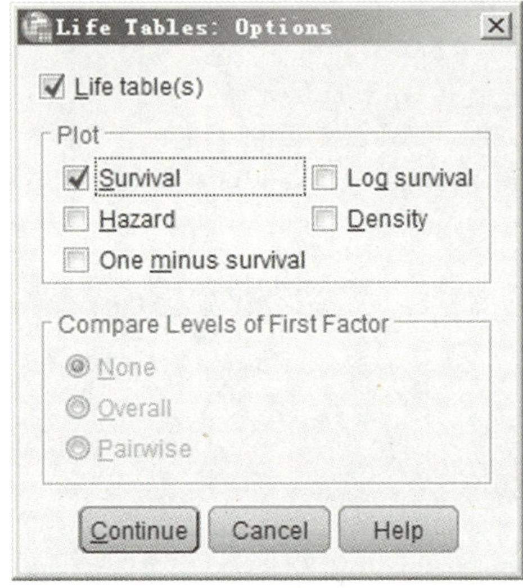

Figure 11-3 The Life Tables: Options dialog box

☑Life table(s) (system default): Displays life tables in the output.

◇Plot: Generates plots of the survival functions.

☑Survival: Displays the cumulative survival function on a linear scale.

□Hazard: Displays the cumulative hazard function on a linear scale.

□One minus survival: Plots one-minus the survival function on a linear scale.

□Log survival: Displays the cumulative survival function on a logarithmic scale.

□Density: Displays the density function.

◇Compare Levels of First Factor: Performs the Wilcoxon (Gehan) test, which compares the survival of subgroups either on the first-order factor if you have defined a first-order factor or for each level of the second-order factor variable if you have defined a second-order factor.

⊙None (system default): No comparisons.

◎Overall: Compares all factor levels in a single test.

◎Pairwise: Compares each distinct pair of factor levels.

11.1.5 Reading the output

The life tables as shown in Figure 11-4. The related explanations are listed.

1) Interval Start Time: The time period that marks the beginning of the interval.

2) Number Entering Interval: The number of surviving cases at the beginning of the interval.

3) Number Withdrawing during Interval: The number of censored cases in this interval.

4) Number Exposed to Risk: The number of surviving cases minus one half the censored cases, that is,

the number of valid observations. This is intended to account for the effect of the censored cases.

5) Number of Terminal Events: The number of events (terminal events) in this time interval.

6) Proportion Terminating: The ratio of terminal events to the number exposed to risk. Also termed as the death rate.

7) Proportion Surviving: One minus the proportion terminating. Also termed as the survival rate.

8) Cumulative Proportion Surviving at End of Interval: The proportion of cases surviving from the start of the table to the end of the interval. It is shown that the cumulative chance of survival to the end of week 100 is 53%, that is, the proportion of patients surviving up to the end of week 100 is 53%.

9) Std. Error of Cumulative Proportion Surviving at End of Interval: The standard error of the estimated cumulative chance of survival.

10) Probability Density: An estimate of the probability of experiencing the terminal event during the interval.

11) Std. Error of Probability Density: The standard error of the probability density.

12) Hazard Rate: The hazard of the event of interest during this time interval.

13) Std. Error of Hazard Rate: The standard error of the estimated hazard rate.

14) The median survival time is 160.000 0: In the Example 11-1, the median survival time is 160.0 weeks. From the cumulative survival function, the survival curve does not intersect the horizontal line crossing 0.5 at the vertical axis (Figure 11-5). There are 53% of all patients surviving to the end of this study.

Life Table[a]

Interval Start Time	Number Entering Interval	Number Withdrawing during Interval	Number Exposed to Risk	Number of Terminal Events	Proportion Terminating	Proportion Surviving	Cumulative Proportion Surviving at End of Interval	Std. Error of Cumulative Proportion Surviving at End of Interval	Probability Density	Std. Error of Probability Density	Hazard Rate	Std. Error of Hazard Rate
0	20	0	20.000	2	.10	.90	.90	.07	.005	.003	.01	.00
20	18	2	17.000	3	.18	.82	.74	.10	.008	.004	.01	.01
40	13	1	12.500	1	.08	.92	.68	.11	.003	.003	.00	.00
60	11	1	10.500	1	.10	.90	.62	.12	.003	.003	.01	.00
80	9	3	7.500	1	.13	.87	.53	.13	.004	.004	.01	.01
100	5	3	3.500	0	.00	1.00	.53	.13	.000	.000	.00	.00
120	2	0	2.000	0	.00	1.00	.53	.13	.000	.000	.00	.00
140	2	1	1.500	0	.00	1.00	.53	.13	.000	.000	.00	.00
160	1	1	.500	0	.00	1.00	.53	.13	.000	.000	.00	.00

a. The median survival time is 160.0000

Figure 11-4 The output of life table

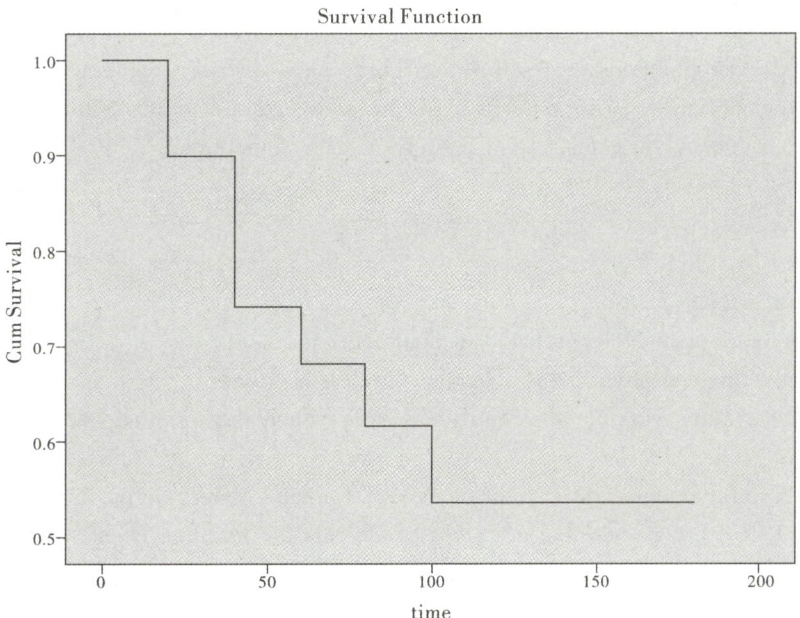

Figure 11-5 The Cumulative Survival Function for the Example 11-1

11.2 Kaplan-Meier estimate

11.2.1 Description

The estimate using exact failure and censoring times is known as the Kaplan-Meier estimate, and is based on a similar argument to that used in deriving life tables.

11.2.2 SPSS data format

The SPSS data file for Kaplan-Meier method requires three variables in SPSS including a time variable, a status variable and a factor/group variable. The time variable should be a continuous variable, the status variable and the factor variable should be a categorical variable.

11.2.3 Example

Example 11-2 The data file "survival_2. sav" is used as the Example 11-2. Table 11-2 shows the response time of 66 leukemia patients receiving one of three different therapies. Is there any difference among the treatment effects of the three therapies?

Table 11-2 Response time data from 66 leukemia patients response time data from 66 leukemia patients (days)

Therapies	The response time
Therapy A	4,5,9,10,11,12,13,28,28,28,29,31,32,37,41,41, 57, 62, 74, 100, 139, 20+,258+,269+
Therapy B	8,10,10, 12, 14,20,48,70,75,99, 103, 162,169, 195, 220,161+,199+,217+,245+
Therapy C	8,10, 11, 23,25,28,28,31,31,40, 48,89,124,143,12+,159+,190+,196+,197+,205+,219+

"+" indicates a censored case.

11.2.4 Running the command

The name of the survival time variable is "time", the status variable is "status" and the factor variable is "group". There are two situations for "status" variable: one is disease progression (a terminal outcome, coded as 1), the other is censored (coded as 0). The variable "group" indicates the therapy group for each case, and it has three dummy variables (1 = "therapy A", 2 = "therapy B", 3 = "therapy C"). The running process is listed.

Analyze

Survival

Kaplan-Meier

The dialog box of Kaplan-Meier is listed in Figure 11-6.

◇Time: Select a time variable. In the Example 11-2, it is "time".

◇Status: Select a status variable to identify cases for which the terminal event has occurred. In the Example 11-2, it is "status(1)".

Click "Define Event" button, and the dialog box of Kaplan-Meier: Define Event for Status Variable pops out (Figure 11-7). Enter the value or values to indicate the terminal event.

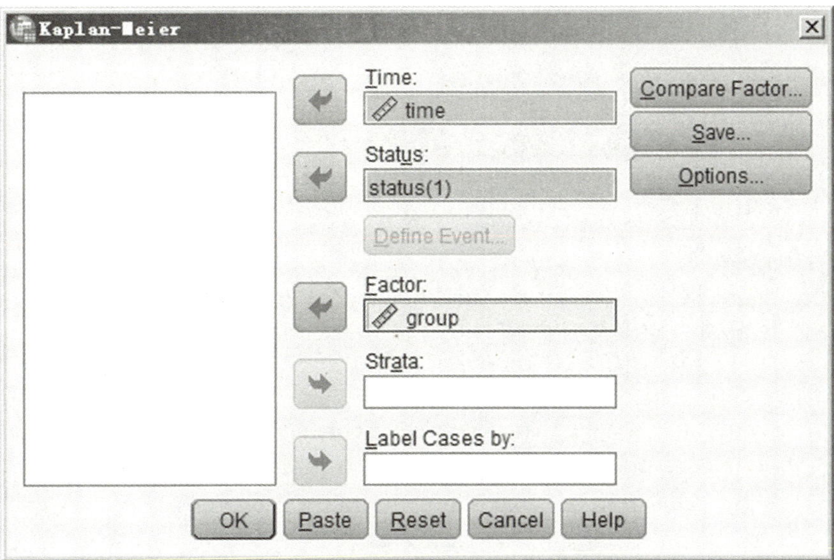

Figure 11-6 The Kaplan-Meier dialog box

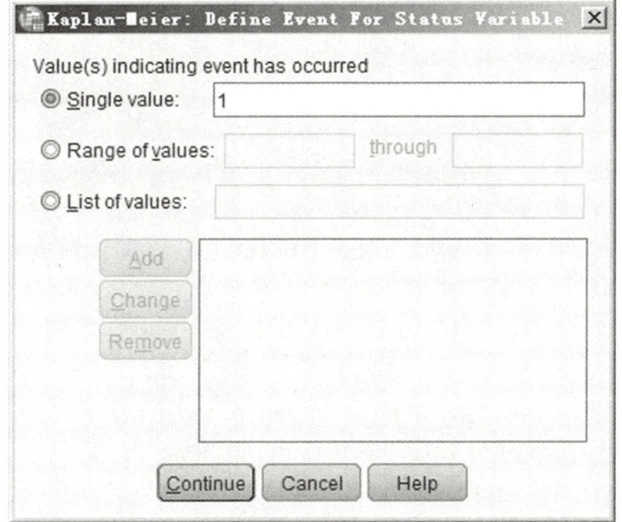

Figure 11-7 The Kaplan-Meier: Define Event For Status Variable dialog box

◇Value(s) indicating event has occurred: Indicate that the terminal event has occurred for those cases.

⊙Single value: [1]: Enter a single value to identify the event of interest. In the Example 11-2, the terminal event is disease progression, which is coded as "1" in the example. Therefore, "1" is entered in the box.

◎Range of values [ ] through [ ]: Enter a range of values that identifies the event of interest.

◎List of Values [ ]: Enter a list of values to identify the event of interest by clicking "Add" button after entering each value.

◇Factor: Select a factor variable to examine group difference. In the Example 11-2, "group" is selected.

◇Strata: Select a strata variable.

◇Label Cases by: Select a label variable to label the cases.

★Compare Factor: To examine group difference. Click "Compare Factor" button (Figure 11-6), and the dialog box of Kaplan-Meier: Compare Factor Levels pops out (Figure 11-8).

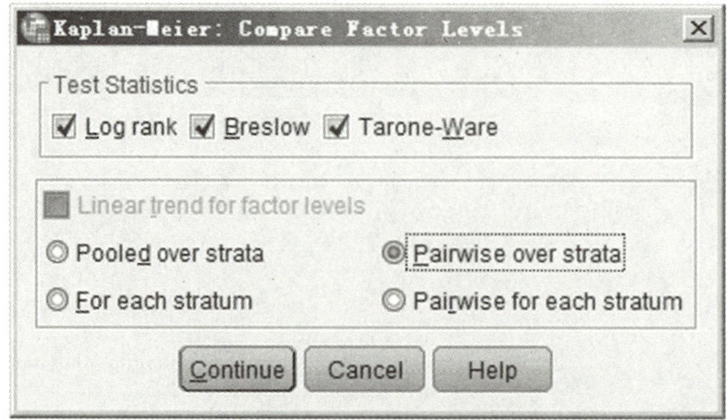

Figure 11-8 The Kaplan-Meier: Compare Factor Levels dialog box

◇Test Statistics: Statistic(s) testing the equality of the survival distributions for the different levels of the factor.

☑Log rank: A test for comparing the equality of survival distributions. All time points are weighted equally in this test.

☑Breslow: A test for comparing the equality of survival distributions. Time points are weighted by the number of cases at risk at each time point.

☑Tarone-Ware: A test for comparing the equality of survival distributions. Time points are weighted by the square root of the number of cases at risk at each time point.

□Linear trend for factor levels: Test for a linear trend across levels of the factor. The factor variable should be ordinal if this option is selected.

◎Pooled over strata: Compares all factor levels in a single test to test the equality of survival curves.

◎For each stratum: Performs a separate test of equality of all factor levels for each stratum.

⊙Pairwise over strata: Compares each distinct pair of factor levels.

◎Pairwise for each stratum: Compares each distinct pair of factor levels for each stratum.

★Save: Save information from your Kaplan-Meier tables as a new variable, which can then be used in subsequent analyses to test hypotheses or check assumptions.

Click "Save" button (Figure 11-6) to open the dialog box of Kaplan-Meier: Save New Variables (Figure 11-9).

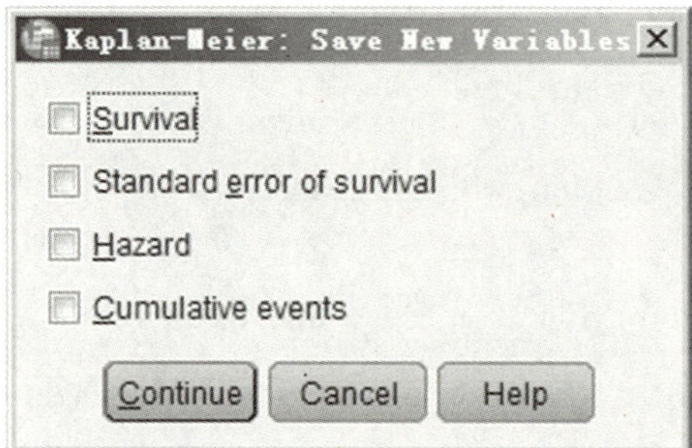

Figure 11-9 The Kaplan-Meier: Save New Variables dialog box

□Survival: Cumulative survival probability estimate.

□Standard error of survival: Standard error of the cumulative survival estimate.

□Hazard: Cumulative hazard function estimate.

□Cumulative events: Cumulative frequency of events when cases are sorted by their survival times and status codes.

★Options: Kaplan-Meier Options. Click "Options" button (Figure 11-6), and the dialog box of Kaplan-Meier: Options pops out (Figure 11-10).

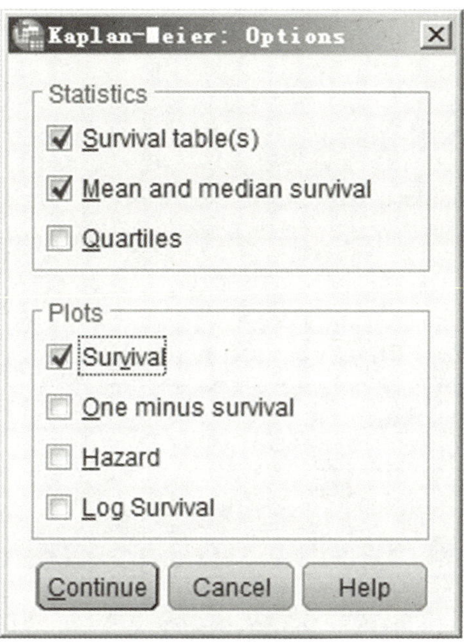

Figure 11-10 The Kaplan-Meier: Options dialog box

◇Statistics: Select statistics displayed for the survival functions computed.

☑Survival table(s): An overall survival table or survival tables for each group.

☑Mean and median survival: The mean and median survival times, their corresponding standard errors and confidence intervals.

□Quartiles: Quartiles (25th, 50th and 75th percentile) and their corresponding standard errors for the survival time variable.

◇Plots: Statistical plots.

☑Survival: Displays the cumulative survival function on a linear scale.

□One minus survival: Plots one-minus the survival function on a linear scale.

□Hazard: Displays the cumulative hazard function on a linear scale.

□Log Survival: Displays the cumulative survival function on a logarithmic scale.

Here is the running process for the Example 11-2:

Analyze

Survival

Kaplan-Meier

▸**Time: time**

▸**Status: status**(1)

▸**Factor: group**

Compare factor

Test Statistics

☑**Log rank**

☑**Breslow**

☑**Tarone-Ware**

□⊙**Pooled over strata** /⊙**Pairwise over strata**

Options

Statistics

☑**Survival table(s)**

☑**Mean and median survival**

Plots

☑**Survival**

11.2.5 Reading the output

(1) Basic information about subjects is shown in Figure 11-11. The numbers of censored cases in therapy A, B, and C are 3, 4, and 7, respectively. The corresponding censoring rates are 12.0%, 21.1%, and 31.8%, respectively.

Case Processing Summary

therapy	Total N	N of Events	Censored	
			N	Percent
therapy A	25	22	3	12.0%
therapy B	19	15	4	21.1%
therapy C	22	15	7	31.8%
Overall	66	52	14	21.2%

Figure 11-11 Basic information about subjects

(2) Survival table is shown in Figure 11-12. The table is very large, so only the section corresponding to the first 25 cases to respond to therapy A is shown. Here are some related explanations.

1) Time: The time at which the event or censoring occurs, with a minimum and a maximum of 4 days and 269 days, respectively.

2) Status: Indicates whether the case experiences disease progression (terminal event) or is censored.

3) Cumulative Proportion Survival at the Time: The proportion of cases surviving from the start of the table until this time (Estimate) and the standard error of this estimate (Std. Error).

4) N of Cumulative Events: The number of cases that have experienced the terminal event from the start of the table until this time.

5) N of Remaining Cases: The number of cases that, at this time, have yet to experience the terminal event or be censored.

Survival Table

therapy		Time	Status	Cumulative Proportion Surviving at the Time: Estimate	Cumulative Proportion Surviving at the Time: Std. Error	N of Cumulative Events	N of Remaining Cases
therapy A	1	4.000	progress	.960	.039	1	24
	2	5.000	progress	.920	.054	2	23
	3	9.000	progress	.880	.065	3	22
	4	10.000	progress	.840	.073	4	21
	5	11.000	progress	.800	.080	5	20
	6	12.000	progress	.760	.085	6	19
	7	13.000	progress	.720	.090	7	18
	8	20.000	censored	.	.	7	17
	9	23.000	progress	.678	.094	8	16
	10	28.000	progress	.	.	9	15
	11	28.000	progress	.	.	10	14
	12	28.000	progress	.551	.101	11	13
	13	29.000	progress	.508	.102	12	12
	14	31.000	progress	.466	.102	13	11
	15	32.000	progress	.424	.101	14	10
	16	37.000	progress	.381	.099	15	9
	17	41.000	progress	.	.	16	8
	18	41.000	progress	.296	.094	17	7
	19	57.000	progress	.254	.089	18	6
	20	62.000	progress	.212	.084	19	5
	21	74.000	progress	.169	.077	20	4
	22	100.000	progress	.127	.068	21	3
	23	139.000	progress	.085	.057	22	2
	24	258.000	censored	.	.	22	1
	25	269.000	censored	.	.	22	0

Figure 11-12 Survival table for therapy A

(3)The means and medians for survival time as shown in Figure 11-13.

1)Mean is the arithmetic mean for survival time. The means of patients receiving therapy A, therapy B, and therapy C are 57.111, 112.263, and 94.831, respectively.

2)The 95% confidence intervals for means of therapy A, therapy B and therapy C are (28.417, 85.805), (72.225, 152.301) and (58.135, 131.527), respectively.

3)Median is the median survival time, that is, the survival time at which the corresponding survival probability is 50%. The median survivals of patients receiving therapy A, therapy B and therapy C are 31, 99 and 40, respectively.

4) The 95% confidence intervals for medians of group A, group B and group C are (24.726, 37.274), (52.076, 145.924) and (17.734, 62.266), respectively.

5)Estimation is limited to the largest survival time if it is censored: The survival time estimation is limited to the largest survival time if it is censored.

Means and Medians for Survival Time

therapy	Mean[a] Estimate	Mean[a] Std. Error	Mean[a] 95% Confidence Interval Lower Bound	Mean[a] 95% Confidence Interval Upper Bound	Median Estimate	Median Std. Error	Median 95% Confidence Interval Lower Bound	Median 95% Confidence Interval Upper Bound
therapy A	57.111	14.640	28.417	85.805	31.000	3.201	24.726	37.274
therapy B	112.263	20.427	72.225	152.301	99.000	23.941	52.076	145.924
therapy C	94.831	18.722	58.135	131.527	40.000	11.360	17.734	62.266
Overall	90.864	11.845	67.648	114.081	41.000	9.609	22.167	59.833

a. Estimation is limited to the largest survival time if it is censored.

Figure 11-13 Survival time estimation

(4) Overall comparisons: After select "Pooled over strata" in the "Compare Factor" dialog box, the output (Figure 11-14) pops out. Since the significance values of the tests are all greater than 0.113, you cannot determine a difference between the survival curves.

Overall Comparisons

	Chi-Square	df	Sig.
Log Rank (Mantel-Cox)	4.311	2	.116
Breslow (Generalized Wilcoxon)	3.672	2	.159
Tarone-Ware	4.348	2	.114

Test of equality of survival distributions for the different levels of therapy.

Figure 11-14 Overall tests of the equality of survival times across groups

(5) Pairwise comparisons: After select "Pairwise over strata" in the "Compare Factor" dialog box, the output (Figure 11-15) pops out. The significance values of two tests are all greater than 0.055, except for a P value of 0.050 for the Tarone-Ware method. Pairwise comparisons are usually performed when a significant result has been shown from the overall comparisons. Otherwise, pairwise comparisons cannot be performed even if a significant pairwise comparison results obtained.

Pairwise Comparisons

		therapy A		therapy B		therapy C	
	therapy	Chi-Square	Sig.	Chi-Square	Sig.	Chi-Square	Sig.
Log Rank (Mantel-Cox)	therapy A			3.650	.056	2.844	.092
	therapy B	3.650	.056			.028	.868
	therapy C	2.844	.092	.028	.868		
Breslow (Generalized Wilcoxon)	therapy A			3.232	.072	1.772	.183
	therapy B	3.232	.072			.066	.797
	therapy C	1.772	.183	.066	.797		
Tarone-Ware	therapy A			3.848	.050	2.264	.132
	therapy B	3.848	.050			.065	.798
	therapy C	2.264	.132	.065	.798		

Figure 11-15 Pairwise comparisons of survival times across groups

(6) Survival curve (Figure 11-16): The survival curves in this figure give a visual representation of the life tables. The plot for therapy B over that of therapy C and therapy A, which suggests that therapy B may have better treatment effect than therapy C and therapy A. But these differences are not statistically significant according to the statistics tests.

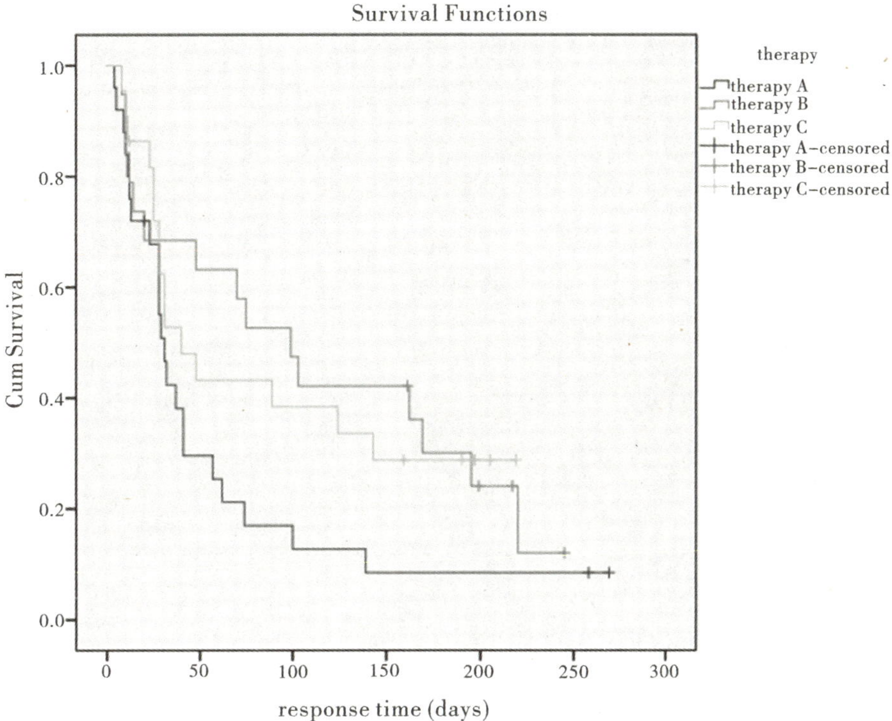

Figure 11-16 Survival curves by therapies

11.3 Cox regression

11.3.1 Description

The Cox regression procedure is useful for modeling the time to a specified event, based upon the values of given covariates.

11.3.2 SPSS data format

The SPSS data file for Cox regression requires variables including a time variable, a status variable and covariates. The time variable can be quantitative, but your status variable can be categorical or continuous. Independent variables (covariates) can be continuous or categorical.

11.3.3 Example

Example 11-3 The data file "survival_3. sav" is used as the Example 11-3. In order to test hypotheses regarding the effects of some potential factors on survival of inpatients with malignant bowel obstruction, related data for 95 inpatients are collected from three hospitals from the year 1995 to 2000. The meanings of entered variables are shown in Table 11-3. Please try to construct a Cox regression model for survival analysis.

Table 11-3 The meanings of variables from data file "survival_3. sav"

Name	Label	Coding	Name	Label
ID	Patient ID		Age	Age in years
Group	Type of stent	1 = metal; 2 = plastic	Cost	Cost(Chines Yuan)

Continue to Table 11-3

Name	Label	Coding	Name	Label
Gender	Gender	1 = male; 2 = female	Time	Survival time in days
Duration	Hospital days		Hb	HB
Status	Status	0 = censored; 1 = death	Stb	STB
Complica	With complications	0 = no; 1 = yes	Alt	ALT
Obstruct	Obstructed position	1 = upperpart; 2 = middle part; 3 = lower part	Ast	AST
Size	Tumor volume (cm^3)		Alp	ALP
Stage	Disease stage	1 = stage Ⅰ; 2 = stage Ⅱ; 3 = stage Ⅲ; 4 = stage Ⅳ	Rgt	RGT
			Wbc	WBC

11.3.4 Running the command

To run a Cox regression analysis, from the menus choose:

Analyze

Survival

Cox Regression

The main dialog box of Cox Regression pops out (Figure 11-17).

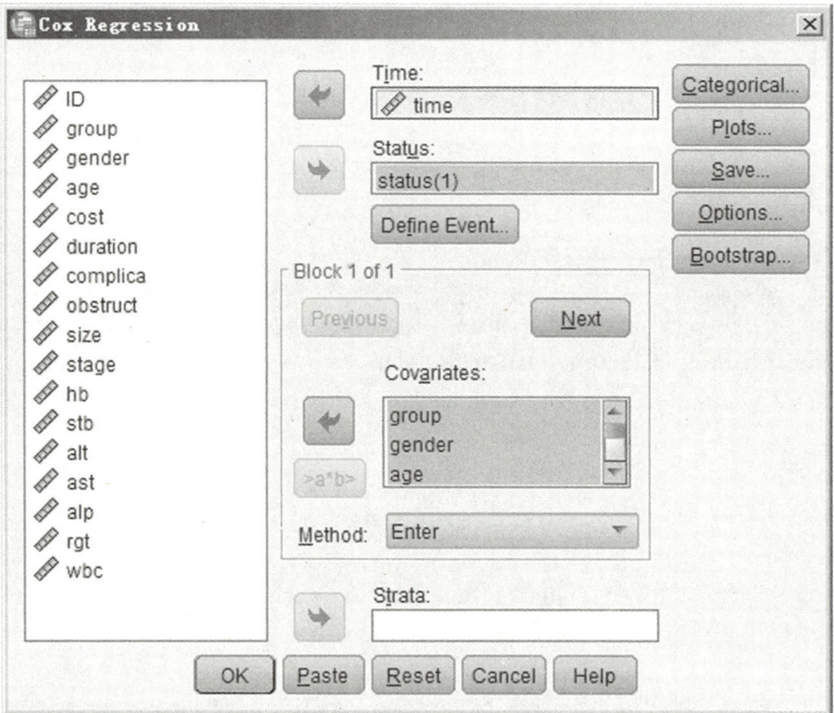

Figure 11-17 The Cox Regression dialog box

◇Time: Select survival time in days ("time") as the time variable.

◇Status: Select status ("status") as the status variable.

◇Covariates: Select one or more covariates.

◇Method: The order of processing and the manner in which the covariates enter the model.

1) Enter: All covariates are entered in a single step.

2) Forward Conditional: Covariates are tested for entry into the model one by one based on the significance level of the conditional statistic.

3) Forward: LR. Covariates are tested for entry into the model one by one based on the significance of the change in the log-likelihood.

4) Forward: Wald. Covariates are entered into the model one by one based on the significance of the Wald statistic.

5) Backward: Conditional: Backward method based on the conditional statistics.

6) Backward: LR: Backward stepwise method based on the likelihood ratio.

7) Backward: Wald: Backward stepwise method based on the Wald statistic.

◇Strata: Identifies a stratification variable. A different baseline survival function is computed for each stratum.

★Categorical: Identifies variables declared to be categorical.

★Plots: To request specific plots to be produced. Click "Plots" button, and the dialog box of Cox Regression: Plots pops out. (Figure 11-18).

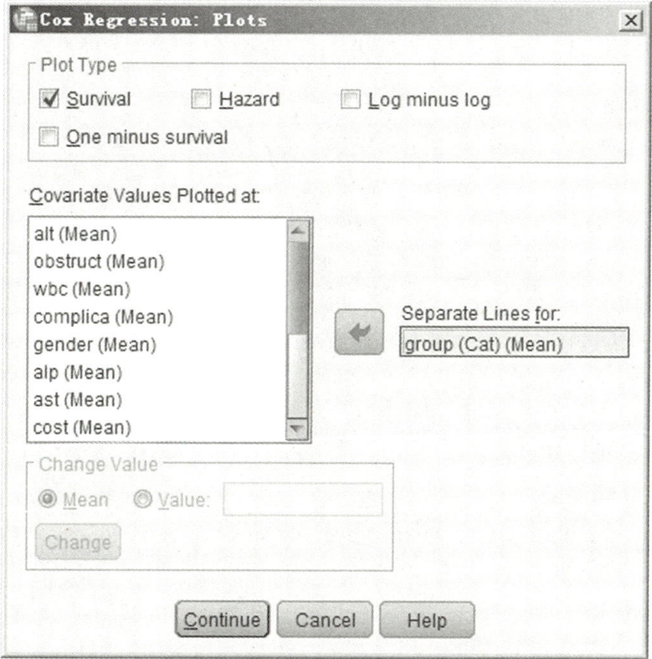

Figure 11-18 The Cox Regression: Plots dialog box

◇Plot Type.

☑Survival: Plots the cumulative survival distribution.

□Hazard: Plots the cumulative hazard function.

□Log minus log: Plots the log-minus-log-of-survival function.

□One minus survival: Plots the one-minus-survival function.

◇Covariate Values Plotted at: Covariate values to be used for the requested plots. The default is the mean of the covariates. You can change the pattern of covariate values by selecting a variable and then selecting "Value" under the activated "Change Value" section and entering a specified value in the blank box right to "Value".

◇Separate Lines for: Choose to have separate. Choose to have separate lines produced for each level of a variable. Note that only variables that have been declared to be categorical can be selected. In the Example 11–3, separate lines produced for each level of group is chosen, that is, plot two separate survival curves for two types of stent.

★Save: Saves the temporary variables created by Cox regression analysis.

Click "Save" button (Figure 11–17), and the dialog box of Cox Regression: Save pops out (Figure 11–19).

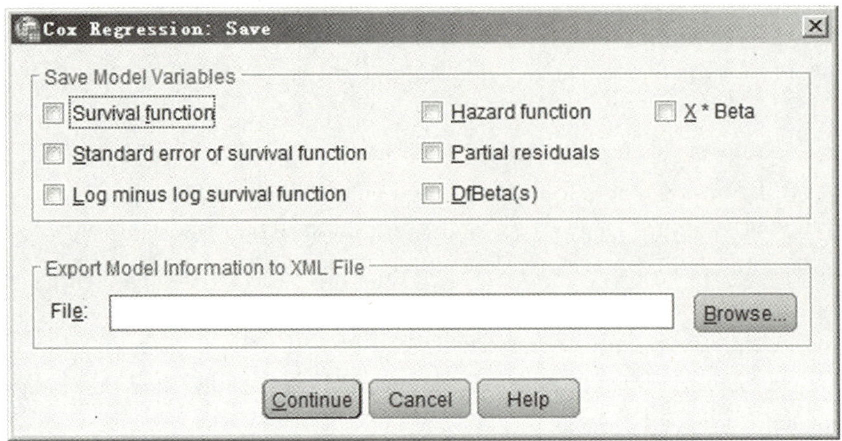

Figure 11–19 The Cox Regression: Save dialog box

◇Save Model Variables.

□Survival function: Survival function evaluated at the current case.

□Standard error of survival function: Standard error of the survival function.

□Log minus log survival function: Log–minus–log–of–survival function.

□Hazard function: Cumulative hazard function evaluated at the current case. Also known as the Cox–Snell residuals.

□Partial residuals: There is one residual variable for each covariate in the final model. If a covariate is not in the final model, the corresponding new variable has the system–missing value.

□DfBeta(s): Change in the coefficient if the current case is removed. There is one DfBeta for each covariate in the final model. If there are time–dependent covariates, only DfBeta can be requested. Requests for any other temporary variable are ignored.

□X * Beta: Linear combination of mean corrected covariates times regression coefficients from the final model.

◇Export Model Information to XML File: Specifies that the data for each split–file group can be held in an external scratch file during processing.

★Options: Click "Options" button (Figure 11–17), and the dialog box of Cox Regression: Options pops out (Figure 11–20).

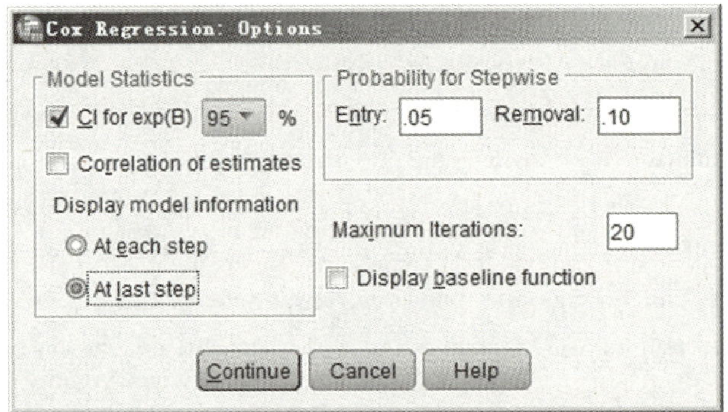

Figure 11–20 The Cox Regression: Options dialog box

◇Model Statistics.

☑CI for exp(B): 95 %: Confidence interval for e^{β}. Specify the confidence level in parentheses. The defaulted value is 95.

☐Correlation of estimates: Correlation matrix for parameter estimates.

◇Display model information.

◎At each step: Print a full regression report for each step.

⊙At last step: Print the final model with full detail.

◇Probability for Stepwise: The statistical criteria used in building the Cox regression models. The default value for probability of statistic for variable entry is 0.05, and the default value for probability of statistic to remove a variable is 0.10. That is, a variable whose significance level is greater than 0.05 cannot enter the model, and a variable whose significance level is less than 0.10 cannot be removed.

◇Maximum Iterations: Maximum number of iterations. If a solution fails to converge after the maximum number of iterations arrived, SPSS displays an iteration history showing the last 10 iterations and terminates the procedure. The default number of maximum iterations is 20.

☐Display baseline function: For each stratum, a table is displayed showing the baseline cumulative hazard, survival, standard error, and cumulative hazard evaluated at the covariate means for each observed time point in that stratum.

Here is the running process for the Example 11-3:

Analyze

Survival

Cox Regression

▸Time: time

▸Status: status(1)

▸Covariates: group / gender / age / cost / duration / complica / obstruct /size / stage / hb / stb / alt / ast / alp / rgt / wbc

Categorical

Categorical covariates: group(Indicator(first))/obstruct(Indicator(first))

Method: Enter / Forward LR

Plots

Survival

Separate line for: group

Options

CI for exp(B): 95 %

At Last step

11.3.5 Reading the output

A full model containing all covariates and a final model based on a stepwise variable selection method are presented here.

(1) The result shows that 20 of 84 cases are censored. Eleven cases censored before the earliest event in a stratum are not used in the analysis (Figure 11-21).

Case Processing Summary

		N	Percent
Cases available in analysis	Event[a]	64	67.4%
	Censored	20	21.1%
	Total	84	88.4%
Cases dropped	Cases with missing values	0	0.0%
	Cases with negative time	0	0.0%
	Censored cases before the earliest event in a stratum	11	11.6%
	Total	11	11.6%
Total		95	100.0%

a. Dependent Variable: survival time in days

Figure 11-21 Case Processing Summary

(2) Categorical Variable Codings: Data file values of 1 for "group" are coded as "0" in the regression, which is the reference category; and data file values of 2 for "group" are coded as "1" in the regression. For "obstruct" variable, the category of upper part is the reference category, and is coded as "0". Each other category of "obstruct" is compared to reference category (Figure 11-22).

Categorical Variable Codings[a,c]

		Frequency	(1)	(2)
type of stent[b]	1=metal	61	1	
	2=plastic	34	0	
obstructed position[b]	1=upper part	39	1	0
	2=middle part	9	0	1
	3=lower part	47	0	0

a. Category variable: type of stent (group)

b. Indicator Parameter Coding

c. Category variable: obstructed position (obstruct)

Figure 11-22 Category Variable Codings

(3) Omnibus Tests of Model.

1) Model includes all variables. Select enter in the box right to method in the "Cox Regression" main dialog box to build a model including all variables. The corresponding omnibus tests of model is shown in Figure 11-23.

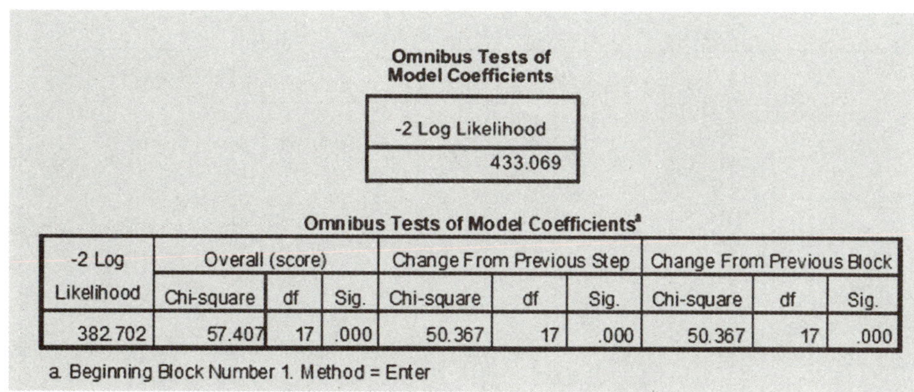

Omnibus Tests of Model Coefficients

-2 Log Likelihood
433.069

Omnibus Tests of Model Coefficients^a

-2 Log Likelihood	Overall (score)			Change From Previous Step			Change From Previous Block		
	Chi-square	df	Sig.	Chi-square	df	Sig.	Chi-square	df	Sig.
382.702	57.407	17	.000	50.367	17	.000	50.367	17	.000

a. Beginning Block Number 1. Method = Enter

Figure 11-23 Omnibus Tests of Model includes all variables

The significance value of the omnibus test of model is significant ($P<0.001$), that is, there is at least one variable's coefficient is not equal to 0. There are 3 different kinds of methods for omnibus test of model.

Overall (score): A likelihood-ratio Chi-square test of the current model versus the null model. The significance value of less than 0.05 indicates that the current model out performs the null model.

Change From Previous Step: The difference between the −2 log-likelihood (−2LL) of the model at the previous step and the current step. If the variable selection method of enter is selected, change from previous step is the same with the change from previous block.

Change From Previous Block: The difference between the −2 log-likelihood of the model including variables in the previous block and the current block. For the Example 11-3, the first block (block 0) includes only the intercept (−2LL=433.069); the current block (block 1) includes all variables (−2LL=382.702). Therefore $\chi^2=433.069-382.702=50.367$.

2) Model using stepwise selection (Forward LR): Select "Forward: LR" in the "Method" drop-down list. Specify Enter 0.05 Removal 0.10 in the "Options" dialog box. Results of omnibus tests of model indicate that the model fit omnibus test for the final model after the 4th iteration ($P<0.001$). The current model outperforms the null model (Figure 11-24).

Omnibus Tests of Model Coefficients^a

Step	-2 Log Likelihood	Overall (score)			Change From Previous Block		
		Chi-square	df	Sig.	Chi-square	df	Sig.
4	394.513	47.245	5	.000	38.555	5	.000

a. Beginning Block Number 1. Method = Forward Stepwise (Likelihood Ratio)

Figure 11-24 Results of model fit omnibus test for stepwise case

(4) Parameter estimation (Figure 11-25)

1) Model includes all variables.

- *B*: Partial regression coefficients.
- *SE*: Standard errors of the coefficients.
- *Wald*: The Wald statistic is a measure of whether the overall partial regression coefficient is equal to 0. This statistic is Chi-square which is calculated by squared of the result of partial regression coefficient divided by its standard error, with a degree of freedom of 1. In the Example 11-3, for "group", its Chi-square value is $7.672=(1.234/0.446)^2$. The power of the Wald test is poor when the absolute value of the partial regression coefficient is large.

Variables in the Equation

	B	SE	Wald	df	Sig.	Exp(B)	95.0% CI for Exp(B)	
							Lower	Upper
type of stent	1.234	.446	7.672	1	.006	3.436	1.435	8.229
gender	-.036	.427	.007	1	.932	.964	.418	2.226
age in years	-.018	.013	1.978	1	.160	.982	.958	1.007
cost (Chinese Yuan)	.000	.000	1.012	1	.314	1.000	1.000	1.000
hospital days	.010	.007	2.102	1	.147	1.010	.997	1.023
with complications	.021	.419	.003	1	.960	1.021	.450	2.320
obstructed position			6.492	2	.039			
obstructed position(1)	.678	.605	1.257	1	.262	1.970	.602	6.444
obstructed position(2)	-.532	.366	2.117	1	.146	.587	.287	1.203
Tumor volume(cm3)	.019	.006	9.656	1	.002	1.019	1.007	1.032
disease stage	.776	.248	9.790	1	.002	2.172	1.336	3.530
HB	-.012	.009	1.691	1	.194	.988	.970	1.006
STB	.000	.001	.205	1	.650	1.000	.997	1.002
ALT	-.001	.002	.636	1	.425	.999	.995	1.002
AST	.001	.002	.409	1	.522	1.002	.997	1.006
ALP	-.001	.001	1.251	1	.263	.999	.998	1.000
RGT	.000	.001	.626	1	.429	1.000	.998	1.001
WBC	.100	.054	3.384	1	.066	1.105	.993	1.229

Figure 11-25 Parameter estimates for model with all variables

- Exp(B): The value of Exp(B) indicates the hazard ratio (HR), also named as the relative risk (RR). It equals the inverse logarithm of the partial regression coefficient, with a value farther from 1 indicating a stronger effect.

The significance values of the effects for "group" "obstruct" "size" and "stage" are all less than 0.01. The values of coefficients are all larger than 0, which means that their hazard ratio are larger than 1. It can be concluded that the death hazard for a patient who has larger values for these 4 variables is higher.

2) Model based on stepwise selection (Forward LR, Figure 11-26). The death hazard for a patient with plastic stent is 3.189 (95% CI: 1.785-5.699) times of that of a patient with metal stent. The regression coefficient for the obstructed positions of middle part and lower part are relative to the reference category (upper part). The hazard for middle part patients is the highest, which is 2.506 (95% CI: 1.007-6.239) times of that for the upper part patients. The significance value for this coefficient for the lower part is not significant ($P=0.101$), so any observed difference between this category and the reference category can be due to chance. The regression coefficients for "size" and "stage" suggest that the death hazard is increased for patients with large tumor volume and advanced tumor stage.

Variables in the Equation

		B	SE	Wald	df	Sig.	Exp(B)	95.0% CI for Exp(B)	
								Lower	Upper
Step 4	type of stent	1.160	.296	15.330	1	.000	3.189	1.785	5.699
	obstructed position			9.266	2	.016			
	obstructed position(1)	.919	.465	3.899	1	.048	2.506	1.007	6.239
	obstructed position(2)	-.470	.286	2.694	1	.101	.625	.356	1.096
	Tumor volume(cm3)	.018	.005	11.820	1	.001	1.018	1.008	1.028
	disease stage	.718	.239	9.015	1	.003	2.051	1.283	3.278

Figure 11-26 Parameter estimates for model based on stepwise selection

(5) Figure 11-27 displays the average value (in the column named Mean) of each covariate in the final equation, plus a pattern for each level of covariates (in the columns under Pattern). The figure is a useful reference when looking at the survival plots, which are constructed for the mean values and each covariate pattern.

Covariate Means and Pattern Values

	Mean	Pattern 1	Pattern 2
type of stent	.345	.000	1.000
gender	1.250	1.250	1.250
age in years	57.369	57.369	57.369
cost (Chinese Yuan)	49640.767	49640.767	49640.767
hospital days	38.131	38.131	38.131
with complications	.333	.333	.333
obstructed position(1)	.107	.107	.107
obstructed position(2)	.524	.524	.524
Tumor volume(cm3)	16.462	16.462	16.462
disease stage	3.119	3.119	3.119
HB	107.651	107.651	107.651
STB	248.591	248.591	248.591
ALT	133.567	133.567	133.567
AST	136.060	136.060	136.060
ALP	539.810	539.810	539.810
RGT	545.298	545.298	545.298
WBC	8.421	8.421	8.421

Figure 11-27 Covariate Means and Pattern Values

(6) Survival curves (Figure 11-28) is the basic survival curve for all patients with malignant bowel obstruction, which is a visual display of the model-predicted time to death for the "average" patient whose covariate values are all close to the mean. Figure 11-29 is the plot of the survival curves for each covariate pattern which gives a visual representation of the effect of "group" (type of stent).

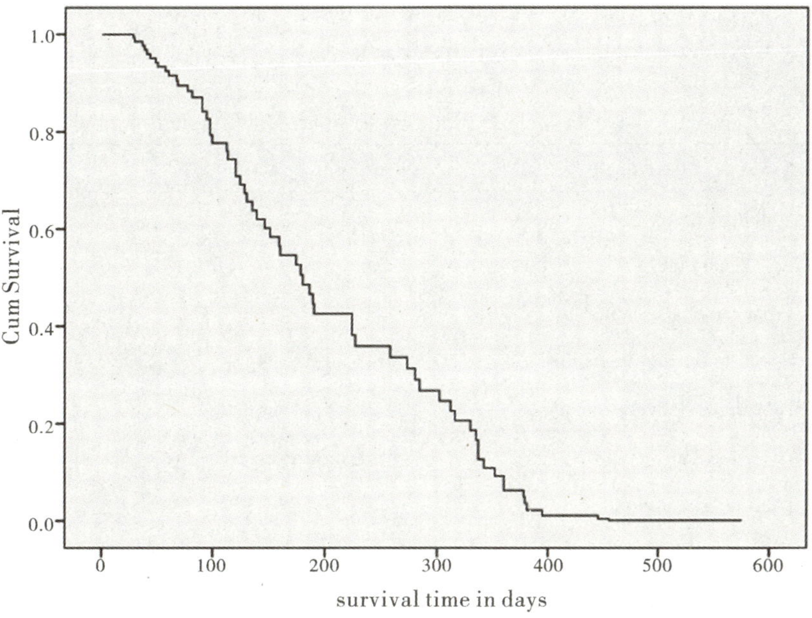

Figure 11-28 Survival curve for "average" patient

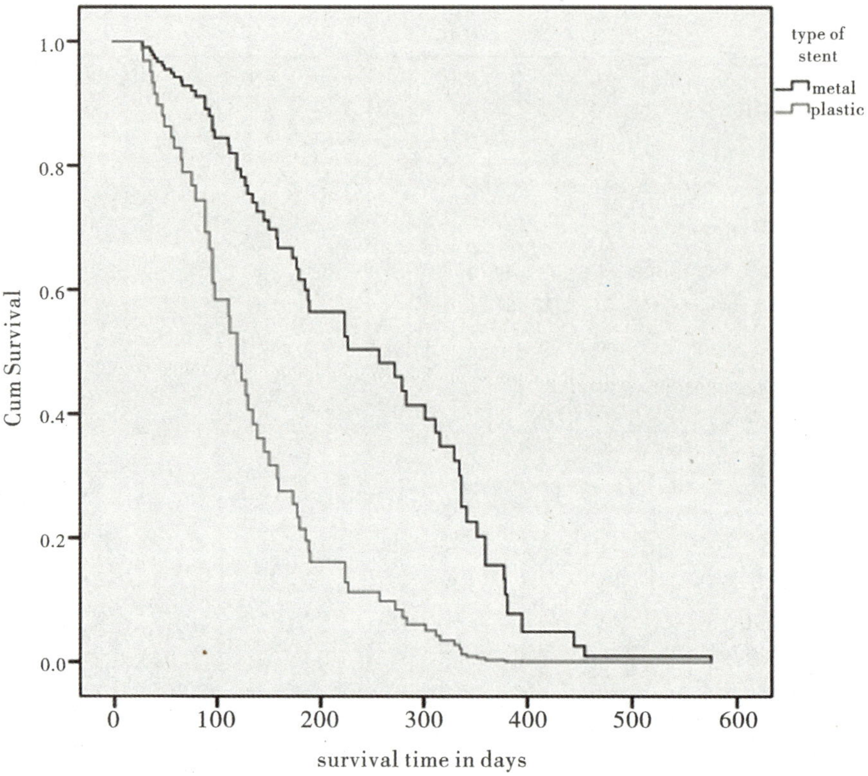

Figure 11–29 Survival curves by group category

The data file "survival_4. sav" is used as the Example 11–4. The data save the collected data from 56 subjects in a 1–1 matched case–control study for the potential factors of low birth weight. The basic information for variables is shown in Table 11–4. Please try to obtain the results of conditional logistic regression model by running a Cox regression analysis for this example.

Table 11–4 Variable information for data file "survival_4. sav"

Name	Label	Coding
Pairid	Matching group	
Age	Age of mother	
Lwt	Pregestational weight	
Smoke	Smoking during pregnancy	0:no;1:yes
Ptd	Premature delivery history	0:no;1:yes
Ht	Hypertension	0:no;1:yes
Ui	Uterine stimulation	0:no;1:yes
Low	Low birth weight	0:no;1:yes

This study should be analyzed by fitting a conditional logistic model. Since a specific module for this model is not provided by the IBM SPSS, a Cox regression can be used to obtain an identical result. To obtain such an analysis, you need to create a survival time variable by specifying an unchanged value for all the "low = 1" cases and specifying another unchanged but smaller value for all the "low = 0" cases. Here in this example use the "Compute Variable" module to compute a new variable "time=low+1", that is, the values of survival times for cases of "low=1" are 2 and for cases of "low=0" are 1. The running process is listed.

Analyze

Survival

Cox Regression

▶**Time: time**

▶**Status: low(1)**

▶**Covariates: age / lwt / smoke / ptd / ht / ui**

Method: Forward LR

Strata: paired

Options

CI for exp(B): 95 %

Last step

11.3.6 Reading the output

(1) The result shows that 56 of 112 cases are censored, which is the number of control cases in this study (Figure 11-30).

Case Processing Summary

		N	Percent
Cases available in analysis	Event[a]	56	50.0%
	Censored	56	50.0%
	Total	112	100.0%
Cases dropped	Cases with missing values	0	.0%
	Cases with negative time	0	.0%
	Censored cases before the earliest event in a stratum	0	.0%
	Total	0	.0%
Total		112	100.0%

a. Dependent Variable: time

Figure 11-30 Case processing summary

(2) Test of model. The corresponding omnibus tests of model as shown in Figure 11-31. The significance value ($P=0.002$) indicates that the current model after 2nd iteration outperforms the null model.

Omnibus Tests of Model Coefficients[a]

Step	-2 Log Likelihood	Overall (score)			Change From Previous Block		
		Chi-square	df	Sig.	Chi-square	df	Sig.
2	63.677	12.383	2	.002	13.956	2	.001

a. Beginning Block Number 1. Method = Forward Stepwise (Likelihood Ratio)

Figure 11-31 Results of the Omnibus Test of Model performance

(3) Estimations (Figure 11-32). The final model based on stepwise selection includes "smoke" and "ptd". The results suggest that mothers having smoking habit during pregnancy and having history of premature delivery are two risk factors for low birth weight. The hazard ratios are 3.078 (95% *CI*: 1.267-7.474) and 4.326 (95% *CI*: 1.310-14.284), respectively.

		B	SE	Wald	df	Sig.	Exp(B)	95.0% CI for Exp(B)	
								Lower	Upper
Step 2	smoke	1.124	.453	6.168	1	.013	3.078	1.267	7.474
	ptd	1.465	.610	5.774	1	.016	4.326	1.310	14.284

Variables in the Equation[a]

a. Constant or Linearly Dependent Covariates S = Stratum effect. age = 45/2 + S ;

Figure 11-32 Final Variables after stepwise selection

11.4 Time-dependent Cox model

11.4.1 Description

The Cox model assumes that the ratio of the hazards for any two cases is the same for all time points, that is, the covariate effect is the same for all time points. This is the proportional hazards assumption. If you want to estimate an extended Cox regression model that allows non-proportional hazards, you can do so by fitting a time-dependent Cox model. Such a model can also be used to test whether the proportional hazards assumption is reasonable.

11.4.2 SPSS data format

The format of SPSS data file for time-dependent Cox regression is the same with that for a regular Cox regression.

11.4.3 Example

Example 11-3 The Example 11-3 mentioned above is used for this analysis. Use Cox regression with a time-dependent covariate to assess the proportional hazards assumption with respect to the type of stent in inpatients with malignant bowel obstruction.

11.4.4 Running the command

(1) To run a time-dependent Cox regression analysis, from the menus choose:

Analyze

Survival

Cox w/Time-Dep Cov

The dialog box of Compute Time-Dependent Covariate pops out (Figure 11-33), and type "T_ * group" is chosen as the time-dependent covariate.

◇Expression for T_COV_. The expression for the time-dependent covariate. The variable list on the left box contains an automatically created variable named "Time[T_]". If you think that some variables may have different effects at different time, you need to define a time-dependent covariate, which can be done by multiplying "Time[T_]" with this covariate or using more complex expressions. You can use the syntax command language to create other time-dependent covariates. Here, a time-dependent covariate is created as "T_ * group" in this example.

Then click "Model" button to open the Cox Regression dialog box (Figure 11-34). Note that the created time-dependent covariate should be added to the model by selecting it as "Covariates".

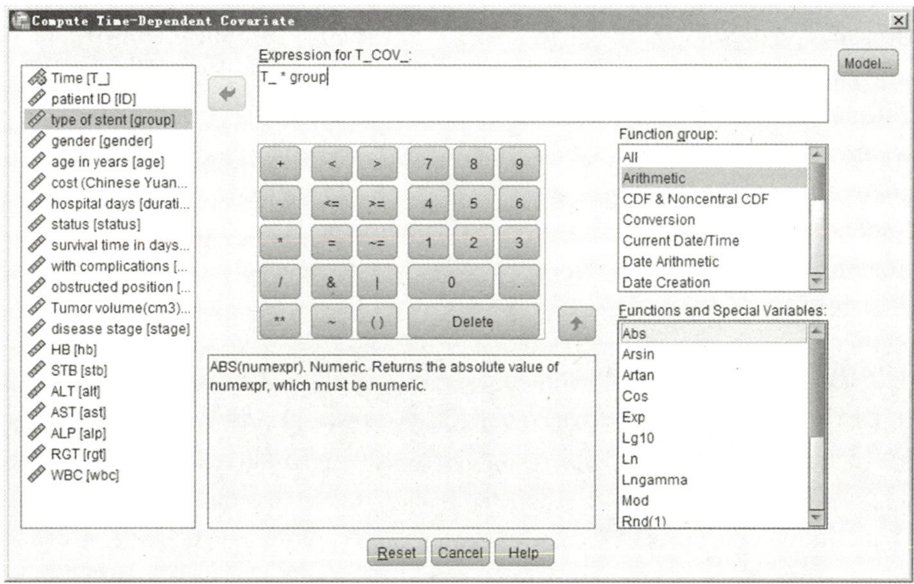

Figure 11-33 The Compute Time-Dependent Covariate dialog box

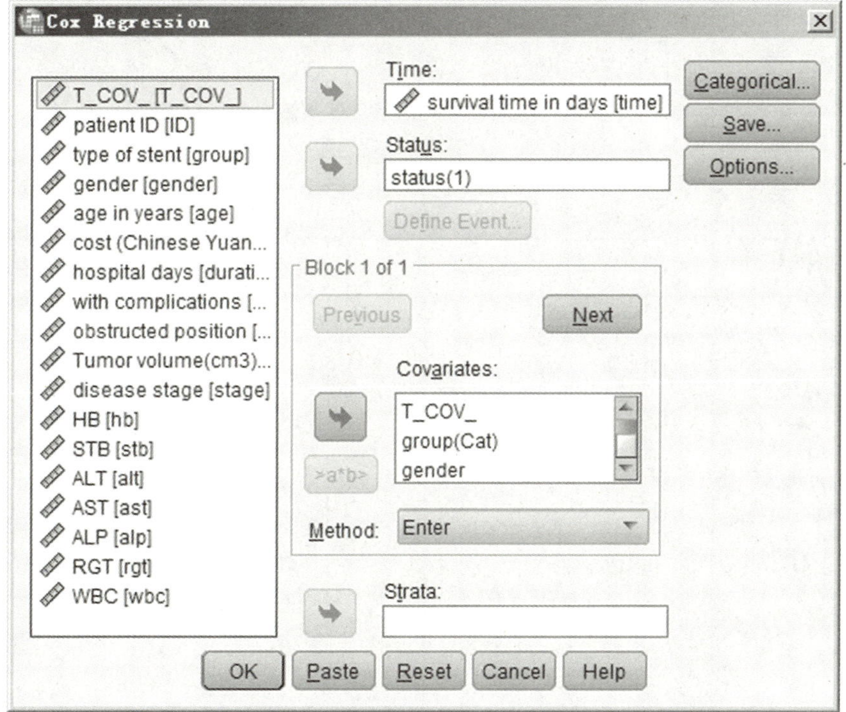

Figure 11-34 The time-dependent Cox Regression dialog box

Here is the running process for this example:

Analyze

Survival

Cox Regression

▸**Expression for T_COV_:** ***T_ * group***

Model

▸**Time: time**

▶Status:status(1)

▶Covariates:group / gender / age / cost / duration / complica / obstruct /size / stage / hb / stb / alt / ast / alp / rgt / wbc

Categorical

Categorical covariates:group(Indicator(first))/obstruct(Indicator(first))

Method:Enter / Forward LR

Options

CI for exp(B):95 %

At Last step

11.4.5 Reading the output

(1) A full model containing all covariates is shown in Figure 11-35 and Figure 11-36. The significance value ($P=0.294$) of the corresponding omnibus tests of model indicates that the current model outperforms the null model. The significance value for the coefficient for the time-dependent covariate is 0.294, which indicates that the effect of type of stent on death is not time-dependent. A regular Cox regression assuming proportional hazards can be used.

Omnibus Tests of Model Coefficients[a]

-2 Log Likelihood	Overall (score)			Change From Previous Step			Change From Previous Block		
	Chi-square	df	Sig.	Chi-square	df	Sig.	Chi-square	df	Sig.
381.561	58.015	18	.000	51.507	18	.000	51.507	18	.000

a. Beginning Block Number 1. Method = Enter

Figure 11-35 The Omnibus Tests of Model Coefficients

Variables in the Equation

	B	SE	Wald	df	Sig.	Exp(B)	95.0% CI for Exp(B)	
							Lower	Upper
T_COV_	-.003	.003	1.101	1	.294	.997	.991	1.003
type of stent	1.745	.665	6.877	1	.009	5.724	1.554	21.086
gender	-.034	.424	.006	1	.937	.967	.421	2.221
age in years	-.017	.013	1.763	1	.184	.983	.959	1.008
cost (Chinese Yuan)	.000	.000	1.283	1	.257	1.000	1.000	1.000
hospital days	.009	.007	1.967	1	.161	1.009	.996	1.023
with complications	.114	.422	.074	1	.786	1.121	.491	2.562
obstructed position			6.648	2	.036			
obstructed position(1)	.570	.617	.853	1	.356	1.768	.527	5.930
obstructed position(2)	-.609	.370	2.704	1	.100	.544	.263	1.124
Tumor volume(cm3)	.021	.006	10.453	1	.001	1.021	1.008	1.034
disease stage	.725	.248	8.526	1	.004	2.065	1.269	3.359
HB	-.010	.010	.983	1	.321	.990	.972	1.009
STB	-.001	.001	.355	1	.551	.999	.997	1.002
ALT	-.002	.002	1.058	1	.304	.998	.995	1.002
AST	.002	.002	.418	1	.518	1.002	.997	1.006
ALP	.000	.001	.474	1	.491	1.000	.998	1.001
RGT	-.001	.001	.838	1	.360	.999	.998	1.001
WBC	.091	.054	2.807	1	.094	1.095	.985	1.218

Figure 11-36 Coefficients of model with all covariates

(2) The model based on a stepwise selection method (Forward:LR) as shown in Figure 11-37 and Figure 11-38. The final model after 4th iteration does not include the time-dependent covariate, and then the output is the same as that in section 11.3 in this chapter.

Omnibus Tests of Model Coefficients[a]

Step	-2 Log Likelihood	Overall (score)			Change From Previous Block		
		Chi-square	df	Sig.	Chi-square	df	Sig.
4	394.513	47.245	5	.000	38.555	5	.000

a. Beginning Block Number 1. Method = Forward Stepwise (Likelihood Ratio)

Figure 11-37 Results of model fit omnibus test for stepwise case

Variables in the Equation

		B	SE	Wald	df	Sig.	Exp(B)	95.0% CI for Exp(B)	
								Lower	Upper
Step 4	type of stent	1.160	.296	15.330	1	.000	3.189	1.785	5.699
	obstructed position			9.266	2	.016			
	obstructed position(1)	.919	.465	3.899	1	.048	2.506	1.007	6.239
	obstructed position(2)	-.470	.286	2.694	1	.101	.625	.356	1.096
	Tumor volume(cm3)	.018	.005	11.820	1	.001	1.018	1.008	1.028
	disease stage	.718	.239	9.015	1	.003	2.051	1.283	3.278

Figure 11-38 Parameter estimates for model based on stepwise selection

Wu Ying

Chapter 12

Graphs

"Graphs" in the main menu compose of "Chart Builder" "Graphboard Template Chooser" and "Legacy Dialogs", *etc*. The legacy dialogs keep the charts in the previous SPSS version and include Bar chart, 3-D Bar chart, Line chart, Area chart, Pie chart, High-Low chart, Boxplot chart, Error bar chart, Population Pyramid chart, Scatter plot and Histogram. The main menu and submenu of "Graphs" can be seen in Figure 12-1.

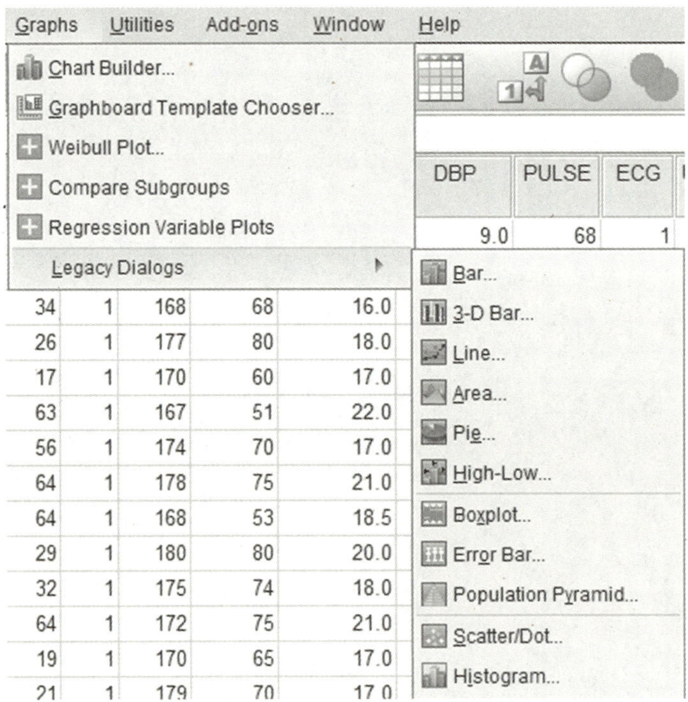

Figure 12-1　The submenu in Graphs dialog box

12.1　Chart builder

The data file "clinical trial. sav" is used as the Example 12-1 to describe the clustered bar.

Graphs

Chart Builder

The dialog box of Chart Builder is listed in Figure 12-2. This dialog box suggests that the measurement level should be set properly for each variable in this chart, especially for the value labels for categorical variables.

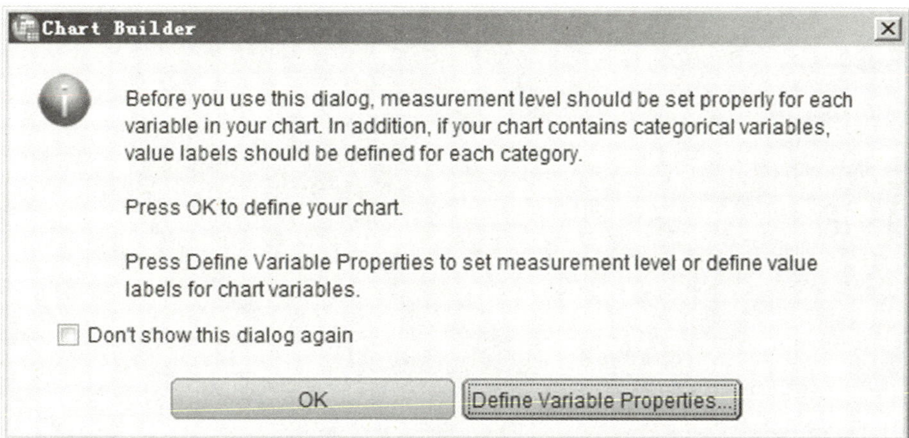

Figure 12-2 The dialog box of Chart Builder

Click "Define Variable Properties" button, and the dialog box of Define Variable Properties pops out. Choose "GROUP" and press "Continue", then pop out Figure 12-3. In the "Measurement Level" box, click "Scale", and then press "OK". The property of variable "GROUP" is transferred from nominal variable to quantitative variable.

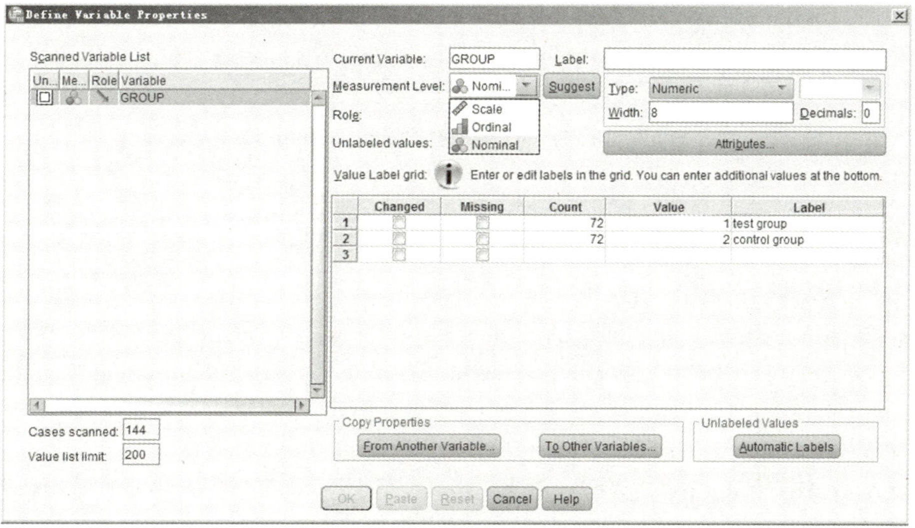

Figure 12-3 The Define Variable Properties dialog box

In the data file "clinical trial. sav", "GROUP" is a nominal variable, so the above procedure can be canceled. Click "OK" button, and the dialog box of Chart Builder pops out (Figure 12-4).

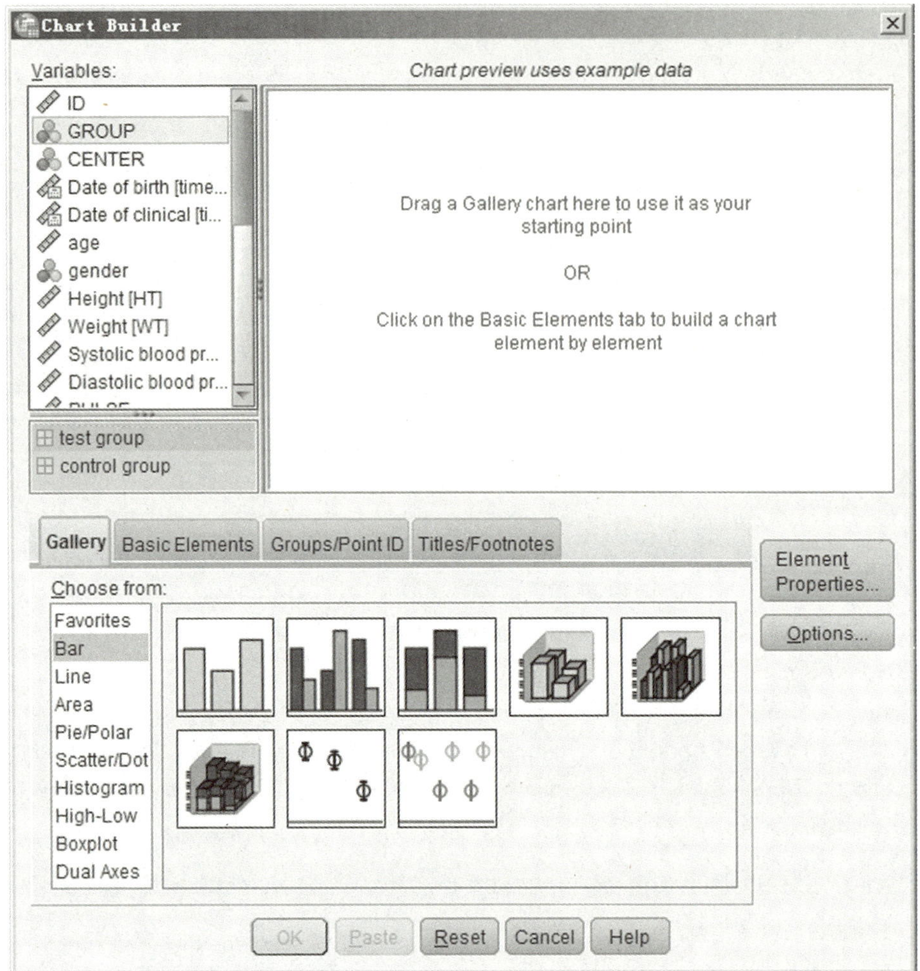

Figure 12-4 The Chart Builder dialog box

In the Figure 12-4, some contents are listed.

◇Variables.

◇Chart preview uses example data.

1) Gallery: In this gallery, Bar chart, Line chart, Area chart, Pie chart, Scatter/Dot plot, Histogram, High-Low chart, Boxplot and Dual Axes can be chosen. Click on the basic elements tab to build a chart element by element.

2) Basic Elements (Figure 12-5).

◇Choose Axes: Horizontal axis (X-axis), horizontal and vertical (X-axis and Y-axis), 3-D three axes, circumferential axis, and double vertical axes can be chosen.

◇Choose Elements: Ten geometries can be chosen.

★Transpose: Transpose the status of drawing the graph.

3) Groups/ Point ID.

◇Checked items add drop zones to the canvas to assign the variables.

□Clustering variable on X.

□Clustering variable on Z.

□Grouping/stacking variable.

□Rows panel variable.

□Columns panel variable.

□Point ID label.

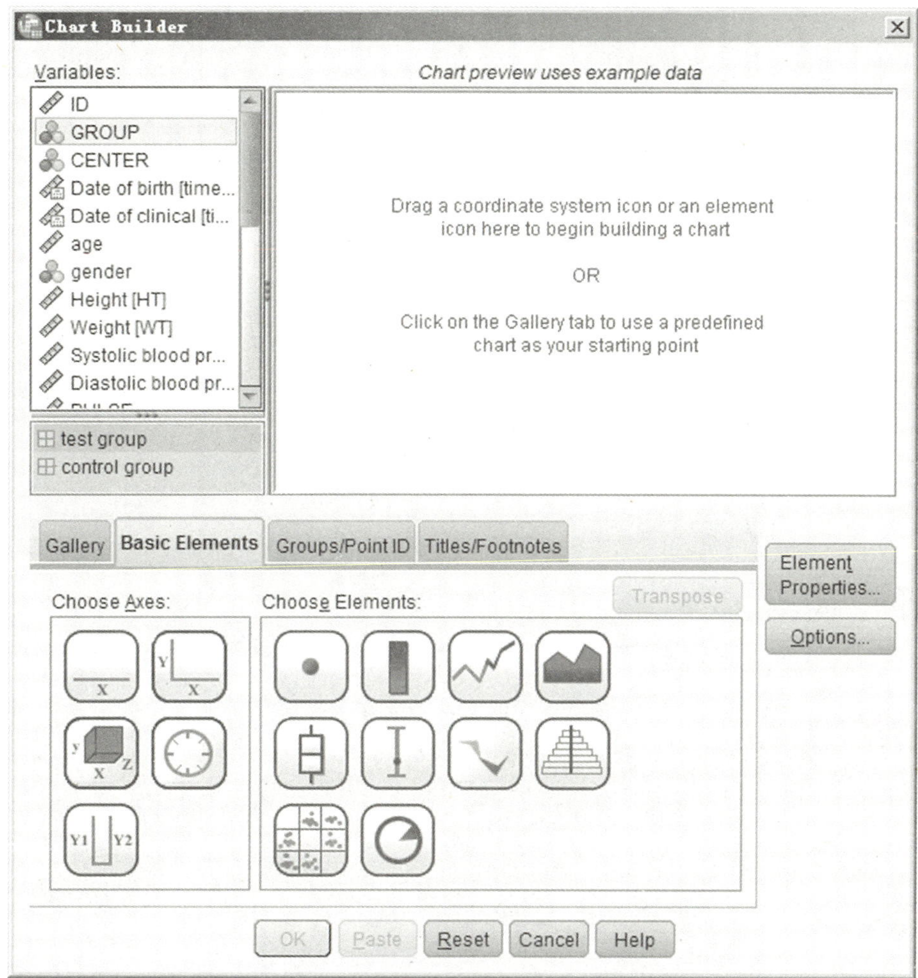

Figure 12-5 The Chart Builder: Basic Elements dialog box

4) Titles/Footnotes.

◇Checked items add titles and footnotes to the chart. Edit the text within Properties.

□Title 1.

□Title 2.

□Subtitle.

□Footnote1.

□Footnote2.

★Element properties. Click "Element properties" button, and the dialog box of Element Properties pops out (Figure 12-6).

◇Statistics: In this section, 20 statistics can be calculated, such as Mean, Median, Standard Deviation, Mode, Minimum, Maximum and so forth.

★Set Parameters: Some statistics can be set parameters. Once you choose these statistics, "Set Parameter" button is activated and then the corresponding parameters are set based on the real data.

□Display normal curve (continuous variable only).

□Display error bars: Confidence intervals, standard error, standard deviation of error bars can be chosen. The default error bar is 95% confidence interval. Two standard errors and standard deviations are default in corresponding error bars.

◇Bar Style: Bar, I-beam and Whisker can be chosen.

Set all the parameters and then press "Apply" to finish the variable properties setting.

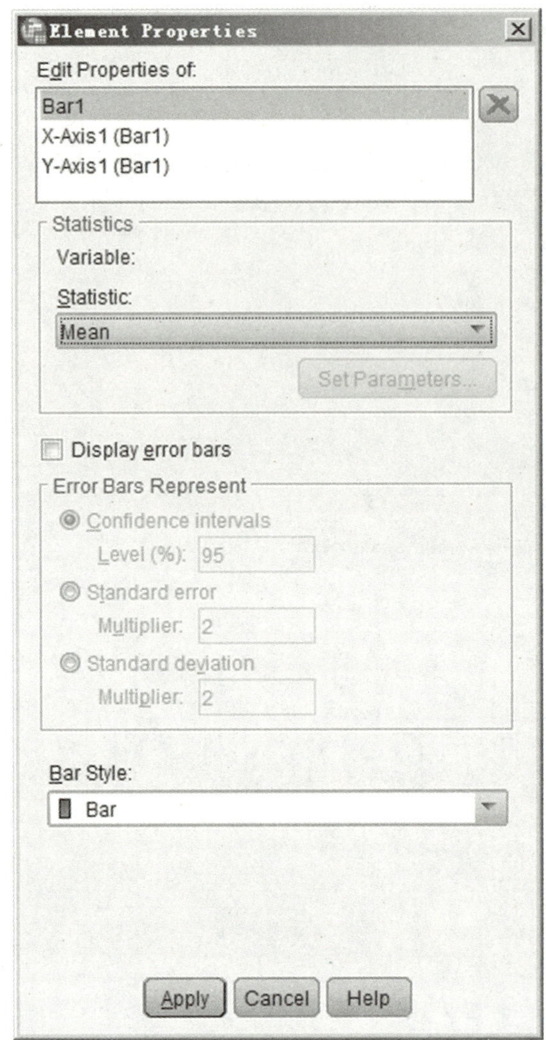

Figure 12-6 The Element Properties dialog box

★Options. It contains how to handle missing values, Template options, Chart size and panels (Figure 12-5).

Describe the age comparison stratified by gender for two medications with clustered bar (as in Figure 12-7). Running the commands:

Graph

 Chart Builder

OK

Gallery

 Bar

  Clustered Bar (the second one in the bar)

 ▸X-Axis: group

 ▸Y-Axis: age

 ▸Cluster on X: gender

 Element properties

 ☑Display error bars

  Confidence inters level (%): 95

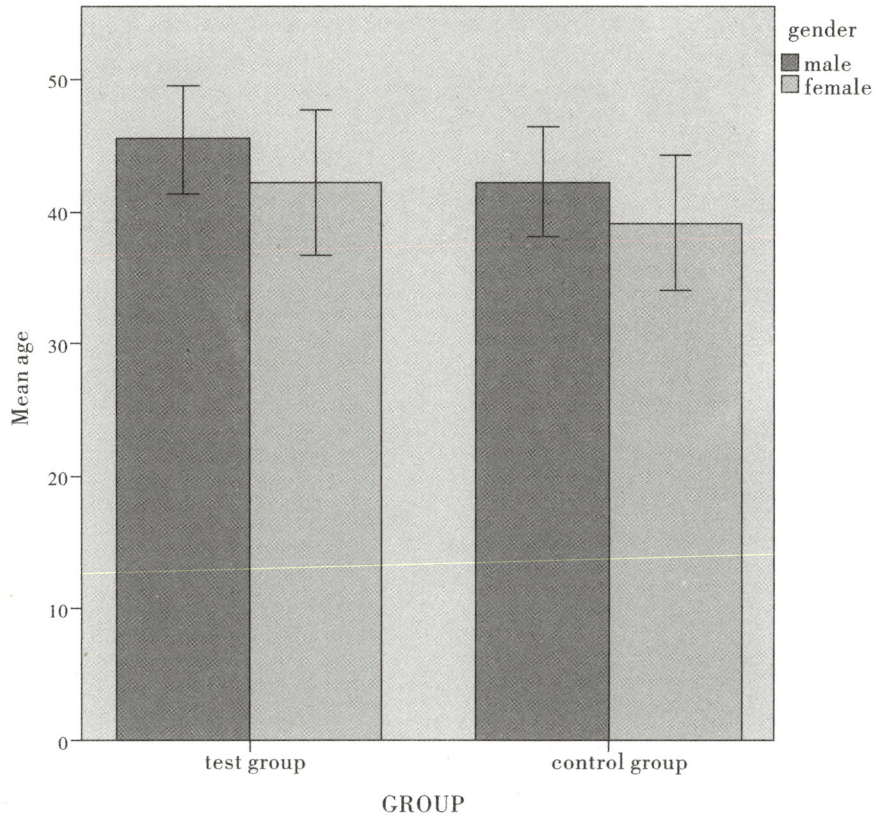

Figure 12-7 Age comparison stratified by gender for two medications

The data file "clinical trial. sav" is used as the Example 12-2. Define "GROUP" and "gender" as numeric values at the beginning. Compare the "PULSE" stratified by "gender" for two medications with 3 D bar chart, and then add the animation to this chart. Running the commands.

Graphs

Graphboard Template Chooser

The dialog box of Graphboard Template Chooser pops out (Figure 12-8).

1) Basic.

⊙Natural: Rank the variable name through entry.

◎Name: Rank the variable name by the alphabetical order.

◎Type: Rank the variable name by the data type.

△Rank from the top to bottom, rank the variable name from Z to A in English.

▽ Rank from the bottom to top, rank the variable name from A to Z in English.

Visualization of: Variable labels automatically appear.

◇Summary: Calculate the statistics based on the variable type, such as Count, Mean, Minimum, Maximum, Mode, Sum and so on.

★Manage: Click this button and pop out local templates and patterns. The users can still import, export, rename and delete the templates and patterns.

★Location: Where the templates and patterns are saved. The default saving location is local computer and the users can still relocate its location.

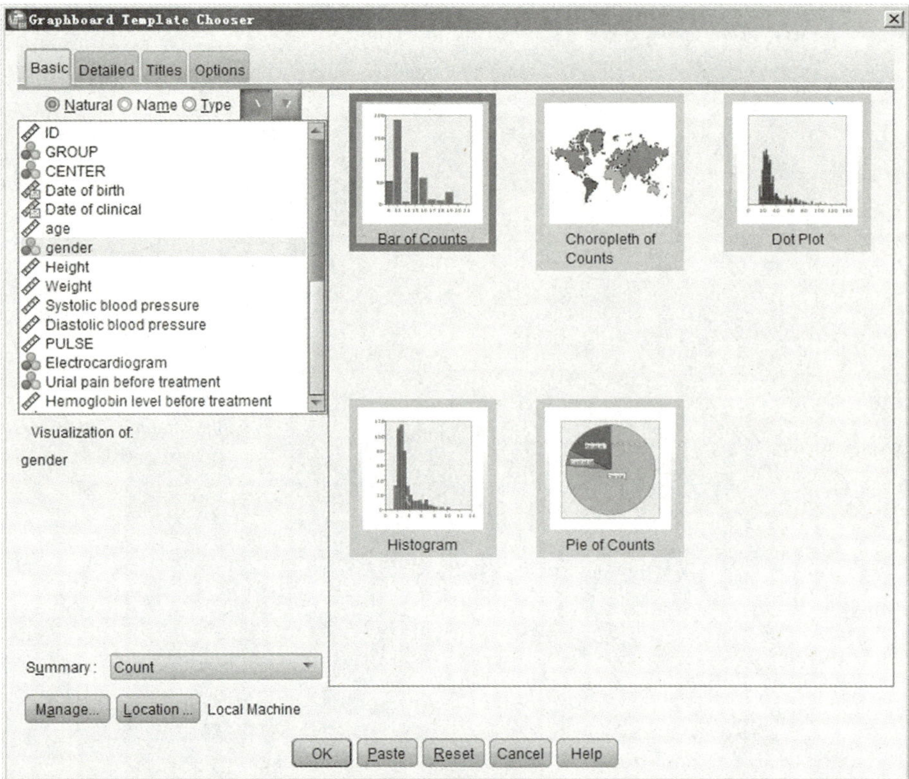

Figure 12-8 The Graphboard Template Chooser: Basic dialog box

2) Detailed (Figure 12-9).

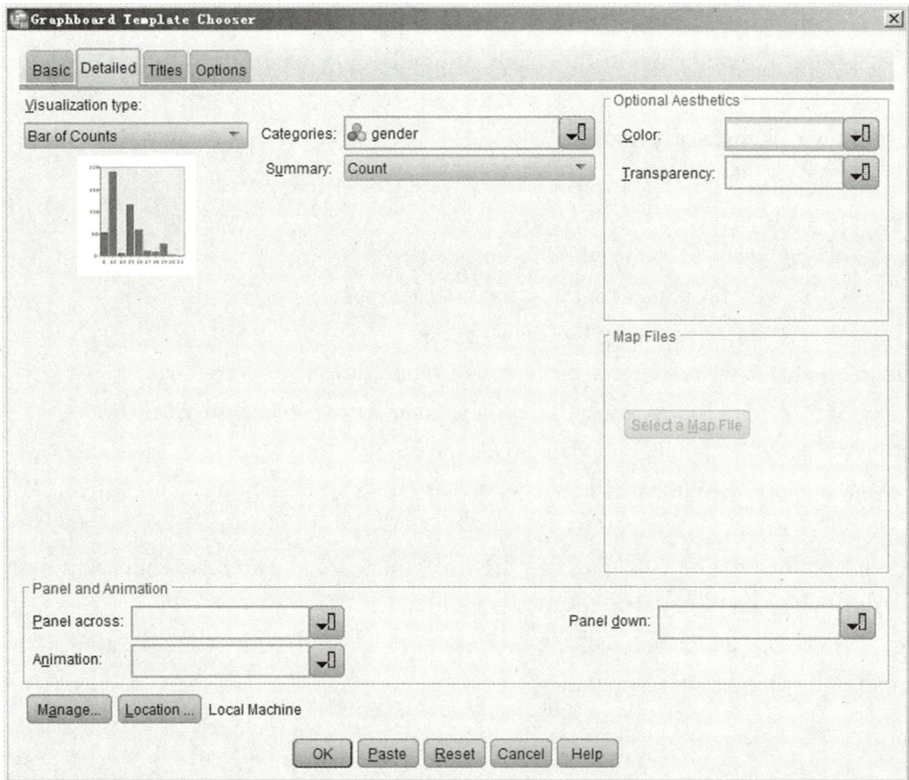

Figure 12-9 The Graphboard Template Chooser: Detailed dialog box

3) Titles(Figure 12-10).

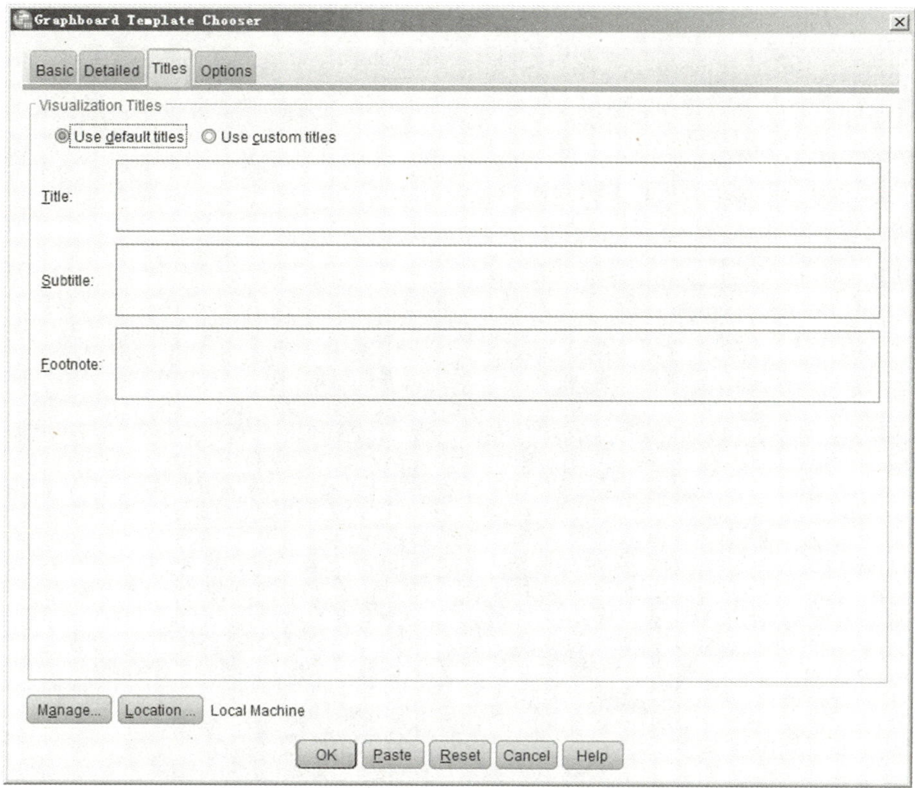

Figure 12-10 The Graphboard Template Chooser: Titles dialog box

4) Options(Figure 12-11).

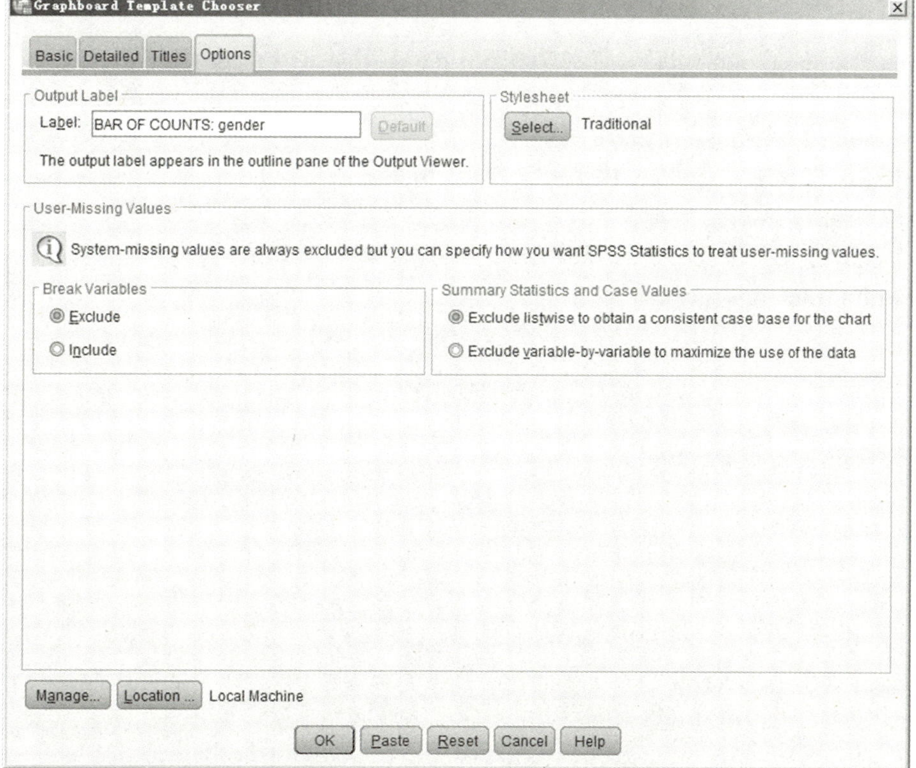

Figure 12-11 The Graphboard Template Chooser: Options dialog box

Compare the "PULSE" stratified by gender for two medications with 3 D bar chart, and running the command.

Graphs

GraphboardTemplate Chooser

▶**Basic: GROUP/gender/PULSE--3-D Bar**

▶**Summary: Mean**

▶**Detailed: x--gender, y-PULISE, z--GROUP**

The output is listed in Figure 12-12.

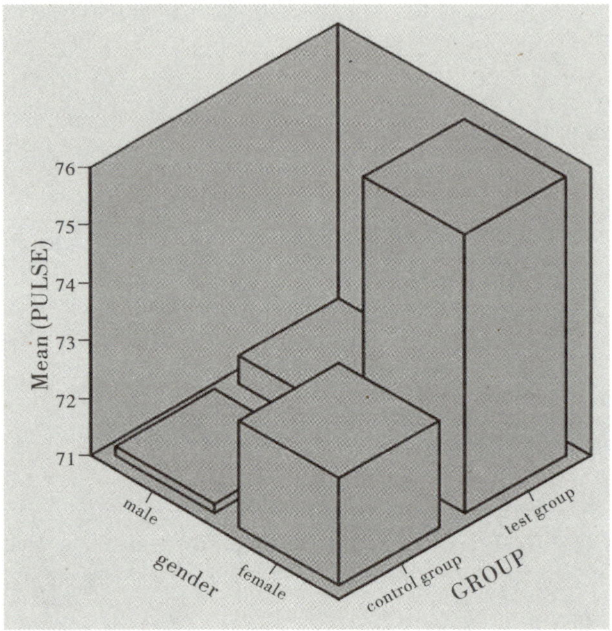

Figure 12-12 3 D bar chart for the Example 12-2

If the animation is needed for Figure 12-12, run the commands and produce Figure 12-13.

Graphs

Graphboard Template Chooser

▶**Basic: GROUP/gender/PULSE--3-D Bar**

▶**Summary: Mean**

▶**Detailed: x--gender, y-PULISE, z--GROUP**

▶**Animation: age_group**

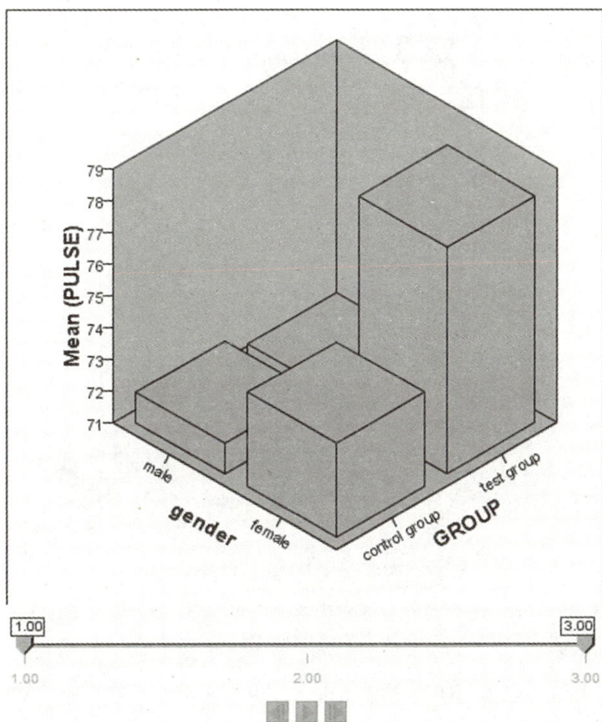

Figure 12-13 Animation char for Example 12-2

12.2 Bar chart

Bar chart is used to describe the measurement for each variable stratified by categorical variable. The data file "clinical trial. sav" is used as Example 12-3, and to describe: ①The mean and standard deviation of age in two groups with simple bar chart; ②The gender distribution pattern in two groups with clustered bar chart; ③The proportions for each age group in two groups with stacked bar chart. The running process is listed as follows:

Graphs

Legacy Dialogs

Bar

The main dialog box Bar chart pops out (Figure 12-14).

◇Bar Chart.

□Simple.

□Clustered.

□Stacked.

◇Data in Chart Are.

⊙Summaries for groups of cases: To describe the number of cases for each group of specific response variable, or descriptive measurements for each group (e. g, mean, median, sum, *et al*). The simple bar chart is for one categorical variable; clustered or stacked bar chart is for two categorical variables.

◎Summaries of separate variables: To describe multiple response variables. The units for response variables should be consistent. The simple bar chart is for one categorical variable; clustered or stacked bar chart is for two categorical variables.

◎Values of individual cases: To describe individual value for cases.

★Define: Click "Define" button, and the dialog box of Define pops out. The Define for three type of

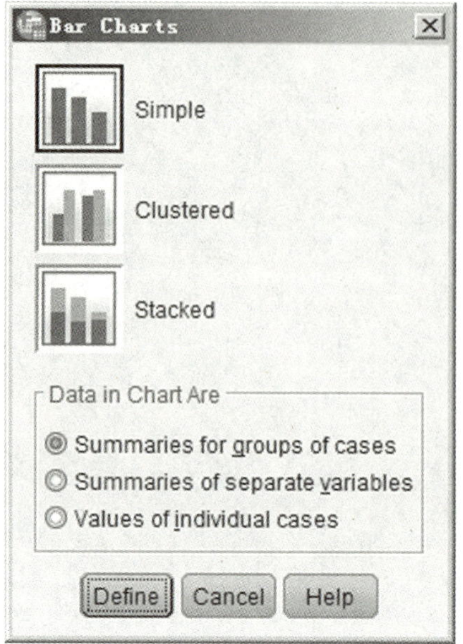

Figure 12-14 The Bar Chart dialog box

bar charts is similar, and just one categorical variable is missing for "Define Simple bar" dialog box. Here, we take Define Clustered Bar: Summaries for Groups of cases dialog box as an example (Figure 12-15).

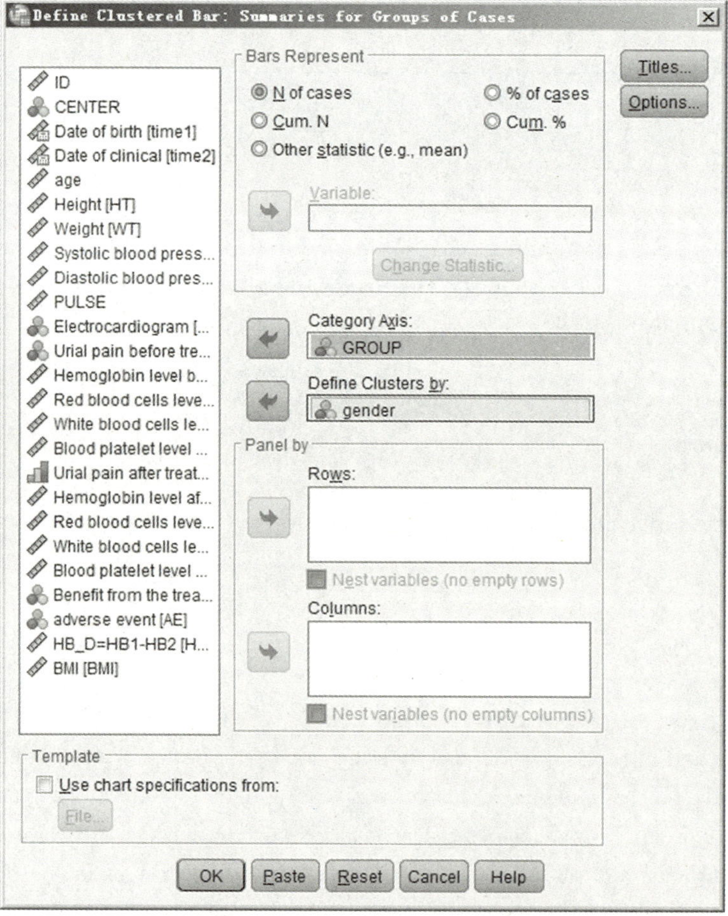

Figure 12-15 The Define Clustered Bar: Summaries for Groups of Cases dialog box

In this dialog box, you can see:

◇Bars Represent.

⊙N of cases (system default).

◎% of cases.

◎Cum. N.

◎Cum. %.

◎Other statistics: Click "Other statistics (e. g., mean)" to activate "Variable box". Choose one variable to activate "Change Statistic" button. A total of 18 statistics can be chosen, including Mean, Median, Standard Deviation, Maximum and Minimum and so forth.

◇Categorical Axis: *X*-Axis.

◇Define Clusters by: A categorical variable and use figure legend to indicate this categorical variable.

◇Panel by: Stratified variable, including a row variable and a column variable.

◇Template.

□Use chart specification from: Click this button to activate "File" button. Choose the existing template as the current graph template.

★Options. Click "Options" button, and the dialog box of Options pops out (Figure 12-16)

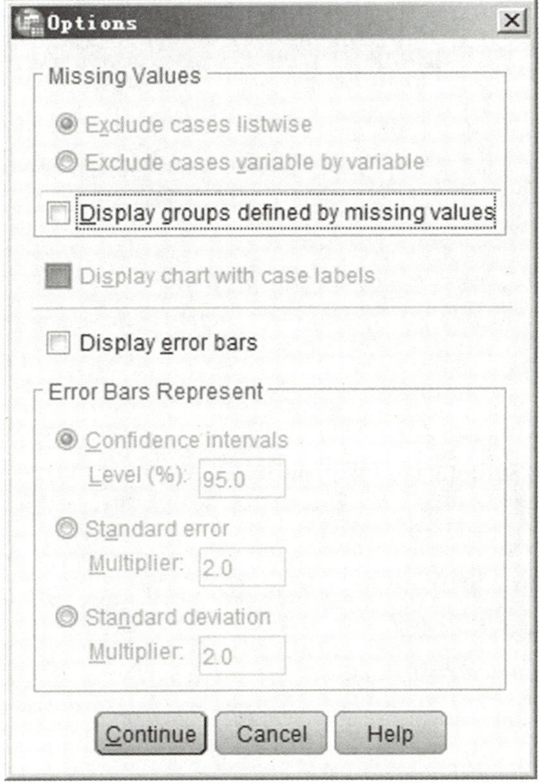

Figure 12-16 The Bar Chart: Option dialog box

□Display groups defined by missing values.

□Display error bars: Confidence intervals, standard error and standard deviation of error bars can be chosen. The default error bar is 95% confidence interval. Two standard errors and standard deviations are defaulted in corresponding error bars.

(1) Simple bar chart: Describe the mean and standard deviation of age in two groups.

Graphs

Legacy Dialogs

Bar

Simple & ⊙Summaries for groups of cases
Define
⊙Other summary function (Mean)
▸Variable: age
▸Category Axis: GROUP
Options:
☑Display error bars
⊙Standard deviation: Multiplier 1.0

The output is listed as Figure 12-17.

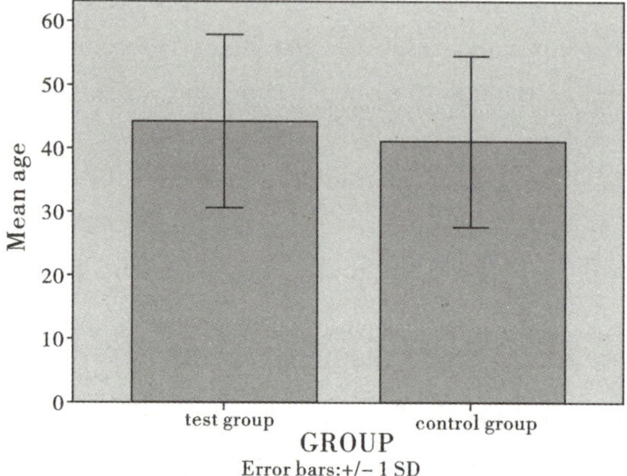

Figure 12 - 17 Age comparison between two groups (simple bar chart)

(2) Clustered bar chart: To describe the gender distribution pattern for two medications. Running the commands:

Graphs
Legacy Dialogs
Bar
Clustered & ⊙Summaries for groups of cases
Define
⊙N of cases
▸Category Axis: GROUP
▸Define Clusters by: GENDER

The output is seen as Figure 12-18.

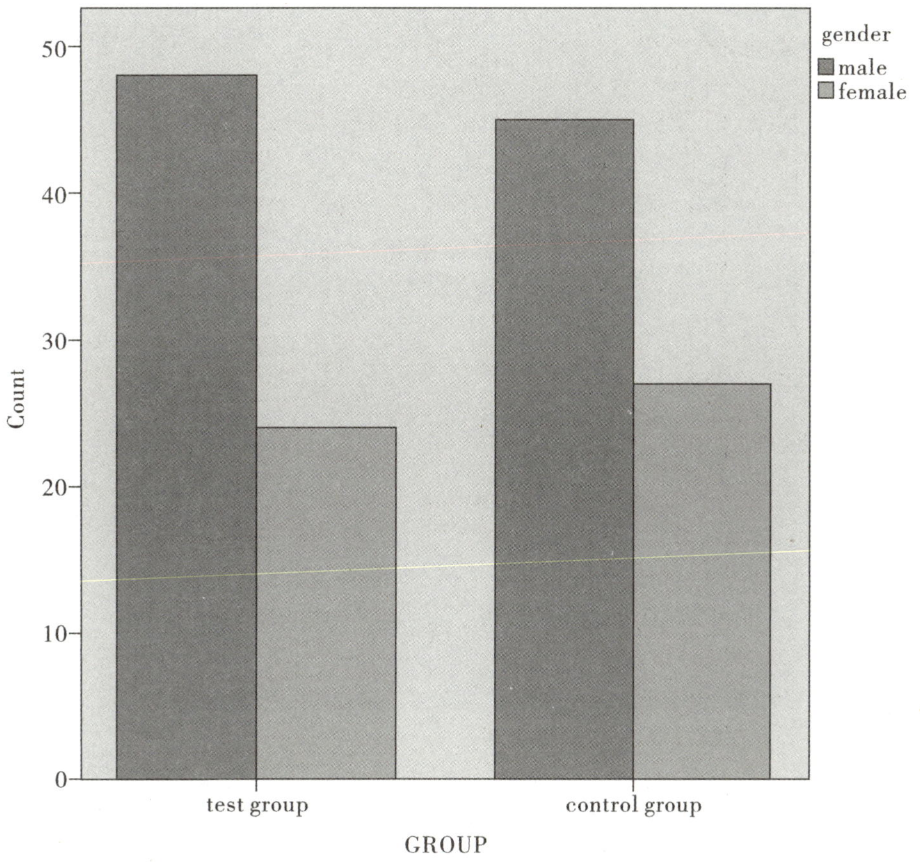

Figure 12-18 Gender comparison between two groups (clustered bar chart)

(3) Stacked bar chart: This chart is to describe the age comparison for two medications. Running the commands:

Graphs

Legacy Dialogs

Bar

Stacked & ⊙Summaries for groups of cases

Define

⊙N of cases

▸Category Axis: GROUP

▸Define Clusters by: AGE-G

The output is listed as Figure 12-19.

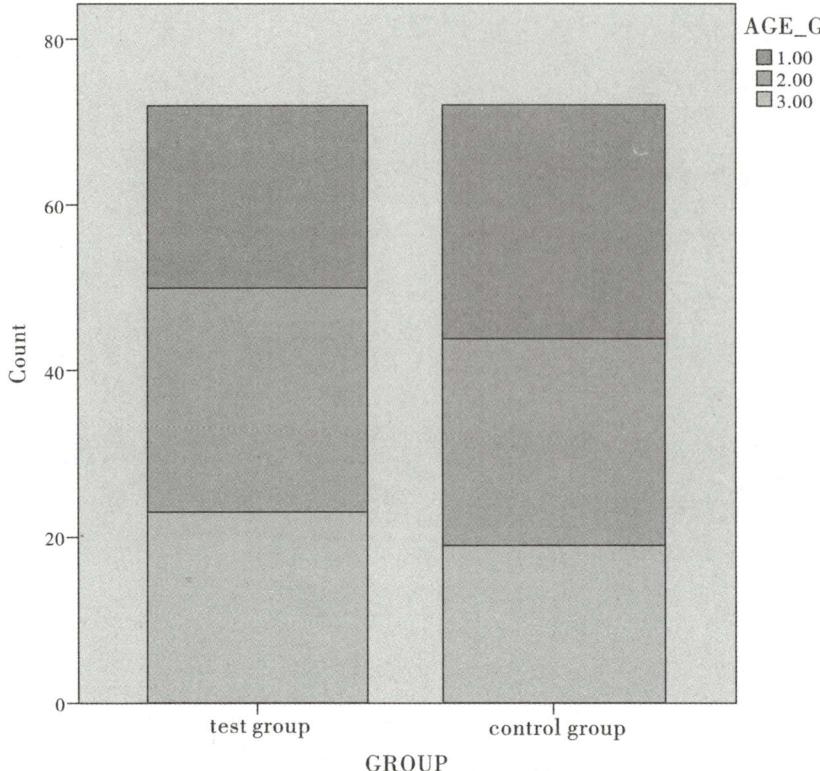

Figure 12-19 Age comparison for two medications (stacked bar chart)

12.3 3D bar chart

The 3D bar chart is the three-dimensional presentation of stacked bar chart. The data file "clinical trial. sav" is used as the Example 12-4 to draw 3D bar chart presenting the gender distribution. Running the commands:

Graphs

Legacy Dialogs

3-D Bar

The main dialog box of 3D Bar Charts pops out (Figure 12-20). Click "Define" button, and the dialog box of Define 3D Bar: Summaries for Groups of Cases pops out (Figure 12-21). The meaning for "Options" is the same as the one of bar chart. Input variable "GROUP" into "X Category Axis", and variable "gender" into "Z Category Axis". In the 3 D bar chart, *Y*-axis indicates descriptive statistics. The output is as Figure 12-22.

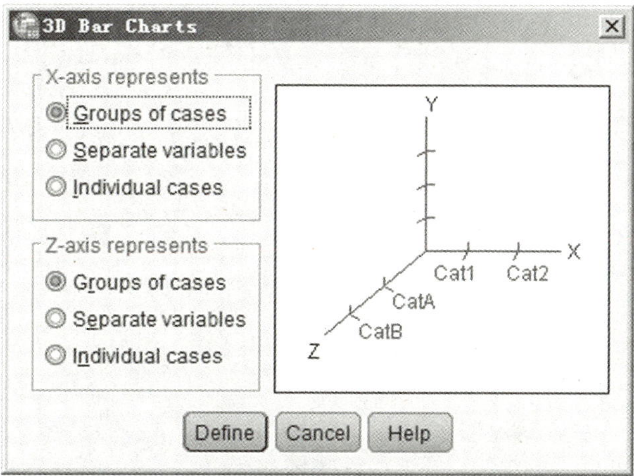

Figure 12-20 The 3D Bar Charts dialog box

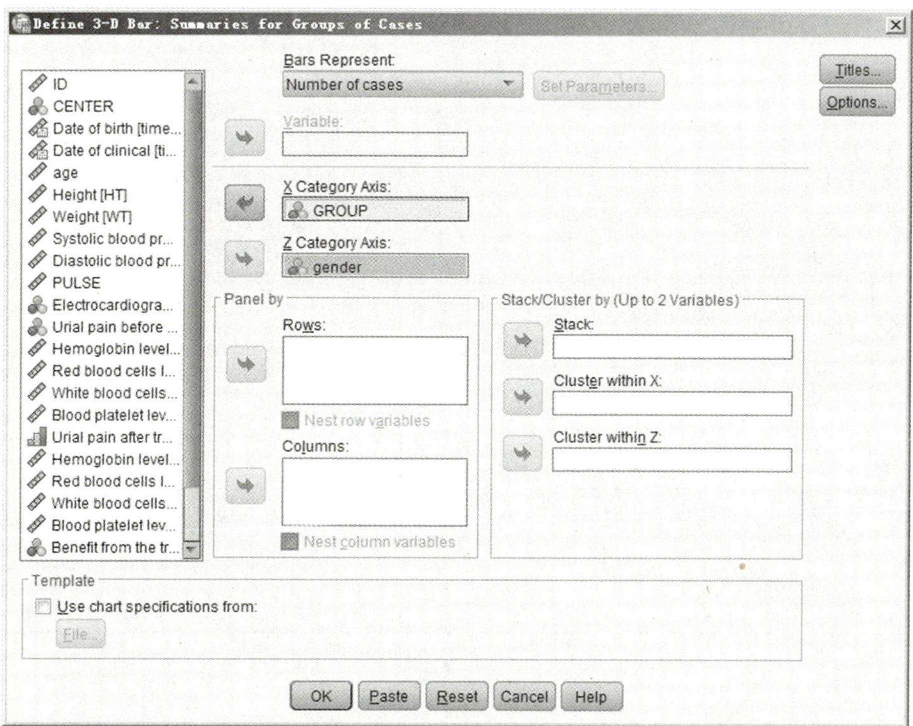

Figure 12-21 The Define 3-D Bar :Summaries for Groups of Cases dialog box

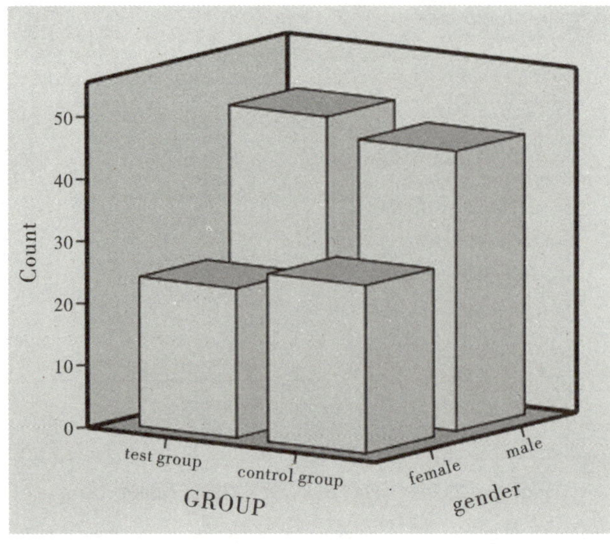

Figure 12-22 3D Bar Chart of gender distribution for two medications

12.4 Line chart

Line chart is typically used to describe the change of specific measurement over time. In general, horizontal axis (X-axis) is time variable and vertical axis (Y-axis) is the response variable. The data file "line. sav" is used as the Example 12-5. Data are displayed in Table 12-1. Describe the mortality rate of typhoid alone and together with tuberculosis over time with line charts, respectively.

Table 12-1 The mortality rates of typhoid and tuberculosis between 1950 and 1966

Year	1950	1952	1954	1956	1958	1960	1962	1964	1966
Typhoid	31.3	22.4	18.0	9.2	5.0	3.5	1.6	0.8	0.3
Tuberculosis	174.5	127.1	142.0	127.2	97.7	71.3	59.2	46.0	37.5

(1) Running the commands:

Graphs

  Legacy Dialogs

  Line

The main dialog box of Line Charts pops out (Figure 12-23).

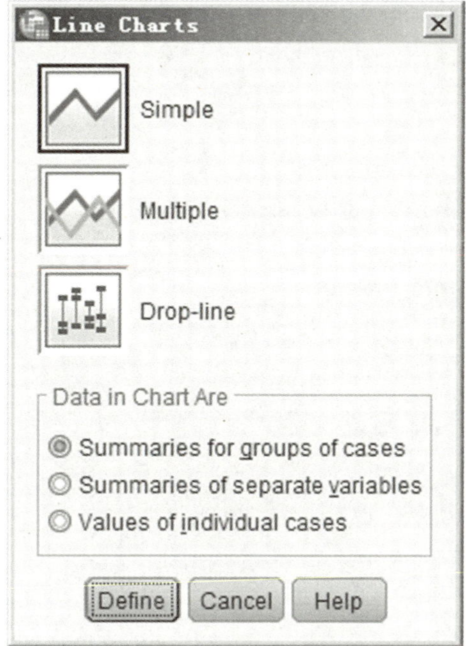

Figure 12-23 The Line Charts dialog box

Type of line charts:

□Simple:Two-variable line chart.

□Multiple:Multi-variable line chart.

□Drop-line:Vertically drop line chart.

◇Data in Chart Are:Data types,refer to section 12.2.

(2)Simple line chart:To describe the mortality rate of typhoid fever over time. Data type is time (categorical variable) and one measurement. Running the command:

Graphs

Legacy Dialogs

Line

Simple & ⊙Summaries for groups of cases

Define

⊙Other statistic (e. g mean)

▸Variable:psh

▸Category Axis:year

The output is seen in Figure 12-24.

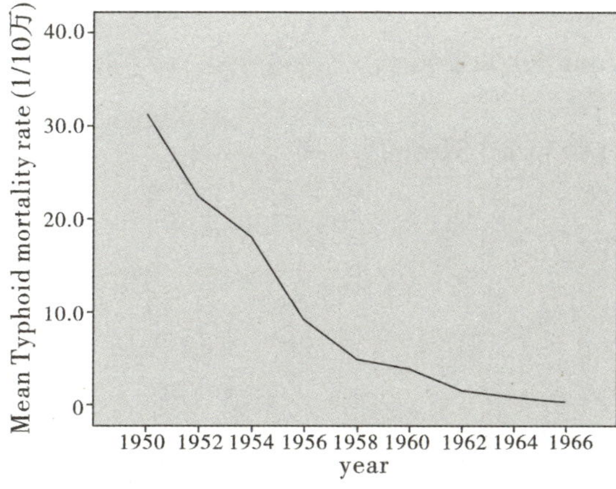

Figure 12-24 Typhoid mortality rate over 16 years

(3) Multiple line chart: To describe the mortality rate of typhoid and tuberculosis over time. Data type is time (categorical variable) and two measurements.

Graphs

Legacy Dialogs

Line

Multiple & ⊙Summaries of separate variables

Define

▸Lines Represent: psh/ptb (Mean)

▸Category Axis: year

The output is seen in Figure 12-25.

Figure 12-25 Typhoid and tuberculosis mortality rates over 16 years

(4) Drop-line chart: Data type is time (categorical variable) and two measurements. Running the commands:

Graphs

Legacy Dialogs

Line

Drop-line & ⊙Summaries of separate variables

Define

▸Points Represent: psh/ptb (Mean)

▸Category Axis: year

The output is seen in Figure 12-26.

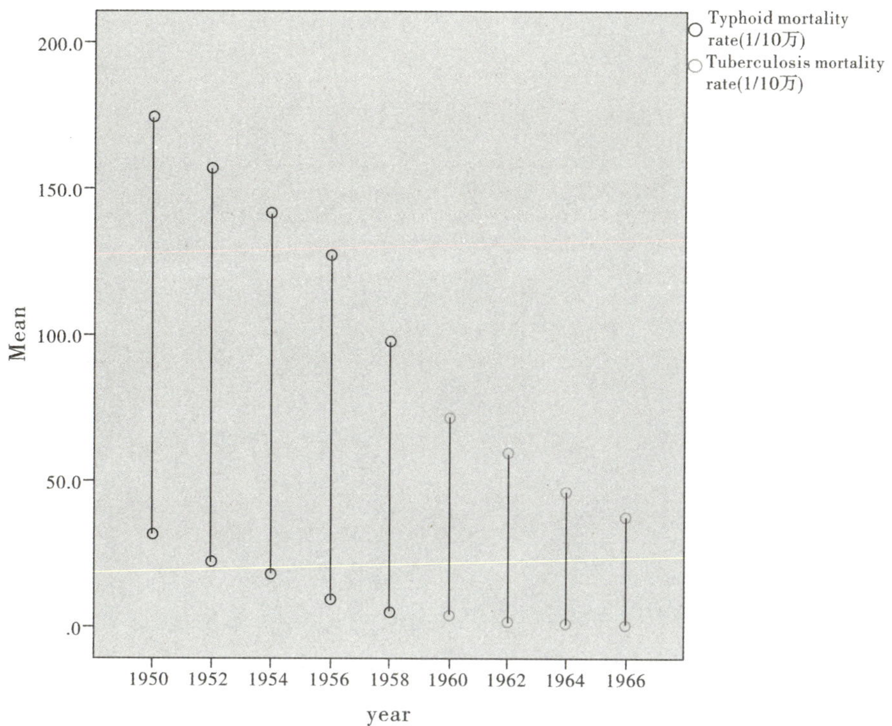

Figure 12－26 Typhoid and tuberculosis mortality rates over 16 years (multiple line charts)

12.5 Area chart

Area chart is typically used to describe the change of a variable(s) over the a continuous variable. In general, the continuous variable is horizontal axis (X-axis) and define the categorical variable. The data file "line. sav" is used as the Example 12-6.

Graphs

Legacy Dialogs

Area

The main dialog box of Area Charts pops out (Figure 12-27).

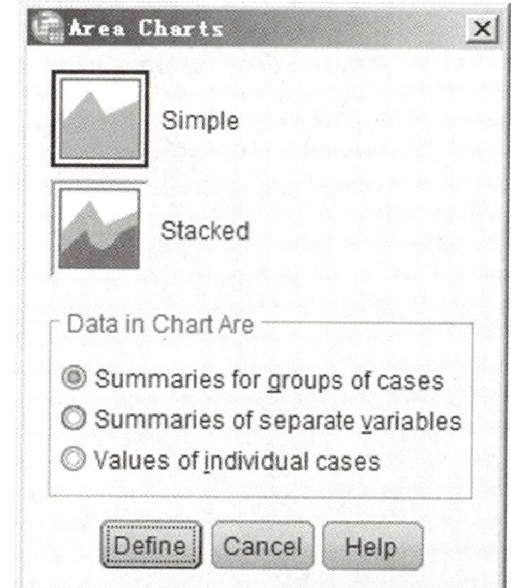

Figure 12-27 The Area Charts dialog box

Type of area charts.

□Simple.

□Stacked.

◇Data in Chart Are: Data types, refer to section 12. 2.

(1) Simple line chart: One continuous variable (considered as categorical variable, horizontal axis) and one measurement.

Graphs

Legacy Dialogs

Area

Simple & ⊙Summaries for groups of cases

Define

⊙Other statistic (e. g mean)

▶Variable: psh

▶Category Axis: year

The output is seen in Figure 12-28.

Figure 12-28 Typhoid mortality rate over 16 years (simple area chart)

(2) Stacked line chart: One more stacked variable than simple area chart in datatype. Each stack is presented with different color or filling. All the shadow area is the sum statistic.

Graphs

Legacy Dialogs

Area

Stacked & ⊙Summaries of separate variables

Define

▶Areas Represent: psh/ptb (Mean)

▶Category Axis: year

The output is presented as Figure 12-29.

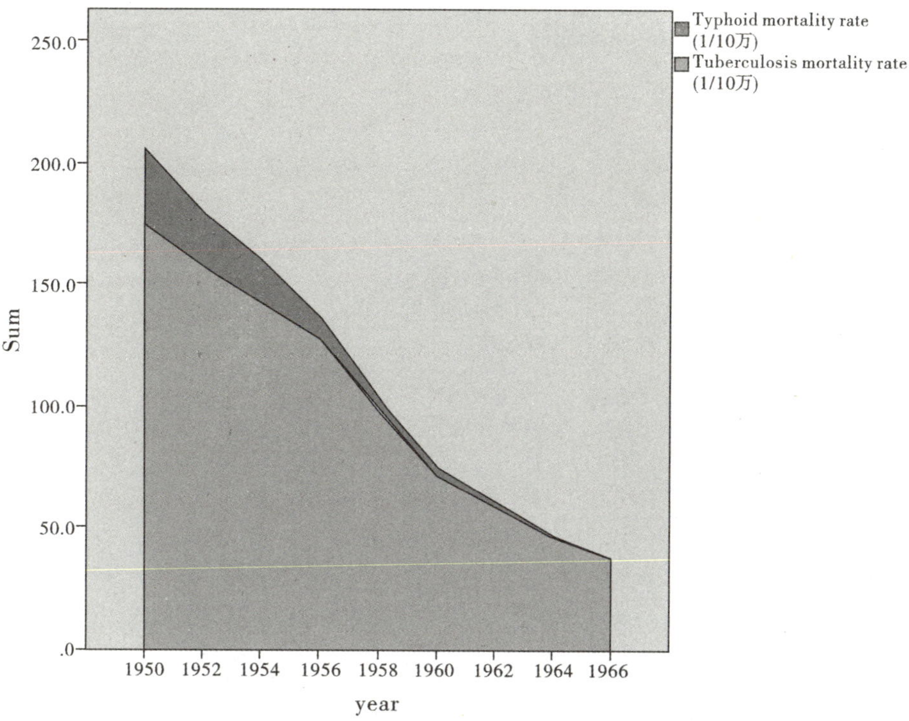

Figure 12-29 Typhoid and tuberculosis mortality rates over 16 years (Stacked area charts)

12.6 Pie chart

Pie chart is used to describe the percentage or proportion of data. The data file "nurse_surve. sav" is used as the Example 12-7 to describe age (variable name is "age_gr") proportion with pie chart.

Graphs

Legacy Dialogs

Pie

The main dialog box of Pie Charts pops out (Figure 12-30).

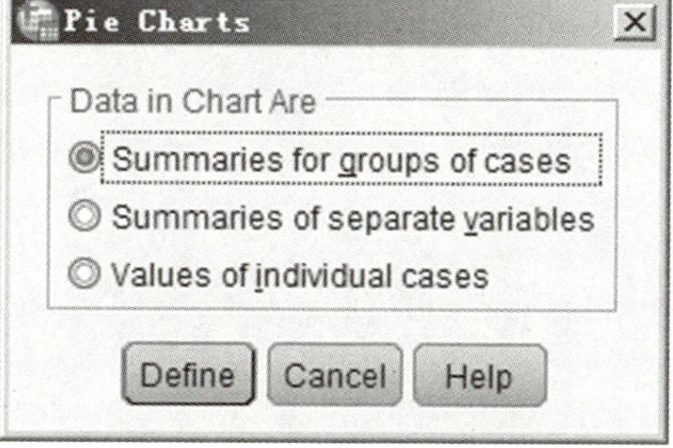

Figure 12-30 The Pie Charts dialog box

◇Data in Chart Are: Data types, refer to section 12.2.

Graphs

LegacyDialogs

Pie

⊙Summaries of separate variables

Define

⊙N of cases

▶Define Slices by: age_gr

The output is presented as Figure 12-31.

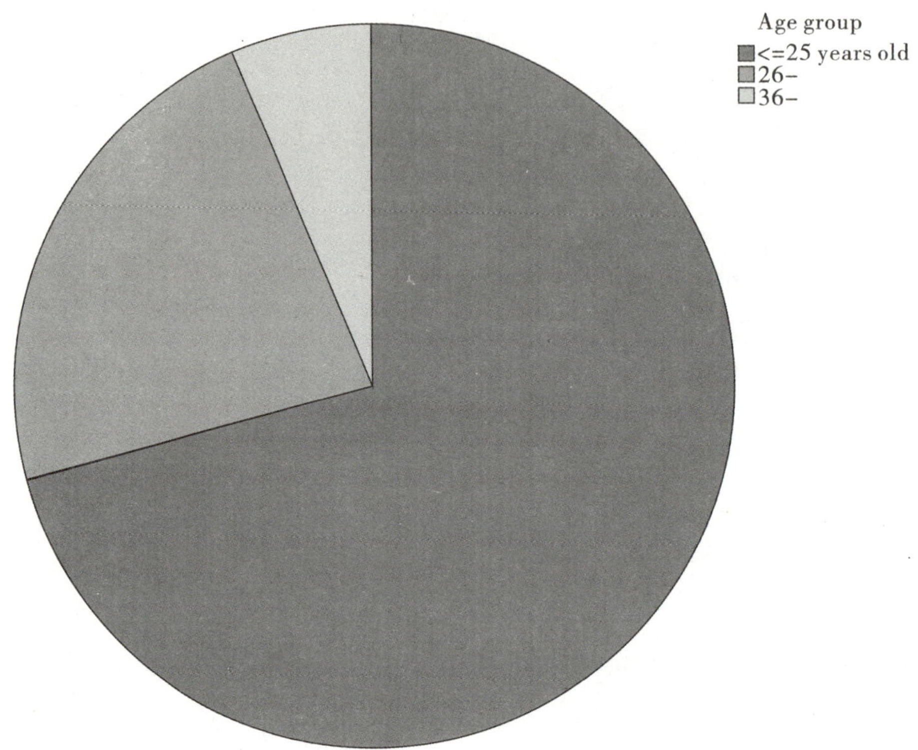

Figure 12-31 Age proportion of nurses (Pie chart)

12.7 High-Low chart

High-Low chart is typically used to illustrate the long-term trend and short-term variation of the variable over time. For example, this chart can be used to depict the closing, the highest and lowest prices over one day in the securities market.

Graphs

Legacy Dialogs

High-low

The dialog box of High-Low Charts pops out (Figure 12-32).

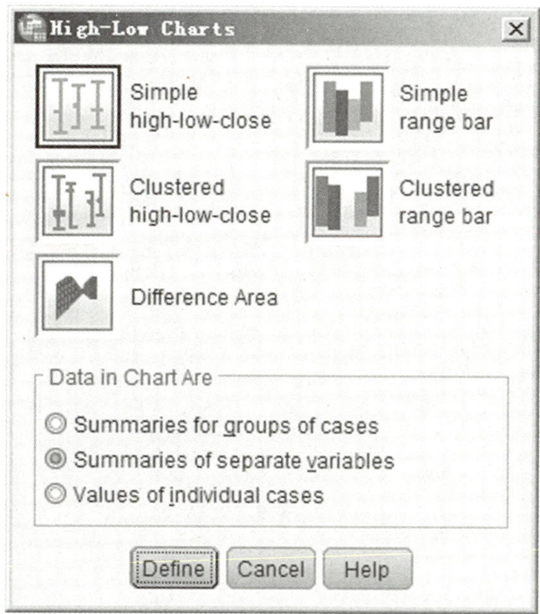

Figure 12-32 The High-Low Charts dialog box

Types of the "High-Low Charts":

□Simple high-low-close: It is mainly used to describe the movements in the price of a financial instrument over time, involving two variables: one is for the time frame, e. g. one day or one hour, and one is for the price range (the highest, the lowest and the closing prices). When the price data is a binary variable, this chart is equivalent to the simple range bar.

□Simple range bar: This chart is used to display the market price over time, but price data is binary variable (the highest and the lowest prices).

□Clustered high-low-close: This chart can present one more categorical variable than the simple high-low-close chart.

□Clustered range bar: This chart can present one more categorical variable than the simple range bar chart.

□Difference Area: This chart is used to display the time trend of two quantitative variables. The area between two lines is indicated as shadow area.

◇Data in Chart Are: Refer to the data introduced in section 12.2.

When the highest, the lowest and closing prices are saved as separate variables, the "Summaries for groups of cases" cannot be selected, but the "Summaries of separate variables" or "Values of individual cases" can be chosen.

(1) Simple high-low-close: The data file "ONE-WAY-1. sav" is used as the Example 12-8. In order to display the maximum, minimum and mean of the trabecular area (%) across three treatments, there are two steps.

First, produce the maximum, minimum and average values of the three treatments.

Data

Aggregate

The dialog box of Aggregate Data pops out (Figure 12-33). Then, produce the average, minimum and maximum of the trabecular area (%), and save these data as "tbar_mean" "tbar_min" and "tbar_max" variable, respectively. This process can refer to the Figure 12-33.

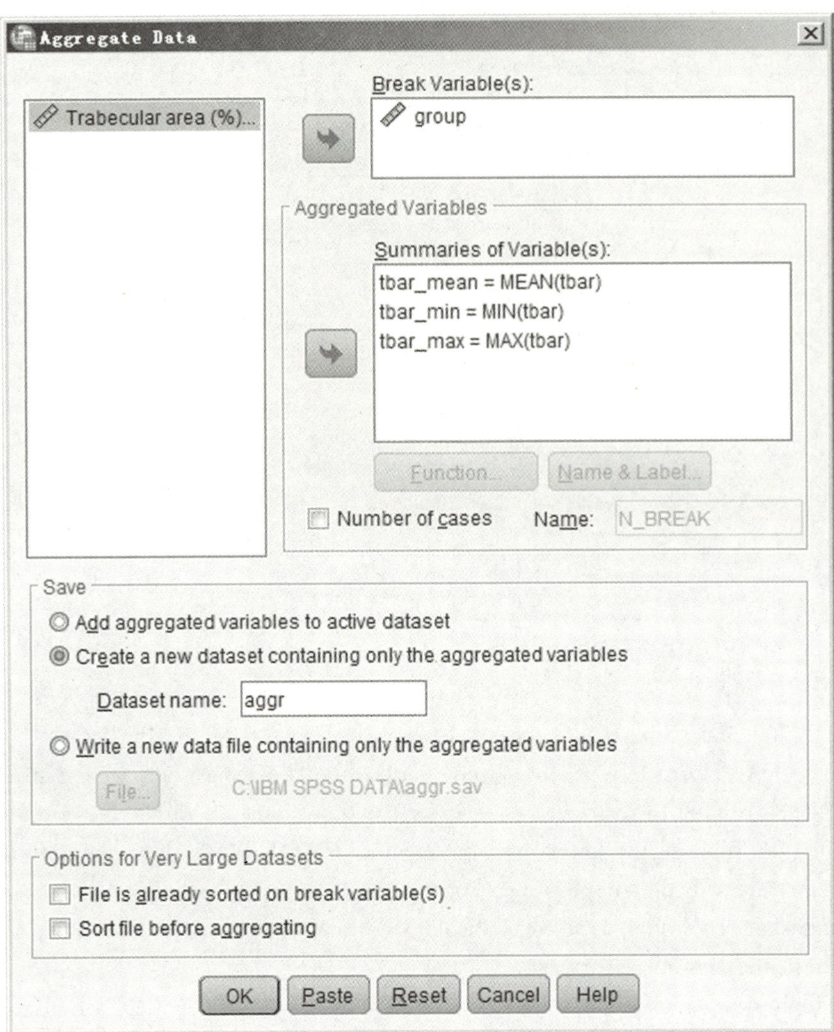

Figure 12-33 The Aggregate Data dialog box

Second, the process of plotting High-Low chart is as follows:

Graph

Legacy Dialogs

High-low

Simple high-low-close & ⊙Summaries of separate variables

Define

▸High: tbar_max

▸Low: tbar_min

▸Close: tbar_mean

▸Category Axis: group

The output is listed in Figure 12-34.

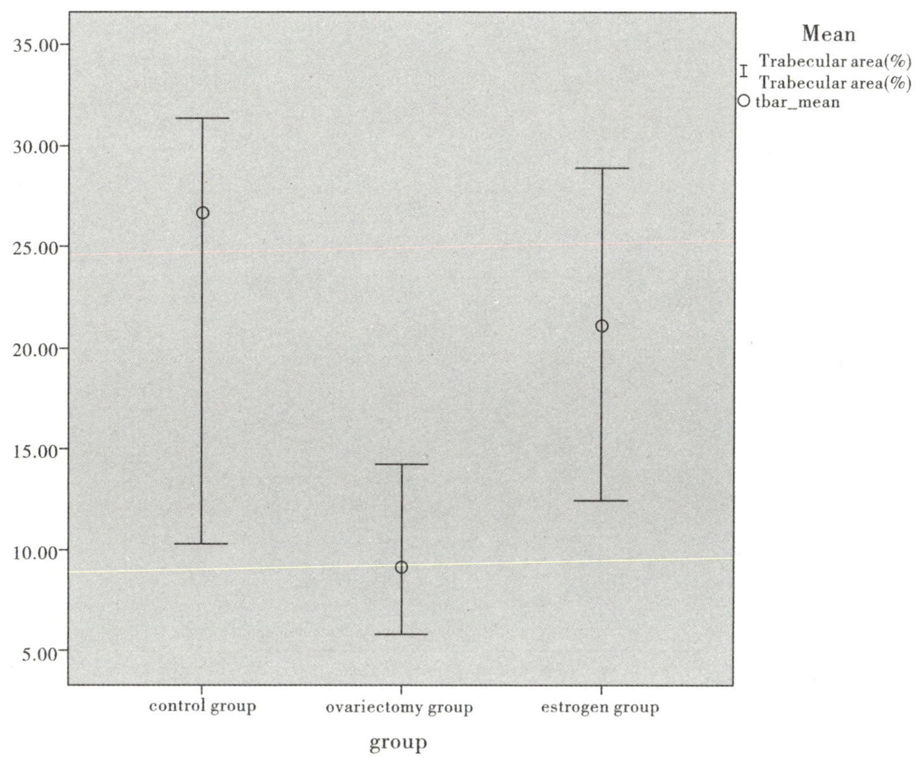

Figure 12-34 The High-low charts of trabecular areas (%) among three treatments

(2) Difference Area: The data file "line. sav" is used as the Example 12-9 to describe the trends of mortality rates of typhoid and tuberculosis between 1950 and 1966.

Graph

Legacy Dialogs

High-low

Difference Area & ⊙Summaries of separate variables

Define

▶1st: psh

▶2nd: ptb

▶Category Axis: year

The output is listed in Figure 12-35.

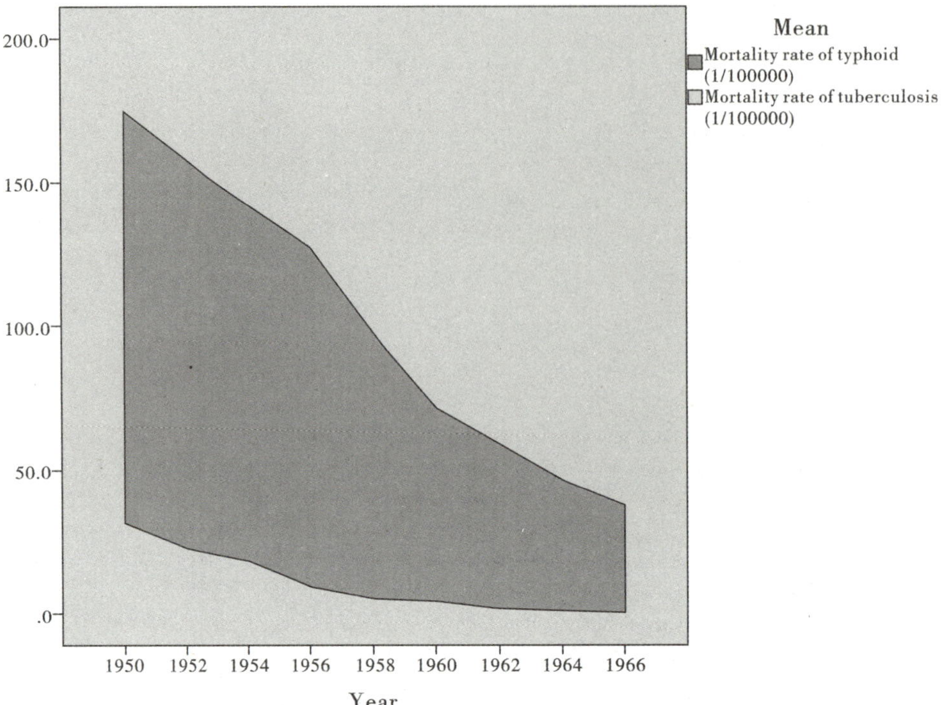

Figure 12–35 The trends of mortality rates of typhoid and tuberculosis presented by difference area High–Low chart

12.8 Boxplot

The boxplot, also known as box–and–whisker diagram, is mainly used to depict the statistical distribution of numerical data through their quartiles, including the 2.5th, 25th, 50th, 75th and 97.5th percentiles. The body of the boxplot goes from the first quartile (25th percentile) to the third quartile (75th percentile); the band inside the box represents the second quartile (50th percentile); the 2.5th and 25th percentiles, and 75th and 97.5th percentiles are separately connected by lines; outliers are plotted as individual points outside the ends of the box.

The data file "clinical_trial.sav" is used as the Example 12–10. Firstly, uses the "Simple" boxplot to display difference in the pre–treated hemoglobin level among the treatment group, and then uses the "Clustered" boxplot to display difference in the pre–treated hemoglobin level among the treatment group and gender.

Graphs

Legacy Dialogs

Boxplot

The dialog box of Boxplot is listed in Figure 12–36.

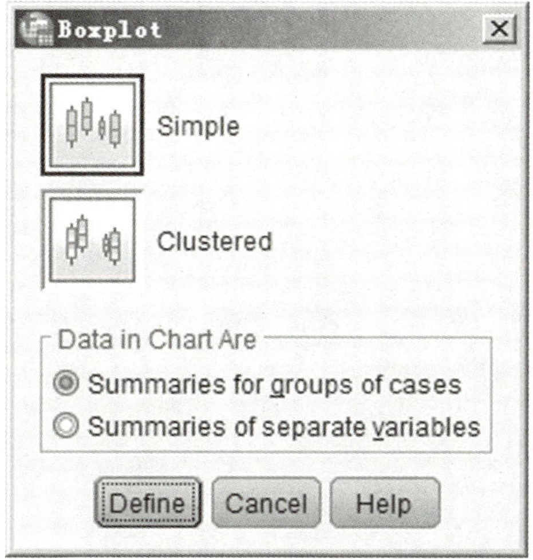

Figure 12-36 The Boxplot dialog box

Types of boxplot:

□Simple:Only one categorical variable.

□Clustered:Two categorical variables.

◇Data in Chart Are:Types of data.

⊙Summaries for groups of cases:Default.

◎Summaries of separate variables

(1)Simple boxplot is used to depict the pre-treat "hb1" by group. The steps as follows:

Graphs

Legacy Dialogs

Boxplot

Simple & ⊙Summaries for groups of cases

Define

▶**Variable:hb**1 (Indicator variable)

▶**Category Axis:group** (Categorical variable)

(▶**Label Cases by:** Label the outliers and extreme value by the Category variable;no content is required for this option by default)

The output is listed in Figure 12-37. The "37" in the figure means that the 37th line of Hb is an outlier, with value of 193 g/L.

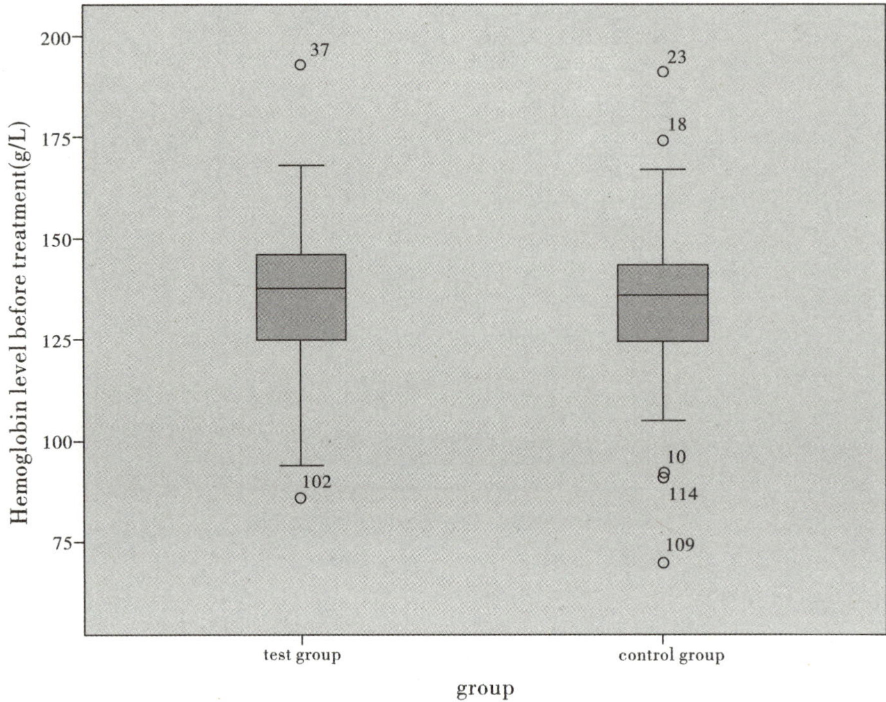

Figure 12-37 The simple boxplots of the pre-treated hemoglobin level (g/L) among test and control groups

(2) Clustered boxplot is used to depict the pre-treated "hb1" by "group" and "sex" together. The steps are as follows:

Graphs

Legacy Dialogs

Boxplot

Clustered & ⊙Summaries for groups of cases

Define

▸**Variable: hb1** (Indicator variable)

▸**Category Axis: group** (Categorical variable)

▸**Define Clusters by: sex** (Categorical variable)

The output is listed in Figure 12-38.

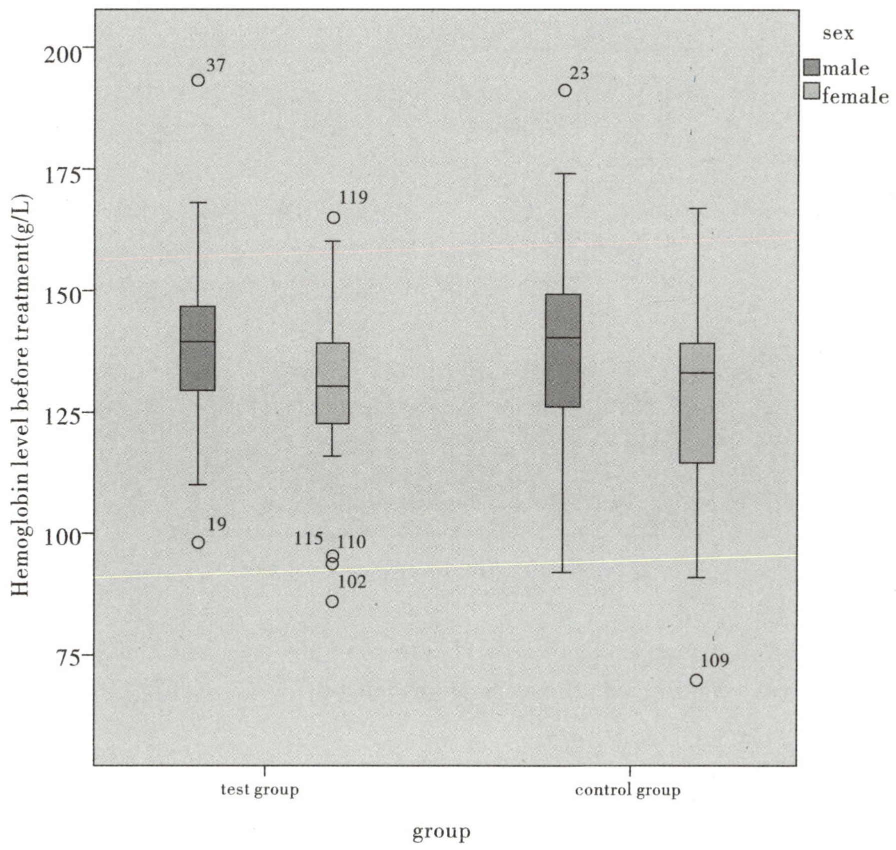

Figure 12-38 The clustered boxplots of the pre-treated hemoglobin level (g/L) across two treatment groups and gender

12.9 Error bar

Error bar is mainly used to present the variability of numerical data, based on three combinations (mean and confidence interval, mean and standard deviation, mean and standard error).

The data file "clinical_trial. sav" is used as the Example 12-11. Firstly, uses the "Error Bar" to display difference in the pre-treated hemoglobin level among the treatment group, and then uses the "Clustered Error Bar" to display difference in the pre-treated hemoglobin level among the treatment group and sex.

Graphs

Legacy Dialogs

Error Bar

The dialog box of Error Bar is listed in Figure 12-39.

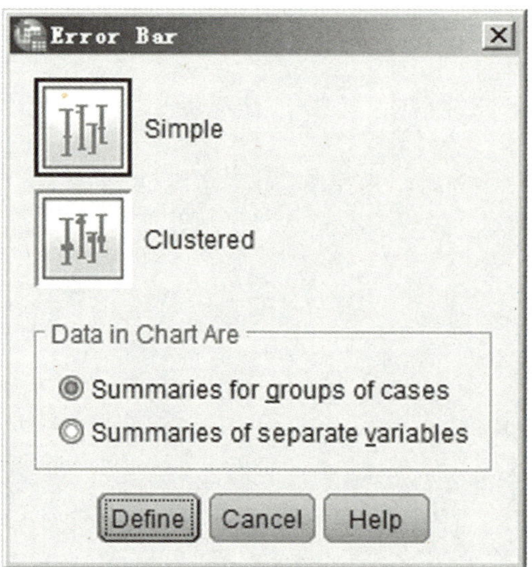

Figure 12-39 The Error Bar dialog box

(1) Simple error bar: It is used to compare the difference on the pre-treat "hb1" between two groups, with respective 95% confidence interval. The steps are as follows:

Graphs

Legacy Dialogs

Error Bar

Simple & ⊙Summaries for groups of cases

Define

▸Variable: hb1 (Indicator variable)

▸Category Axis: group (Categorical variable)

Bars Represent

Confidence interval for mean

Level: 95 % (95% Confidence interval; Default)

(Not only the confidence interval, the bars can also be used to present the standard deviation and standard error.)

The output is listed in Figure 12-40.

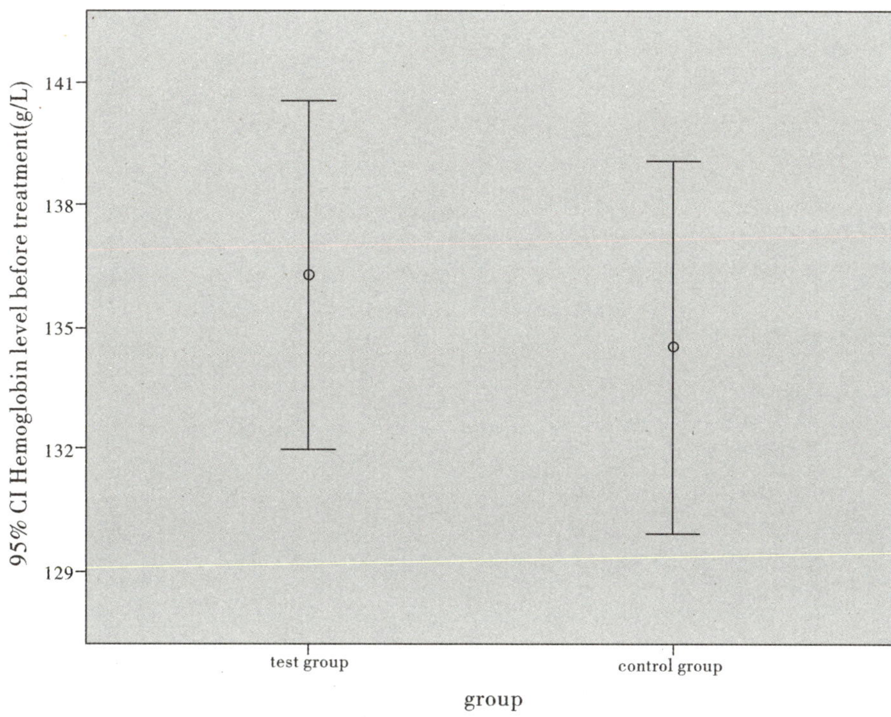

Figure 12-40 The simple error bars of pre-treated hemoglobin level (g/L) and 95% CI among test and control groups

(2) Clustered error bar: It is used to compare difference on "hb1" by "group" and "gender", with respective mean ± standard deviation. The steps are as follows:

Graphs

Legacy Dialogs

Error Bar

Clustered & ⊙Summaries for groups of cases

Define

▸**Variable: hb1** (Indicator variable)

▸**Category Axis: group** (Categorical variable)

▸**Define Clusters by: sex** (Categorical variable)

Bars Represent

Standard deviation

Multiplier: 1

The output is listed in Figure 12-41.

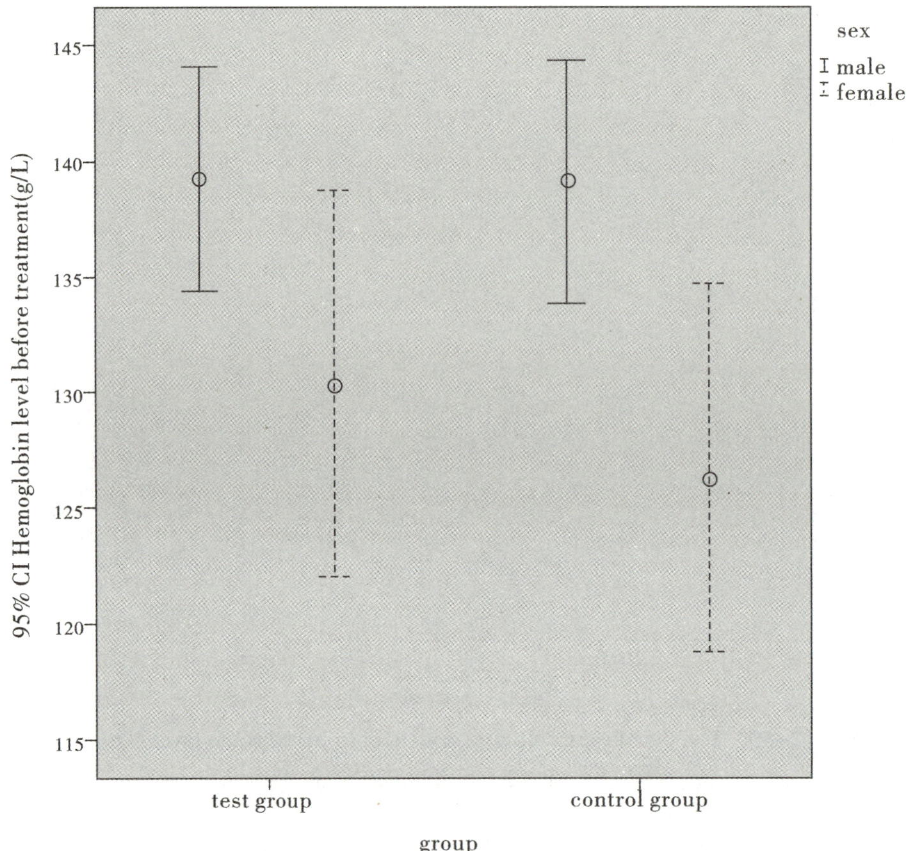

Figure 12-41 The clustered error bars of pre-treated hemoglobin level (g/L) across two treatment groups and gender (Mean±SD)

12.10 Population pyramid

Population pyramid is used to depict the frequency distribution of the variable by the other categorical variable. The data file "clinical_trial. sav" is used as the Example 12-12. Population pyramid is used to depict the frequency distribution of the pre-treated hemoglobin level by the treatment group and sex.

Graphs

Legacy Dialogs

Population Pyramid

The dialog of Define Population Pyramid is listed in Figure 12-42.

◇Counts.

⊙Compute counts from data: Default.

◎Get counts from variable.

The steps are as follows:

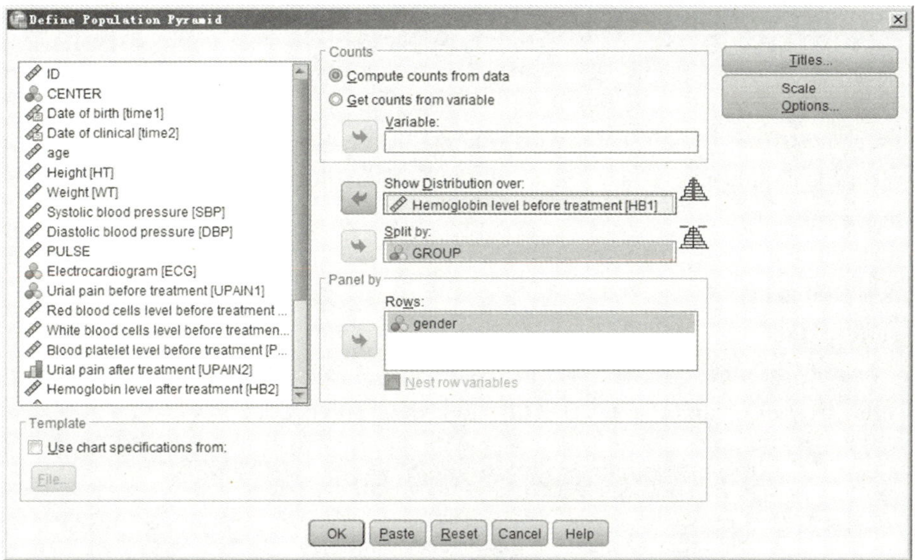

Figure 12-42 The Define Population Pyramid dialog box

Graphs

Legacy Dialogs

Population Pyramid

Define

⊙Compute counts from data

▸Show Distribution over: HB1

▸Split by: GROUP

▸Rows: gender

The output is listed in Figure 12-43.

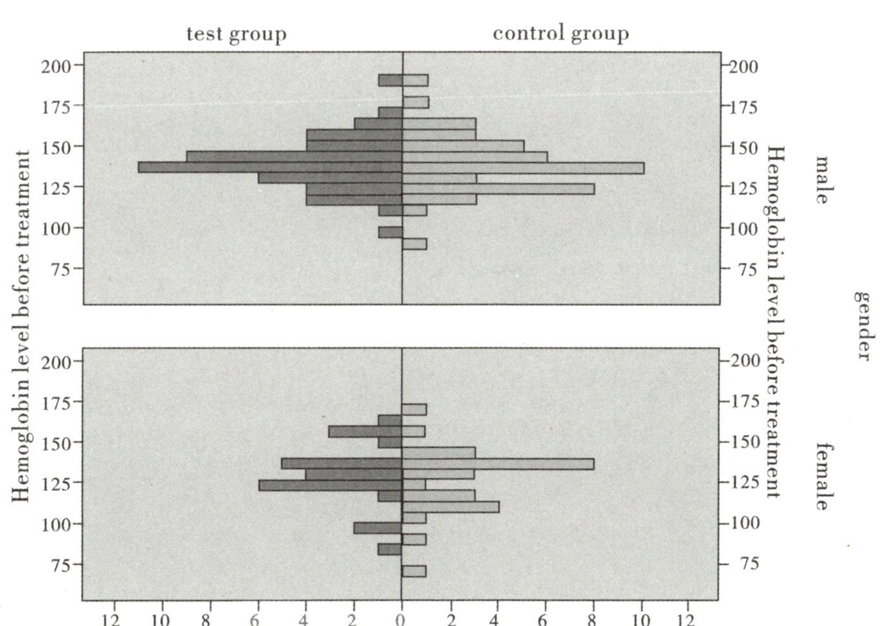

Figure 12-43 The population pyramid chart of pre-treated hemoglobin level (g/L) across treatment groups and gender

12.11 Scatter plot

Scatter plot is mostly used to present the distribution of the data and correlation between two numerical variables. The data file "clinical trial. sav" is used as the Example 12–13 to get the scatter plot of the patients' blood test results.

Graphs

Legacy Dialogs

Scatter/Dot

The dialog box of "Scatter/Dot" is listed in Figure 12–44, including five types of scatter charts (Simple Scatter, Overlay Scatter, Matrix Scatter, 3-D Scatter and Simple Dot).

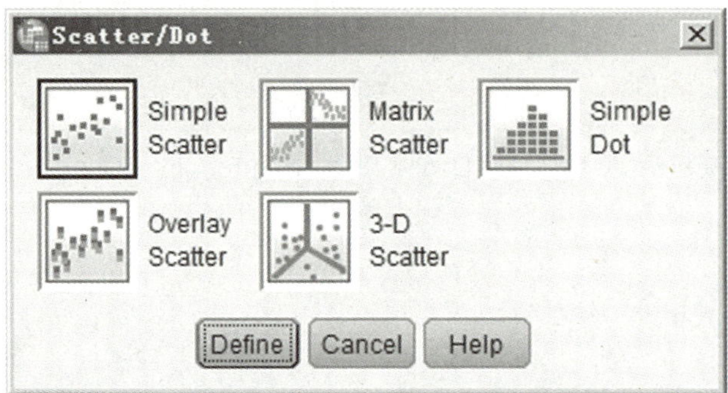

Figure 12–44 The Scatter/Dot dialog box

(1) Simple Scatter plot: Each point represents the value of one variable determining the position on the horizontal axis and the value of the other variable determining the position on the vertical axis. The scatter plot of pre-treated hemoglobin level ("hb1") and red blood cell count ("rbc1") is produced by the following steps.

Graphs

Legacy Dialogs

Scatter/Dot

Simple Scatter

Define

▸**Y Axis: hb1** (pre-treated hb1 as *Y*-axis)

▸**X Axis: rbc1** (pre-treated rbc1 as *X*-axis)

▸**Set Markers by: sex** (sex variable as marker)

The output is listed in Figure 12–45.

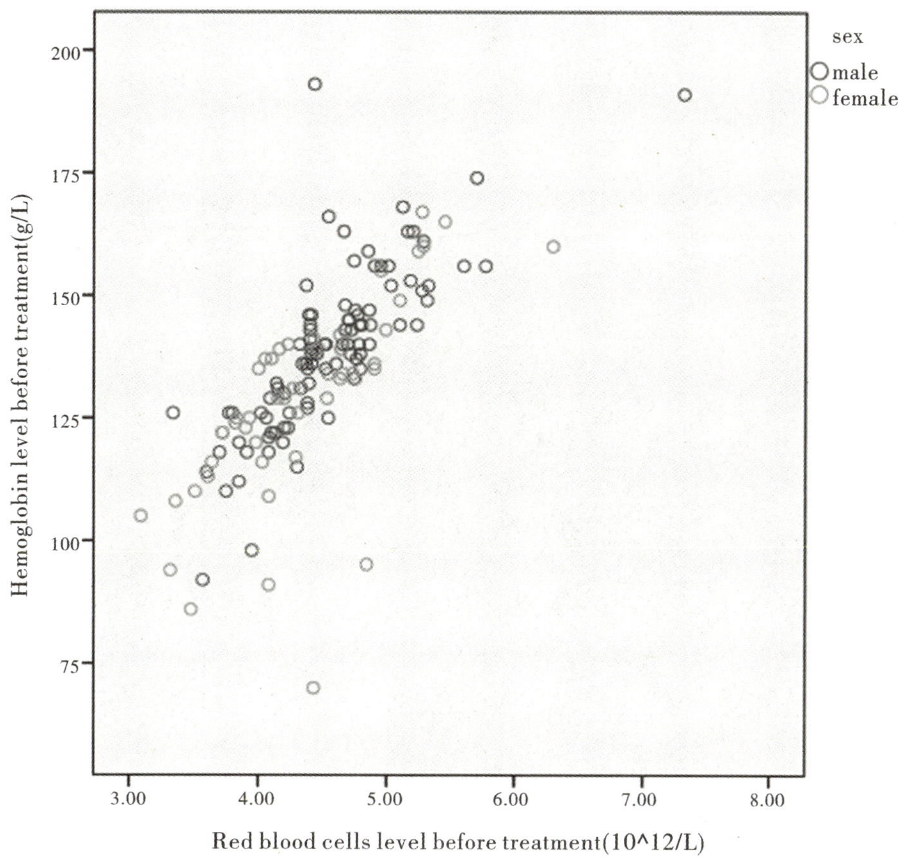

Figure 12-45 The simple scatter plot of pre-treated hemoglobin level (g/L) and pre-treated red blood cell level (10^12/L)

(2) Overlay scatter plot: It can show the pairwise simple scatter plots of multiple variables; to be noted, all the variables to be drawn on the scatter plot should have the same unit. The following example will produce the overlay scatter plot of SBP and DBP by age together. The steps are as follows:

Graphs

Legacy Dialogs

Scatter/Dot

Overlay Scatter

Define

▸Y-X Pairs: SBP-age / DBP -- age

(Age as *X*-axis; SBP and DBP as *Y*-axis together)

The output is listed in Figure 12-46.

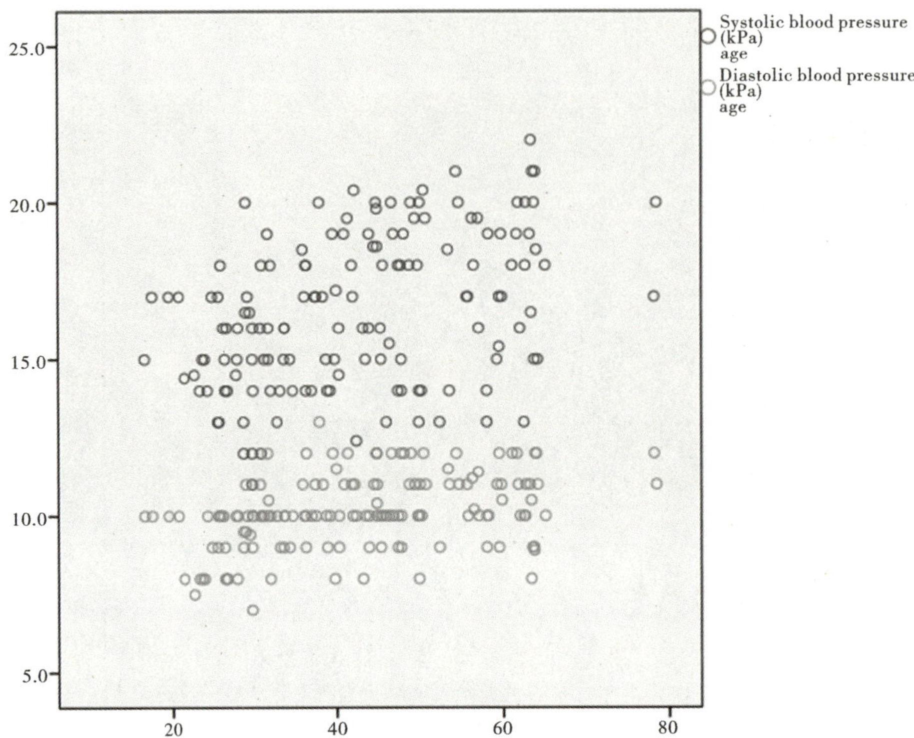

Figure 12-46 Overlay scatter chart of systolic blood pressure and diastolic blood pressure by age

(3) Matrix Scatter plot: It depicts all the pairwise scatter plots of the variables in a matrix format. Four types of routine blood test is described using this method by the following steps:

Graphs

Legacy Dialogs

Scatter/Dot

Matrix Scatter

Define

▸Matrix Variables: hb1 / rbc1 / wbc1 / plt1

The output is listed in Figure 12-47.

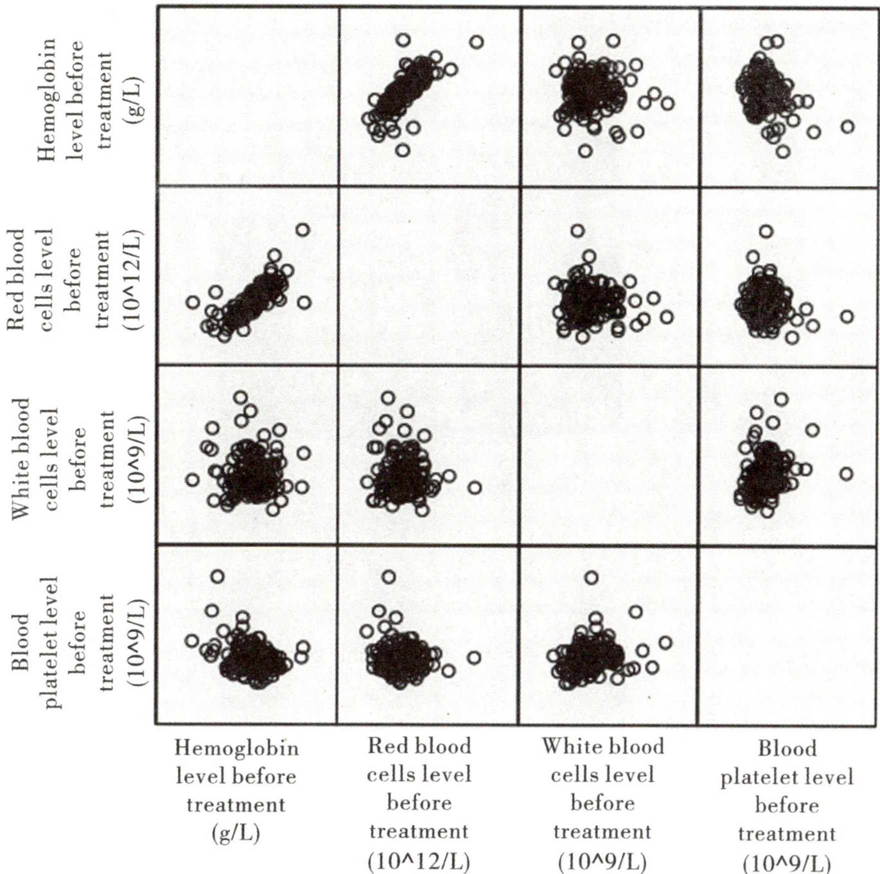

Figure 12-47 The matrix scatter chart of four types of pre-treated blood test

(4)3-D Scatter plot: Shows the visualization of correlations among three variables. The 3-D scatter plot of SBP, DBP and age is produced by the following steps:

Graphs

Legacy Dialogs

Scatter/Dot

3-**D Scatter**

Define

▸**Y Axis: SBP**

▸**X Axis: age**

▸**Z Axis: DBP**

The output is listed in Figure 12-48.

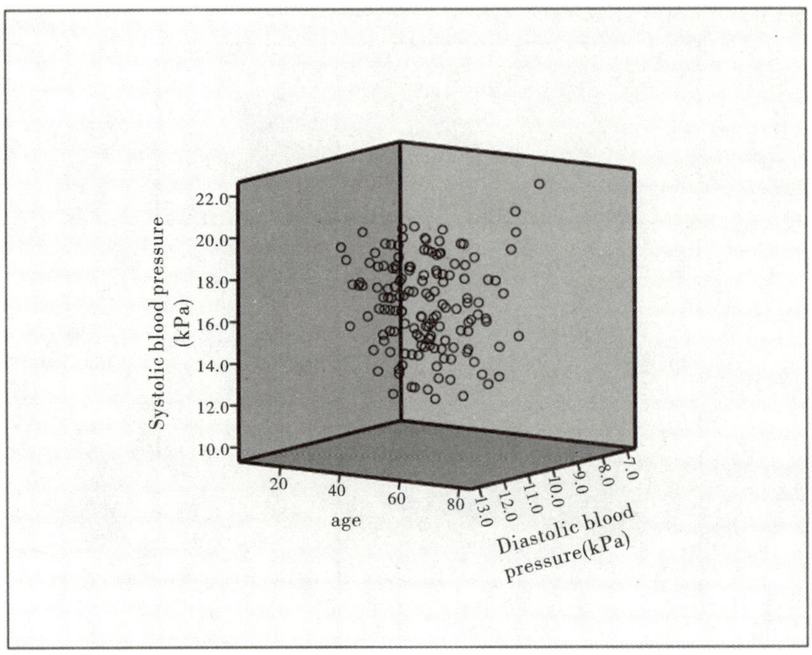

Figure 12-48 The 3-D scatter chart of associations among systolic blood pressure and diastolic blood pressure and age

(5) Simple Dot: It is used to show the number of each value of the data. The following example will produce the simple dot of the height (ht). The steps are as follows:

Graphs

Legacy Dialogs

Scatter/Dot

Simple Dot

Define

▸X-Axis Variable: ht

The output is listed in Figure 12-49.

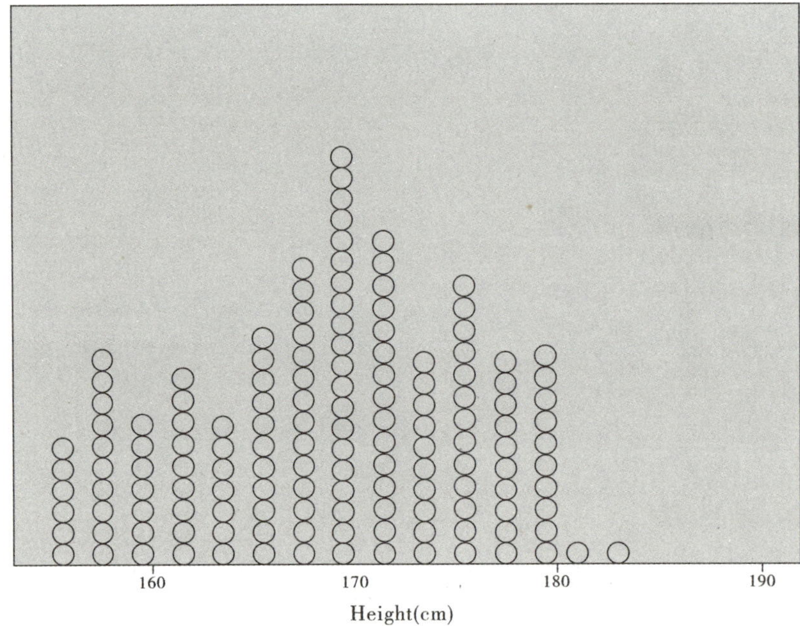

Figure 12-49 Simple dot chart of height (cm)

12.12 Histogram

Histogram chart is mainly used to show the frequency distribution of the numerical variable. The data file "diameter_sub. sav" is used as the Example 12-14 to draw the histogram in order to display the frequency distribution of "trueap_mean" variable.

Graphs

Legacy Dialogs

Histogram

The dialog box of Histogram is listed in Figure 12-50.

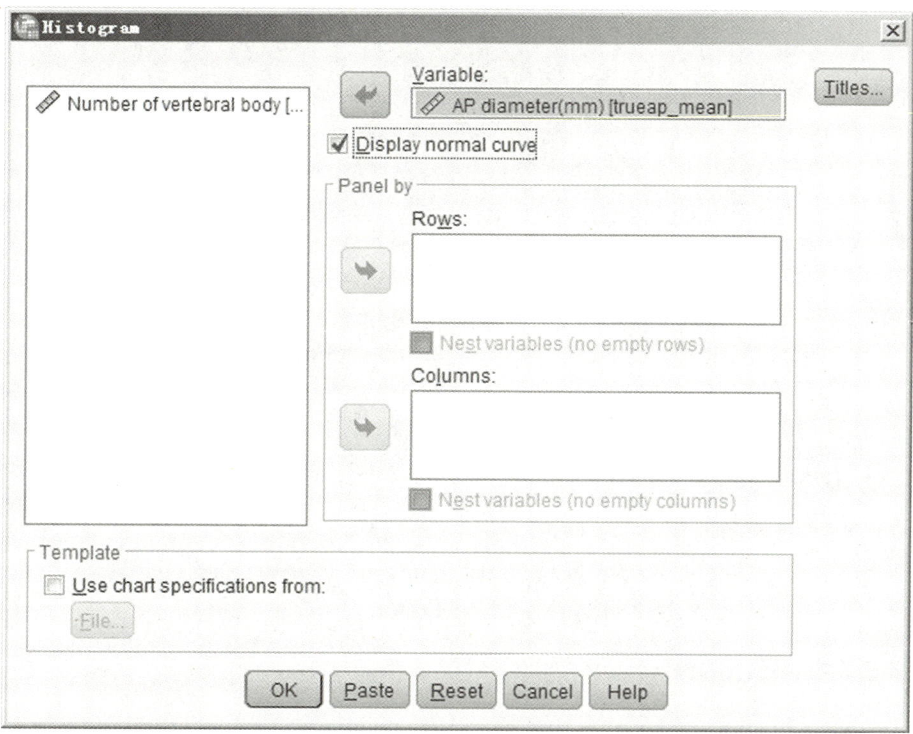

Figure 12-50 The Histogram dialog box

☑Display normal curve: The normal distribution curve is plotted using the sample statistic as the parameter.

◇Template.

□Use chart specifications from: If selected "Use chart specifications from", the "File" button is activated for selecting the existed templates. The steps as follows:

Graphs

Legacy Dialogs

Histogram

▶Variable: trueap_mean

☑Display normal curve

The output is listed in Figure 12-51.

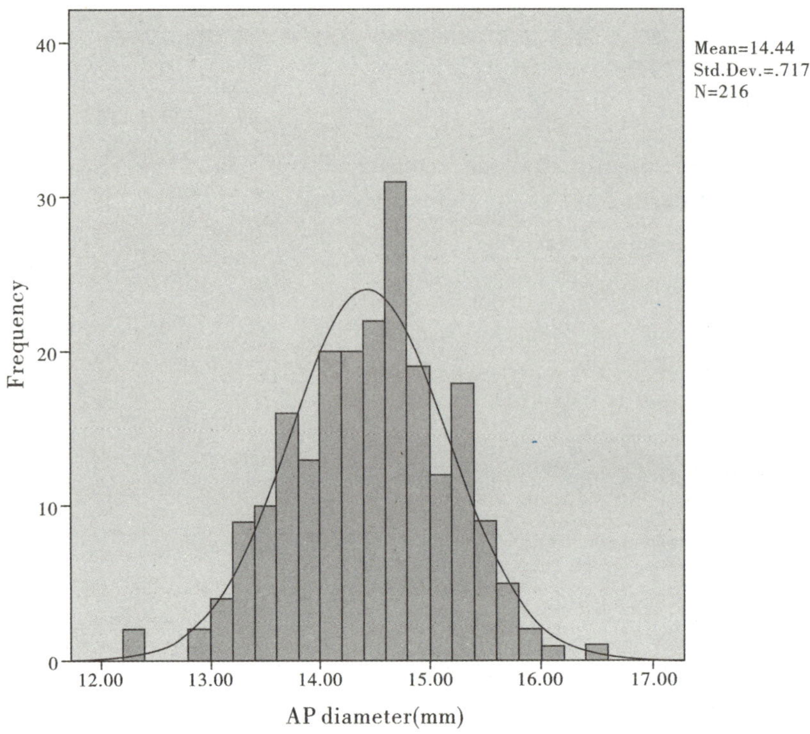

Figure 12-51 The histogram and normal distribution curve of AP diameter (mm)

12.13 Chart editor

When the statistical graphical output is produced using above mentioned charts, we can edit it according to different requirements using the following Chart Editor.

12.13.1 Chart Editor

Before editing the graphs, the Chart Editor must be activated via the following three ways:

1) Double-click on the selected graph directly.

2) Right-click on the selected graph to bring up the dialog box, then follow the below steps:

Edit Content

In Separate Window

3) Left-click on the graph to be edited, then follow the below steps:

Edit Content

In Separate Window

The activated Chart Editor is listed in Figure 12-52. The graph in the shaded background means that it is still in the editing and activated status, and can be applied and edited at any time from the bottom of the screen. If too many Chart Editors are activated simultaneously, the computer running speed may be affected.

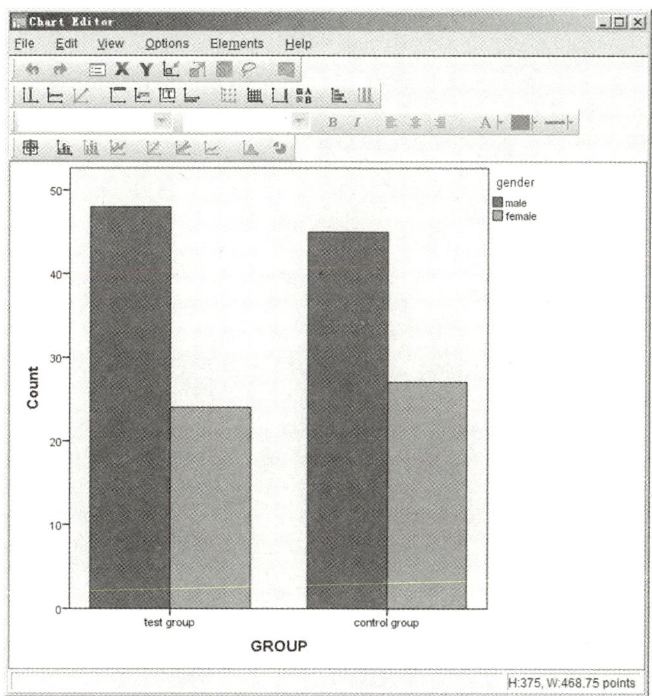

Figure 12-52 The Chart Editor dialog box

(1) File: Refer to Figure 12-53.

1) Save Chart Template: Save the chart as template file.

2) Apply Chart Template: Apply the existed chart template file.

3) Export Chart XML: Export the chart as XML file.

(2) Edit: The most important function here is "Properties". Other functions include editing the X-axis, Y-axis and Z-axis (Figure 12-54).

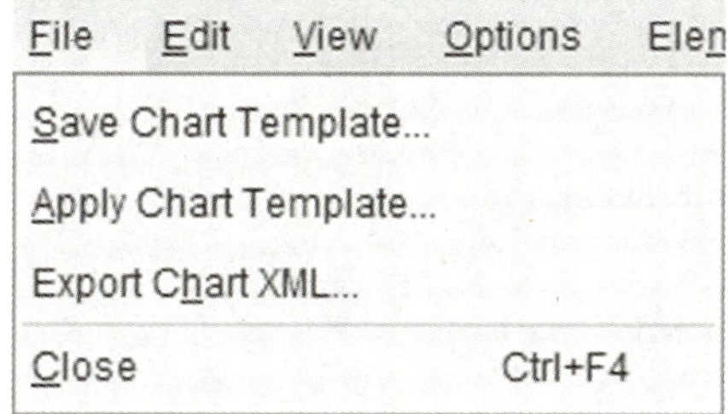

Figure 12-53 The File menu dialog box

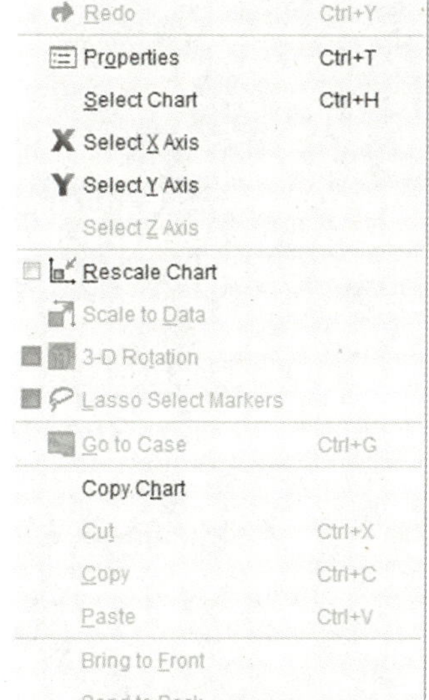

Figure 12-54 The Edit menu dialog box

(3) View: Includes the "Status Bar" "Edit Toolbar" "Options Toolbar" "Element Toolbar" "Format

Toolbar" and "Large Buttons" (Figure 12–55).

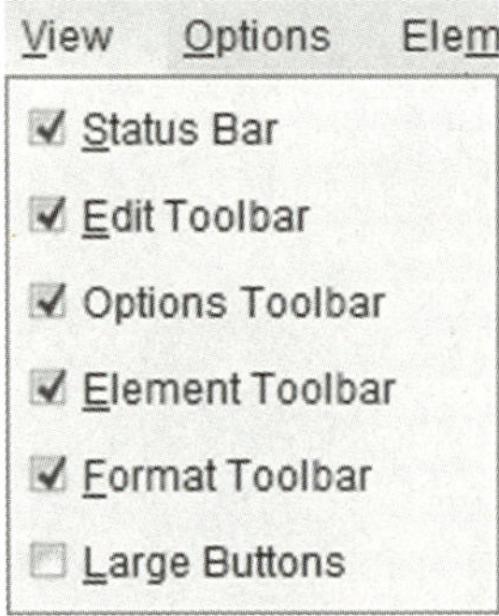

Figure 12–55 The "View" menu dialog box

(4) Options: Includes the "X Axis Reference Lines" "Y Axis Reference Lines" "Title" "Annotation" "Text Box" "Footnote" "Show Grid Lines" "Show Derived Axis" "Show Legend" and so forth (Figure 12–56).

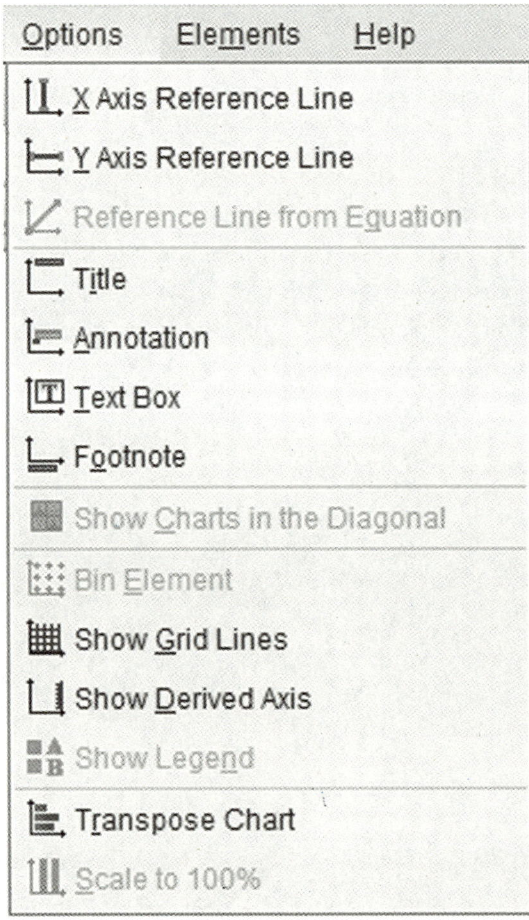

Figure 12–56 The Options menu dialog box

(5) Elements: Includes the graphic elements editing (Figure 12–57)

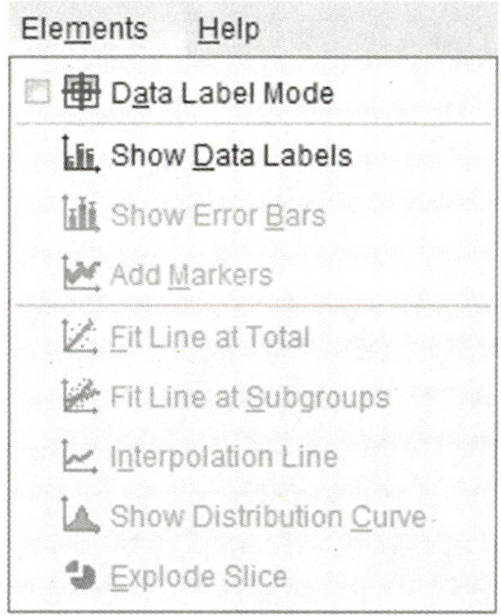

Figure 12-57 The Elements menu dialog box

12.13.2 Chart property editing

12.13.2.1 Chart property editing

(1) In general, when the "Chart Editor" is activated, the Properties dialog box can be opened through the usual Edit/ Properties, or just double-click anywhere in the chart. This dialog box has three sub-dialogs, which are listed from Figure 12-58 to Figure 12-60.

1) Chart Size: Define the height and width of the chart. If "Maintain aspect ratio" is selected, the height or width is modified automatically according to the default ratio.

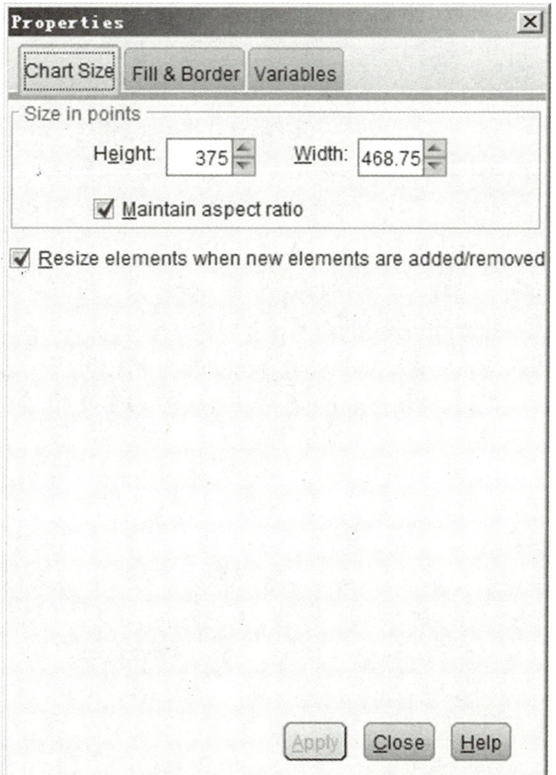

Figure 12-58 The Properties: Chart Size dialog box

2) Fill & Border: Refer to Figure 12-59.

Fill: Fill in the color.

Border: Define the color of the border.

Pattern: Define the background pattern.

◇Border Style: Define the width and type of the border lines, such as solid line, dotted line and broken line.

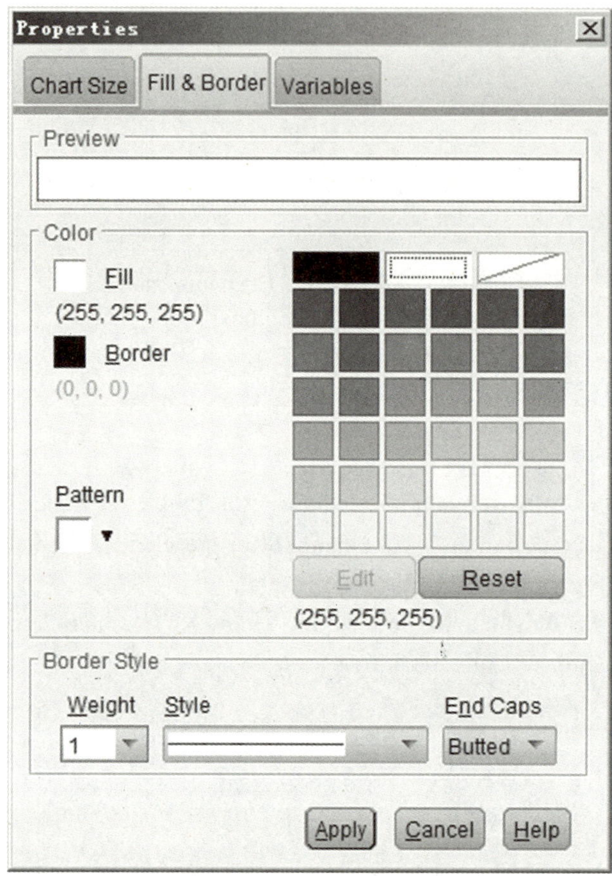

Figure 12-59 The Properties: Fill & Border dialog box

3) Variables: The combination of the variables can be updated (Figure 12-60).

Double-click the "graphic element" on the editing chart, e. g. , the bar, line, scatter point, the "Properties" dialog box pops out. This dialog box includes common properties for all charts (from Figure 12-58 to Figure 12-60) and some special properties for different charts, which is introduced as follows.

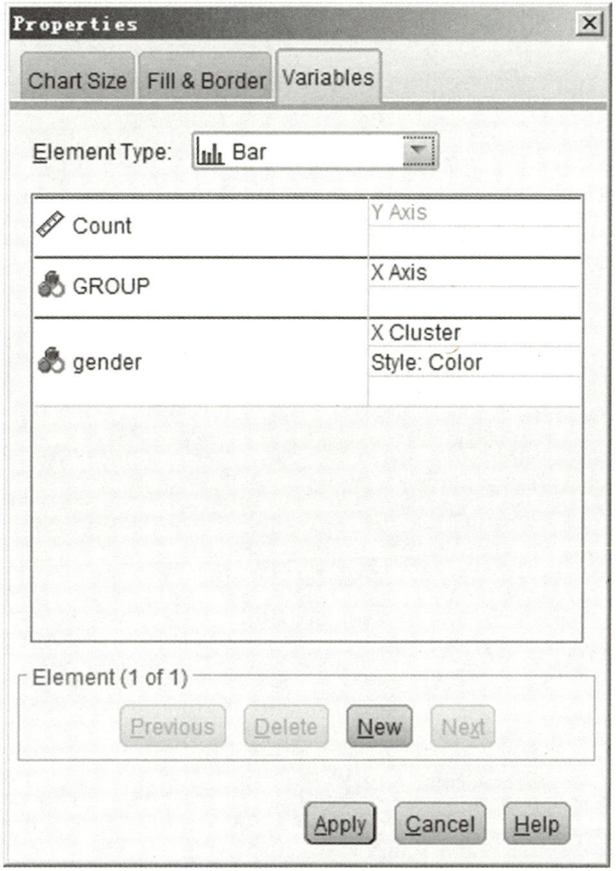

Figure 12-60 The Properties: Variables dialog box

(2) Bar chart: Double-click the body of the bar after the chart editor is activated, "Properties" dialog box pops out. Apart from three common dialog boxes, there are another three special boxes, which are listed from Figure 12-61 to Figure 12-63.

1) Bar Options: Refer to Figure 12-61.

Bars: Specify the ratio of total bar widths on X-axis.

Clusters: Specify the ratio of width between and within bars in the cluster bar graph.

☑Link the box, median line, and error bar widths.

□Scale boxplot and error bar width based on count.

Boxplot and Error Bar Style: Select the types of boxplot and error bar, including T-type, Line-type and Bar-type.

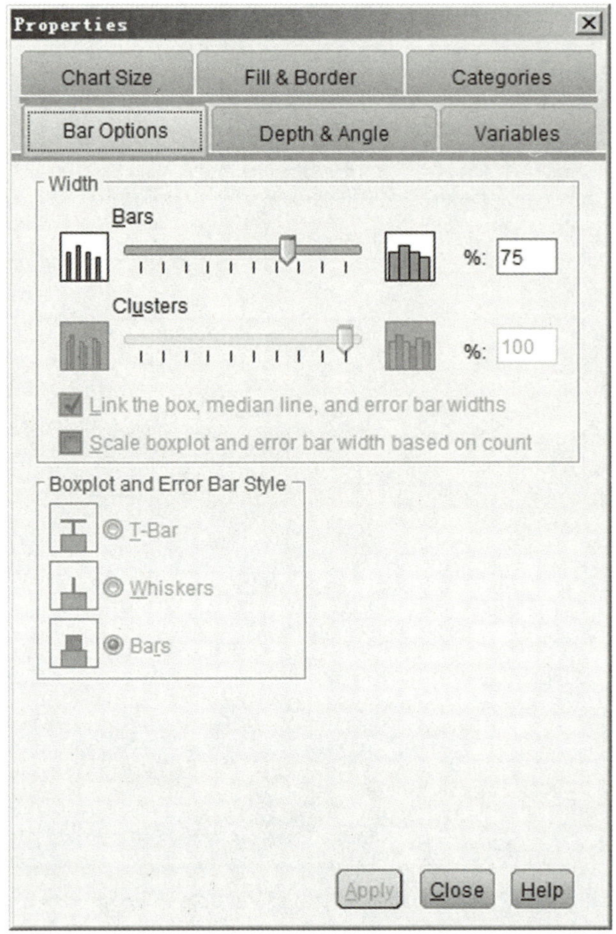

Figure 12-61 The Properties: Bar Options dialog box

2) Categories: Order the levels of the categorical variable, or just add or delete one (some) of them (Figure 12-62).

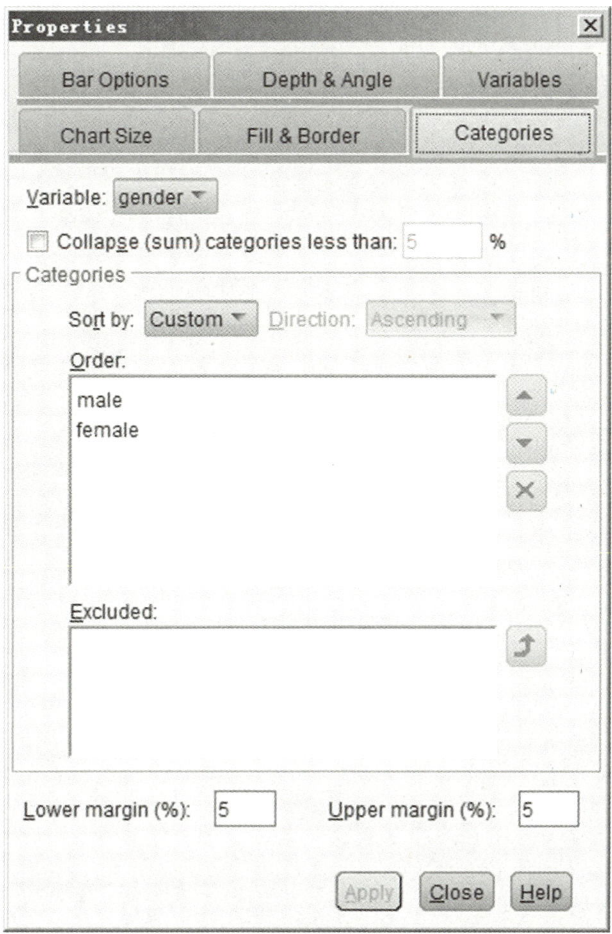

Figure 12-62 The Properties: Categories dialog box

3) Depth & Angle: Specify the visualization of the bar, including the Flat Effect, Shadow Effect and 3-D Effect (Figure 12-63). When the last two effects are selected, the angle of projection is activated and can be adjusted by sliding the mouse. In addition, the viewing distance from the 3-D effect can be changed.

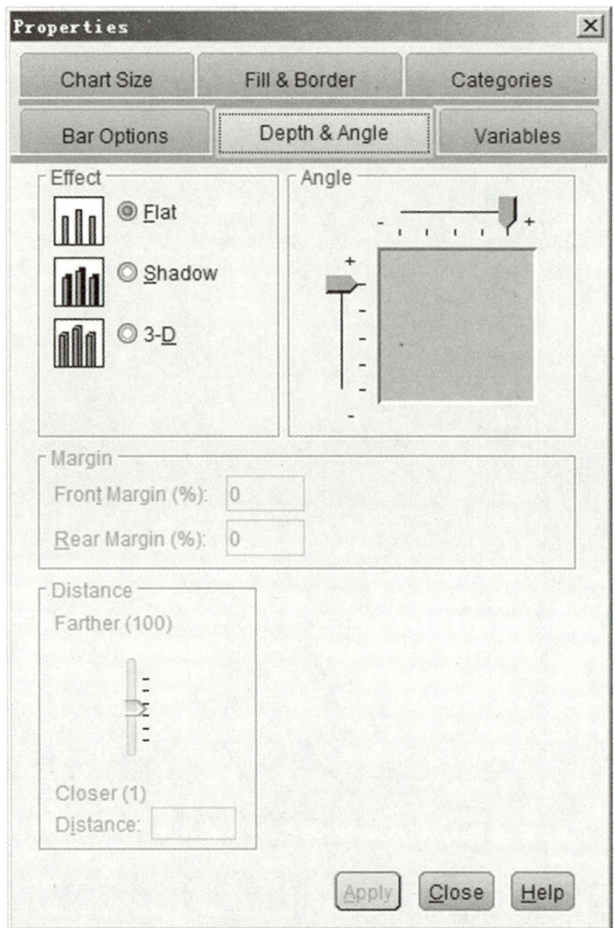

Figure 12-63 The Properties: Depth & Angle dialog box

(3) 3-D Elements: In addition to the properties for the 2-D bar, the dialog box of 3-D Elements is particularly added for 3-D bar (Figure 12-64).

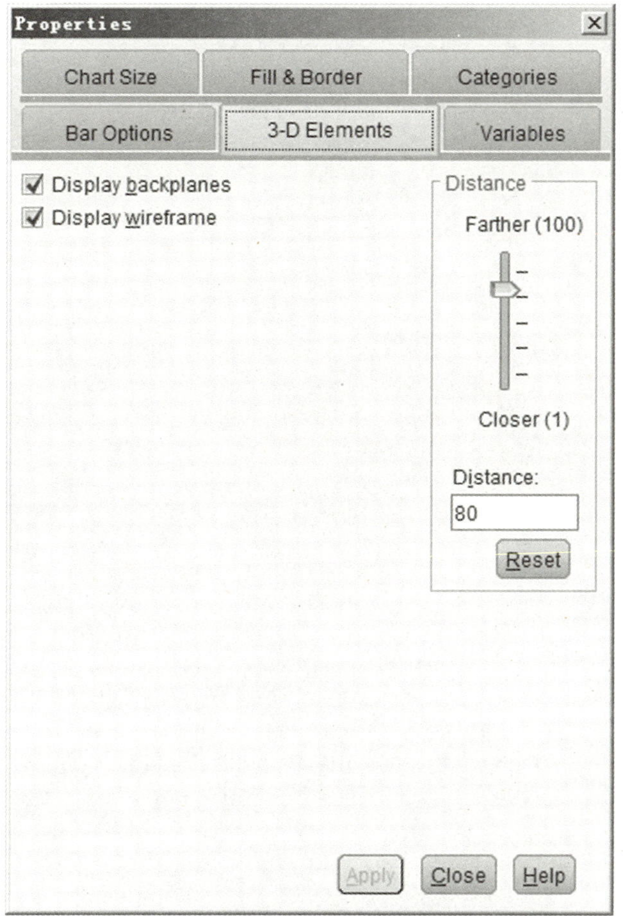

Figure 12-64 The Properties:3-D Elements dialog box

(4) Line chart: The dialog boxes for "Line chart" are listed from Figure 12-65 to Figure 12-67.

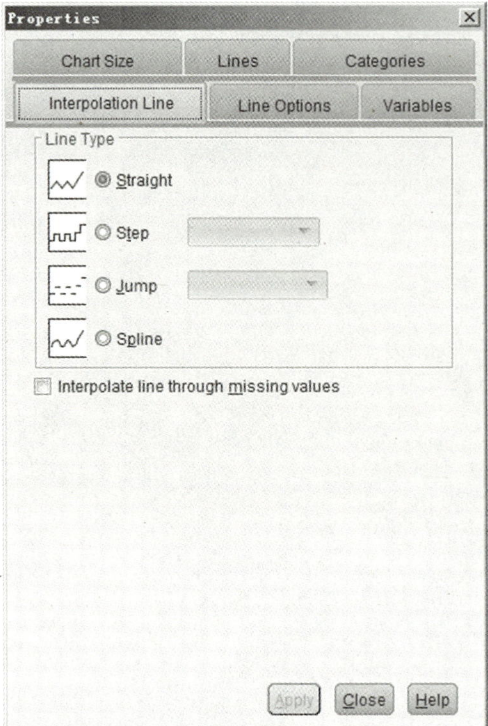

Figure 12-65 The Properties: Interpolation Line dialog box

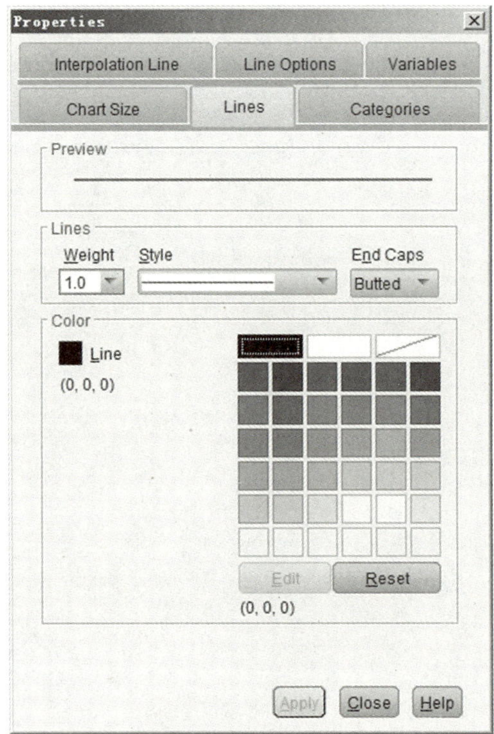

Figure 12-66 The Properties: Lines dialog box

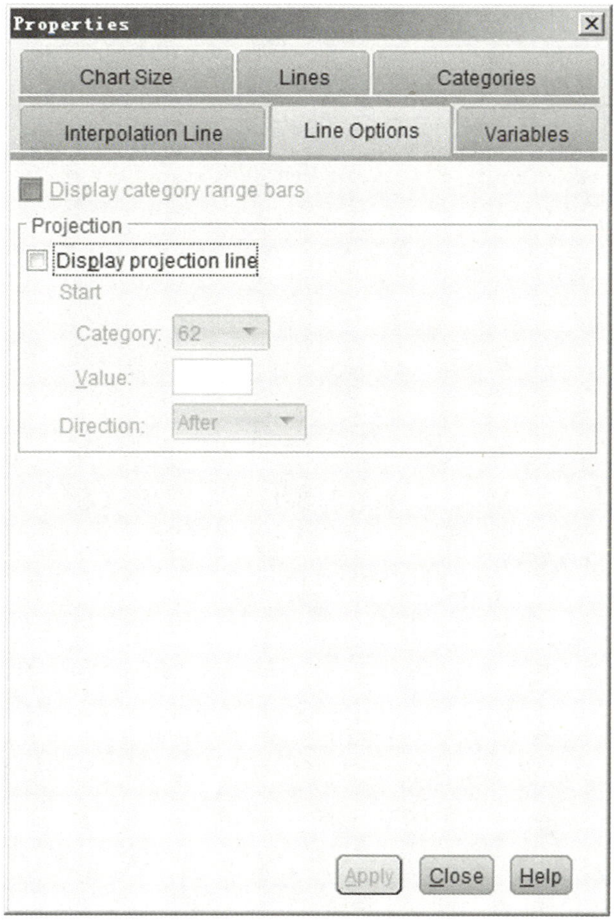

Figure 12-67 The Properties:Line Options dialog box

1) Interpolation Line: An interpolation line connects data values, including four types (Straight, Step, Jump and Spline).

2) Lines: Line editing options, including the color, weight and style of line (Figure 12-66).

3) Line Options: Refer to the Figure 12-67.

□Display category range bars: If selected this button, the segments at each time point are connected by a vertical line.

◇Projection.

□Display projection line: Mark the important time period. If selected, the boxes of "Start" and "Direction" are activated. For instance, Start 1952 and Direction After indicates that the line after 1952 will be highlighted in order to mark the importance of the range.

(5) Pie chart: The dialog box is listed in the Figure 12-68.

◇Effect: There are three types of effects, including Flat, Shadow and 3-D. When the last two effects are selected, the angle of projection is activated and can be adjusted by sliding the mouse. In addition, you can change the viewing distance from the 3-D effect.

◇Position Slices: Specify the First slice (clock position), with 12 o' clock as default. There are two directions, including Clockwise and Counterclockwise.

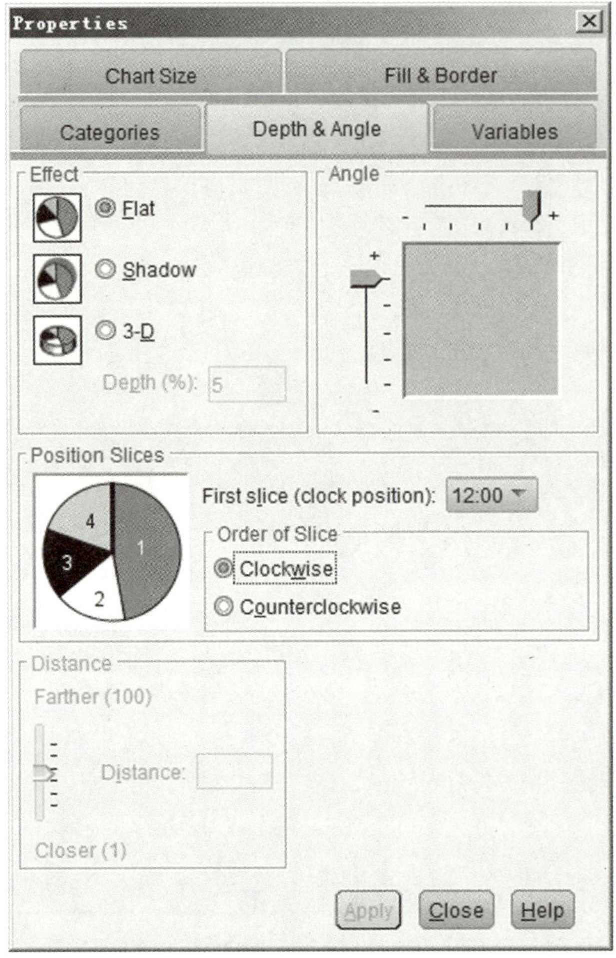

Figure 12-68 The Properties: Depth & Angle dialog box

(6) Scatterplot: The dialog boxes are listed in Figure 12-69 and Figure 12-70.

Marker: Specify the properties of point maker, including the type, size, border width and border color, and the filled color.

Spikes: Specify the spikes, including None, Floor, Origin and Centroid.

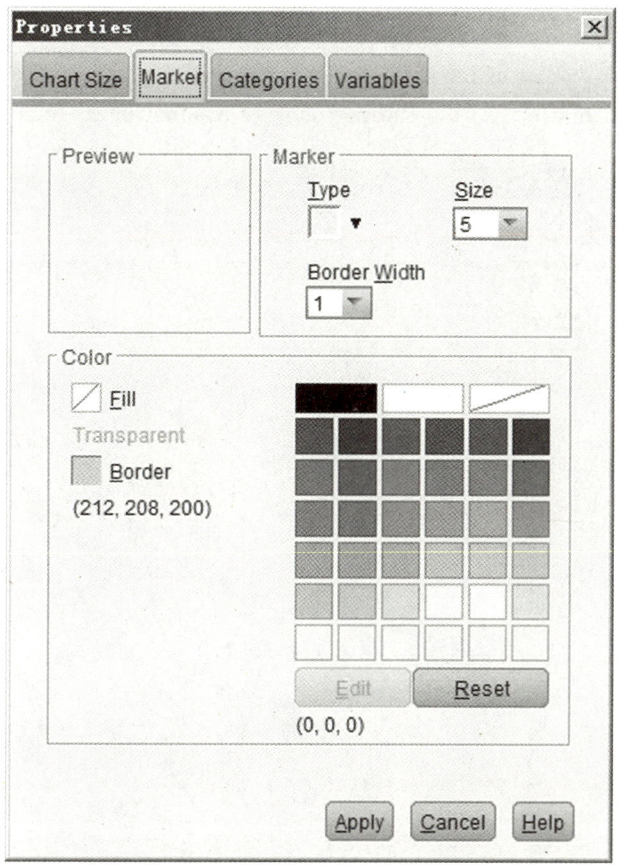

Figure 12-69 The Properties: Maker dialog box

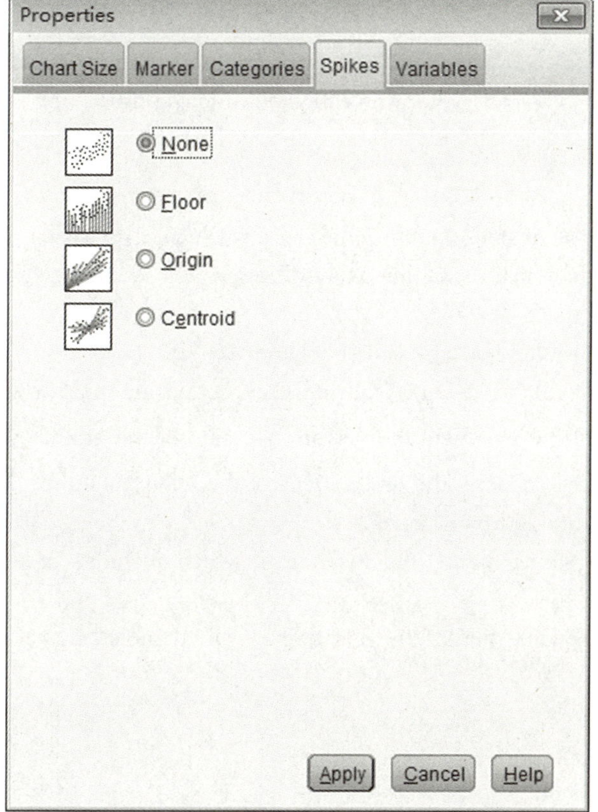

Figure 12-70 The Properties: Spikes dialog box

(7) Histogram: The dialog box is listed in Figure 12–71.

⦿Automatic: The width and number of the intervals are set by default.

◎Custom: Specify the number of intervals and interval width.

□Custom value for anchor: Define the starting point of the first bar.

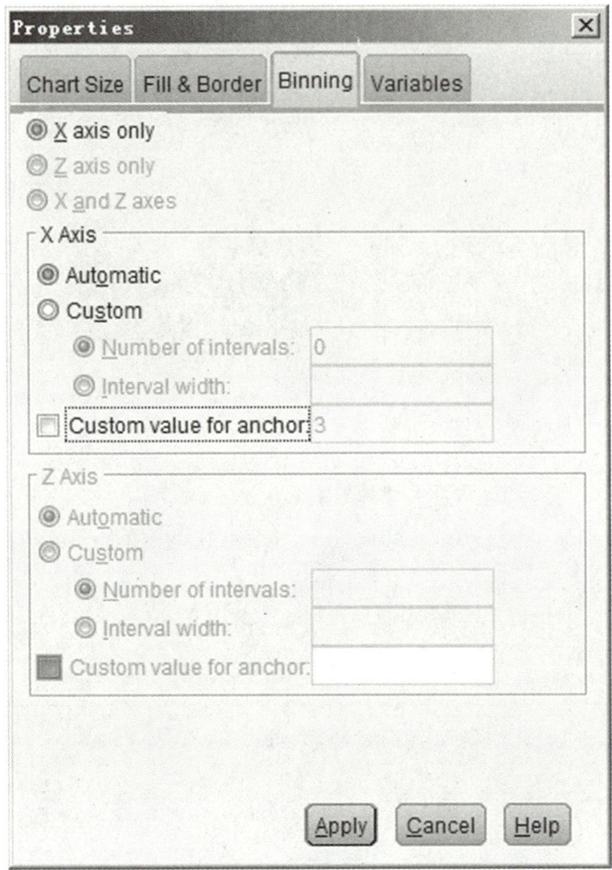

Figure 12–71 The Properties: Binning dialog box

12.13.2.2 Axis editor

After the chart editor is activated, double-clicking any place of the axes of chart to activate "Properties" dialog box. There are four main tabs for axis editing, which are listed from Figure 12–72 to Figure 12–75.

1) Labels & Ticks: The dialog box is listed in Figure 12–72.

☑Display axis title: The title is default placed in the bottom or the left side. If choosing the Display axis on the Opposite, the title moves to the top or right side of the graph.

◇Major Increment Labels: Specify the orientations of the label, including Automatic, Horizontal, Vertical and Diagonal, Staggered and Custom Degrees.

◇Major Ticks: Large spacing marks, the location of which includes the medial, lateral and bilateral options.

◇Minor Ticks: Small spacing marks, the location of which includes the medial, lateral and bilateral options.

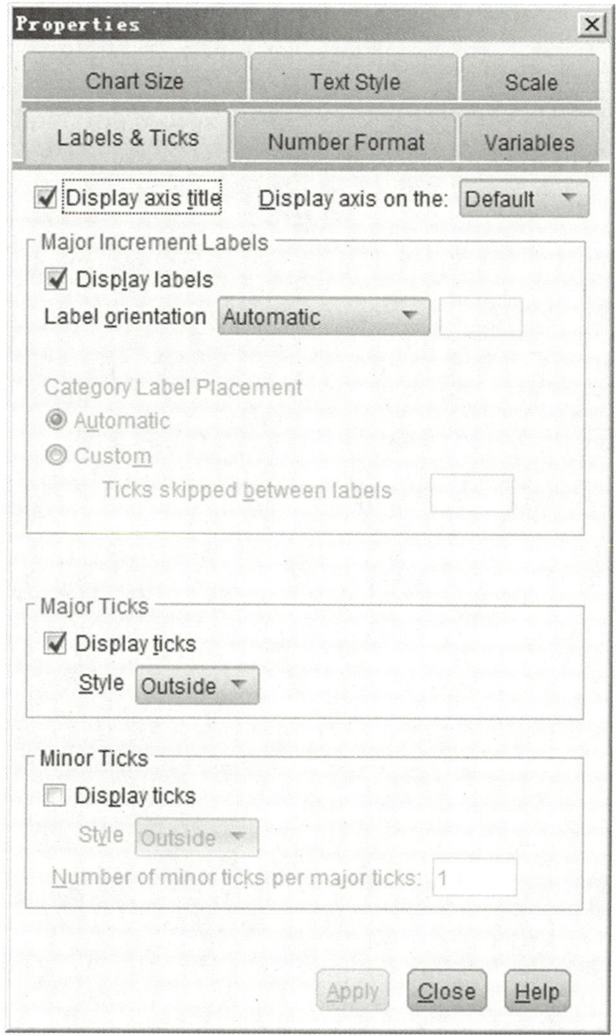

Figure 12-72 The Properties: Labels & Ticks dialog box

2) Number Format: Refer to the Figure 12-73.

- Decimal Places.
- Scaling Factor: If the number is entered, the scale of the original axis will be divided by the number. The default value is 1.
- Leading Characters: Add the character in front of the original mark.
- Trailing Characters: Add the character behind the original mark.

☑Display Digit Grouping: Add the thousands symbols.

◇Scientific Notation: Includes Automatic, Always and Never.

3) Text Style: Specify the style, font size and color of the text. The dialog box is listed in Figure 12-74.

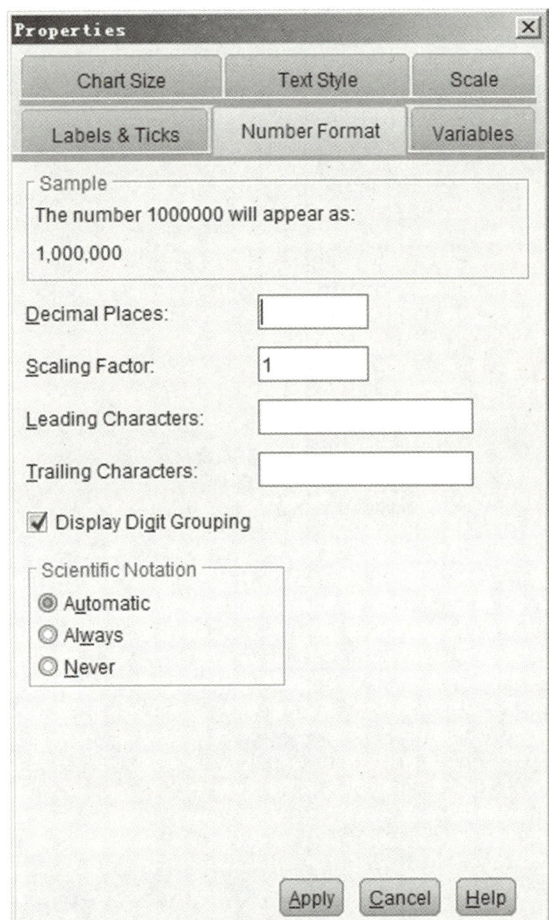

Figure 12-73 The Properties: Number Format dialog box

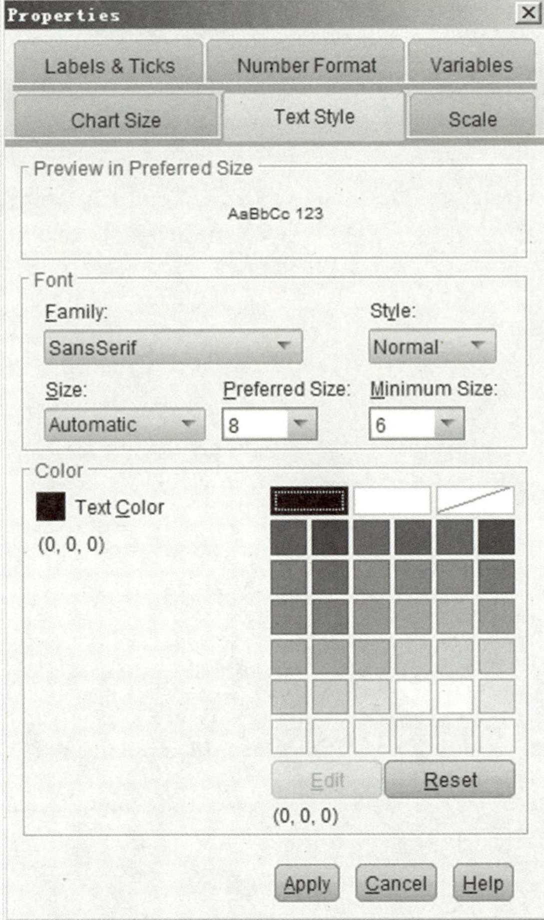

Figure 12-74 The Properties: Text Style dialog box

4) Scale: Refer to Figure 12-75.

◇Range: Specify the minimum, maximum, width and starting point of the axes.

◇Type: Measurement types, including Linear, Logarithmic and Power types. If you want to change the linear chart to the semi-log chart, just transform the axis scale from the Linear scale to the Logarithmic scale.

- Lower margin (%): 5 : Add 5% (system default) of the defined axis length to the bottom or the left of the scale axis.
- Upper margin (%): 5 : Add 5% (system default) of the defined axis length to the top or the right of the scale axis.

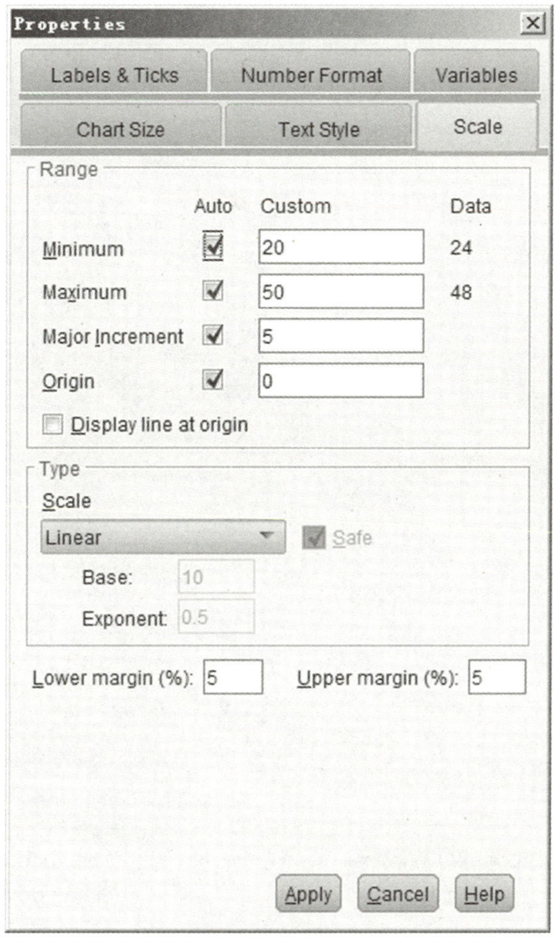

Figure 12-75 The defining the axis scale dialog box

12.13.3 Add and display chart elements

Right-click the activated chart, and the dialog box of Properties Window pops up (Figure 12-76 and Figure 12-77). For different charts, there may be slightly different in the Properties Window. The chart element will be added to the chart, after it is selected in "Properties Window", and at the same time the option particularly for this chart will also be added in the Properties Window dialog.

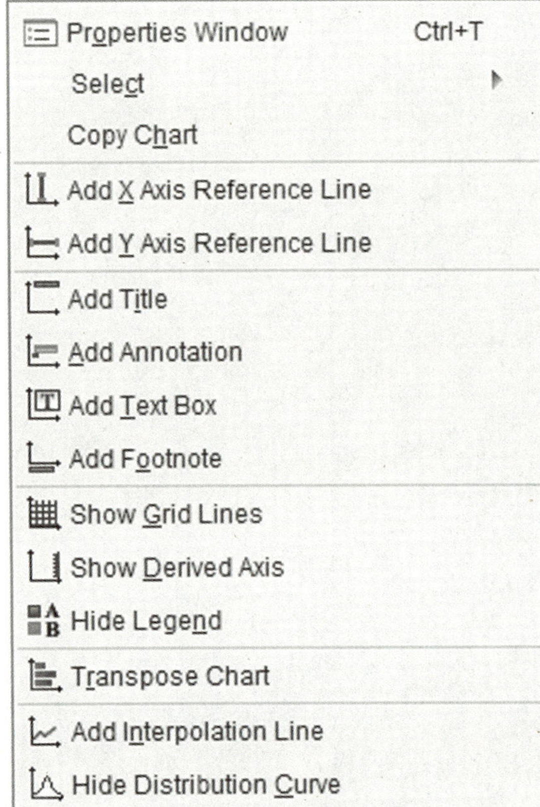

Figure 12-76 The menu of Properties Window dialog box(1)

Properties Window Ctrl+T
Select
Copy Chart
Add X Axis Reference Line
Add Y Axis Reference Line
Add Reference Line from Equation
Add Title
Add Annotation
Add Text Box
Add Footnote
Show Grid Lines
Show Derived Axis
Hide Legend
Transpose Chart
Add Fit Line at Total
Add Fit Line at Subgroups
Add Interpolation Line

Figure 12-77 The menu of properties window dialog box(2)

1) Add X Axis Reference Line: If selected this item, a vertical line is added in the middle of X-axis. The option for reference line editing is added to the "Properties Window" dialog box. The placement of X Axis Reference Line can be changed by dragging the line directly, or setting it in the corresponding dialog.

2) Add Y Axis Reference Line: If selected this item, a horizontal line is added in the middle of X-axis.

3) Add Reference Line from Equation: If selected this item, a diagonal line from lower left to upper right is added.

4) Add Title: If selected this item, a text dialog for title inputting pops out above the editing chart.

5) Add Annotation: If selected this item, a text dialog for annotation inputting pops out in the centre of the editing chart. Its placement can be changed through dragging the dialog.

6) Add Text Box: Select the text to be edited, the text box pops out outside the text.

7) Add Footnote: If selected this item, a text dialog box for footnote inputting pops out in the bottom of the editing chart.

8) Show Grid Lines: If selected, the grid lines is added.

9) Show Derived Axis: If selected, another vertical axis is added to the right side.

10) Hide Legend: Show or hide the legend of the chart. If selected, the chart legend is added to the right side, and it can be moved arbitrarily. And its status can be changed from the Show to the Hide.

11) Transpose Chart: Transpose the horizontal and vertical axes. This function can be used to transform the horizontal bar to the vertical bar chart and vice versa.

12) Add Interpolation Line: If selected, an interpolation line will be added to connect the scatter points along the horizontal axis from the minimal to the maximal data. Includes four types of interpolation lines, which can be found in the above mentioned Line Editor.

13) Show / Hide Distribution Curve.

14) Add Fit Line at Total: Add the Fit Line based on the total scatter points. If selected, in addition to add the fit line, the dialog box of Fit Line is also added, which is listed in Figure 12-78.

□Display Spikes.

◇ Fit Method.

◎Mean of Y: Mean value of the dependent variable.

⊙Linear: Fitting linear regression curve.

◎Quadratic: Fitting quadratic regression curve.

◎Cubic: Fitting cubic regression curve.

◎Loess: Fitting locally scatterplot smoothing curve. If selected this item, you need to specify the percentage (1%-99%) of points to be fitted. And there are seven core functions in the Kernel dialog for option.

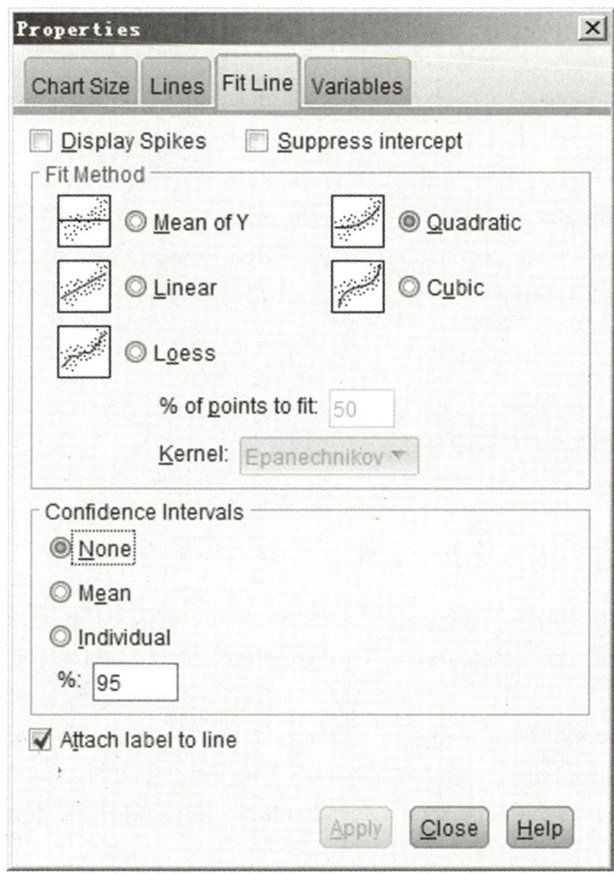

Figure 12-78 The Properties: Fit Line dialog box

Hou Yan, Yang Jun

Chapter 13

Comprehensive Data Analysis

In this chapter, a comprehensive analysis based on the data of a real clinical trial is performed. The data file "clinical trial. sav" used in this chapter is collected in a clinical trial verifying the effect of a new analgesic drugs for urinary tract. In this study, 144 individuals are randomly assigned to either control or intervention group. The individual's age, height, weight, blood pressure, ECG (Electrocardiogram) and pulse are measured at baseline. Urine pain, hemoglobin, RBC (Red Blood Cells), WBC (White Blood Cells) and PLT (Platelet) are measured before and after treatment. Adverse event of any kinds is recorded for scientific evaluation.

13.1 Data verification

13.1.1 Description

Data verification focuses on the detection of logical problems existing in current data set. It includes the exploration of the range, maximum and minimum value, variation and other logistic issues of certain variables.

In data verification, descriptive analysisis performed. The descriptive analysis provides the mean, range, maximum, minimum, variance (standard deviation) as well as other descriptive statistics of the variables for identifing any logical problem exists (i. e. individual's age lower than 0 or the height is taller than 3 meters).

13.1.2 SPSS data format

The requirement of SPSS data file for the descriptive analysis is illustrated in the previous chapter.

13.1.3 Example

Example 13-1 According to clinical trial protocol, the age of individuals included in clinical trial should no older than 80. In this part, we need to check the descriptive statistics of age for checking any protocol violation.

13.1.4 Running the command

The data file of "clinical trial. sav" is used in this analysis. The descriptive analysis is located in the "Descriptive Statistics" submenu, under the "Analyze" menu:

Analyze

Descriptive Statistics

Descriptives

The dialog box of Descriptives pops out (Figure 13-1). The dialog box for the descriptive analysis requires that we transfer the variable representing the current set of "age" to the "Variable(s)" section. Then, select the descriptive statistics required in the "Options".

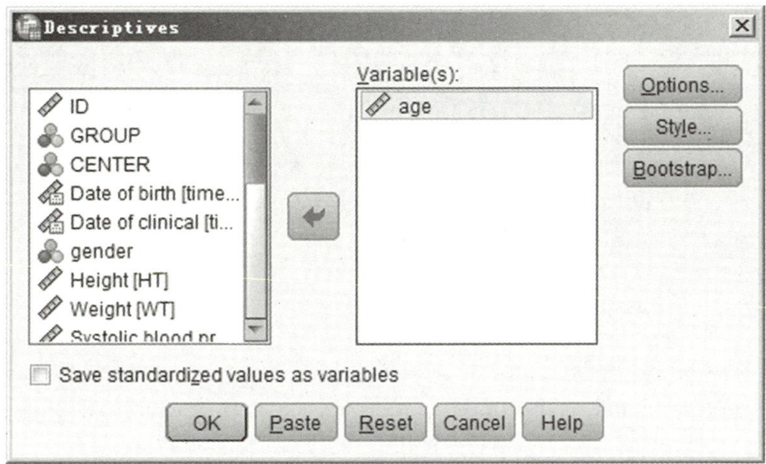

Figure 13-1 The Descriptives dialog box

★Options. Click "Options" button, and the dialog box of Descriptives: Options pops out (Figure 13-2).

☑Mean: Displays mean for the variable(s) selected.

◇Dispersion.

☑Std. deviation: Displays standard deviation for the variable(s) selected.

□Variance: Displays variance for the variable(s) selected.

☑Range: Displays range for the variable(s) selected.

☑Minimum: Displays the minimum value for the variable(s) selected.

☑Maximum: Displays maximum value for the variable(s) selected.

□S. E. mean: Displays standard error of mean for the variable(s) selected.

◇Distribution.

□Kurtosis: Displays kurtosis for the variable(s) selected.

□Skewness: Displays the skewness for the variable (s) selected.

◇Display Order.

⊙Variable list.

◎Alphabetic.

◎Ascending means.

◎Descending means.

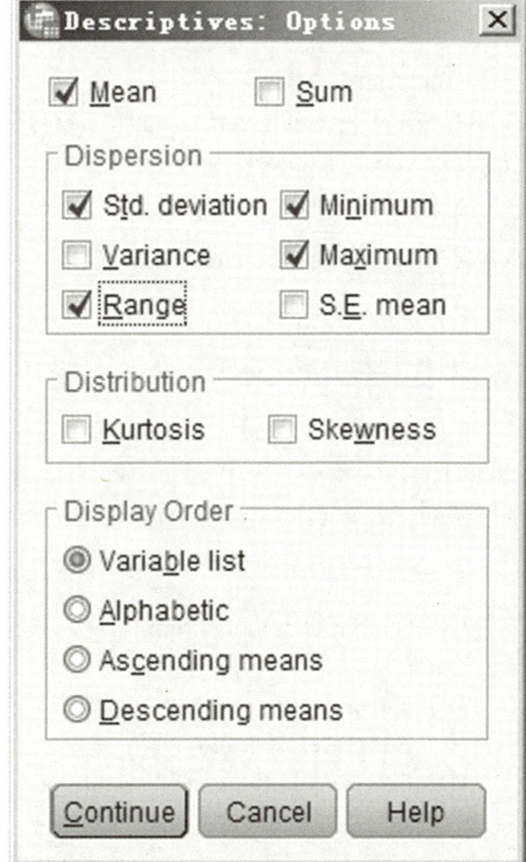

Figure 13-2 The Descriptives: Option dialog box

13.1.5 Reading the output

The output for the descriptives consists only one section. This section lists the sample variable and some basic descriptive statistics which we selected in the Options dialog. The results show that the sample size, range, minimum, maximum, mean, and standard deviation are 144, 62, 17, 78, 42.72, 13.579 for age, respectively (Figure 13-3).

Descriptive Statistics

	N	Range	Minimum	Maximum	Mean	Std. Deviation
年龄	144	61.95	16.51	78.47	42.7197	13.57864
Valid N (listwise)	144					

Figure 13-3 Descriptive statistics of the example

13.1.6 Drawing conclusions

The range for age is 62 (17-78), and the sample mean and standard deviation of age is 42.72 and 13.579, respectively. No individual in the study with an age beyond age limitation.

13.2 Data reduction

13.2.1 Description

Data reduction is about to make the raw data fit the demands of statistical analysis. In data reduction, variable transformationis performed. It includes the generation of new variable based on existed variables (i. e. to compute the BMI based on height and weight), and the data recoding of variables (i. e. recode BMI from continues variable to ranked variable).

13.2.2 SPSS data format

The requirement of SPSS data file for the data reduction is the same as for descriptive analysis.

13.2.3 Example

Example 13-2 Fat or overweight is general risk factor to almost all kind of illness. According to nutritional requirements, the BMI for Chinese adult is recommended no to exceed 24. Calculate the BMI for individuals included in the study base on height and weight measured at base line.

13.2.4 Running the command

The data file of "clinical trial. sav" is used in this analysis. Variable compute is located in the "Transform" submenu:

Transform

  Compute Variable

The dialog box of Compute Variable pops out (Figure 13-4). The dialog box for Compute Variable requires that users define and enter the new variable's name (BMI) into the "Target Variable" section. Since the unit of height used in the calculation of BMI is meter, the variable representing height in the data set is measured in centimeter. So, the data is transformed in the calculation process through dividing height by 100. Transfer the variable need transfer representing the current set of "weight" and "height" to the

"Numeric Expression" in the form of "weight/height(in meters)^2" according to the definition of BMI.

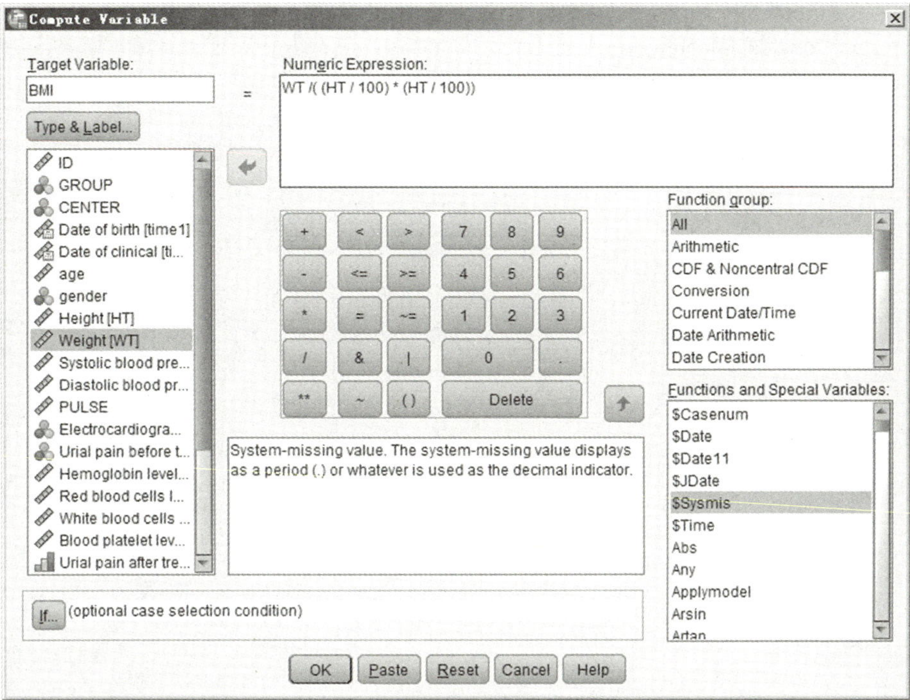

Figure 13-4 The Compute Variable dialog box

★Type & Label. Click"Type & Label" button, and the dialog box of Compute Variable: Type & Label pops out (Figure 13-5).

◇Label.

⊙Label: BMI : Define label for the new generated variable.

◎Use expression as label.

◇Type.

⊙Numeric: Type of new variable is "numeric".

◎String: Width: 8 : Type of new variable is "string" with width 8.

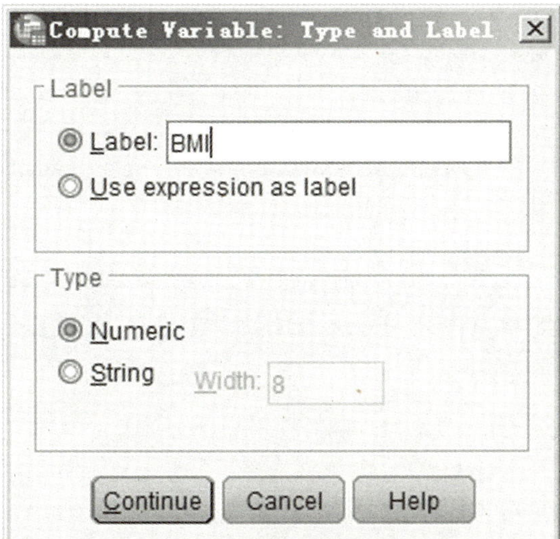

Figure 13-5 The Compute Variable: Type and Label dialog box

13.2.5 Reading the output

There is no any output for compute variable. The generated variable is saved in the activated data set automatically (Figure 13-6, Figure 13-7).

	?2	RBC2	WBC2	PLT2	benefit	AE	HB_D	BMI	var
1	140	4.75	7.00	275	0	0	-1.00	16.73	
2	139	4.44	9.70	232	0	1	17.00	21.47	
3	99	3.32	9.30	399	0	0	6.00	19.63	
4	123	4.18	4.40	229	1	0	36.00	20.08	
5	107	3.60	11.00	277	0	0	19.00	23.94	
6	118	3.69	6.80	240	0	0	7.00	20.45	
7	92	3.98	6.60	332	0	0	43.00	22.49	
8	156	5.60	5.10	242	.	.	.00	24.09	
9	161	9.90	5.44	242	0	0	-12.00	25.54	
10	130	4.40	6.40	212	1	0	7.00	20.20	
11	123	4.40	4.60	312	1	0	-29.00	27.34	
12	151	5.46	8.70	362	0	0	-26.00	20.76	

Figure 13-6 Variable generated of the example (data view)

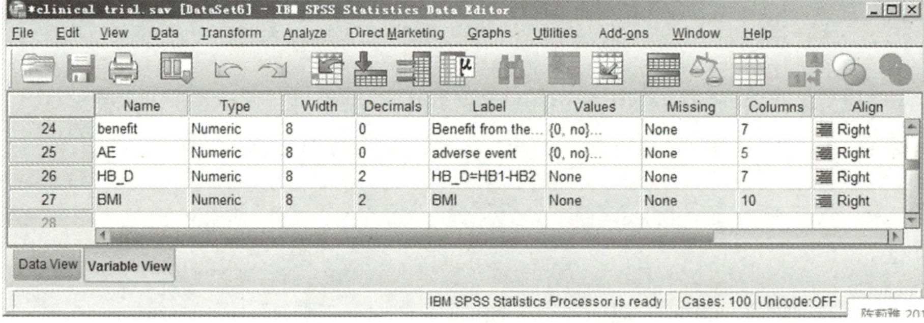

	Name	Type	Width	Decimals	Label	Values	Missing	Columns	Align
24	benefit	Numeric	8	0	Benefit from the...	{0, no}...	None	7	Right
25	AE	Numeric	8	0	adverse event	{0, no}...	None	5	Right
26	HB_D	Numeric	8	2	HB_D=HB1-HB2	None	None	7	Right
27	BMI	Numeric	8	2	BMI	None	None	10	Right

Figure 13-7 Variable generated of the example (variable view)

13.3 Equilibrium test for baseline characteristics

13.3.1 Description

Homogeneity of baseline characteristics yields great importance in data analysis. It guarantees the comparability of interest variables among groups. In practice, the homogeneity of baseline characteristic are verified through the equilibrium test between groups.

In equilibrium test, hypothesis test is performed to test if the sample mean or proportion are homogeneous among groups (i. e. to verify the individual's age and gender are homogeneous among groups).

13.3.2 SPSS data format

The requirement of SPSS data file for the equilibrium test is illustrated in previous chapters.

13.3.3 Example

Example 13-3 In order to achieve good comparability between groups, equilibrium test to verify if the "age" "gender" and "urine pain" before intervention are homogeneous between intervention and control groups.

13.3.4 Running the command

The data file of "clinical trial. sav" is used in this analysis. The equilibrium test for "age" "gender" and "urine pain" is located in the "Compare Means" submenu under the "Analyze" menu:

Analyze

Compare Means

Independent-Samples T Test

The dialog box of Independent-Samples T Test pops out (Figure 13-8). The dialog box requires that users transfer the variable "age" to the "Test Variable(s)" section. Also, transfer the variable "group" to the "Grouping Variable" section and define the groups with numbers through the "Define Groups" option.

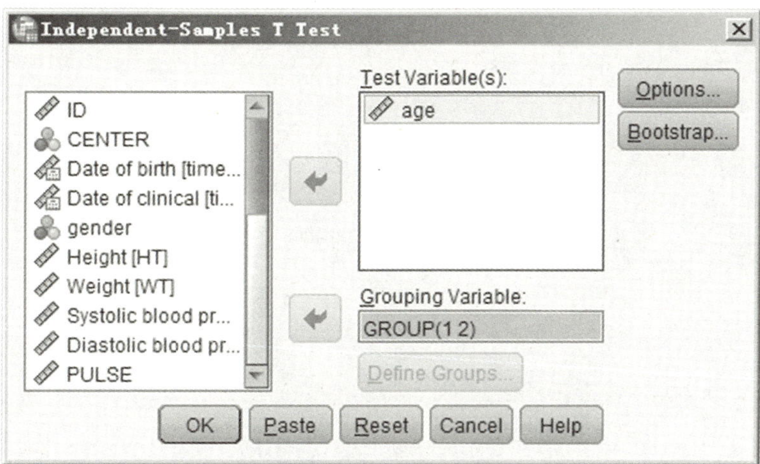

Figure 13-8 The Independent-Samples T Test dialog box

★Define Groups. Click "Define Groups" button, and the dialog box of Define Groups pops out (Figure 13-9).

⊙Use specified values

Group1: [1] : Cases with the group variable equal to 1 are in group 1.

Group2: [2] : Cases with the group variable equal to 2 are in group 2.

◎Cut point: [ ] : If group variable is continues or multinomial then cases can be grouped according to the cut value.

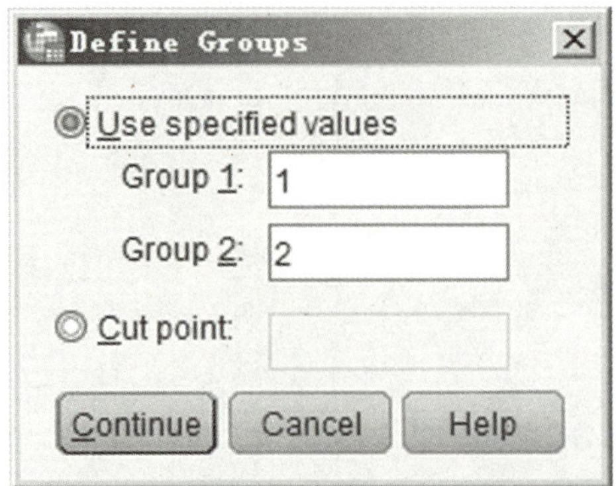

Figure 13-9 The Independent-Samples T Test: Define Groups dialog box

★Options. Click "Options" button, and the dialog box of One-Sample T Test: Options pops out (Figure 13-10).

Confidence Interval Percentage: 95 %: 95% confidence interval for the difference between sample mean and population mean.

◇Missing Values.

⊙Exclude cases analysis by analysis.

◎ Exclude case listwise.

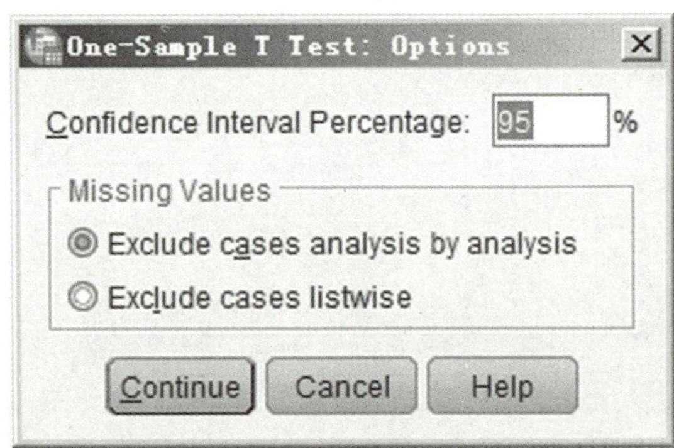

Figure 13-10 The One-Sample T test: Option dialog box

The equilibrium test for "age" "gender" and "urine pain" is located in the "Descriptive Statistics" submenu (for gender) under the "Analyze" menu:

Analyze

Descriptive Statistics

Crosstabs

The dialog box of Crosstabs pops out (Figure 13-11). The variables of "gender" and "GROUP" are transfer to the Row(s) and Column(s) Vsections, respectively. In "Statistics" options, the Chi-square test is selected.

★Statistics. Click "Statistics" button, and the dialog box of Crosstabs: Statistics pops out (Figure 13-12).

☑Chi-square: Chi-square test for R×C contingency table.

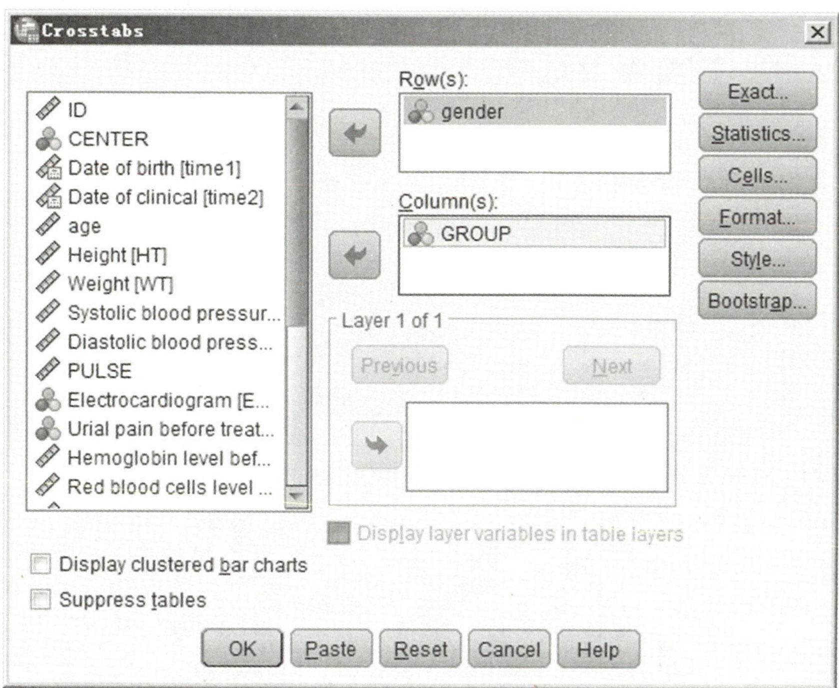

Figure 13-11 The Crosstabs dialog box

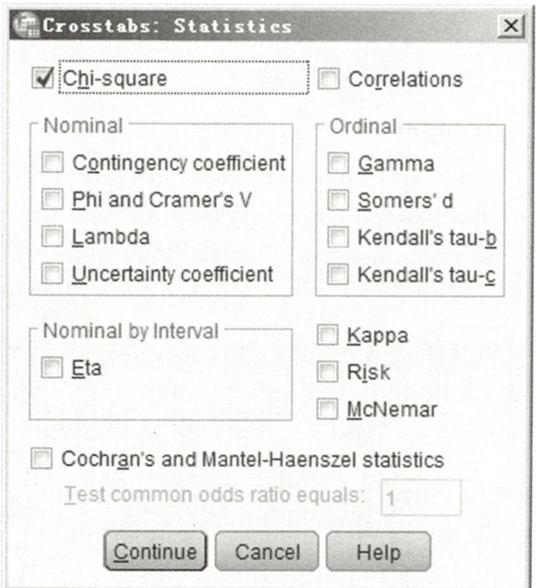

Figure 13-12 The Crosstabs:Statistics dialog box

★Cells. Click"Cells" button, and the dialog box of Crosstabs:Cell Display pops out (Figure 13-13).

◇Counts.

☑Observed: Displays the observed frequency of the contingency table.

☑Expected: Displays the expected frequency of the contingency table.

□Hide small counts.

◇Percentages.

□Row.

☑Column: Shows the percentages calculated by column.

□Total.

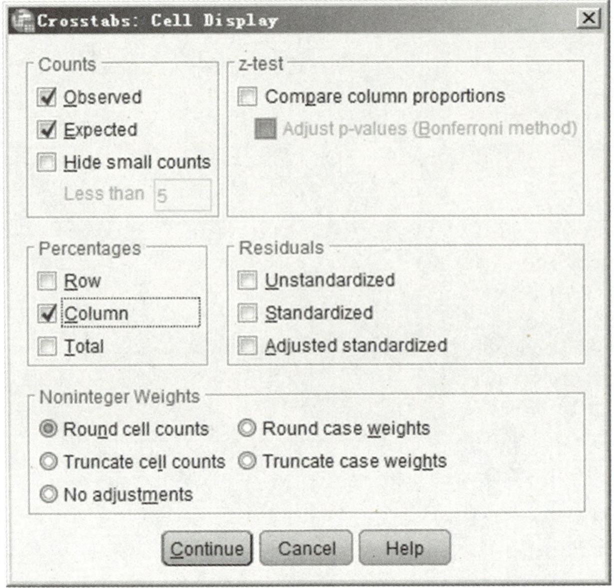

Figure 13-13 The Crosstabs: Cell Display dialog box

The equilibrium test for "urine pain" is located in the "Nonparametric Test" submenu (for urine pain) under the "Analyze" menu:

Analyze

Nonparametric Tests

Legacy Dialogs

Two-Independent Samples

The dialog box of "Two-Independent-Samples Tests" pops out (Figure 13-14). The variable of "Urine pain before treatment" is transferred to the "Test Variable List" section. The variable "group(12)" is transferred to the "Grouping Variable" section and defined the groups with numbers through the "Define Groups" option. Also, "Mann-Whitney U" test is selected at the "Test Type" section.

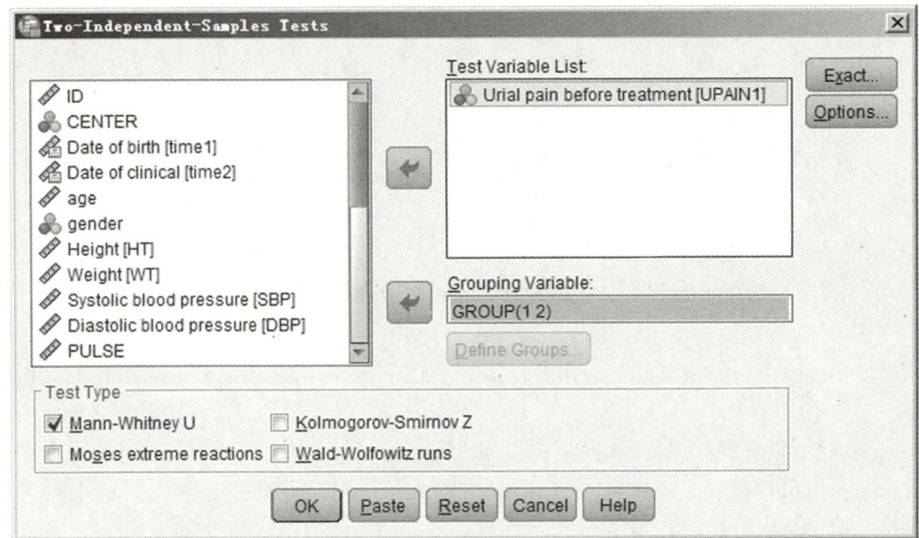

Figure 13-14 The Two-Independent-Samples Tests dialog box

◇ Test Type.

☑Mann–Whitney U: Two–Independent Samples Mann–Whitney U test is conducted.

□Kolmogorov–Smirnov Z.

□Moses extreme reactions.

□Wald–Wolfowitz runs.

◇ Define Groups. Click "Define Range" button, and the dialog box of Two Independent Samples: Define Groups pops out (Figure 13–15).

Group1: [1]: Cases with the group variable equal to 1 are in group 1.

Group2: [2]: Cases with the group variable equal to 2 are in group 2.

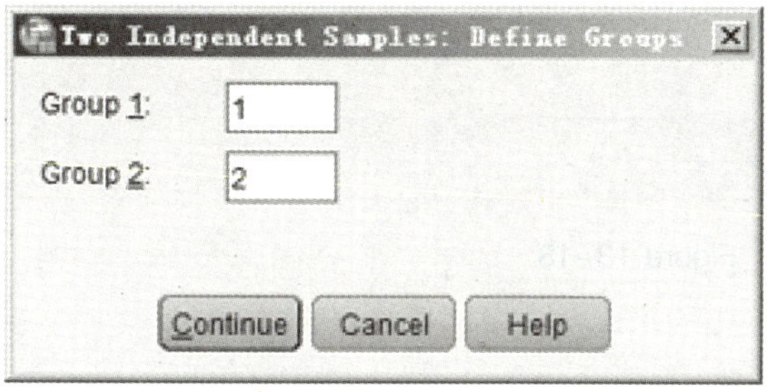

Figure 13–15 The Two–Independent Samples: Define Groups dialog box

★Options. Click "Options" button, the dialog box of Two–Independent–Samples: Options pops out (Figure 13–16).

◇Missing Values.

⦿Exclude cases test–by–test.

◎Exclude case listwise.

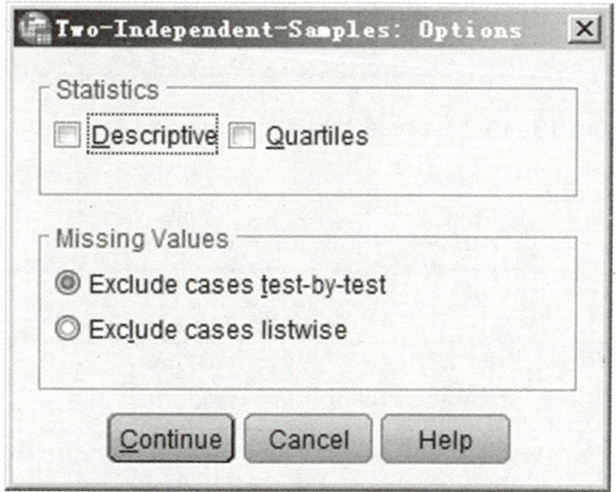

Figure 13–16 The Two–Independent–Samples: Options dialog box

13.3.5 Reading the output

The output for the two independent t–test consists two sections. The first section lists the sample variable and some basic descriptive statistics including sample size, mean, standard deviation and standard error mean of each group (Figure 13–17). The second section lists the result for Levene's test for equality and the independent samples t–test and the 95% CI for the mean difference between two independent samples

(Figure 13-18).

Group Statistics

	GROUP	N	Mean	Std. Deviation	Std. Error Mean
age	test group	72	44.3622	13.59996	1.60277
	control group	72	41.0772	13.45084	1.58520

Figure 13-17 Descriptive statistics of the example

Independent Samples Test

		Levene's Test for Equality of Variances		t-test for Equality of Means						
									95% Confidence Interval of the Difference	
		F	Sig	t	df	Sig. (2-tailed)	Mean Difference	Std. Error Difference	Lower	Upper
age	Equal variances assumed	.089	.766	1.457	142	.147	3.28504	2.25427	-1.17122	7.74130
	Equal variances not assumed			1.457	141.983	.147	3.28504	2.25427	-1.17123	7.74131

Figure 13-18 Result of *t*-test of the example

The output for the two independent *t*-test consists two sections. The first section shows the sample size and number of valid and missing cases in the data (Figure 13-19). The second section presents the cross tabulation of the data. In each cell, the first line represents for the observed frequency of certain combination of the grouping variables for row and column, the second line is the expected frequency and the third line the percentage of certain category within column class (Figure 13-20). The third section shows the results of Chi-square test (Figure 13-21).

Case Processing Summary

	Cases					
	Valid		Missing		Total	
	N	Percent	N	Percent	N	Percent
GROUP * gender	144	100.0%	0	0.0%	144	100.0%

Figure 13-19 Sample size information of the example

gender * GROUP Crosstabulation

			GROUP		Total
			test group	control group	
gender	male	Count	48	45	93
		Expected Count	46.5	46.5	93.0
		% within GROUP	66.7%	62.5%	64.6%
	female	Count	24	27	51
		Expected Count	25.5	25.5	51.0
		% within GROUP	33.3%	37.5%	35.4%
Total		Count	72	72	144
		Expected Count	72.0	72.0	144.0
		% within GROUP	100.0%	100.0%	100.0%

Figure 13-20 Cross tabulation of the example

Chi-Square Tests

	Value	df	Asymptotic Significance (2-sided)	Exact Sig. (2-sided)	Exact Sig. (1-sided)
Pearson Chi-Square	.273[a]	1	.601		
Continuity Correction[b]	.121	1	.727		
Likelihood Ratio	.273	1	.601		
Fisher's Exact Test				.728	.364
Linear-by-Linear Association	.271	1	.602		
N of Valid Cases	144				

a. 0 cells (0.0%) have expected count less than 5. The minimum expected count is 25.50.

b. Computed only for a 2x2 table

Figure 13-21 Result of Chi-square test of the example

The output for the two independent samples nonparametric test consists two sections. The first section shows the information of sample size, mean rank and rank sum of each group (Figure 13-22). The second section gives the results of two independent samples nonparametric test (Figure 13-23).

Ranks

	GROUP	N	Mean Rank	Sum of Ranks
Urial pain before treatment	test group	72	79.83	5747.50
	control group	72	65.17	4692.50
	Total	144		

Figure 13-22 Sample size and rank information of the example

Test Statistics[a]

	Urial pain before treatment
Mann-Whitney U	2064.500
Wilcoxon W	4692.500
Z	-2.465
Asymp. Sig. (2-tailed)	.014

a. Grouping Variable: GROUP

Figure 13-23 Result of two independent sample nonparametric test of the example

13.3.6 Drawing conclusions

(1) For the age of two groups at baseline, the mean age for two groups is 44.36 and 41.08 with standard deviation 13.600 and 13.451, respectively. Levene's test for equality of variances ($F = 0.089$, $P = 0.766$) indicates the homogeneity of variance between two groups. The independent t-test result ($t = 1.457$, $P = 0.147$) indicates that the difference of means between two independent groups is not statistically significant.

(2) For the gender of two groups at baseline, the expected frequencies for all cells are above 5, so any adjustment is not be needed in the testing procedure. The proportion of male (female) in test and control

group sare 66.7% (33.3%) and 62.5% (37.5%) in control group, respectively. The result of Chi-square test ($\chi^2=0.273$, $P=0.601$) indicates that there is no statistical significance in the gender difference between the two groups.

(3) For the urine pain before intervention of two groups at baseline, the mean rank and sum of ranks are 79.83 and 5 747.50 for intervention group and 65.17 and 4 692.50 for placebo group. The result ($Z=-2.465$, $P=0.014$) indicates that a statistically significant difference in urine pain before intervention of two groups.

13.4 Efficiency analysis

13.4.1 Description

Efficiency analysis includes the comparison of pre-intervention and post-intervention measurement between and within groups. In the efficiency analysis, data are splitted, and then paired t-test and two related samples nonparametric test is performed.

13.4.2 SPSS data format

The requirement of SPSS data file for the efficiency analysis is illustrated in previous chapters.

13.4.3 Example

Example 13-4 The data file of "clinical trial. sav" is used in this analysis. Hemoglobin and urine pain are considered as the primary outcome for evaluation of efficiency in the clinical trial. If the hemoglobin level and urine pain are different before and after intervention between and within groups?

13.4.4 Running the command

"Split File" is located in the "Data" submenu:

Data

Split File

The dialog box of Split File is listed in Figure 13-24. The dialog box for the split file requires that user defines the rules of splitting and transfer the variable which the splitting based on into the "Groups Based on" section.

Since the within comparison is about to test the difference before and after intervention within each study group, the "Organize Output By Groups" option should be chosen and the variable representing treatment group in this data should be transferred into the "Groups Based on" section.

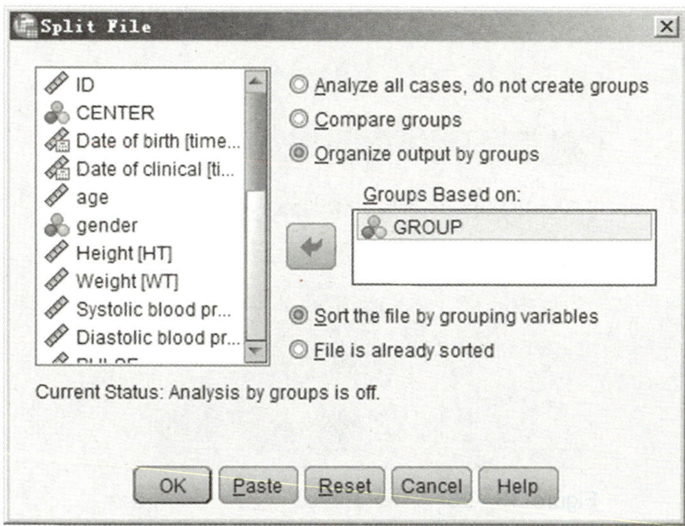

Figure 13-24 The Split File dialog box

◎Analyze all cases, do not create groups.

◎Compare groups.

⊙Organize output by groups.

⊙Sort the file by grouping variables.

◎File is already sorted.

The paired samples t-test is located in the "Compare Means" submenu, under the "Analyze" menu:

Analyze

Compare Means

Paired-Samples T Test

The dialog box of Paired-Samples T Test is listed in Figure 13-25. The dialog box for the paired samples t-test requires that user transfers the variables representing the current set of hemoglobin level before and after treatment to the "Paired Variables" section.

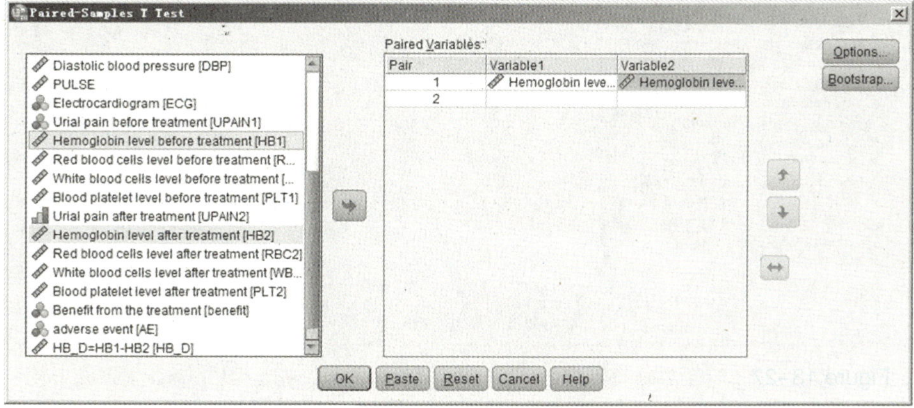

Figure 13-25 The Paired-Samples T test dialog box

★Options. Click "Options" button, and dialog box of Paired-Samples T Test: Options pops out (Figure 13-26).

Confidence Interval Percentage: 95 %: 95% confidence interval for the difference between sample mean and population mean.

◇Missing Values.

⊙Exclude cases analysis by analysis.

◎Exclude case listwise.

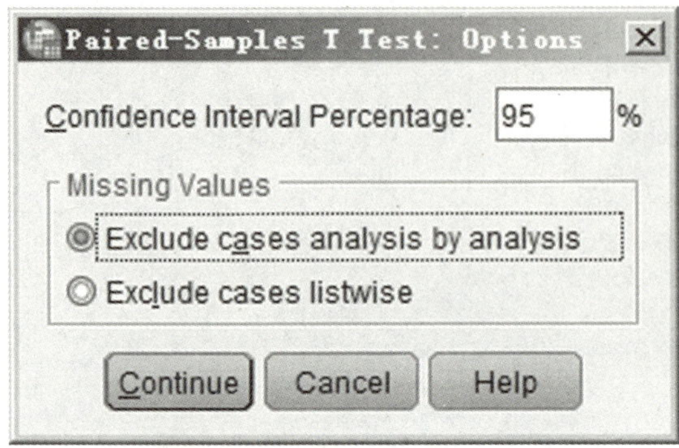

Figure 13-26 The Paired-Samples T test: Options dialog box

The two related samples nonparametric test is located in the "Non parametric Test" submenu, under the "Analyze" menu:

Analyze

Non parametric Test

Legacy Dialogs

Two-Related Samples Tests

The dialog box of Two-Related-Samples Tests is listed in Figure 13-27. The dialog box for the two related samples nonparametric test requires that we transfer the variables representing the current set of urine pain before and after treatment to the "Test Pairs" section. The Wilcoxon signed rank test is performed for this example.

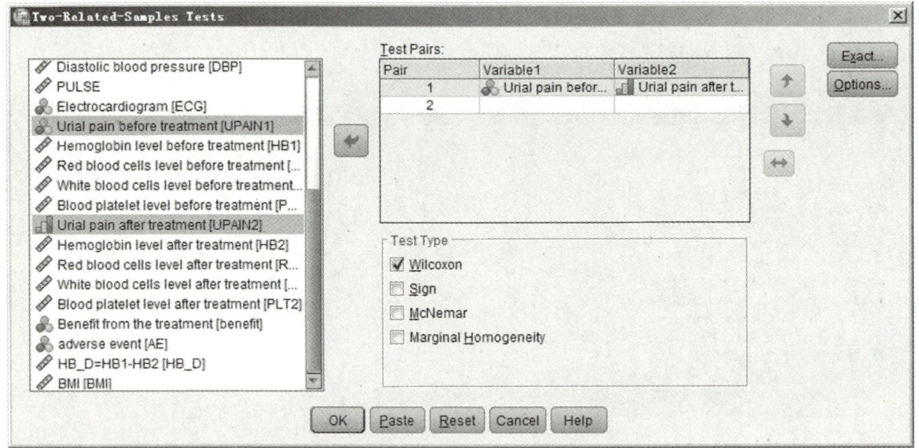

Figure 13-27 The Two-Related-Samples Tests (nonparametric test) dialog box

◇Test type.

☑Wilcoxon.

☐Sign.

☐McNemar.

☐Marginal Homogenity.

13.4.5 Reading the output

Since the analysis are performed with data file splitted, all outputs are organized and presented by groups. Here, the results for test group is explained in details. The output for the paired samples t-test consists of three sections. The first section lists the sample variable and some basic descriptive statistics. The sample size N, mean, standard deviation, and standard error mean are 72, 136.28, 18.156, 2.140 and 72, 133.01, 17.014, 2.005, respectively (Figure 13-28).

Paired Samples Statistics[a]

		Mean	N	Std. Deviation	Std. Error Mean
Pair 1	Hemoglobin level before treatment	136.28	72	18.156	2.140
	Hemoglobin level after treatment	133.01	72	17.014	2.005

a. GROUP = test group

Figure 13-28 Basic descriptive statistics for intervention group of the example

The second section presents the correlation results of the example. The Pearson Correlation Coefficint (r) of hemoglobin between pre-treatment and post-treatment for intervention group is 0.571 (P<0.001) (Figure 13-29).

Paired Samples Correlations[a]

		N	Correlation	Sig.
Pair 1	Hemoglobin level before treatment & Hemoglobin level after treatment	72	.571	.000

a. GROUP = test group

Figure 13-29 Correlation analysis for intervention group of the example

The third section presents the results of the paired t-test. The example presented above indicates a t value of 1.699 (t=1.699), with 71 degrees of freedom (ν=71) and P value of 0.094. The mean difference of between pre-treatment and post-treatment hemoglobin level is 3.267 with 95% CI (-0.567, 7.100).

Paired Samples Test[a]

		Paired Differences					t	df	Sig. (2-tailed)
		Mean	Std. Deviation	Std. Error Mean	95% Confidence Interval of the Difference Lower	Upper			
Pair 1	Hemoglobin level before treatment - Hemoglobin level after treatment	3.267	16.314	1.923	-.567	7.100	1.699	71	.094

a. GROUP = test group

Figure 13-30 The result of paired t test for intervention group

The results of paired samples t-test for placebo group (from Figure 13-31 to Figure 13-33) can be read in the same way as above. The detailed explanation is ignored.

GROUP = control group

Paired Samples Statistics[a]

		Mean	N	Std. Deviation	Std. Error Mean
Pair 1	Hemoglobin level before treatment	134.51	72	19.420	2.289
	Hemoglobin level after treatment	131.50	72	18.323	2.159

a. GROUP = control group

Figure 13-31 Basic descriptive statistics for placebo group of the example

Paired Samples Correlations[a]

		N	Correlation	Sig.
Pair 1	Hemoglobin level before treatment & Hemoglobin level after treatment	72	.722	.000

a. GROUP = control group

Figure 13-32 Correlation analysis for placebo group of the example

Paired Samples Test[a]

		Paired Differences					t	df	Sig. (2-tailed)
		Mean	Std. Deviation	Std. Error Mean	95% Confidence Interval of the Difference Lower	Upper			
Pair 1	Hemoglobin level before treatment - Hemoglobin level after treatment	3.014	14.097	1.661	-.299	6.326	1.814	71	.074

a. GROUP = control group

Figure 13-33 The result of paired *t*-test for placebo group

The output for thetwo related samples of nonparametric test of intervention group consists of two sections. The first section lists rank and sample size information. From the results, the sample size N, mean rank and sum of ranks for negative ranks (urine pain after int. -urine pain before int.) are 31, 31.74, 984.00 and 25, 24.48, 612.00 for positive ranks, respectively (Figure 13-34).

Ranks[a]

		N	Mean Rank	Sum of Ranks
Hemoglobin level after treatment - Hemoglobin level before treatment	Negative Ranks	31[b]	31.74	984.00
	Positive Ranks	25[c]	24.48	612.00
	Ties	16[d]		
	Total	72		

a. GROUP = test group

b. Hemoglobin level after treatment < Hemoglobin level before treatment

c. Hemoglobin level after treatment > Hemoglobin level before treatment

d. Hemoglobin level after treatment = Hemoglobin level before treatment

Figure 13-34 Rank and sample size for intervention group of the example

The second section presents the test results of the two related samples nonparametric tests of the example. The result presents above indicates a Z value of -1.518 ($Z=-1.518$), with P value $=0.129$ (Figure

13–35).

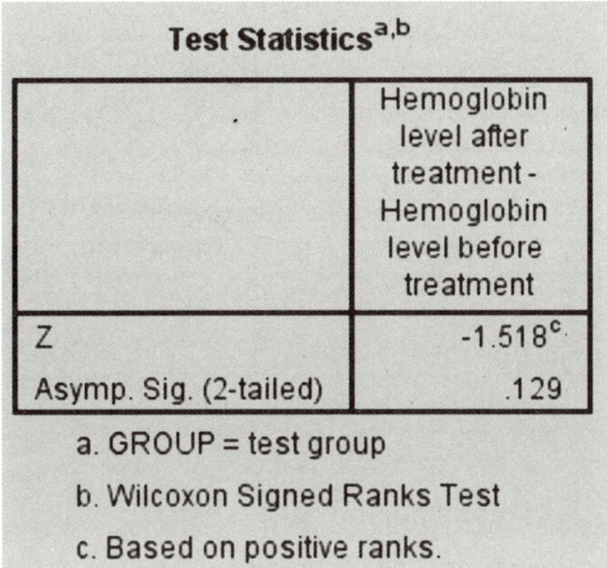

Test Statistics[a,b]

	Hemoglobin level after treatment - Hemoglobin level before treatment
Z	-1.518[c]
Asymp. Sig. (2-tailed)	.129

a. GROUP = test group

b. Wilcoxon Signed Ranks Test

c. Based on positive ranks.

Figure 13–35 Test results of two related samples nonparametric test for intervention group

The results of paired samples t–test for placebo group (Figure 13–36, Figure 13–37) can be read in the same way as above. The detailed explanation is ignored.

Ranks[a]

		N	Mean Rank	Sum of Ranks
Hemoglobin level after treatment - Hemoglobin level before treatment	Negative Ranks	37[b]	37.03	1370.00
	Positive Ranks	30[c]	30.27	908.00
	Ties	5[d]		
	Total	72		

a. GROUP = control group

b. Hemoglobin level after treatment < Hemoglobin level before treatment

c. Hemoglobin level after treatment > Hemoglobin level before treatment

d. Hemoglobin level after treatment = Hemoglobin level before treatment

Figure 13–36 Rank and sample size for placebo group of the example

Test Statistics[a,b]

	Hemoglobin level after treatment - Hemoglobin level before treatment
Z	-1.445[c]
Asymp. Sig. (2-tailed)	.149

a. GROUP = control group

b. Wilcoxon Signed Ranks Test

c. Based on positive ranks.

Figure 13 – 37 Test results of two related samples nonparametric test for placebo group

13.4.6 Drawing conclusions

(1) For the paired t-test. No significant difference is found [$t=1.814$, $\nu=71$, $P=0.074$ (two-tailed test)]. The sample mean difference of pre-treatment and post-treatment for (3.014) is not significantly different from 0, indicating there is no difference in hemoglobin level between pre-treatment and post treatment in intervention group. The result for placebo group can be drawn in similar way.

(2) For the two related samples nonparametric test. No significant different is found [$Z=-1.518$ $P=0.129$ (two-tailed test)]. The results indicate that urine pain after intervention is not significant different from that before intervention.

13.5 Multivariate analysis

13.5.1 Description

Multivariate analysis is an extension and always performed following the univariate and bivariate analysis. It is useful in adjusting potential confounders and determining if the factor of interests is still statistically significant given certain covariates.

13.5.2 SPSS data format

The requirement of SPSS data file for the efficiency analysis is illustrated in previous chapters.

13.5.3 Example

Example 13–5 The data file of "clinical trial. sav" is used in this analysis. A clinical trial has been conducted to study the effect of a new medicine's on urine pain. The urine pain after treatment has been selected to be the primary outcome. However, to make rational comparison, it is necessary to take the urine pain level before treatment into consideration. Try to compare the level of urine pain after treatment with that before treatment as covariate.

13.5.4 Running the command

The analysis of covariance is located in the "General Linear Model" submenu, under the "Analyze" menu:

Analyze

General Linear Model

Univariate

The dialog box of Univariate is listed in Figure 13–38. The dialog box for the analysis of covariance requires that we transfer the variable representing the current set of "Hemoglobin level after treatment" and "Group" to the "Dependent Variable" section and "Fixed Factor(s)" section, respectively. The hemoglobin level before treatment is defined as the covariate by transform "Hemoglobin level before treatment" into "Covariate(s)" section.

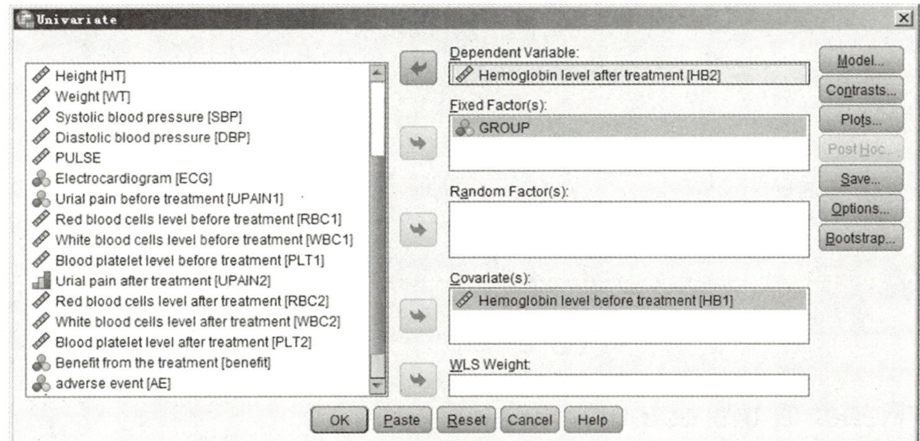

Figure 13–38 The General Linear Model Univariate dialog box

★Options. Click "Options" button, and the dialog box of Univariate: Options pops out (Figure 13–39).

Transform the variable representing the current data set of treatment group from "Factor(s) and Factor Interaction(s)" section to "Display Means for" section.

◇Display

☑Descriptive statistics.

Significance Level: 0.05 % ; Confidence intervals are 95.0%.

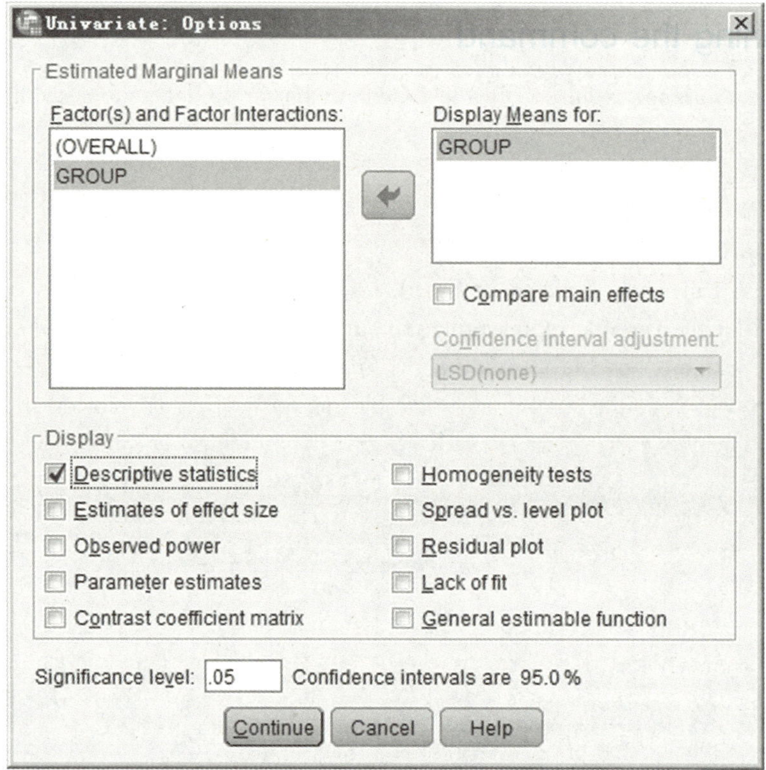

Figure 13-39 The General Linear Model:Univariate:Options dialog box

13.5.5 Reading the output

The output for the analysis of covariance consists of four sections. The first two sections list the sample variable and some basic descriptive statistics. From the results, the mean, standard deviation and sample size for test group are 133.01, 17.014, 72 and 131.50, 18.323, 72 for control group respectively (Figure 13-40 and Figure 13-41).

Between-Subjects Factors

		Value Label	N
GROUP	1	test group	72
	2	control group	72

Figure 13-40 Before subjects factors for ANCOVA

Descriptive Statistics

Dependent Variable: Hemoglobin level after treatment

GROUP	Mean	Std. Deviation	N
test group	133.01	17.014	72
control group	131.50	18.323	72
Total	132.26	17.635	144

Figure 13-41 Descriptive statistics for ANCOVA

The third section of output contains the results of the ANCOVA test. The statistics for Hb1 (F = 104.382, P<0.001) indicates the hemoglobin level before treatment is a covariate for the hemoglobin level after treatment. The statistics for Group (F=0.037, P= 0.848) indicates no significant difference between groups (Figure 13-42).

Tests of Between-Subjects Effects

Dependent Variable: Hemoglobin level after treatment

Source	Type III Sum of Squares	df	Mean Square	F	Sig.
Corrected Model	18964.937[a]	2	9482.469	52.419	.000
Intercept	6503.056	1	6503.056	35.949	.000
HB1	18882.430	1	18882.430	104.382	.000
GROUP	6.647	1	6.647	.037	.848
Error	25506.556	141	180.898		
Total	2563305.000	144			
Corrected Total	44471.493	143			

a. R Squared = .426 (Adjusted R Squared = .418)

Figure 13-42 Test of between subjects effects for ANCOVA

The last section lists the estimates of marginal mean, standard error and 95% confidence interval for the dependent variable (hemoglobin after treatment) in two groups adjusted by the covariate (hemoglobin before treatment). The marginal mean, standard error and 95% *CI* for test group are 132.472, 1.586, (129.337, 135.607) and 132.042, 1.586, (128.907, 135.177) for the control group respectively (Figure 13-43).

GROUP

Dependent Variable: Hemoglobin level after treatment

GROUP	Mean	Std. Error	95% Confidence Interval Lower Bound	95% Confidence Interval Upper Bound
test group	132.472[a]	1.586	129.337	135.607
control group	132.042[a]	1.586	128.907	135.177

a. Covariates appearing in the model are evaluated at the following values: Hemoglobin level before treatment = 135.40.

Figure 13-43 Marginal estimates for ANCOVA

13.5.6 Drawing conclusions

No statistical significance achieved for the difference between test and control group with hemoglobin before treatment as the covariate variable.

Chen Fangyao, Guan Ying

References

[1]陈平雁,黄浙明. IBM SPSS 19 统计软件应用教程[M].2 版.北京:人民卫生出版社,2012.

[2]EVERITT B S. The Cambridge Dictionary of Statistics in the Medical Sciences[M]. Cambridge:Cambridge University Press,1995.

Appendix

Data
N
Ordinal or
N
R × C Table
Could become
T<5
Y
1、Enlargesamplesize；2、Combinesomecolumns
N
Y
N
Y
Draw
Corrected Chi-square
Y
N
N>40
Y
T>5
Y
Y
N
N
T>1
N
Y
N
Y
McNema
Fisher' s Exact
Corrected
N
N
N
Y
Kruskal-W alli
Y
N
Wilcoxon Signed
Mann-Whiney
N
P< α
Y
Y
Y
Post Hoc Test with
N
Y
N
N
Y
Y
N
One way
N
Y
Y
Y
P< α
P< α
Y
Post Hoc Test for Group factor
N
N
Draw
Draw
Paired t test
N
Corrected t test
Y
Independent t test

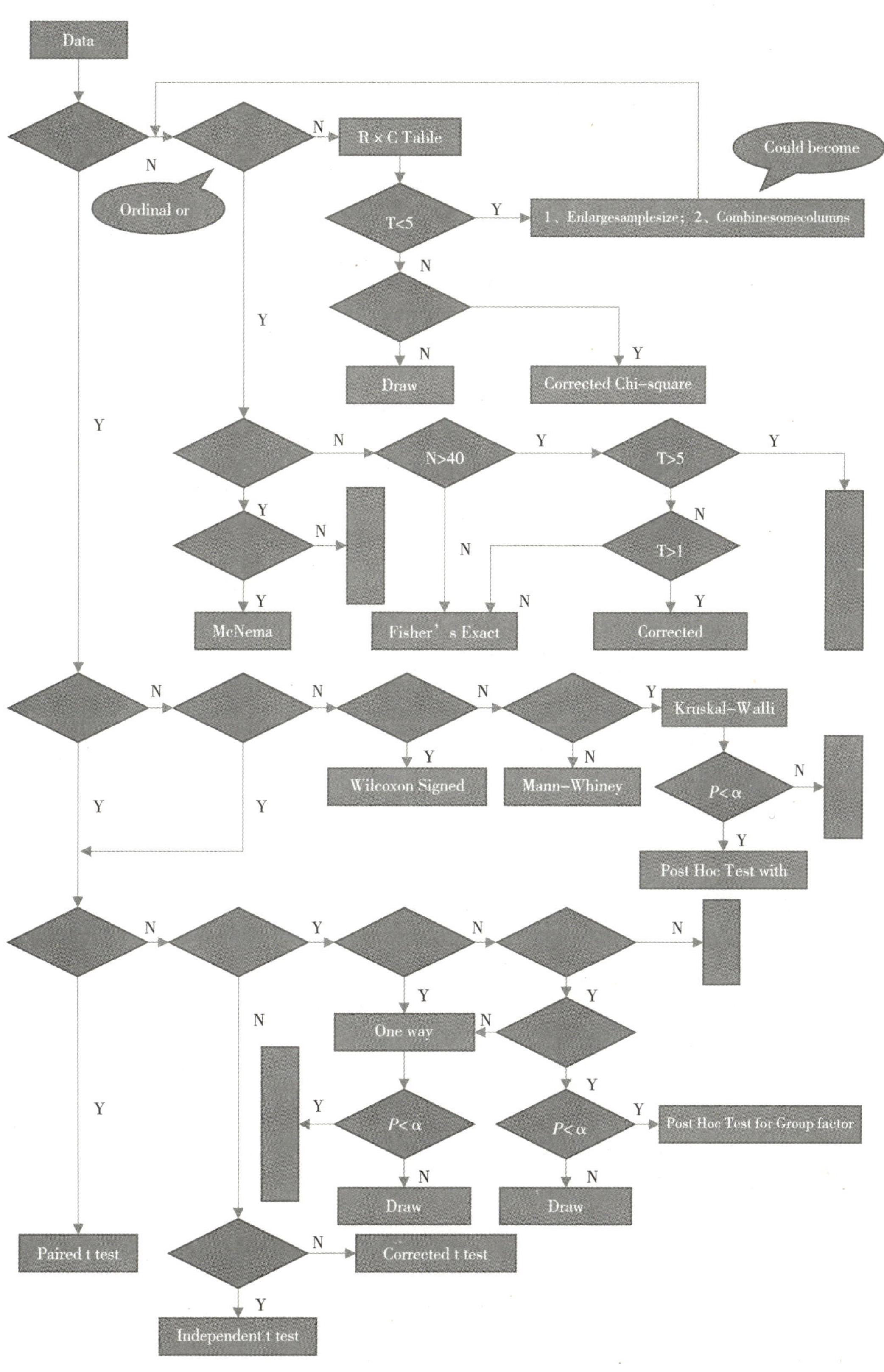